# Letters of H. P. Lovecraft

## VOLUME 10

## LETTERS TO C. L. MOORE AND OTHERS

*Harold Gauer and Robert Bloch with C. L. Moore and Henry Kuttner,*
*visiting from California, in front of the apartment of Bloch's parents*

# H. P. LOVECRAFT

# LETTERS TO C. L. MOORE AND OTHERS

## EDITED BY DAVID E. SCHULTZ AND S. T. JOSHI

Hippocampus Press

New York

# Contents

# Introduction

H. P. Lovecraft's legendary and voluminous correspondence encompassed people of many different ages and from many different backgrounds, but nearly all his correspondents were writers. (His aunts are, of course, an entirely and understandably different audience.) Throughout his life he corresponded with fellow amateur journalists—for he was at heart an amateur—and with professional writers alike. The principal lifelong professional correspondents included Robert E. Howard, Clark Ashton Smith, E. Hoffmann Price, Frank Belknap Long, and August Derleth, all peers, more or less. In the 1930s, Lovecraft found himself corresponding increasingly with young fans of his work who were also aspiring writers. The present volume contains his letters to three great science fiction writers of the mid-twentieth century, although in his day they were basically novices. Unlike some of Lovecraft's other protégés, they were not slavish imitators of his work. Some approached writing as a hobby, others as their future careers. At the time Lovecraft first wrote C. L. Moore, she had already published six stories and was something of a fixture, and a popular one at that, in *Weird Tales*. Henry Kuttner had not published much when he first wrote to Lovecraft, but he already had several acceptances of verse and fiction and in 1936 alone he published eight stories and three poems. Fritz Leiber had sold a few children's stories to a religious magazine, but his ambition was to write fantasy fiction. For several years Leiber and Harry Otto Fischer had been working on heroic-fantasy yarns about Fafhrd and the Gray Mouser, but Leiber was unsuccessful at getting *Weird Tales* to publish "Adept's Gambit," and Fischer himself published no stories. Jonquil Stephens, who became Fritz Leiber's wife, was a poet, although she seems to have published little. Frederic Jay Pabody, though not in the weird or science fiction arena, was writing stories but finding it difficult to get into both the name and even the little magazines. Only one of these authors felt moved to write in a Lovecraftian style, and then only for a short time. In short, all these writers wrote from the onset in their own distinctive voices.

Lovecraft read the unpublished work of some of these writers and offered criticism and encouragement where he could. In the case of Kuttner and Fritz Leiber, they were fairly skilled, needing mostly factual accuracy and verisimilitude in their work. It does not seem C. L. Moore ever sent stories to Lovecraft, for she was selling her work steadily, but she did include numerous poems in her letters. It must be remembered that, except for several letters written to Moore in 1935, virtually all the letters in this volume date to 1936, and a few to early 1937. Some of the letters are quite long, containing the fruits of considerable research that Lovecraft did for the benefit of his young associates. See the long discussion about Childe Roland in his letter to Moore and the discourse on the changing use of *which* vs. *who* over the years, the lengthy listing of books provided to Fritz Leiber to aid him in researching background for a proposed novel, the description of Salem to Kuttner, replete with sketches of typical tombstones, architectural styles, and even a hand-drawn map. There are some 92,000 words in the letters to the six correspondents, and that is only the surviving text—he may well have written 125,000 words all told. And so in 1936, Lovecraft wrote perhaps 100,000 words to only six individuals, at a time when he was in poor health. And yet the magnitude of his total correspondence at the time utterly dwarfs this small fraction of it.

Lovecraft's correspondence with Catherine Lucille Moore (1911–1987) of Indianapolis began in uncommon fashion, for Lovecraft wrote to *her* first. With her first story in in *Weird Tales,* "Shambleau," Moore created quite a stir among the readership, including Lovecraft who wrote favorably to the editor:

> "Shambleau" is great stuff, too. It begins *magnificently,* on just the right note of terror, and with black intimations of the unknown. The subtle evil of the Entity, as suggested by the unexplained horror of the people, is extremely powerful—and the description of the Thing itself when unmasked is no letdown. [. . .] it has real atmosphere and tension—rare things amidst the pulp tradition of brisk, cheerful, staccato prose and lifeless stock characters and images. The one major fault is the conventional interplanetary setting. That weakens and dilutes the effect both by introducing a parallel or rival wonder and by removing the episode from reality. Of course a very remote setting had to be chosen for so unknown a marvel—but some place like India, Africa, or the Amazon jungle might have been used . . . with the horror made more local.[1]

Despite some immaturities and inadequacies, Lovecraft admired the story's originality and the author's potential. Unlike many, Moore successfully stormed *Weird Tales* on her first attempt. Few realized that Moore was a young woman; for, after all, at the time few women wrote for the weird and science fiction magazines, and because she used only her initials, her gender was not evident. Moore used the initials to conceal her identity from her employer, a bank where she worked as a secretary, which had taken pains to try to keep all its staff employed during the Depression. She felt that if her employer knew she had another means of income, she would lose her job to someone in greater need than she. Her first stories, published in college, are signed Catherine Moore.

As a child, Moore was chronically ill (as she confides in a particularly vivid episode in her letter to Lovecraft of 27 May 1935), and in her absence from school she spent much of her time reading literature of the fantastic. Her favorites were *Alice in Wonderland,* the Oz books, the work of Edgar Rice Bur-

---

1. HPL to Farnsworth Wright, 21 November 1933; *Lovecraft Annual* (2014): 38–39.

roughs, and pulp magazines such as *Adventure, Amazing Stories,* and *Weird Tales.* Her family looked down on the pulp magazines, but she obtained and read them on the sly. At the age of eighteen, Moore enrolled at Indiana University–Bloomington, where she attended only three semesters from the fall of 1929 through the fall of 1930. During that time, three of her stories appeared under the byline Catherine Moore in the *Vagabond,* a student publication: "Happily Ever After" is a reworking of the Cinderella story; "Semira" is part of the Lorain mythology described in detail in her letters to Lovecraft; "Two Fantasies" comprises two vignettes, one about the Duchess of Penyra, a country in her mythological realm.[2] Before declaring a major, she withdrew from the university because of the financial hardships of the Depression and returned to Indianapolis to work at the Fletcher Trust Company.

R. H. Barlow, Lovecraft's young friend, began corresponding with Moore in March 1934, initially to express admiration for "Shambleau," but ultimately (as was his wont) to ask Moore for the draft manuscript of the story. Moore did not have the draft, but promised to provide manuscripts of her future work. Barlow was soon giving or lending her books and magazines, which she vastly appreciated. They corresponded for a year, before Barlow asked Lovecraft to write her on his behalf as part of a subterfuge to dissuade Moore from allowing William L. Crawford, another aspiring young publisher, to publish a book of her stories, for Barlow wanted to issue some of her stories himself. Barlow, who had grand plans to publish books by Henry S. Whitehead, Clark Ashton Smith, H. P. Lovecraft, Robert E. Howard, and Edith Miniter (and produced nothing but booklets of Lovecraft's "The Cats of Ulthar" and Frank Belknap Long's verse), also wanted to lay claim to publishing Moore's first book. Because he was somewhat behind the game, he enlisted Lovecraft to persuade Moore to let Barlow have her best stories and to let Crawford have lesser material, just as Lovecraft himself had done. (Somewhat contradictorily, Lovecraft let Crawford publish "The Shadow over Innsmouth" as a small book.) Barlow, apt pupil of Lovecraft, also sought to dissuade Moore from pursuing the path taken by so many promising writers for the pulps—forsaking sensitivity, realism, and craftsmanship in order to make easy money by catering to the demands of the pulp editors and readers who craved action-packed thrillers. Who better than Lovecraft to speak to this? Lovecraft's description of Barlow's feelings on the matter echoes his own:

> Little Ar-E'ch-Bei—the premier Moore fan—is quite concerned about the slipping of the new luminary; & is urging the gang to find some excuse to shoot her tactful words of advice counteracting the tradesmanlike recom-

2. In June 1939, R. H. Barlow mentioned to August Derleth that Moore was "still submerged in her Arthurian book" (ms., WHS), a book that possibly derived from her early Penyra writings.

mendations of Satrap Pharnabazus . . . . . & the philistinic suggestions of Prince Effjay of Akkamin, who has been volunteering collaboration![3]

To another correspondent Lovecraft wrote:

> As to the work of C. L. Moore—I don't agree with your low estimate. These tales have a peculiar quality of cosmic weirdness, hard to define but easy to recognise, which marks them out as really unique. "Black God's Shadow" isn't up to the standard—but you can get the full effect of the distinctive quality of "Shambleau" & "Black Thirst". In these tales there is an indefinable atmosphere of vague *outsideness* & *cosmic dread* which marks weird work of the best sort. How notably they contrast with the average pulp product—whose bizarre subject-matter is wholly neutralised by the brisk, almost *cheerful* manner of narration! Whether the Moore tales will keep their pristine quality or deteriorate as their author picks up the methods, formulae, & style of cheap magazine fiction, still remains to be seen. A. Merritt fell for the pulp formula, hence never realised his best potentialities. Miss Moore may do the same. But at present she certainly belongs in the upper tier of W T contributors along with Smith, Howard, &c.[4]

For a young writer to be placed on "the upper tier" of *Weird Tales* authors along with Clark Ashton Smith and Robert E. Howard (and, incidentally, H. P. Lovecraft) was high praise indeed.

And so, after mulling over for several weeks what he thought he should say, Lovecraft drafted a letter to Moore around 1 April 1935 on a used envelope, revising it here and there before preparing a fair copy and sending it to Moore. Lovecraft was not in the habit of drafting letters and revising them before sending them, but, as he told Barlow, "it takes time & thought to phrase a letter of *unsolicited advice*—to neutralise with tact the implication of depreciation & flaw-picking, & guard against an air of arrogant superiority & officious meddling."[5] It appears, however, that Moore did not simply receive an identical fair copy of the draft contents, for the second letter included herein seems to be the actual first letter that he sent. As part of a somewhat backhanded compliment, Lovecraft suggests that he and Barlow hope Moore will not follow the path taken by so many other promising writers who ultimately turned into pulp hacks, as so many of his colleagues had been tempted to do. Having completed the task requested by Barlow, Lovecraft considered the matter finished, but Moore replied. She seemed somewhat taken aback by the suggestion, admitting that she enjoyed writing pulp thrillers. In a later let-

---

3. HPL to CAS, 26 March 1935, *Dawnward Spire* 595. Moore and Forrest J Ackerman collaborated on "Nymph of Darkness," which HPL suspected had been a collaboration between Moore and E. Hoffmann Price.

4 HPL to William Frederick Anger, 28 January 1935; *Letters to Robert Bloch and Others* 227.

5. HPL to RHB, [25 March 1935], *O Fortunate Floridian* 228.

ter, Moore expressed disagreement with suggestions Lovecraft quoted from "Some Notes on Interplanetary Fiction," his dictum for the composition of effective science fiction stories. Despite Lovecraft's general defense of her work, he did find some weaknesses, though he never broached these to Moore. Stuart Morton Boland wrote that Lovecraft

> went on to declare that Catherine Moore wrote as "an incurable optimist rescuing man from an ill-omened fate by the means of a 'Star-destined fortune-favored' element; and that she would take over these old Mexican gods and dispose of them one by one through the valor, courage, and will power of her characters." He said she believed that the animal "man" had the undeniable ability to recover from the most hell-shattering catastrophe. The immortal potentialities of mankind, as she saw them, were too enormous a factor to be submerged or intimidated by mere "terror-gods." Such would make excellent straw-men for her heroes to vanquish.[6]

Moore's letters to Lovecraft give us a rare look at what Lovecraft received in the mail, for unlike letters from some of his fellow writers, hers are not primarily about writing but about anything that occurred to her—much like Lovecraft's typical letters. Most of the letters Lovecraft received from youth were somewhat immature and fannish, but Moore's are vivacious and thoroughly engaging. The state of the correspondence of Lovecraft and Moore is somewhat in reverse of his correspondence with others. We have probably all Moore's letters to Lovecraft, yet only a very few of his to her. Moore told August Derleth, who after Lovecraft's death sought to obtain Lovecraft's letters for transcription and ultimate publication, that she had nearly *two hundred pages* of letters from Lovecraft. We know that Lovecraft tended to write far more to his correspondents than they did to him, and the length of some of Moore's typed letters surely inspired lengthy replies from Lovecraft. This volume also contains Lovecraft's notes written on two envelopes for letters received from Moore to aid him in preparing suitable replies. (One imagines that Lovecraft applied the practice on similarly long missives from others, though examples of this are rare.) As noted, surviving letters from Lovecraft to Moore are inexplicably few. Some examples bear notation by Moore stating that the opening and closing pages are lacking, but why that is so is unknown. Most letters that do survive exist only in the Arkham House transcripts. One can only wonder how the starchy Lovecraft responded to comments from Moore about "a girl in a high-waisted Empire gown of eggshell satin, stepping delicately into the mud of an unpaved street on a rainy night" or about Moore's new bathing-suit with its "little flared skirt" and "rubber-fabric briefs as I now take pride in possessing," for he rarely left any

---

6. Stuart Morton Boland, "Interlude with Lovecraft," In *A Weird Writer in Our Midst,* ed. S. T. Joshi (New York: Hippocampus Press, 2010), 31.

comment from a correspondent unaddressed. It is deeply regrettable that we do not have Lovecraft's complete replies to her charming letters.

After Lovecraft's death, Moore enjoyed a long career as a writer of science fiction, mysteries, and westerns, mostly in collaboration with Henry Kuttner, whom she married in 1940. After Kuttner died in 1958, she became a script writer for television and dropped out of science fiction writing.

It is somewhat surprising that Henry Kuttner (1915–1958), the youngest of the writers in the group and also the shortest-lived, ever became a correspondent of Lovecraft. He was the son of Henry Kuttner and Annie Levy. The father ran a bookstore, which Hank haunted as a youngster. Henry Sr. died when Hank was four, and so he and his two older brothers grew up in relative poverty. Like C. L. Moore, Kuttner grew up reading the Oz books, Edgar Rice Burroughs, and pulp magazines. After graduating from high school, he worked in Los Angeles for the literary agency of a first cousin by marriage. His first published story, "The Graveyard Rats," appeared in *Weird Tales* for May 1936, though his first appearance there was the poem "Ballad of the Gods."

The September 1934 *Weird Tales* published a somewhat smart-alecky letter by the then nineteen-year-old Kuttner taking Lovecraft to task, and finding C. L. Moore to be Lovecraft's superior:

> Here's a letter of comments and criticism, inspired chiefly by "Through the Gates of the Silver Key" in your July issue. I wonder if it has not occurred to you that sheer thorough explanation of the weird may rob a subject of weirdness. It seems to me that mystery is an essential of the weird, and when, in such a story as Lovecraft's, the author tries to cover Heaven and Hell, humans and non-humans, explaining everything in one colossal sweep, the story falls flat and becomes more preachy than interesting or weird. Little need be said about the surprising ending of the yarn. Lovecraft at one time could supply a good ending, but now he is getting trite as hell. It is a bad example of a forced surprize [*sic*] ending that he has on that story. Lovecraft's earlier stories, "The Hound", "The Rats in the Walls", "The Call of Cthulhu", "The Dunwich Horror" and one of the best, "The Horror at Red Hook", were far more truly weird than his later stories, which go past the weird and mysterious, and, throwing a cold light of scientific reason onto non-human affairs, result in a science-fiction story. If you will bring to mind Lovecraft's best stories (not his most successful ones), you will find that mystery, not calculating science, provided the fillip of true weirdness. That is why C. L. Moore seems to me a better writer than Lovecraft—the *present* Lovecraft.[7]

Lovecraft surely read the letter when it was published, but apparently he took no offense because he himself thought "Through the Gates of the Silver

---

7. "A Slap on the Wrist," *WT* 24, No. 3 (September 1934): 398–99.

Key" a poor story. On 10 February 1936, Kuttner wrote a cordial letter to Lovecraft, presumably at the behest of Robert Bloch:

> Yes—I have heard from Kuttner—& day before yesterday snatched the time to drop him a line with a few geographical, architectural, & necropolitan remarks about *Salem,* which he seems to favour as a locale. I congratulate you upon discovering him, for he really seems to be a very unusual find—his prose & verse alike having remarkable force & fluency. His fiction does, as you suggest, display a little imitativeness—& a certain lack of adequate motivation & gradual development—but it has excellent atmospheric qualities & a promising sense of climax. I have an idea that Kuttner will be a rapid learner— whose work will acquire polish & maturity through a series of quick leaps.[8]

At the time Kuttner wrote Lovecraft, his first piece to be published in *Weird Tales,* "The Ballad of the Gods," had appeared, followed the next month by "The Graveyard Rats," a story in which many believe Lovecraft had a hand but which had been accepted before Kuttner first wrote to Lovecraft. Before long, Lovecraft was reading and commenting on a new story set in Salem that *Weird Tales* had rejected but then published the following year. Having lived his entire boyhood in California, Kuttner had only a vague idea of what New England and Salem might be like, and so his descriptions were not entirely accurate. Lovecraft lent Kuttner pictures of the area and also described various features at length which Kuttner had described erroneously. Lovecraft then asked Kuttner to forward to C. L. Moore the "Salem and Marblehead miscellany" that Lovecraft had lent him. At the time, Kuttner thought Moore to be male, but he soon learned otherwise. Lovecraft's chance instruction was the beginning of a correspondence that in time led to Kuttner and Moore collaborating in February 1937 on "The Quest of the Star Stone," which united Moore's characters Northwest Smith and Jirel of Joiry for the first time, and ultimately their friendship and joint career.

Lovecraft genuinely praised Kuttner's apprentice work and encouraged him (along with Robert Bloch) to borrow from the mythic elements in Lovecraft's own writings. Imagine Kuttner's reaction to admonitory letters from August Derleth, telling him he should *not* do so. We do not have Derleth's exact comments, but Kuttner's responses clearly indicate what Derleth had written to him:

> As no doubt you realized, I sinned through ignorance rather than intention. My use of the Lovecraftian milieu was a direct result of steeping myself in HPL's stories until I could nearly talk the ancient tongue. Too, I've been in correspondence with Bob Bloch, and he's rather encouraged me to use Lovecraft's settings, gods, and tricks. . . . It will be wiser, as you suggest, to

---

8. HPL to Robert Bloch, 14 March [1936], *Letters to Robert Bloch and Others* 165.

follow my natural bent rather than slavishly copying—although Lovecraft has had a profound effect on my stuff. . . . what about using the gods of Lovecraft and Smith (Tsathoggua, Yog-Sothoth, Cthulhu—or even mentioning them) to get atmosphere? Unethical? . . . While I appreciate the importance of such props, I naturally don't want to do something I shouldn't, and I'm very inexperienced at the writing game. I'd greatly appreciate any comments you care to issue from Delphi.[9]

[. . .] thanks for your last missive giving me the dope on keeping clear of Lovecraftiana. Ironically enough, Wright has just taken my SALEM HORROR, and I am expecting vials of wrath from you.[10]

Very glad for your most recent comment on the Lovecraft affair. I have never thought of it in the light of being unfair to HP. But since you make the point I can readily understand how this may be so, and I rather wish I'd figured it out before. I have a profound admiration for Lovecraft, whom I think is one of the two great masters of weird literature (Blackwood is the other; nuts to Machen, who talks too much)—and I never would have imagined that either Bloch's work or mine would militate against HP's chances of acceptance. [. . .] It would certainly be a hell of a dirty trick on my part to try to cut out HPL—I owe him much for his influence upon my work; and the idea is thoroughly distasteful to me. If I can't sell stuff without stealing Lovecraft's thunder I don't care to sell at all. Now that the reasons behind the case are known to me, you may be sure that Farnsworth will get no more "cheap imitations" from me.[11]

We mention this at length to show not only Kuttner's profound admiration of Lovecraft's work, but also that even in Lovecraft's lifetime August Derleth had appointed himself Lovecraft's literary watchdog, even though his discouragement of others borrowing from Lovecraft flew in the face of Lovecraft's own avid encouragement, and also belied his own heavy borrowing from, and blatant imitation of, Lovecraft and his work, particularly for his own personal gain in later years. Derleth's gall in referring to Kuttner's work (and that of others), but not his own, as "cheap imitations" of Lovecraft is beyond credulity. And it is ludicrous to suggest that by borrowing Lovecraft's mythic elements and even aping his style somewhat, Kuttner or Bloch or anyone else would jeopardize Lovecraft's ability to sell a story to *Weird Tales*. In any case, Kuttner was content to dispense with the Lovecraftian trappings in his work. He focused on developing his own writing style and saw the wisdom of setting stories in a locale with which he was familiar.

In April 1937, Kuttner wrote: "There is really nothing I can say about

---

9. HK to August Derleth, 14 March 1936 (ms., WHS).
10. HK to August Derleth, 9 May 1936 (ms., WHS).
11. HK to August Derleth, 19 May 1936 (ms., WHS).

Lovecraft's death. I don't want to think about it; the news made me ill. HPL was my literary idol ever since I was a kid, and I can't realize that he's gone."[12] In his grief, Kuttner wrote an elegiac piece "For H. P. Lovecraft" (unpublished). The acrostic poem by Kuttner on Lovecraft's name that appeared in *Weird Tales* in September 1937 had been written and accepted while Lovecraft was still alive. Kuttner had considered withdrawing the poem under the circumstances, but Robert Bloch urged him not to. In the coming months, Kuttner wrote many stories for *Terror Tales, Horror Stories, Thrilling Mystery,* and the like; but in time, at the suggestion of his agent, Julius Schwartz, he began writing science fiction.

In 1938, Kuttner began to visit Moore in Indianapolis on trips between New York and Los Angeles. He quit his job at the literary agency in 1939 and moved in with his mother in New York, where he could write full time. On 7 June 1940, Kuttner and Moore married in New York. They soon became a powerful writing team, publishing dozens of science fiction stories of great merit. So close was their collaboration that they could easily slip into whatever the other had written and continue or revise it.

In the 1940s, Kuttner also wrote for *Green Lantern* and other superhero comic books (at the instigation of Schwartz.) But his legacy is that he emerged as one of the great writers of science fiction's Golden Age, or perhaps we should say Kuttner and Moore together, for much of their writing at that time was collaborative—so much so that they could not recognize their own hand in their efforts. The fact that they used at least eighteen pseudonyms, each having specific personal attributes, including Lewis Padgett, Lawrence O'Donnell, Paul Edmonds, and Will Garth, besides their own bylines, makes it difficult to give either author individual credit. In time, the pair tired of science fiction and turned to other genres. They moved to California because of Kuttner's health. Kuttner went to the University of Southern California under the G.I. Bill, earning a bachelor's degree, working toward a master's degree (his thesis being on the works of H. Rider Haggard), and also teaching creative writing at USC, but he died of a heart attack in Los Angeles before attaining his degree. Moore obtained her own bachelor's degree from USC in 1956 and took over Kuttner's writing classes following his death, and obtained her Master's in 1964.

In November 1936, Lovecraft received a letter from Jonquil Leiber, forwarded from Street & Smith, publishers of *Astounding Stories,* where his *At the Mountains of Madness* and "The Shadow out of Time" had appeared earlier in the year. Lovecraft must have been surprised to have received a letter from the daughter-in-law of the Shakespearean actor whom he had seen on stage many times. Jonquil Stephens Leiber (1907–1969) was the oldest of the young

---

12. HK to August Derleth, 5 April 1937 (ms., WHS).

correspondents herein in this group. Unlike the others, she was not a budding fiction writer. At the time, she and her husband Fritz, Jr. (1910–1992), had been married ten months and were living in Beverly Hills. Fritz and Jonquil had met while attending the University of Chicago. After college, Fritz briefly acted in his parents' company and served a short stint as a lay reader and minister in the Episcopal church.

It is difficult to imagine any writer being more profoundly affected by Lovecraft than Fritz Leiber. He received only five letters from Lovecraft in the last four months of his life. In that time, Leiber, a college graduate, received from Lovecraft the education of a lifetime in the very field in which he himself became a titan. In his foreword to *The Book of Fritz Leiber* (1974), Leiber called Lovecraft "the chiefest influence on my literary development after Shakespeare."[13] Fritz Leiber was a rare person who recognized the significance of what Lovecraft accomplished in his own fiction. Leiber pointed out to Lovecraft some shortcomings in his work, and Lovecraft acknowledged the defects, noting that in future work he needed to improve. When others, such as August Derleth, Clark Ashton Smith, Donald Wandrei, and E. Hoffmann Price, commented on Lovecraft's work, Lovecraft ignored their suggestions, because they mostly had missed the point. Leiber did not. He revised his early story "Adept's Gambit" per Lovecraft's suggestions, and on his own removed some of the Lovecraftian allusions he initially had included in the story. The story was not published until 1947, when it appeared in Leiber's first book, *Night's Black Agents*.[14] Leiber's writing was slow in gaining traction. His first published story, another in the Fafhrd–Gray Mouser cycle, was "Two Sought Adventure" (*Unknown*, August 1939).

Reflecting back on a long life, Leiber named four people as being profound influences on him. Three of them were his wife Jonquil, his son Justin, and his colleague Harry O. Fischer, who devised the characters of Fafhrd and the Gray Mouser—the main characters in seven volumes of short stories. The fourth was a man he never met; whom he corresponded with for merely four months. How many of us can say that one of the greatest influences in our lives was a man with whom we exchanged maybe only half a dozen letters? Lovecraft's letters to Fritz and Jonquil no doubt comprised more than the nearly 26,900 words presented herein, in five letters to Fritz (19,675 words) and four to Jonquil (7,200 words). Leiber surely was awed by the length and detail of Lovecraft's guidance. As he later recalled, "When I merely mentioned to him my intention of writing a novel set in Roman times, he sent me

---

13. Cited in Bruce Byfield, *Witches of the Mind: A Critical Study of Fritz Leiber* (West Warwick, RI: Necronomicon Press, 1991), 11.
14. An earlier version—not necessarily the one that Lovecraft read, but one that does contain some references to Lovecraft's Mythos—has been published as *Adept's Gambit: The Original Version*, ed. S. T. Joshi (Welches, OR: Arcane Wisdom, 2014).

several thousand words of highly pertinent advice, including a longer and shorter bibliography for researching the period. Now, setting to work on such a novel twenty years later, I am helped by his remembered instructions."[15] That novel, *The Big Time* (1958), is not set entirely in the Rome era, for Leiber's Change War series of tales covers all time. It won a Hugo Award for best novel.

Leiber's careful study of Lovecraft's fiction has offered the greatest insight into Lovecraft's literary legacy. Much as Lovecraft was, as Leiber so felicitously named him, a "literary Copernicus," Leiber himself was something of a Copernicus in shifting the false portrait of Lovecraft painted by the view of a parochial "self-blinded earth-gazer" of the man's work—as propounded by one incapable of seeing it for what it was—to a much grander, far-reaching perspective. It is astonishing that the writer who ham-fistedly tried to force Lovecraft into an ill-fitting straitjacket fabricated from his own earthbound conceptions published another's view of Lovecraft's work antipodal to his own, one that has proved to be the more accurate. August Derleth once bestowed on Lovecraft the backhanded compliment of calling him a major writer in a minor field. (Derleth's implication about his own standing in literature is far from subtle—and has turned out to be erroneous.) Fritz Leiber, however, perceived that Lovecraft was in no field at all. Lovecraft was not a pulp writer or a horror writer or a science fiction writer, but *a writer*. And his accomplishments led Leiber to name him—correctly—"a literary Copernicus." The Copernican Revolution was a great scientific paradigm shift from the long-held Ptolemaic model of the heavens, in which the earth was stationary at the center of the universe, to the revolutionary heliocentric or Copernican model, with the sun at the center of the solar system. So profound was Lovecraft's influence that the standard tropes of supernatural fiction were shattered by his shift from a dread excited by ghosts and vampires and haunted houses to dread of the unknown cosmos itself and its unimaginable denizens.

With his friend Fritz Leiber, Harry Otto Fischer (1910–1986) developed the characters Fafhrd (based on Leiber) and the Gray Mouser (based on Fischer) and the heroic-fantasy genre. Fisher is another of the rare correspondents who was first approached by Lovecraft. Leiber had supplied Lovecraft with Fischer's address after Lovecraft had expressed admiration for the fragment of text in a letter to Leiber in which Fischer had supplied colorful information about the developing Fafhrd–Gray Mouser myth-cycle. Fischer created the characters and named their home city of Lankhmar, as detailed in a letter to Leiber in September 1934. Fisher and Leiber fleshed out the fantasy in their letters, much as C. L. Moore and her girlfriend developed their own mythical realm and characters. In 1936, Leiber finished the first Fafhrd–Gray Mouser novella, "Adept's Gambit," and began work on a second, "The Tale

---

15. See "My Correspondence with Lovecraft" in the appendix.

of the Grain Ships," while Fischer was writing "The Lords of Quarmall." Lovecraft mentions being in touch with Fischer as early as 27 January 1937, calling him "a remarkable imaginative genius."[16] The two could not have exchanged many letters, for by late February Lovecraft could no longer write. Of perhaps three letters to Fischer, we have the partial contents of only one.

Fischer was the primary force behind the growing myth-cycle, around which he and Leiber developed a board game,[17] but despite writing much about the primary characters and their adventures Fischer published very little. Leiber himself wrote virtually all the Fafhrd–Gray Mouser tales and finished "The Lords of Quarmall," first published in 1964 as by the duo. Fischer's wife, Martha McElroy Fischer (1912–1991), an artist in various media, prepared a map of Lankhmar and painted a portrait of Ningauble of the Seven Eyes, one of two wizards in the Lankhmar tales.

Lovecraft had suggested to Helm C. Spink—a correspondent and fellow amateur journalist, and an officer in the National Amateur Press Association—that he attempt to contact Fischer, since both lived in Louisville. It does not appear that Spink did so, or if he did that anything came of it. Lovecraft had thought Fischer a potential NAPA recruit and described him to Spink thus:

> Thanks immensely, by the way, for the tip anent 3515 W. Kentucky St., where my correspondent Harry O. Fischer lives. Fischer is an extremely brilliant chap, with one of the most fertile imaginations I have ever encountered. He is the author of reams of unpublished fantasy, & one of the most appreciative students of fantastic literature alive. I have had no word from him since the coming of the waters—& up to Feby. 3 his closest friend & correspondent (in the Los Angeles region) [= Fritz Leiber] was equally uninformed. I owed him a letter, & have been adding gradually to one for some time; but have hesitated to mail it in the absence of definite information. He is employed in some minor executive capacity by the General Box Co., & I had thought of addressing him in care of that firm with a view to more certain delivery. I would probably send a postcard ahead to make sure before entrusting a long letter to the mails—but meanwhile I'd certainly be grateful for any information which might come through you. Don't, however, undertake any laborious detective work on my account. If you do get in touch with Fischer, I think you'll probably find him very likeable & congenial. He is a relatively new correspondent of mine, but his letters point to a remarkably brilliant & distinctive personality. As a writer of fantasies out of the commercial rut, unwilling to make concessions to cheap market demands,

---

16. HPL to RHB, 27 January 1937; *O Fortunate Floridian* 397.
17. In 1976, TSR published *Lankhmar*, a redeveloped version of the initial fantasy board wargame.

he might be good material for N.A.P.A. recruiting—although he would have little patience with the more puerile products of amateurdom.[18]

Even though Fischer wrote "reams of unpublished fantasy," he published none of it.

Fischer's correspondence with Lovecraft was even briefer than Leiber's, but he was no less moved by Lovecraft' untimely death, as related in the following anecdote by C. L. Moore:

> A letter from a young man named Leiber, in California, received recently, quoted his friend Fischer, of Louisville [. . .] in the following paragraph which seem to me quite nice indeed. He speaks of HPL, of course: "But rather is he striding, browned by the sun and elements, with short sword at his back toward some Dover shore at the head of his cohort. When the campaign is over and the barbarians quelled he will return to his scrolls and his villa-library. And even as he marches he jots on a small waxen tablet notes of the peculiar land, this foggy island outland. . . . He seems to me an albatross—a lonely bird soaring over icy wastes over pathless tropic seas—searching for a land on which he would not settle if it were found."[19]

It was Fischer who suggested that he and the Leibers conspire to get Lovecraft fresh vegetables, but they were unable to follow through; and in any case, good nutrition at this stage of Lovecraft's life would have been of little use.

Of Lovecraft's late correspondent Frederic Jay Pabody (1910–1993), little is known, save that he only completed his third year of college, was of similar age to the others represented herein, and like them was an aspiring writer. His initial letter to Lovecraft was genealogical in nature, for he wondered how Lovecraft came to use the name "Pabodie" in the recently published *At the Mountains of Madness,* thinking that Lovecraft knew a person of that name. As usual, Lovecraft discoursed at length—on the name, its variants, a resident of Providence named Pabodie whom he did not know but for whom he supplied an address, and his own general principles in assigning names to characters in his fiction. He even volunteered to do genealogical research into the name *Pabodie* at the Rhode Island Historical Society!

By way of reply, Pabody sent Lovecraft a story he had written, a work unlike those by the other authors addressed in this book, for he had written a mainstream piece, not a weird or science fiction story. Like other young readers of the pulps, Pabody was interested in the occult, the compendia of unusual phenomena assembled by Charles Fort, and other pseudoscientific topics. Lovecraft encouraged Pabody with advice about his writing and where

---

18. 11 February 1937 (ms., JHL). Fischer was out of touch with his correspondents at the time because of severe flooding of the Ohio River.
19. CLM to August Derleth, 13 May 1937 (ms., WHS).

he might try to have it published, but he also divulged numerous points about his personal life, including his inability to find a job and his perilous finances (which he also discussed with the Leibers, showing that these issues were very much on his mind at the time). And of course he attempted to steer the young writer away from the pulps for weird writing toward the masters: Blackwood, James, Machen, Hodgson, and others. Although Pabody had some light verse published in E. M. Robinson's "Philosopher of Folly" column in the *Cleveland Plain Dealer,* he seems to have published nothing and became not a professional fiction writer but worked in the insurance industry.

—DAVID E. SCHULTZ

S. T. JOSHI

## *A Note on the Texts*

As has been the case with some other volumes of Lovecraft's letters, this volume derives from less than ideal though probably satisfactory sources. C. L. Moore seems to have lost 80 percent or more of Lovecraft's letters to her, and the few that survive are incomplete. The loss seems to have occurred before she sent the letters to Arkham House for transcription. At first she wrote August Derleth: "there must be nearly two hundred pages in all, written closely on both sides in the familiar Lovecraft chirography."[20] Upon searching for the letters to send for transcription, she observed: "There seems to be an inexplicable gap in the chronology of my letters, several being missing which HPL had illustrated with a sort of frontispiece of the scene before him as he wrote. Many of his poems must have been in these, for the only ones I now find are titled respectively, 'March', 'A June Afternoon', 'August'—all of these presented as examples of his juvenile work—and 'To Mr. Finlay Upon His Drawing for Mr. Bloch's Tale, "The Faceless God"', and 'To Clark Ashton Smith, Esq., Upon His Phantastick Tales, Verses, Pictures and Sculpture' [. . .]."[21]

Therefore, Lovecraft's letters to Moore derive primarily from the Arkham House transcripts of his letters. Leaves from only a few individual letters are held at the John Hay Library and privately. A draft of Lovecraft's first letter to Moore exists, but he may well not have sent that letter to her as a fair copy. The final version of the letter, and the typescript Moore prepared of it are lost. (See p. 29; quite likely CLM 2, taken from the Arkham House transcripts, derives from Moore's transcript of only part of Lovecraft's letter.) It is not known why Lovecraft's letters to Moore exist only in fragmentary form. J.-M. Rajala has pointed out that in the transcripts, pages of different letters had been intermixed, presumably because many were lacking their introductory and concluding pages. These errors are noted in the designation of

---

20. CLM to August Derleth, 12 April 1937 (ms., WHS).
21. CLM to August Derleth, 12 April 1937 (ms., WHS).

sources in the letters. The John Hay Library also holds Moore's typed letters to Lovecraft, published herein, and also to R. H. Barlow. Moore's poetry in the appendix is taken from letters to Robert Barlow, both among the papers Barlow deposited and also on George Smisor's microfilm of papers among Barlow's effects at the time of his death.

In the case of Lovecraft's letters to Henry Kuttner, we rely entirely on nine transcripts prepared by Kuttner and one photocopy of a handwritten letter, all held at the Wisconsin Historical Society among the August Derleth Papers. Kuttner's transcripts are not part of the Arkham House transcripts (which, incidentally, the Historical Society does not have). Kuttner's transcripts contain a few explanatory notes intended for Arkham House's benefit; they are reproduced herein. What became of Lovecraft's actual letters to Kuttner is unknown.

Lovecraft's letters to Jonquil and Fritz Leiber derive from the Arkham House transcripts, except for a single letter owned by the John Hay Library. It is unknown how the library came to have that lone letter, for Leiber stated that "The entire correspondence was later borrowed and retained, permanently as yet, by . . . [an] individual who shall remain nameless here." The Leibers requested that Annie Gamwell return their own letters to Lovecraft, and those, too, have never surfaced. The letter to Leiber's associate Harry Otto Fischer also derives from the Arkham House transcripts. Fischer's son once told the editors that he had Lovecraft's letters to his father, but copies of these were never obtained. Lovecraft's letters to Frederic Jay Pabody derive entirely from manuscripts recently obtained by the John Hay Library.

The common perception—in large part true—is that Lovecraft did not keep letters from correspondents, for among his papers there are few complete or even long runs of letters. What survive are probably all the letters from E. A. Edkins, most of the letters from Robert E. Howard, E. Hoffmann Price, Frank Belknap Long, and Henry George Weiss, a good number (though not even half) of those from Clark Ashton Smith—and, mirabile dictu, all the letters from C. L. Moore! Lovecraft observed late in life: "I was forced by the prevailing chaos to devote 4 solid days (including 2 nights of sacrificed sleep) to the devastating process of file-cleaning. I must have thrown away a couple of tons of old letters, cuttings, &c."[22] Surely "a couple of tons" is something of an exaggeration, but Lovecraft may well have retained letters for a long time, until he simply could not find storage space for them all. Just as Annie Gamwell returned the Leibers' letters to them, she may have returned other letters—how else to account for Donald Wandrei having all his letters to Lovecraft in his possession? It seems that Lovecraft valued Moore's letters, for they survived the file cleaning bout. The fact that they survive at all is because they probably came into the hands of R. H. Barlow. Given Lovecraft's propensity to deluge

---

22. HPL to HK, c. 15 June 1936.

correspondents with lengthy letters, it is truly astonishing that more of Moore's letters (which are fairly long) to Lovecraft survive than his letters to her.

Naturally, the reader gains much from having both sides of two writers' correspondence at his or her disposal. When only one side can be found, one must infer what the other writer may have written based solely on the sender's comments. We can only imagine what Elizabeth Toldridge may have written Lovecraft, for example. But in the case of C. L. Moore, we have virtually all she wrote Lovecraft. Her letters are from a time well covered by Lovecraft's letters to others who were close to Moore in age at the time. It should not be difficult to imagine what Lovecraft may have written her, although certain comments unique to their correspondence must remain unknown. But we are fortunate to have the opportunity to see what sort of mail Lovecraft must have received daily from the growing hordes of fans and would-be writers.

*Acknowledgments*
The editors wish to acknowledge the assistance of Christopher Geissler of the John Hay Library, the staff of the Wisconsin Historical Society, Richard Bleiler, Stefan Dziemianowicz, Kenneth W. Faig, Jr., Donovan K. Loucks, Eileen McNamara, and Christopher M. O'Brien in providing information for this volume, and especially J.-M. Rajala who helped establish the sequence of, and decipher, Lovecraft's letters to C. L. Moore.

*Abbreviations*

| | |
|---|---|
| CE | *Collected Essays* (2004–06; 5 vols.) |
| CF | *Collected Fiction* (2015, 2017; 4 vols.) |
| FF | *Fantasy Fan* |
| FM | *Fantasy Magazine* |
| LL | S. T. Joshi, *Lovecraft's Library: A Catalogue* (2002; rev. ed. 2017) |
| SL | *Selected Letters: 1911–1937* (1965–76; 5 vols.) |
| WT | *Weird Tales* |
| | |
| CAS | Clark Ashton Smith |
| CLM | C. L. Moore |
| HK | Henry Kuttner |
| HPL | H. P. Lovecraft |
| RHB | R. H. Barlow |
| | |
| AHT | Arkham House transcripts |
| ALS | autograph letter, signed |
| ANS | autograph note (postcard), signed |
| JHL | John Hay Library, Brown University |
| TLS | typed letter, signed |
| TNS | typed note, signed |
| WHS | Wisconsin Historical Society |

*C. L. Moore, some time after October 1935*

# Letters: H. P. Lovecraft and C. L. Moore

[1]    [ALS (draft), JHL]

[late March 1935]

[. . .]

My brilliant young friend Robert Heyward [*sic*] Barlow—an arch-devotee of your work & connoisseur of weird writing in general—has been urging me to back him up in the task of persuading you to let him republish some of your choice stories (perhaps in slightly revised form) in a series of carefully edited & privately printed brochures which he is contemplating. ¶ He tells me that William Crawford of *Marvel Tales* is also a contender for this honour, & asks me to help him point out—so far as I am able—the reasons why his own plan is more suited to the nature of your material & of your literary future than is Crawford's. ¶ Hence this otherwise unsolicited & apparently meddlesome bulletin of comment from a stranger—albeit a stranger admiringly familiar with all your published fantasies, & enthusiastic regarding the advent to the weird firmament of its first new major luminary since Clark Ashton Smith. How much might the added opinion may possess, I cannot say—though Barlow tells me you have read some of my own occasional attempts at fantastic creation.

Now as to the matter in question—I can be very sincere indeed in sustaining Mr. Barlow's plea. The fact is, he & his enterprise represent a level & quality of endeavour utterly removed from the sordid arena of tradesmanlike hack work typified by the wood-pulp magazines & their sickening standards. It is his design to choose those specimens of your fiction which are *actually*—not popularly or commercially or saleably—best, & to issue them in a dignified format & fashion suited to their quality—circulating them among readers of real discrimination, who would not be likely to take seriously such tawdry rags as *Weird Tales* & its fellow-news-stand pulps. He would thus be paving the way for the development of your genius along the right instead of the wrong line—preparing you to follow the sincere, spontaneous, purely artistic course of real fantaisistes like Poe, Dunsany, Arthur Machen, Algernon Blackwood, M. P. Shiel, Walter de la Mare, Montague Rhodes James, Ambrose Bierce, H R Wakefield, & their congeners, instead of the mob-catering, insidiously charlatanic course of the cheap-magazine idols who sacrifice sincerity & aesthetic quality to the arbitrary herd-motivated demands of the callous business men who control the popular periodical press. ¶ Of course, it may seem a bit impertinent in Barlow to fear that a first-rate genius ever *could* be permanently sidetracked in this way—but when you reflect on the number of splendid writers whom he has *seen* thus alienated from literature, you will probably be disposed to forgive him. ¶ Consider the case of A. Merritt—a

25

man with natural fantastic endowments unsurpassed in the 20th century—stranded in the cheap & sterile best-seller field, & grinding out unctuous gallons of pap containing the mechanical "adventurous young hero", "beauteous heroine", "black villain", "sweet love interest", "showing conflict"[,] "triumph of good" &c. &c. &c. of kitchen & summer-porch popularity. Consider "Single-Plot Hamilton", lured by persuasive editors & the chink of gold from the heights represented by "The Monster God of Mamurth"[1] to the soporific swamp of listless quantity-production now so sadly familiar to his readers—or would-be readers. Consider my friend E. Hoffmann Price—beckoned from the djinn-like artistry of "The Stranger from Kurdistan" & "The Dreamer of Atlanaat"[2] to the rubber-stamped "action" novelettes & "detective mysteries" which he now rattles feverishly into a dictaphone. Eheu fugaces! Barlow has seen them come & go—& he wants to be sure that the latest major dawn is a permanent one!

Well—the point is, that while Barlow's plan is to feature your best work & encourage the most authentic phases of your genius, Crawford would undoubtedly be just like the other pulp exemplars in fostering whatever of ready *saleability* your work might contain—irrespective of actual merit. He would feature just the *wrong* things & ignore or subordinate just the *right* things. All of which, though perhaps beneficial to your purse, would be far from beneficial to a natural literary genius far more important—& far harder to duplicate or recover if crushed—than any mere purse-furniture.

*Notes*

1. Edmond Hamilton, "The Monster-God of Mamurth" (*WT,* August 1926; rpt. September 1935).
2. E. Hoffmann Price, "The Stranger from Kurdistan" (*WT,* July 1925); "The Dreamer of Atlanaat" (*WT,* July 1926). The former story slightly influenced HPL's "The Horror at Red Hook."

[2]     [AHT]

[c. 31 March 1935]

[Dear Miss Moore:—]
                    [. . .]
It takes some time to realise that there are actually *two* worlds of literary endeavour—as far apart as the poles in essence & motive, despite occasional outward resemblances & certain fortuitous overlappings. One is the realm of sincere aesthetic expression—the saying of what the author actually has to say in the best possible way, regardless of audience or commercial results. To this world belong all the figures in standard literature—& such practitioners of fantasy as Blackwood, Machen, &c. This is the only world which Barlow & I can take seriously, & we don't see why any genuine artist should bother with

any other if he has any honest means of obtaining the essentials of food, clothing, shelter, warmth, & a civilised environment apart from the sacrifice of his talents. The other world is the realm of "popular" writing—not the saying of what one has to say oneself, but the saying of what a callow, under-educated public wants to hear, & therefore of what commercial editors will pay for. This latter world—or underworld—is of course simply a matter of gauging low-grade popular psychology & mechanically following the pitifully few & childishly unreal & oversimplified formulae which suit that psychology in such matters as plot, incidents, atmosphere, assumed values, & characters. It is easy to distinguish a typical popular product from a typical work of litera-ture—for there are always the damning stock properties—bold, handsome hero, fair maid, adventure, conflict, good-&-evil values, &c. &c. &c. to mark it out. The real work of literature, on the other hand, is likely to have few or none of these. In the weird field, a *genuine* story is more likely than not to con-sist simply of a pageant of baffling shadows seen—without conflict—by some kind, obscure, middle-aged house-holder. The "hero" of such a story is never a *person* but always a *phenomenon* or *condition*—the "punch" or climax is not what *happens to anybody,* but *the realisation that some condition contrary to actual law as we understand it has (fictionally) had a brief moment of existence.* For the object of weird fiction is purely & simply emotional release—a highly specialised form of emotional release for the very small group of people whose active & restless imaginations revolt against the relentless tyranny of time, space, & natural law. It must, if it is to be authentic art, form primarily *the crystallisation or symbolisation of a definite human mood—not* the attempted delineation of *events,* since the "events" involved are of course largely fictitious & impossible. These events should figure *secondarily*—atmosphere being first. All real art must somehow be connected with *truth,* & in the case of weird art the emphasis must fall upon the one factor representing truth—certainly not the events (!!!) but *the mood of intense & fruitless human aspiration typified by the pretended overturning of cosmic laws & the pretended transcending of possible human experience.*

But I digress. The gist of the matter is that a following of popular van-dals—the sort of thing represented by the pulp-magazines who cluster fawn-ingly around them, not only *does not help* a genuine literary aspirant, but actually *harms* him to a small degree by leading him in the wrong direction. The laws of one world cannot operate successfully in another world—& any-one seeking commercial success of the Merritt–Edgar Wallace–Bedford-Jones–R. W. Chambers–*Saturday Evening Post* type, must bid farewell to the hope of succeeding in the sincere field of Poe, Hawthorne, Coleridge, Black-wood & Machen. It is a matter of choice—& Barlow (very justly, I think) be-lieves that your work is of a sort which indicates the advisability of the Poe–Hawthorne kind of choice in your case.

This, though, is not to say that sincere work is one hundred percent un-remunerative & unacceptable to popular editors—or even necessarily unpopular with the herd. As you see, Poe & Blackwood & Dunsany *have* managed to get into professional print, while even the miserable pulps print some of Clark Ashton Smith's & the late Henry S. Whitehead's sincere work . . . as well as your own productions! The fields overlap, & it is quite possible for a genuine artist to become a popular idol as well—if *by chance* his work, (or part of his work) coincides with something the stupid rabble are gaping for. The important thing is simply for the author to retain his artistic integrity—to think only of sincere expression & ignore the herd & the hope of profit. Then, if profit & popularity come to him *incidentally*, all very well. *That* will not hurt his genius. He will not make as much money, or be such a darling of the proletariat & petite-bourgeoisie as if he had chosen the popular road of Mammon; but he will have saved his own personality & enriched literature with an artist who would otherwise have been sacrificed.

[. . .]

[3]  [TLS, JHL]

April 3, 1935

Dear Mr. Lovecraft:

Your letter has impressed me tremendously. It's awfully nice to be flattered, and Mr. Barlow's compliments in particular have pleased me a great deal, but not until yesterday when I read your letter did it really occur to me that my "pulp"-published and extrav[ag]ant romances might actually, after all, contain a nucleus of worth which should be taken seriously. Of course I realize I have Mr. Barlow to thank for your interest, but when one of your standards and ability takes the trouble to write at all I think it behooves me to stand off and look at myself with some awe.

Everything you say is so true that I am somewhat terrified when I consider it seriously as applied to myself. But I'm wondering just how possible it's going to be for me to maintain a place in that "overlap" you spoke of between the worlds of aesthetics and commerce.

I'm in no position to turn my back on profits, and somewhat doubt my ability to forego the temptation of easy money even if the choice were entirely mine. As Mr. Barlow knows, it isn't. I have responsibilities which can't be evaded, and the little money I can make by writing is so desperately essential to their fulfilment that at present—and I hope temporarily—there can be no hesitation for me between the high road and the low road if the necessity for choosing should come.

All that, though, seems to me not a matter so much of choice as of chance, or circumstances, or whatever it is which puts ideas into one's head and drives one to work them out. Surely no one deliberately degenerates. It must be involuntary, and those writers you mentioned who have slipped must have tried as hard as I shall try to maintain their place in the "overlap".

For what it's worth, I can promise never to write anything I don't enjoy writing. A labored production from me wouldn't come up to any standards at all. But it must be admitted that my present standards include some pretty low ones. I do get a tremendous lot of pleasure out of dealing in a slap-dash, wild-western manner with just the basics of cheap fiction you so dislike. All this juggling with other civilizations and impossibly Earth-like other worlds, and hair-breadth escapes and handsome heroes is such fun I would probably do it whether it sold or not. In time I'll outgrow that definitely adolescent phase of writing. I'm only twenty-four, and my standards are still shifting perceptibly. If you'll bear with me until I can get this florid slap-stick out of my literary system maybe whatever basic merit I possess will show through.

When the degeneration does come, I probably won't know it. You wouldn't have taken the trouble to write as you did if I hadn't written some good things, and I know that part of my work has been poor—but which is which I couldn't tell when I wrote it and can't be sure even now. I write blindly, following no rules, and am no judge whatever of the work I turn out. (Still cherish a lurking suspicion it's all trash and people will suddenly wake up and realize it someday soon. That's a nightmare I've had more than once.)

All this is one reason why I've just made a typewritten copy of your letter. I'm going to be referring to it often. The points you outline in explaining the essentials of good weird fiction came as completely new ideas to me—the sort of things I somehow never learned in college or in any reading I've done. They give a new dignity to what I'd heretofore regarded as something akin to wild-west fiction—a lot of fun, and popular with a certain class, but of no literary merit and with no connection to the world of Machen and Dunsany and the rest. If anything can save me from the abysses of hack-writing, I think it will be the ideas I have just absorbed from your letter. (I have been guilty of flattery from time to time—but just now, however fulsome that may sound—I'm quite sincere.)

If Mr. Crawford will be content with my poorer tales, I'll offer them to him as you suggest. It's a way out of the dilemma I hadn't thought of. I have very little rejected work, since I've been writing so short a time, but with what I have and what future trash I'm bound to produce perhaps he can be kept busy along with Mr. Barlow. All this, of course, if he ever gets around to publishing the booklets he plans.

I'd like to thank you not only for being kind enough to write, but for opening my eyes to the possibilities of dignity in the type of writing I enjoy, and in the possibilities of merit in my own work, which is so florid and splashy in contrast to your own and that of the other great weird-fiction writers that until now it has been impossible for me to take it very seriously.

And a whole row of apologies for the countless I's in the foregoing.

Very sincerely,

Catherine Moore

[4]    [AHT]

April 12, 1935

[Dear Miss Moore:—]

[. . .]

As for the serious possibilities inherent in fantastic fiction—there is no question about them (though, of course, the literature of the unreal is admittedly a narrow & specialised field). The mood of revolt against nature is as old as the human race—as the whole existence of religion & its mythology proves. Weird elements have permeated literature since prehistoric times—flourishing in Elizabethan drama & forming a distinct school since the middle of the eighteenth century. (cf. "The Tale of Terror" by Edith Birkhead; "The Haunted Castle", by Eino Railo; "The Supernatural in Modern English Fiction", by Dorothy Scarborough—all presumably obtainable at the public library . . . . but perhaps you know some or all of these works) Algernon Blackwood ("The Willows", "John Silence", "Incredible Adventures", "The Centaur") is—despite deplorable unevennesses & lapses into the namby-pamby—probably the greatest & sincerest living exponent of this form of expression. My own bunglings are not to be taken seriously. There are merely well-*meant*—but are in the main definite failures. I grow more & more dissatisfied with them, & write less & less as my inability to say what I want to say becomes increasingly apparent.

Yrs most sincerely,

H. P. Lovecraft

[5]    [TLS, JHL]

April 24, 1935

Dear Mr. Lovecraft:

I've just written Wm. Crawford offering him any of my stories except Shambleau, Black Thirst and Black God's Kiss, which are the three Mr. Barlow wants. I didn't know exactly how to offer my lesser tales without offending him, and don't yet know what I'll say if he writes insisting on having these in his book. I can't very well use the "pearls before swine" metaphor to him, and feel very awkward about the whole matter.

He is doing one good thing, anyhow—getting some of your work in a form available to people like me, who discovered fantasy too recently to have read those of the classics of weird literature which don't appear in book form. I've read so few of the stories you've written, and they've all been so excellent that it's infuriating to think how many more just as grand I'll never even see.

Speaking of which, it makes me a little angry to hear you decrying your own work. Only you, of course, know how far short of what you wanted to say the actual writing fell, but to us who never glimpsed the heights in your mind the stories themselves seem too splendid to be criticized at all, even by their writer. (Fulsome, perhaps, but perfectly true!) The best weird story I ever read was, I think, your "The Outsider" which I ran across in a volume of bound copies of WT which Mr. Barlow forwarded to me.

And close to that, for me anyhow, runs Robert E. Howard's "Worms of the Earth". Perhaps it was because that was the first of his stories I had read, and brought home to me very vividly the possibilities of that type of fiction, even when it appears in the pulps. I am a tremendous admirer of Mr. Howard's work. At his best he is very near perfection, it seems to me, and even at his goriest and blood-and-thundery-est there's a lusty vitality about everything he writes that makes the story engulf one in the vividest, most living sort of way.

Also have just written Clark Ashton Smith for a copy of his "Double Shadow, etc." the advertisement for which you enclosed in your last letter. He is another fantasy writer whose work it is such a pleasure to read, and for almost opposite reasons from those that make R. E. Howard's writing so good. Exquisite and fantastic enough to lift one clear out of the present. I'm awfully glad of the opportunity to get more of his work to read.

Mr. Barlow loaned me some of the CAS drawings—just little tentative sketches and preliminary water colors mostly—that were a revelation. It's possible, with words, to create an illusion of incredible and impossible things actually happening, but I would never have believed it possible to create the same effect with pen and ink and color. Some of these dreadful little heads were so horribly *possible,* even in their incredibility. It happened that I was ill the day I received them, and had a little fever that night, and those gargoyle faces and little animal and insect heads that somehow had so strong a hinting of humanity about them peered at me around the bedposts most of the night. I can still see them! Br-r.

I haven't yet had an opportunity to read The Golem.[1] Have been awfully busy, and want to devote a whole evening to it when I can be sure I won't be interrupted. And an evening when I'm not going to be alone in the house! I'm a very suggestible and credulous female, and believe implicitly most of the things I read, at least while reading them.

Thanks again for your advice. I wish I could tell you how I appreciate it, and how much it means to me to know that one of your standing thinks enough of my writing to take an interest in it. I'm much encouraged.

Sincerely,
Catherine Moore

*Notes*

1. By Gustav Meyrink.

[6]    [AHT 9.1]

66 College St.,
Providence, R.I.,
April 27, 1935.

Dear Miss Moore:—

Regarding the quality of my efforts—I don't think I'm too severe in my latter-day judgments. Considering the *length of time* I've been trying to do this kind of thing, I certainly ought to be able to produce something passable—yet how abysmally even the best of my products falls below Blackwood's "Willows" or Shiel's "House of Sounds" or Machen's "White People" or de la Mare's "Seaton's Aunt" or James's "Count Magnus" or Poe's "Usher" or (apart from the really macabre vein) Dunsany's "Idle Days on the Yann" or "City of Never"! "The Outsider" is not one of my own favourites—it is too mechanical to suit me . . . too much of a cheap Jack-in-the-Box ending. Of my stuff, I like "The Colour Out of Space", "Erich Zann", "The Picture in the House", "Dagon", "At the Mountains of Madness", "Pickman's Model", "The Cats of Ulthar", "The Strange High House in the Mist", & perhaps one or two others. Some of my effusions are so bad that I've disavowed them—stricken them from my list—& others (such as "The Hound", "The Tree", "Herbert West", &c.) will probably follow sooner or later.

Howard's "Worms of the Earth" is certainly a tremendous thing—which captivated me profoundly despite the way the Roman civilisation is traduced. I have a curious feeling of kinship & identification in connexion with the Roman world—so that (despite a lack of any blood link) I feel myself instinctively a Roman in surveying any historic era behind A.D. 500. My own Nordic forbears become, in my imagination, "those barbarians beyond the Rheno-Danubian frontier"—& I literally see red when anyone attacks the Respublica of the Scipiones & the Caesars . . . . as Howard most savagely & repeatedly does. But in the case of this story my admiration outweighed my resentment, & I was prepared to forgive any of the anti-Roman digs . . . . . even though my own perspective of Britannia Romana is that of a legionarius in the ranks of Legio XX under C. Suetonius Paullinus, or of Legio II Augusta under Sextus Iulius Frontinus . . . . . . which latter, by the way, is the one that in A.D. 78 established the camp of Isca Silurum forming the nucleus of Machen's "Hill of Dreams". "Two-Gun Bob" will never be a hack because he puts so much of himself into his work—even his most ostensibly mercenary work. He *is* King Kull or Conan or Bran—or whatever may form the subject of any given tale. And not even what Clark Ashton Smith calls his "monotonous manslaughter"[1] can spoil the vividness of his results. Nor do I know of anyone else who can throw such an aura of unholy, palaeogean antiquity about a lonely jungle ruin or a Cyclopean crypt beneath some mouldering, aeon-weighted city of horror & decay. Of all R.E.H.'s work I think I like the "Kull" stories most—though some of the newer things are fine. That "Queen of the Black Coast"—which appeared last spring or summer—flowered out into sheer poetry in places.

But for sustained magic & subtle colour it is hard to touch Klarkash-Ton, High-Priest of nighted Tsathoggua. Poet—artist—fantaisiste—nobody else has yet produced such an exhaustless & exuberant stream of rich, maturely polished fantasy of every sort. I am sure you will find the contents of "The Double Shadow" highly impressive. My favourite items are "The Maze of the Enchanter", "The Double Shadow", & "A Night in Malnéant". Has Barlow ever lent you any volumes of C.A.S.'s poems—especially "Ebony & Crystal", with the stupendous "Hashish-Eater"? If not, ask him—or me—to do so. C.A.S. the poet would be a revelation to those who know only C.A.S. the fictioneer. Glad you have seen some of his drawings—which are like nothing else on earth . . . . except the efforts of his admiring imitators. They certainly are diabolically well-adapted to haunting the couch of fever!

By the way—has Barlow ever shewed you any of his *own* drawings . . . much on the order of C.A.S.'s? They are astonishingly clever, & if he has not sent any, I'll be glad to supply the deficiency with a representative loan. He started as a Smith disciple, but has developed a distinct method of his own. His present art studies at the Corcoran Gallery will probably give him a better technical grounding than Smith has. Some of his clay modelling, too, is extremely good. Has he ever sent you photographs of the Cthulhu bas-relief he made for me, or the elephant-god statuette modelled for good old William Lumley of Buffalo?

Another weird artist—& perhaps the most technically advanced of all— is Howard Wandrei, brother of Donald & author of many good stories of his own. His work is in a totally different vein from Klarkash-Ton's & Barlow's—in the tradition of Sime & Harry Clarke.[2]

[. . .]

*Notes*

1. It is not clear that Smith ever said these words in regard to Howard's work. In a letter to HPL ([11 September 1931]), he wrote: "Robert E. Howard's omnipresent gore-spattering is surely getting monotonous, but I fear it will prove a hard fault to eradicate" *Dawnward Spire* 324. Later (20 June 1936), HPL wrote to Smith: "Two-Gun's serial is really splendid despite the 'monotonous manslaughter' & confusing nomenclature" *Dawnward Spire* 644.

2. HPL refers to the celebrated weird artists Sidney H. Sime (1867–1941), who illustrated many of Lord Dunsany's books, and Harry Clarke (1889–1931).

[7]    [TLS, JHL]

Tuesday May 7, 1935

Dear Mr. Lovecraft:

I wish I could tell you what a gorgeous prospect it is to be looking forward at last to reading your stories that I've missed. I've checked on your list those I've seen. Also, since I assume you do not type, I've given myself the pleasure of making three copies of the list for you in the event you want to use it again. It was fun—I get a tremendous kick out of typing lists and drawing red lines, and it's actually a pleasure to write the names of those stories. There's only one other thing I ever typed just for the enjoyment of feeling those beautiful words slip under my fingers—Thornton Wilder's one-act play "Child Roland to the Dark Tower Came". Have you read that? There's a queer, dark enchantment about it like nothing I've ever read anywhere else.

On the subject of titles, I envy you your ability. The most painful part of writing, so far as I'm concerned, is naming the stories. Mr. Wright more or less takes it out of my hands sometimes, as in the case of a story scheduled for mid-summer sometime, which he is calling "The Cold Grey God". I'm getting a regular spectrum of colored gods, staring with black and working slowly upward thru grey toward goodness knows what.

The other day I got desperate about this book-publishing idea, and since I didn't seem to be getting anywhere trying to decide for myself, went over to Bobbs-Merrill one noon and talked to an assistant editress who of course had never heard of Crawford, but suggested I should have a contract to avoid any chance of trouble later. Also said they'd be very glad to see my stories, though warned me there was very little chance of their wanting to do anything with them themselves, since books of that type so seldom sell. In this case, don't you think Crawford himself could do a better job of selling, since he can reach the limited audience directly, as one of themselves? Have you thought about having a contract? Have you thought we have no real way of checking up to see how many he actually sells? The Bobbs-Merrill woman told me he would simply have to be trusted, since there's no way of being sure he's splitting the profits on all that are sold. She offered to go over the contract and see that it is OK when I get it.

I am still quite sure that you are not giving your own stories their due. Even the few I've read convince me of that. Eric[h] Zann needn't yield second place to *anything*, by anyone. That's final! And I'd rank any one of your stories against any of Poe's. I don't like him. He's dank. You can get that same dark horror without the miasmic clamminess that simply drips from everything he did. And I'm perfectly sure that as I read more of your work I'm going to grow more and more set in my opinion. Some of those titles are so very promising—Beyond the Wall of Sleep, or The Whisperer in Darkness, or The Strange High House in the Mist. Lovely!

Isn't it queer what a curious pride one has in ancient Rome? I've felt it too, at odd times, about the oddest things. In Sherwood's "The Virtuous Knight", for instance, in the scene where the old monk is pointing out to the boy from the castle-top the Roman road which still runs thru the English countryside, and the boy makes some remark about how God's river takes the easiest path, while the road the Romans build runs straight over every obstacle, in an arrogant, unbroken line. I've put all that badly, but perhaps you can understand the odd little thrill of pride that went over me when I read it? And I've devoured all of Naomi Mitchison's books and stories—do you know them?—and Robert Graves' two Claudius books. For some reason am remembering Don Byrne's line "Roman legionaries swinging northward with their brazen helmets and their bear-skin tunics and their songs of farewell to Romans and the red mouth of Lalage".[1] Surely Roman soldiers didn't wear bear-skins? but it's a lovely sentence. "When I left Rome for Lalage's sake, by the Legions' road to Rimini—She vowed her heart was mine to take With me and my sword to Rimini—till the Eagles fly from Rimini."[2] And didn't you feel a delicious little thrill of recognition and pleasure when in that "ASTOUNDING" story "Sidewise thru Time" (was that it?)[3] in the overlaps of various eras a detachment of Roman soldiers came marching down a modern suburban street? They looked so blessedly familiar!

I am expecting the CAS "Double Shadow, etc." any day now. I had a note from him Saturday saying it was on the way. Yes, Barlow has lent me "Ebony and Crystal" and the "Hashish-Eater" is haunting me still. I am so sorry for people who don't like that sort of thing—they miss such an awful lot! There must be very few people who can produce prose, poetry and drawings of such superlative quality.

No, I've never seen any of Barlow's drawings, but am awfully anxious to—hadn't known he'd really done any. He's spoken of scribblings and sketches, but somehow left the impression he'd never turned out a finished pictures. Could you let me see some of them? And the Cthulhu bas-relief and the elephant god? I've missed too much!

I'm returning the Wandrei drawings reluctantly. Barlow had sent me a photographic enlargement of one of them, but I'd never seen any of the others. The photos are only a tantalization—you just realize the details there, without being able to make it out clearly. In colors they must be breathtaking.

Please don't say nice things about my attempts at drawing, or I'll disbelieve what you say about my writing. For I've no illusions about my pictorially artistic products, and I *am* beginning to cherish a budding hope that the things I write may be better than they'd seemed to me. With infinite labor I can occasionally turn out a *fairly* accurate anatomical drawing, but there's nothing meritorious about the things I sketch and I know it. Wish I did have the ability to do so many things well—like CAS.

You were right about "The Golem". Reading it in broad day was no insurance against its subtle assaults upon reality. "No actual monsters jump out of its pages", but even tho I read it on a sunny Sunday afternoon, in a deck-chair in the sunshine, it left me cold and chilly inside, and a bit glassy-eyed. I remember so vividly having wakened somewhere in grey night and seeing dusty moonlight falling thru bars on just such a littered floor as P.[4] awakened to see in the Golem's room. I can't have, of course, but the book is so vivid I do remember it clearly. It was ugly. I haven't quite finished, but will forward it to Miss Sylvester soon, as Barlow has requested.

I'm looking forward with the highest pleasure—and an almost unbearable impatience!—to seeing your work that I've missed. The Recording Angel is no doubt setting down in a golden book your good deed in offering me the opportunity to read it!

Sincerely,

Catherine Moore

[P.S.] You'll find the list of your stories probably needs correction, and I've left blanks in one or two places where I wasn't sure about a name.—O dear! It's just occurred to me you may be one of the many who dislike typed work except when it's absolutely necessary. If so, please forgive my gratuitous offering! It is meant well, anyhow.

C M.

*Notes*

1. CLM refers to the Irish novelist Donn Byrne (born Brian Oswald Patrick Donn-Byrne; 1889–1928). The work in question is *A Party of Baccarat* (New York: Century Co., 1930), viii; as *The Golden Goat* (London: S. Low, Marston & Co., 1930), 3.

2. Rudyard Kipling, "Rimini," ll. 1–4.

3. Murray Leinster, "Sidewise in Time" (*Astounding Stories*, May 1934).

4. Athanasius Pernath, ostensible protagonist of *The Golem*.

[8]  [from AHT 9.3]

[c. mid-May 1935]

[. . .]

Another thing that always interested me was De Quincey's recurrent opium-dream in which the words Consul Romanus (more impressive to him than "King" or "Emperor") were constantly repeated, whilst there "came sweeping by, in gorgeous paludaments, Paullus or Marius, girt around by a company of centurions, with the crimson tunic hoisted on a spear, & followed by the alalagmos of the Roman legions."[1] This interests me the more because, without the aid of the poppy, I have always had very curious Roman dreams—invariably laid in some western *province* rather than in Italy itself (though *I* am always (unlike my waking self) a native Roman of the old hawk-nosed, broad-templed Italic stock . . . Latian, Sabine, Samnite, Oscan . . . ), & with myself generally a minor civil or military official. The *detail* & apparent duration of some of these dreams is exceedingly singular—& their lifelike vividness is impossible to exaggerate. Perhaps the most vivid of all occurred late in October 1927, when I dreamed I was a provincial quaestor in Hispania Citerior—at some time vaguely placeable as late in the republican age . . . say

B.C. 60 or 70. The dream seemed to cover three days in continuous succession, & had a terrific nightmare ending. My name was L. Caelius Rufus, & I seemed to be in the small city of Calagurris on the Iberus. I was having all sorts of trouble adjusting a matter which had been referred to me by Tib. Annaeus Mela, the half-Iberian aedile of the village of Pompelo at the foot of the Pyrenees. There had been some hideous threats from a strange race who dwelt in the mountains, & Mela wanted a cohort of the XIIth Legion (encamped at Calagurris) for protection. Cn. Balbutius, legatus of the legion, wouldn't let him have it, but he had appealed to the proconsul P. Scribonius Libo at Tarraco, & Libo had ordered Balbutius to accede to the request. Or rather (the dream is rusty after nearly a decade) he asked me to appeal to Libo, & I had done so. The *worry* I felt at all these moves was distressingly real. Finally Balbutius gave Mela the fifth cohort under Sextus Asellius, and we all rode north to Pompelo (I was in a litter with six Illyrian bearers), whither Libo had preceded us. I can see that village yet—with crude, whitewashed houses, wooden amphitheatre, & new Corithian-columned curia—the only decent building in the place. The population was a curious mixture of Roman colonials, Celtiberi, Greeks, Carthaginians, & assorted foreigners. There were all sorts of arguments among Libo, Mela, Balbutius, Q. Trebellius Pollio (Libo's secretary) & myself, and in the end we decided to send the cohort into the hills on the night before the Kalends of November when the strange dark people (Miri Nigri) were expected to give trouble during their semi-annual rites to the *Magnum Innominandum* they worshipped. It was, by the way, a cavalry cohort. Well, we went—with a young half-Spaniard named T. Accius as a guide. After a while it grew so steep that we had to leave our horses with a guard of ten men and climb the narrow defile on foot. Then—very suddenly—we heard the horses we had left behind us *screaming* with hideous terror. The young guide seemed to know *why* they screamed, & instantly killed himself with a sword snatched from P. Vibulanus the centurio. Then blackness descended & snuffed out the stars; hellish laughter sounded on the hills; monstrous fires burst out atop distant peaks; shapeless titan shadows leaped in the sky; & a cold wind wound around us like a snake. There was screaming & trampling & delirious panic then—everybody but old Publius Libo seemed to go mad. He said: *"Malitia vetus—malitia vetus est—venit—tandem venit—"* And then I woke up—as thoroughly scared as I had ever been in my life or have ever been since. Not long afterward I wrote up the entire dream in some detail in the course of a letter to Long—& it impressed him so much that he asked permission to incorporate it into a story he was then writing. I let him do it—& the completed narrative ("The Horror from the Hills"—*Weird Tales* Jan. & Feb. 1931) contains my epistolary account in the original wording . . . put into the mouth of a character.[2] Some day I may write a tale with a Roman background—perhaps about some primal horror unearthed in Africa by the southerly expeditions of C. Suetonius Paullinus (A.D. 41) & of Maternus. Or

I might get back at Two-Gun by having a single cohort of the VIth Legion decapitate & otherwise dismember an entire tribe of his precious barbarians! S. P. Q. R.! Alala!

## Notes

1. From Thomas De Quincey (1785–1859), *Confessions of an English Opium-Eater* (1821), Part III, Section III.

2. HPL's account of the dream (as contained in a letter to Donald Wandrei, 3 November 1927) was published as "The Very Old Folk" (see *CF* 3.494–500).

[9]    [TLS, JHL]

Monday May 27, 1935

Dear Mr. Lovecraft:

You can't possibly imagine how delighted I was to get those two packages, enclosing so many delicious tales by HPL! I have read nearly all of them by now, and will be returning them soon. Read CTHULHU yesterday in a half-hour literally wrenched out of the day's program (I never have half the time I need and am always away behind in everything. And your stories do demand leisure to get the full savour of their artistry. They're one thing you don't want to hurry over.) Anyhow, you really had me reeling and dizzy with the geometry of Cthulhu's city. You are almost too vivid sometimes!

Some of those Barlow sketches were quite up to CAS standards—or almost, anyhow. I had no idea he was so good at it. And the sculp[t]ing was good too. I'm returning the Cthulhu plaque. He's a holder-outer—never mentioned a word of all that to me.

I would very much like to have a complete file of the late *Fantasy Fan*, of which I've heard so much and seen so little. I'm feeling a bit abject at accepting so much from you—will have to look over that packet of typed stories before I return them and see what I can do. Really, typing isn't bad once you've developed the requisite set of shoulder-muscles. And when it's bread-and-butter for you, there's no choice in the matter. Once you've got used to the physical effort, there's as much pleasure in turning out a neat copy as in producing a fine bit of embroidery or a sketch or a short story. All this applying to something brief, of course. I do extra typing work when I can get it, and by the time you've finished a 150-word [*sic*] MS the pleasure of production wears a little thin.

Lately I've been working on a family record for one of the local 400, and it's intensely interesting. Some of it goes back to very ancient Wales, 960 or thereabouts, and the names in it are simply incredible. I wish I'd made a note of some of them; the imagination boggles at even attempting to reconstruct a sample. In the 12th Century the name God's-Hill began an evolution which passed through stages of Tot-hill and Totyl and eventually became Tuttle. And the Ayres family name originated when their earliest forebear pulled a smashed-in helmet off William the Conqueror's face, restoring "The ayer which I breathe" to the Duke. Then there are any number of wills dividing slaves and feather beds and stills and silver, and several sons and daughters scattered through the centuries cut off with literally one shilling "and no more". I'm still full of the subject, and experiencing vague stirring of ideas in the back of my mind, though nothing definite to write about yet.

Anyhow, I'm glad *you* were glad to get the lists I typed. The pleasure was all mine—really. Those lovely names—it was as much fun to write them as it is to—oh, feel satin or fur or run your fingers thru sifted flour.

Which brings us around to the subject of CHILDE ROLAND TO THE DARK TOWER CAME. I must blushingly admit knowing nothing whatever about Childe Roland save a fragment of unidentified verse, "Dauntless, the slughorn to his lips he set, And blew 'Child Roland to the Dark Tower came.'"[1] Will have to look Browning's lines on the subject. Where shall I find them? [*marginal note:* (What do you know about the Roland to the Dark Tower legend?)] Possibly that quotation is from his poem. Also have wept bitterly over Roland's death when, in my angel infancy I read—something. Can't remember. Chanson de Roland? It was all so long ago. I'm enclosing a copy of Wilder's play for you—for keeps. I have my own here. No, he doesn't seem to know anything at all about the origins of the legend, simply accepts it in its entirety, like manna from the ravens, toys lightly with it for one act and dismisses it again. The whole thing is extremely shadowy—almost non-existent—and the charm of the play lies wholly in its magical atmosphere. Even that, I'm afraid, isn't as breathlessly lovely as it was when I read it first, about five years ago.

Whenever I recommend anything, you must bear in mind that probably my view of it was obscured by Wordsworthian trailing clouds of glory. In my teens so many things were almost unbearably lovely. I was damp-eyed with pure bliss over Dunsany's "King of Elfland's Daughter"—reading it on a hot, still, summer afternoon full of a thick enchantment so exactly like the book I was in danger of getting lost in the story and never finding my way out. It's a pity that era of painfully acute perception doesn't last forever. Or maybe a mercy!

I had a very severe illness at 15—scarlet fever, measles and mastoiditis all mixed up together—and at that most impressionable age went through a long while of delirium and fever and twisted impressions of the most commonplace things that, perhaps, explains my aversion to the Poe type of writing. You see, I *know* what it's like to experience that horrible, dank, miasmic atmosphere for hours together, and don't like to be reminded of it even in the words of a genius. There were times when the vine-leaves across the window and the step of the nurse on the carpet-nap were unbearably loud; and sometimes the sunshine was the ugliest, garish shade of yellow you ever saw, and the green grass looked like poison. And I know what it must be like to be mad, when everything is all muddled and horrible, and you're just conscious enough to know that everything's awfully wrong, and can't do anything about it. So my case against Poe is, after all, a strictly personal one. The point is, I suppose, that he's too terribly adept at creating the atmosphere he affects. I dislike him because he *is* a genius. (There! That proves the immortality of genius. I spoke of him all the way thru my little speech in the present tense.)

That reminds me, too, why I couldn't quite enjoy your CALL OF CTHULHU yesterday. In my lexicon of ailments must be included the early infant disorders that must somehow have induced the awful dreams I used to have of a place—no, nothing so localized as a place—an *existence* wherein I used to get lost, sometimes even just by shutting my eyes, without going to sleep—where nothing was at all describable in terms of physical things, because I wasn't aware thru the senses at all. There was a greyness over everything that was a greyness of the mind, not of the light, and nothing had size, yet there were awful *bignesses* outside the bounds of any mere dimensions. And there was an instability of the ground underfoot—only it wasn't ground and there was no "underfoot"—it was rather like an instability of anything basic in which to build one's consciousness. And your description of the men crawling around the edges of the acre-sized door that was neither inclined nor horizontal nor perpendicular brought on, somehow, a vivid remembrance of those almost forgotten dreams. You'll have to forgive the detail in the above. I never really worked the thing out in words before. Heretofore it just *was*—and Mother couldn't understand why I didn't want to go to bed. Well, will probably cash in on my early distresses—that paragraph has all the earmarks of a story nucleus.

Your own Roman dream was one of the most impressive and vividly horrible things I remember reading. The moment when the horses screamed and the young guide instantly killed himself! When you talk about Rome I do get so burstingly patriotic. And homesick. Like the hero of Mason's "The Three Gentlemen"—have you read it?—presenting three incarnations of the same person, one as a Roman legionary, one as an Elizabethan gentleman and one as a modern. The original, to whom live [*sic*] wasn't worth living outside Rome, was sent abroad to serve and never saw home again, and the ache for the Eternal City lived down the centuries in his descendants. The Elizabethan dreamed of a slanting, shop-lined street in a city he never saw or identified even in dreams, and the modern, visiting Rome for the first time, pointed to the dome of St. Peter's and said "What's that *new* thing?"

There's only one incident in dreams that I connect with Rome, but it's intensely vivid, tho only a snatch wherein I was being carried down a road, broad and wet with late rain and the sunset shining red in the puddles. The road wound around a long orchard hill, and on the right side the land dropped away to a city in the middle distance where the lights were beginning to bloom mistily. The slaves had just lighted torches. Then I stopped the litter and got out and ran up through a blooming apple orchard with thunder rising purple behind the trees, and I was choking and bursting with a violent and unidentified emotion so great I didn't stop to pick up the sandal I lost, but ran on thru the cold, wet grass without it, my skirt-hem all draggled with the rain, toward someone who was waiting out of sight behind the trees. I woke up in violent excitement, and am still wondering what it was all about.

You will enjoy the Claudius books when you get them. And by all means read Naomi Mitchison's "The Corn King and the Spring Queen". It's an enormous volume not much shorter than Anthony Adverse,[2] and deals in the most vivid and convincing detail with a barbarian girl (who incidently [sic] works casual magic now and then) all her family and friends, a Spartan girl et al., and their experiences in Rome, Sparta, Alexandria and the barbarian hinterlands. The thing is as good, almost, as a real tour of the places she tells about. You have the feeling of having actually lived in Sparta and Alexandria. It must have taken years to get together. I don't know just how accurate it is—she calls her barbarian heroine Erif Der, which when spelled backward doesn't exactly impress one as a genuine name. But it's well worth reading just for the experience. (Warning—I haven't read it since about 1929. But later books of hers still impress me vividly with the reality of her characters and background, so it can't fall much short of my memory's ecstasies.)

Incidently—now I'm off!—Mrs. Mitchison has a curious ability to invest her stories with a sort of material, physical *horror* worlds removed from the Poe–Machen–*Lovecraft* school, yet real as a slap in the face. Her latest book, one I've read this year, tho the name escapes me just now—deals with a Spartan family living just the sort of modern, matter-of-fact, vividly detailed life as we lead now.[3] She does that so awfully well, putting in the roast-beef-on-Sunday, dishes-in-the-sink touches until you could step right into a Spartan day without even noticing the change. And then suddenly a political situation goes wrong or something—I'm hazy on details there—and the whole family is sold into slavery. *Bang,* just like that. It couldn't be more of a shock if the same thing happened to me right now, she'd got the casual daily life so exactly that it didn't seem there could ever be a change. What happened afterward is not pleasant reading, but it certainly does drag you right into the midst of events. And that's where the horror comes in. You suffer vividly with the cruelly abused slaves. The book goes on to show how three or four of the members of the family adapted themselves to their new condition—how the young wife rose above the degradation of slavery to a brutal barbarian farmer, how her husband reacted to the environment he was too strong to break under and too stubborn to accept, how the brother's vicious nature prompted him to rise, through cunning and avarice, to freedom and slaveholding himself and to visit upon his own slaves all the tortures he had undergone. Oh, it's a grand book. But as I say, not pleasant reading, nor are any of her stories, especially if you're susceptible to the sort of dull horror that attends most of the situations she presents.

     \*\*\*                     \*\*\*

Yes, I've finished the "Double Shadow" by now. And you were right, as I knew you'd be. It was all I had expected of it. I'd like to see "The Star-Trader" [*sic*]. If it's even related to "Ebony and Crystal" I know what to expect.

I've read the "Bal Macabre"[4] you mentioned. No, I've never read anything of Hodgson's. I'll write to Mr. Koenig, I think, and get in on the circulation list. What a lot I've been missing!

Thanks again, any number of times, for the grand installment of stories you sent. They're almost spoiling me for the coarser fare presented in WT and Astounding—the only two of the pack I read now. In fact, haven't finished my last Astounding yet. It's mediocre this month, anyhow. I shall be returning the group soon and hoping hard for more.

Very gratefully,

Catherine Moore

P.S. I do hope the enclosed Wilder one-act play won't be too much of a disappointment to you. The more I look at it the frailer it seems, and there are only shreds of the lovely dark magic that veiled it when I first read it years ago. It will be interesting to see how it strikes you. Incidently, Wilder was in the bank here a year or so ago. He's a friend of our young president, and was spending a few days with him. A sandily brown, moustached, youngish man.

cm

[HPL's notes, on envelope (front). Underscores indicate obliterated text:]

Childe Roland to the D. T. came
    Thornton Wilder

HPL stories
genealogy—Welsh names
Barlow drawings   printing
     daemoniac & _____ry blocks
FF (Hornig visit)
Lumley letter
Koenig books &c.
typing _____ &c.
Childe Roland
Dunsany
Star-Treader—Double Shadow—Bal Macabre
impressions & dreams
               fever—
Rome _____

_____ _____
_____
     photographs—keep
Kentucky _____

_____ Renaissance _____
Travels generally—
photographs
Moe episodes—

_____

Florida

notes ____n't

Ansd.

[(back):]
Many knights sought to take D. T. but failed
Browning's poem 1st person

The round squat turret, blind as the fool's heart
Built of brown stone, without a counterpart
In the whole world.[5]

Roland (Orlando)—Count of Mans & Knight of Blaives—Son of Duke Milo of Aiglant & Bertha, sister of Charl. Sword—Durandel (Durandal) Horse—Veillantiff (Veglian[tino] brave, loyal, simple. Comm. rear guard when return from Spain. A[mbushed] in Pyrenees (Roncesvalles) & perished [with] all his men—the M[erovingian?] Ch's army. (778):

Therouldes Chanson
Boiardo's Orlando
Ariosto's Orlando

Enchanted horn

Dark Tower

Childe Rowland young[est] brother of one Helen, g[uided] by Merlin, he undertook [to] bring his sister back from [Elfland] whither she has been taken [by] fairies—He succeeded.

repellent landscape

*Notes*

1. The epigraph to Part V of Naomi Mitchison's *The Corn King and the Spring Queen.* It comes from Browning's "Childe Roland to the Dark Tower Came" (1855), stanza 34, ll. 5–6.

2. A bestselling historical novel by Hervey Allen.

3. Apparently *Black Sparta.* The book was first published in 1928, but reprinted in 1933.

4. By Gustav Meyrink.

5. Browning, "Childe Roland to the Dark Tower Came," ll. 182–84.

[10]    [TLS, JHL]

June 21, 1935

Dear Mr. Lovecraft:

First, thank you more than I can say for all those grand stories. I am returning them to Providence, reluctantly, and hoping hard for more when you get back. I can't remember anything more exquisitely *horrid* than that "Picture in the House". Reminded me of a dream I had not long ago of an icebox full of pieces of people. Don't I have delicate dreams? But perhaps your "Rats in the Wall" [*sic*] was a shade more horrible even than that. It takes real ability to deal with such subjects as deftly as you do.

That reminds me—remember in the end of "Rats in the Wall" when the man's speech went through a sharp reversal of Colonial English and Old English and on back through Sanscrit and to the caveman's grunts? (that was a beautiful touch!) Well, I've come across some Welsh names that seems really little more than primitive grunts and snorts—Cwyr, for instance, and Vron and Wenll. Then there's Afflech, Afflach, Gorddufu, dyffimysk, [*sic*] Tegayayr, Gwillim Gam, and lots of others, positively incredible. I suppose Gwillim is the forerunner of William. Gwillim Gam and Wenll were husband and wife along about 100 AD, but which was which would be hard to say. Wonder if Afflech and Afflach were twins? Neat names for twins, anyhow. In the Sat. Eve. Post years ago was a silly little poem that has haunted me ever since— "There's a city in Wales spelled C-W-M. A populous place as one counts it. I'd sing of its beauties except that—ahem—I do not know how to pronounce it." I have an awful weakness for the silliest verses. You might warn Mr. Barlow that I think I shall inflict some upon him the next time I write—I have an idea he might be amused.

That packet of postcards was delicious. I'm glad someone else has an affection as strong as mine for that sort of thing. I got such utter joy out of an advertising folder that railroad company with the air-conditioned cars put out last summer—you know, the "George Washington" and the "Lincoln" (was it?) cars and all the hysteria of self-admiration that they flooded the country with. (My syntax is perfectly appalling, I know.) Anyhow, these folders were filled with scraps of historical information, and pictures of Colonial houses and places where Washington had slept, and so forth. The house built for the "Lowlands Bride" was so lovely.

That "Old Gateway to Simonton House"[1] was so particularly beautiful that I wanted—O, the whole thing, gate and wall and trees and house and all. I wonder how long it will be before our modern architecture takes on that air of antiquity and irretrievably lost loveliness. One wouldn't really want to go back into those days—did you see Leslie Howard in "Berkeley Square"?[2] It illustrated so vividly the drawbacks to going backward into past times—but even knowing what an unsanitary, coarse-customed, non-bath-taking era it was doesn't help much when you look at the lovely old houses and feel the leisure and the peace that still haunt them and are lost forever now.

Not long ago we drove down thru Kentucky and stopped at the house where Foster wrote "My Old Kentucky Home", and it was so eloquent of the lost beauty of 1800 and the beautiful, sunny, courtly leisure that once paced American life. I'd love to have had slaves and worn hoops and ruffles and lived in as perfect a house as that—for about a week. Probably not longer!

Then there's a State Park about 80 miles south of here where an old pioneer village of about 150 years ago has been restored. It has age, but it's still raw and ungracious, tho intensely interesting. They say wolves and bears used to come down occasionally into the streets, and drunken trappers from the town tavern made the village quite unsafe for children to run about alone. (I never visit the place, and stop at that tavern where the most innocuous soft drinks are sold now, without thinking of that delicious and ridiculous song, "There is a tavern in the town!")[3] The mill has been made into a museum full of things so vivid of the past you'd almost think the pioneers who lived there would be turning in their graves, all restless because they left so much of themselves behind in the still preserved clothes, and the shoes that are stretched to the shape of their feet, and the pans and pots they cooked in and the worn saddles they used.

Before leaving that topic, I do want to ask if you saw the movie "Pursuit of Happiness".[4] It expressed so perfectly the atmosphere of delightful Revolutionary-days charm with which one automatically invests that period and which very likely it didn't possess at all. The movies can do that very skillfully sometimes—tho one suspects that when they do succeed as beautifully as they did in that it is pure accident.

Another thing I want to tell you about is the Rand-MacNally chart I've bought called a "Histomap" or something.[5] It shows the comparative power of all the nations of the world from 200 BC on down, done in map-colors and representing goodness knows what agonies of research. Somehow I had always had the complacent idea that the United States of America was the greatest of all earthly powers. If I'd stopped to think I'd have known better, but somehow never did until I saw with a shock the little blue wedge about four inches long on the five-foot chart which is all there is to the mighty USA. But Rome was tremendous, by far the greatest of all recorded historical nations, a vast pink blob spreading clear across the page and crowding everyone else of their time into little squeezed-up blue and purple patches. From 800 BC to 1500 AD that enormous pink expanse spreads. Assyria was huge too, in its day, and Egypt, up near the top, almost rivaled Rome. But the really startling thing is that from the very beginning, clear up among Ur and Chaldea and old, forgotten nations in history's dimmest dawn, and all down the page past Assyria and Egypt and enormous world-swallowing Rome, and past the Huns and the beginnings of European powers, and right down alongside

England and America—clear along the right-hand margin in one unbroken stream since history's first beginning come the Chinese. As it was in the beginning, is now and ever shall be. Tremendously impressive. I hadn't realized. All those little patchy peoples coming and going, pink and blue and green among the changing nations, Assyria starting and swelling and dwindling away, and Egypt, and huge Rome, and England coming, and the United States swelling out from 1776—and past all this in a yellow flood, China's ageless history pouring unbroken.

————

You must be having a grand summer. You can't imagine how I envy you traveling through just the country I want so much to visit myself. And then to Florida! Such luck! I'm green with envy.

Give Mr. Barlow my regards. It must be so nice for both of you, getting to spend a few weeks together. I'm keeping the postcards until I know whether you want them sent to Florida or Providence.

Enviously,

Catherine Moore

22d

P.S.

I just remembered the letter from Mr. Koenig saying he'd get in touch with you about letting me have some of his books, and mentioning the catalog you have. I'm looking forward to seeing the Hodgson books particularly.

*Notes*

1. "Old Gateway to Simonton House Built 1776 Charleston SC."

2. *Berkeley Square* (Fox Film Corp., 1933), directed by Frank Lloyd; starring Leslie Howard, Heather Angel, and Valerie Taylor. Based on the play by John L. Balderston. HPL saw the film four times, and it clearly influenced "The Shadow out of Time."

3. "There Is a Tavern in the Town," a traditional song and the anthem of Trinity College, Dublin, first appearing in William H. Hill's *Student Songs* (1883).

4. *The Pursuit of Happiness* (Paramount, 1934), directed by Alexander Hall; starring Francis Lederer, Joan Bennett, Charlie Ruggles, and Mary Boland.

5. John B. Spark, *The Histomap: Four Thousand Years of World History; Relative Power of Contemporary States, Nations and Empires* (Chicago: Histomap, Inc., 1931; printed and distributed in the U.S. by Rand McNally & Co., Chicago). 158 × 31 cm. HPL himself owned a similar map—the *Adams Synchronological Chart or Map of History* (Cincinnati: Strobridge & Co., 1871).

[11]    [AHT 9.3, 10.2]

℅ R. H. Barlow

Box 88

De Land, Florida

July 2, 1935

Dear Miss Moore:—

As I begin once more to catch up with my travel-disorganised correspondence, I have both of your highly interesting letters before me. It certainly pleases me immensely to learn that my more or less "complete works" did not prove disappointing. Later—when I get time & at my archives—I'll send some of the other items which you have not read. "The Picture in the House" expresses my feeling of horror at the curious air of mystery & alienage which pervades certain backwoods New England houses I have seen. Many people wonder why I don't exploit the traditional element of weirdness in the South—the brooding cypress swamps, the mouldering plantation-houses, the whispered negro lore, &c. &c. The fact is, however, that I can't feel the same deep, Gothic horror in any mild & genial region that I can in the rock-strown, ice-bound, elm-shaded hillsides of my own New England. To me, whatever is *cold* is sinister, & whatever is warm is wholesome & life-giving. . . . an echo, no doubt, of my own tropic-loving constitution. "The Rats in the Walls" was suggested by a very commonplace incident—the cracking of wall-paper late at night, & the chain of imaginings resulting from it. As for the *languages* represented in the atavistic passage—I don't recall including *Sanscrit,* though I did lift a sentence of *Celtic* (of which I know not a single word) from another story, "The Sin-Eater", by "Fiona McLeod" (William Sharp). This sentence, incidentally, was what brought me into correspondence with Robert E. Howard. It was—since I swiped it from a Scottish story—a *Gaelic* specimen, whereas of course the Celtic language of southern Britain was *Cymric.* R.E.H.—as an expert Celtic antiquarian— noticed the discrepancy, & thought I had adopted a minor theory that a Gaelic wave had preceded the coming of the Cyrmi to Britannia. He wrote Wright on the subject & Wright forwarded the letter to me—whereupon I felt obliged to drop a line to the mighty Conan exposing my own ignorance & confessing to my rather inept borrowing.

After your labours in the field of Welsh genealogy you must be a close rival of Two-Gun Bob so far as Celtic etymology is concerned. I have a Welsh line in my ancestry—Morris (of Clasemont, Glamorganshire)— Parry—Jenkins—Rhys—Parcell—&c. &c.—which purports to go back to some mediaeval monarch yclept Owen Gwynedd (if that's the way to spell it), but I have not studied its ramifications in detail. The bits of folklore & nomenclatural paradox which you have unearthed as by-products are surely delightful—even more so, no doubt, than many of the objects of your main research. The evolution of Tuttle (a common New England name) is especially interesting. As a supplement to the *building-up* which you cite, I can cite a case of *degeneration* occurring in the stagnant central-Massachusetts backwater which I once put into fiction as "Dunwich". Here a retrogressive family which sprang (or dropped) from the *Tuttle* tree has come to spell & pronounce its name as *Tootil* . . . . . certainly without any conscious reversion to the mediaeval Totyl! Many Welsh names certainly look as if they were not far from the troglodytic grunts concocted in the "Rats"! Whether Afflect & Afflack ((a) *Affleck* is a common New England surname. (b) Barlow insists—on good authority, he says,—that the family seat of James Boswell (Avchinleck) is *pronounced* "Affleck".) were twins I couldn't say—but *Gevillin* (or *Guillaume, Guglielmo, Guillermo, Liam,* &c. &c) is certainly *William*. I have an idea that the name of my regal forefather—Gwynedd or what-have-you—is an early form of the common name Gwinnett (Button *Gwinnett*, Georgian signer of the Dec. of Ind. . . . . . . Ambrose Gwinnett Bierce, &c. &c. &c.). That limerick on *Cwm* is surely brilliant—it delighted young Barlow, who will be equally appreciative of the other whimsical verses which you intend to show him. Old wills are always interesting—I have one of an eighteenth century ancestor who bequeathed endless *puter* dishes & cups, copper *kittles,* & *linning* (linen) & *woolling* (woollen) wheels to his numerous progeny. Incidentally, this document is in bad shape, & I intend to let Barlow (a wizard in all mechanically creative & restorative operations) fix it up in a skilled way with something he calls Japanese tissue.

You may be interested to know that on May 25, I had an agreeable visit from young Charles D. Hornig, erstwhile publisher of the ill-starred venture. He is a very pleasant & intelligent youth—reminding one slightly of Donald Wandrei except for a vaguely quasi-Semitic turn of features. He seemed to appreciate the archaic charm of venerable Providence quite keenly (it is not unlike his own Elizabeth, N.J.), & I showed him most of the historic high spots—including the hidden churchyard on the ancient hill, from among whose spectral tombs Poe first saw his fiancee Mrs. Whitman in her garden by moonlight. (I presume you know the Poe lore of Providence as well as of other places). I like Hornig very much—& certainly admire the competence which enables him to serve as editor of a full-fledged magazine—*Wonder Stories*—at the age of eighteen. He looks about twenty-two or twenty-three.

[. . .]

Glad to hear that you were not disappointed in "The Double Shadow". There's nobody quite like good old Klarkash-Ton! "The Star-Treader" (TREADER—not TRADER) includes C.A.S.'s early poems—written at & before the age of seventeen. It is just as remarkable as "Ebony & Crystal", even though it does not contain any such *tour de force* as "The Hashish Eater".

[. . .]

[12]    [TLS, JHL]

July 19, 1935

Dear Mr. Lovecraft:

This is one of those nasty, moist days in the 90°s when everyone simply welters in misery, and I shall try to forget my gelatinous surroundings in letter writing. I am returning the enclosures in your last letter, with considerable gratitude for having let me see them. Those photos of the hidden churchyard graves were particularly interesting. I was surprised at the windmills. Hadn't realized that they were once in use in New England. Not in that "Little Dutch Mill" form, anyhow. To me there is something infinitely fascinating in the very bricks and mortar of old buildings, somehow as if they had soaked in age and radiated it out again in all but tangible waves. There was a curious satisfaction in putting my hands on the worn old spongy bricks of the slave quarters at the "Old Kentucky Home" house I mentioned visiting in Kentucky. They *feel* interesting, full of soaked-in sunshine and antiquity. And there is no lovelier color than the mellow browny-red of very old bricks.

I certainly envy you your trip through southeastern New England. I shall do that myself someday if I have to wait until I'm 90. Isn't it fun just to ramble that way? I haven't had much opportunity to get off the beaten paths as you have. There isn't much country around here that isn't overrun with tourists and hot-dog stands. But there has come to be, for me, a certain delight in the smell of gasoline and hot concrete and middlewestern summer dust, simply because they typify the week-end trips we occasionally make with no particular end in view. Going up to the Fair last year and the year before was a sort of mixed pleasure—fun in the trip, and in the gay and gaudy Fair itself, even though so much of it was so very cheap. There was a gusto and garishness and wholeheartedness about that Fair that I've never met anywhere else. A pity it's over.

The trip to Kentucky was taken during a weekend of continuous rain, and there can't be anything anywhere much more beautiful than those great soft-looking, thickly wooded hills, mountainously steep, seen thru veils of slanting rain. That was once when we were really outside modernity. We saw ox-teams in actual use once or twice, and everyone goes about on horseback as a matter of course.

But there are so very few really old buildings within several days' journey from here that most of my admiration of ancient architecture has to be done at second or third hand. My grandmother's house, about 70 years old, was one of the real antiques of the town before it burned several years ago. I remember that when it had rained hard and the ground was soaked you could make out the tracks of a sunken wagon road that had once curved through the front yard, and that used to seem to me like the very breath of antiquity. For Indianapolis 70 years ago was a little muddy-streeted village, and there's nothing in the whole countryside but a moribund little log cabin or two that is any older than 75 at the most.

What an awful pity about the row of houses on your street that are to be pulled down. It makes me a little sick to think about such things. It's a blessing at least that the building to replace it isn't to be too awful. When I look at some of our local examples of ancient architecture—the gingerbread and scrollwork and monstrous little turrets, and think of the delicious little houses being pulled down there it becomes clearer than ever that there is no justice in this world.

I'm so anxious to see the views of Quebec you intend to get. That and New Orleans are my most passionately desired goals. Quebec in particular. How heavenly that great rock of houses must be. And I think there's nothing more eloquent of pure romance than streets broken by flights of steps, unless it's houses whose rooms are on different levels, so that you have to go up and down stairs on the same floor. Silly, but I've always connected streets and houses like that with my loveliest daydreams of perfection. Sometime, in about five years from now, when Prosperity has returned and I've quit my job and married and saved up the money, I'm going to drive to Quebec or perish in the attempt. In the meantime notice all the details and tell me about them.

I suppose you watched the eclipse of the moon the other night. Somehow I had expected it to go out completely, and was surprised at the translucency of the shadow, and particularly at the saffron-red that crossed the tarnished silvery surfaces that were still in shadow. Reminded me of—wasn't it King Charles?—who saw blood on the moon at the Battle of Naseby or somewhere?[1] And *that* reminds me of the Crosbie Garstin[2] poem which has always impressed me with its lovely rhythm:

A prince he went a-courting a princess of the Spains,
They decked Madrid in flags for him and bade the bugles sound,
The gallants rode before him with their black and scarlet trains,
The donnas wore their farthingales and curtsied to the ground.
But Olivares fooled him, and Steenie Vil[l]iers ruled him,
And the apple-bloom Maria, she was cold, ah, cold!
The pink and white Infanta, she did as she was told.

A king he stood a-waiting at a window in Whitehall,
They decked the town in black for him, the drums beat slow and stern—
. . . . the king, he looked upon his troops—the troopers looked away.
"I will uplift my heart," he said, "on this, my wedding day;
Heigh-ho—I go to meet a dark queen, who will not say me nay."[3]

In that, I think, is one of the most quietly eloquent lines I ever read—Charles, going out to be beheaded and "the king, he looked upon his troops—*the troopers looked away*." Almost, if not quite, as effective as my favorite of all lines ever written, that one about "Stout Cortez with his men—silent, upon a peak in Darien." Tho wasn't it really Balboa?[4] Such ignorance. I don't know anything. But anyhow— *"silent . . . upon a peak in Darien."* Isn't it lovely? You want to hold your breath. Or have I expressed myself about that before?

However, to get back to the moon, imagine how magnificent the eclipse must have looked from there. Wouldn't it have been a vision of a black Earth ringed with rainbowy haloes of atmosphere? I hope so. It sounds well, anyhow. Are you familiar with Dunsany's poem on that topic—Earth from the moon? His verses are not, of course, as magical as his prose, but sometimes he produces things almost as lovely. In this one the faulty metre somehow gives the poem a charm that smoothness would never have. Do you know it? the one that goes—

> It's dark tonight in the moon countries
> On the far side of its girth;
> It's dark in all the moon countries
> Where none see Earth.
>
> They never see Earth's splendor
> Rise like a silver hill
> Monstrously over the seabeds
> That no waters fill,
>
> —continents bright, and the seas
> Lucid as palest sapphires
> Sold by the Cingalese. . . .[5]

I can't remember the rest, but just now I think it's the loveliest poem ever written. Seas lucid as palest sapphires, sold by the Cingalese. . . .

I do envy you having seen and heard Dunsany, even though his thespian powers aren't equal to his—odear, that started out to be such a noble sentence, and now I can't think of the word I want to finish it. Anyhow you know what I mean. A better writer than actor. Is it in "Poltarne[e]s, Beholder of Ocean" that "—with solemn ceremony, they curse the tides of sea, and the moon looks down and hates them"? But I shall always remember as the very best of all that—"King of Elfland's Daughter" which I mentioned reading in my teens on that lovely summer afternoon. I can remember it now quite clearly, and the long shadows across the grass (it was at my grandmother's house that's burned now) and beyond the acre of lawn a high hedge with beeches drooping over it, and an actual haze of golden mist around everything in haloes, so that everything was blurred with gold. I have wondered since if the same scene would look half so beautiful to me now. There was something rather Wordsworthian, Trailing-clouds-of-glory about that afternoon that I think could never be recaptured. Things really *are* more enchanted in one's early teens than ever again afterward. Heaven—in short—lies about us in our infancy.

That reminds me—are you by any chance familiar with the Oz books?[6] I think it must have been them more than any other one thing that started me on a career of fantasy writing. They are, of course, a set of children's books, but so full of a delicious, engaging, solemnly real fantasy that I read them even yet with almost as much interest and certainly more deeply loving appreciation than I did in my childhood. I have the dear old battered set I accumulated at Christmases and birthdays from about five on, full of crayon scribbles and early attempts at drawing, and there is nothing pleasanter even now than a trip as nearly actual as a reader can embark on, into the Land of Oz again. I wonder if even now you wouldn't like them. If you enjoy Alice I'm sure you would.

Thanks for the information about Childe Roland and the Dark Tower.[7] I'm somehow glad there isn't much to be found on that subject. It's at its best half hidden in darkness. Awfully glad the Wilder playlet appealed to you. It's such a frail little thing, and yet so powerful[l]y and evanescently enchanting, at a first reading, anyhow.

Mr. Koenig has written several letters on the subject of my prospective entry to his library. He has sent me a list of recent additions and I am somewhat appalled by the immensity of the field—like a six-year-old in a candy shop. I want it all at once, and don't know where to begin. I have told him that I shall probably have to depend on you and him to select what I would enjoy, because for the most part titles are so unilluminating, and if you don't know the author either it's just guesswork. I am anxious to see the Summers works on vampires and witchcraft,[8] tho should warn you I'm extremely suggestible and hope the books aren't *too* vivid. I had some wisdom teeth pulled a month or so ago and went about for a couple of weeks, all together, with the taste of blood so constantly in my mouth that I almost—well, every time I looked in a mirror I didn't expect to see anything there at all. And whenever a bat went by I wondered if it was me.

I was so pleased with the sample sheet of the Frank Belknap Long book.[9] I wouldn't tell, even if I were in correspondence with him. It'll be a grand surprise. I was particularly impressed by the poem called, as I remember it, "The White People". "Out of the grass when the dew is wet Their houses lean and their hoards are set Deep in the woods that are not yet." and "—across the grass They crawl like shadows on a glass".[10] Reminds me somewhat of a poem I once ran across by, of all people, Eugene Manlove Rhodes—[11]

> Across the moonlit meadow we saw our lady pass,
> A silver singing shadow upon the shadowed grass,
> Her way was to the dim woods that lie along the sea
> Where we can never follow. *Aie,* lonely folk are we.

22d

(Slight intermission) Julius Schwartz has inveigled me into one of these chain-story things in which you are also scheduled to be drawn.[12] I wrote a first installment and mailed it to him on the 18th. Certainly not a brilliant thing by any means—it's hard to get very brilliant in three pages, especially if they're chiefly devoted to setting the stage—but the best I could think of just then. If it comes to you next, as I think it will, perhaps you can do better on the second installment. If you want to be bothered.

William Lumley must be a good soul. I was immensely pleased at his tribute, especially by the sentiment to the effect that success hadn't spoiled me. Bless him, do you suppose he pictures me enshrined in a palatial studio with secretaries circulating in the background and the public clamoring at the door? What about him, anyhow? Who is he and what does he do?

23d

That "Histomap" I was telling you about costs only $1.00, is put out by Rand-McNally and can be ordered through any stationery store, I imagine. I inquired at several here and was told that they could get it for me in a few days, but finally located one in the book department of a department store. If you can't find any I'll be glad to get one here and sent it on.

What a pity you missed seeing "Pursuit of Happiness". There was such a delicate naivete and charm about it that I was afraid to see it twice, tho I'd have liked to. And another picture with the same air of gayety, tho in a much robuster mood, was "Naughty Marietta".[13] I suppose the music in that was good—being tone-deaf and utterly uneducated in musical lines I can't say for myself—but it was the lightness and the laughter in the story that appealed to me, even over its background of conventional tragedy. (It's a misfortune to miss as much as I must do in the way of music, but it does give me a keener appreciation of the marching, thumping rhythm which is all I get out of songs, and the only kind that appeal to me are the strongly accented sort. Even in poetry—*vide* "A prince he went a-courting a princess of the Spains"—I get a keener and more sensual enjoyment out of the beating kind than from the sort that's purely "mental" like "The white mares of the moon Are rushing along the glass heavens"[14] which must be one of the loveliest of all poems. But then I suppose all that is true of most people?)

I started out to talk about "Berkeley Square", though. Do you think, too, of what you'd do if you were suddenly snatched back through time as happened in that? Ever since I read "The Connecticut Yankee"[15] in my early infancy I've had daydreams of how I'd manage in various centuries if something like that were to happen. How to arrange a comfortably livable house in the 17th century, or back in the 12th. How you'd manage eatable food and a decent amount of cleanliness without being burnt for a witch or put into a madhouse. (anachronism!) It's a fascinating thing to think about.

What fun you must be having in Florida. I am desperately jealous of your leisure and your work and your nearness to unlimited amounts of water. People who have lived near an ocean can't begin to understand the queer, overpowering-ness it can have on those unaccustomed to seeing such things. When I saw Lake Michigan several years ago for the first time since I was about 6, it knocked me breathless and speechless for all of five minutes, and the girl I was with actually wept a few tears in her surprise. It was a lovely bright blue, windy day, and I had those five minutes of nameless and trans-cendent emotion which comes only in youth. Trailing clouds of glory again. I'll probably never again experience so keenly that lovely lightness and brightness and tremulous-ness inside. It just doesn't happen after you've grown up. (There's something a bit ungainly in a young woman of 24-going-on-25 getting thrilly and rapturous over mere scenery. Reminds me of "And by him sported on the green His little daughter Wilhelmine, Who'd just turned twenty-eight.")[16]

I'm so anxious—to get back to the subject—to see some more of RHB's work. Don't forget that I'm to see a photograph of his latest "Thing" which you mentioned. Those little linoleum prints on the envelope were splendid. Which reminds me, how effective the Clark Ashton Smith dinosaur-bone sculpture must be. I don't want to miss reading "The Star-Treader", either.

Well, this had better be wound up before it takes on any more aspects of an endless diary. Three days' installments are enough. Write again soon, and at as great a length as you can possibly find time for. I can't tell you how I enjoy reading your letters.

Sincerely,<br>Catherine Moore

P.S. Haven't properly thanked you yet for the FF complete file. What a pity it had to stop. Surely there's a real need for something like that, without the strong science slant of FM. I enjoyed reading the copies you send immensely and was much annoyed because just it began to catch up with the stories and writers I'm familiar with it had to stop.

*Notes*

1. The Battle of Naseby, part of the English Civil War, was fought on 14 June 1645 be-tween King Charles I's Royalist army and the Parliamentarian New Model Army com-manded by Oliver Cromwell and Sir Thomas Fairfax. Cromwell's forces were victorious.

2. Crosbie Garstin (1887–1930), British poet and bestselling novelist.

3. "The Last Love" in *The Coasts of Romance*. CLM omits ll. 5, 13–14, and 16–17 in her transcription and also misquotes the poem quite a bit.

4. CLM refers to Keats's sonnet "On First Looking into Chapman's Homer" (1816), which tells of the author's astonishment at reading Homer as freely translated by the Elizabethan playwright George Chapman. The lines in question do indeed refer to the

Spanish conquistador Hernán Cortés when they should have referred to the Portuguese explorer Vasco Nuñez de Balboa, who crossed the isthmus of Panama in 1513 to glimpse the Pacific Ocean.

5. "At the Time of the Full Moon," *Saturday Evening Post* 201, No. 10 (8 September 1928): 74. In *Fifty Poems* (1929).

6. HPL does not seem to have read any of the seventeen Oz books by L. Frank Baum (1856–1919).

7. See letter 9 for HPL's preparatory notes on CLM's letter postmarked 22 May 1935.

8. Probably *The Vampire: His Kith and Kin* (1928) and *The Geography of Witchcraft* (1927).

9. HPL had sent a page proof from Long's *The Goblin Tower,* a small collection of poetry published by R. H. Barlow. HPL helped set the type when he visited Barlow in the summer of 1935.

10. "The White People," *WT* 10, No. 5 (November 1927): 633, ll. 1–3, 11–12.

11. Eugene Manlove Rhodes (1869–1934), American writer known as the "cowboy chronicler."

12. CLM refers to "The Challenge from Beyond," a round-robin story written with A. Merritt, HPL, Robert E. Howard, and Frank Belknap Long.

13. *Naughty Marietta* (MGM, 1935), directed by Robert Z. Leonard and W. S. Van Dyke; starring Jeanette MacDonald, Nelson Eddy, and Elsa Lanchester. Based on the operetta *Naughty Marietta* by Victor Herbert.

14. Amy Lowell, "Night Clouds," ll. 1–2. The lines actually read "The white mares of the moon rush along the sky / Beating their golden hoofs upon the glass heavens;".

15. Mark Twain, *A Connecticut Yankee in King Arthur's Court* (1889).

16. Robert Southey (1774–1843), "The Battle of Blenheim," ll. 5–6 (the last line quoted is not in the poem).

[13]    [AHT 10.2][1]

[c. late July 1935]

[Dear Miss Moore:—]
                    [. . .]

Yes—in the Chapman's Homer sonnet Keats really meant Vasco Nuñez de Balboa when he said "Cortez". But the effect is the same. The image is magnificent & unsurpassed in its way.

Old Bill Lumley certainly is a rare character. I really know nothing about him personally—except that he believes in all sorts of naive superstitions, & professes to have visited mysterious places in remote parts of the earth when a seaman long ago. Nepal, Angkor, interior China, Burma, India . . . all these places, he says, are old stamping-grounds of his. Once he slept in the ruins of a pre-human jungle temple & awoke twenty years older. He has a correspondent in the East whom he calls "The Oriental Ancient", and who once sent him a book which he dared not read save after ceremonies of purification which included the donning of a white robe. Bill has read all the occult books which exist, & most of those which don't exist. Every now & then he visits a place near Buffalo called "Ghost Valley", where a thin misty wraith appears & reveals to him secrets which may not be repeated. Old Bill is an author, too. His poems have a certain elusive, cryptic charm even before revision, & some day the world will behold his magnum opus in prose—"The City of Dim Faces". Bill is as generous as the day is long—& has twice made me presents of books .... once the Mahlon Blaine "Vathek",[2] & another time E. L. White's "Lukundoo". A rare child of nature—who undoubtedly believes most of the marvels he unfolds. Last year Barlow made him a clay model of an elephant-god which tickled him immeasurably—elephant-images being a specialty of his. I don't know what Bill's occupation is—although he refers to one now & then. His health is none too good, & he seems to be well along in years. I fancy he really was a mariner once upon a time, & wouldn't be surprised if some of his knowledge of Eastern seaports were real. He is genuinely—if less than critically—erudite in fantastic folklore, & even as proficient a scholar as Clark Ashton Smith finds his discourse on serpent-gods & other elder phantasms eminently worth listening to. His taste in weird fiction is really sound & discerning—so that you may consider his enthusiastic opinion of your work a genuine compliment. Good Old Bill!

[. . .]

*Notes*

1. Text here is part of AHT 10.2. See also CLM 11.
2. HPL refers to an edition of William Beckford's *Vathek,* illustrated by Mahlon Blaine.

[14]   [TLS, JHL; to R. H. Barlow and HPL]

(Postman's fingermark)

August 20, 1935

Gentlemen:

To your boundless amazement I shall now take typewriter in hand and write you a letter. Still further to shock you, I am enclosing the story you so kindly inquired about, and also—did I or didn't I send you WEREWOMAN? This burning question has haunted me all day, ever since I delved industriously into the stack of boxes and bales which I laughingly term my files and produced every story I ever wrote with the exception of the famous WW. I am probably being even more hen-brained than usual, but will enclose the carbon of WW which I have somewhere around, tho lurking in the back of my subconscious is a suspicion that I have already sent you the original. If so, pay no attention. Surely you have sufficient aplomb to withstand a sudden deluge of werewomen.

I'm sending the entire mass along with a temporary birthday gift for HPL and letters to both of you. According to your last letter HPL is responsible for nagging you into writing, after a brazen lapse of some years, while it was you originally who bullied him until he wrote me. A vic[i]ous circle for you two, but extremely convenient for me.

This GOBLIN TOWER sounds delicious. Don't forget you promised to let me have a copy. I've got that in writing, so don't backslide. Also all this about your most recent masterpieces sounds very enticing. I am very interested in seeing all but the boils you mentioned. You have my sympathy, but being not even a co-sufferer (I've never had one—knock-knock) I just can't work up the same interest which I confess to feeling over the sketch entitled A DREAM and the watercolor WITCHES' SABBAT, to both of which I look forward hopefully but without much hope, if that mean's [*sic*] anything to you. (I am purposely not erasing the apostrophe with which I just decorated means. It's so lovely I want you to see it. I can make some very amusing mistakes sometimes. Like the time I misspelled "where" to the intense delight of the person who caught it.)

Your printing office hath a lovely sound. Mention of the boat strikes a kindred note—my beloved bought himself a motor boat at the beginning of the summer, and has no time now for golf or any of his former loves. We spend our Saturdays chugging up and down the river which is usually very like so much thick soup, but really quite lovely a mile or so up from the boathouse where the millionaires' mansions back down to the water and picnic baskets and paper napkins no longer bob about in midstream.

I am simply bursting with aimless gossip about this and that, but I must mail this package and at least get it postmarked August 20 for the HPL birthday.

So, come Michaelmas, maybe I shall get a letter from you. Until then—
    Adieu.
        KAT

           CLM [signed]


[15]   [TLS, JHL]

                  Indianapolis, Indiana
                  August 20, 1935

Happy Birthday!

I'm sending a sort of Indian-gift birthday present in the form of that Histomap. Take your time about returning it. Also I'm enclosing a couple of stories which RHB wanted to see.

Thanks so much for the Florida postcards. Next best to visiting a place is seeing lots of pictures and hearing all about it. You must tell me which of the cards you want returned. I'm looking forward to seeing the Charleston, Quebec, New Orleans and Natchez cards too. Natchez always reminds me of tough old Captain Waterman and his *Natchez* and *Sea Witch*.[1] ("Old" in reference to the time since his day, for I understand that the clipper ship officers were usually amazingly young. 18 and 19 sometimes, and ready to retire at 25. Is that really true? From what one hears about the brutality of discipline aboard the clippers it doesn't seem that boys as young as that would be phys- ically capable of commanding ships.) To get back to the subject, we're plan- ning a three-day trip over Labor Day, and if we go down into Kentucky again I'll see if I can pick up any worth-while cards for you. I don't believe I've ever visited Vincennes, but if I do will look for cards there too.

I haven't a great deal of interest in middlewestern antiquity, because it's all—what there is of it—concerned with pioneers and log cabins and Injuns, which subject hasn't enough variety to interest anyone very long, I should think. Only where it touches family history can I find anything worth dwelling on, and that's purely personal. My father's pioneer ancestor was a black sheep from a (we think and hope) distinguished Virginia family, who came north with his wife and baby, a covered wagon, a side of bacon and a sack of corn meal to start life in the wilderness. We still have a couple of the spoons which, in the widespread local tradition, he is said to have beaten out of silver dollars that his family might eat with silver. They're so soft they bend in your fingers, so can't really have been much use.

Well, if you don't care particularly for the sea *per se*, at least we share a weakness for seaports and ships. Meaning by ships, of course, nothing later than the clipper era. I conceived a great literary passion once for Crosbie Garstin—another of my obscure but intensely admired authors—and ab- sorbed from him a love for the days of the clippers that affects me still with faint nostalgia as if I'd lived then and was homesick. There's a scrap of verse I read somewhere that expresses it exactly—

> It's a long, long road for the Natchez,
> A blowy, beating way
> With silks and teas from China
> For the girls by Boston Bay.
>
> Lonely the road from Boston,
> The long road to Foo Chow,
> Empty the road to China
> Of ships like the Natchez now.
>
> Would I were back with the Natchez
> And Waterman's cheering men,
> Greeting the drifting whale-ship
> On the China Road again.

You know, to one who's always been intimate with the sea, there must be something you never realize. Long familiarity blinds one. (For instance, the view from our home is probably one of the loveliest in middle Indiana. We're on a low hill above a park around which Brookside Pkwy. curves, and nothing can be seen in any direction but woods and treetops and rolling grassy spaces beyond the boulevard. Yet we very seldom really look at it. Really look, I mean. I've sat on the porch and stared glassily out for several minutes, and then suddenly and rather shockingly realized what I was looking at and how lovely it really is.) You must be that way with the ocean. That can be carried a little farther. I remember the first time I ever saw a large body of water—Lake Michigan, when I was about six. And it had no resemblance to water as it looks to me know. I saw it first from a distance, and I can see it now just as clearly—a wide expanse of intensely blue, roughened surface like a plane tilted up against the sky, dotted at fairly regular intervals in a polka-dot pattern of dazzling white triangles. Perfectly solid and motionless. It wasn't until later that I began to see it as it really was. I read too, somewhere, an account of a man who had been blind from birth and suddenly had his sight *restored,* and how queerly different from what other people saw things looked to him, until he became accustomed to sight. For instance, perspective drawings looked like buildings that really staggered, instead of diminishing into distance, and shadows in pictures were black blots instead of aids to the depth-illusion. I wonder if sights on a new planet wouldn't all look utterly different from what they really were, just at first. Well, I'm getting somewhat involved; better start a new paragraph.

Speaking of houses, yours must be delicious. The perfect place for you, especially. I hope you can stay there! It's rather odd that you should have so strong a leaning toward the New England of colonial days, yet find so much pleasure in hot climates. I can't share your delight in temperatures of 90°. It's queer that up to about 20 I did, and loved nothing better than basking in the violent heat of our Indiana summers. Four years ago all that changed, and now I'm in utter misery anywhere from 85° on up.

I'm returning to Mr. Koenig the Summers book on witchcraft and Provost's "Ghosties and Ghoulies".[2] The Summers book was interesting perhaps not so much as a textbook but as a revelation of the writer's character. How very seriously he takes it all! I was quite convinced—until I put down the book. As I remarked to Mr. Koenig, I'm like the White Queen and can quite easily believe six impossible things before breakfast, temporarily at least, until someone comes along with more positive ideas to the contrary, whereupon I swing over to the opposite view.

I'm in a hurry to get this off today, so it will at least have been mailed on our birthday, but want first to effuse a bit about the book I read last night, "Dew in April",[3] 600 pages and I read it from cover to cover last night. It will always be a mystery to me how I ever accomplished it, for I didn't skim thru it either. Have a headache today in consequence, but it was well worth it. As you probably know, it's all about a renegade nun and convent life in 1212 when the world was expecting Doomsday on the 12th day of the 12th month of the 12th year of 1200. The expectation of the End of the World colors everyone's actions and thoughts, and there is such vivid detail and such an understanding viewpoint of what life among a community of 13th century women must have been like. And all thru it the author has such deft touches of the supernatural. The convent is built next to the ruins of the Roman bath, and the gods of the past and the terrors of paganism are lurking just under the surfaces of everyday life. I wish I had the book here now. I'd like to quote some of it. Do read it if you get a chance—but not at one sitting.

Will mail this now. Don't hurry over the Histomap. I gave it to my father for a Father's Day present, but am proving Indian-giver all around. Again, Happy Birthday.

Cordially,

C. L. M.

*Notes*

1. Robert H. Waterman (1808–1884), American merchant sea captain known as "Bully Bob Waterman." He set three sailing speed records.

2. Actually Francis C. Prevot.

3. By John Clayton.

[16]    [HPL, nonextant]

[c. late September 1935]

[17]    [TLS, JHL]

Tuesday, October 8, 1935

Dear Mr. Lovecraft:

So glad you were pleased with the typing. As I explained, I really enjoyed the stories I typed better than those I didn't, for the work forced me to read them word by word instead of phrase by phrase, and I caught things in the typing that I'd missed in the mere reading.

I wish our Kentucky trip had taken us through places where I could have bought cards showing some of the old homes with their slave quarters and family cemeteries. Unfortunately for that purpose, the sights we saw were chiefly scenic, and postcards do such awful things to landscapes and views from mountains that I almost hesitated to inflict them on you.

I've never seen Mammoth Cave, but intend to someday. Caves give me a slight touch of the horrors anyhow. I think of the terrible Floyd Collins case.[1] The feeling of tons and tons of earth pressing down and in and around on all sides—brr! I know how a person afflicted with claustrophobia must feel.

We didn't get to visit the caverns in Lookout Mountain. It seems perfectly feebleminded to drive all that distance and then not take time to see what you really made the trip to visit, but that's what we did. We spent so much time going through the Smokies that there wasn't much left when we reached Chattanooga. Someday I want to go back and really see the mountain.

Isn't it a heavenly feeling to be up that high? I have a vague idea that ozone is somehow connected with the sense of bursting wellbeing, but I'm sure part of it is sheer animal pride at being up above everyone else and having the whole world spread out at your feet. There's a poem that used to be in all the school books which I always think of when I'm on a mountain—

> He clasps the crags [*sic*] with crooked hands
> Close to the sun in lonely lands,
> Ringed by the azure world he stands.
> The wrinkled sea beneath him crawls,
> He watches from his mountain walls. . . .[2]

Your own peregrinations make mine seem very small. What a glorious summer you've had! I hope your weekend trip with the Boston friend[3] proved as pleasant as the rest of your journeys. But I suppose you're glad to be home.

The one great thing that's happened since I wrote last won't mean a thing to you but it looms so large in my own life that I just have to mention it—I've had my hair cut! I've worn it waist-length ever since I was old enough to put it up at all, and the sensation of being shorn is so deeply distressing that I've wondered since if there mightn't be something more than superstition in the old Biblical injunction not to let the shears touch one's hair. It's so instinctive and deepseated a feeling. Frank Belknap Long Jr. in one of his poems has a line, "They loved thee as a woman loves her hair",[4] and I'd never realized how apt it was until I had mine cut. Afterward, wondering just what the Biblical rule was on the subject of hair, I looked it up, and ran across a whole series of rules and regulations which are astonishingly accurate in the matter of quarantine and sanitation and treatment of contagious diseases. Before the discovery of modern science so many of those old laws must have seemed sheer superstition, and not until the present generation can people really have understood why the injunctions were so wise. So, I thought, mayn't there be other rules there that seem pointless now but which future science will prove quite sensible? And if so, how did the old Hebrews know it? One could build up an ancient and lost civilization from just those sets of ancient Hebrew law. After all, how *did* they know? Just from observation of cause and effect over long periods of time, I suppose, but Europe from the beginning of the Dark Ages up to the last generation or so didn't seem to reach any sensible conclusions from watching exactly the same series of cause-and-effect. (I read an account of a surgical operation of some fifty years ago, the other day, describing the well-meaning surgeon stropping his scalpel on the sole of his *shoe* before making an incision!!)

On second thought, this senseless affection for one's crowning glory is probably the result of countless generations which have admired long hair; a Chinese accidentally breaking his long finger-nail would probably feel the same sentimental loss. It's all a matter of environment—but if you were in the mood you could build up a towering structure of unknown and undiscovered natural laws, lost civilizations whose far-advanced scientific achievements come down to us veiled in the injunctions of ancient Hebraic law—a whole vanished culture from the simple fact that I had about a yard of hair cut off the other day.

What a mix-up about that serial story for Fantasy. I hope you haven't had too much trouble over your installment.[5] Mr. Schwartz asked me to be as weird and original as possible in starting it out, and I was notably neither. At least there was a vast expanse of room for improvement as the story advanced. Frankly, if I'd been able to think up something strikingly weird and new I wouldn't have given the idea away for nothing. Anyhow, it will be interesting to see what the others have done with such a poor start.

You mention lots of work piled up awaiting you. I do hope some of it includes a new story. It's been ages since you've had any and your most ardent admirer is getting very restless for more. On this inspiring appeal I think I'd better close.

Hopefully,
Catherine Moore

O my, I almost forgot—didn't I recognize you in Bloch's tale in a recent WT?[6] The student of occult and obscure sciences, friend of the speaker in the story, who died a frightful death in Providence at the hands (or feet or claws or something) of a Terrible Monster?

*Notes*

1. William Floyd Collins (1887–1925), American cave explorer in central Kentucky. On 30 January 1925, trying to discover a new entrance an underground cave system, Collins became trapped underground and died about 14 days later.
2. Alfred, Lord Tennyson, "The Eagle," ll. 1–5. Tennyson has written "crag" in l. 1.
3. Samuel Loveman.
4. "Florence," l. 7.
5. After CLM had written the opening segment of "The Challenge from Beyond" and Frank Belknap Long the second, A. Merritt complained to the editor about where the story had led and insisted that he be given the second berth. Schwartz acceded to Merritt's demand, and so Frank Belknap Long had to write a new piece (the fifth).
6. "The Shambler from the Stars" (*WT,* September 1935).

[18]   [HPL, nonextant]

[c. 12 October 1935]

[19]   [TLS, JHL]

2547 Brookside Pkway., S. Dr.
Indianapolis, Indiana.
Tuesday, Oct. 16, 1935

Dear Mr. Lovecraft:

First of all—thanks so much for the New Orleans, etc., material. I spent a very pleasant hour poring over it. Was indignant because the New Orleans folders devoted so much space to proving with pictures and statistics what a modern, up-and-coming manufacturing center the place is, and so little to the places for real interest. But what photographs and information there was (were?) on the real New Orleans as everyone thinks of it were satisfying enough to make up for the profusion of factories and shipping data which infested the rest.

The thing about the New England pictures which appealed most to me was the glimpse or two of little lanes, hollyhock bordered, stone-paved, leading between delicious old houses. Little lanes are another of my weaknesses, and these were perfect.

Somehow the New England photos appealed to me so much more than the New Orleans. (Two "News" that are really so very old!) I hadn't realized before until I had the two side by side how much better I like the New England than the exotic oriental-ness of so much of New Orleans. That picture of the Spanish Garden of the Two Sisters, or something, as contrasted with the little New England lane painted too sharp a contrast to overlook. I cannot share your passion for the tropics.

Another thing I realize from looking at the material is how widely our view points differ in respect to—O, just how we look at the past. New Orleans is a lovely and ancient city, and living record of a past comprised of the clash of two races for supremacy, and their blending there. But to me—well, when I think of New Orleans I think of a girl in a high-waisted Empire gown of eggshell satin, stepping delicately into the mud of an unpaved street on a rainy night, with the balconies of a building dimly seen above her in the dark. I don't know why, but that's the picture that always comes into my mind when I think 'New Orleans'. I see the past only as a background for the individuals who lived in it and went through the same emotional experiences as ourselves. Somehow it fascinates me to think of that. No sense in it, but I can gloat for hours over old family trees and wills and marriage licenses and such, just thinking of who the people were and what they looked like, and the sort of a day it was when the document was written, and how the men and women recorded in the "tree" happened to meet and marry, and the clothes they wore and—O, all sorts of things like that. Utterly trivial, but completely fascinating. And it doesn't leave much room of the sweep of the windy centuries and the march of races that means so much more to you.

Somehow that reminds me of a poem, all of which I can remember is a line or two to the effect that women are content—"in the hot, tight houses of their hearts to eat bread".[1] Implying that they can't see any farther than the daily round of individual duties—even in their dreams.

I saw the motion picture "The Crusades"[2] the other day, and haven't quite recovered yet. Naturally unspeakable as the Middle Ages were, there was about them a lusty and gorgeous spaciousness that has quite vanished from the earth, recaptured now and then only in fiction and on the screen. And only through such mediums, I suppose, can they seem so violently delightful. I read in a comic strip, of all places, the explanation of why that's so. Someone in the funnies was lamenting that life isn't romantic and exciting like the movies, and a philosophical soul pointed out that when you compress a lifetime into two hours of entertainment you're bound to hit only the high spots, and that any life probably contains just as much excitement and romance as a play, only spaced over about seventy years. And that, of course, is what makes the moving picture version of the Crusades such a rich and satisfying pageant. In life such a man as Richard Lion-Heart would be perfectly maddening, and to live in his time one would have to drag through such morasses of dirt and disease and discomfort that the spacious gorgeousness of the age wouldn't register at all. But despite all that the picture infected me with such a great, windy lustiness and splendor and smashing glory that I'm moving still in the trailing clouds of it. That, as I've said before, is the movies' real contribution to civilization. They can recapture an age and the best aspects of it and recreate them so vividly that one goes for days afterward in a pleasant fog of remembrance. By the way, before I change the subject—what do you think about the contention that the men of those days were smaller in stature than modern men? I read an article in The American Weekly not long ago declaring that the men and women of today are taller than any since the Norseman and the Cro-Magnon, and showing a photograph of Tunney standing beside a suit of armor that came only to his shoulder, in proof of their theory. Do you think it's true? One is generally led to believe that anything the Sunday supplements print is rank fantasy, but this particular idea is just disappointing and disillusioning enough to be true.

Do you know G. K. Chesterton's "Lepanto"? All about Don John of Austria, and one of the must luxuriously satisfying poems I've ever read. That, of course, was much later than the Crusade with which Coeur-de-Lion marched to Palestine, but it has to do with strife between Saracen and Christian just the same, and the description of Don Juan might apply to Richard—

> "Don Juan laughing with [*sic*] the brave beard curled,
> Spurning of his stirrups like the thrones of all the world!"

Part of it in particular has a marching, smashing, climactic swing that would have you shouting if you recited it aloud, by the time you reached the end—

"He moves a mighty turban on the timeless houri's knees,
A turban that is woven of the sunsets and the seas,
He shakes the peacock gardens as he rises from his ease
And he strides among the treetops and is taller than the trees!"

And—"It is he who knows not Kismet, it is he who fears not fate,
It is Richard, it is Raymond, it is Godfrey at the gate!"

And—"The Pope has flung his arms abroad in agony and loss
And called the kings of Christendom for *swords about the Cross!*"

And then it's full of fragmentary lines that are simply perfect, such as— "Temples where the yellow gods shut up their eyes in scorn." and "They rise in green robes soaring from the green hells of the sea", and in particular, "And dead is all the innocence of anger and surprise". I had to think about that for awhile before it meant anything, but it's beautifully put.

What I started on that for was to quote the one line that expresses the movie aspect of the Middle Ages so well—"Scarlet running over on the silvers and the golds"[3]—but as usual I wandered pretty far off the subject. However, it serves to elaborate on the fact that I can't agree with your exceedingly apt phrase to the effect that the Middle Ages are 'one long stench'. That's so well put I wish I could agree just to do proper obeisance to the phrase. So you really get no pleasure out of the splendor and sound and fury of the Middle Ages? Does their dirt and squalor, for you, eclipse their gorgeousness?

And that brings me to a quotation I want to try out on you. It's from a book I read so long ago I've forgotten the name, but the paragraph impressed me so as being written with absolute precision and all the delicacy and exquisiteness of a jeweler cutting a diamond—that I copied it to keep. The author—a woman as you'll know from the wording—was writing about Rennaissance [*sic*] Italy:

"This mysterious mortal mind, so variably housed, refuses to fail before the idea of the ultimate destruction of Earth, when, a snow of scintillating atoms, she drifts down the solar gulfs. Indeed, so aware of the long intensities of its immemorial history is our imagination that it seems as if this lovely, desperate planet, this little castle of fire and wind and water, shaped like a star, must in vanishing leave on the quivering ether some fiery ghostly imprint of its shape of passion and beauty."[4] One adjective more and it would be overwritten, but as it is I think it's as near perfection as anything I've read. And speaking of overwriting reminds me of the classic example, a sentence I ran across in a volume of Don Marquis' short stories, probably written in his early youth. "Dawn came up the sky like a wild, fair woman with blood-stained feet."!![5]

On rereading that Rennaissance (I think I've misspelled that) Italy paragraph, there doesn't seem to be much connection with either Italy or the Rennaissance. But does it seem overwritten to you? I find my tastes are still changing so that I can never be sure that what appealed to me a year ago will be admirable at all after a little time has elapsed. And I've a bad tendency to crowd in adjectives myself, so would naturally admire the flamboyant. Just as a matter of curiosity, what do you think of the quotation?

And speaking of G. K. Chesterton and quotations, a recent Father Brown story I read contained a couple of paragraphs so apt in the light of your last letter that I saved them for you:

> "Three men came out from under the low-browed Tudor arch in the mellow façade of Mandeville College into the strong evening sunlight of a summer day which seemed as if it would never end. *** They were conscious of a contrast. They themselves, in a curious quiet way, were quite harmonious with their surroundings. Though the Tudor arches that ran like a cloister round the College gardens had been built four hundred years ago, at that moment when the Gothic fell from heaven and bowed, or almost crouched, over the cosier chambers of Humanism and the Revival of Learning—though they themselves were in modern clothes (that is in clothing whose ugliness would have amazed any of the four centuries) yet something in the spirit of the place made them all at one. The gardens had been tended so carefully as to achieve the final triumph of looking careless; the very flowers seemed beautiful by accident, like elegant weeds; and the modern costumes had lent any picturesqueness that can be produced by being untidy."[6]

I do indeed envy the students at Yale who move amidst such surroundings as you describe.[7] They probably don't appreciate them now, but I don't see how even the most callous of them could be wholly uninfluenced, and I don't doubt that in fifteen or twenty years from now they'll look back and remember the beauty of the place, though they may not realize now that they see it at all.

My own humble college, the state university, had one of the loveliest campuses—I mean campi, don't I?—anywhere. It is—or was at that time—utterly untouched save to clear away the underbrush from the forest, and you could walk for ten or fifteen minutes through woods that might have been a thousand miles away from any buildings. Indiana's only real beauty is in its trees, and these were glorious—straight and tall and at the time of year sifting down shower upon slanting sower of colored leaves until you felt like Danae when you went walking. My windows looked into a beech woods that turned bright gold, and it was like staring straight into heaven whenever I looked out. If you can't have perfect buildings such as you describe it's next best to leave the place in its original perfection, untouched.

That makes me think of two friends of ours who were married recently, on an income of little more than nothing a year, and who are living in a little cabin in the woods south of town. We were out there to dinner last week, and the place is delightful. They've done nothing to spoil the background of their log cabin, and the trees rise straight and slim and tall, colored gloriously, behind the squat little two-room hose. Certainly I wouldn't want to change places with the bride, but from a purely aesthetic viewpoint the place is enchanting. The bridegroom went out to cut wood for the fire, and standing at the door, hearing the ring of his axe and looking out into impenetrable wilderness, I might have stepped back a hundred and fifty years, for there was nothing anywhere to destroy the illusion that unexplored and pioneer Indiana lay just outside the door. Perhaps, after all, I do envy them a little. It must take a lot of courage, to do a thing like that.

I was glad to have your explanation of the old Hebrew laws that had puzzled me so. It had never occurred to me that the injunction against hair-cutting had their root in the danger of infection. Quite logical, though.

I can sympathize with your mother's sorrow over the loss of your infant curls. I wonder why so many males are blessed with curly hair, while naturally curly women are as scarce as hen's teeth. There is no justice in this world. I'm going to let my hair grow again. I can't abide it this way. Long howls of protest go up from all sides when I declare that I'll have no further association with barbers, for it seems it's becoming this way—but I am determined.

Your expeditions in September must have been delightful, despite the funereal errand you had to perform in Wilbraham.[8] Your description of the "Dunwich" scenes is reminiscent of G. K. Chesterton. Have you ever noticed that almost every one of his stories occurs in a red and stormy sunset? And there must be a sort of dark, brooding, twilight tinge to the places you visited there. They sounded as if they'd be at their best in a Chesterton sunset.

Your reference to Gothic architecture recalled to me a million-dollar mansion I explored last Monday. The owner is dead, the place being prepared for sale, and I was helping to tag the library for auction. Anyway, in the basement between the 50-foot swimming pool and the billiard room paneled in oak and leather, was a little Gothic chapel so exquisite with its lovely pointed arches and stained glass and carven panels that it was several moments before I realized the hilarity of the figures in the glass and carvings and saw that the room was a bar.

The place was almost incredible. Twenty years old, and complete with marble conservatory and sunken fountain, music room one wall of which was a great carven grille with organ pipes lurking behind it, the floors of the entire place of intricate parquetry. The bathrooms of the master bedroom had *three* lavatories and I have been wondering ever since why—also a *fireplace*. I wish I had known that man just long enough to ask him a few questions. And the entrance hall, with a gallery running round on which the upper story opened, was solid with carving. I think there was said to be $300,000 of carving in the whole place, and it gave somewhat the effect of thunderclouds hanging ominously and heavy just overhead. O yes, the upper walls of the gallery were covered with cut velvet above the carved panels. Most of the furniture had been sold, but from what was left I greatly fear that it too was a riot of carving. The place must have been rank horror when fully furnished. Like living in a heavy-roofed cavern crammed with stalagmites. (While I think of it, I'd very much like to read Howard's description of his Carlsbad Cavern explorations.)[9]

The King Lear quotation was magnificent. It had not impressed me before—my excursions into Shakespeare are very limited as yet. Voluntary excursions, that is. The only play I ever read of my own free will, entirely through, was Romeo and Juliet, and enjoyed it enough so that when the mood seizes me I shall be encouraged to continue. Did you ever think how interesting a person Rosaline, Romeo's first love, must have been? Someone refers to her as "that pale, hard-hearted wench, that Rosaline", and later "stabbed by a white wench's black eyes".[10] She must have been a very striking individual, too much so to be completely eclipsed by the conventional Juliet. And I was fascinated by Mercutio. Such a gay and ribald soul, dying so lightheartedly as he says of his wound, "Why, no, [']tis not so deep as a well nor so wide as a church door, but [']tis enough—'t will serve. Who seeks me tomorrow will find me a grave man."[11] (The pun is awful, but one must make allowances for the dying.)

I haven't seen the *Phantograph*, [sic] and feel very much neglected that Crawford overlooked me. It sounds most interesting. And I shall certainly have to see the Conan the Reaver world-history.[12]

When I think of that I remember some stanzas of Kipling's which have always given me such acute pleasure. Do you recognize these—?

> See you the ferny ride that steals
> Into the oak-woods far?
> O that was where we hauled the keels
> That rode to Trafalgar.
>
> See you the windy levels spread
> About the gates of Rye?
> O that was where the Norsemen fled
> When Alfred's ships came by.
>
> See you after rain the brace
> Of mound and ditch and wall?
> O that was a legion's camping place
> When Caesar sailed from Gaul.
>
> See you lines that show and fade
> Like shadows on the downs?
> O those where the lines the Flint-men made
> To guard their wondrous towns.[13]

I'm so glad you approved of my "Cold Grey God" (which is Wright's title, not mine.) And am looking forward eagerly to seeing your new story "The Shadow".[14]

I returned Mr. Koenig's last batch of books recently. He's been giving me the Summers text-books on witchcraft and vampirism, and every time I read them I get so boiling angry I could bite someone. How any man can *be* that way! I never before read any book through whose text the author's personality shows so vividly or so infuriatingly.

I was so sorry to hear about Mr. Smith's mother.[15] I had a debate with myself whether to write, since we have exchanged a note or two, but decided not to both because our correspondence has been so brief and formal, and because in his place I think I'd rather not hear from anyone or be reminded at all of such a bereavement.

With my indefatigable interest in individual emotional reactions I am reminded of the Dowie Houmes of Yarrow ballad, wherein the widowed Sarah replies to her father's attempt at comfort, "O haud your tongue, my father dear, Ye mind me but of sorrow."[16]

I want to thank you once again for those lovely cards and folders of New Orleans and Salem and the rest. I looked at them until I could smell the Atlantic and feel the sand under my feet. And those old houses and lanes were delightful. Pick me out some of your 'antiquarian iconography' and I'll promise to return it promptly.

Very gratefully yours,<br>Catherine Moore

## Notes

1. Louise Bogan (1897–1970), "Women," *Measure* No. 12 (February 1922): 14 (ll. 3–4).

2. *The Crusades* (Paramount, 1935), directed by Cecil B. DeMille; starring Loretta Young, Henry Wilcoxon, Ian Keith, and Alan Hale.

3. CLM has quoted from "Lepanto" by G. K. Chesterton (1874–1936), ll. 29–30 ("in" for "with"), 38–41, 64–65, 9–10 ("cast" for "flung"), 49, 50, 81, and 130.

4. See letter 21n11.

5. Don Marquis (1878–1937), "Behind the Curtain," in *Carter and Other People* (New York: D. Appleton & Co., 1921), 281.

6. "The Crime of the Communist," in Chesterton's *The Scandal of Father Brown* (1935).

7. HPL had recently visited Yale University in New Haven, CT.

8. HPL and Edward H. Cole had gone to Wilbraham, MA, to scatter the ashes of the amateur journalist Jennie E. T. Dowe (1840–1919). HPL had drawn upon the locale for the setting of "The Dunwich Horror" (1928).

9. As found in Howard's letter to HPL ([c. July 1934]); *A Means to Freedom* 780–84.

10. Shakespeare, *Romeo and Juliet* 2.4.4, 12–13 (both said by Mercutio).

11. *Romeo and Juliet* 3.1.90–92.

12. "The Hyborian Age," *Phantagraph* (February–November 1936). The publisher was Wilson Shepherd.

13. Kipling, "Puck's Song," ll. 1–4, 25–28, 33–40. CLM makes a few minor errors in transcription.

14. I.e., "The Shadow out of Time."

15. Clark Ashton Smith's mother, Fanny Gaylord Smith, died on 9 September 1935.

16. Anon., "The Dowie Dens of Yarrow," ll. 65–66.

[20]    [HPL, nonextant]

[early November 1935]

[21]    [TLS, JHL]

Thursday Nov. 7, 1935

Dear Mr. Lovecraft:

Following your example, I present above a view from my window. We are having one of our celebrated local smogs—equal parts of mist, fog and smoke, with gentle showers of soot drifting thru the thick of it and every breath you draw feels like sand. The whole outdoors is perfectly solid, and getting that fragment of Howard's Carlsbad letter and a card from Price in Mexico and remarks from you about Boston and late fall excursions doesn't help a bit. It's bad enough having to live in such a climate, without having other people gloating over their travels.

Your little sketch of Quinsnicket was charming.[1] "Crude diagram" in deed! And I loved the horrid bearded demon illustrating your youthful preferences for impersonation. Reminded me of letters my cousin and I used to exchange in our angel infancy. Like so many somewhat introspective children, we had constructed for ourselves an elaborate mythical-kingdom, and used to send back and forth between Memphis and Indianapolis newspapers of the doings of our respective nations. They frequently contained rotogravure sections with the visages of our better-known villains, heroes and heroines, and I remember in particular one wicked conspirator who, my cousin explained, had very luxuriant eyebrows through which he was in the habit of running his fingers in moments of abstraction, a habit encouraged by his fellow-plotters because he decidedly did not have a poker face. Just the other day I was engaging in one of my sporadic fits of cleanliness and delving into ancient boxes with a view to putting them in better order, ran across a couple of microscopic notes which had been exchanged between two of our villains, "Dear Rupert: What about Villany [*sic*] #892" Answer: "I don't know about Villiany #892, but think so." It sounds very competent, but the passages of the years has robbed it of any meaning at all, if it ever possessed any.

To get back to my topic—Quinsnicket must be a delightful place. And the verses of your teens after the manner of Pope were surprising. It's hard to realize that a seventeen-year old boy wrote them. At this point I cannot resist quoting a poem I wrote in the 8th grade, when I was about 11—at the request of the teacher who excused me from recitation until I had finished the eight lines to fill in a blank in the school publication:

> O March, although thy blusters ring
> Thou art the herald of lady spring;
> Tho with thee rain and thunder comes
> And thy angry wind on his wild harp strums,
> Tho thy voice resounds thru the shivering trees
> We know that winter before thee flees
> So we love thee, for thy winds remind
> That our lady spring comes close behind.

I shall never forget the luxury of sitting there scribbling rhymes while the rest of the class struggled through a recitation. Never before or since have I felt so completely the splendid isolation of the poet!

However, the "Quinsnicket Park, by a Gentleman of New England" has all the glittering polish of a Pope poem, and I loved the carefully conventional scenes and phrases which even in their most elaborate conventionality could not wholly disguise what a lovely place the park must be.

Pope as a poet I have no use for at all. Poetry ought, I think, either to flow spontaneously—as rain from the clouds of summer, or tears from the eyelids start (excusit please)—or else be rigidly and epigrammatically forced into set forms, such as the triolet or the sonnet or rondeau. And even the sonnet I don't care a lot for. It's always seemed to me rather a dull verse-form, too long to be crisply clever, too short to be sincere. I do love triolets—used to turn them out by the gallon in my school days—

> "Our shadows kissed upon the moon-white wall,
> Though he and I so primly stood apart
> Our shameless shadows did not heed at all,
> I saw they [*sic*] sway together on the wall
> Soft grey against the quiet moonlight's fall
> And smiled a quiet smile inside my heart.
> Our shadows kissed upon the moonwhite wall
> Though he and I so primly stood apart."

Or— "Under my window an old love's laughter
> Startled me from my sleep,
> Ringing from wall and beam and rafter,
> I heard my heart in my old love's laughter,
> And knew too late what I hungered after—
> Quiet, my heart, and weep—
> Under my window an old love's laughter
> Startled me from my sleep."

And if you can't cling to these purposely insincere and crisp verse-forms, then let loose and just ramble. Like this—from some of my mythical-kingdom literature—

> She closed her eyes in weariness and pain
> And turned into the shadowed room again
> Where gilded hangings glimmered on the wall.
> She heard the singing fountain's rise and fall,
> She heard the night wind in the swaying trees.
> She closed her eyes.
>
>           In silence, on her knees,
> Her forehead bowed against her folded hands,
> She learned these sounds as landsmen know their lands,
> Seeking through pain the bitter road to peace.
> She found no magic for her soul's surcease,
> The Blessed Mary turned Her eyes away.
> Deep in her heart she knew she did not pray
> The haloed God so many ages dead,
> Deep in her heart that other haloed head
> Ringed with its coronet of deadly gold
> Glimmered behind the slipping beads she told.
>
> "O Holy Maiden, give my prayers thy heed
>   From Heaven's high throne, in this my hour of need. . . ."
> *(These are the arms that closed his shoulders' spread,*
>  *To this dark hair he bent his gilded head. . . .)*
> "Dear Lord, thy mercy like a fountain streams,
>   Guard me from sin by daylight and by dreams
>   Of His dear sake, who died upon the Tree—"
> *(Send my crowned lover back again to me!)*

How I love doing things like that—probably because it's so easy. Pope's method, besides being hard work, I really don't admire at all. No doubt because my own viewpoint is diametrically opposed to yours—it's emotion and not reason that seems to me so important. However poetry is primarily emotional, and any verses which disregard emotion entirely are just rhymed prose. Or am I wrong?

I shall have to inquire more diligently into the late Mr. Shakespeare's celebrated writings. I have a Complete Works left over from school days, into which I dip occasionally, continually amazed how full of quotations it is. And by the way, speaking of school books, are you fond of Chaucer? He seems so gloriously alive, after so many centuries, that I love to get out the chewed-looking old book we studied in Eng. Lit. III and read again the very human things his people say in their peculiar talk. There's something positively juicy and luscious in "Whanne that Aprille with his shoures sote The droughte of Marche hath perced to the rote".[2] And wasn't it the Pardoner who sang "Come hider Love to me"?[3] I can hear him.

And do you care for Spencer [*sic*]? I should think you'd like him better than dear old Geoffrey. My room-mate and I took the same literature course and went halves on buying the books, so when the end of the term came she took Spencer home and I kept Chaucer, and I remember very little of Spencer now—just a vague, blurred parade of page[a]ntry and symbolism, with two or three highlights such as Death riding on a tiger—"For as the wing-ed wind his Tigre fled",[4] and one incident wherein a running fugitive who keeps looking back over his shoulder gasps, "For God's dear love, Sir Knight, do not me stay—For lo, he comes! he comes fast after me!"[5] There's something very terrifying about that.

(slight intermission occasioned by
Armistice Day) Nov. 12

I am returning herewith all your stories contained in the last bundle except those I'm forwarding to Koenig. Am keeping the catalogue of his library for awhile, if you don't mind, as I haven't had time to go over it and make a list of what I want.

It would be hard to say which of those stories I enjoyed most. They were all so splendid. "The Strange High House in the Mist" was reminiscent of Dunsany, of course, but more satisfying, because Dunsany doesn't always carry out his fantasies far enough to satisfy—just leaves you dangling and tantalized. But in this you strike exactly the happy medium, explaining just enough and not a bit too much of what lived in the House. Somehow that title has intrigued me for a long time, and I'm happy to say I wasn't in the least disappointed.

The "Shadow Over Innsmouth" had me all but pounding the chair-arm in excitement. I've always been interested, too, in the idea of the union of human and unhuman, that you have so beautifully worked out in several stories. Wonder what their home life would be like! And "The Thing on the Doorstep" made something clear to me that I never understood before. I know now why my fiance looked at me in that peculiar way after he'd read "Shambleau"—the first and only one of my stories he was ever persuaded to read. I know now what he was thinking. *What kind of a person is this who can think of such things?* The changing-bodies idea is so old that it's strange no one has thought before to put a living mind into a decaying corpse. Unquestionably it's the most ghastly thing I ever read. Congratulations.

The postcards and pamphlets you send were most enjoyable, too. Particularly your "Some Dutch Footprints" and the description of "Shakespare's [*sic*] Head". You know, all this is going to be of immense value to me someday. For years I've had vague ideas about a New England 18th Century series of stories I want to write, and when they've incubated long enough I'll be needing just the sort of background in pictures and descriptions which you've been furnishing me. So, aside from being so interesting in themselves, all this is doubly welcome for the use I hope to put it to someday.

How grand about your two ASTOUNDING sales.[6] The lovely thing about ASTOUNDING is the promptness of their checks. And I'm so pleased they've taken your stories because that means they must be letting down their rigid bars against anything but the strictly "scientific" and I'll be able to sell them some more of my own attempts. Yes indeed, I'm a regular reader of the magazine. It and WT are the only two I've been buying out of that field. ASTOUNDING often has some splendid stories in it, and I'll certainly be looking forward to yours. I suppose they'll be published next spring sometime? It's usually about six months from the date of acceptance, or has been in my case. It'll be a long wait, but worth it I'm sure.

You must be sure to see "Crusades" if you haven't already. Unquestionably it takes history by the forelock and leads it down paths it never trod before, but the result is really gorgeous. Like you, my sympathies were chiefly with the Saracens. No matter if our blood forebears were on the other side—the civilization of the infidel was surely so much more closely related to our present one than that of the Crusaders that our sympathies would naturally be on the other side. Which is a somewhat involved sentence, but I'm sure you follow me. To quote RHB "Sentence obscure, but fraught with meaning". You should read Don[n] Byrne's book whose title I can't remember—all about a young Crusader captured by the Saracens and coming over to their point of view.[7]

The whole idea of the Crusades was a dazzling one, but surely it was only the rank and file who went with the sole idea for rescuing Jerusalem? I mean, though I know nothing at all about the politics of the era, it doesn't seem natural that the Kings of Christendom hadn't some ulterior motive.

"Berkeley Square" was splendid, wasn't it? Saturday evening I found myself listening to a radio presentation of "The Amateur Gentleman" with Leslie Howard in the leading role,[8] and got a great deal of pleasure out of just hearing the voices without paying much attention to what they were saying, and picturing the scenes of that lost and lovely world through which the characters moved.

"Clive of India"[9] was good too. Wasn't it historically accurate? It made no attempt to maintain a plot or even the usual continuity of a movie romance, and I had supposed that the reason was that it was simply picking out the highlights of his career. You must have had much satisfaction in your dream when you so efficiently snubbed Gen. Burgoyne. I'm glad to know he finally received his just deserts.

And speaking of movies, I saw "The Last Days of Pompeii"[10] the other afternoon. A good picture, but what impressed me most was a moment when

Basil Rathbone as Pontius Pilate came out on a marble terrace in his purple-bordered toga, and I realized for the first time the sheer beauty and dignity of the Roman dress. Funny that, though all my life I've seen similarly dressed men in countless drawings and photoplays, I never until that moment realized how infinitely superior the toga is to any masculine dress before or since in dignity and beauty. What a pity that people ever got to buttoning their clothes instead of draping them. Perhaps a mercy for the women, though, for unless one's dignified and matronly and of a definitely hefty build the garb of the Roman lady would be anything but becoming.

Thanks for the information on racial types, relative heights, etc. That too may come in very conveniently someday for some more dim ideas which are circulating in the back of my mind. You're a gold-mine!

I'm so glad you didn't think my "purple passage" too colorful. The book, as I have finally succeeded in recalling, was "Invitation to Rennaissance [*sic*] Italy",[11] a sort of impressions of the place by one who has been there. It was beautifully written, and quite as vividly as if its eloquent author had just returned from a visit to the time and place she described. I'd love to read the W. Compton Leith book.[12] It sounds delightful. And no, I've never seen the catalogue of the weird section of your library. I'm looking forward to it.

Yes, there was as you surmised a definitely melancholy effect in the cataloging of the library in that Gothic mansion I described. Indeed the whole house was full of a wistful and forlorn desolation. All that lowering and thunderous carving, all the lavishness of marble conservatory and velvet-covered walls and the elaborate rest of it must have been the man's pride and joy for years and years—and now intruding us, prowling through his cherished treasures. Reminds me of an estate in southern Indiana which I have visited several times with an acquaintance who is receiver for the place. The occupants left it with no suspicion that they'd never return—accidents and sudden death wiped the whole family out—and the house is exactly and rather creepily as they left it, with the latest novels of ten years ago open on the bedside tables and the blanket in the dog basket all rumpled up just as it must have jumped out when its mistress whistled. For some obscure reason the whole house is being kept as it was left, and a very queer experience it is to wander through the rooms whose occupants must surely have simply stepped out and will be back at any moment. There are little cards tacked on pillars "Visitors not allowed on this porch in Captain English's absence" and the like. Notices in the servants' quarters which rooms they're not to enter unless summoned. And there were we, prowling through the holy of holies. The lion and the lizard keep the courts where Jamsheyd gloried and drank deep.

However, in cases like that the forlornness is wholly in the deserted inanimate objects which have somehow lost all significance with the withdrawal of the human mind that invested them with meaning. It seems to me that nothing has any value except in the mind which values it, and—just as nothing can really be lost, since its only true worth is in the mind itself, which can never lose anything—so that disbanded library evoked melancholy only because it no longer had any significance. The owner took with him all the value which had once dwelt in the books. Which is very stumblingly put. The same ideas must have been worked out in great detail and much more lucidly by someone, somewhere. It's impossible that they should have occurred only to me. Someday perhaps I'll run across them in someone else's words.

I loved the little sketch marked "LOVECRAFT—1715". Surely not a self-portrait?[13] It's a pity your childhood was blighted by Mrs. Burnett's saintly infant hero,[14] but if the possession of curls was what helped in turning your attention to the 18th Century and its myriad fascinations perhaps they weren't wholly in vain. It's a great blessing that modern mothers are influenced by more wholesome ideals of child-garb. My fiancé's little new nephew, now three months old and perfectly square, is already tending toward rompers and such, his mother declaring that she hates to see even a very new baby boy in skirts. You were born too soon.

I simply must curb my babbling fingers now and stop, though am not in the least talked out yet. Speaking of fingers, over Armistice Day I somehow managed to gouge deep grooves in both of my thumbs with sharp pins, and it's hard to believe until one's so crippled how essential thumbs are in the performances of civilized life. Do you suppose if we had our thumbs all cut off we'd sink back into savagery?

Thanks for the *Phantagraph* information. I want to see one. And I'm glad CAS is getting back to normal after his loss. That has to happen to everyone, and in a way it must be somewhat of a relief to have it over with, and not be dreading it any longer.

I'm returning the Carlsbad letter and folder. They were extremely vivid and I am fired with the necessity of visiting the place myself.

Thanks again for the five stories, and looking forward happily to the next bundle,

Gratefully,

Catherine Moore

*Notes*

1. Quinsnicket Park (now Lincoln Woods State Park), about four miles north of Providence, was one of HPL's favorite haunts. See "Quinsnicket Park" (written 1913).

2. From the "General Prologue" to the *Canterbury Tales,* ll. 1–2.

3. From the "General Prologue," l. 671.

4. Edmund Spenser, *The Faerie Queene* 11.26.1.

5. *The Faerie Queene* 1.25.1–2.

6. Julius Schwartz sold *At the Mountains of Madness* to *Astounding Stories,* Donald Wandrei "The Shadow out of Time."

7. Presumably *Crusade* (London: Sampson Low, 1928; Boston: Little, Brown, 1928).

8. Leslie Howard (1893–1943), English stage and film actor, director, and producer, who starred in *Berkeley Square* an in the serial *The Amateur Gentleman* (which became *Leslie Howard's Matinee*), which featured a weekly broadcast of a new play adapted for radio.

9. *Clive of India* (20th Century Pictures/United Artists, 1935), directed by Richard Boleslawski; starring Ronald Coleman, Loretta Young, and Colin Clive.

10. *The Last Days of Pompeii* (RKO Radio Pictures, 1935), directed by Ernest B. Schoedsack and Merian C. Cooper (uncredited); starring Preston Foster, Alan Hale, and Basil Rathbone.

11. By Rachel Annand Taylor.

12. I.e., *Sirenica*.

13. See *SL* 2.9 (facing).

14. CLM refers to Frances Hodgson Burnett (1849–1924), Anglo-American author of the novel *Little Lord Fauntleroy* (1885–86), whose popularity led to the development of the "Fauntleroy suit" for little boys.


[22]   [HPL, nonextant]

[c. late November 1935]


[23]   [TLS, JHL]

Dec. 7, 1935

Dear Mr. Lovecraft:

I do get some of the most interesting things to do. Friday I spent the afternoon with a history teacher from one of the local highschools taking down a brief history of American taxation, a lot of which I hadn't known before. Slowly but surely I am getting an education.

For instance, I had never realized that the Revolution was so inevitable. Somehow I'd always supposed that the Colonies here and England abroad were simply two sections of the same sort of people. Apparently the colonists were almost entirely of the lower classes, who had been forbidden to own land at home and who in America, in their ignorance of English law, had developed a much simpler and more natural system of landowning and taxation than that of the British courts. It seems to have been perfectly awful in English eyes, and you can't blame either side for their attitude, but according to my history-teacher the English in England treated the English in America in much the same way as they did their Indian and Egyptian colonists. (Or did they have India and Egypt in those days? I don't know from nothing.) Anyhow the American colonists very naturally hated being treated like stepchildren. The English officials of those days must have been incredibly stupid not to realize what they were getting into. Here's what the history teacher says, in part:

"It was only natural that when the colonists came to this country from a region where most of them could not own land, they should immediately desire to own land using their own methods of certifying to the possession of land. This custom opened up an enormous field for objectionable action by the English government, because from the English point of view practically all colonial land titles were illegal. Moreover, by a somewhat similar twisting of facts which were facts and which were entirely legal, it was made to appear that all colonial laws from about 1710 to 1750 were illegal. This of course meant that all marriages in the colonies during that forty year period were illegal, that the children of such marriages could not inherit and that consequently all colonial lands should revert to the crown. It was no wonder that the colonists were frantic with anxiety and that the Revolution did not come until 1776 is a miracle. Miracle is the proper word to use, for the stage was all set for the Revolution in 1676, although it was a hundred years later before it really came."

What is the real truth about all that? Can England have been so short-sighted as not to realize where her actions were leading, or were the colonists not so abused as they thought? Just as a matter of curiosity I'd like to have your views on the subject.

Incidentally, it's so interesting to speculate on what might have happened if America hadn't revolted. I believe I've mentioned before that story some while ago in ASTOUNDING[1] in which it was predicated that any given situation has infinite numbers of possible results, and that each individual result is carried out to its final decimal in a separate pocket of time. The story presented a sketch of what might happen if the various times got mixed up. There was a man driving thru Kentucky who suddenly found himself in a South which had *won* the Civil War. And another startled group of moderns blundered into an America which was under the rule of a Rome that had never fallen.

Speaking of Rome reminds me of mention of it in my taxation history which should appeal to you. "Through all of this long story one fact stands out, that since the crash of the Roman Empire the world has progressed enormously, but it is necessary to realize that we are still in the process of recovering from that crash. There are certain ways in which progress is notably great, as in the lines of science and invention, medicine and surgery, but in this one line of finance and taxation our progress is not in the least comparable to those lines mentioned. We have gained in religious toleration, altruism has expanded beyond belief, but we have lost the devotion to law and legal systems that characterize the Roman Empire*** but we still need a public spirit comparable perhaps to that which makes the Community Chest possible, a genuine willingness on the part of everyone to bear his share of public expenses and a willingness to believe that the officials appointed or elected to do this work are actuated solely by that spirit of devotion that led Cicero to proclaim to all Rome that the duty of the consuls was to see to it that the Republic suffered no harm."

If Rome really possessed that spirit of public willingness to share the burden of the government sensibly and willingly it must mean that most of the public officers were sincere and honest, which, I have just realized, is one point on which your equally beloved Rome and 18th Century were widely at odds. It has just been made clear to me in this taxation history how naively and frankly *awful* the system of public offices and public funds was from the days of Pepys on. It seems to have been so completely rotten that it paradoxically acquires a sort of brazen honesty, since everyone knew and took as casually as the coming of day and night the fact that public officers stole as fast and as much as they could. And this argues a wide variance in the general public outlook in the 1700s from that of Rome. I am looking forward to your discussion of this.

I'm thinking now of the results of going back, like the man in "Berkeley Square". He didn't like it, you remember. And I wonder if you really would. There's no doubt that the tempo of the times in 1700–1800, and in ancient Rome, was immeasurably more attractive than that of our own is. (Reminds me of a story in the latest Cosmopolitan that you should read, of a man in just such a situation, hating the pace of modern life and longing for the peace of the past, and how he went back for awhile.)[2] But unquestionably the individual is much happier and safer in his happiness today than has ever been true before? Such incredibly awful things happened to people at the whims of officials and emperors and kings. Nobody could be sure that his happiness was secure from one moment to the next—well of course that's true today, but we can be surer that we'll have a measure of justice if anything happens to us that's someone else's fault, and no malice or injustice or caprice of a more powerful individual can ruin us today, as it could so easily in the past. I think your longing for earlier days is done in the same spirit in which you regard the past—panoramically, not individually. And it's very true that the general atmosphere of the 1700s or of Rome seems much more attractive than that of today. (I'm getting in deep there, for the argument carried out means—much more attractive in that it's conducive to individual peace and happiness, and that's just what I'm trying to disprove.) The only way out is to say that all other things being equal, those days would have been better ones in which to live. Other things obviously not being equal, I believe I'll stay in the 20th Century.

Your argument, I suppose, will be that it's only the cases of injustice and mistreatment which history records, and that the vast majority of citizens lived then as now in peace and some happiness, the more so because the tempo of their era was adapted to the enjoyment of greater peace and happiness than we have today. But at least today I can live in the certainty that no government is going to declare illegal the laws which permit me to possess what little I have; and I can go out on the street in the pleasant security of knowing that no fat and hideously depraved noble in a toga and wreath is going to take a fancy to me and snatch me out of the bosom of my family. And I think I've somewhat ridden this subject to death, so let's change it.

For instance, here are three cards I picked up in Valparaiso, Ind., where I spent a few days of my last week of vacation the third week in November. We went on to Chicago from there, and I looked for more cards, but found nothing. Not that these are worth much. Their chief value lies in their evidence that I am a well-meaning woman and that the spirit is willing even if the resources hereabouts are singularly weak.

The lily-pond view for some reason reminds me of a queer little experience my brother and I had about five years ago, when we were very young indeed and took a trip by ourselves up around the Lakes region and into Canada. The moment we got one foot firmly planted on foreign soil we instantly sent torrents of postcards to everyone we were on speaking terms with, creating the impression that we'd spent a week in Canada, though as a matter of fact returned into Detroit the same day.

The queer thing, though, was this. We had a passion for wide expanses of water and would drive all night rather than pitch our pup-tent on a site from which we could not see a lake. (We had an old Chevvie and a battered little pup-tent, which constituted our entire camping equipment.) One evening we'd driven for hours looking for a lake-side tourist camp, and finally just at sunset found a weatherbeaten sign announcing the presence about a mile off the road of a bathing beach. We decided to chance finding a camp site there and turned into a narrow little rutted road that might not have been traveled by anyone in the last fifteen years. It led off into wildernesses of swamp thick with pulpy green reeds, and laced here and there with open canals in which the sunset was gorily red. We drove and drove and drove, through all that bloody water and dark green swamp of reeds, and by the time the sun was almost down we came out into a scrubby little clearing on the edge of Lake Erie, where a frame building and an expanse of rocky shore constituted the bathing-beach we'd been hunting. There was only a little space of clear water, for all along that part of the Lake it's so shallow that as far out as you can see clumps for reeds stick up out of the brown water. And here except for that little clear space thickets of grass and those pulpy green reeds clogged the water for a dozen yards out from the shore, the Lake so shallow that the waves broke almost out of sight and came crawling in among the roots of the green thick things that grew there, making them shiver and rustle together as if snakes were crawling through them.

There were three or four people in the building, apparently the owners settling down for the night. We asked what they'd charge to let us camp there, and to our stupefied amazement they said we could do it for nothing. They were not pleasant looking people, and this generosity almost overcame us. So while my brother was pitching the tent I went down along the shore looking for firewood. And the farther I went and the darker it grew the more uneasy I became. It was so lonely there, miles away from anyone but those most unpleasant looking people and their unbelievably generous ways, and the ugly lake was fading out into darkness and all along the shore those fat thick reeds moved continually together and the ripples lapped among their roots. There wasn't even honest grass among the rocks, but a sort of crawly moss, and I couldn't find any firewood. When I got back to the tent I was definitely afraid. My brother laughed at me. But I was in a state by then when even the generosity of the beach's owners was a matter of grave suspicion—after all it isn't normal to turn down a chance to make 50¢ or so when people are practically waving it under your nose, and we hadn't encountered any other camp-owners, pleasant or unpleasant, who didn't want payment for the use of their ground. And it was getting darker and darker, and stiller and stiller everywhere except for the ripples crawling invisibly among the reeds, and panic is a very contagious thing.

It all ended by our packing our tent again and tearing out of there like a couple of bats out of the usual place, and every time I see water with reeds growing in it I remember that singularly pointless and definitely silly experience. Partly, I suppose, it was caused by our unaccustomedness to solitude and the utter quiet of such places as that, and partly by the dreary and depressing landscape. I don't suppose there was any real point in our alarm and flight, and we did feel very foolish—but we left.

There are places like that which make one afraid just by their presence. And it does seem that there are places which—well, I'm thinking of a road near here I may have mentioned before. There have been at least five murders on it, one early this summer. And all, of course, quite unassociated with one another. One was the death of a hitch-hiker who was killed and burned in the car of the man who had picked him up. One was a poisoning in a house one the road; one the murder of a girl by a negro who threw her off a high bridge a few miles from the poisoning house. I forget the fourth, but the fifth was the death of a young child found below the same bridge from which the girl was thrown. It does seem odd that all five of the murders should have happened on one road. There are lots of other dark and lonely ones nearby, and why the five murderers should have chosen this one is beyond comprehension, and certainly a little beyond coincidence.

Dec. 9th

I have just taken the liberty of making a typewritten copy of your library catalogue. I do feel tremendously guilty doing so little to earn your generosity in lending me your books and stories, and I'm glad of a chance now and then to repay my obligations in such little ways as this. In places where I've been uncertain as to the spelling of titles I'm not familiar I've left blanks to be filled in in ink by you, rather than attempt guesses of my own. (I'm reminded of an anecdote about Eugene Manlove Rhodes, relating that his writing was at times so difficult to decipher that once a quite intelligent reader translated "faith and honor" as "filth and horror"!) Not, of course, that your writing is particularly difficult to read once one's used to it. Really! If you could see some of the handwriting I'm called upon to transcribe in the course of my daily tasks you'd be astonished. Lots of it looks like the tracks of demented angleworms squirming across the page.

I've checked lightly the books I've read on the list. I should be extremely grateful if someday you'd let me see some of the Dunsany books I haven't yet read, and I'd love to get the Merrit[t] "Through the Dragon Glass" and "Face in the Abyss". Have you read his "Burn Witch Burn"? I happen to have a copy of that which is at your disposal if you should ever want to see it. And *that* reminds me remotely of an Arabian lovesong I read once, somewhere—

> "As an ant brought to Soloman [*sic*] the King
> The thigh of a grasshopper as an offering,
> So do I bring my heart to thee, beloved . . .
> I have laid my heart upon your doorsill—
> Step lightly, child!"[3]

The first two lines of that seem to fit the case very well. I do wish I had some better opportunity to repay your generosity than the finding of one book which you don't have. Perhaps "there'll come a day".

The other books in your catalogue all look intensely interesting, but as I've so often said it's impossible to judge by titles what's in the book. I'll keep one copy of the list and make a few meek requests now and then which I hope you'll ignore completely if it's in the least inconvenient for you to comply.

I was extremely pleased at your most flattering remarks about my pomes. It's so lovely to be complimented on things you do only fairly well. It makes little impression on me when people say I can write pretty well or make good biscuits—I know that. But when my coffee or my poetry or my drawings are flattered I purr like a kitten. I'm never very sure of them. You are thrusting your head into the lion's mouth when you ask to see some of my poetic mss. The only thing that saves you from being completely engulfed in mountains of mss. is the fact that I haven't much. (I suspect that "engulfed in mountains" is not a very happy choice of words, but let it go.) I'll enclose a few specimens. No, I've never attempted narrative verse, chiefly because I'm probably the laziest of all created things, and could never drive myself to finish such a work. That's one reason I incline to set verse-forms—you *have* to finish to get the effect right. I'd never even finish writing a story if I didn't know I had to or forego the check.

It will be grand to get your criticism on my Collected Works. Certainly you are qualified by experience as a critic as well as by native ability, as shown very brilliantly in your own verse, to give a verdict on poetry. RHB has seen a few of my efforts. However I have never written anything that might come within the wide scope of the fantastic and weird, and I believe that this is what interests him chiefly.

Yes, I received a copy of "The Goblin Tower" recently, and was very much impressed. The Long poems are well worth preservation, and as the work of an amateur the book was surprisingly well done. It had a charm about it that the slick, stereotyped professional printing completely lacks, and can't even imitate without looking strained. My favorite of all the Long verse, however, is still "Out of the grass when the dew is wet The houses lean and their boards are set Deep in the woods that are not yet."[4]

At the age of 11 you had apparently already formed the tastes which have been with you all your life since. The Ode to Selene is perfectly astonishing for a child of that age, though perhaps not so much so as if one hadn't read the efforts of your cradle days about the cure-all.[5]

(I haven't nearly said all that I want to about verse, but the name Selene reminds me of something I'll forget if I don't tell you about it now. I can see that this letter is going on forever. I've been writing a story about moon-dwellers lately, and at the start of it cast blankly around, as usual, for a name for the race.[6] My eye fell upon the words "Remington Noiseless" inscribed across the façade of my typewriter and following my custom I lifted out of the "Noiseless" the name "Seles". Thought I'd better look it up in the dictionary to see if it meant anything already, and was astounded to find that it meant moon-dweller. Or anyhow, that "selenite" means that. I have never run across "Selena" as an alias of Diana, and was completely stunned by the coincidence.)

You were certainly fortunate in your early youth to have access to such books as you mention. And more fortunate to have the intellect, even at that age, to appreciate them. I begin to understand why the Pope form of verse seems natural to you, incredible though it seems to me that the polished and revised and re-revised poetry of that era can seem to anyone a more natural form of poetic expression than the spontaneous outflow which is my own preference. I suppose I'm not old enough yet to see another's viewpoint, but even to realize that such a thing exists is a step in the right direction.

Your sufferings among Victorian poetry must have been awful. As one who was left severely alone from infancy to form my own tastes in literature, I extend commiserations. However you mustn't condemn Victorian verse in one great sweeping damnation? [sic] There are fragments that are rather lovely. Even those hackneyed lines from Tennyson about magic casements and faerylands forlorn, Ruth in tears among the alien corn,[7] and the horns of elf-land faintly blowing[8]—they all have a charm which constant repetition has dulled, but which is still there. The Idyls of the King have a tapestried beauty which even forcible reading in high school couldn't wholly spoil, and The Lady of Shalott has for years furnished me with a much more effective way of going to sleep than sheep-counting. You recite it very slowly, visualizing each scene in detail, and you never get beyond the third stanza. It's soporific magic. And each time you do it you see the thing more plainly, until you're as nearly as possible to *being* there. Willows whiten, aspens quiver, little breezes dusk and shiver, in the wave that runs forever round the island in the river. . . . You can hear the water breaking against the island, and feel the little cool breeze off the river and see the quivering and twinkling of the leaves in the sun. I have a great weakness for that poem. And simply must quote, with apologies, a paragraph from the peculiar sort of diary which I keep intermittently, as the continuation of letters I used to write to my childhood companion of the mythical kingdom days—"Also that lovely windy moment in the Lady of Shalott's life when She left the web, she left the loom, she made three paces through the room; and out flew the web and floated wide, the mirror cracked from side to side. Such tumult after years of watching reflections in a mirror. I know just how she felt. I can see it. The shadow of Lancelot swimming brightly up through the dim glass, and she starting up, not realizing until she was on her feet that she would do it at all—and the three long paces while her tapestried skirts swirled about her legs, and in one breathless, agonizing vivid moment *She looked down on Camelot.* And then a wild rush in the room behind her, and *out* flew the web and bang went the mirror, and she knew what she had done! And she claps a hand to her side and shrieks "The curse has come upon me!" and that ecstatic moment is gone forever."

Then there are fragments such as "The stern, black-bearded kings, with wolfish eyes, waiting to see me die",[9] and "O, you tamely died! you should have clung to Fulvia's waist and thrust the dagger through her side!"[10]— which are full of a lovely colorful life. However I must admit they're in the minority. [handwritten note:] What about "Lotus Eaters" and "Ulysses"? Surely you don't dislike them?

I simply must change the subject or I'll never in the world finish this letter. Must take time to appreciate the Gentleman of New England's "On an Unspoiled Rural Prospect" with its illustrations, though. And that frontispiece was darn good, too, while I'm on the topic. Mother saw it and went into a mild spasm of admiration.

I am glad you share my enjoyment of Chaucer. Through him, as well as through some of the genuine ballads, there speaks more clearly and vividly than I can well describe the voice of the eternal and changeless *human*. I wonder if that doesn't describe pretty well my real interest in any given past—just to search out the evidences that in any era, in any dress or land or language the man and the woman are no different from ourselves. I don't know why— unless it's explained by humanity's eternal groping after immortality—it gives me such acute pleasure to hear my own voice in stanzas out of the remote past. In different phrases but the same mood, haven't you heard "I would I were dead and in my grave, And the green grass growing over me!"[11] that some long-dead Scottish dame's deathless voice is still crying in an old ballad. Or the Wife of Bath's shrugging off regret for her lost youth, "Lat go, farwell, the devel go therewith!"[12] and you can hear, fullthroated and vigorous and clear, the voice of the Binnoirie heroine as she struggles in the mill-race, shrieking, "O, sister, sister, reach me your hand!"[13] And I could go into endless raptures over the vividness of "The Bowie Houmes of Yarrow" and the emotions of Bonnie Sarah as she "rins down yon hie, hie hill"—stumbling over the wet stones, catching her heels in her draggled skirt-hems, blind with the burning of her tears, her throat one intolerable ache of dread, for she knows even before she reaches the Yarrow what she'll find there—seeing him lying among the dead men, just as he lies in his sleep with one cheek turned to the wet grass, and his blood bubbling thickly around the knife-hilt standing in his back. O, poor Sarah! I don't have to experience a thing like that to know how it must feel, and I'm so desperately sorry for her it's a shame she'll never appreciate it.

And I must mention that casual line out of Chaucer "For she was wilde and yong, and he was old",[14] which is so brutally eloquent of a still living human problem. There surely hasn't been anyone since Geoffrey's day who made so clear that though times change man is eternally the same.

It never occurred to me to call Spencer [*sic*] the first of the Victorians, but I see now that it's beautifully apt. He is a bore, but only in that too much of anything is a bore. Almost any given tableau out of his endless pageant is lovely, but anything cloys if it goes on forever. (I'd better take that to heart and curtail this letter.)

I'll be looking forward to the next package from you. And am hoping I haven't yet seen all your stories. I wish I could take your advice about introducing my fiance to the type of literature which is so fascinatingly represented by your own writing—but it's no use. He's so completely my opposite in everything that he'd simply be bored and revolted. In a way it's good for me that his interests circle around golf and base-ball, automobiles and motor-boats, poker and bridge and detective yarns. I need someone like that to counterbalance my leaning toward the opposite side of life, and I've learned to enjoy ball-games and everything they represent in a way that I would have thought incredible a few years ago. I'll tell you someday of the joys of baseball and basketball that I think very few fans really appreciate who didn't serve an apprentice-ship like mine among books.

I'm looking forward to "The Haunter of the Dark". It sounds splendid. Glad you have your revenge upon Bloch. And I'm so pleased about the Lumley tale.[15] It was awfully kind of you, and I know how grateful he must be.

Dec. 11

Your information about the Crusades was intensely interesting. You should have been a history teacher. You can make such stuff sound fascinating—the lack of which ability among all the history teachers who struggled with me accounts for my ignorance. As I said at the beginning of this letter, I'm gradually acquiring an education, and a large portion of it is due directly to your knack of making dry facts burgeon into vivid life when you recount them.

I was especially interested in your hatred of the bigotry and blind antagonism toward the spread of knowledge which characterized the Middle Ages, in the light of a book I once read that presents a view of that bigotry and blindness which was entirely new to me. It was "Lest Ye Die", by someone called Hamilton,[16] and told the old story of the fall of modern civilization through modern warfare, with such new highlights and original ideas that I think I'll quote some of it:

"How many times—how many times since the world began to spin has man, in his eager search for truth, rushed blindly through knowledge to the ruin that means chaos and savagery? How many times, in his devout, instinctive longing to know his own nature and the workings of the infinite Mind that created him, has he wrought himself weapons that turned to his own destruction? Ignorance of the powers and forces of nature is a condition of human existence as necessary to the continued life of the race as the breathing of air. . . . Man, so long as he is fighting man, must limit his knowledge; which, applied to warfare, means slaughter not only of human bodies but of human institutions, of all we have created through the centuries. The race that would seek science and pursue it without halt must be such a race as the world has not yet seen, composed of men and women balanced and forebearing [*sic*]. Men and women whose passions are so reigned [*sic*] and controlled that they will not flare to action even in a cause most righteous; not even in the name of the God they worship, or at the wrong done others, the helpless. Science, in return for her power and munificence, demands a sacrifice of humanity's virtues as well as of humanity's vices. . . ." And, referring to the days after the fall of civilization, as mankind began the upward struggle again, "— somewhere in the vastness of the great round world the beginnings of a priesthood, a scientific caste, might be building unconsciously on the lines of ancient wisdom and laying the foundations of yet another Egypt or Chaldea, a State whose growth would be rooted in the mystery of knowledge and the fear of human passion, whose culture and civilization would be moulded by a living and terrible tradition of catastrophe through science uncontrolled. And, so long as the tradition was living and terrible the initiate would stand guard before his mysteries, that the world might be saved from itself. Behind the bench of zealots who judged Galileo lay the dumb race-memory for ruin, ruin perhaps many times repeated. They stood, the zealots, for that ignorance which, being interpreted, is life, and Galileo for that knowledge which, being interpreted, is death. Behind the injunction to devout ignorance, being the ecclesiastical hatred of science and distrust of brain, lay more than prejudice and bigotry; the prejudice and bigotry were but superficial and outward workings of instinct and the first law of all—the law of self-preservation."

No doubt the theory could be picked full of holes, but anyhow, it's very original and new, to me at least. Thou shalt not eat of the Tree of Knowledge, "lest ye die". What is your reaction?

Your information about Roman names was well worth knowing. It's a shame the Pompeii movie was spoiled for you just because you knew too much. That "Marcus" abbreviation must have seemed flagrant to you. Surely even the Average Movie Fan would have had enough intelligence to follow the picture even if its hero had had a more convincing name. I've sometimes wondered what mental age is set as the limit for the movie audience intelligence. It can't be more than six.

Didn't the F.F. [*sic*] "Challenge from Beyond" turn out well, considering? Yours was by far the best installment insofar as originality and workmanship are concerned. You had the hardest section, too—having to explain all the unconnected ramblings of your predecessors. Several of the installments, including mine, were carelessly written and loosely phrased, but yours, as usual, was a miracle of exact wording. And wasn't it interesting to see how the personality of each writer colored his installment.

I wish I could debate with you at first hand on the ultimate goal of that form of energy called life. It is so hard to talk this way. It seems to me that there's one fallacy in your argument seen in the light of your own reaction to it. (There she goes, dragging in personalities.) But doesn't it seem logical that if you were convinced down to the very core that death of the body meant the end of that *mode of motion* you speak of, and that all conscious life goes out like a candle, forever—then your own life would have been lived very differently? If the physical things of life are all we're ever to have, and if the mind ceased with the body, then eating and drinking are fully as important as study and knowledge. I'm putting it awkwardly, but do you see a gleam of what I'm trying to get at behind the morass of words? Of course "eating and drinking and carousing" are very important factors in life, and of course knowledge is after all a need in itself and not necessarily a preparation for an "after-life", but in spite of all my argument's frailties I do think that behind your devotion to a life of intellectual culture rather than a life of debauchery and physical excess lies some deeply buried confidence that your own mode of living is not to be wasted as the other mode would be. Is the pursuit of knowledge as wholly futile as the pursuit of physical pleasure? And is it logical to believe that all a man endures in a lifetime is endured to no purpose? Is all the misery and unspeakable hardships and grief of all the past generations only a contribution to the physical betterment of their remote descendants, and not a promise of individual recompense somehow, somewhere, even if it's only in strengthened character and strengthened ability to go on into some unimaginable future. (I can hear you snort!)

But it's very difficult for me, even in my innocent ignorance of what I'm talking about, to believe that there isn't some purpose behind everything that happens, and some future for the "form of energy" beyond the death of the body it animates. Not an individual future, perhaps, but surely we can grant the "soul" at least the immortality its body has—the immortality of atoms going back into the earth and taking on other forms that disintegrate again while the component parts live forever.

I wrote a story once, which I don't believe you ever saw—starting out as my story "Greater Glories" started with a man lost in the interior of a giant body, being swept into its brain-chamber and finding himself in the presence of a god whose people have almost completed their race-goal. The people are of a peculiar physical structure which permits their amalgamation into one immense and rather horrid-looking mass, like a great vine budded with individuals who by now have sunk their individuality into the whole, being drawn together by a common race-love which through the milleniums [*sic*] of life has grown out of and taken the place of all other forms of attraction between individuals. The race has become a unit, but incomplete as the god is incomplete, because each lacks the essential attributes of the other. They are reaching their ultimate goal, which is the union of god and united people, into a perfect whole which is to go on, perhaps, as no more than an atom at the bottom of some tremendous scale of unknown evolution—somewhere. I didn't sell the story, and finally cut it up into "Greater Glories" and "Bright Illusion" and another mass which I haven't tried to recast.

All this not for any particular purpose except to illustrate what I mean by a future not necessarily individual or in any form we know or could understand— but surely *something!* The mind refuses to accept blankness as its only goal, however illogical any other future than that can be made to seem. And mightn't that universal, root-deep determined and unreasoning faith in some ultimate future beyond death be proof in itself that something like that must exist?

Let's argue about your devotion to your library and treasury of personal possessions. The value they possess is admit[t]edly in yourself—beauty in the eye of the beholder, so to speak—yet you say quite sincerely that you'd prefer physical destruction to life without them. And that is defeating your own purpose if you actually believe that life ends with the body, for you'd be destroying not only your own person but the library, since its true, intrinsic worth is in your own destroyed intellect. Only by believing that the intellect goes on could such a self-destruction take on purpose, because by the act of dying you'd remove yourself from a world where the actual books and papers and articles had worth to an actual flesh-and-blood body, and transport yourself to a plane where their intrinsic value is apparent without the medium of tangible paper and ink. I'm sorry if that conjures up a picture of you floating ectoplasmically about in a long misty sheet among the spirits of the psychic world. But I hope you get at least a glimmer of what I'm trying so awkwardly to say—it being the first time I've ever put it down in words.

Also, since I'm disagreeing with everything today, I'll have a shot at your dislike for romance contrasted with your love and understanding of fantasy. You don't have to take Dumas any more literally than you do Dunsany. Of course lots of people probably do look persistently through rose-colored glasses, but then dear, sincere old Lumley believes implicitly in his phantasms. To me it's just as pleasant to imagine during the duration of the story that there is a lovely springtime world peopled exclusively by handsome heroes and exquisite heroines and life is one long romp of adventure with no unpleasant attributes at all, as it is to believe for the length of the story that time, space and natural law can be elastic enough to permit the existence of a Shambleau or a Cthulhu (have I spelled him right?). Your point, of course, is that to be acceptable as release-literature the happenings must be incredibly *outside*, not *against* the phenomena of nature. Does that mean that you can't, with self-respect, enjoy Howard's gorgeous Conan sagas, which are surely pure romance for the most part?

Well, I've been disagreeable enough, so had better change the subject.

Thanks so much for the new cards. The Montcalm house was lovely as an old painting—perhaps because of the unusual finish of the postcard. And the Russell house interior—well, someday I'll have a room just like it. Someday, too, I simply must see the results of the work mentioned in your clipping. It sounds heavenly.

Funny about the Henry Ford windmill of incredible antiquity.[17] I suppose not one in any number of people would know any better than to take the newspaper date for honest fact—certainly not I.

Haven't heard of the new Unusual Stories magazine. Who puts it out? It sounds interesting.[18]

What a pity about Long's aunt.[19] I'm so sorry—admiring his poems gives one a sort of vicarious acquaintance and brings such happenings as the aunt's death a bit closer than simply an accident to a totally unknown.

I have three Koenig books to be sent on to you, and could start a whole new letter talking about them. As you say, when you write in installments it is almost impossible to stop each time, but I'll be firm with myself and still the babbling for this particular letter.

Oh yes, and merry Christmas.

CLM [signed]

Catherine Moore

[P.S.] Lord help us, this is without end. I *am* sorry, but I just couldn't find a stopping place.

[Note by HPL:] mention Dark Land & illus.

[Enclosure: assorted poems by CLM]

POMES

I stumbled in the dance. Beneath my feet
The red-hot flags of hell-pave scorched my soles.
Where others danced on hardwood, smooth and sweet,
The hell-coals turned beneath my stumbling feet,
And brimstone, bitter through the music's beat,
Blinded me hotly from the flame-washed coals.

I stumbled in the dance. Beneath my feet
The red-hot flags of hell-pave scorched my soles.


Here is an end to all that tragic
Blinding sweetness and glimpse of magic,
And feet that mounted the rainbow's bend
Come down to earth at the farther end,
And heart's desire is a tale long told,
And spring is ended and love is old!


Sold—for a penny. Here is all you buy:
A bubble moon adrift across the sky;
A dim regret for other nights and moons,
And half-heard dancing tunes.
Indifference, and quietude and peace,
And half-regrets that cease,
And leave no scar.
How cool the stars across your shoulder are
The while my throat is bent beneath your kiss,
All I am thinking of is this, and this.
What matter? Though my lips may prate of love—
This I am thinking of.

THE DOGS SHALL EAT JEZEBEL BY THE WALLS OF JEZREEL
The white walls of Jezreel are splattered in the sun;
The mongrels of Samaria are howling as they run.
Underneath the splashed walls Jezebel is lying,
Jezebel, the white queen, dead upon the stones.
There shall be none to bury her,
To lift her up and carry her,
But only dogs to harry her
And scuffle for her bones.

Traitors in the queen's house, harshly Jehu calls,
O white queen of Jezreel, flashing as she falls!
Jehu's shodden horses trample by the walls.

The white walls of Jezreel are splattered in the sun;
The mongrels of Samaria are howling as they run.


(And I'm not entirely guiltless of the pseudo-comic, as thus:) (The scene being the bank where I work)

Mary is a lady—a lady not too slim,
With deep, bewitching dimples and a fatal lure for *him*.
I sit and watch them daily from the balcony above
And grind my teeth to splinters as I see her with my love.
She's pink and white and pearly, and she billows where she should,
And her hair is always perfect, and I'd kill her if I could.
O, it's hell to sit and watch her as she ambles past his cage,
And her cream and peaches buxomness brims up my soul with rage
As she furls her flowing lashes with a slow and honeyed guile
And flashes all her dimples in that perfect, pearly smile.
It's murder that I'm plotting if she goes his way again—
I hate a girl who poaches, and the world is full of men,
So I serve this timely warning—let her heed it while she can:
It is murder, murder, MURDER if she doesn't leave my man!

But most of my versifications have been on the various topics of the Mythical Kingdom:

High o'er Alisia's level land
The castled crags of the Sun-born strand;
And over the country, near and far
The blood tracks of the Dragon are!

———

If I were lord in Aralie,
Larali, Larali,
Why then the ground your feet have pressed
Should be a shrine forever blessed,
And every print should be inlaid
With polished ivory and jade
To be small shining shrines to thee,
If I were lord in Aralie—
Laralie, Laralie!

———

When last we rode this way
The woods were blossoming into May,
And knee to knee we rode that day,
Your brown boot to my velvet gown,
The sunlight dappling softly down
In changing patterns to our pace.
The angle of your downbent face

Sidelong beneath my lashes caught
Turned the whole world to less than naught,
And heaven and earth revolved for me
Round one whose brown boot touched my knee
Once, on a May-tide, long ago,
When time was younger.
                          Dreaming so,
Almost I think the world a-May
And time turned back to yesterday,
The hour when last we rode this way,
The tear-sweet hour we rode this way.

———

(In the year 2000 A.D. the islands which comprise our kingdom are scheduled to sink beneath the main, and the situation then has spawned many a
lamenting song:)

The salt tide sweeps through Rivah Town,
Where once the war-tide swept;
Blue peace broods over Rivah Town,
Where peace as never kept.
The windows of the tower look down
On fishes swimming through;
And sea-weed furls the castle walls
Where once the Dragon flew.
Through Rivah Town in sounding swells
The tide of war has rolled,
But rust is on the sleeping blades
And Dragon blood runs cold,
And Rivah dreams her splendid dreams
Beneath the quiet deep—
Dream on, dream on, O Rivah Town,
Forever in your sleep!
Sing a dirge for the Dragon King
Who never wore a crown,
Toll the bells for the Black Lorane,
The Monarch of the Drowned.
For I was lord of a golden land
That slumbered on the deep,
But to and fro o'er the Dragon Throne
The tides of ocean sweep.
And nevermore shall my maidens dance
To the music of the *laar*,

And nevermore shall the Lydragon
Go sweeping forth to war.
For over our green and golden land
The headlong ocean broke,
And I am lord of the drowned and dead—
My gay and gallant folk!
I hear them call when I lie to sleep
And the moon is at the round,
Dwellers all in a sea-swept land,
In a kingdom of the drowned.
I know their beds in the tideless dark
Where the twilight glooms and gleams—
Their faces pale and their foam-jeweled hair
And their voices in my dreams.
O, sing a dirge for the Dragon King
Who never wore a crown.
Toll the bells for the Black Lorane,
The monarch of the crowned.

———

The girls who died for Dalmar,
Tonight they sleep a-chill,
The honey lips are dust now,
The throbbing throats are still,
And peace is on the high hearts
That beat for him so warm,
And peace is on the sleek heads
That lay on Dalmar's arm.
Their hearts have ceased from sorrowing,
Their tears no longer fall,
The narrow bed, the cold bed,
The grave enfolds them all.

———

And there's just room for my latest and perhaps last of the countless stanzas which have been written since I was old enough to hold pen in hand, a lament that I've grown up out of the old days, and inspired by the juvenile ballad about "Far and few are the lands where the Jumblies live":[20]

Far and few the Islands are,
Few and Far, few and far.
And I shall never walk again
The highway of l'Mal Lorane,

Or see, save dimly, from afar,
The Lydragon go forth to war,
Or hear the bugles, clear and keen
Save faintly, o'er the gulf between,
For I have come too far to turn,
And though I know the watch-fires burn
Along Alisian's hilltops still
Where once the sons of Ildrinil
Were cradled for their wakening.
And all the bells of Avar ring,
No sight or sound can bring me back
To walk again the Dragon's track.[21]
For I, who loved it far too well,
Shall nevermore see Coronel
Save briefly, for a moment's space.
O lost and well beloved place,
Farewell. Your lovely islands are
Too few and far, too few, too far!


And thank you kindly for reading this far. You have my sympathy.


*Notes*

1. "Sidewise in Time." See CLM 7n3.
2. Mildred Cram (1889–1985), "Time Found Again." *Cosmopolitan* 99, No. 6 (December 1935): 22–25.
3. Tcherkess Khan, "An Afghan's Love" (tr. Achmed Abdullah [1881–1945]), *Harrisburg* [PA] *Telegraph* (29 July 1925): 6; *Golden Book Magazine* 2, No. 8 (August 1925): 197.
4. "The White People," ll. 1–3.
5. HPL had sent CLM the ms. of his juvenile poetry volume *Poemata Minora, Volume II* (1902), containing "Ode to Selene or Diana," "To the Old Pagan Religion." "On the Ruin of Rome," "To Pan," and "On the Vanity of Human Ambition."
6. "Lost Paradise," a Northwest Smith story.
7. Actually lines from Keats, "Ode to a Nightingale."
8. Tennyson, "Blow, Bugle, Blow," l. 10.
9. Tennyson, "A Dream of Fair Women," ll. 111–12.
10. Tennyson, "The Lotos-Eaters," ll. 259–60.
11. Anon., "The Forsaken Bride." In Francis Turner Palgrave, ed., *The Golden Treasury*.
12. "The Wife of Bath's Prologue," l. 482.
13. From the English fairy tale "Binnorie."
14. "The Miller's Tale," l. 3225.
15. HPL had revised Lumley's story "The Diary of Alonzo Typer."

16. A rewritten, retitled version of *Theodore Savage: A Story of the Past or the Future* (1922). The author, Cicely Hamilton (pseudonym of Cicely Mary Hamill) was a British suffragist.

17. Farris Windmill (formerly known as Cape Cod Windmill, built in 1633) stood at the road to West Yarmouth, MA. The windmill was a gift to Henry Ford from his Ford dealership employees, who had it moved it from the Cape to Greenfield Village.

18. *Unusual Stories* (1934–35; 3 issues) was William L. Crawford's companion magazine to *Marvel Tales*.

19. Frank Belknap Long's only aunt, Cassie Doty Symmes, died in a motor accident near Miami on 20 October 1935.

20. Edward Lear (1812–1888), "The Jumblies," ll. 11–12.

21. The couplet is oddly similar to the opening lines of HPL's "The Ancient Track": "There was no hand to hold me back / That night I found the ancient track."

[24]    [HPL, nonextant; Christmas card]

[mid-December 1935]

[25]    [AHT][1]

[January 1936]

The revolution of 1775–83 certainly did involve blame on both sides—& the separate elements are almost impossible to disentangle & appraise. But the one thing I cannot forgive is the act of the rebels in withdrawing wholly from the Empire. There is no question but that the course of civilisation in these colonies would have been much smoother & higher-grade if a close connexion with the Mother Land had been maintained. Firmer educational ties, more colonists from home & fewer immigrants from the scum-deposits of Southern & Eastern Europe, better maintenance of British standards of order & reasonableness, sounder development of the literary & aesthetic tradition—a thousand different things would have been better if the hotheads & greedy pushers of 1776 had not rushed through their treasonable secession. The bad results of the break were instantly evident—America having a reign of wholesale demoralisation & chaos from about 1780 to nearly 1800 which few today seem to realise. Then around 1820—when the last of the cultivated colonial generation began to die off—there was a profound & pervasive drop in the niceties of general culture. Architecture began to glide down hill, & language & manners acquired unheard-of extravagances. By the 1840's the dominant atmosphere was one of barbarism, grotesqueness, & infantile sentimentality—as Poe knew to his cost. Then, after a slow climb a trifle upward, the rise of a parvenu plutocracy in the 1870's—the Gilded Age—gave American culture another cataclysmic backward push . . . . . a thing which could not have happened in a region closely joined to English life. From the insipid '80's onward, there has been a certain improvement—but a very uneven one, with heavy losses in certain fields to subtract from general gains. Since the

World War there has been a vast decadence in everything but the sciences & the novel & drama. America is wiser but cruder. England of course has had its parallel ups and downs, but the troughs are not so deep there. I wish your history teacher & good old McGavack could be rounded up for a debate! An auditor would learn much from the resultant pyrotechnics!

*Notes*

1. In AHT, this text is dated 8 March 1936.

[26]   [TLS, JHL]

Thursday, January 30, 1936

Dear Mr. Lovecraft:

I meant to begin with a perfect paean of thanks for those lovely books. That large a dose of Dunsany at one time was almost too much for me. The urge to try something similar in the way of fantasy and description is almost irresistible, and yet somehow it never turns out to be worth the paper it's written on. No one can imitate Dunsany, and probably everyone who's ever read him has tried. The Merritt books were delightful, too. I had read "Face in the Abyss" once years ago and had been trying for a long while to find it and reread it. And I think I enjoyed "Through the Dragon Glass" more than anything else of his I've read. His description of the Glass itself was extremely powerful, and the incidents in the enchanted land beyond it were done so deftly and lightly that they kept just the air of delicious impossibility which such a story needs. Its brevity, I think, was what made it so good. If he'd stretched it out to book-length and piled adventure on adventure and fantastic scene upon scene it would have lost all its lightness and charm. Thanks so much.

I'll be looking forward to the next Dunsany books. I do hope you can get the "Sword of Welleran" with the S. H. Sime illustrations. Wasn't it he whose frontispiece in "King of Elfland's Daughter" showed the man and the unicorn struggling together on the hilltop with planets blazing in the sky behind them? If so, no one else should ever illustrate Dunsany. I've always connected that drawing with my earliest impressions of Dunsany, and like the Tenniel (spelling?) illustrations for Alice in Wonderland, the artist and the author belong together. (My sentences do get so involved.)

I'm glad you are pleased with the typed copy of your catalogue. It seems little enough return for all your generosity, and I'm still deeply indebted to you. Thanks for the list of corrections, and of the suggested items to be borrowed. As nearly as one can judge from the titles and the authors all of them sound extremely interesting. I shall leave it to you, however, which are sent. You're a better judge, since you've read them. Whichever books you can spare and which aren't too much trouble to send I shall appreciate seeing very much indeed. There are so many of them and they all sound so interesting.

It's somewhat appalling to consider how many books there are which I should love to read and which I may never get to. And all the others that I may never even hear of. That is bad enough now, when the writing of imaginative fiction on a very prolific basis, in our language, is still comparatively recent in origin. But imagine the plight of people like me several hundred years ahead, with centuries of literature piling up behind them so deeply they know they'll never in one lifetime be able to read all the delightful stories they'd like to read. And also, think of all the new books and new authors who will flourish after we're dead. It's most discouraging. Reminds me of a Dunsany poem I read once—"Who are they, leaning out of golden air, [/] These people of the morning?"[1] and continuing to say that they're the Lancelots and Arthurs and Quixotes whom we'll never live to read about.

It was gratifying to find "Astounding" publishing your "Mountains of Madness" so promptly. I'm experimenting on the strength of my will power by trying not to read it until I have the complete story, but the strain is terrific. Oh yes—that "might have been" story in "Astounding" would, if carried out fully, not only have included a future in which Tremaine had rejected and Wright accepted the "Mountains of Madness" tale, but also included other futures in which it was both accepted and rejected by every publication in the world, printed in every issue of every one of them instead of the February issue of Astounding, and not only that but futures wherein every separate idea you weighed and rejected in writing the story was incorporated, separately, with resultant changes in the course of the plot. I suppose, if you really take the idea seriously, you'd have to have a train of events shooting off into separate times every split second of one's life, as every possible action that might be taken at every instant during the day and night was carried out to its ultimate goal. Heavens, I think I'll change the subject.

I was extremely interested in reading your summary of your own views on the Revolution. As you say, the controversy over which side was to blame will probably never be decided, and from your outline it looks as if—like all quarrels—both were much to blame. But from a purely selfish standpoint it does seem, for our own good, that we shouldn't have broken entirely away from England. It's fun to think how differently modern civilization might have developed in America if we hadn't. It seems to my untutored mind that the country would have had a much more uniform and well-balanced growth if it had had a center of government as strong and conservative, comparatively speaking, as the English rule it cast off. The situation here must have been much like that of a colony of children setting up their own government and managing fairly well without adult supervision. Not, of course, that I know anything about it, but that's the impression my scattered and meagre information leaves.

McGavack's "Genesis of the Revolutionary War"[2] is certainly a violent antidote to the information the local history teacher gave me. The fur would fly if those two ever came together! He surely must be exaggerating to some degree, though I don't doubt that both he and my own informant could point out any number of authentic cases to prove their contentions. There must have been enough individual incidents on each side of the argument to prove almost anything either for or against.

Your quotations from old and new press opinions were delightful. It's a very old truth, and yet always interesting to re-prove, that people have been saying the same things for a good long while. Whenever that subject is mentioned I remember the fragment of clay tablet from—as I recall it—Babylonia purporting to carry part of the diary of a dancing-girl whose account of her breathless waiting one night for a certain man-at-arms to arrive at her place of business was almost too modern in its ageless and familiar tableau. The thing may have been a fake—it seems rather unlikely that a dancing-girl would be able to write at all—but I've always got as much pleasure out of thinking about it as if I knew it were gospel truth.

The Roman politics you sketch sound awfully familiar too. I'd like to quote the French proverb about the "plus ce change, le plus c'est la même chose" or something vaguely like that, but my French limps so pitifully that you probably don't even recognize I'm trying to say that the more it changes, the more it's the same thing.

Speaking of Rome, let me warn you never to read Talbot Mundy's "Tros of Samothrace", a 900-page opus which I've been slowly wading through for weeks and weeks—slowly because I'm enjoying it so much I don't want to finish, though Mr. Mundy's attitude toward all things Roman strikes even me as somewhat prejudiced. According to him, nothing in any way connected with Rome, Romans in general and Julius Caesar in particular, can have anything good said about it. He pictures Caius Julius as the epitome of everything treacherous and cruel and disgusting, though conceding him a personal charm which I suppose even he couldn't quite deny. The book, as far as I've gone, concerns the efforts of Tros of Samothrace to keep the Romans out of Britain, knowing what frightful things have happened wherever else the rule of Rome has spread. I suppose when you put petty overlords of any race in possession of high, low and middle justice over a conquered people you have to expect a certain amount of tyranny, but it did seem to me he exaggerated. He cited Caesar's cutting off the hands of thirty thousand rebellious Gauls, for instance. It sounds very dreadful today, but I doubt if it did to the Britains whom "Tros" was represented as addressing. The modern viewpoint must be much more squeamish than that of Caesar's time. According to Mundy, Rome itself was a hotbed of political rottenness and personal vice, and that it was spreading its poisonous unpleasantness as fast and as far as Caesar could manage, and that every colony he established would in no time at all be a little Rome, as full of tyranny and corruption as the original. Was it all as bad as that? Do you think Rome's colonization was justified from the point of view of eventual benefit to the conquered people? (A distinct flavor of Mussolini-vs.-Ethiopia there, further illustrating "le plus ce change").

Mundy presents Britain before its conquest as a barbaric paradise peopled by brawny and noble folk whose simple pastoral life was guided by wise, benevolent Druids. He even has his Druids aware that the world is round and that the earth goes round the sun, ca[l]culating tides and such from their astonishing astronomical knowledge. Incidentally his hero is a Samothracian whose mystery apparently had initiated him into similar knowledge. Out of that paragraph a whole flock of questions arises. Just how much do you suppose the Druids did know about science and medicine and so on? Does anyone know what were the secrets behind the Samothracian and other Mysteries? Also, going back to the Druids, I've heard of them as a gang of bloodthirsty warlocks going about with their golden sickles offering up human sacrifices left and right; and here they're a cult of gentle, benevolent sages. Just where does the medium of truth fall between those two concepts? Another interesting "might-have-been" here—what would British culture have been like today if Roman had never conquered the islands?

Mundy's description of the little town of Lundon on the river Thames sounds so delightful that though I know I'd run shrieking in horror from the very thought of living there if I could once walk through the place and smell the smells and see inside the doubtless bug-ridden thatched houses with their smoking fires and bare timbers—still it did sound idyllic from his description. And the little footnotes scattered through the book wherever a brooklet flowing through the town or a spot along the river is mentioned, announcing that this stream now flows through a sewer under Fleet Street, and the old London Bridge was located at about this spot on the Thames centuries later—give a curious sort of pleasure to reading and the visualization that I can't quit define. Makes it seem so authentic, perhaps.

I shouldn't advise you to read the book—it would make you so furious you couldn't enjoy it—but I'm having a lot of fun out of it myself. Speaking of books, did you ever get around to the two Claudiuses by Robert Graves. You must do so someday. Graves, like yourself, has the knack of making history come so vividly alive that it's like paying an actual visit to the era he's talking of.

Just remembered something I saw this morning that made me think of you and your contribution to the Fantasy "Challenge" story. It's been unspeakably cold here—the lowest has been 20 below, but it [is] 8 below outside right now and fluctuates up and down from there (I suppose [it] is even worse in Rhode Island)—and I passed on the street a man carrying a baby all wrapped up in a blue blanket so tightly, and with the end of the covering folded over its face completely in so curious a way, that the child looked exactly like a small blue worm swaying upright in the man's arms. I remembered your worm-race, and wondered if the man himself might not have been a distant connection, whose tainted blood had betrayed him in the shape of his child, and that the baby was indeed what it looked so startlingly like.

Continued Feb. 1

Recently I attended one of the local celebrations of the President's birthday dance—desperately formal, dripping gardenias, amid much acreage of bare feminine backs and stiff masculine shirtfronts—and the formality of it and the nation-wide celebration had a very pleasantly feudal flavor. Whatever one may—or mayn't—think of FDR the birthday celebration is an enjoyable rite and one which I hope will be taken up by the next incumbent for some worthy charity or other. Beside the formal affairs there was a dance in the colored district for all the negroes, and a Labor Union assembly for, presumably, the various unions, thus embracing practically all walks of life. I like the idea.

You can't imagine how much I enjoyed reading your "Further Criticism of Poetry".[3] It was actually the first critical analysis of verse that I have ever read. I have, I think, been following more or less, and quite unconsciously, your outline for the avoidance of too-bad verse, but shall keep the brochure (and thank you!) so that I may hereafter guard myself from such lapses as I'm sometimes guilty of. (I hope sentences ending with prepositions don't annoy you. I get perfectly rabid whenever I see a split infinit[iv]e, so can understand I might possibly be giving offense. Prepositional endings are a weakness of mine which I make little effort to correct. Now that I think of it, there is to me something rather pleasing about them, a definite, blunt end to a sentence that gives sharp emphasis to the fact that you're *finished*.) Back to the subject: the other day I spent a dusty and highly entertaining evening digging through an old chest of drawers full of the effusions of my early teens. The first stories I wrote were there, and scores of notebooks full of "History" and bales upon bales of early verses. I am somewhat distressed to find that I certainly have not improved any in the last ten years or more so far as my poetry is concerned. I unearthed some old love-songs that Dalmar j'Penyra sang to the girls of Coronel a timeless while ago on the fair blue islands of History that made me very homesick. What utter *fun* that used to be! I'll never again be able to enter into anything with the absolute abandon of those infant days when the islands of Coronel were far more real for hours at a time than anything else on earth. I'd like to quote just for the pleasure of quoting, but can recall just now only the first stanza of one song:

> The earth lies warm in the arms of night,
> The stars in the sky's embrace;
> The dark bay breathes in the harbor's arms
> With stars upon its face;
> The trees bend down to the night wind's kiss,
> His breath more sweet than wine;

> The old moon leans on the young moon's arm—
> And why not you on mine?

(It just occurs to me how tactless it would [have] been of Dalmar, in consideration of the second from the last line, to sing that song to a lady somewhat older than himself! I hope he never did.) Aside from the Historical aspect of my late discoveries, there were a few echoes of highschool crushes for various football heroes and the like, such as—

> I saw you walking in the snow
> (With one than I more blessed)
> And you were walking in the snow
> And laughing at some jest,
> Your hat pulled low upon your brow,
> Your eyes with mirth alight,
> And you were smiling in the snow
> And O, your smile was white!
> I know not what your jesting was,
> And yet when you were gone
> I laughed a happy laugh myself
> And happily went on,
> Remembering your flashing smile
> Beneath the snowy skies,
> The hat pulled low upon your brow,
> The laughter in your eyes.
> And so I laughed as I went on,
> A happy laugh, and low,
> Because I passed you once today,
> Laughing in the snow.

And here's one that rather surprised me, I'd forgotten it so completely, and am not exactly sure yet if the peculiar jerky rhythm is a fault or a virtue. What do you think? I had somewhat tritely labeled it "Mad Shepherd's Song"—

> The snow-white queen goes walking through her hall,
> As white as the snows and as cold as the snows.
> In her diamond slippers she stands very tall,
> And she looks not to the left nor to the right as she goes.
> A diamond crown shines on her coiffed hair,
> Her silk robes rustle along the dark floor;
> Proud ladies walk behind her, none are half so fair;
> A priest who swings a censer paces on before.

*   *   *

She shall near the window, a pace or two along,
The tall queen, the proud queen, so rich with nations' art—
I shall lift my voice up and sing a gypsy song,
She shall feel the wild strains tugging at her heart.

The priest will chant an anthem to drown my voice away,
The maids will draw the shutters and let the curtains fall.
The tall queen, the proud queen, she will not say them nay,
But she will hear my love-song ring above them all.

I shall leave my post then, and go beyond the town,
Out where the wild bird carols to its mate,
Out where the white road ribbons through the down,
All in the night-time I'll sit me down and wait.

When I hear the dawn wind ripple through the grass,
When the sun rises, and the night birds are dumb,
When I see the east sky glimmering like glass,
Down along the white road I shall see her come.

She is in her white shift, her narrow feet are bare,
She wears a wreath of daisies, no other gems at all,
The little breathless dawn wind tosses up her hair,
And without her silver heels she is not very tall.

Out along the woodlands where the leaves are green,
I shall come in triumph, walking with the queen.

It's very reassuring that you liked the samples of verse I afflicted you with. Thanks for calling my attention to the "drowned–crown" flaw in rhyme. I don't know why I never noticed that. Perhaps because in the eight or ten years since I wrote it I've become so accustomed to it that I no more notice or question the wording than I would "Our Father Which* art in Heaven", though that too needs a little work on the pronouns, don't you think? It's more or less a key line in the poem—do you think its alteration into a slightly less pleasing wording is justified by the correction of the rhyme? I actually

---

[*note by HPL] *which* & *who* interchangeable—persons or things & interchangeable (as now) with *that* from beginning of 16th century to well into 17th. *That* used from 13th century was relative. *Which* from 14th in. *Who* from 16th. "Our Father *which* art . . ." all right when K. James bible was written.

By 18th century most had forgotten that *who* & *which* had been interchangeable, so that in 1711 Steele complains in the Spectator (#78 "humble Petition of Who & Which") of the use of one for the other (& of the excessive use of *that*), & cites the Lord's Prayer as an instance of error.

can't tell—have known it as it is for so long that any change, however badly needed, seems somewhat vandalistic to me. (If there is such a word.)

Your infant "Ode to Selene" becomes more surprising the more I read of it. Not only is the workmanship of its metre and wording and general form above any criticism I could make, but the idea it expresses is rather more subtle than one would expect from a child of such tender years. If you remember any more of it, let me know.

Feb. 5

Still on the subject of poetry, I come blushingly to my shocking blunder in confusing Keats and Tennyson. I cannot, however, truthfully say that I'm sure I knew better. When I was a little bookworm brat my discoveries among the poets were wholly haphazard and quite unguided, and at that early age I paid little attention to the authors themselves, grouping the snatches of verse I learned by content rather than by writer. Tennyson *did* write "sweet and far, from cliff and scar, the horns of Elfland, faintly blowing—", didn't he? I suppose I've always, ever since I could read, attributed to him everything in that mood written in verse. All of which explains but does not excuse.

I had a lot of fun in my early reading days discovering poetry. Some of the very earliest I shall always remember in pictures rather than words. I suppose children must visualize things more automatically than adults. At any rate I shall always *see* the Lady of Shalott on her river island, when I think of that poem, in the split second before the words themselves come into my mind. I've often thought what fun it's going to be introducing my children to literature, but perhaps after all it's more fun for them to discover for themselves, as I did, all the excitement and beauty of poetry and prose.

A co-employe at the Bank has been regaling me with meritorious quotations from Tennyson, and I've been thinking all day today of his favorite lines from "Idyls of the King" (I'm certain I'm not confused there!) which describe Arthur's death, and the carrying of his armoured body down a rocky hillside by his knights, all the harsh, clanging, consonantal words as the steel-clad body bangs and clashes on the stones—and then the scene changing—"and on a sudden, lo, the level lake. . . ."[4] That is a very beautiful line, spoken aloud. Incidentally, the same co-worker claims proudly that some of his ancestors were burnt for witchcraft.

Speaking of the Arthurian legends, Dunsany's mention of all the lost cities—Camelot and Illion and the rest—in one of his tales roused in me a never very latent interest in Arthur's city, and the other day I got from the library a volume of the Morte d'Arthur with a vague idea of doing something with it. I may be mistaken, but the Lancelot–Guinever[e] romance has always seemed to me rather startlingly authentic in contrast with the usual type of love story in that era. I mean, there's not much idyllic and romantic about it—it might so easily have happened. Lancelot loving Guinever[e] and remaining sincerely

Arthur's best friend, and feeling rotten about it and not being able to help himself. And the gradual let-down in the affair as the years passed, with everyone but Arthur knowing, and the lovers gradually growing sick of each other, yet unable to separate, and the inglorious end of the whole thing. One doesn't as a rule encounter such realism in any literature save the ultra-modern. After the first of the Lancelot–Guinever[e] affair, when the bloom of it had somewhat worn off and the long ride through the springtime woods and the first blazing romance of the sub-rosa lovemaking at King Arthur's court had slipped behind them, I don't like to think about the affair at all. It gets too unpleasant.

About games, I do agree with you heartily. There's a certain flavor of other days in chess and chessmen that I appreciate—the galloping leap-move of the Knight, and the ponderous, lumbering rush of the Castle, and the rather wickedly ironic protection of the King and use of the Queen in the battle, and above all the Bishop's cloven head which I like to connect with Thomas a'Becket's [*sic*] martyrdom, though there may be no relation at all. Chessmen have a glamour which the actual playing of the game lacks. Cards, too, are pleasant to look at—the stiff Kings and Queens and Jacks in their funny heraldic clothes, and the symbolism of the suits and numbers are rather fun. And there is in outdoor games a wild exhilaration that unfortunately fades before the event is half over and leaves one squirming and restless. If baseball had four innings instead of nine or more, and basketball lasted half an hour and football two quarters instead of four I'd enjoy them immensely. As it is, the picturesqueness of the crowds and the contagion of enthusiasm make it almost worth the going.

I shall remember for a long while the State finals of the Indiana basketball tournament which I attended a year or two ago. The game itself is long forgotten, but it was held in the fieldhouse of one of the local colleges, seating about 15,000 or 20,000. It was jammed to the eaves that night, and from where we sat I could look up and up and up at tier after tier of intent faces that made a queer sort of pattern in the haze of floating cigarette smoke that hung in layers, giving the enormous place a yet more tremendous vastness, as if actual clouds were floating in midair under the sky-high roof. Masses extending into dim distance, almost to infinity, was the illusion. And a lovelier tapestry cannot be imagined than the panorama of that crowd. Rows and rows of close-packed white ovals, each faintly patterned with eyes-nose-and-mouth design, and a gorgeous smoke-blued background of brown and red and purple and green and blue, all blending richly in the hazy dimness. And between halves when everyone lit cigarettes the effect was startlingly beautiful as little points of brilliant light broke out of and faded and bloomed again twinklingly all over the moving tapestry, like the glitter of tiny starts. The whole panorama was a bit larger than the eye could grasp. I kept trying to compass it all, and had the baffling sensation of just missing it. And the odd, unsymmetrical pattern was just distinct enough that I knew it existed, yet couldn't define it.

There was a touch of extreme barbarity at the end, when the winning team hoisted its captain to its shoulders and he hacked down both nets from the baskets with a knife, amid the earsplitting shrieks of the entire 20,000. One felt that a very few layers of veneer removed would have treated us to the spectacle of the winners hewing the heads from the vanquished with exactly such howls of triumph.

And then there was a baseball game last summer that was rather impressive too, chiefly for the singing which, between games (it was a "doubleheader") would rise faintly in one corner of the stands and gather strength as it rose, and go sweeping across the bleachers in deepening floods until one was almost drowned in cyclopean melody. Ten thousand people rolling out "The Man on the Flying Trapeze" makes quite an impressive noise. And in the last half of the inning with the home team making a desperate effort to even the score the noise in the stands was almost unbearable, not human at all, the voiceless roar of a typhoon, on a very much larger scale than the merely mortal. The earth shook as somebody swung and hit and the ball soared up against the black sky. It must be intoxicating to have ten thousand people agonizing on one's swing, and to evoke such more than mortal roaring when one hits. And then in the midst of that thunderous, stunning tumult the loudspeaker would cough preliminarily, and a hush like death would fall instantly upon the splitting throats of the ten thousand, and down from the darkness overhead, beyond the blazing batteries of lights too strong to look into, rolled the voice of the oracle naming the play and calling the batter's name. Exactly like the voice of the Lord thundering out of a blinding light in the dark sky, disembodied, unhuman, vaster than any throat of flesh could utter in its magnified volume, coming from all points of the compass at once in the echoing night overhead and silencing the crowd like magic. The yells that followed its cessation were distinctly reminiscent of the shrieks of savage warriors surging forward to battle after a direct message from on high. Something very evocative of the first ancestor in crowds and games and music.

Speaking of the panoramic, un-definable pattern of the basketball crowds recalls to me my still stubborn though quite untutored insistence that there *should* be, behind living, a purpose and pattern quite ungraspable, perhaps, but it *ought* to be there. I do not, of course, know what I'm talking about exactly, and I've not, like you, read any of the authorities you quote, but the viewpoint of my uninformed mind still insists upon some purpose in everything that happens. I hope I didn't drivel about good and evil and justice in my last letter, for I didn't intend to, but I have the impression that for every force in nature there's an opposite force, and that balance and proportion exist everywhere in the physical world, that even in history there's a sort of compensatory force so that even the most dreadful things that happen eventually work out to benefit the human race, and the most beneficial things that happen have their balancing detrimental effect, eventually. So it seems to me that everything one goes through in a lifetime tilts the scales heavily off level if there's no purpose to it. I can see, reading over that, how childish it must sound to you, and perhaps I'm wrong and a few years from now will look back on it in deep shame at every having been such a Pollyanna. However, right or wrong, there's nothing to be done to change things, so I shall change the subject instead.

I'm glad you didn't miss the movie "Crusades". It muffed the history it portrayed rather badly, but it did catch the roistering swagger and color of the times perfectly. I saw another lately, "Captain Blood"[5] which was pure melodrama and romance, but very pleasing. It portrayed James II as a monster, which rather shocked me since, reared on Browning's Cavalier Songs, I've always been a strong Jacobite without knowing a thing about the Stuarts. I've always seen them in the glow of the Bonnie Prince Charlie, King-Over-the-Water toast, and am now curious to know the truth about them. I suppose it's the contrast with Cromwell rather than any inherent virtue of their own that makes the Stuarts shine so in comparison. What's your opinion?

How thoroughly horrid the Roger Williams discovery was!

By the way, your Christmas card was involved in quite a coincidence. I'd been saving to show you one with the same picture, and a note on the back, "The Old Fairbanks House, Dedham, Mass. This rambling, picturesque old house is believed to be the oldest frame house now standing in the United States. After a lapse of three centuries it is still owned by lineal descendants of Jonathan Fayerbanke who were made a corporation in 1903 to preserve and perpetuate this historic spot."[6]

By now you've probably, at long last, received the Charles Williams books along with the returned Dunsany and Merritt things. I enjoyed "The Greater Trumps" and "Place of the Lion" tremendously, but for some reason went suddenly flat when I came to the third book and simply could not read it. I envy the writer his ability to say exactly what he wants to say, in as great detail and just as obscurely as he pleases, without a single qualm about the lag in the motion of his story. I never read anything written with such utter disregard for the reader. It seems to be written for his own pleasure and no one else's, with a sort of take-it-or-leave-it attitude, and it's surprising how readable, after all, the books, are if you're in the mood for it and can keep yourself thoroughly submerged and read slowly and deeply enough to see what he's talking about. I think that even then you could go back and reread the book several times, discovering new things at every trial.

I was glad to see the clipping showing the proposed new buildings on College Street. They look pleasantly authentic despite their newness. And the slant of the street itself gives me great joy. Reared in the utter flatness of the middle west, I react violently to angles and altitudes. And it was interesting to see #66 in the Rhode Island pamphlet. I think I recognized the trees from one of your frontispiece drawings for a letter not long ago. My fiancé and I enjoyed the songs in that pamphlet, too. He was immensely tickled by "Hurray for Little Rhodie!" and the rhyme, "Rhode Island, Rhode Island, I love each bay and highland" almost drove me insane before I could get it out of my head. Reminds me of the Rhyme of the Year in "Roberta"—"Heaven rest us, I'm not asbestos!"[7] Close harmony!

The First Baptist Church folder as interesting too. You must have rocked the place to its foundations when you proclaimed yourself a Mohammedan.[8] The steeple is certainly as beautiful as you say, and the wooded hills behind it set it off perfectly. All steepled churches should be built in valleys to give them the proper background. I envy your aunt so handsome a building for her church-going. I was born and reared a Methodist, my grandfather having been a Methodist pastor, and occasionally attend church myself even now for the deep and aweful religious calm which exists nowhere save in churches. There's something very restful and full of peace in the interior of a huge dim church on a Sunday morning with sunlight slanting through stained glass and the organ rolling and the choir singing and the chimes floating down from very high above and the smug feeling of conscious virtue which one can't escape in a church. Very pleasant.

Enjoyed very much the first installment of EHP's[9] Mexico trip, though in mid-winter, with months before me before I can hope to travel anywhere it was rather maddening to read. And the circular announcing the new Loveman poems[10] was very enticing. If the lines you quoted are a fair sample of his work I shall *have* to read all of it. I don't know when I've been more delighted. Do quote some more! And talking of travel, Koenig's letter and cards from Florida, received lately, were almost more than I could bear, congealing here in sub-zero weather. He didn't mention how long he intended to stay away from home, so I shall have to guess at where to address my reply. To New York, I suppose, if he's moving about much in Florida.

And now you with your New York trip. The whole world is agin me. If I get another letter from anyone telling of recent travels I shall probably burst. Yours sounded delightful. Someday I should like to meet all the people you mentioned, with whom I've corresponded and of whom I've heard so much. And I'm fired with enthusiasm to visit the planetarium. There was one at the Chicago Fair[11]—one of the countless things I didn't get to see there—but nothing like [*sic*] so elaborate as the one you describe. Thanks for the card with the view of Mars from Deimos. Another thing that distresses me is that I shall be long dead before mankind can hope to know—if it ever does— what causes those canals. If I could just manage to live that long! Though by then would probably have lost all interest in anything. Living forever would be an awful thing. There's a story in some collection of fantastic tales—I think Dorothy Sayer[s]'s latest Omnibus in the fantasy section—telling of an island whereon no one can die, and the dreadful weariness of the ship-wrecked inhabitants who have lived for centuries and face eternity together. And that reminds me of a thoroughly awful story I read once long ago, about a ship lost in a fog at evening and a boat rowing thru the dimness and a voice warning them off from the island they're near, and telling its own experiences there, and how grey moss grows on everything and everyone who lands—and at the end a rift in the fog showing the boat rowing away and a greyish mound of shapelessness bending between the oars.[12]

Glad you liked "The Dark Land". I made the drawing a long time ago, a and wrote the story so I could bring it in, with the addition of a cadaverous head and a swirl of vagueness. I'm delighted at the reprinting of some of your old stories in WT. They are well worth rereading.

Yes, I received the Christmas copy of "The Cats of Ulthar". As I've said before, there's a charm about the work of the Dragon Fly Press that gives it personality and vividness, and this little booklet was a splendid example of what I mean. I was very glad indeed to receive my copy.

Somehow, someday I should like to get together all my Historic data into compact form, simply for the pleasure of doing it. All the songs and epic poems and odes and hymns. All the myths and legends and all the Historical sequence from the dawn of time down to that moment in 2000 A.D. when the crashing seas burst headlong over the earthquake-shaken shores, and under the cities of the Coronels the Islands shuddered and sank. Oh dear, I wish I didn't have to do it. I can hardly bear to see Rivah go. However I don't dare tamper now with History's ordained course, and in sixty-four years from now all that will remain of that wreath of shining blue islands will be the great widening circles upon the Pacific and lots of bubbles rising. Meanwhile if I ever have a year or two to spare I'm going to collect all the data into about ten volumes and preserve it for my grandchildren.

I hope you've received the Williams books and your own by now. Thank you again for the hours and hours of enjoyment I had from the Dunsany and Merritt stories. I only wish there were some more adequate way of repaying you than by an occasional few minutes of typing.

Gratefully,
CLM [signed]
Catherine Moore

P.S. I think I'm returning everything you wanted back, but if not be sure to tell me.

C. M.

*Notes*

1. Lord Dunsany, "The Shining Faces," *Saturday Evening Post* 204, No. 2 (11 July 1931): 112; rpt. in Dunsany's *Mirage Water*.

2. Henry Clapham McGavack, "The Genesis of the Revolutionary War," *Conservative* 3, No. 1 (July 1917): [1 3]. HPL's amateur journal.

3. See Bibliography under "Notes on Verse Technique."

4. Tennyson, "Morte d'Arthur," l. 191.

5. *Captain Blood* (Warner Bros., 1935), directed by Michael Curtiz; starring Errol Flynn, Olivia de Havilland, and Basil Rathbone.

6. HPL wrote an essay about the house, "An Account of a Trip to the Antient Fairbanks House . . ."

7. Dorothy Fields, "I Won't Dance" (1935). The song is in *Roberta* (RKO, 1935), a musical directed by William A. Seiter; starring Irene Dunne, Fred Astaire, Ginger Rogers, and Randolph Scott. It was lifted from the musical *Three Sisters*.

8. "Sunday school—to which I was sent when five—made no impression on me; (though I loved the old Georgian grace of my mother's hereditary church, the stately First Baptist, built in 1775) and I shocked everybody with my pagan utterances—at first calling myself a Mohammedan and then a Roman pagan." *E'ch-Pi-El Speaks* 6.

9. I.e., E. Hoffmann Price.

10. *The Hermaphrodite and Other Poems,* his forthcoming book from the Caxton Printers.

11. CLM refers to the Century of Progress Exposition, or the Chicago World's Fair (1933–1934).

12. William Hope Hodgson (1877–1918), "The Voice in the Night" (1907). The story was reprinted, not in any of Dorothy L. Sayers's three *Omnibus of Crime* anthologies, but in Colin de la Mare, ed., *They Walk Again: an Anthology of Ghost Stories* (London: Faber & Faber, 1931).


[27]　[TNS, JHL]

Daytona Beach, Thurs. Feb. 20[, 1936]

Dear Mr. Lovecraft:

Am here with mother, moving on today toward Miami and then up around west coast. Intend to make side-trip to DeLand in an effort to see RHB, but neglected to write him and may not be able to locate. My fiance was killed a week ago today while cleaning a gun, and we're just moving pointlessly along around Florida by bus, with no definite plans as yet. Saw St. Augustine yesterday, and thought of you there last summer. Would very much enjoy receiving one of your long letters (doubtless now in progress) as soon as I have address. Will write later.

　　Regards,　　C. L. Moore


[28]　[part of AHT 9.3][1]

[24 February 1936]

[. . .]

But as to *pattern in the universe* as related to "purpose"—I just don't get the connexion. *Of course* pattern exists & dominates everything. With whirlpools of force mutually interacting over an infinite area of stresses, it would be impossible to conceive of anything but ultimate balance—pull corresponding to pull, & temporary equilibria attained & broken according to rhythms which are definite in relation to the collective mass. But what in thunder has this to do with "purpose"? *Purpose* is a distinct emotion of a certain highly-organized form of nitrogenous matter—a narrowly specialised function of an exceedingly scarce & local type of energy-formation & transformation. It depends on the peculiar sort of force-whorls constituting so-called matter, upon the quasi-electrical excitation of that matter into the metabolic pattern called "life", & the accidental evolution of that pattern into a particular complex force possessing the intricate impression-registering apparatus called "consciousness", & the especial combination of glandular & neural action linking that consciousness with varied desire-reflexes—both unconditioned and conditioned. In other words, it is a special material set-up so distinctive & complex that it could not be imagined as forming a nebulous, diffusive "principle" floating around in space & existing without anything for it to exist in. It demands *consciousness & emotion*—which in turn demand *an organic body*—which I turn demands *special material organisation.* We can't think of a stone, or a quart of milk, or a cubic yard of vacuum, or an automatically functioning galaxy, or the whole darned total of existing galaxies (= the universe), as having *consciousness & purpose. To be sure* the forces of the universe are *balanced* . . . . . but what in Pharaoh's name has that to do with the *wishes or fortunes* of an infinitesimally insignificant organic parasite—the human race—to whose existence the cosmos as a whole is oblivious    for the simple reason that it has no consciousness to make it non-oblivious? What *balance & proportion* does to human beings is to twist their electrons, atoms, & molecules into certain natural pattern-sections which have nothing to do with the accidental "wishes" & feelings aroused in these beings for a moment by the action of nerves & glands on the fortuitous cell-arrangement called consciousness. That is to say, the consciousness, nerves, glands, & feelings of organic beings—& these beings themselves—are so completely accidental & negligible in the universe, that it would be absurd to regard them as any foci, criteria, or measures for the vast, unconscious, indifferent, automatic forms of balance which act on & determine the paths of electrons & atoms (*as* sheer electrons & atoms; *not* as parts of temporary & accidental aggregates such as organic beings, or aspects of organic beings) in the vast, blind, unconscious, eternal flux of symmetrical energy-tides. The cosmos has not mind, doesn't know anything, acts regularly merely because it hasn't the special volitional organisation to act otherwise, is headed simply in a blind circle, doesn't give a hang about the organic beings on any of its infinite dust grains, & doesn't know that the beings or the dust-grains exist. At least, that is the *reasonable probability* which strikes us after we examine what little of the cosmic mechanism lies without our limited range of vision. But what the devil of it? Man doesn't need to fancy that the whole universe worries about him—or has plans for him   in order to evolve a rational organisation for himself. Suppose the cosmos *doesn't* know he exists?

*He* knows he exists, & it's up to him to work out a plan to get the maximum amount of pleasure & harmony from the accidental spots of consciousness & sensitiveness with which the fortuitous events of evolution on a particular planet have saddled him. The world of his perceptions & desires & ego-expression & symmetry-seeking is real enough *to him,* even though it doesn't mean a damn thing cosmically. Let him then cease trying to pretend that he is the pet kitten of some imaginary kindly magnification of himself coterminous with the universe, & settle down to the worthy practical job of adjusting himself to his chance environment, & smoothing out as many as possible of the inconsistencies & disharmonies which exist between separate parts of his accidental consciousness-&-sensitiveness-&-desire equipment. That's a full-time job, & brings in all the standard ethical, scientific, political, & aesthetic principles which he has learned through millennia of experience & has hitherto attributed to shadowy mythical volitional forces outside himself. Let him forget the primitive myths, but keep hold of the solid, experience-derived, scientifically justifiable substance of the principles. It will be worth the trouble, for good sense can help man to work out a programme much less inharmonious than any hitherto achieved. As things are, wishes clash with wishes to the tragic extent. They always will clash more or less, but plain reason can make them clash a lot less. Utopia is unattainable—but we certainly could manage to stumble over ourselves a damned sight less than we do at present! And what have the fancied "wishes" or "purpose" of a non-existent "cosmic mind" got to do with all this? . . . . . . . . Yuggoth, how the old man does run on!

[. . .]

Notes

1. AHT 9.3 also contains parts of letters 8 and 11.

[29]   [TNS, JHL]

Sarasota, Fla. Feb. 29, 1936

Dear Mr. Lovecraft:

I promised my address so I could luxuriate in one of your nice long letters while here in Florida, but am moving about so much I think I'll have to forego it. Leaving Sarasota tomorrow for Tampa, and will then head home, I think. I didn't believe them when I left and they told me I'd be back within three weeks, but am so sick of doing nothing that already I'm anxious to be back at work. Expect to be home about Weds. or Thurs. Weather is rather chilly, but lots of sun and I am burned.

Regards,

C. L. Moore

[30]  [TLS, JHL]

Tuesday May 26, 1936

Dear Mr. Lovecraft:

The rarefied air of Olympus is so dazzling all around me that I can scarcely write, for I have recently been made secretary to the president of the bank, and sit here effulgent among the immortals. The confusion occasioned by the re-arranging of office furniture to accommodate me, the clearing out of old desks and files and the reorganization of an entire system has just been one more riot in the madhouse which the bank has been for the past week. They're re-wiring the telephones and desk lamps and surveying for electric fan sites, and I do feel too important for words. The State Bankers Convention held in Indianapolis last week was brightened by my presence as hostess and organizer of a suite of rooms at the convention hotel for the convenience of wives of correspondent bankers, and for two entire days I did nothing but say gushingly, "How do you do, I'm Miss Moore, won't you come in and let me give you a corsage, wouldn't you like a coca-cola, have some mints, I'd like you to meet Mrs. Brown of South Bend and Mrs. Smith of Evansville, and we'd love to have you sign our guest book, and be sure to stop in again—" over and over to droves of perfect stranger until my tongue hung out. Most exhausting, extremely confusing and lots of fun. Anyhow, these are just samples of the way life has been going lately in Indianapolis. The 500-Mile Race is next weekend and I appear to be going, somewhat to my surprise because heaven knows how deadly it is after the first half hour or so. But somehow in this town May 30 is always a brilliant blue day with the air simply dancing with excitement, and you just *have* to go somewhere, because everybody else is.

Well, at long last, to your letter dated (I blush to admit) February 24th. More than three months later, I finally get around to answering it. You must, in spite of my inexcusable neglect in writing, know how extremely welcome that delightful long letter was, exactly what I needed with its rambling dissertations on countless interesting topics, leading the mind off into scores of by-paths outside the unhappiness attending homecoming. When I think how busy you must have been and how much time you spent in writing me, words of thanks rather fail me.

Thank you for your sympathy. I can't yet dwell on this topic without becoming a bit maudlin, so had better change the subject.

Reading over your comments in Florida, I realize what we missed in our three weeks. In a way, though, am rather glad we did, for I was of course in no state of mind to appreciate anything external. Later perhaps I can go back and see all the places I missed, in a much more appreciative frame of mind. I shall call upon you for guide information when the time comes. Traveling as we did by bus, of course we missed most of the worth-while things. The down-town sections of most cities look alike, and that was about all we saw. And taxis are so darn expensive. We spent most of one day in St. Augustine, and did hire a cab and take an hour's trip around the city, visiting the Creole graveyard, the Fort, that enormous hotel, the slave market and several other places. And then spent the rest of the stay walking around, managing to see most of the sights. But I have only the dimmest recollections of the Oldest House, the little school-house, the narrow street and all the rest of it. In fact my memory of the entire trip is very hazy, and what I do remember is perfectly silly—the way the earth was raked so neatly around the shrubs and trees in southern cities, the wild white cranes in the Everglades, porpoises rolling in Sarasota bay. The whole trip is vaguely horrible to look back on, and I think I shall change the subject again.

Before I go any farther, I must tell you how delightful the two stories in Astounding were. I'm so glad the illustrations seemed accurate to you—and am wondering how you liked those for "Shadow Out of Time". About both of those stories there was such an air of meticulous accuracy that the sensation of perfect conviction prevailed all through them. I'm not quite sure yet that you weren't drawing from life. Somehow the detailed descriptions and matter-of-fact presentation of other-world habits lends a particularly horrible tinge to the tales. So unpleasantly convincing. Did you notice the ridiculously funny letter of criticism in the latest Astounding, in which the writer indignantly complains that the Mountains of Madness are haunted by a monster which even the author couldn't describe?[1] Visions arise of the way he must like his horrors, complete with specifications, samples and photographs—so many bristles on its tail, so many fangs and dripping four drops of venom, eyes emitting a specified voltage of glare, exact length in feet and inches—odear, words fail me. "Even the author couldn't describe it"!! It does take a considerable amount of genius to know just when to go into meticulous details, as you did in both stories, and when to hint breathtakingly at utterly indescribable horror.

My own writing is practically at a standstill. Am making rather feeble efforts to write for the horror-tale and sugary love-story markets to get some money, and have finished one story of the former type which Kline has very competently criticized for me and suggested specific revisions. I may get around to it someday. I have neither time nor inclination to write about anything any more. I suppose it will come back, but the hour is not yet. Though there has been one opus of about 2000 words or so which I wrote about a month ago, with no thought of sale. All about mysterious doings in a holly wood. Once when I was very small a letter from relatives in California around Christmas time reported that someone had gone down to Hollywood to get some holly, and I quite naturally thought, how lovely and convenient, and pictured the aunt in question wandering thru the deep, dark, glossy wood of holly, with the growing scarlet light of the berries reflecting from the shining leaves, a place of gloom and greenness and glows of crimson. The image has returned to me time and again, and I finally had to do something about it.

Incidentally, thanks for Edkins' *Causerie*. I was much interested in his remarks about "The Goblin Tower"[2] and the Dragon-Fly Press, though naturally not agreeing with him on many points. He misses a great deal of the
beauty and power of the Long poems, though of course much of his criticism
is justified. Certainly he's pitilessly witty at the expense of amateur poets all
through the little paper. I think a little unnecessarily so, even if his wit is undeniable. However I did enjoy reading the pamphlet. Most of it was fun.

Did you get the manual on English grammar and usage properly revised
by April 1?[3] And is there anything you haven't had a hand in at one time or
another?

Thank you for the information about the new Wonder Stories. I shall
certainly remember it and someday may profit by the new magazine. Have
you had time to write anything for them yet yourself? I do wish you would,
though certainly you sound busy enough as it is.

June 4

Yesterday morning Charles Hornig stopped by on his way to San Francisco. We had a very pleasant conversation. He mentioned having seen you,
as I think you told me at the time, and showed me a little photo of the graveyard you visited. I recognized it, of course. Would love to see it myself someday, and may yet. If I can ever force myself to write enough to buy that car
I've been wanting. I was so glad Hornig had succeeded in finding another position, and in such marvelous surroundings. What wouldn't I give to land a
job in California! It was Merritt who got him the place on the San Francisco
paper, and I hope it turns out well.

I was much interested in your description of Merritt and his poison garden. How utterly appropriate! Yes, I knew he was connected with the American Weekly, and never read it without thinking him responsible for the
moon-rockets and castle-haunting ghosts and so on detailed in its pages. As
you say, the thing is utterly trashy, but lots of fun. Our Sundays are not complete without the Chicago Herald-Examiner with its countless comics and its
American Weekly. Incidently I am a connois[s]eur of comics, or do I mean
connoiseuse? anyhow, [*sic*] have found in the funnies subtleties both of drawing and of dialect which seem to me supremely funny. The "Snuffy Smith"
series,[4] taking place in the feud-country of Tennessee or thereabouts is full of
the most delightfully apt colloquialisms. Consider the bearded ancient who
cocked an eye aloft at a lowering sky and remarked, "Hit's a-clabberin' up fer
a shower". And "do-less" is such a descriptive adjective. And "Time's a-
wastin'" has become a by-word at our house. The artist must have spent quite
a bit of time and effort collecting such gems of dialect—must be authentic,
for no one could make up so many such apt ones. And nowhere but in the
comic strips and funnies does one encounter such deft subtlety in delineating
moods and expressions with a few strokes. The grotesque little characters can

assume marvelously apt attitudes—bewilderment, despair, speechless confusion—all achieved with a few dots and lines. I think if the funnies could be preserved for a few thousand years and shown to a new civilization, they'd convey in fewer words and pictures, and such more accurately than anything else could do, the daily life of our present age. Certain selected funnies, of course—one in particular that I have in mind shows with exquisite aptness the ridiculous things that happen to all of us—the day when everything goes wrong, the time when the phone rings with an important message and you run downstairs losing your slippers in the process, stumble over chairs, trip on rugs, and reach the phone to find the baby has just hung it up. And then there's the dry humor of "Skippy",[5] the timeliness of "Mr. and Mrs.",[6] and the vividly familiar dilemmas of "Out Our Way"[7]—certainly the funnies have progressed a long way since the "Bang-Powie-Plop" era.

However, it seems to me we were talking of Merritt. I was just coming to your offer of the original "Moon Pool" which I would very much enjoy seeing. And by the way—I hereby register a solemn vow that I will this day, come weal, come woe, pack up the Dunsany books which you sent me nigh onto eighty years ago and return them. So help me, I will. The additions to your library, of which I am making notations on my own catalogue-copy, sound very interesting. If you feel you can ever trust me again with your books I'd love to read a few more when your own work lets up enough for you to send them. Did you ever get around to the Williams books? I am curious to know what you think of them.

I was extremely interested in your summary of the Roman morals vs. Celtic virtues question. And the consequences of the Roman conquest. I had never realized before the difference still apparent between those of us whose ancestors were Romanized and the races which remained independent of Rome. Russia in particular, now that you mention it, seems the perfect example of a country that, like Topsy, jest growed.[8] I wonder what will eventually become of them? In time will they achieve, through trial and error, a stable civilization utterly different from the sort the rest of the world, under different conditions, developed? Or will they finally reach the same goal, having gone the "long way 'round"?

Your mention of Crete and the Minoan civilization interests me too. I have always been utterly delighted with the mysterious influences which, in an age when everyone else was draping their garments flowingly from the shoulders in long strips and robes—caused the development in Crete of the wasp-waisted ruffled skirts and poke-bonnets of the Cretan women. Come to think of it, styles are very queer and interesting things. I wonder what duplicating influences two thousand years apart made Cretan women and Europeans of the 18th and 19th centuries wear dresses do remarkably alike. There can't have been any connection between the two, yet the mysterious causes of styles must have had some similarity to produce such similar results. In short, what happened in pre-Roman Crete and in 1750 AD to produce the same result in feminine fashions? Queer, too, how voluminously (though with some rather startling lapses) the women were clothed, while the men went about in funny little kilts and nothing more. And then the cripplingly tight belts both wore. Didn't they go about leaping over bulls' horns for recreation, too? Must have been a singularly hardy race. A very fascinating folk, the Cretans. What do you know about them?

After re-reading what you tell me about the Druids (*Druid!* the very word sounds like mistletoe dripping off ancient oaks and long beards dripping from venerable chins) and about the various mystery-cults, I realize perhaps for the first time what a lucky person I am. All I have to do is say, "What about this?" and presto, there is a world of fascinating, comprehensive, clearly-stated information forthcoming. I should treasure your letters if for no other reason than that in time I shall have a complete library of knowledge on every subject that interests me, all without any more effort on my part than that entailed by typing the query. Real luxury, I calls it. And very deeply appreciated.

Londinium as you describe it sounds heavenly. Wouldn't it be lovely to live in a place as intoxicatingly full of the past as that? Walking the same streets where the Legions marched, living in houses built over Roman graves—over the actual bones that once wore the flesh of life and spoke living Latin and hailed Caesar! I can get gooseflesh of delight just thinking of it. You can imagine what pleasure the thought of that coin with the actual view of Londinium gave me. I have gloated deeply over your little sketch. I shall probably never understand fully why the thought of everyday life, much as we know it now, existing so far in the past should give me such illogical delight. Perhaps because of the illusion of immortality it gives, bespeaking a deeply-rooted uncertainty about the permanence of present existence, and taking pleasure in the knowledge that two thousand years ago people were doing exactly what we do today. Anyhow, the thought of those Roman relics dug up out of modern London—the actual pots and pans they cooked in, the sandals they wore out on the Roman streets of Londinium, the mirrors that once reflected their living faces . . . . it makes me feel good.

And how eloquently the non-Roman objects they find too speaks of the power of Rome! And how illogically and foolishly proud it makes one feel! What earthly reason for pride have I in the thought that

> "Rome's imperial Eagles flew
> From Scythia and Timbuctoo
> To seas without a name"?[9]

You might like to hear a bit more of that pome, origin long forgotten—

> The sea lies over Lyonesse,
> Proud Lyonesse, lost Lyonesse,

> Grey waves wash over Lyonesse, where pulsed the heart of Rome.
> The dogfish drive the mackerel
> Where once the Saxon shield-walls fell—
> —No more the Empire's lances ride
> In thundering squadrons through the tide
> Of ravening heathen spears;
> Ten fathoms down her topmost towers,
> Her fragrant, rose-entangled bowers
> Dream the eternal years.

(Not so sure I can appreciate the thought of fragrant, rose-entangled bowers dreaming ten fathoms deep in salt water, but the general idea is pleasant.)

Well, back with a jerk to modernity. I hope you got through the winter without too much distress during the cold weather. I wish I had as good an excuse as yours for remaining indoors in sub-zero weather. In fur coat, fur muff, fur-lined boots and with a scarf pulled up over my nose so that every inhalation was scented with wool, I managed to navigate the storms even at 10 below, when it was so cold that breathing was absolute agony, the very center of one's head congealing and aching with the bitterness of the air breathed in, and one's nostrils froze together with the moisture of one's breath. But no doubt in a month's time the very memory of that distress will be a pleasure, when we're gasping like fish trying to force the superheated air into our lungs. It gets so hot here that when one comes out of a cooled place into the full midday heat of the downtown district it takes several gasps before the air can be pulled into one's lungs—like trying to breath warm sheet-rubber. Nice country.

I must protest against your impatience with your own youthful efforts at poetry. I liked the gentleman of New England's "March" very much. In fact, I doubt if you could show me anything from Pope which I'd like much better. I'd love to see some more of the Gentleman's couplets.

You inquire in some puzzlement about the chronology of the Coronel saga, and will doubtless be amazed to learn that somewhere off the coast of—I think—Africa or someplace—at this very moment the Islands lie, and if you just knew the proper passwords and the right people to consult, you could take a ship for the exclusive shores tomorrow. Fortunately only the proper people know how to get there. We don't welcome foreigners. However those of us who have once been there never quite recover, and, as a lyric exile of ours once lamented,

> "Jocelle! my heart turns homeward from abroad
> To that dear land upon the sky-blue sea,
> The sea-blue sky high-arching over me . . .
> Jocelle! my heart turns home!"

Queer that during the past three years of my preoccupation with my fiancé the Islands became as misty and unreal as they really are, though of late I actually get homesick for them, as if I'd once lived there. You say you hate to think of Rivah sinking to join Lyonesse and Mu, but think how it breaks the heart of the city's builder to allow that submersion. However it must be done. I don't know why we were quite so firm about it, but the entire cycle has to end in 2000 A.D. It's as mysteriously necessary as the cycle's origin, and to allow it to continue forever would spoil the whole thing. I think Rivah is particularly dear to us because of its location. It's rather an ugly little town, grey-walled and grim, with narrow streets not half so lovely as the bubble-domed whiteness of Aralie and Trochan. But it guards the straits through which our bitterest enemies, the Lavalanese, were constantly trying to invade us, and Rivah has been so desperately defended so often that it becomes the very symbol of our independence. The straits are colloquially known as The Postern Door, and are mentioned even in nursery rhymes as being vitally important to the nations's integrity. And it was to Rivah that the Red Prince rode on that tragic day which really ushered in the "Twenty is Plenty" revolution. (I hate that note of levity in the really terrible events of that day of massacre, but the twentieth king of the Lorane line was on the throne at the time, and the people just couldn't stand it any longer, so "Twenty is Plenty" has fixed itself immovably in my mind as the name of the revolution.) The story of the Red Prince is one of the most delightfully tragic and tender romances in history. He was a Lorane, and he met Felici of Lé who was unfortunately already married. There was a scandal that rocked the Islands to their foundations when she left her husband, for he was a great nobleman, but she went off with the prince and they lived in the country until the gossip had somewhat died down. Afterward for some reason I've forgotten the Prince began to gather an army—oh yes, a threat of Lavalanese invasion—and all the young men in the country came flocking to join it because of the fun they had. The threat of danger passed, but the army was enjoying itself too much to disband and the court was practically depopulated because everyone wanted to go out to Caramin and join the Prince's army. There was a lot of family trouble about it, stern fathers commanding their sons to come home and the sons putting off departure for just another week-end with the Prince. The Lé Lady was there with her attendants, and there were dances every night and hunts and rides every day into the mountains, and a grand time was had by all. Until one night a messenger came galloping up to announce that the enemy was at the gate. Whereupon the army collected itself and rode to Rivah, by forced marches, arriving just in time to save the day, though the Red Prince was killed, and most of his men. Isn't that a lovely melodramatic tale? There's a song about it, and historians have said that the most tragic line in all our history is the simple statement, "The Red Prince rode to Rivah" because it was in his day that the Loranes were just beginning the arrogance and extravagance which a few generations later was to climax in the "Twenty is Plenty" disaster, and the prince was always trying to curb them and show them the error of their ways.

I've just thought of something. It occurs to me that only in time of war, when men are actually marching to battle, is the great dragon flag ever flown. It's called the Lydragon, and the curious reason is that tradition has it the Loranes are descendants of the Sun-God, whose symbolical form is that of a dragon. The Loranes occasionally are victims of a berserk rage in battle which superstition attributes to the dragon fury showing through. "From under the sloughed veneer of the Dragon Prince came roaring forth the Dragon!" as one writer flamboyantly puts it. Anyhow, I was trying to think of a technical name for it. Lycanthropy means turning to a wolf, so why not "Lydragon-thropy"? I looked up dragon in the dictionary and found "Drakos". Apparently "lycanthrope" is a combination of "lykos", wolf, and "anthropos", man. So Drakonthrope would mean man-into-dragon. Anyhow, "Lydragonthropy" starts off with the lovely word "Lydragon" and evermore that will mean the Dragon Flag to me. As I was saying, however, only in actual battle is the Lydragon ever unfurled, and a magnificent sight it is, the great golden dragon rolling back tremendously over the marching soldiers. The peasants turn out for miles around just to see the terrible sight. Ah! I know! The reason it's only flown in battle is this. In early history when the Loranes were just beginning they were a pack of robbers living in a mountain castle and worshipping the sun, whose altars were always alight with carefully guarded flame. When they felt a fight coming on they would light a huge torch at the holy fire and go careering at breakneck pace down the mountain on their half-wild horses, the great torch streaming fame and sparks at their head, and the villagers below, hearing the wild yells and the thunder of hoofbeats down the mountain would look up and see that terrible blaze rushing down upon them. Whereupon they would scream "L'mal L'orane! L'mal L'orane!" and run frantically in circles, knowing that doom was upon them. The Lorane idea was to fire the village with holy flame, sending it up in smoke as an offering to the Sun-God. Doubtless as the years passed the Lydragon took upon itself the symbolism of the original torch, and is flown only when the Loranes are on the warpath and blood is about to be spilled. In fact I imagine that a certain superstitious awe still clings to it even in the minds of our nobles, for its kinship with the long-ago torch of holy flame kindled at the Sun-God's altars. Our people are all good Catholics, but the heathen legends are too deeply ingrained in them ever to be rooted out entirely. Once I remember when a boat-full of noblewomen was caught in a storm and the terrified ladies started a prayer to the Holy Virgin they discovered in the midst of it that they were chanting a plea to Léolyne the Sea-Maid, not even realizing how it happened. And they went right on and finished it, eyeing each other in terror as their lips moved in the familiar old phrases, yet not daring to stop.

Well, heavens, look how I've been carrying on. It's been a long, long time since a new idea struck me in that connection, but I'm glad I thought of the Lydragon legend. The whole thing simply reeks of melodrama and gore and flamboyance, and I do enjoy it so much! Sorry to have inflicted a whole page of it on you, though.

I was very much interested in your explanation of "Our Father *Which* art in Heaven" and the who–which–that evolution. Aren't words interestimg? Wonder how the language will have changed and refined in another few hundred years? I noticed a book not long ago in which "that" was spelled thatt to distinguish in usage. It looked perfectly horrible and spoiled the book for me, but really isn't such a bad idea. I'd love to see the Lounsberry "History of the English Language". I think nothing is more fascinating than the origin of idioms and the growth and formation of words. It's fun to notice the archaic forms of common words like "break-fast" and "be-ware", if you only think to notice. "Wel-come", too, and "Fare-well". I like to read over my old school copy of Chaucer just to see the words they used and the odd ways they used them. Wasn't it the Pardoner who sang "Come hider, love, to me"? Probably a popular song of the day. Isn't it odd to think of people that long ago humming fragments of the current song-hits, even as you and I? (There I go again.)

I wonder if you wouldn't enjoy Malory if you read him with an eye for the naivety and the sidelights on customs of the times. You don't have to admire the era to be amused by the odd little phrases they used and the queer things they did so matter-of-factly. I surely must have mentioned the scene wherein the lady is dragged by the hair, screaming and protesting, out of Arthur's hall, "And when she was gone the king was glad, for she made such a noise"! And the amazing way in which two knights would stand up to each other and back away with their swords for hours and hours and hours, until their armour must have been filled with blood and the ground they were trampling turned into red mud. It sounds very improbable to me. I can see, though, why you can work up no enthusiasm whatever for Sir Thomas and his writings—it's the era and not the dwellers thereof that interests you, and the era is undeniably ugly and cruel and stupid. While to me the really fascinating thing about it is the people and their reactions to events.

I was glad to learn of the various contributing legends which went together to make up the Arthurian cycle. It does seem that no great story-group, whether its hero is a god or a mortal, and whether the epic is religious or secular, is complete without having the hero immortal. It's queer that I have no urge to endow Dalmar j'Penyra with immortality. As you say, all rooting in the cycle of the seasons and representing the solar myth. It might be fun to know what affect [*sic*] upon a race's mythology the lack of a sun would have—such as the case must be on Venus if that whiteness around it is clouds and not simply sun-baked deserts, and if it were inhabited. Or if there were two or more suns, so that one was always up and the primitive races had never known the terror of darkness or the rigors of winter. And what would become of me if there were no such word as "IF"?

It was very depressing to read your account of the barbarism which overtook England. You think of it simply as a great pity, and the loss to the world of a marvelous civilization, but I can't help thinking of the wretched people affected, and the long darkness and unspeakable cruelty of the Middle Ages. It's really a shame that anyone had to live at all in those centuries. Such awful things happened to them. In Coronel there's a stone carved roughly to represent a kneeling woman, and a spring dripping from the rock provides the tears which she is traditionally supposed to weep for the world's sorrows.

As usual, you provide me with information, this time in regard to playing cards, which I've always wanted and was never sufficiently energetic to look up. If by this time you've read the Williams book, "The Greater Trumps" you'll have encountered the taurots [*sic*] there and the amazingly skillful and beautifully written account of their occult significance. Remembering that book is even greater pleasure than reading it, I find now. The dancing "They" and the golden mist that blinded the household at the book's climax, and the storm that would not end. . . . I am so curious to know your own reaction to Williams.

As to games themselves, your points against them are clearly logical and incontrovertible, but darnit, I still enjoy a game of bridge! And say what you will, I do believe that an occasional hour or so in which the mind is given entirely over to abstract problems entirely outside the realm of daily life is in most cases beneficial. The mind as well as the muscles needs relaxation from its usual tasks, and games are a very pleasant means of relaxation. Oh well, what's the use of finding excuses to play, anyhow. It's its own excuse for being. Incidentally, there's a card game going on at this very moment in the guard room of the Lorane castle in Trochan, which has not been broken for a thousand years. Odear, I wonder if during the revolutions it mustn't have broken up? Such a pity, I had always thought that the guards waiting their turn on duty played, and dropped out and others sat in, and the same game which Dalmar of Penyra played, waiting his duty at the King's door, is still going on at that guard room where soldiers have worn the Lorane dragons on their chests for more centuries than I dare set down for fear of being called a liar. What a pity about those revolutions breaking it up. I shall have to think that over.

I suppose, as you so lucidly point out, that the Stuarts were pretty messy, and goodness knows the Jameses rouse no patriotic feelings in me. (Incidentally, I just realized the other day that the young movie actor, James Stewart, has a really surprising resemblance to his royal namesake, just the long, dark, horsey face that the original had.) The glamour of the Stuarts lies in their traditions and not in their persons, really, I suppose. But how pleasant the traditions are!

Thanks so much for the booklet and cards illustrating the 1742 Providence house.[10] They are welcome additions to my collection. It's rather appalling to think of the circumstances attending the erection of the Fairbanks house, on an unknown continent full of terrors, hemmed in by the dark woods. Imagine Jonathan Fayerbanks glancing over his shoulder at utterly unimaginable perils as he worked. It seems incredible that the same house is still standing, or that three centuries could see such changes. How awfully *young* America is!

Thanks also for the Loveman verses, which I am returning. I enjoyed them tremendously, and am somewhat haunted by fragments. The poem "Foes" for instance, and the line "Butterflies and moths are there with gold upon their anthers" seems curiously lovely to me. (I notice it's been changed to "—and flowers with golden anthers",[11] but I think the original line is much nicer. Somehow the image of those fluttering, powdery-winged things with anthers dusted in gold is much richer and more—O, different—than the flower-image.) And the one beginning "When I stood in mid-heaven" is utterly lovely. It takes a real master to write "My face with joy was riven, Mine eyes with starlight crost"[12] and rise as sublimely above the faintly ridiculous connotations of the lines as he does. It's full of unbearable bliss and blinding radiance and music so sweet that ecstacy reaches heights too high to scale and falls back into the beautiful quiet of the last line "And lovelier than the dew". And the lines "—the cry that the dead man cries, Once, e'er the darkness fills his eyes—"[13] were too vivid. Yet in none of the poems you send did I find quite the beautiful excitement of the fragment you quoted in your last letter   "A hundred years they (something)— a hundred years they bound me while they strove to make me speak—[. . .] found me, in all things, still a Greek!"[14] I don't know why that gave me such intense pleasure. I'd like to know the rest of it. Is it included in "The Hermaphrodite"? Whether it is or not, I should very much like to read the book.

Well, it seems to me high time to conclude this manuscript, which might well be entitled, "Maunderings of a Moron". On looking over the Loveman poems again I realize that they are showing their years somewhat—I mean the paper—and that a typewritten copy would doubtless enable you to preserve the autograph originals and use the new pages for reference. Anyhow it will be a pleasure to go over the lovely lines again—as I've often said, typing words like those is as much a joy as reading them. And it will be a small return indeed for all the kindness you have shown me. I wonder if you realize what a blessing that long letter was, particularly at the time I received it, and the Dunsany books just when I wanted something of the sort most.

As for me, I am keeping very busy and will doubtless survive, willy-nilly. (Isn't that a ridiculous expression? The origin being, I believe, "Will he, nil he", but contracted now into the silliest imaginable form.)

I hope your aunt is recovered by now,[15] and that you aren't allowing your many activities to interfere with your own health. Are you planning any travels for the summer? It would be very pleasant if you could arrange to pass through Indianapolis, though I don't know of any scenic attractions to bring you in this direction. Please forgive my long delay in writing, though I know you'll understand it was not lack of appreciation or interest that caused it.

Humbly,

Catherine Moore

P.S. EHP asked me to forward the enclosed racing data.
C M.

*Notes*

1. In the June 1936 issue of *Astounding Stories*, Cleveland C. Soper, Jr. wrote in the letter column: ". . . why in the name of science-fiction did you ever print such a story as *At the Mountains of Madness* by Lovecraft? . . . If such stories as this—of two people scaring themselves half to death by looking at the carvings in some ancient ruins, and being chased by something that even the author can't describe, and full of mutterings about nameless horrors, such as the windowless solids with five dimensions, Yog-Sothoth, etc.—are what is to constitute the future yarns of Astounding Stories, then heaven help the cause of science-fiction." Rpt. in *A Weird Writer in Our Midst: Early Criticism of H. P. Lovecraft*, ed. S. T. Joshi (New York: Hippocampus Press, 2010), 114.

2. [Ernest A. Edkins], "The Goblin Tower," *Causerie* (February 1936): 2–4.

3. HPL was helping Anne Tillery Renshaw with her treatise on English usage, *Well Bred Speech*. Because of HPL's illness and other factors, the project was not finished until September.

4. *Barney Google and Snuffy Smith* (originally *Take Barney Google, F'rinstance*), an American "tout de suite" comic strip created by cartoonist Billy DeBeck (1890–1942), that debuted in 1919.

5. *Skippy*, a comic strip written and drawn by Percy L. Crosby (1891–1964), published from 1923 to 1945 and adapted into movies, a novel, and a radio show.

6. *Mr. and Mrs.*, a comic strip created by Clare A. Briggs (1875–1930) that first appeared in 1919.

7. *Out Our Way*, an American single-panel comic strip series by Canadian-American comic strip artist J. R. Williams (1888–1957) that ran from 1922 to 1977.

8. Topsy is a girl in the novel *Uncle Tom's Cabin* (1851–52) by Harriet Beecher Stowe. When asked if she knows who made her (i.e., whether she has heard of God), she replies "I expect I grow'd."

9. Farnham Bishop and Arthur Gilchrist Brodeur, "The Altar of the Legion," *Adventure* 50, No. 4 (10 January 1924). The story (first part of a three-part serial) contains a poem titled "The Lost Land," which CLM quotes.

10. The Stephen Hopkins House.

11. "Foes," l. 5. In *Out of the Immortal Night* 73.

12. "Music," ll. 1, 3–4. In *Out of the Immortal Night* 112.

13. "Bacchanale," ll. 15–16. In *Out of the Immortal Night* 65.

14. "Lineage," ll. 5–8. In *Out of the Immortal Night* 59. The words CLM could not read are "held me."

15. Annie E. P. Gamwell had been hospitalized for breast cancer, which resulted in a mastectomy. HPL generally told correspondents that she was suffering from "grippe."


[31]    [nonextant postcard]

[16 June 1936]

[CLM had sent HPL a postcard informing him of the death of Robert E. Howard.]


[32]    [AHT]

June 19, 1936

Dear Miss Moore:—

[. . .]

As for various civilisations—I certainly think that the line between once-Roman & never-Roman lands will continue to be manifest. All will change as the stresses of mechanised industry force a showdown in social, economic, & political matters, but the *direction & extent* of change will be vastly conditioned by historic heritage. The countries under the sway of the Roman idea—law, orderly processes, logic—will become gradually socialised through the public ownership of large-scale industries & utilities, & the responsibility of the state toward its citizens—but will have no cultural upheaval. Italy may experiment in dictatorships, England may cling to its well-beloved monarchy (& I for one uphold it & account myself a loyal subject of King Edward!) while redistributing wealth, Spain may try varying degrees of popular control, France & the United States may test the progressive possibilities of their existing political frameworks, & so on—but in none of these countries will sudden & sensational changed in daily life, public education, aesthetic taste & practice, intellectual habits, or philosophic background occur except through unforeseen calamities such as foreign conquest or desperate revolution. These nations have a potent & deeply ingrained way of thinking & feeling—rubbed into them through the practices of three thousand years of cultural ancestry beginning with Hellas & intensified by the Roman imperium. For the others, other traditions inherent in their blood-heritage are constantly cropping out to compete with the diffused influence of the classic world-civilisation of the west. Teutonic tribalism, which with us survives only in the *ethical* field (our *real* ethical motive-force is the Germanic honour concept based on the *exhibition of strength & superiority,* rather than the aesthetic-utilitarian classic concept or the divine-will concept incongruously borrowed from the Semites), is in Germany a vital & persistent force transcending logic & recent tradition. And in Russia the concept of justice & collectivism is as old as the mystical Slav himself—something quite like a Soviet state having existed at Novgorod in the Middle Ages. Outside the Roman circle the unpredictable may always occur. Within it, certain probabilities are seldom absent. Regarding Russia's future—I think it may be very bright in the end, despite the damage wrought during the decade 1917–27. Nor do I think its differences from the rest of western civilisation will be as extreme as many imagine. Or course it will never represent the cautious, balanced, logical culture of the Roman world (any more than sentimental, tribal Germany will); but it will probably achieve a high type of civilisation according to its own standards, & bring to fruition in a new way that remarkable Slavic genius which gave the old Russia figures like Dostoievsky, Turgeniev, & Tchaikovsky. The economic system toward which Russian is slowly & unconsciously gravitating—a lapse from the pure communism originally aimed at—is probably not very far from the rational socialism which every nation must ultimately approach (with equal slowness, albeit from the opposite direction) if it is to survive at all. And anyhow it is absurd to fancy (as do the bolsheviks & the Hooverite nitwits, with equal & paradoxical naivete!) that the really essential parts of civilisation—the daily habits, the choice of artistic media, the tradition of scholarship, &c.—need to be tied up with the mere mechanics of resource-distribution. The best aesthetic tradition of the past—that of the aristocracy—was completely divorced from economic & other material considerations. Why this same tradition cannot continue when an even larger part of the population (ideally, the whole population) ceases to make the mere mechanics of acquisition its primary concern, is a question which neither the Marxians nor the Republican mummies seem able to answer despite their oft-ululated insistence on the interdependence of economics & culture. Russia's period of greatest divergence from western culture is over. Since 1928, & more especially since 1932, she has been slowly swinging back toward the main stream. Today her art & architecture are actually *less radical* than those of many reactionary nations. While the plutocrat-controlled architects of the U.S.—Frank Lloyd Wright, the late Raymond M. Hood (of Pawtucket, R.I.—just North of Providence), &c.—were conceiving the repulsive and insane horrors of the Chicago Century of Retrogression, Stalin was approving plans for many buildings of classic or Renaissance design, in addition to some of a moderate functional modernism. Last year Russian schools quietly dropped the freakish & ill-proportioned "proletarian" curricula adopted with the revolution, & restored a balanced array of courses based on the general European tradition—so that by 1950 we shall see again among the young what today we see only among the elderly . . . the *Russian gentleman* (although he won't *call* himself that, since his broad culture will not represent the narrow segregation of one part of the population from the rest). Furthermore—*this* year the Soviets have abolished the political & economic disabilities hitherto imposed upon families of patrician & bourgeois origin, & are now taking steps toward the institution of parliamentary government—including the consideration of geography as distinguished from "class" or occupation in apportioning representation. In the end, the Russians will have achieved—in about thirty years, & at an appallingly high cost—just what the rest of the world is trying to achieve at a vastly lesser cost though with much less speed . . . . a civilised nation in which resources are collectively controlled, & in which the individual is assured security & the opportunity to enjoy rewards reasonably proportioned to his individual merits & without reference to his origin, affiliations, sheer luck, or coarse acquisitive rapacity. The great drawbacks are twofold—the appalling cost above mentioned, & the atmospheric residue of the eccentric Marxian philosophy which guided the revolution. The advantages are such as derive from *completeness* of reform. Thus much of the insidious *psychology* of competitive greed has been crushed out, whereas it will long form a persistent evil in the western world. Likewise—much of the *low-grade tawdriness of taste* which so cheapens rabble-plutocracies (the taste which nourishes tripe, tinsel, & charlatanry all the way from the tabloids to the *Saturday Evening Post*) has been cut out through the now-relaxing government supervision of creative effort . . . . . a supervision which was bad in principle, & destructive in major effects, though it had this one good effect. Thus, all told, I think poor old Muscovy will be able to meet the west pretty much on its own terms twenty-five to fifty years hence. Of course, *sheer chance* plays a great part. No one knows what the next war will do. Such a war will mean the instant collapse of the west if it develops far—though communist revolutions in some of the combatant nations (like that in embattled Russia in 1917) will probably cut it short. Much, again, will depend on the location & outcome of such revolutions. It is a sad possibility that many of the western nations may have to repeat the ordeal of Russia—with local variations depending on heritage & precise conditions. It is amusing to reflect that what is developing in Russia is not at all what the old bolsheviks of 1917 wanted. The international Utopia of absolute equalitarianism at which they aimed could never have existed. Lenin—one of the world's truly great men, & a *conservative* in art & general philosophy—knew this, & would probably be satisfied with the fruition of his labours. Trotsky, on the other hand, remains the irreconcilable firebrand preaching world revolution in exile. A great war leader, he never became quite the statesman. Stalin is a really major figure—probably comparable only to Mussolini among living leaders.

But even so, I am definitely opposed to orthodox communism as a solution of the western nations' problems. In spite of the shrill thundering of my little grandchild Belknapovitch Longievsky (a true young Trotsky who loves the proletariat except when the maid burns the sirloin or is slow in answering the bell!) I have three major objections to bolshevism which leave me relatively cold toward his cherished Briffault & Strachey & Calverton.[1]

(a) Orthodox Marxian communism is founded on a basic philosophy and metaphysics whose erroneousness is virtually certain—a system involving false and artificial values, postulating non-existent linkages and interdependencies between different fields of human consideration (as economics, literature, science, & art), & maintained with just as emotional and unintelligent a dogmatism as is the supernatural religion it repudiates.

(b) It aims (outside Russia, where the callow phase is disappearing) at extreme and international goals which are not only incompatible with the normal situation of mankind in nature & in the present world of groups & races, but which violate profound psychological principles (such as the maintenance of a certain continuity in folkways, attitudes, aesthetics, intellectual discipline, etc., and the exercise of independent thought & art without restriction or ulterior motives) on which the basic happiness, proper adjustment, & maximum life-rewards of sensitively organised persons depend.

(c) It sanctions and encourages methods so violent, unlawful, illiberal, arbitrary, intellectually unsound, and irresponsibly destructive, that any application of them is likely to produce infinitely more harm than good—a harm to be measured not merely in cultural & material damage, but in a subtler and more irreparable damage to human habits in though, emotion, ethics, and social polity.[2]

Thus I stand today somewhere among the Fabian socialists—having ideas in common with Wells, Shaw, Norman Thomas, Bertrand Russell, &c., but still believing that the only way to put rational ideas in force is to hammer them little by little into the programmes of the existing major parties & bring about their adoption through traditional avenues of legislation. If the socialist party of Thomas (or its almost indistinguishable right wing which lately split off) had a chance of winning, I'd advocate efforts toward its election to power. Since it *hasn't* such a chance, I advocate throwing all progressive votes to whatever potentially successful party may have made (under popular pressure, to retain the votes which the smaller parties & the sporadic mass movements like Coughlinism, Townsendism, & Huey-Long-ism would otherwise capture)[3] the most concessions in the direction of a planned economy, a guaranteed social security, & a public ownership of large resources & processes. This year I'm for the New Deal. If the La Follette party were national in scope I'd probably be for that.[4] Little by little. Old doddering judges will die off, & new vigorous men will demand new interpretations—or amendments—of the Constitutional Sacred Cow of 1790. Methods of administration will improve when the capitalists understand that their system will never again receive public support, & release their technical experts for socially constructive purposes. England is slowly moving in the same direction, & Scandinavia is even further advanced. With patience & judgment, a rational order can be secured (barring destructive wars, or revolutions precipitated by such wars or by capitalistic reaction) in the United States in from fifty to one hundred years—& without any of the blows & setbacks to general culture which Russia has experienced. Belknap, like Trotsky, will be disappointed—but I fancy the grief of the few is less important than the welfare of the many! Scarcely had I completed the preceding postscript when your card of the sixteenth arrived—with its depressing & staggering news from Cross Plains. I'm surely glad the books look interesting—but for the moment am engulfed by the melancholy bulletin. It seems incredible, as you say. I had a long normal letter from R.E.H. written May 13. He was worried about his mother's health, but otherwise seemed perfectly all right. If the news is indeed true, it forms weird fiction's worst blow since the passing of good old Whitehead in 1932. Scarcely anybody else in the gang had quite the driving zest & spontaneity of Brother Conan. Crom, what a year of disaster is '36! This loss will seem especially real to E.H.P., since he was the only one of the group to have seen Two-Gun Bob in person. But if he can feel any worse than I do about it, he'll be going some. Mitra, what a loss! R.E.H. had gifts of an order even higher than the readers of his published work could suspect, & in time would have made his mark in real literature with some folk-epic of his beloved southwest. He was a perennial fount of erudition & eloquence on this theme—& had a creative imagination to make old days live again. It is hard to describe precisely what made his stories stand out so—but the real secret is that *he was in every one of them*, whether they were ostensibly commercial or not. He was greater than any profit-seeking policy he could adopt—for even when he outwardly made concessions to the mammon-guided editors & commercial critics he had an internal force & sincerity which broke through the surface & put the imprint of his personality on everything he wrote. Seldom or never did he set down a lifeless stock character or situation & leave it as such. Before he got through with it, it always took on some tinge of vitality & reality in spite of editorial orders—always drew something from his own experience & knowledge of life instead of from the herbarium of sterile & dessicated [*sic*] pulpish standbys. He was almost alone in his ability to create real emotions of fear & of dread suspense. (Crom, those vine-hung paleaogean ruins in forgotten jungles . . . & those primal vaults beneath accursed cities older than man!) Contrast his "Black Canaan" with the pallid synthetic pap comprising the rest of the current *Weird Tales*. Bloch & Derleth are clever enough technically— but for stark, living fear . . . . . the actual smell & feel & darkness & brooding horror & impending doom that inhere in that nighted, moss-hung jungle . . . what other writer is even in the running with R.E.H.? No author can excel unless he takes his work very seriously & puts himself whole-heartedly into it—& Two-Gun did just that, even when he claimed & consciously believed that he didn't. And this is the giant whom Fate had to snatch away whilst hundreds of insincere hacks continue to concoct phony ghosts & vampires & space-ships & occult detectives! I can't understand the tragedy—for although R.E.H. had a moody side expressed in his resentment against civilisation (the basis of our perennial & voluminous epistolary controversy), I always thought that this was a more or less *impersonal* sentiment—like Sonny Belknap's rage against the injustices of a capitalistic world. He himself seemed to me pretty well adjusted—in an environment he loved, with plenty of congenial souls (like the "Pink" Tyson & Tevis Clyde Smith of whom he spoke so often) to talk & travel with, & with parents whom he obviously idolised. His mother's pleural illness imposed a great strain upon both him & his father (the latter a physician, as you probably know), yet I cannot think that this would be sufficient to drive his tough-fibred nervous system to self-destructive extremes. Nor was his financial state at all desperate so far as I know. I wonder if he was alive when my last letter arrived—that must have been a week ago. Probably he never saw its thirty-two pages, that ended with an enthusiastic tribute to his serial & to "Black Canaan", which I had then just read. Well, anyhow, I think he realised how keenly his work was appreciated. I hope the *Phantagraph* boys had told him about their plan to issue his "Hyborian Age" as a separate pamphlet. That ought to prove popular among Conan's thousands of admirers. Incidentally—since E.H.P. Was the only one of us who ever talked with R.E.H. in person, I'm telling him that he ought to prepare a brief obituary & appreciation for *Weird Tales* as I did when good old Whitehead (whom I alone had met personally) died. Some such word is a necessity—& he is the logical author.

All good wishes—

Yr oblig'd & obt Servt
E'ch-Pi-El.

*Notes*

1. HPL refers to such historians and sociologists as Robert Briffault (1876–1948), John Strachey (1901–1963), and V. F. Calverton (pseud. of George Goetz, 1900–1948).
2. A draft of these paragraphs exists at JHL under the title "Objections to Orthodox Communism." See *CE* 5.140.
3. HPL refers to radical politicians and agitators in his day: Charles Edward Coughlin (1891–1979), Francis E. Townsend (1867–1960), and Huey Pierce Long, Jr. (1893–1935).
4. Robert M. La Follette, Sr. (1855–1925) and his sons, Robert M. La Follette, Jr. (1895–1953) and Philip Fox La Follette (1897–1965), were members of the Wisconsin Progressive Party.

[33]   [TLS, JHL]

Begun: June 24, 1936
Ended: July 27, 1936

Dear Mr. Lovecraft:

Your letter arrived yesterday, in the wake of numerous highly welcome packages. I have been having the time of my life flitting about among books and clippings like a butterfly with gold upon its *anthers*. Incidentally, I adored your similes of the cat with petals and the hoofed roses. I don't know why a petaled cat should be such an attractive thought to dwell upon. Imagine it, licking down its fragrant fur. Has it fine petals like ragged-robin, or thick-growing, curled petals like a rose? A beautiful thought, indeed. Oh heavens, speaking of cats brings back to mind a dream last night which until this moment I had forgotten—a nondescript sort of young man with reddish hair and the usual ruddy freckles that accompany such coloring, but with eyes of a clear green whose pupils were slits instead of circles! And the horrible way they expanded in the dark to great staring rounds of blackness! I remember he wore glasses. And recall a story read long ago about a nearsighted cat whose master had glasses made for it, and the remark that the oculist must have had a prescription to grind that made the hair stand up on his head! I shudder to think of the emotions of the oculist who fitted my horrible dream-youth with spectacles! How very clearly, now, I can remember those green eyes with their slit pupils, expanding to ovals and contracting to narrow lines with horrid facility as the light changed. By the way, don't a cat's eyes turn quite black in full light, the pupil blotting out the iris? It's been a long time since I looked a cat in the eye, and memory somewhat fails me. Somehow, harking back to the first of the paragraph, there's nothing very incongruous in thinking of a cat with petals. I mean, they're so fastidious and dainty that if any animal could wear petals properly it would be a cat. Did you ever meet a cat by night, slinking along as pantherishly as any real panther in a dark jungle, and speak to it and have it put its tail up and rub against your legs, shedding in a split second all the jungle ways? Isn't the change startling? And doesn't it illustrate perfectly the deceptive and scornful cat nature? I always feel a bit inferior in a feline presence anyhow. One can admire cats wholeheartedly without growing sentimentally fond of them. I was reared with a dog from my sixth year, and until my sixteenth loved it somewhat as I did any other member of the family. Since it died I have no more wanted to replace it than I'd want to replace a dead brother with some adopted boy. Obviously a one-dog woman. However of all the countless cats I have had the privilege of associating with I've not felt a spark of human affection for any of them after they grew out of their babyhood, when all things are lovable. It's a privilege and an honor to live with cats, but their aloofness really wards off any undue familiarity.

Ye gods, look at that paragraph.

Had you not heard of the Cross Plains tragedy until I wrote you? By the way, I must apologize for sending all of my news of disaster on postcards, blatently, [*sic*] for the mailman to read. Somehow I just didn't feel up to writing a letter, yet wanted you to know if you didn't already. I am enclosing the clipping of his death which came in the letter announcing it, from Thurston Torbett of Marlin, Texas. So far as I know he is not in correspondence with any others of the gang, though the was a fairly close friend of Howard's. I wasn't sure just where my duty lay in spreading the news of the tragedy, so contented myself with informing you. (May I have the clipping back, please?) I have since received a letter from Dr. Howard, his father, enclosing a note dated May 14 which REH had apparently been saving to send me. He died on the 12th,[1] and may possibly have received your letter.

The news was like a blow in the face. It's amazing how real he seemed even through the medium of his letters. I had hoped to see him next year when and if I get that much-talked-of car and make the California trip, but he could scarcely have become more vivid had I known him personally. As you say, he seemed to live in every story he wrote, breathing life and color and vitality in the pages until sometimes it was a little surprising the paper itself was not sodden and bright with blood and vocal with bugles and the sounds of battle. The end of every story was like the slamming of a door in one's face upon such a world of color and vividness and peril as never existed anywhere else. He recreated such immensities of aeons in his tales of the past that the mind reeled a little trying to grasp them, and he put into his long-dead lands such shuddering peril in the midst of such brilliantly colored reality as surely no one will ever be able to do again. I am desperately sorry for his father, who has lost his entire family in one blow, but almost as sorry for ourselves who will never read again such stories as Howard wrote.

I had come in from a bridge party the night I received that letter, and had bought a new bathing-suit and tried it on for the benefit of the girls who brought me home, and we were having such a good time. And then they left and I opened the letter. I can't tell you how horribly—oh, *hollow*—it made the whole past evening of laughter seem. I was ashamed of the fun we'd had, and that suit with its silly little flared skirt. Had that all-gone feeling like going down too fast in an elevator—and yet it didn't seem possible at all.

It seems to me that there's something wrong with a civilization that permits such men as Howard to be drive[n] to suicide, yet simply swarms with writers of trash. People like REH ought to be kept in glass and guarded from all danger, mental or physical. But of course it was from his own turbulent life that he drew so much of his writings' color. I have had this mood before, of glaring about at nonentities and wondering what earthly right they have to draw the breath of life when men so much finer in every way are dead. Oh, well, another fifty or sixty years and we won't care a bit.

I shall lighten the atmosphere by discoursing on bathing suits. I'm so pleased that the present trend is not, as it has been for the past many years, toward less and less and *less*. Apparently the irreducible minimum was reached at last, for this year they're selling them with little pleated shorts that stand out like skirts. The introduction of rubber-fabric which will retain some will of its own even when wet seems to have opened vast fields of possibility to designers. Hope they don't get too ornate. There was once in the family a bathing-dress of the incredible past, complete with long ruffled bloomers and long-sleeved dress. Horrible as it was, the mind shudders from the thought of its aspect when wet. I hope the world will be spared from such afflictions in the future. Though quite possibly the 21st Century will shriek with glee at the sight of just such handsome rubber-fabric briefs as I now take pride in possessing.

Your speculations concerning the arising of slim-waisted fashions in Crete and in Europe thousands of years apart were fascinating. To me nothing is more interesting than fashions, past, present and future. Those ruffled skirts, low bodices and tight corsets on the women of ancient Crete bring them mysteriously close to modernity, despite their unknown origins and their age-shrouded history. (Incidentally, what an unbearably exciting experience it must be to have an entire lost civilization exhumed practically before one's eyes! I think I should probably have blown up and busted with sheer excitement.)

I have heard it said somewhere that the silhouette of feminine fashion for any given period represents woman's status at the time. For instance, from the 15th Century to the 19th the outline was more or less pyramidal, the broad base tapering up to wasp-waist and narrow shoulders, and denoting the sedentary life which women led. Thereafter the silhouette took on narrower proportions at the base as such vigorous pursuits as croquet and badminton engaged feminine attention and the hour-glass outline arrived. During the War women were apparently expected to be giddy and entertaining for the pyramid silhouette was inverted and the hobble-skirt came into fashion. And then everyone must have gone utterly crazy, and the flapper-era ushered in knee-length skirts and utterly shapeless dresses and sauce-pan hats. Looking back over the styles which I imitated when I first began to follow fashions I simply can't believe it. Waistlines low around the hips, about twelve inches of straight skirt, and then legs. Surely the world has never seen such hideous fashions since the first cavewoman donned a bear-skin. In all their styles, however horribly exaggerated, the lines have at least somewhat followed the figure. Elizabeth's farthingale and stomacher may have made her look like something from the far side of the moon, but at least the exaggeration did hint at a narrow waist and full hips and shoulders such as the normal human has. And the bustles and leg-o-mutton sleeves and all the braid and ruffles and beading of my own mother's day may have strained poor taste to the last elastic limit, but the outlines were burlesques of the feminine shape. But heaven preserve us, what do you suppose the 1920s were imitating? There was nothing human in any of their fashions. I get gooseflesh looking back over snapshots of my teens.

Returning momentarily to Crete, I am particularly grateful for the information about collections of Cretan artifacts in the Metropolitan Museum of New York. I shall certainly see it someday. Seems a bit incredible that such actual remains should be available, for the island seems like something half-fabulous, very ancient, sunk in the past with only a few spires leaning above the sands to remind us that once upon a time there was a myth called Crete. Did you ever see the moon at mid-day, looking like a pale and badly worn disk half-sunk in blueness like a shell in sand? Something real, but so remote and fabulous that I think I should be no more surprised to see actual relics from the moon than to see real Cretan statuettes and other evidences of the lost civilization. Speaking of statuettes reminds me of the horrid little figure of the Snake Goddess which the American Weekly reprints every so often. I suppose it's authentic. Surely no faker could produce that air of utter horror with which the snake-head, eyes deeply slanted, blunt snout thrust forward, rises above the human shoulders in their bodice and the slim-waisted ruffled skirts.

[Marginal note:] I'd very much like to read Audrey Haggard "The Double Axe" which you mentioned.

No less than the information itself about Crete did I enjoy the little excursion with the Romans to the conquest of the island. You have been in Rome no less than I in Coronel, and probably far more often. I don't doubt that your own footprints would be discoverable in the Italian dust if some mystic force could have frozen ancient Rome into Pompeii's eternal tableau.

I am glad you enjoyed the lines about Lyonesse. For me too Cornwall furnishes a little corner of exotic romance in the matter-of-fact field of English legends. Tintagel, Igerne and Tristram and all the rest are pure magic out of that fabulous place. The names themselves have always seemed to me a little like mosaics of colored syllables. Remember Don[n] Byrne's account of the ghostly cavalry that fell in some Atlantean battle and now haunts the Cornwall coast, thundering down on the hapless traveler with lances at rest? But when they pass him by all he feels is a cold wind blowing in his face.[2]

Incidentally, I believe you are not familiar with Crosbie Garstin and his stories and songs of Penzance and the Scillies.

> "The Isles of the Indies are rare isles and fair isles
>    With sweet odors blowing from garden and tree;
>    The Isles of the Scillies are poor isles and bare isles,
>    But it's there where my home is, ah, there would I be.
>    I would I were far from Port Royal, Jamaica,
>    I would I were stepping ashore at Hughtown;
>    My true love should have a gold ring for her finger,
>    A gay coral brooch and a taffety gown.
>    My love on my arm, I would walk on Pen—(something)
>    Where the grey gulls are flying like tatters of spume,
>    On Salakee Downs I would walk with my pretty,
>    On Salakee Downs when the gorse is in bloom.
>    The isles of the Indies are rare isles and fair isles,
>    The isles of the Scillies are poor isles and drear,
>    But fain would I trade all the blossoms and sunshine
>    For the sea-pink that blooms in the cheeks of my dear."[3]

Not great poetry, but rather pleasant. The Garstin picaresque novels about Ortho Penhale of Penzance[4] have created in my tenacious memory a love not only for that part of the English coast but for the period of which he wrote— "Eighteen Hundred and Wartime". I had a grand time in Penzance in Eighteen Hundred a few years ago.

Mother and I are reading Lounsbury's history of the English language with intense interest. It forms another link with the past that brings us very close to unimaginable antiquities, to realize that the words we speak today had their origins so far away in space and time. I shall hereafter cherish an especial tenderness for "oxen" and "children", knowing their survival from the obsolete -an plural. "Hosen and shoon" too, not so very long abandoned in general usage, appear to be examples. I was amazed to learn what a place French held for so long in England. Ap[p]arently even in Elizabeth's time it had not entirely been discarded as the speech of culture. And I had heard before of Bacon's low regard for his native tongue, so that he translated his writings into Latin to preserve them for posterity. Why do you suppose English has survived so strongly and spread so widely, in spite of all its set-backs? Is it purely because of the supremacy of the English-speaking people, or is there in the language an adaptability that fits it to such universality? I wonder if it's hard to learn? Certainly it's ugly. Our Island speech is the loveliest imaginable, not only in imagery and symbolism, but in its liquid, lilting sounds. When you listen to a roomful of our people talking you have to think twice before you can tell if they're not singing softly. Yet there's nothing sing-song about it. The phrases and sentences are so constructed that no matter what you're saying or what sequence they come in, there's a measured rhythm which flows through the sentences, accenting every fifth or seventh syllable or—well, I shall think it over and let you know later. Just thought of it, and the idea is not worked out yet.

What you say about English usage degeneration, and the horrors of modern pronunciation made me very dubious about my own speech. For instance, I never heard harass pronounced with the accent on the first syllable. I looked it up instantly in the dictionary and found you were perfectly right. Well, that's just another thing to remember. I have had to pick up my grammar piecemeal that way, in its finer points at least. If these are taught at all in public schools, which I doubt, I missed them in my leaping to and fro among the grades, and have had to discover for myself the charms of the intact infinitive, the differentiation between "like" and "liable", the use of "so—as" in a negative phrase, and "shall" instead of "will". I feel sure, however, that even in infancy I never said "Different than" or "he don't" or "If I was you". Thus, though the spirit is eagerly willing, the flesh is somewhat weak occasionally in the fine points of speech. I hope you'll call my attention to any flagrant errors you observe. Slovenliness among the masses in their usage of the language is, I suppose, to be expected, but there must be thousands of people like me who leap avidly upon every point of grammar which their educations missed and make it their own. The fault is with the schools, surely.

Incidentally, have you noticed ASTOUNDING's astounding propensity for "if you was he"? That's been done several times to stories of my own. Their vandalism to your "Shadow" and "Mts. of Madness" is not surprising. The subject is at least somewhat lightened by the "For gracious' sakes!" substitutions for slightly sturdier ejaculations. I mean, it does give you something to laugh at.

Returning for a moment to the subject of speech, its usage and its history, a group of New Yorkers were here during Memorial Day for the Races, and in their company I attended one of the very few dances to which I yet find it tolerable to go. (What an involved sentence!) At any rate, they insisted that we middle-westerners live up to their conception of our diction by talking in the idiom of Si the Hired Man.[5] "We're a-goin' to a dance tonight". Spent the entire evening a-dancin' and a-talkin' and a-usin' similar verbs, but I didn't realize until I read Lounsbury how authentic the use of the prefix a- was, or how old a custom it was. Oh yes, and I noticed that "hit" for "it" and "they be" were once quite correct. I had always understood vaguely that the Kentucky mountaineers were using purer English than ours, I never knew why until now. "They be a-doin' hit bettern us."

I do notice, too, the far superior voices of easterners, and wish I possessed such crisp, clearly enunciating tones instead of the slovenly and somewhat nasal drawl which I suppose I share with the rest of the middle-west. Another thing which should be taught in schools is voice-culture simply for the purposes of everyday speech.

I saw the movie version of Wells' "Things to Come"[6] the other day, and was tremendously impressed. Mere size is quite overpowering sometimes— those incredibly huge planes roaring through the clouds with 20th century ships buzzing infinitesimally as hornets against their wheels! Probably such monsters wouldn't fly, but they did produce a tremendous effect. And the scenes of warfare with little bat-winged planes swarming through the clouds so thickly that the air was black with them. And I think I shall remember for a long while the scenes in the city of the far future, panoramas so vast that the eye couldn't quite take it all in, the towers of windowless buildings rising pure and sleek into the air, webbed with crystal spans for traffic, and through the bright air crowds of people in remotely Grecian robes moving over the shining streets. You should see the picture if you have a chance.

The buildings reminded me remotely of the Chicago Fair, which you mention. I suppose most of it was pretty awful, though we had such fun both years when we visited it that the whole memory is wrapped up in positively Wordsworthian clouds of glory, through which the horrors had to be very horrible to reach me. And there were some beautiful buildings. The General Motors tower, for instance, a shaft of pure white rising austerely above the riot of colors with the giant gold initials G.M. crowning it. We came upon the Fair first in the late twilight, with Chicago a black bulk against the darkening sky and twinkling bewilderingly with lighted windows, and the Fair itself was an incredible and somewhat garish fairyland of colored buildings in inconceivable shapes and shades, outlined brilliantly against the dark. Above it the G.M. tower soared, white as an angel, and the letters that topped it looked so much like C.M. that I thought, "This is heaven and there is my heavenly mansion all monogrammed for me."

But out of the gaudiness and tawdriness I do remember some rather lovely things. I may have mentioned them before—the shafts of amber light, glowing golden from within, that illuminated the frightful Midway, the little shop on the Children's Island that was festooned with huge dim morning-glories three feet across, lighted inside so that each of them glowed softly with luscious shades of purple and rose and blue, a little bit like something Dunsany might have written—a morning-glory bower seen from the viewpoint of a humming bird.

As you say, most examples of the so-called "modern architecture" are definitely horrible, but there is in it a nucleus of considerable beauty and when time has—or if time does—refine away the needless angles and unnecessary ugliness there may emerge buildings of greater loveliness and purity than anything the world has seen yet. I wonder if there isn't a beauty of utter simplicity, from which absolutely everything unnecessary has been stripped, that might surpass even the beauty of Gothic churches with their countless spires and windows or of Grecian temples with many columns. Probably that sounds like heresy to you, but it's fun to think about. And I at least react to such architecture as was depicted in the "Things to Come" movie with a more breathless awe than even to Gothic or Grecian beauty. Those long, white planes of utter purity swooping up unbroken to reeling heights—it does catch at one's breath. This must have been what—was it Dickinson?—meant when she said that "Euclid alone has looked on Beauty bare—."[7]

July 1st

I have just been sweating blood over a sonnet whose last line refuses to turn out right. I need help.

> In your cool tomb whose carven pillars rise
> So calm against the ages, do you learn
> Still peace at last, or does that fever burn,
> Unslaked, the white bones that your flesh denies?
> Could death itself bring quiet to your eyes?
> Did those long years whose heat consumed you earn
> Surcease at last? The wheeling ages turn
> Above the tomb wherein your silence lies.
> Death was a kinder lover if he stripped
> The aching flesh which that strong fever scarred
> Down to the cool bones, ivory and unmarred
> On which no flame could batten, fever-lipped.
> God knows your pain was all you had to keep:
> *I clasp it like a lover in my sleep.*

[By HPL:] Is it your claspèd lover as you sleep?

It's no masterpiece, but I hate to leave it that way. Having climaxed the octave by announcing that nothing but silence answers the preceding questions, I rather hate to have the dead lady suddenly become vocal in the last line, but there simply is no other way to do it without remodeling the line, and any revision I can think of weakens it until it can't hold up the heavy burden which always falls on the last line of a sonnet. "Perhaps you clasp it, even in your sleep"? I give up.

I am just discovering the sonnet, and have written several apostrophizing various ladies of my Histories, as, of course, the preceding one does. Here's another, rather feeble in spots, but I quote it to illustrate the need of the last line for something of a kick—

> Through all your dreams one breathless night would flame
> Had you grown old and withered with the years.
> All else might fade to limbo whence it came,
> But not that evening's passion and its tears.
> The kiss that kindled flame upon your mouth
> Struck deeper than you dreamed, or ever learned
> Although you knew hot foretaste of the drouth
> So many knew. Its deadly sun-blaze burned
> Beneath the love that to the day you died
> You thought a shield against the fever's craze.
> Age would have taught you what your youth denied—
> All else might fade but that devouring blaze.
> You never learned the heartbreak and the truth;
> The gods were good who slew you in your youth.

July 3d

I have just seen a cartoon in a late magazine which has had me in stitches for about five minutes. A severe man confronts the workman who has been lettering doors, demanding, "Is this your idea of a joke?" and indicating three doors labeled respectively, "One,['] "Two" and "Buckle My Shoe". To my feeble intellect that seems almost overpoweringly funny, though you have to see the cartoon and have the full force of the joke dawn upon you to realize its greatest effect. (Incidentally, is it true that nursery rhymes of that sort—surely you played "One, Two, Buckle My Shoe, Three, Four, Shut the Door, Five Six, Pick up Sticks" and so on—once had ritual meaning? [And I defy you to produce a more involved sentence.] Eenie, meenie, minie mo, and similar gibberish, however, must have originated somehow, and it would be pleasant to think that once high priests chanted it over the spilled blood of sacrifice.)

Cartooning must require a much higher degree of ability than one might think at the first glance. I remember one in Collier's not long ago wherein two small choir boys confront an ecclesiastical looking gentleman, one complaining, "And every time I sing 'Halleluia' he whispers 'You're a bum!'"[8] [Marginal note: To appreciate that you must be familiar with the Jolson song, "Halleluia, I'm a bum."] Not just awfully funny, but the expressions upon the two boys, somehow achieved with a few lines and dots are marvelous. The small plaintiff had such a perfect look of serious, aggrieved indignation that his voice was all but audible in exactly the tones of querulous complaint that small boys use. It was a marvelous drawing of a voice. And the defendant's face was a miracle of smug self-satisfaction—a picture of a mood which everyone at one time or another has been lucky enough to experience—you know—"Gee, I'm smart!"

And there was a cartoon in the same magazine portraying a judge leaning over his bench and transfixing a prisoner with a look of smug joviality, the caption reading, "Thirty days hath September, April, June and you for speeding".

All three of those, I suddenly realize, illustrate the surprise element which you suggest as one component of humor; each depends upon a preconceived phrase with an unexpected ending, or in the choir boy case an unexpected implication. Very similarly, last winter a series of nursery rhymes were going the rounds (somewhat like the hilarious finger-charades now) in such simple forms as:

> Simple Simon met a pieman going to the fair;
> Said Simple Simon to the pieman—
> "Hello."

Or:

> Little Miss Muffett sat on a tuffet,
> Eating her curds and whey.
> Along came a spider and sat down beside her
> And said, "Is this seat taken?"

Or:

> Pease porridge hot, pease porridge cold,
> Pease porridge in the pot nine days old.
> PFOOI!

I am somewhat at a loss to classify the humor of the type that depends for its point on misprinted words in newspaper quotations, unless it would be the feeling of subtle superiority which it arouses. For instance, the other day I myself saw in a country newspaper and item, "LOST, half hound dog"!! And one from the New Yorker sends me into spasms whenever I think of it:

Wilkes-Barre, Pa. Times-Leader: "Sometime during the night Miss DiAngelo, described as being of a troublesome nature, strangled the older woman." And the footnote: Not really troublesome, just pesky.

The choice of that word "Pesky" is what inevitably convulses me. It's perfect.

And Eugene Manlove Rhodes is credited with a remark that, while it's too subtle to make one want to laugh out loud, is still worth recording. He was sending a photograph of a young lady to a friend. The girl was in bathing suit and had sat down just as he snapped the picture. He explained, "The legs are silent, as in mermaid."

### JULY 20

Very cautiously I emerge from the state of completely suspended animation which has been my only refuge from the heat of the past two weeks. Words fail me when I consider the temperatures. By comparison anything under 100 seems cool. We have had summers when the heat was like thick soup, smothering and clammy, but never before a time when it was as malevolent and alive and purposeful as heat under a frying pan, dry, determined, sizzling all animation out of the wretches who are so inert as to live in Indiana. The grass is like shredded-wheat, and even the trees are dropping their leaves, and no flowers bloom in the garden I've toiled over all spring and summer. I wonder if it's true that unwise farming is turning these united states into a desert. One hears fearful warnings that the west was meant for grazing lands, and farming it drains off moisture until nothing but dust results, that modern drainage even in the middle west is lowering streams to the vanishing point (and it really is—even in the last ten years that's been noticeable) and that in good time America will be another Gobi. Or are such droughts as in 1934 and 1936 simply things that happen occasionally and always have? They say this last heat wave here was the worst ever recorded. By the way, how have you enjoyed it? It can't have been so unbearably hot in Providence, but I suppose temperatures up to 100 are your particular joy.

### 24th

Recovering from a mild attack of summer flu, I realize that this letter has been dragging on for exactly a month. This will never do. Steps must be taken, as thus:

To continue:

I have been enjoying the books you sent immensely. The two James volumes are miracles of subtle, unspoken horror. I think perhaps the worst is the scene wherein the young boy leads his hellish beasts through a graveyard at night, nothing being visible of them but the quivering of the grass.[9] Reminds me of the title of a story by McKinlay Kantor "The Grave Grass Quivers".[10] Nothing in the story itself is at all eerie, but the title never fails to give me cold chills. And the nameless hairy *thing* which the man patted, thinking he patted his dog, was particularly frightful. James has a shocking talent for juxtaposing indescribable horror and matter-of-fact everyday things in a way to produce frightful results. Remember the two boys poking their rolled-up sheet music into the hole underneath the altar, and bringing it out all black and wet in the end where the horror that dwelt there has seized it? And they thinking until then that it was a wild animal of some sort! O, heavens, and when the woman sat down on the altar the thing inside tore a piece from her skirt! Imagine sitting there in all innocence, while black horror clawed at one's clothing! The thing was a lamia, I believe. Reminds me of a dream I had once wherein two tall, willowy-bending creatures with deeply slanted eyes stood about in our living room, saying nothing, and I was talking and trying to conceal the fact that I was petrified with terror, knowing all the while that the silent, snaky things were lamiae. Br-r-r! Well! Just looked "lamia" up in the dictionary, and find that they are "a class of blood-sucking monsters, half woman, half serpent". Now that I recall, they *were* definitely serpentine.

The Vathek books were interesting and most unusual, full of color and a strange sort of enchantment. I was glad of the opportunity to read them. The Dunsany book I need not tell you I appreciated. And the Loveman "Hermaphrodite" was truly marvelous. I found my favorite lines in the poem "Lineage" and was very pleased with them. I shall return all these shortly.

Thank you too, most copiously, for the antiquarian material enclosed with the "Moon-Pool", which latter I found all that you said it was. It's a depressing thing to reflect that whenever even the loveliest mystery is explained it loses most of its beauty. The Dweller should have remained veiled in beauty and silence—and I wish I'd read this original version first

Kuttner forwarded the Salem and Marblehead miscellany, and I have done a lot of gloating over the lovely old houses and streets. (By the way, while I think of it, what do you suppose sets architectural styles? Gabled roofs to shed snow and rain, I suppose, but were there as material reasons for the beautiful door details, for instance? Is it all simply following the fashion? Why flat roofs in hot countries? Why the Grecian pillars in such profusion? Was there a climatic reason?)

Apart from the fascination of architecture and legend in the pamphlets included in the bundle was the utter joy of the old-fashioned advertisements which appeared in their front and back pages. The blissful naivity [*sic*] with which they were worded! I wish I had them here and could quote examples. They were definitely appealing, quite apart from the appeal of modern ads which one knows are worded according to a carefully charted science, all tabulated and worked out according to norms and averages and word-values until they have no human appeal at all. The old Salem and Marblehead ads were almost vocal with the sound of the advertisers themselves, speaking ordinary everyday words in recommendation of their wares. Nowadays when an advertisement speaks in homely phrases you know it's cunningly planned. Somebody's thought as he wrote it, "There, that's the way the yokels talk among themselves, it ought to get 'em!" But the old ones were genuine.

Oh yes, eating an ice-cream soda (or should I say drinking?) this morning, I remembered the drug-store ads of old Marblehead, "Ice-cold soda water with fresh fruit flavors"! The early beginnings of the modern soda-fountain, bulging with variations of the root whence they all spring—ice-cold soda water with fruit flavor! (A soda in the morning sounds rather horrid, doesn't it? *vide* the first sentence of this paragraph; but I'm on a diet and practically live on ice-cream and oatmeal.) And the Salem and Marblehead material will return home in due course. Maybe I'd better charter a box-car!

I was delighted with the newspaper sheets picturing and describing the Tercentenary pageantry. It must have been grand to watch. I envy you your vantage-point during the proceedings, and don't wonder that you came near hissing the speakers. It's just as well for you that you weren't present during the original session of the legislature. You'd have gotten into serious trouble with your neighbors, I fear.

I was, of course, particularly interested in the account of the Colonial Dames' costumes, so many of which were resurrected from attics by great-granddaughters of the original wearers. There surely can't have been any garments of the 18th century actually surviving, but it must be fascinating enough to wear clothing which one's great-grandmothers wore. I do wish our own families had lived long enough in the same houses to make such attic-collections possible. Though of late modern fashions seem to be duplicating Quaker styles in delightful fragments. Have you noticed the white linen and pique Quaker caps which every other woman on the street is wearing this summer? And the square-toed, flat-heeled slippers with big buckles which came into fashion last winter are very pleasant things to wear.

And I do hope Roger Williams feels better now![11]

The clippings about the two museum houses were delightful, and made me wish for that nebulous and hoped-for car, and about a month's freedom from work! There'll come a day, as the eminent Mr. Penner[12] says, but I wish it were closer when I see such photographs as were reproduced of the John Brown House.

(Incidentally, the fragment of Gluyas Williams[13] cartoon in the Carringtown House clipping is a pretty good illustration of what I've been trying to say about cartoons. With how few lines the artist has conveyed the awkwardness of small boys, the round, fluffy heads of near-infancy, the faces that laboriously put on adult expressions, only to fall in repose into the round-mouthed vacuity of babyhood. The cartoonist's art isn't half so simple as it looks. And the subject matter here is immortal. Cretan boys probably solved the same problem as confronts the Gluyas Williams children, with just such arguments and yellings back and forth and injury to ears and shoulders.)

I envy you your walk to visit the Clemence house of middle 17th century architecture. The sketch looks interesting; I should like very much to see the place myself, even with its disfiguring later additions. The huge chimney reminds me of one of my mother's early recollections of visits to her grandparents when she was about six years old. She says they had a big chimney and a fireplace like a small room, with swinging cranes whereon they cooked food sometimes when they didn't want to build a fire in the stove. And her grandmother, who had run away from slave-owning parents in her sixteenth year to marry an eighteen-year-old suitor and didn't dare return until their first child was several months old, for fear of having the marriage annulled or something—her grandmother always wore severe black with lace cap and apron and a jingling bunch of keys at her belt, with which she unlocked cupboards and doled out cups of sugar and spoonsful of butter to her daughters and hired-girls, evidently a hang-over from the slave-owning days.

Reflecting on the chimney-cooking, it occurs to me how queerly time has moved westward over this continent. I don't suppose even your great-grandparents cooked so primitively, yet here it must have been a common thing. And farther west camp-fires for a long while must have been the only means of cooking. Perhaps Robert Howard's great-grandparents lived in wagons and tents and cooked over open fires. So one present generation can look back into varying degrees of antiquity ranging from stone-age living to cultured entertainment in hundred-year old mansions. If the continent extended just a little farther west perhaps we'd find contemporaries whose great-grandparents lived in caves and gnawed raw bones.

I told Mother about your discovery of a new nine-times-great-grandfather, the astronomer Field, and she was devoured with envy of one who has records tracing his ancestry back beyond immigration to America. Since my work last year in typing the genealogical data for a local matriarch both of us have been deeply interested in such research, and Mother has been delving back into her own ancestry. We know that my great-grandmother Coggeshall was a descendant of the Coggeshalls who were one of the four families settling Newport (or so I've been told), and that they came over in the ship *Lyons* from England where I think there's a Coggeshall county; and there are vague rumors of a sir Thomas de Coggeshall who rode to Jeruselem [*sic*] in, I think, 1166. But the intervening generations are anonymous. Starting with only the names and birth-dates of her grandparents she's performed wonders in the last several months, and is burning now to make a trip to West Virginia and investigate records there in an attempt to find who the parents of her father's great-great-grandparents were. She's written to ancient family connections in all directions, urging them to rack their memories, and is having the time of her life. In fact, has importuned several elderly ladies so urgently that her conscience hurts her and she had a dream the other night wherein she thought she received a postcard from one of her victims saying, "I know nothing more than I've told you. DO NOT *PRESUME* TO VISIT ME!" I shudder to think of her symptoms when she finally traces the various lines back to their arrival in America, and begins to cast yearning glances across the ocean.

I shall be interested to hear what more you learn about the astronomer. And hope no more ecclesiastics return to haunt you.

I was very glad to learn that your aunt has at last recovered. I hope the dreadful summer weather has not been bad enough there to affect her health. A friend vacationing in Norwalk, Connecticut gloatingly reports having slept under blankets for the past several weeks, so perhaps you too have not suffered such temperatures as afflicted the rest of the country.

Oh yes, and thank you exceedingly for the clippings of your verses. And particularly for the second volume of H. Lovecraft's *Poemata Minora*, which I enjoyed hugely, from cover to cover. I was vividly reminded of similar publications of my own at a like age, though mine certainly didn't display a fraction so much erudition. I still maintain that for a child of twelve the "Ode to Selene" is remarkable. Your illustration depicting the Child of Israel is delicious, and I would give anything to read some of the H. Lovecraft works advertised in the back pages of Vol. II. "The Noble Eavesdropper" sounds fascinating, as does "John, the Detective", and that even then the twig was bent is evidenced by the titles of your remaining fictional works, particularly "The Secret of the Grave". And how eloquent of twelve-years-old's mature condescension is "Mythology for the Young".[14]

Your "Ode for July Fourth, 1917" was a masterpiece of equivocation, and I enjoyed your sallies into other fields than iambic pentametre. I am returning the clippings, and particularly the *Poemata Minora*, reluctantly, inspired thereby to delvings in my own bales and boxes of juvenile publications. It should be most entertaining.

My recent writings seem to have bogged down completely. In the last five months I have produced one trashy horror which Kline ages ago asked me to rewrite, thinking he could sell it in a revised form and which I haven't touched since, and a drippy love-story which languished away and ceased half-finished some six weeks ago. The weather is partly responsible, but I must admit a sort of mental vacuum which shows no promise of change. I devote seven and a half hours daily to my secretarial duties and spend the rest of the time sewing desultorily, knitting on a very handsome afg[h]an, attending about three movies weekly, indulging in endless gossip with friends. How long this cloistered and nun-like seclusion will continue I wish I knew. I suspect that if my brain were functioning I would find myself bored to a horrible death, and rather dread the awakening. The few non-commercial attempts which I mentioned I should be very happy to have you read if I could ever get them finished to my satisfaction. I am writing and rewriting them over and over, in moments of comparative consciousness, and am far from satisfied even yet. However, to quote Mr. Penner once again, There'll come a day.

I received a copy of *Causerie* not long ago, and am not sure whom to thank for it. I haven't it here, and my sluggish mind is tormented by the thought that there was in it something which I wished to discuss. I could probably do clearer thinking with a head full of oatmeal than with that which now so inadequately fills the cerebral cavities. Edkins' caustic criticisms of the amateur poets is no doubt more than justified, as you say, but to my mind quite futile and therefore needlessly cruel. Surely these people are either poets or they're not, and no power on earth or from heaven could turn the doggerel-writers into Miltons, so why hurt their poor little feelings so brutally? They'll never be any better; one might as well let them drivel along, happy in their ignorance. No more use to try to save their souls than to argue with a religious fanatic or a rabid and wild-eyed strict-prohibitionist.

Your views on the probable future of the various nations were extremely interesting. You don't think, then, that Roosevelt is rushing Utopia at the expense of the taxpayers? What did you think of Landon's speech of acceptance the other evening? Ideas seem to struggle up through my oatmeal brain with all the reluctance of bubbles bursting "plop-plop" in a pan of the cereal cooking, and my knowledge of the political situation scarcely deserves to be dignified by the use of the word. But I am curious to know your reactions to the present situation.

Thank you effusively for the etymology of the word *hydragon*. It's helpful to know the Greek derivation of the term and makes me feel much more authentic. As for our early Islands history, I must confess to considerable haziness. I seem to recall vague rumors of sinking Atlantis and mountain heights of comparatively limited breadth to which flocked the survivors of the immemorial catastrophe. All that, of course, is pure legend and not offered as a serious suggestion, but surely the surviving myths of a great continent, sunken in the western sea, are significant. It seems to me that the story ran that the Atlantean nobility, who spent certain seasons indulging in mountain sports, and a group or two of sheep- and goat-herds were the survivors of the submersion, and, together with the comparative few who managed to reach the safety of the heights by various means, comprised the original population of the Islands. But as to their actual origin I cannot say. I much resent the suggestion that they're a mixture of any sort. Herr Hitler himself could be no more rigid than I on the topic of racial purity. I think they must be dolichocephalic, from a purely aesthetic point of view. But as to their connections with prehistoric Mediterranean races I know very little. Perhaps fugitives from the Great Submersion escaped to or were at the time traveling in southern Europe, and share racial origins with my own people. The language too is apparently unrelated to any known today, though I must admit the introduction of several words with distinct Romance Language origins. Our people are apparently Caucasian, chiefly dark in coloring, though blonds are not unknown and the occasional "Fair Lorane" born into the royal line has hair that is almost red, definite proof that Ildrinil the Sun-God's divinity still runs in the blood of his remote descendants.

As I've indicated, neither history nor legend itself goes back far enough to tell of colonization of the Islands. So far as anyone knows we've always lived there. The social systems apparently are attributable to the Loranes, originally a piratical and brigandish family who levied tribute on a whole island from their mountain stronghold. This family originated in Lavalon, but a breach in the turbulent family relations resulted in a schism which sent a shipload of angry rebels across the Narrow Sea to Coronel, where in the Alisian mountains they set up a duplicate of their original home and mode of life. The Lorane physical and mental characteristics seem to be so vivid and strong as to overcome all other hereditary traits, and like the Hapsburg lip which I think has persisted for about six hundred years or so, despite all intermarrying strains, appeared in a large percentage of the Lorane children. The brigands had a bad habit of waylaying caravans and carrying off women from traveling parties and from the raided villages. The mountain stronghold was populous with harems, and though the strict laws of the family insisted on monogamy insofar as the Loranes themselves were concerned—I mean, the name descended through the children of the Lorane wife of a Lorane nobleman, and he could have only one wife of his blood at a time—the children of the harem women displayed a high percentage of Lorane attributes; so high, in fact, that before many generations the mountaintop became too small to hold them and the turbulent and brawling family began to spill down the sides of the mountains, to travel over the island and set up castles of their own and finally to cross the inner sea to the other islands and subdue the dwellers there. They seemed to take a particular pleasure in provoking battle and quelling the resultant uprisings, and it wasn't long before the whole Island group was overrun with them. A generation or two after that sufficed to weaken the family ties between the various branches, and for a long while the Islands were a hotbed of feuds and discord. I think this is why the feudal system, much later to develop in Europe, grew up in the Islands. To protect themselves the wretched peasants had to ally themselves with the nearest Lorane lord, and no Lorane has ever been known to relinquish any advantage which he ever gained over anyone.

Gradually the descendants of—perhaps—other Atlantean noblemen trapped on the mountaintops long ago, began to assert themselves, adopting the feudal system in self-preservation, and after centuries of struggle the Loranes finally drew together again on the choicest island of the group, the fertile, rolling, river-ribboned hills and meadows of Avar. Here they founded their present capitol, Trochan, and from here they subdued one by one the upstart families which deserved the honor of their attention. There were four of these, and as time went on they were sufficiently downtrodden to become obedient, and were entrusted with the rule of four large outer islands, under

Lorane leadership. However they've never really become reconciled to such subordinate stations in life and keep things interesting for the Loranes by being almost continually on the verge of rebellion. About once a generation one family or another will attempt an insurrection. This state of affairs is still continuing, and probably will until the "pale-green, bitter waters of the sea"[15] quench forever the fires of their rebellions.

However we've never had much to do with Europe, or indeed with any of the outside world. Our islands are so perfect that we have no urge toward colonization. We know that nowhere else on the face of the earth is there a land half so lovely as ours, and I think we couldn't find sufficient numbers of our people who could be driven out of the country into foreign climes to colonize any other land. In early days war kept the population down so that there was no overcrowding, and more recently the intensely close-knit system of inheritance and land-division has prevented the noble families from over-prolific-ness. If a man knows he's got just so much land to divide up among his sons, and that any shortage is liable to cause violent social upheaval in his duchy or whatever grant and title he holds, the tendency is doubtless to small families. In England the younger sons didn't seem to mind much going abroad to seek their fortunes while the older brothers inherited the family lands, but among us the reluctance to live in foreign lands, among barbarians, in the cold, foggy countries of northern Europe or the hot, smelly southern countries, was so strong that younger sons were liable to attempt insurrections in order to stay at home. And in a lesser degree this was true of the lower classes. There was room for just so many farmers and cattle herds and fishermen, and any superfluous sons and daughters were liable to get into serious trouble. In fact the northernmost of our islands, Umar, was the hang-out for so many pirates that life on it for law-abiding citizens was one long, never-ending battle. I never thought of it before, but of course the smallness of the island group and the limited fields for employment caused such an abundance of pirates. They're really one of our major industries. And apparently the field was sufficient to absorb the overflow of forgotten men, because we've never had a population problem and the mortality rate among pirates is of course very high indeed. Up to the 19th century piracy among us has been a recognized profession. We preyed on other shipping as well as our own. In fact I imagine much of our contact with the outside world was made through our pirates, who brought back the interesting things of Europe and Asia and sold them in markets of Avar. Until the "Twenty is Plenty" revolution on the Lorane kings rather encouraged piracy. Subsidized by the reigning king, pirates were very handy indeed in reducing the power of over-ambitious families without openly bringing the monarch into the case at all. Bandits on the roads were used for the same purpose, until the whole country was over-run with lawlessness and it's no wonder the Revolution finally came.

However, I'm getting off the subject. As I say, our connections with Europe were very limited. Travelers abroad went incognito, making no mention of their homeland, and though we knew as much as was worth knowing about the various races and civilizations as they came and went, we weren't much interested by anything that took place outside. And visitors were so rudely and sternly snubbed that they almost never got past the island which guards the entrance into our island ring, in whose center like a green jewel lies Avar. I think no one ever came in force to invade us. We kept ourselves in such strict seclusion, fearing just that, so that not even the most drunken pirate ever babbled of home, and no foreign seamen ever manned the ships that came past our guardian fortress into the Inner Sea. If people did hear rumors of us they put it down to legend, and I have no doubt that the tales of the Hesperides and the Fortunate Isles and Hy-Brasil and all the rest had their origins in the Coronels.

I should not be at all surprised if travelers, searching through Europe and Asia for news of interest to take back home to Lorane, came into Averoigne. Perhaps whispers of the *Livre d'Eibon* drifted back into the sunny lands of Coronal from the dark places of that haunted land. And there may have been cults of Tsothoggua [*sic*] hidden here and there among the mountains. But for the most part there was little of the sort among us. We were sunnily religious, taking our gods from the sun and the sky and the sea and taking them lightly enough as a rule, tho as I have mentioned before the countless centuries of their reign in the hearts and minds of Coronel have rooted them so deeply that devout Catholics of today will sometimes, under stress, find themselves chanting hymns to Leolyne or Mayola. The latter is our goddess of evil, who walks clothed in flame, beautiful as fire itself. The few mortals who saw her, stepping lightly across the fields of earth and leaving behind her wherever her feet pressed prints that forever afterward were barren in the midst of the fertile meadows, were struck blind on the instant, that they might carry behind their eyes all their lives long the blazing beauty of Mayola. Her hair was flame too, and rushed up from her lovely and evil face in tendrils of golden fire, and sheets and quavers and rushes of flames blue and yellow and scarlet move continually in changing flickers over the beauty of her body. Wherever a fire burns opens a gateway into the land of Mayola, and the shadows are her servants, dogging mankind through all his days and nights and reporting to the goddess his sins whereby she may seize him when he dies. Shadows dance wildly in firelight because they pay tribute to the nearness of their goddess, who dwells always in flame everywhere. And much evil is done by night because the sinners think their shadows lost. But in darkness, invisible, as well as visibly by day, the shadow stalks the man, and every sin he does Mayola knows. Hell is a sort of darkness lit by flames, not physically uncomfortable but horribly monotonous and as different as possible from the lovely lands of the living. The ghosts of sinners go wailing up and down forever through the flame-shot darkness, gloated over by Mayola's evil smile. And Heaven for some unaccountable reason I know nothing about.

Perhaps you may have run across some ancient reference which could throw light on some of the mysteries which shroud our origin. I wish I knew more about our race and language.

And I'm still brooding intermittently over the "crowned–drowned" rhyme, with no more result than in anything else I try to do of late.

Thank you for the kind words about the Coronel saga. I'm pleased to know that they proved of some slight interest to you. Lately I've experienced an awakening of interest in the old Histories, and perhaps in time may produce something for publication.

And now at long last I shall try to get this in the mail. Really I'm sorry to have kept it drifting on so long. The weather and my mental apathy are the only excuses. I hope it won't happen again. Your books and other things will be returned soon, with my most sincere thanks.

Best wishes for your aunt's complete recovery and for your own health and comfort in these incredible temperatures,

>Sincerely,

>Catherine Moore

Glancing through your letter again I find I have unaccountably missed mentioning how much I enjoyed your "A June Afternoon". Say what you will, it has all the drowsy, murmurous charm of June itself and the last two lines are delightful

*Notes*

1. Actually 11 June.

2. Unidentified.

3. Unidentified.

4. The Penhale trilogy: *The Owls' House* (1923), *High Noon* (1925), and *The West Wind* (1926).

5. Silas is a character in Robert Frost's "The Death of the Hired Man."

6. *Things to Come* (London Film Productions, 1936), directed by William Cameron Menzies; starring Raymond Massey, Edward Chapman, and Ralph Richardson. Based on H. G. Wells's novel *The Shape of Things to Come* (1933). Wells wrote the screenplay.

7. The poet was Edna St. Vincent Millay, the poem "Euclid Alone," l. 1

8. CLM refers to "Hallelujah, I'm a bum!," a song of the Industrial Workers of the World, a radical labor group.

9. In "An Episode of Cathedral History," in *A Thin Ghost and Others*.

10. *Elk's Magazine* (July 1931). Cited in *O. Henry Memorial Award Prize Stories* (1932).

11. CLM responds to HPL's comment (made to numerous correspondents) regarding Massachusetts Governor James Michael Curley's presentation to Governor Theodore Francis Green of R.I. a copy of the recent resolution of the Massachusetts General Court, rescinding the banishment imposed upon Roger Williams in October 1635. HPL noted wryly that after 300½ years Williams doubtless appreciated the gesture. See HK 4.

12. Joe Penner (1904–1941), American vaudeville, radio, and film comedian of the 1930s. CLM quotes one of his catch-phrases.

13. Gluyas Williams (1888–1982), American cartoonist, notable for contributions to *New Yorker* and other major magazines.

14. Moore refers to one of HPL's youthful publications, which contained notices of other of HPL's juvenile writings. Of the works mentioned, only one survives. "The Secret of the Grave" is HPL's mistitling of the extant story "The Mystery of the Grave-Yard" (*CF* 3.484–88).

15. G. K. Chesterton, "The Doom of the Darnaways," in The Incredulity of Father Brown (1926).


[34]   [AHT]

[August 1936]

[Dear Miss Moore:—]

[. . .]

As for American politics—while I think the platform of Norman Thomas & the Socialist Party has more real sense & vision than any other in sight, I know darned well that the torpor & ignorance of the people leave it without a chance to become the administrative law of the land. Therefore I turn to the only reasonably sane & more or less contemporaneously conscious political mechanism in sight which *does* have a chance to get adopted & play its part in the needed social & economic evolution—The New Deal. Yuggoth knows it has its faults & inefficiencies—but what else *is* there for an historically literate adult to favour? "Rushing Utopia at the expense of the taxpayers"? Mehercule! I hardly call it *rushing* to *begin* that series of desperately necessary revisory steps which every civilised European nation has *already* been through, & which make England & the Scandinavian nations relatively well-balanced today while the U.S. still wallows in indecision & archaic delusion & sentimental memories of town-meeting & pioneering days! What do the taxpayers expect—a stable nation while millions starve & move toward justified revolt because of an obsolete governmental policy favouring individual accumulation by the few people lucky enough to get any of the decreasing number of jobs? If such taxpayers aren't willing to let their net incomes be lowered for the sake of greater national stability I hope to Gawd some new government will withdraw the protection whereby their artificial ideas of what they "ought" to earn were formed! Of course, this is not to say all tax laws—passed hastily & against savage & selfish opposition—are theoretically perfect in their equitability, or that the disposition of funds is always wise & efficient. What does one expect in an age of bewildered transition & novel situations—an age when neither men nor methods can be thoroughly appraised in advance of suddenly-needed steps? The most faults of the New Deal are those to which the stupid mass of voters force it. Certainly, it is a desperate matter to get the money needed for civilised governmental activities when vast amounts are hoarded & diverted into socially useless channels as private profits. *That* is the true "waste"—allowing the large-scale commerce & manufacture of the nation to corral for useless private gain the resources & profits which logically & ethically belong to the public for social use. But so far the herd is too dull to back up any sudden & universal acquisition of basic industry by the government. It demands that resources still be wasted in private channels. Hence no government can get in power unless it attempts seemingly incompatible things—the feeding of the people on the one hand, & the continuance of private industry & profit on the other hand. For years it will be necessary for governments to continue this farce—socialising industry imperceptibly & under cover without using the *name* of "socialism" (how my doddering generation of has-beens shudders at the name!), & voluntarily acquiescing in waste & inefficiency for the sake of the dying ideal of capitalism. We can't blame them for this—for if any party *called* itself "socialistic", the herd would turn against it & vote in a gang of blind reactionaries who would quickly starve them into a red revolution ten times more radical & sanguinary than the peaceful change they rejected! That's merely human nature ... what a piece of work is man! It is, then, absolutely necessary that imperative changes be adopted *slowly & half-secretly*—just as the wise Octavianus Augustus established a vitally imperative imperium Romanum whilst preserving in every outward detail the forms & rituals & nomenclature of the obsolete & unworkable senatorial respublica. Shrewd ol' Gus—he had himself "elected" consul of the "republic" year after year, whilst the conscript fathers doddered emptily on in the old Hooverite (or Catonian or what-have-you) way without any further power to cause poverty & mischief & revolt! Well—if anybody is treading the common-sense Via Octaviana any better than the consul Franclinius is treading it today, I have yet to recognise him. He has what no mere profit-grabber on the one hand, or sullen peasant or artisan on the other hand, could possibly have—the *historick perspective* of the scholar & gentleman. It is not by chance that the best popular leaders (Agis, the Gracci, Caesar,—take your pick!) come from the educated, far-seeing, & relatively disinterested gentry as opposed to the trading & working classes. It is one of the great excuses of aristocracy that it educates well-perspectived leaders capable of curtailing its own privileges—& those of the plutocracy—in favour of the whole social fabric. F.D.R. may have his weak points—love of approval, choice of tortuous methods where boldness might succeed, &c. &c.—but I certainly think he has three essentials which make him the only rational choice of the nation at this juncture: (1) *A genuine conception of the changes needed at this historic period;* (2) *A clear determination to work toward a goal historically right rather than momentarily expedient;* & (3) *a sensible willingness to humour the stupid herd & work slowly & imperceptibly—thus making his reforms actually possible in the long run.* The Lemke[1]–Coughlin–Townsend move is wildcat stuff—a hopeless jumble of incompatible & unfulfillable promises, spiced with left-overs of the most nauseous Republican sentimentalities & misleading catchwords ("individualism", "Constitutionalism", "economic freedom", &c. &c.)—yet it will unfortunately draw votes from the New Deal & create an actual danger of a Republican victory. Much of it is based on the specious fallacy that a successful economic order could arise from an artificial restoration of *small trading & localised industry in the present mechanised world* . . . . as if such a restoration were now possible, & as if it would not represent a howlingly flagrant waste & inefficiency even if it *were* possible. It is about as sensible as the King Canute gesture of the old Knights of Labour in the nineteenth century, who urged the destruction of man-displacing machinery instead of the remodelling of society to receive the leisure-bringing benefits conferred by such machinery. Lemkeism & Coughlinism get the ignorant lower middle class who know that some change must occur, yet cherish all the slogans & delusions of an obsolete pioneer plutocracy unalterably opposed to that imperative change. As for the Republicans—how can one regard seriously a frightened, greedy, nostalgic huddle of tradesmen & lucky idlers who shut their eyes to history & science, steel their emotions against decent human sympathy, cling to sordid & provincial ideals exalting sheer acquisitiveness & condoning artificial hardship for the non-materially-shrewd, dwell smugly & sentimentally in a distorted dream-cosmos of outmoded phrases & principles & attitudes based on the bygone agricultural-handicraft world, & revel in (consciously or unconsciously) mendacious assumptions (such as the notion that *real liberty* is synonymous with the single detail of *unrestricted economic licence*, or that a rational planning or resource-distribution would contravene some vague & mystical "American heritage"*) utterly contrary to fact & without the slightest foundation in human experience? Intellectually, the Republican idea deserves the tolerance & respect one gives to the dead. With the physically surviving corpse—now & then a menace as it appeals to greed, timidity, inertia, ignorance, & dissatisfaction—one must take such steps as one usually takes against social obstacles. The facts are plain. We know today that the conditions of intensively mechanised industry, swift transportation, & wide-area commercial organisation are such as to intensify & accelerate a thousandfold the natural tendency of free capitalism to concentrate resources & opportunities in the hands of a few persons of exaggerated greed & shrewdness, while stripping more & more persons of any chance whatever to exchange their services or abilities for the basic necessities of life. Throughout history—even in agricultural-handicraft times—the general drift toward explosive concentration has existed & has had to be checked by periodic New Deals with "government in business"—hence Agis, Cleomenes, the Gracchi, &c. Any sane person over five ought to know this—& to recognise also how hideously & stupendously this drift is magnified &

---

*Economic oversight, price-fixing, "government in business", &c. recur often in American colonial history.

speeded up when automatic machines, administrative consolidation, "high-pressure salesmanship", & other developments of recent years become more & more universal. The laissez-faire economics of Adam Smith, Herbie Hoover, H. L. Mencken, et al. offer not the slightest hope of relief or the slightest inkling of solution. The natural curves of the "business cycle" become exaggerated until each inevitable depression is a world wide calamity for countless millions, & the mechanisation of industry throws more & more workers *permanently* out of all employment as processes of indefinite duplication make it possible for a minimum of man-power to supply every conceivable human demand in *indefinite quantity.*\* Never again in a laissez-faire mechanised world will any person have more than a gambler's chance of being able to exchange his skill & services for the necessities of life. For millions—more millions every decade—there will never be any "natural" jobs—not even at the wildest peaks of "business prosperity" when the lucky part of the people are riding on the crest. There were 900,000 unemployed in 1928–9, at the height of the American boom, & of this vast number only a modest fraction were bums or "unemployables". Most of them were decently able citizens for whom no place could be found under a business-man–Republican scheme of things. Since then mechanical efficiency has doubled & trebled. If tomorrow we were to have a boom of Coolidge proportions, with all the rich & their lucky employees rolling in luxury, there would be at least 5,000,000 unemployed under a regime traditionally Republican. Landon would throw them crumbs.[a] Hoover would starve them out by turning the problem of relief over to local communities whose funds would soon be exhausted. This in days of *prosperity.* And when the *next* depression came—as inevitable as the ebb tide under a government which does not "meddle in business"—the result might be imagined. Amid such chaos communism would seem like an Utopia! And yet this madhouse policy of nationally suicidal laissez-faireism is what the Republicans & the D.A.R. (what a piece of irony!) & the prominent bankers & the comfortably fixed citizenry call the "noble American scheme of life" which must be protected (along with The Flag, The Constitution, Religion, Home & Mother, Freedom, &c., &c., &c.) from the nefarious (communistic-fascistic) designs of the Moscow-paid, Jew-guided, atheistic, immoral, tyrannical, laziness-fostering New Dealers!! *American scheme* . . . . I'll say it is! Since not a single civilised nation outside the United States has failed to abandon such insanity through the pressure of sheer necessity! Whatever countries have not evolved *ahead* like England, Denmark, Sweden, &c. (or *stampeded* ahead like Russia), have had to evolve *laterally* into rigid systems of fascism equally antagonistic to laissez-faire . . . as in Italy, Germany, &c. *But has not America also begun to evolve?* Is the old scheme indeed any longer the "American" one? Is it not a fact that the old scheme *could not work anywhere today?* Why indeed is

---

\*Increases in demand do not mean corresponding increases in necessary man-power.

America so different from the more progressive Nordic nations which have visibly moved with the stream of history? Is it not true that the New Deal simply followed the inevitable mandates of natural law, applied the first aid which other nations had known enough to apply long before, & enabled the nation to survive peacefully when the old scheme would have led it into immediate collapse & bloodshed? We know absolutely today—as absolutely as anything can ever be known—that *nothing* will ever provide employment for the entire population of a nation save the direct governmental supervision of large-scale industry & the deliberately artificial allocation of jobs to an increased number of individuals through drastic curtailments of working hours *irrespective of profits*. Governmental supervision has to be provided because private profiteers have shown their stubborn unwillingness—if not inability—to take such a line of action themselves. If private industry can meet the needed governmental terms, it can conceivably survive despite the essential silliness (tolerated, like supernatural religion, only because vestigially surviving from an earlier & obsolete milieu) of private profit. If it cannot or will not, it must be taken over (preferably peacefully—or through freezing-out by government competition) by the government & operated for the public benefit. That is a later stage—which supervision in the form of the N.R.A.,[3] but was so savagely opposed (& perhaps so lacking in boldness) that the effort was defeated before attaining fruition. Hence the Republican boasts of N.R.A.'s failure. Yet some precisely similar attempt will be absolutely necessary if the millions of reliefers are ever to be returned to regular industry. What have the Republicans done to provide for this problem? As usual, nothing—except to boast that their regime would restore employment . . . which it didn't do in 1928 & could do even less today! The truth is that no nation can ever survive in the future except through a strong centralised government with full control over economic & industrial processes. To call such centralisation & control "oppressive tyranny", or to claim that it postulates a corresponding oversight over the details of private life, opinion, expression, art, intellect, &c., is simply to lie or be a fool. I do not think the Republicans can delude many when they try to claim that a decent economic control by the government implies a Nazi-like cultural purge or interference with free scholarship & utterance & general individual folkways. That is as silly as their claim that a rationalised world would not allow distinguished ability to reap a fairly-proportioned reward—as if even Soviet Russia did not pay her executives & scientists more than she pays her ditch-diggers! But then, Republicans seem to resent the loss of *unearned* rewards (profit to merely sharp & lucky grabbers) more than any possible loss of *earned* rewards! Another irony . . . when Dr. Tugwell[4] tries to help certain families by aiding their voluntary settlement in new regions, Republicans howl about the invasion & control of private life by the state. How about the slavery in which *private corporations* hold their victims until they finally cast them adrift penniless? How about the arbitrarily assigned cottages, company stores, &c. &c. encountered by industrial vassals in mining & mill villages? Is this freedom? Perhaps not, but the staunch Americanism of the Republicans never seems to rebel at slavery imposed by their private business favourites. Business is the beloved juggernaut beneath which anything—even "freedom"—may properly be sacrificed. Supervision or aid in private life offends Republicans only when rendered by the state for decently humane ends. When similar supervision, colonisation, regimentation, &c. are imposed by greedy private corporations for indecent & inhumanly acquisitive ends, no good Hooverite ever takes offence! Thus it goes—the Republican principle always standing squarely in the way of all necessary progress. It is the principle of retrogression, chaos, & death—demanding the retention of vicious & meaningless values & practices which must be superseded if the nation is to escape explosion. Its only remaining appeals are those of sentimental yearning for vanished & impossible social adjustments; ignorant efficiency-respect based on the neatness with which its favourites & officials (because of long training) serve their respective limited (not the people's) ends; & frank private greed of the *"apres moi, le deluge"* type. As ultimately crystallised, it is the heritage of the vulgar "Flesh Age" of coarse & traditionless cut-throatism which followed the Civil War. Its greatest contemporary need is a decent burial.

Such is Republicanism in all its theoretical purity. But how about the ambiguous & benevolent platitudes of this well-meaning ex-New Dealer Mr. Landon? Well—we here have a sample of the real sources of whatever progressivism the Grab Our Profits party ever acquires. Mr. Landon's acceptance & other speeches, besides parroting some of the stock gags about "freedom", "individualism", & "business", show a quite unprecedented solicitude for social security. So does the Cleveland party platform adopted over the groans of the old guard. Unlike Mr. Hoover, Mr. Landon does not wish people to starve. He promises to put everybody to work through magic (for only magic could enable mechanised laissez-faire industry to reabsorb more than half of the present unemployed), but also promises a dole (a highly efficient & economical dole consistent with the budget-balancing sought by Business) to the trifling few whom the magic might overlook. And—his intelligence having reached the early 1900's in its survey of history—he would like to break up the big trusts & restore free competition. A sort of Bull Mooser—& somewhat suggestive of his rival Mr. Lemke in lack of logic regarding the incompatibility of small business on the one hand & intensive mechanisation & nation-wide commercial organisation (secret or open) on the other hand. But whence this unexpected retreat from Hooverism toward the New Deal? Whence this copying of some of the New Deal's psychology and principles? The answer is obvious. Even the Republicans know that the nation would sooner have a revolution than a Hoover-like regime. Let-'em-starve Old Guardism is *out*. But since the New Deal has not—amidst its harassment by reactionaries—brought the millennium in four years, vast masses of ignorant sufferers are dissatisfied. They are ready—though they wouldn't swallow Hooverism—to veer to any set of cheap catchwords opposite to the New Deal's provided they keep on getting the dole which the New Deal won for them. Hence the Republican strategy . . . . . mouth some vivid slogans about Americanism, the Stars & Stripes, the Constitution, Liberty, &c. to catch the fickle mob; don't cut off their dole as yet; copy enough of the New Deal to ward off general strikes, hunger marches, &c.; ride on the crest of a provincial, nationalistic wave; & if victorious, gradually tone down the promised reforms & give predatory business a free hand to flourish & buy legislation as of yore, irrespective of current historic trends & ultimate consequences. Such is current Republicanism—the wolf in sheep's clothing. It is plain to see that anything really civilised in Landon of the platform was plagiarised from the New Deal. The Republicans promise all the New Deal's advantages plus other "advantages" really incompatible with these basic & necessary ones . . . the while *they blame all the principles which made the New Deal's advantages possible.* They want the advantages without the very background which alone brought such! Well—the wise man will vote for Roosevelt & the real thing rather than for Landon & the fake article. I doubt if the danger of a Republican victory is extreme, even though Lemke will cut into the Democratic vote. Even if Landon did win, there would be no immediate catastrophe. He would have a Congress on his hands, & when business tried to put the screws on him there would be a healthy reaction. The pressure of the New Deal would continue to exist & mould Republican policy against the latter's will—& after a miserable four-year struggle a New Deal landslide in 1940 would be almost a certainty.

But I am far from uncritical of the present administration. It seems to me to have the twin faults of poor coördination & timidity. It has held over too much of traditional political methods—Farleyism[5] &c.—& has tolerated distinct incompatibilities & inefficiencies. It is also too subservient to capitalism. Probably even now, despite an instinct in the right direction, President Roosevelt is unwilling to introduce the amount of real socialism demanded by circumstances. He probably speaks the language of capitalism even more than the temper of the public demands. Nor has he met the Supreme Court & other reactionary influences as boldly & decisively as he might. He knows the way & follows the people in it, but is not quite a leader. However—what better man is on the scene? What other party has even approximately the right goal? If the New Deal isn't moving the country forward *much,* what other system seems likely to move it forward *at all,* or even to keep it from retrograding & going on the rocks? History—both ancient & contemporary—shows what is taking place. Socialism is inevitable in an industrially mechanised world. How shall we achieve it? By revolution, & perhaps with a chaotic upheaval destructive of our choicest traditions, or by gradual development, with a full preservation of our way of life & cultural heritage? It is for the people to choose. The voter may look about, analyse, & decide for himself what major organised party (i.e., what party with any chance of seating its nominees) represents least imperfectly the line of social & economic evolution which the nation certainly *must* follow in the end.

[. . .]

*Notes*

1. William Lemke (1878–1950), a politician from North Dakota who ran as a third-party candidate in the presidential election of 1936. He was supported by Coughlin and Townsend.

2. Alf Landon (1887–1987), the Republican candidate for president in 1936.

3. The National Recovery Administration, a major New Deal program.

4. Rexford G. Tugwell (1891–1979) served in various capacities in FDR's administration during his first term (1933–37) but resigned at the end of 1936 and became vice president of the American Molasses Co. He subsequently served as governor of Puerto Rico (1941–46), then taught at various universities.

5. James Aloysius ("Jim") Farley (1888–1976), Postmaster General (1933–40), who managed FDR's presidential campaigns of 1932 and 1936.

[35]  [TLS, JHL]

Finished Oct. 6, 1936

Dear Mr. Lovecraft:

You were quite correct in your prophecy of coming events. RHB, complete with moustache, has come and gone. The adornment may not be a permanent one, but it must be fun to be able to experiment with facial additions and subtractions. I always wanted a moustache. He declares that he would have cherished a beard were it not quite so outlandish a decoration to modern eyes. I presume small boys would have followed him in groups and dogs barked wherever he went if he'd tried it. The only beards I've ever seen on young men adorned a race driver who until his death this year competed yearly in the local Speedway races, and the Italian airman who lead [*sic*] the armada a year or so ago. I really rather like them, within stern limits. They add a touch at once distinguished and dashing to an otherwise unremarkable face.

RHB, knowing of Mother's passion for family research, brought along a portfolio of charts which entertained her greatly. And how curious that the great-great-great-great-great-grandsons of John Rathbone should have met across so many miles of continent without even suspecting their relation![1] Strange, too, to think that our remote progenitors in Newport were probably well acquainted. I wonder if in centuries to come on some wild outpost of civilization's far-flung borders, on a moon circling Saturn or in a space-ship flaming between Mars and the asteroids, two strangers, comparing reminiscences to while away the hours, will find that their far-away ancestors, named Lovecraft and Moore, once knew one another?

Mother is extremely grateful for your generous offer to check the Coggeshall hiati? (hiatuses?) which interrupt her records. I shall enclose a table of names and dates, and our gratitude will be unbounded if you can find anything at all within the next few years, whenever leisure permits you to investigate the records.

M. de Castro sounds like a most entertaining companion. It must have been pleasant to have the three generations represented by you, him and RHB so closely linked in interests and together in such absorbing surroundings. The Poe acrosticks, written in such a perfect setting, must have been a lot of fun.[2] As the products of no more than half an hour, and that frequently interrupted, they seem surprisingly well done. De Castro's reference to "Leonore" reminds me of the most gloatable (sorry!) lines I've yet found in Poe—

> Lo, on yon drear and rigid bier, *low lies thy love Lenore.*
> Come, let the funeral rites be read, the funeral songs be sung,
> An anthem for the queenliest dead that ever died so young,
> A dirge for her, the doubly dead in that she died so young.[3]

I think that "low lies thy love Lenore" is a masterpiece, really funny in its ululating perfection. Reminds me of the most beautiful of all names—Leona Maloney—which looks quite commonplace in print, but when spoken ripples as smoothly and musically as water over stones, the liquid lilt of vowels rising and falling over the break of the consonants in a totally un-English euphony. I defy you to find another name in any language that can even equal that for pure rippling beauty. (And must apologize for this ribbon, which is very new and smeary.)

The line about "doubly dead in that she died so young" reminds me of Housman, for whom I have recently contracted an intense admiration. He takes entirely an opposite viewpoint, and though his philosophy is eternally adolescent, love and death his only themes, still he deals with them so beautifully that his craftsmanship makes up for his lack of versatility. You probably remember his apostrophe to the Athlete Dying Young—

> Now you will not swell the rout
> Of lads that wore their honours out,
> Runners whom renown outran
> And the name died before the man.[4]

He rings the changes on that theme countless times, but always beautifully. By the way, do you know anything of change-ringing?[5] (Slight digression here.) Since reading Sayers' "Nine Taylors" [*sic*] I have been much interested in that ancient and honorable profession. It seems that a chime or peal of bells is rung to a mystic system of their own, not to produce a tune but to follow every bell up and down through their courses, so that of nine each rings first, second, third, and so on up and down the range. All very complicated and mystifying, and rather interesting to consider the odd use to which a succession of bell-tones can be put, other than in tunes. I wonder what other uses there are for—oh, colors, for instance, or odors—than those to which we put them? Do you happen to know the origin of this strange system of bell-ringing?

Returning to Housman, one of his most effective change-ringing on the time-honored topic is—(and don't you like the queer, difficult rhythm?)

> The lads in their hundreds to Ludlow come in to the fair;
> There's lads from the mill and the field and the forge and the fold,
> The lads for the girls and the lads for the liquor are there,
> And there with the rest are the lads who will never grow old.[6]

> ———

> And many the handsome of face and the handsome of heart,
> And few that will carry their looks or their truth to the grave.[7]

> ———

> I would we could know them; I wish there were some way to tell
> The fortunate fellows that now we can never discern,
> For then we could talk to them friendly and wish them farewell,
> And watch them depart on the way that they will not return.

> But [. . .]—nothing to scan,
> And brushing our elbow unguessed at and not to be told
> *They carry back bright to the coiner the mintage of man,*
> *The lads who will die in their glory and never be old.*[8]

[Marginal note:] ˘ − / ˘ ˘ − / ˘ ˘ − / ˘ ˘ −
what is it, anyhow? Anapestic pentameter? Or—
˘/− ˘ ˘/− ˘ ˘/− ˘ ˘/− ˘ ˘/−
dactylic?

Another of his scanty store of themes is I think beautifully put in this:

> Farewell, my lad, for naught's eternal,
> No league of ours for sure.
> Tomorrow I shall miss you less,
> And ache of heart and heaviness
> Are things that time shall cure.

> Over the hill the highway marches,
> And what's beyond is wide;
> And soon enough will pine to naught

> Remembrance and the faithful thought
> That sits the gave beside.
>
> The skies cannot be always raining

Or grey the twelvemonth through,

> And I shall meet good days and mirth
> And range the lovely lands of earth
> With friends no worse than you.
>
> But oh, my man, the house is fallen
> That none shall build again. . . .[9]

His line "They mow the field of man in season"[10] I think particularly lovely in his queer, matter-of-fact, euphonious way. And in at least one poem he echoes a very old way of verse-writing, far beyond the modern urge to rhyme—

> His *f*olly hath not *f*ellow
> *B*eneath the *b*lue of the day
> That gives to man or woman
> His heart and soul away.
> Ah, *p*ast the *p*lunge of *p*lummet
> In *s*eas I cannot *s*ound—[11]

However to admire Housman one has to have a feeling for his verse which cannot point to any line or phrase or rhyme to support its contention. There is a peculiar magic in certain combinations of word and thought which strikes me on some spot of extreme mental sensitivity. I've had the feeling of intense reaction to lines with no visible literary value whatever—random phrases to fragmentary to possess meaning, but full of an indescribable power to evoke a pleasure for which no words were ever invented. Probably we are just bulging with senses which our lives never stimulate enough to make us aware of them, and it's only on rare occasions that something strikes a flash from bafflingly delightful brain-centers which we can't even fully enjoy because we don't know enough about them to cultivate the pleasure. Consequently picture my surprise and pleasure upon coming across the following in "Hill of Dreams":

"Words have a far higher reason than the utilitarian office of imparting man's thought. Language is chiefly important . . . by its capacity when exquisitely arranged, of suggesting wonderful and indefinable impressions perhaps more ravishing and farther removed from the domain of strict thought than the impressions excited by music itself . . . the art of causing delicious sensation by the use of words. He who reads wonderful prose or verse is conscious of suggestions that cannot be put into words and which do not rise from the logical sense, which are rather parallel to than connected with the sensuous delight . . . a world disclosed beyond all expression or analysis, neither of the intellect nor of the senses. . . ."

I suppose everyone has certain phrases to which he reacts in the way Machen describes. I think for me one of the strongest is Kipling's "Lalage" song, of no intrinsic worth at all, but unutterably delightful for its connotations:

> When I left Home for Lalage's sake
> By the Legion's road to Rimini,
> She vowed her heart was mine to take
> With me and my sword to Rimini,
> Till the eagles fly from Rimini.[12]

And did I ever confide in you my epic composed on a streetcar about ten years ago, in a gentle daze induced by the motion of the car, the beat and an ad in a newspaper across the aisle, "Sale—Hardy Shrubs"?

> Sale, hardy shrubs, against the midnight sky;
> What eye can pierce thy solitude, what tongue describe
> Thy myriad fantasy?
> The seasons roll their endless course throughout all time,
> But thou, companion of the sunlit day,
> May mark thy course unaided through the sky,
> Or in the silent darkness fade away.

The meaning is very obscure indeed, but it does have a Thanatopsian ring to it and really, despite its jargon, induces in me at least a fleeting mood of philosophical introspection. Most impressive for a moment.

The other day I happened across a recent edition of the Indiana Historical Society monthly publication, in which were some—to me—utterly fascinating excerpts from records of Fort Knox, Indiana, quoted for your edification:

Capt. Thomas Pasteur, Commanding Officer, Fort Knox
Garrison Orders, Aug. 3, 1793

Danl Burr, private, was this Day examined on a charge of Sleeping on his post on the Night of the 2nd Inst, it appears that the testimony was Not Sufficient to Support the Charge fully, but the prisoner is guilty of Setting Down on his post & ommitting to pass the word *alls Well*, being a breach of article 5th Section 13th of the Rules and articles of war. In consequence of which the Commanding officer orders him 35 Lashes *&* Directs the punishment to take place this Evening at Roll Call.

Aug 12th, 1793
***—it is not the furst time Corpl Halkerston has been found blameble on the Same accation, & if the feelings of the Corpl was not callous the com-

manding officer would endeavour to tuch them, but for the present he shall only observe that it is the Last time that Corpl Halktn may exspect the smallest glimps of lenity. He will return to duty.

Aug. 17, 1793
In consequence of the unsoldierly, and riatus behavour of William Curten private on the evening of the 14th Inst the Commanding officer orders him thirty five lashes. . . .

Mar. 16, 1794
Tomorrow being St. Patrick day all the Irishmen in the Garrison will be exempt from duty and will receive one gill of Extra whiskey per man.

May 3, 1794
On enquirey made this Day, Corpl Ludlow was found guilty of Variety of misconduct when Corpl of the guard on the 2d Inst, & for makeing use of imporper expressions respecting the Commanding Officer, in consequence of which, together with Corpl Ludlows general misconduct for some time past, the Commanding Officer orders him reduced to a private Sentinel.

Aug. 16, 1794
Corporal Benjamin Palmar was found guilty of being drunk on guard on the 16th Inst. In consequence of which the Commanding Officer orders Corpl Palmer Reduced. . . . he is sorry for Palmars feelings if he has any, on reflection of his Shameful and unsoldeirly conduct.

March 26th, 1795
On enquirey this day made into a Charge against Peter Moore, Private in the Detachment, for haveing wilfully Killed a Hog, the property of some person in or abought the Garrison, when on his post in front of the Same, It appears that positive proofs Cannot be had to Support the Charge, but the presumption is Strong and forcable. But to lay that a side, the negligence of a Sentinell Suffering Such a peace of violence to be Commited actually on the ground of his walk, is Sufficient, Cause for the Commanding (Officer) to Order four dollars and a half to be Stoped out of his next three months pay.

Apr. 4, 1795
Corpl Francis Lucas was this day found Guilty of gitting Drunk and pirmitting the Men under his Immediate Conduck in the Village to get drunk also in the 11th Inst. It being directly in violation of the order of the 26th day of June 93, the Commanding Officer orders Corprel Lucas Reduced to a privet Sintinel. (I quote this chiefly to illustrate how badly Capt. Pasteur's spelling went haywire on April 4. He must have fortified himself with a small snort too before sitting down to write.)

13th Jany, 1796
The Non Commissioned officers and Privates will provide themselves with materials to appeare on the Parade from and after the 20th inst. with their hair cued at least 10 Inches long from the tie, which will be uninformly cloase to the head.

There was a lot more, but these were the choicest items. The whole thing brought back to vivid life the "unsoldierly and riatus" men who garrisoned the west, and the troubles their officers had in subduing them. How clearly I can see Corpl Ludlow muttering improper expressions respecting the Commanding Officer—Corpl Francis Lucas gitting drunk and pirmitting his men to git drunk also—Private Peter Moore wilfullly Killing a Hog—riatus Wm. Curten on an August evening 250 years ago incurring thirty five lashes by his high spirits—Corpl Halktn of the feelings too callous to tuch. The matter-of-fact records of daily life, set down with wretched spelling and limping grammar, bring back to life the color and noise and confusion of those long-gone days more vividly than the finest writing in the world could do.

The records were one long account of drunkenness on duty. I wonder what sort of people the solders could have been, anyhow. Every day recorded some infractions of ordinary rules of order, and subsequent punishment.

I have always been mildly curious about the odd spelling of that period, but never became acutely interested until now. Was it lack of education, or a general custom? And by what rules did they govern their capitalization? At any rate the phonetic spelling adds another touch of realism to the records. We know exactly how they pronounced "conduck", "sintinel", "corprel", and "git".

Which brings us directly to the question of modern speech, and my one-woman campaign to improve the "aow" whine of this locality. I have been going about chanting, "How now, brown cow?" and consciously pronouncing all other "ow" sounds with desperate precision. I am assured that it doesn't sound the least bit affected, especially since I never get it right the first time and have to repeat at least once. And on those very rare occasions when an initial attempt does result in the proper sound I pause and say it over in fascinated admiration. However the spirit is willing, and no doubt in time I shall be a better woman for the effort.

That reminds me that somehow in RHB's diction I fancied I could hear an echo of your own. So often a youngster is unconsciously influenced by the inflections and voice-tricks of a much admired elder. I remember a professor in college whose exact speech was so echoed by his group of satellites that it was funny to hear them. At any rate RHB's diction had somewhat crisped and quickened since I talked with him in Florida last February, and I fancied it was your doing. The speech one hears has such a strong influence on one's own—I have come out of a movie after listening to George Arlis[s] or Charles Laughton[13] and caught myself thinking with an English accent on the way home.

The clippings you enclosed were extremely interesting. It's a shame to think of the Cockney dialect being eliminated, even though its only virtue is its link with the past. How rapidly the time approaches when every living human will speak, think, dress and act in conformance with one rigid pattern! Reference to the English accent, however, reminds me of a newspaper account of Winston Churchill's son, on arrival in New York, remarking that he was very glad to be in Ameddica. And somewhere recently I read an observation to the effect that it was marvelous how many Oxford undergraduates wrote and published books, until one reflected that no doubt the Oxford accent had been so cultivated there that the students couldn't understand one another and had to resort to writing. Too, the differences in accenting and pronunciation between American and English use of the same words was fascinating. Speech must be the most malleable and mutable thing in the world. The wonder is that in the days before international communications had spread to the common people many more languages did not develop than we have now. I don't know, though—perhaps not, for the root-sounds would probably remain, and it is possible even now to glance through a passage of written Spanish or Italian or German and from one's knowledge of French, Latin and English piece together a rough outline of its meaning. However, think how many languages would have developed from English—would yet, in fact—if progress had never united the States and blended all the dialects. It's fascinating to speculate on what small nations of widely varying speech and customs and styles would develop if all communication save the unaided human voice and travel afoot or by horseback were suddenly to cease in North America. However the trend is so much the other way that I am trying to slay my local accent and produce the rounded "ous" of England, and in a few hundred years no one on the continent will be able to guess by a stranger's speech from what locality he comes—no doubt. The Linguistic Atlas[14] which you mention will be precious beyond words in a few generations if present tendencies are not interrupted.

Speaking of slang, have you noticed in the October Reader's Digest a condensation of (I think) H. L. Mencken's on the subject?[15] It is interesting to learn from him, for instance, that "hoosegow" and "rodeo" were introduced into the language from the Spanish at about the same time, but that since we had so many other words for "jail" the expression "hoosegow" remained hopelessly slang, living only through a sort of fantastic wildness of its own, while "rodeo", being a term for which we have no substitute, long ago was accepted into the best linguistic circles. "The Study of Words"[16] sounds extremely interesting. I should appreciate an opportunity to read it.

Thank you for the pleasant remarks about my sonnets. I like your suggestion for a last line much better than any I succeeded in thinking up, but any transposition to the second person seems to weaken it lamentably. Nor has the crowned–drowned rhyme been solved as yet. I think it over occasionally and may still produce a solution.

The article you mentioned on the history of rhyme sounds fascinating. Just when did it replace the other forms of versifying—alliteration and so on—and why, do you know? How surprised people would have been to whom poetry meant such forms as Housman so anachronistically uses—"His *folly* hath not *fellow*"—to hear a modern poem built on some desperately close rhyme such as the couplet from "Top Hat" which I think I've mentioned before—

> "Heaven rest us,
> I'm not asbestos!"[17]

And I wonder what future surprises literature has for us in the way of versifying as new and strange to modern ears as ours would have been to Beowulf. Reflection calls to mind any number of trick rhyming schemes. There was a popular song of five years or so ago the refrain of which has haunted me ever since with its catchy and obscure internal rhythms—

> "From the lily white
> To the black as night,
> They all fall in love."

There seems to be in "lily white" and "black as night" a rhyme even deeper than actually exists. I don't quite know why. And the catch and drag of "all—fall in love" with its internal rhyme is most effective. An implied rhyme of the lily-white-black-as-night variety exists very strongly in the French nursery rhyme which goes, as nearly as I remember,

> "Sur le pont d'Avignon,
> Tout le monde y dans en ronde".

and a line from a French song, "O douce printemps d'autrefois" illustrates a system in which every beat rhymes with the next.

I must put in a word for Mickey Mouse, too. His popularity I suppose is chiefly with the juvenile portions of the audience, but there's a subtlety in the execution of the cartoon figures which makes the reactions rather than the actions of the characters the great value of the program. The utter horror expressed by the dog Pluto's up-shooting ears and widened eyes is a marvel of drawing and action (incidentally, there we have cartooning acquiring a third dimension of continuous action, in which as great a skill is required as in the inanimate "stills" of yore.) Mickey's thin-voiced braggadocio and Donald Duck's belligerency after all danger is past, is (are—is) an eloquent commentary of human frailty, and the astonishing deftness with which chickens and ducks and dogs and other fauna are invested with marvelously human actions by the slightest shrug of feathered shoulder or inclination of canine head. The Popeye the Sailor cartoons are not very good—depend upon the comic strip published in the newspapers for their value, but the Disney Symphonies and cartoons are better in action than inanimately. (That's almost a pun, though unintentional.) I hadn't realized until now the third dimension of cartooning which has grown up so strongly in the last few years—the ability to put life itself into the motions of its characters on the screen. It's a brand new art which has developed so recently that artists of fifteen years ago couldn't even have imagined it. I do wonder what surprises the future holds!

I can think of one possible innovation. Ever since I discovered while idly scribbling on a telephone pad one day that since shorthand is a system of phonetic writing rhymed sounds are similar symbols. I've speculated on the possibilities of such a pattern of sounds. One might recite a poem and at the same time write it, and the rhythm of the spoken words would be echoed in the rhythm of the written ones. One could produce an harmonious pattern or freize [*sic*] of written poetry. For instance—

Low lies thy love Lenore—is in shorthand:

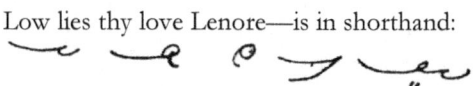

the long "l" symbols could easily be made into a recurring pattern. And the other lines I quoted "From the lily white to the black as night" would be represented by—

The other languages have had a system of writing based on phonetics, and would rhymes have worked in this way with them? Or did they have rhymes?

Of juvenile games and songs, I think I once read an account of a primitive custom which, if authentic, could have been the forerunner of many of them. It was a custom which must have been the precursor of the rituals described in Mitchison's "Corn King and Spring Queen" which I still hope you will find time to read someday—a pageantry with a priest impersonating the corn, a priestess the spring, and the ritual depicting the death and resurrection of the grain. The still older ritual—I can't remember where I read of it—must have been the original of the Corn King and Spring Queen pageant, in which a chosen couple was actually killed each year at sowing time and another pair selected by priestly rites to reign as king and queen of the crops for the ensuing season. The account told of the eligible young men and women circling round the priest, who with a divinely inspired wand somewhat like a water-diviner pointed out the chosen couple as they danced round him. If there is any basis of truth in this legend, then Ring Around the Rosy and Farmer in the Dell and Little Sally Walker and countless other circling and choosing games are of immemorial antiquity. Eenie-Meenie might assume ritual significance too in that light. In fact, now I think of it, almost all childish games involve either a choosing or a wild pursuit, or both. If they are imitative of stone-age adult games carried out in deadly earnest then my well remembered chills of delicious terror as I flew around the Drop-the-Handkerchief circle with "It" in mad pursuit have roots a million years deep. Incidentally, how ominously abstract "It" is as the designation of the principal figure in the game. Wonder how it got started. Oh heavens, the more one thinks of this the more awesomely it goes back into prehistoric times. Wood-tag, remember? with "It" hunting one from sanctuary to sanctuary—hide-and-seek, with "It" coming nearer and nearer to the place where one cowers with thumping heart, choking back the laboring breath not to betray oneself, and then the inevitable discovery, the wild shrieks of triumph from the hunter and terror from the hunted, and the frantic dash for the starting place with "It" in horrible pursuit. All that must have begun when man was a half-human, timorous thing shuddering in caves, flying for his life from shelter to shelter with monstrous beasts in close pursuit. Br-r!

How long will it take, I wonder, before the games of our children forsake the stone age? Or will the collapse of civilization be echoed in some childish ritual of the future, as the 500-year-old catastrophe of London Bridge? All games are apparently imitative, and what at first glance seems to be as modern as the minute, the current game of G-Men and Gangsters, as played in the park across from 2547[18] by vociferous youngsters, was formerly cops and robbers, and before that cowboys and Indians, and before that heaven knows what, but the same game exactly. It would be fascinating to trace back to their beginnings in history or politics such games as London Bridge. I've heard too that many nursery rhymes had their origin in political satires. Hey Diddle Diddle, the Cat and the Fiddle, for instance. I've always wondered about it. And there is immense irony in "Pussycat, pussycat, where have you been?" (It always puzzled me to rhyme "been" and "queen" in my infancy.) (Another illustration of the value of children's games and rhymes in preserving old forms of custom and speech which in daily life are replaced and forgotten.) (And that reminds me of the Housman poem rhyming "fair" and "were".[19] I was repeating it to my brother's intended, and she murmured something about "fur lady" to comply with local pronunciation of the verb. Which made me think of a newspaper story about a Philippino [*sic*] who wrote to a well-known blonde movie actress, "I am Inglis learning to tell you your fur is like brass sunshine.") Anyhow, to return to the subject, someday I shall devote my attention to tracing back to their origins children's games and rhymes, and expect to come across mines of fascinating information.

One last memory returns to trouble me as I close the subject—the custom of acquiring immunity from pursuit by crossing the fingers and shouting "King's Ex". Could that have arisen from the charm against witchcraft of crossed fingers? And the "King's Ex" sounds vaguely familiar, but I can't place it. All very baffling.

It is certainly astonishing how men persist in cutting down trees and ruining farming land for the brief immediate benefits of a few acres more of grain. Surely anyone in his right mind and with any foresight at all could realize the inevitable results. Apparently an offence [sic] against aesthetics is an offense against nature, and it makes one feel very smug and righteous when, opposing the destruction of willows along streams, and clumps of woodland, from a purely selfish sensory viewpoint, one finds the vast forces of nature arrayed solidly behind one. All this, probably, because what seems right and beautiful to us is what is natural. The trend away from the country, as you say, is producing a whole new system of literature and beauty ideals about which it is rather alarming to speculate. It would be perfectly all right—I mean, beauty is in the eye of the beholder, and not in the object beheld, and in a few generations our standards of admiration could change from wood and stream and landscape to steel and iron and cement, with no real lost computable from human standpoints, since what seems beautiful to the race *is* beautiful—but such a criterion isn't safe. What you call "ghetto literature" is obviously artificial, its fundamentals too perishable for men to build upon them to the exclusion of everything else. If it should go on for a couple of milleniums, [sic] until all memory of the beauties of nature were wiped out of human minds, there would come a day when civilization collapsed and the whole race would be very, very unhappy about it, having to live in the midst of nasty wet grass and hideous trees and huge, lumpy mountains, with nothing but nostalgic memories of the beautiful cement streets and lovely trash dumps to sustain them.

Incidentally, I wish you could experience a middle western summer. Perhaps even you would satisfy your almost *reptilian* love of heat! I would hate to think that the weather itself is being so affected by injudicious farming and wasting of natural resources that we would have to confront the prospect of such heat and cold every year as marred 1935–36.

The loss of REH is—though very faintly—alleviated by the prospect of a collection of Conan tales. The P. Schulyer Miller history of Conan sounds delightful, and I hope Wright decides to publish it. The comparatively few Howard stories which I have read are so consistently good that I wish it were possible for me to collect and read them all. Obviously it couldn't be done except by someone with more ready access to long past files of magazines, but I do wish someone would do it. The Robert E. Howard Memorial Collection is a splendid idea. Your "Shunned House" will be a valuable addition. I do hope RHB finally succeeds in publishing the Howard poems.[20] It's sickening to think of all that grand material lying about loose, and me helpless to do anything about it.

I wonder if anyone will ever succeed in filling the void left by REH's death. Such ability as his is lamentably rare, but surely of all the millions who speak English there must be others who in time will produce just such vital prose as his. I suddenly realize what that heretofore meaningless Tennysonian line from the Idyls means: "The old order changeth, yielding place to new, and God fulfils himself in many ways, lest one good custom should corrupt the world".[21] I fail to see the application of the last phrase, though.

Speculations about the survival of Norman French and Latin in childish rituals are fascinating. All sorts of jargon rises to the mind which may have deep significance in some other language than ours—hickory dickory dock (tho that may have deep onomatopoeia; it sounds vaguely like a clock ticking), eenie-meenie-minie-mo, (sounds a bit like one-two-three-four in some out-landish tongue), hey diddle diddle, the Drop-the-Handkerchief chant, iski-tiski-taskit, and many more. It all ties up the present with the past in such a comfortable way, somehow. This recurrence to the topic caused by re-reading your observations on the survival of French in England. And as you say, in many ways it's a pity that no universal language for works of science and lit-erature now exists. Any written language so constantly referred to as such a tongue would be could scarcely suffer the fate of losing its vividness because of sinking into the disuse of a dead language. And I have often regretted the barriers which lie between us and enjoyment of great works of literature in French and Russian and Italian and other unfamiliar tongues. They can never be translated in a wholly satisfactory manner, for the personality of the trans-lator is certain to color the text. If everything were written in some Esperanto of the arts, how much nicer it would be.

What you say of English as the dominant tongue is interesting, and full of speculative possibilities. How would the language be affected, I wonder, if the Russians for instance, or the Orientals, overthrew our civilization and we lost our proud supremacy as a free and conquering people. I was wondering the other day, too, whether if the Negroes should take their place in the sun as a conquering race, they would continue to sing their plaintive ballads of oppression. Rulers singing the songs of slaves. Probably not, though, since I understand their songs are very largely composed on the spot, being highly topical. My father tells of experiences in bossing gangs of niggers loading riv-er boats in his youth, and the way they would make chants as they worked about the most trivial incidents. And then it's highly unlikely that the Negro race will dominate for some time to come. Though interesting to observe the effect of two or three generations of highly intensified culture imposed upon the raw savage out of African jungles. Who knows to what further heights they may rise in a few more generations?

I much enjoyed the pamphlets and further information about the John Brown and Carrington houses.[22] Someday I shall see them. It must be very satisfying and deeply enjoyable to know that generations of one's family have lived under the same roof. The progress of science bestows so many new comforts and luxuries upon us that it is only in rare moments, such as this, that one realizes the price of change and impermanence exacted. Well, it's too late to do anything about it for myself, but I believe I shall found a dynasty and be a matriarch like G. B. Stern's character,[23] only much nicer.

Thank you for the privilege of reading that early publication of the Royal Atlas Company, "Wilks' Exploration", [*sic*] and for the ode to August. Interesting to see how even then you "choose the August days as mine".[24] Was heat so pleasant to you even then? It's most unfortunate for you that your physical and mental makeup will not allow you to be entirely happy anywhere. The only thing we can do about it is to apply to "science-fiction" to change the course of the Gulf Stream or tilt the planet a bit more on its axis to produce a tropical climate in Providence, which would, I think, be simpler than the other alternative—moving Providence bodily to the West Indies or central Africa. I am returning "Wilks' Exploration" with a sigh for my own juvenile publications, still *un*-unearthed. It was fun in those days. And harking back for a moment to "August", I can't understand your scorn of your earlier verse. The line "The frankincense of new-mown hay"[25] is a very pleasant one, and the whole poem is sufficiently lush and summery to prove genuine ability on the part of the poet.

As for your outline of daily life, it sounds very pleasant indeed. To be able to do with one's time exactly as one pleases must be heavenly. It's such fun to stay up as late as one likes, in the night quiet when somehow awareness of oneself is so much stronger than in the day, and to sleep luxuriously late in the mornings. Such pleasures are mine only on weekends, and I envy you your freedom. But perhaps leisure palls as much as lack of it. When enjoyment of full freedom has to be concentrated into a few hours a week the pleasure is probably proportionately concentrated, and I suppose it wouldn't be half so much fun to stay up late and sleep till noon if I could do it every day. I liked very much your expression "—as time passes repeated waves of fresh impressions come and go", leaving deposits of alluvial soil out of which new reactions grow. (Pome.)

I was sorry to hear of Edkins' illness, and hope he is improving by now. Your defense of his merciless criticism of his amateurs is logical and unanswerable; except that it seems to me the vicious attacks upon incompetence would be more convincing and constructive if it were not obvious how much enjoyment he gets out of them. In my opinion the "this hurts me worse than it does you" type of chastisement, in all sincerity, is the only kind of much value. It is fatally easy to make any sort of emotional writing such as poetry sound ridiculous, and one has a feeling in reading Edkins' more virulent sarcasms that if they hadn't been so clever he wouldn't have said them— therefore the cleverness and not the criticism was his purpose in speaking— therefore the fault itself is not so bad as he makes it seem. Q.E.D. A milder and more humane critic might carry more conviction. But as you say, perhaps it's true that gentler indictments would not provide the kick in the stomach which the complascent [*sic*] incompetents need.

Your outline of the political situation is horribly convincing, though it left me only with the conviction that the panorama is far too broad for any one person to grasp completely. As usual, you are thinking in terms of the entire population over sizable periods of time, while to me the only vividness exists around my immediate situation, in a strictly personal sense as representative of the individual who suffers or benefits from the broad policies you advocate. It has just dawned on me what must have been apparent to everyone else for generations—the extremely difficult problem which confronts a president who in the four years of his office has to institute changes which can only come about through long, slow, subtly contrived experiments, yet show enough progress to insure his re-election in order that the plan may be continued. Why, of course—that's what political parties are for, to insure a continued policy sufficiently long life for success, even though presidents come and go.

Government control of business seems in theory, as you so convincingly argue, the only solution to many apparently unanswerable social problems. But in practice I can only judge from my own only contact with government officials—the banks['] examiners, federal and state, for whom I have worked from time to time, and I have come nearer to homicide during those periods than in any other hours of my life. Clothed in their little brief authority, the lamentably large majority of them are so arrogant, so puffed up with self-importance, and the knowledge that their social and financial superiors, the bank officers, must do as they recommend, that by the time they've gone the typists who worked for them are verging on hysterics and the officers are in a state of polite insanity. A friend whose husband is cashier in a tiny country bank reports that in small institutions as well as large they are almost unbearable sometimes, openly insulting and rude in their remarks about the modest building and furnishings as well as in their work of auditing. Not all examiners have all these faults, but I have yet to encounter a crew of them in which one member at least isn't so blatantly self-important and gratuitously insulting that you have to count up to ten every time he speaks to you before answering. If this is an example of the sort of people into whose hands authority would fall were the government to take over business, heaven preserve all capitalists.

Everything you say is so clear and convincing that the only possible flaw I can see in it is the inevitable personal element, the people who will administer that centralized authority over industry which you advocate as the only solution to the present problems. From what little I know about it, the political nature of man will have to be changed from the ground up, or else authority will rest in the hands of men with pull, not men who achieve the high places by ability, and from men like that, good Lord deliver us. It must be bad enough in the present situations wherein politicians are in authority—the federal building and departments and so on, where the little man does the work and the big man makes him miserable. I've seen it happen too often. Men in business for themselves are, generally speaking, fair and considerate in their relations with employes, because in the long run it pays, but politicians care only to make a big showing for the short term of their office, après [*sic*] which, as you observe, le deluge. The whole political machinery would have to be changed, or that long awaited revolution would flare close on the heels of governmental taking over of industry.

Probably if you could pick the man, a dictatorship or kingship would be the best solution. We have such a vivid example of that in our bank. I have worked for almost every man here at one time or another, in every department under all their various heads and systems, and the whole thing is startlingly like a cross-section of the country at large, with its multitudinous types of men in authority. We have twelve branches each under a manager, some twenty or so departmental divisions handling every sort of banking industry—bonds, trusts, insurance and rental, loans, checking and savings accounts, safe deposit, travel, foreign exchange, bookkeeping and auditing and many more. There are tremendous feuds among department members, violent dislikes, rivalry between departments, snobbishness sometimes among employes, every conceivable problem which arises when several hundred people are employed under the same roof. But the three men at the head of the bank are so darn nice and considerate and wise that, since keeping one's job hinges on conforming to their own standards, everyone else has to assume tolerance and generosity whether it's his nature or not. We have petty tyrants who would keep those under them working until midnight if they thought the bosses didn't know about it. We have people who occasionally get away with hogging credit for work which others did, but they don't get away with it long. The men in authority have to conform to the highest authority, and so this is the swellest place to work I know of. I'm working for the president now, as I've mentioned, but if he were the lowliest clerk I'd still rather work for him than for anyone else here. I began at the bottom, and it's startlingly true that as you go up among the more important men their pettiness and self-importance and selfish tyranny lessens in degree with their position.

Of course there's much room for improvement, but the majority of the employees are well aware of their luck in working for these bloated capitalists in whose hands the bank is so well managed. We've carried an over-large staff all through the depression, the few discharges coming either in the wake of gross incompetence or, when we just had to cut down, the axe falling on those with a private income who could better afford to go. Pay goes right on through illness and absence. One has only to ask for a day or two off to receive it. Lunch hours are elastic. The officers contribute to a fund from which employes who need money may borrow without interest. And all this is much wiser and more productive of cooperation than one might think. I have never known anyone to take advantage of all these privileges, to stay out week after week with faked illness or take two-hour lunches or ask too many days off—partly, of course, because abuse would probably result in a lost job, but also because one is ashamed to take advantage of generosity. It's a grand place to work because the heads are grand people—and it could be a hell on earth if it weren't. After the 1933 crisis, (through which we came in great triumph, incidentally) another bank just across the street failed and was taken over by federal management. I hear rumors now of tyranny and harshness to employes which bewilders them after the humaneness of their former authorities.

All of which doesn't necessarily prove anything, but it's worth considering.

I'm awfully glad to hear that Wright has accepted your "Thing on the Doorstep" and "Haunter of the Dark". The latter I do not recognize and may not have read, though it's possible the text may prove familiar. I never remember titles. At any rate I am looking forward to re-reading them. Pickman's Model in the latest WT I read again with as much pleasure as before. It made me curious to know just what about certain drawings invests them with terror and strangeness. Doubtless there are countless tricks of the trade which only long study would reveal. I know that an object or figure lighted from *below* acquires an air of seriousness, simply, I suppose, from the reversal of the ordinary. But what it is about Sime or Dore that produces such hideous dolefulness in the latter and such a breathless glamour in the former I can't imagine. Study of their techniques would probably be well repaid. In cartooning, the eyebrows' slant and angle and elevation produce amazing results. I once read that Fontaine Fox, creator of the "Toonerville Trolley" strip,[26] once studied an old drawing of King Charles II hiding in a tree from his pursuers, for a long while unable to discover just why the fugitive Stuart's face had such a look of sheepishness, finally deciding that it was simply because one eyebrow was higher and more tilted than the other. And when one eye of a drawing is slightly larger and darker than the other the face has a peculiarly penetrating stare. But whatever tricks the intrepid Mr. Pickman employed in his drawings from life, I very much enjoyed being horrified by your account of him.

Virgil Finlay's illustrations in WT continue to be some of the best things in it. His drawing for the Jules de Grandin story[27] was delightful, with its swathes and streamers and dazzles of stars shining in the girl's hair and turning the darkness luminous behind her. I wonder what there is about twinkling points of brilliance which has so definitely pleasing an effect. Tinsel and spangles and sequins impart an air of gaiety to any scene, and I have sat and looked at the crumpled-up sheet of tinfoil off a chocolate bar with sensations of conscious delight in the points of silvery brilliance. In the movie, "The Great Ziegfeld"[28] one of the extravagantly magnificent dance scenes takes place on a long runway spiraling down round a gargantuan birthday cake looking fifty feet high, the sky behind it velvety black and winking and glinting with constellations of stars. That spangled sky gave the scene half its beauty. Someday I shall have to sit down and figure out just why this effect is so delightful.

Reminds me of the new cel[l]ophane raincape which I bought the other day. They're the most extravagantly spectacular things I've seen, and I've waited all summer for enough to appear on the streets so I could buy one without feeling as if crowds were following me. Have you noticed them? Red and green and blue and white transparency, hooded and flowing. Mine's colorless, and I feel like a Christmas present walking along caped in transparent sparkling gossamer, miraculously protected from the rain by invisible dazzles which are only apparent to the eye in the sparkles which light strikes from the transparent folds. My very conservative employer gazed at me as I came rustling in wearing it for the first time, rain running in rivulets down the unseeable folds—I felt like someone in a cloak of invisibility—and remarked reservedly that he thought they were rather attractive. Amazing me.

Your chronicle of summer journeyings sounds like such fun that I am greenly envious. A second perusal of the Marblehead and Salem items before returning them makes me very eager for some not too hot summer in the near future, and that hoped-for car of mine. The dinner of ice cream sounds perfectly horrible, and should have killed you. I could probably get away with a pint or so of chocolate, but the very thought of three pints of such varied flavors as you mention is incredible.

Enclosed are several cards illustrating "The Old Kentucky Home", gathered up during my vacation several months ago. You may already have similar scenes, and anyhow these are of no great value. I picked them up in the faint hope that you might be interested.

It will amaze you to learn that I am actually in the process of bringing down to work each day an armload of books and things to be returned to you. When they're all collected I'll have them wrapped and at long last mail them.

Incidentally, I read the "Double Axe" with much interest, and am very grateful to you for the opportunity. I suppose most of the details of daily life must have been supplied by Miss Haggard's ingenuity, since so much of Cretan civilization is lost, but she made the book interesting and convincing, and I enjoyed it. However, upon consideration, I can't help contrasting it with Naomi Mitchison's "Corn King" and other tales of Greece and Rome. The Haggard book was interesting and well done, full of detail and color—but Mrs. Mitchison's books have the breath of life in them so tangibly that it is sometimes almost painful to read them. I don't know quite how she does it. With all this fulsome recommendation you might expect far too much from her work, and perhaps it's just as well you've never read her. Maybe the virtue is in the eye of the reader in this case. Anyhow, I did enjoy the "Double Axe", and thank you.

My excuse for delaying so long in answering your last letter is two-fold— my father was operated on Saturday for inflammation of the peritonium, [sic] and though he's doing very well now his sojourn in the hospital has taken up lots of the family's time. Secondly, it seems that in everything I've talked about in this interminable letter I've had so much to say that I just ran on and on.

This is really all. Your books, etc. will return to you in a day or two, and thank you again for them and for your indulgence.

Sincerely,

Catherine Moore

*Notes*

1. HPL had discovered that he and Barlow were sixth cousins by common ancestry from John Rathbone [or Rathbun] (1658–1723).

2. HPL wrote the acrostic "In a Sequester'd Providence Churchyard Where Once Poe Walk'd," while seated on a tomb at St. John's churchyard in Providence. Barlow wrote "St. John's Churchyard" and Adolphe de Castro "Edgar Allan Poe." These, and others written at a later time by Maurice W. Moe and Henry Kuttner, appear in David E. Schultz, "In a Sequester'd Churchyard," *Crypt of Cthulhu* No. 57 (St. John's Eve 1988): 26–29.

3. Poe, "Lenore," ll. 4–7.

4. A. E. Housman (1859–1936), "To an Athlete Dying Young," ll. 17–20.

5. The ringing of sets of church bells or handbells in a constantly varying order.

6. "The Lads in Their Hundreds," 23.1–4.

7. "The Lads in Their Hundreds," 23.7–8.

8. "The Lads in Their Hundreds," 23.9–16.

9. "The Rain It Streams on Stone and Hillock," ll. 6–22.

10. "The Deserter," l. 19.

11. "There Pass the Careless People," ll. 9–12, 5–6.

12. Kipling, "Rimini," ll. 1–5.

13. CLM refers to the British actors George Arliss (1868–1946) and Charles Laughton (1899–1962).

14. Ed. Hans Kurath.

15. "What Is Slang?" *Reader's Digest* 29, No. 4 (October 1936): 67–70. An extract from *The American Language* (1936).

16. By Richard Chenevix Trench.

17. See CLM 26n7.

18. I.e., CLM's address at 2547 Brookside Parkway, S. Drive, Indianapolis, IN.

19. "XIII. The Deserter" in *Last Poems*: "They mow the field of man in season: / Farewell, my fair, / And, call it truth or call it treason, / Farewell the vows that were." ll. 21–24.

20. HPL sent for the collection *The Shunned House*" (bound by Barlow), Barlow's *Cats of Ulthar,*' the Visionary Press edition of *The Shadow Over Innsmouth*. HPL alludes to Barlow's plan to issue a volume of Robert E. Howard's poems, *Echoes from an Iron Harp,* but the project came to naught.

21. Tennyson, *Idylls of the King* ("The Passing of Arthur," ll. 48–50).

22. CLM refers to the John Brown house (1786–88) at 52 Power Street and the Edward Carrington house (1810, 1812) at 66 Williams Street.

23. Gladys Bronwyn Stern (1890–1973), author of fiction, plays, literary criticism, biographies, and memoirs. CLM refers to her play *The Matriarch.*

24. CLM refers to a juvenile work by HPL, *Wilkes's Explorations* (1902; nonextant), about the Antarctic explorer Charles Wilkes, and quotes from the last line of HPL's "August."

25. "August," l. 8.

26. *Toonerville Folks* (a.k.a. *The Toonerville Trolley That Meets All the Trains*) was a popular newspaper cartoon feature by Fontaine Fox (1884–1964) that ran from 1908 to 1955.

27. Seabury Quinn, "Witch-House" (*WT*, November 1936).

28. *The Great Ziegfeld* (MGM, 1936), musical drama directed by Robert Z. Leonard; starring William Powell, Luise Rainer, and Myrna Loy.


[36]   [AL, JHL; AHT 9.4]

[c. 20 October 1936]

[Dear Miss Moore:]

[. . .]

[from letter fragment, AL, JHL; leaf V:]

[. . .] common literary as well as intellectual & diplomatic medium. This *might* be the fate of English. As to the possibility of some other other [*sic*] language gaining supremacy through the ultimate dominance of the civilisation behind it—that is certainly an interesting field of speculation. Although a conquering nation often *does* impose its language & institutions upon the nations it absorbs—as the Nordics imposed Aryan culture upon the Slavonic & Mediterranean races, & as Englishmen, Frenchmen, & Spaniards have imposed their respective languages on various negro groups in the New World—largely the West Indies—this imposition is by no means the rule. Some cultures, especially the Greek & the French—have proved incredibly tenacious; so that conquerors have seldom been able to uproot them where once they have existed. The Romans never even tried to Latinise the Hellenistic world which they ruled for 500-odd years, & even the all-uprooting Mohammedans could not oust Greek in the neighbourhood of Greece itself. So likewise French is still dominant in Quebec after almost 175 years of British rule—while it perished only with the greatest slowness & difficulty in Louisiana (it still survives there fragmentarily in the rural districts) after 130 or so years of United States control. I have an idea that English speech & culture might prove equally tenacious. It has never been brought to the test, since our race has never retreated from any region over which it has spread its influence. Britons never shall be slaves! Just what great wars of conquest lie ahead of the world—& just how well any sort of continuous civilisation could survive another war—we cannot say. [1]Our western world is at its lowest ebb—with an effete culture & unworkable political-economic system which have sapped many important fundamentals of group-feeling & group-ambition to a perilous extent. The only determined psychological renaissances in the strictly western nations are those in Italy & Germany, & these are so diluted with undesirable elements that their beneficial effect is doubtful. Russia is the only really solid integrated nation today—the only nation which has tried to apply reason to actual life, *& which really believes in the course it is following.* It is the only nation whose present line of evolution leads *directly* anywhere, although Scandinavia & Great Britain seem to be evolving definitely ahead in a more fumbling & dilatory— but less destructive—way. The trouble with Scandinavia & Great Britain is that their evolution is too *imperceptible* to arouse & regenerate the national psychology & create the fresh grip on life which has been achieved in Russia. This also applies to the U.S. so far as the sniping & sabotage of Republican & business interests have allowed it to evolve at all. Today Russia could probably conquer any other one nation on the globe—but she really has no *wish* to do so. Her strength is to be used in defending herself against such enemies as Japan & Germany. I doubt whether Russian control & culture will ever spread westward, although it might spread in various directions in the Orient. Soviet governments will probably be very common in the world a century hence, but I do not believe they will be in any sense tributary to Russia. They will study Russian methods & receive advice from Russian administrators & economists, but each will preserve its own major cultural institutions. The idea that cultures are wholly dependent on economic organisation is altogether silly. In general, the spread of socialism will diminish the incentives both of waging war & of imposing one's culture on other nations. Conquest by Germany or Italy, or by a coalition of the two, would form another story—but I doubt whether such an event could ever take place. Great Britain & France would undoubtedly act together as before—& Russia could probably be counted on as an ally. The same is true in the event of a Japanese war of conquest. Japan has something of the pristine virility & integratedness which the west has lost, but is not yet ready for world dominance. In the end, she will probably form the new conqueror if there is to be any conqueror; for with a little social & economic readjustment at home (the establishment of a sort of military feudal socialism harmonious with the traditional Japanese spirit & fired with the mystical zeal of the emperor-cult) & with the control of China's supine & malleable millions, she could defy almost any possible combination of western powers, unless they all acted together amidst a reborn determination equal to Russia's. Such psychological rebirths, however, are distinctly possible in many nations. When any great nation manages to achieve a really workable way of life in which the people can genuinely believe—whether through socialism proper or through the national socialism of fascistic reaction—it is likely to experience the sort of sudden renaissance or purpose and virility which we have seen in Russia, Italy, Germany, & Kemalist Turkey. Thus reanimated, *England* would once more be the dominant & unassailable world leader which she has been in the past, & all our fears of a tottering culture would be for naught:

"This ENGLAND never did, nor never shall,
Lie at the proud foot of a conqueror,
But when it first did help to wound itself.
Now these her princes are come home again,
Come the three corners of the world in arms,
And we shall shock them. Nought shall make us rue,
If ENGLAND to itself do rest but true!"[2]

BRITANNIA
IMPERATRIX
MVNDI

GOD SAVE THE KING!

I do not believe that either the negro or australoid race will ever rise to power or found an autochthonous civilisation—both being of definite biological inferiority. Each forms a sort of sub-species (not a *separate* species, since interbreeding with undiminished fertility is possible of *homo sapiens;* exhibiting radical departures from the human norm established by the caucasian-mongoloid races, all of which departures are in the direction of the lower primates & of the extinct hominidae or sub-men whose skeletal remains have been so closely studied. As the ground-ape stock behind mankind evolved, it was constantly getting differentiated & throwing off lateral branches of sub-men, some of which seem to have quickly perished, whilst others survived & multiplied (like the neanderthaloids) down to a period on the verge of recorded history. Up to & including *homo neandertalensis,* these sub-men were undoubtedly of a separate species from ours—[3]

[. . .] Despite the niceness of big business-men to others in the same business, the system behind the existence of such (great) businesses as a whole is slowly & relentlessly dispossessing so many individuals in walks of life invisible to "nice business people"—small farmers, miners, factory workers, clothing makers, mechanics, utility operators, &c.—that a continuance of it will not be tolerated by a majority of the population. The concentration & centralisation of business administration, the marketing methods which abolish the small dealer, & the invention of labour-saving machinery for quantity production, have all united to produce a growing class of the permanently unemployed (once every able man could sooner or later get some kind of a job. Today, no matter how able a man is, it is only a gamble whether or not he will be one of the limited number for whom jobs can exist.), whilst the surplus of labour makes it possible for employers & corporations to reduce even those whom they do employ (for not all employers & corporations are as nice as big bankers!) to a state of degrading peonage. The idea of America as a "land of opportunity" has been mocked & dragged in the mud—& by the very people who ululate against those partisans of decency who try to correct the vilest abuses in "our glorious hereditary pioneer American way of life & enterprise". Well—apart from all questions of ethics, this simply can't go on. It hasn't gone on in any other country where a comparable dilemma has developed. The bulk of the people simply won't stand for it. Private control of large resources exists only by accident—as a result of certain past conditions & of public inertia—& is upheld solely by the physical force of the majority. Were the physical force to be withdrawn, the natural resources would again—as in feudal times—be in a a state of constant transfer, through force of arms, among groups of the physically strong & shrewdly organised. Capone & his racketeers gave us an idea of the general tend of an unpoliced modern world. Well—the majority have hitherto lent their physical support to existing capitalism because they believed it gave them a better deal than feudalism did. Probably they were right up to about 70 years ago—for the worst pressure of capitalism is its recent pressure, whilst the techniques of industry & economics did not make practical socialism possible till the last two generations. To-day, however, the masses do not get as much from the capitalistic order as they would get from feudalism. (Capone established free soup kitchens in Chicago when that insufferable entity Hoover was puling against the rudimentary decency which produced federal public relief!); & the bonus march & other events of '32 show how definitely they are preparing to withdraw their physical support from the existing order. The extent to which the masses of the dispossessed idealised racketeers & the kidnappers of rich men is an unmistakable symptom. Sooner or later, the beneficiaries of capitalism are going to lose the physical support of those who have hitherto kept their system in existence—the physical support of the masses they have neglected, ignored, & evicted from the hope of a livelihood. What will they then prefer—anarchy, feudalism, or socialism? Of course the plutocrats will try to delude themselves & the people up to the very last, & are obviously preparing for a sort of veiled fascism with a dole (instead of the logical spreading of honest work under government ownership of resources & federal allocation of jobs) to keep their victims quiet. . . .

The extent to which "nice people" condone the suicidal policy of the Hooverites is an eloquent commentary on the sway of emotion over reason. They have been conditioned to certain moods (as in religion), & are unable to see or think beyond them. Indeed, they suffer from just the same congenital stupidity & mass hysteria which they recognise & deplore in persons of lesser education & pretensions. If the present crisis has taught me anything, it is to ridicule the tragically emotio-traditional & basically anti-intellectual background of genteel "education". God! The utter ignorance & sappiness of the snivelling, myth-swallowing, church-going stuffed shirts who go about cackling dead slogans & spreading the heraldic tail-feathers that proclaim them self-conscious members of a close corporation of "best people"! Not that they're necessarily any *more* stupid & irrational than the rabble they hate, but that they add to an equal stupidity & irrationality the intolerable assumption of some mystical superiority unbased on personal merit. I'm all for personal merit, & used to revere aristocracy because it developed personal merit. Just as you revere your kindly plutocrats, so did I revere my kindly & honourable agrarian squires. But seven depression years in a hotbed of blind reactionaries has taught me things! . . . What some of these birds call *argument & logick!!* Now I'm beginning to wake up & see that what I used to respect was *not really aristocracy, but a set of personal qualities which aristocracy then developed better than any other system . . . a set of qualities, however, whose merit lay only in a psychology of non-calculative, non-competitive disinterestedness, truthfulness, courage, & generosity fostered by good education, minimum economic stress, & assumed position,* & JUST AS ACHIEVABLE THROUGH SOCIAL-ISM AS THROUGH ARISTOCRACY. It was the *fruits,* not the *mechanism,* which were worthy of respect—& today the decadent mechanism functions in vacuo, pavoninely proud of its mere skeletal essence, & no longer producing the fruits which once justify'd its existence. Hell! I'm done with it & its pretences. Best people! Best people my eye! I've reached the stage now where my aunt wants to hush me up in company, & keep me out of the sight of certain old friends. Last month, when she resignedly lamented the advent to the flat below us of a perfectly quiet & well-bred family "whom none of our friends know", I fear that my lack of sympathy was almost obtrusive. I almost went so far as to ask why I could find so little scientific vision, historic perspective, & disinterested logic in some of the precious old hens & unctuous stick-in-the-muds "whom we *do* know"! Goodbye, gentility, naive idol of my callower years! Hallelujah, I'm a bum![4]

The present crisis in America is part of a fight that extends deep into the core of human standards & ideology. The real clash is betwixt two philosophies of life—one of which urges that the people coöperate & employ the fruits of invention & discovery in making the process of living as easy as possible for everyone in order to liberate energies for the real development of human personality, & the other of which urges that the struggle of the jungle be prolonged—life being made very hard for those not happening to inherit resources, so that the less shrewd will be forced into an intolerable position & have a high death-rate while the shrewd & calculative multiply, fight, & cultivate an ideal of dominant shrewdness. Upholders of this second philosophy argue that only by exalting shrewdness & aggressiveness, & trampling down the non-calculative, can a nation develop the hardness necessary to excel or survive in the world-struggle. They have no confidence in the power of education, medical science, hygiene, character-training, & the discipline of legitimate work (i.e., non-profit struggle for the common welfare, or definite & rationally allocated service in exchange for an equitable stipend) to keep the race up to the necessary standard of stamina, material progressiveness, & survival-value. In other words, they ignore the modern world of science & hark back to the world of primitive man & the lower animals; where all the factors of evolution are accidental, & where consequently the prosperity of the acquisitively strong & the subordination & death of the weak are indeed elements making for progress. They evade entirely the question of different kinds of superiority. Then they speak of favouring the "strong & efficient" they mean only the *industrially* acquisitively strong & efficient. The man of science, artist, or philosopher who is not a good money-maker is classed with the shiftless & consigned to suffering & extermination. All values but material values, apparently, are non-existent for these hardy upholders of "our historic pioneer Americanism". Well—I have already made it plain that I have thoroughly repudiated this primitive philosophy in favour of the more scientific & contemporary one. There is really nothing else for a thoughtful & disinterested person to do. I revere tradition—am in fact preëminently an antiquarian—but can hardly see why the coarsest & crudest element in pioneer life should be singled out & worshipped as "historic Americanism". I am likewise no friend of aimless idleness—but do not see why a savage & feverish scramble for bare necessities, *made artificially hard after machinery has given us the means of easier production,* is necessarily superior to a reasonable amount of sensible work plus an intelligently outlined programme of cultural development. Nor is my reluctance to starve & kill off the weak any indication that I worship weakness *per se.* I would advocate the improvement of backward groups through education, hygiene, & eugenics—nor do I think it especially naive or ultra-idealistic in me to prefer these conscious & scientific methods to the blind, brutal, & accidental methods of primitive nature, in which real advances are merely the casual *by-products* of aimless, wasteful forces. The slyly & disingenuously raised question of "freedom" is of course a mere reactionary smoke-screen. Nobody wants to restrict the freedom of the individual in America in anything but his large-scale economic organisation—& everyone who considers this single economic element synonymous with the whole of life stands revealed as occupying a rather crude philosophic plane. What is more—this very economic freedom does not exist any more under the old order than under a possible new one. As things are, the large economic interests completely enslave the small. Reform seeks merely to transfer restriction from one group to another—the reason being that the restriction of the large will have fewer bad effects on the whole social fabric than does the present & past restriction of the small. *Some* kind of change *must* be established; since old-time Hooverism was merely pauperising more & more individuals & piling up the gunpowder for a social revolution. Even the bulk of half-awake Republicans realise that something must be done—as in the times of Agis, Cleomenes, the Gracchi, Caesar, & Diocletianus—but the trouble is that they have no sympathy with a better state of things. All they want is to perpetuate as much of the old economic order as they safely can—their concessions to the needs of the times grudging & inadequate. [. . .]

I hope the coming transition can be accomplished gradually & peacefully, in the manner of the northern nations, rather than in the violent manner of Eastern, Central, & Southern Europe. The most sensible philosophy is that of Norman Thomas—but the only practical avenue actually leading to peaceful transition is the New Deal. It has its faults & limitations—but it is the only course which offers a real chance. Indeed, one of its weaknesses—its constant endorsement of the general capitalistic principle—is likewise one of its practical strong points; since the sheep-like slogan-servitude of the mob is such that voters shy off from the *label* of socialism even when they are most in need of its benefits. By clinging to the outworn shibboleths of a capitalistic vocabulary, the New Deal is able to get its mild medicine down a desperately sick but capriciously recalcitrant patient's throat. I sincerely trust it will be returned to power next month, lest all the forces now slowly set in motion be retarded, & the way paved for another crisis like that of '32. It looks to me as if all will be well—even through the reactionaries are fighting like cornered rats & lying like grammar-school bullies. As mention'd a few paragraphs back, I am amused by the savage bigotry & historick blindness of the Republican mossback element in which I am immersed. All of our old family friends are hysterical Landonites, who regard me as a sort of wild maniac or reprehensible anomaly. They read intelligent articles on the situation in *Harper's* & elsewhere (although the poor old *Atlantic* dodders on as a senile reactionary), & hear sound liberal lectures at the college, but are totally impervious to the logic & historic perspective set forth. They seem to think all authors & professors are hopeless visionaries apart from the real world, & of little use as compared with the "practical business executives" whose ignorance & myopia piled up the crisis of 1932! However—the liberal percentage of the younger generation, especially those who have taken economics, sociology, & history in college since 1930, is much higher, so that the vote of the smug, blinder-wearing second ward will not by any means possess an unbroken sunflower motif. The only young people who do not incline toward liberalism are those conventional parental echoes, or those wholly self-centred pleasure-seekers & main-chancers, who do not think at all. The percentage of non-capitalistic sentiment rises sharply as one surveys a college personnel from its freshman class of papa-parroters to its senior class of independent thinkers. The trouble is that most of the young chaps tend to drift too far, & to become mixed up in the pseudo-scientific dogmata & violent revolutionism of orthodox Marxism. However, they are not beyond reason, & may ultimately decide to cast their lot with the rational liberal socialists & New Dealers to form a Popular Front against black Republicanism & its grotesque Townsendite & Coughlinite allies. Things are going to move more swiftly when the collegians of 1930 & later reach years of influence & take over the key posts of government from the unsettled, rheumy-eyed old bald pates of my generation. It's only the freak specimen of my generation—reared as we all were on dead platitudes in the soporific twilight of pre-war days—who can think straight & unemotionally on the issues of the present & future. All honour to Norman Thomas, FDR, Gov. Green of Rhode Island, & other 19th century products who have broken through the meshes of tradition-clogged education & savage class bias & have headed toward the light regardless of the past, of environmental prejudice, or of material consequences to themselves! There is in this emancipation something of the spirit of the *18th century*—the age of Voltaire, Rousseau, Diderot, d'Alembert, Paine, Hume, & others who cast aside superstition for reason & dared to think of a real application of human intelligence & decent justice to the problems of society & government. Much of this fine old spirit was killed by the resurgent greed & sentimentality of the 19th century, but a few always kept the tradition alive—St. Simon, Fourier, Comte, Robert Owen, Greeley, Dana, Nathaniel Hawthorne, Lassalle, Marx, Engels, Sidney Webb, Oscar Wilde, George Bernard Shaw, William Morris, Jean Jaures, H. G. Wells, Bertrand Russell—till now sentimentality & greed are at least temporarily routed once more by the prophets of an Age of Reason. The greatest peril to civilised progress—aside from an annihilative war— is some kind of basically reactionary system with enough grudging concessions to the dispossessed to make it *really work after a fashion*, & thus with the capacity to postpone indefinitely the demand of the masses for the real rights—educational, social, & economic—as human beings in a world where the great resources should be cornered by none. Laissez-faire Hoover–Mills– Mellon–Menckenism[5] is simply a joke which can be counted out. Unsupervised capitalism is through. But various Nazi & fascist compromises can be cooked up to save the plutocrats most of their spoils while lulling the growing army of the unpropertied with either a petty programme of *panem et circenses*,[6] or else a system of artificially created & distributed jobs at starvation wages on the C.C.C. or W.P.A. idea.[7] A regime of that sort, spiced with the right brand of hysterical flag-waving, sloganeering, & verbal constitution-saving, might conceivably be as stable & popular as Hitlerism—& that is what the younger & more astute babbitts of the Republican party are quietly & insidiously working toward. Preferring the more civilised alternative of socialism, I can't say that I wish them luck!

But the chief indictment of a capitalistic ideal is perhaps something deeper even than humanitarian principle—something which concerns the profound, subtle & pervasive hostility of capitalism, & of the whole essence of mercantilism, to all that is finest & most creative in the human spirit. As mentioned in the preceding pages, business & capital are the fundamental enemies of human worth in that they exalt & reward the *shrewdly acquisitive* rather than the *intrinsically superior & creative*. Pro-capitalists are prone to slobber over the "free competition" in economics which "rewards the worthy & punishes the shiftless". Very well. Let's see how the worthy are rewarded. Let us list a few of the most incontestably superior minds & personalities in the modern capitalistic world & see whether capitalism has given them its highest rewards. Albert Einstein. Romain Rolland. Bertrand Russell. H. G. Wells. George Santayana. Thomas Mann. John Dewey. W. B. Yeats. George Bernard Shaw. M. & Mme. Curie-Joliot. Heisenberg. Planck. Eddington. Jeans. Millikan. Compton. Ralph Adams Cram. Sigmund Freud. Ignacio Zuloaga. Theodore Dreiser. Julian & Aldous Huxley. Prof. G. Elliot Smith. Are these the world's richest people today? And in the past did capitalism award its highest benefits to such admittedly superior persons as Poe, Spinoza, Baudelaire, Shakespeare, Keats, & so on? Or is it just possible that the *real* beneficiaries of capitalism are *not* the truly superior, but merely *those who choose to devote their superiority to the single process of personal acquisition rather than to social service or to creative intellectual or aesthetic effort* . . . . . those, & the lucky parasites who share or inherit the fruits of their narrowly canalised superiority? "Capitalism fosters technological progress, &c. &c. &c." All right, Mr. Hoover, but just answer three questions for an old man: (a) is technological progress very important in the long run? (b) who *makes* the technological progress—the capitalists, or their underpaid inventors & engineers & research scientists? & (c) why has non-capitalistic Soviet Russia exceeded most of the capitalistic nations in technological progress during the past decade? What's that I hear in reply? "Oh, shut up, you goddam bolshevik, & don't ask such seditious questions!" Very well—we'll let history work out the problem in its own way. But as for anything *just* or *beneficent* in capitalism . . . Pfooey! Equine plumage!

I recently took one phase of this subject—the influence of commercialism on art—up with young Finlay, the brilliant new *WT* artist, who thought Grandpa was too severe on the editorial rats who have gnawed most of the merit out of the coming crop of writers. Finlay thought that the obstacles put in the way of good writing form a stimulating "challenge" . . . . . God! As if the ruthless discouraging of true merit & systematic encouragement of cheap & tawdry charlatanism had anything *beneficial* in it! As I told Finlay, the "challenge" offered by commercialism is *not* the true challenge of harder conditions in the right line of development, but is simply a demand for aesthetically harmful *departures from the right line of development*. What is valued & insisted upon by commercial editors is precisely what has no place whatever in authentic literary expression. Whoever consents to aim for the tawdry effects demanded by commerce, is deliberately checking & perhaps permanently injuring his ability in an effort to achieve certain cheap results alien & antagonistic to literature. The literary ruin of brilliant figures like Long, Quinn, Price, Merritt, & Wandrei speaks for itself. *No really fine story would ever be accepted by a modern pulp editor if submitted without the name of a prominent author*. I have no hesitancy in saying that "The Willows", anonymously submitted, would draw a rejection slip from every penny-dreadful editor in England & America combined. When a half-decent story *does* get printed in a pulp magazine, it is generally because of some irrelevant element wholly unrelated to its real merit. The really *best* stories of the same author would be promptly rejected—as the experience of Klarkash-Ton eloquently proves. The one effect of commerce on the writer is to make him stop trying to write good stuff & begin trying to tailor trash to order in conformity with some cheap & anti-artistic formula. This is no proper *challenge.* The *real* challenges are those offered by the various problems of aesthetic expression—the problems of achieving this or that different effect in genuine artistry. Concrete embodiments of these *real* challenges are things like Nobel & Pulitzer Prizes, & the standards set by "quality" magazines & the more substantial & dignified publishing houses . . . standards based on intellectual reputation, not on sales. Those, of course, are a far cry from rampant commercialism. *That,* indeed, is an unmitigated evil which has ruined more potential authors than any other single influence. It is useless to point out that a few tremendously vigorous authors like Two-Gun Bob do somehow find a way to circumvent commercialism in part, & to get a few good stories published in spite of Mammon-standards. Even in this case a cruel *waste* of energy & ability—which might have gone into aesthetic creation—is involved, & the net output of the author is just so much less excellent than it would have been in the absence of commercial pressures. . . .

[. . .] I've recently come into touch with Finlay, & find him a most unusual & brilliant character. He's only 22, & a resident of his native city of Rochester, N.Y. He is a poet of no mean attainments as well as an artist—though of course pictorial art is his primary medium. In future years I feel certain that he will become an artist of distinction, so that the *WT* group will feel very proud of having known him in his youth. . . . All of Finlay's *WT* work is good—especially the designs for your "Lost Paradise" & Bloch's "Faceless God".[9] Bloch tells me that Wright considers the latter the finest illustration ever drawn for *WT,* & that the original hangs framed in the office. The recent illustration for Quinn was indeed clever—the scintillating sparks adding a particular magic. The psychology of twinkling points surely does form an interesting subject in itself. It is probably rooted in the pleasurable & stimulating nature of all *light & warmth,* & everything associated with light & warmth—this in turn coming of course from the life-saving part played by the radiance of the sun, the campfire, & the hearth. Apollo & Vesta are very ancient deities! The especial glamour of *spangles* probably comes from a synthesis of different pleasant associations—the stars, the rising sparks of a comfortable fire, precious stones, &c. [. . .]

\*\*\*\*\*\*\*\*\*\*

About the plural of *hiatus*—in Latin it would be spelled *just the same* as the singular, except that the *u* would be long, since the word is of the *fourth* declension. In English one might use either that plural or the boldly English form *hiatuses.*

[. . .] Meanwhile the "fan" magazines are getting too numerous to keep track of! There must be 10 or 11 of them now—although most are heard of rather than actually seen. You've doubtless received the bulky anniversary *Fantasy* from Leedle Shoolie, plus a couple of *Phantagraphs* from Wollheim or Shepherd. *Fanciful Tales* is slowly taking form, & Conover's *Science-Fantasy Cor-*

*respondent* bids fair to be a rather ample venture despite its small page-size. The latter plans to continue the serialisation of my "Sup. Horr. in Lit.", left high & dry by the suspension of the good old *FF. Some* day Hill Billy Crawford *may* git around to issuin' his long-postpon'd *Marvel Tales* & my "Innsmouth"! I just read some more proofs of the latter. [. . .]

*Notes*

1. At this point begins AHT 9.4, dated as "Oct. 1935."
2. Shakespeare, *King John* 5.7.118–24.
3. The AL ends here.
4. See CLM 33n8.
5. HPL refers to Herbert Hoover (1874–1964), who was president (1929–33) when the stock market crash of October 1929 occurred; Ogden L. Mills (1884–1937), secretary of the treasury under Hoover (1932–33); Andrew Mellon (1855–1937), financier and secretary of the treasury under Harding, Coolidge, and Hoover (1921–33); and H. L. Mencken (1880–1956), journalist who developed a furious hostility to FDR and the New Deal.
6. From Juvenal, *Satires* 10.81: "Bread and circuses" (or bread and games). A superficial means of appeasement.
7. The Civilian Conservation Corps and the Works Progress Administration, two major New Deal programs.
8. "The Faceless God" (*WT,* May 1936).

[37]   [TLS, JHL]

Begun: Oct. 24, 1936
Ended: Dec. 15, 1936

Dear Mr. Lovecraft:

Your very interesting letter arrived yesterday. I had gone to a movie after work and didn't know it had come until about 9:00, and hold you solely responsible for my yawns this morning, since I sat up until nigh onto midnight reading and digesting it.

The movie was the latest Shirley Temple opus,[1] and I am wondering if you have ever seen any of her performances. I am reluctantly compelled to admire her almost incredible ease and self-possession, which represents either dramatic ability far beyond what seems possible for a seven-year-old or genuine detachment and unselfconsciousness that seems equally impossible before the cameras. And when such abilities are combined with conventional doll-like beauty the whole thing becomes even more impossible. There is in the self-possessed and confidential smile with which she favors her audiences a sort of adultness which I had not realized before last night. There is adult humor in it, as if she were capable of realizing the hokum of the story she acted in and were subtly laughing at herself and her audience. All of which is too fanciful and fantastic to credit seriously, but the child herself is fascinating to consider from a viewpoint quite apart from admiration of her dimples and curls and rather hackneyed beauty. She is the only child actor whom I ever saw who wasn't offensive, either through obvious parroting of lines or through showing-off smartiness. Her lines have the conviction and delivery of spontaneous speech, an she does utterly childish things with gave abstraction as she goes thru the sticky hokum of her scenes. I am amazed anew every time I see her.

On the topic of movies, have you yet seen Midsummer Night's Dream?[2] As a movie it was pretty much of a flop—and for the same reason that really good stories flop in pulp magazines. The average pulp reader and the average movie goer regard story and picture in the light of brief entertainment for a short period of leisure. They haven't much time to spare and they want the entertainment to come to the point *now,* to move swiftly and excitingly enough to hold attention which is really not interested in the play or the book half so much as in the individual's wholly uninteresting life itself. The entertainment has got to be of the bang-bang type to keep the self-centered interest at all. A story or a movie that takes time to build up background and atmosphere fails before it starts with that type of audience. The fault is really not, of course, with publishers and editors, but with the people they cater to. And nothing can be done about it.

The movie of the Shakespeare play, however, rather opened my eyes. I had never before heard the bard of Avon's lines recited in any other way than declamatorily, if there is such a word—thundered in measured numbers, you know. Something about Shakespeare seems to bring out the ham inherent in every actor. But the movie Hermia and Lysander and the rest were really marvelous. For the first time I heard the lines spoken conversationally, or impassioned-ly, putting eloquent life into the ancient phrases. I realized for the first time how Shakespeare has been butchered in the last several centuries. He wrote blood-and-thunder and vulgar comedy and impassioned love stories for the masses, with no thought of immortality, presumably, and the mere fact of his genius doesn't alter the fact that the plays were written for and of living, breathing people and deserve interpretation into living, breathing drama again, not thundered recitations that make all the tears and mirth and terror mere wooden elocution.

And Mickey Rooney's Puck was marvelous. He is perfect for the part, and his thin, lanky, half-grown, brown little person carried wonderful and rather chilling conviction, with his elvish, pointed features and wicked grin and the budding horns so delicately hinted at among the tangles of his tow hair. In movies which insistently call a spade a lousy shovel it's wonderful to come upon some such exquisitely inhuman topic kept so vaguely indeterminate, so that though I kept watching all through the picture for a clear view I was never certain the horns were there, never positive they weren't. He played the part so perfectly that I suspected him of changeling-hood himself. Surely no one wholly human could understand or reproduce the goblin glee that rocked him with mirth at things no mortal could consider funny at all. He shrieked his dreadful, soulless, gleeful laughter at tragedy as well as comedy, or at nothing at all, the enchanted woods resounding with his indescribably inhuman mirth, halfway between the chattering of a squirrel and a sound no human ears can ever have heard before. All through the picture he knew no mood but that goblin merriment as the flashed and soared through the forest, winking in and out of visibility with enchanted ease and screaming his chattering, half-animal, half-elfin laughter in a voice inaudible to the humans he was bedeviling. I understood for the first time why goblins and elves are considered malicious by the people they plague. It's because they're motivated by minds that work so differently from human minds as to be quite untouched by any human viewpoint. The things they do aren't deliberately malicious—all this legendary souring of milk and preventing the butter from coming in the churn and pinching the dairy maids and so isn't intentionally cruel. After seeing Mickey Rooney laughing elvishly at tears and tragedy and at nothing at all one can't help understanding how strangely the goblin mind works. The whole performance was marvelous.

The filming itself was beautiful, but somehow marred by having seen a technicolor picture recently so that the whole thing seemed a little flat and quite out of proportion to itself. I mean, spending a million dollars or so on a two-dimensional, uncolored picture, when in so short a time, surely, we will have glowing color and depth in our movies. I even had a vision of the sort of thing my granddaughter will see—three-dimensional movies in clear natural colors, over a much greater scope of screen than ours. Possibly by then odor and touch will have joined sight and sound, or perhaps the movie will seem to be taking place all around her, she herself in the midst of the action, the dim, misty meadows of faeryland stretching haunted in every direction, the odor of mist in her nostrils, the phantom dancers rising from the dim grass at her very feet, their wings brushing her, the thin, clear sound of their piping shrill in her ears. What a strange sensation it would be to stand among crowds and be quite ignored, people of seeming reality brushing by us as if we were the ghosts, not they. Such a pity that I shall probably not live to see it. In fact, the best I can do is weave the above into a tale for Astounding,[3] which I shall proceed to do, I think.

***  ***  ****  ***  ***  ***  ***

This letter has been written so erratically, beginning two or three times on fresh pages as new ideas struck me, that I find myself with half a page of blankness which my Scotch forebears rise up in their graves to forbid me wasting. I think I shall use it to record items that do not require development, as thus:

Thank you, yes, I would very much like to have a copy of the Charleston travelogue if you have one to spare. My car is as far in the future as ever, but

I am collecting such data as I can against the day of its advent, and sometime in the far future I shall put the travelogue to use.

As for "Old 'Dolph" and his canny sale of his Poe acrostic—such stuff! Wright should have waited; he got soundly gypped, for I thought both your pseudo-sonnet and RHB's much superior. The echoes of that summer afternoon certainly reverberated. I shall demand of Kuttner a copy of his own effort.

There is a little old man who comes into the bank occasionally selling honey and cheese, and who must have stepped right out of a Dunsany book. The cottage cheese which he and his wife make is such stuff as dreams are made on—one simply wouldn't believe that so lowly a substance could reach such heights. One spoonful in the mouth and one positively swoons with bliss. I've never tasted anything like it. It seems fairly obvious that the couple lives right on the edge of Elfland, only a narrow border parting their pastures from the fields that know now man. His cows unquestionably have found a door into Paradise and graze the hills of heaven, or else Io herself has somehow strayed into the herd and the enchantment of her magical milk lends the cheese a touch of Olympian splendor. He was telling me today that he uses honey alone to sweeten his coffee and his nightly bowl of mush and milk, and that his wife uses wheat flour ground in a water-mill on Blue River. It's all too idyllic and pastoral and Dunsanyish to be quite real, and nothing but the heavenly lusciousness of the cheese he leaves behind convinces me that I have not imagined the whole thing.

Have you seen the posthum[o]us Housman book, "More Poems"? I haven't read it yet, but have seen fragmentary quotations from it which make me eager to have the book. His immense preoccupation with death seems to be illustrated in almost all the stanzas I have seen:

> Good night. Ensured release,
> Imperishable peace,
> Have these for yours.
> While sky and sea and land
> And earth's foundations stand,
> And heaven endures.
>
> When earth's foundations flee,
> Nor sky nor land nor sea
> At all is found,
> Content you; let them burn,
> It is not your concern:
> Sleep on, sleep sound.[4]

He does it with such marvelous purity of style that it's baffling to try to find just what imparts that peculiar magic to the effect. F.P.A. observes of this phenomenon:

> —and how the songs of scholars
> Are simple songs and sure,
> How utter is the music,
> How true the note, and pure.
> I walked alone in Weston
> The night that Housman died
> And craved the simple courage
> To lay my pen aside.[5]

As you say, he does get pretty sorry for himself and stands back and gazes admiringly on his own resolute fortitude in a good many verses. And there's a sort of a dry, grim smugness in the lines that preface this last book,

> This is for all ill-treated fellows,
>     Unborn and unbegot,
> For them to read when they're in trouble,
>     And I am not.[6]

But despite his faults, there is no one else with that elusive quality of crystal clarity in his verses, so that the simplest words and rhyme-schemes and themes go together into a whole of exquisite perfection.

I was much pleased with your little dissertation on bells, their origin and ringing. My interest in the subject arose from the reading of a novel by Dorothy Sayers, wherein she performs a unique murder by tying up the victim in the bell-chamber while a peal of nine bells is being rung, the unbearable noise finishing him off very neatly. A pleasantly horrid thought. In the book she remarks sapiently that there is about bells, cats and mirrors something indescribably occult.

I am glad to be informed on the question of why misspelling was so rife in the writings of yesteryear. It seems odd that ignorance and illiteracy in spelling and grammar should not extend further into the field of general knowledge. The modern illiterate not only can't spell or speak correctly, but has a very limited vocabulary and no knowledge of literature, while the daily records of Captain Pasteur of Fort Knox, for instance, if read aloud would sound as if written by a well educated and eloquent man with a good command of English. I've noticed that before—well chosen words clearly expressing the thoughts of an obviously well educated person, written with such ridiculous errors in spelling that the whole thing is very baffling. As for capitalization of all nouns, the custom must have been a very deep-rooted one, for ever since I learned shorthand I have inexplicably and consistently "capitalized" every important word except when I watched myself sternly. A page from my notebook would, if translated into longhand, have the appearance of 18th Century writing. "—this however means a serious Loss to the City Government and I fancy it will be a long Time before the Place is filled adequately."

The "ignorant Yankeeisms" you quote were delightful. I can remember having heard "sofy" on childhood visits to the country, and a family anecdote related by the aunt whose namesake I am tells of her own childhood in a neighborhood which said "cheer" for "chair", and her scorn of such ignorance, so that when the Star Spangled Banner was sung she always roared loudly, "Three CHAIRS for the Red, White and Blue"[7] to shame the local illiterates, since she knew that "cheer" was a word used only by the ignorant. (On rereading the above, I'm sure I don't mean the Star Spangled Banner, but some other song whose name I can't think of.)

It is at once interesting and disappointing to learn that the field of juvenile games and their origins has never to your knowledge been thoroughly explored. Your suggestion of an essay publishing details and asking for contributions and comment is a very interesting one, but much as I'd like to do it, I have an unhappy conviction that it's one of the things I'll never get around to.

I can sympathize with your distress to find the city parks gradually losing their natural aspect and succumbing to clipped hedges and flower-beds and marble benches and the like. I think I mentioned having visited Indiana University last summer and finding the beautiful wooded campus being ruined by new buildings, the school evidently being unable to resist the mess of pottage offered by government financing of construction. Of course the buildings are attractive in their way and will certainly be needed, but the lost beauty of those trees and shrubbery and long stretches of woodland is being bitterly lamented. That natural beauty is still appreciated, even by the people who condone its destruction, was eloquently attested by the crowds around one of the exhibits in a garden show last spring, which depicted a corner of woodland that must have wakened in most of the audience memories of childhood as nostalgic as my won. It represented with great skill an utterly untouched fragment of wilderness, carpeted with fallen leaves, a moss-grown grey tree-trunk furnishing a background for spring wildflowers at its roots. Among all the other carefully planned garden arrangements the artless reality of this was doubly effective. As you say, the only way to insure soil conservation and the preservation of natural beauty is to enforce it through national authority. But I read a pamphlet the other day which complained bitterly against WPA and CCC and other alphabetical groups that were 'improving' the country by straightening streams (photographs of before and after illustrating the complaint) until the water, with no bends to slow it, raced off and allowed the stream to dry up. There were other atrocities, but I remember graphically only the brook illustration. I suppose errors are inevitable even on the part of the government with all its good intentions.

I liked your burst of illustrated Anglophilic pride. What tremendous things England would accomplish if the spreading renaissance of national enthusiasm under great leaders reached her shores! I had never before appreciated the line you quoted, "Now these her princes are come home again." It fills one with obscure pride and glory to repeat it. Similar to that wholly primitive pride which suffused me when I realized, as you pointed out, that we belong to a race which has never retreated from any country it has conquered. I feel a strong impulse to thump the tribal drum and howl pridefully. And an equally primitive one to knock wood, for the time will inevitably arrive when another race supplants us. May it be not soon.

Speaking of this spreading renaissance of national unified purpose, am I mistaken in my vague memories that it began in Russia and spread westward thru Turkey, Germany and Italy? (Heavens! I just got out a map to trace the westward course, and to my amazement found a tremendous stretch of yellow, apparently over half the world, labeled Union of Socialist Soviet Russia. It's a little terrifying—that overpowering expanse of the USSR. I haven't been so impressed since sending that "histomap" thing and seeing the mighty spread of Roman civilization compared to our own, and China's serene yellow column pouring down the right-hand margin, unbroken since history began, changelessly while little nations came and went, while Roman swelled incredible over the world and died away, and modern times began.) Well, my original purpose was to point out what I read once somewhere about civilization beginning wherever it did begin, in China or Egypt or India, and moving westward around the world, with Rome through Gaul and Britain, and then from England to New England, and westward across America until the full circle was complete. Wouldn't it be odd if the new enthusiasm were moving westward. I do hope I'm right in thinking it has so far. It will have to come through France and Spain and England before we get it.

I read your treatise on racial characteristics with much interest, and have a few questions on points which you didn't develop and about which I'm curious: for instance, why have the American Indians fallen to such low estate? One would think that with the mighty Mayan and Azetec [sic] tradition behind them they could do something more than herd like cattle in their reservations. However, I seem to recall having read that most of the tribes when the Europeans came were just nomads, with no civilization and no tendency toward it. Why not? Weren't they all of the same race as the Aztecs and Mayas? If so, why the great difference between Mexican Indian civilization and the civilization of the eastern Indians? And why, with such great traditions and background, did the Mexican Indians dwindle away to their present peonage?

The Polynesians are another race that interest and baffle me. I have seen photographs of members of that people in the National Geographic which showed really handsome men and women according to our own standards. I wonder if these were hybrids, or if the pure race stock really produces such ornamental folk. And if physically they resemble us, why haven't they achieved any more socially than African tribes? The enervating weather? The lack of driving necessity? The Lincoln Library of Essential Information,[8] wherein I've just now looked up "Polynesian" informs me that they are the tallest race in the world, with an average height of 5 feet 10 inches, which is interesting. Oh, and the dictionary gives the origin of their name as from the Greek polus, many, and nesos, island. Nice? I did not know before that the Pacific island groups were called collectively "Oceania", but I'm very much pleased about it. It has an Atlantean flavor of wide sea spaces and wide time ranges, all clean and blue and windy and stretching back to history's dawn.

Harking back for a moment to the Indians, I learn from the Lincoln Library that—good heavens!—the Aztecs were cannibals. I have always visioned them on their pyramid temples tearing the hearts from living human sacrifices, but I didn't know they went any farther than that. However the Mayas seem to have had a language whose written symbols represented sounds. I wonder if that means phonetics like shorthand? Oh, and I wonder if they wrote in rhymes? Golly, look at this: "The Maya[n]s had a system of chronology so accurate that no one day could be confused with another over a period of 370,000 years"!!![9] Mustn't that be a misprint? 370,000 years ago weren't we all swinging by our tails? I didn't suppose any recorded history could by the wildest stretch be extended beyond about 6,000 B.C. Or does that simply mean their way of reckoning time could be projected into the past that far, theoretically, without confusion?

Well, now about the negroes. Have I ever mentioned noticing their curious non-resistance to heat? Perhaps it's just because I notice that particularly, but in summer it seems to me that a large percentage of heat prostration cases reported in the papers are negroes. One would think that they wouldn't feel it at all, with their background of steaming jungles. My fiancé once suggested that it was because black absorbs heat, while white reflects it. Since that's true, why do you suppose races in hot countries tend to turn dark? They ought to become more dazzlingly white after every hour in the sun. Something should be done about this.

All you say about the negro race is undoubtedly true, and the only point in their favor which I have to offer is that—one moment—no, I'm wrong. I was going to suggest how extremely pretty negro girls are when they *are* pretty, but a moment's reflection makes me think that the features I admire are more Mongolian. I saw a negro singer in a night club the last time I was in Chicago whom I simply sat and admired for one whole evening. There's such a *smoothness,* flowing and liquid as molasses, in the negroid and mongolian face which the abrupt angles of the white features lack entirely. The space between this singer's eyebrows and upper lashes was sheer beauty, born of shallowly set eyes so that the lids were poems of pure, gently shadowed curves hollowing smoothly down into the pearly darkness of the sockets. (Incidentally, until I began my present study of the human figure in charcoal drawings I had not realized the exquisite beauty of reflected lights into shadows, which impart a sort of pearly softness of light. This almost always occurs beneath the chin, for instance, the reflection from shoulder and chest throwing light up into the shadow. I dwell lovingly on all the reflected lights I can find, much to the disgust of the instructor.) Back to mongolian features, I can understand since seeing that girl the distress with which the orient regards caucasian faces with their deep-set eyes and jutting noses. And I wonder what caused this wide divergence of facial characteristics among the various races. I've read that dwellers in cold climates developed long, narrow, high-bridged noses to warm the air before drawing it into the lungs, while people in hot countries have flat, broad-nostriled nasal appendages to breathe the most, warm air. In that case, pity the Eskimos. I would like to think that their type evolved when the poles were tropical, but I suppose they migrated north long after their physical characteristics were set. But I wonder why oriental eyes are slant and shallowly set, while occidentals are deep and straight. There must be reasons for the evolution of every facial peculiarity of every race, but I suppose no one will ever know them.

Did you read the account in Collier's recently of the effect of food on rats? Rodents of the same family were divided into groups and each group was fed the characteristic food of a different race, and in a few generations, according to the author, the rats took on the aspect and character of the people whose food they ate. Those nourished on rice were small and runty; those who ate the British fare of boiled food were rough and tough; French cooking produced sleek, round little beasts, and so on. If this can be relied on, then food has a tremendous influence on racial characteristics. I am just realizing what a lot of background I shall have to work out for my own private mythology to provide the elements of food and climate and so on which would produce the physical characteristics already decided upon. What an awful lot of details go into the making of a race!

December 5

The newspaper headlines, shrieking of Wallis and the King, declare that he may defy Baldwin and appeal directly to the people, risking the loss of the disapproving dominions rather than the loss of Mrs. Simpson.[10] I wonder what would happen if he did. Perhaps by the time you read this he will have done it, and history will have been made. I can't recall a woman figuring so largely and yet so objectively in English history since Anne Bol[e]yn. If Wallis Simpson changes the course of empire, the whole thing will become even more fantastic and incredible than it is now. If all this were fiction, it would be too far-fetched and in much too poor taste to publish. But as it is, do consider the literary reverberations which will go rolling down time's corridors in the form of immortal prose, deathless verse aching with tears and passion and defiance, novels dripping with authentic romance, dramas without number. Davie and Wallis will join Romeo and Juliet, Lancelot and Guinevere, Heloise and Abelard, as great lovers hard beset by adversity but defying the world to part them. Perhaps a new Shakespeare generations hence will seize upon his drama of love defiant as the vehicle of his genius, and actresses whose great-

great-grandmothers are yet unborn will sweep the stages in the quaint, ancient costumes of 1936, and a King Edward in greasepaint and blond wig will defy an actor Baldwin (by then as villainous a name to students of drama as Machiavelli) and crowds of extras will parade below palace windows painted on backgrounds, shouting "We want Edward!" as the latest papers declare they are at this moment doing, under the actual palace windows, a long way from here. My far descendant granddaughters will read the old romances and sigh for the glamorous days of the 20th century when the world was young and romance blossomed in high places.

Something that I read long ago and had forgotten for years recurred to me this morning and I am moving in a pleasant daze. Where I saw it and who wrote it is gone with the wind now, but I do recall the little fragment of dramatized nursery rhyme, "See-Saw, Marjorie Daw, Sold her bed and lay upon straw".[11] (Wonder what small domestic tragedy of long ago is immortalized in that chant?) made into a poem—

> White feet than lilies tenderer
>> *C'est la sainte Margerie.* . . .
> That scarce upbore the body of her,
> Naked upon the stones they were,
>> *C'est la sainte Margerie.* . . .[12]

and there is something so serene and cool and devout about it that I am delighted at having remembered it. Curiously, there is about the old saintly mortification of the flesh an atmosphere of sanctity and cool austerity which is delightful, though the habits themselves seem senseless and horrible now. I suppose it's the spirit in which they were done that is, in its highest interpretation, so reasonlessly beautiful that the memory of it transcends even the repulsion of the acts it was manifested by. Apparently there is in the human make-up a deeprooted need for fasting and austerity, since almost every religion I can think of insists on it. Even the Indians. In "Man the Unknown" which I glanced very hurriedly through as I was returning it to the library after my father read it, Dr. Carrel dwells upon the strange fact that the intense religious fervor which was as violent and tangible as a disease and which manifested itself in individuals of every generation up to our own, seems to have vanished. Maybe it's gone into the nationalistic fervor of the Fascisti and the Brown Shirts. I think if I'd been given half a chance I would have had it very strongly myself. The intense beauty of the legend of Christ, from the birth in the manger to the cross on Calvary, reduces me to a pulp of sentimental ecstasy every Christmas and Easter, and I think I would have loved being a Catholic and observing all the ritualistic beauty of their church. High Mass and candles burning, the Stations of the Cross, incense, chants and costumes. Life is so matter-of-fact that the Holy Catholic Church seems to offer the last oasis of stately ritualistic living. I don't suppose the Spaniards would be rebelling so violently against the Church if it hadn't been tramping pretty hard on them, but still I kinda wish I had been born a Catholic. It's perfectly possible to join quite sincerely in appreciation of the spirit of religion without having an atom of belief nor faith in the tenets of the religion itself.

Dec. 11

I am positively swooning with shame as I glance over the dates of the innumerable letters I owe. They go back to the middle of September, and people will stop speaking to me if something isn't done soon. At least you will note that I have kept indefatigably at work on this through all the vicissitudes of the past two months. Typewriters come and go, ribbons come freshly to the machines, wear out in pallor and are replaced, and still I do not succeed in finishing. Perhaps I wouldn't enjoy writing to you so much if I could sit down and indulge whenever I wanted to. This last week has been devoted to feverish composition of a story for Klein [*sic*], who says ASTOUNDING is clamoring for grist. I wrote the three-dimensional movie theme up into a tale so basically weird that they may have to refuse it.

Which brings us to the memory of your distress over the butchery of your two tales in that magazine. I had somewhat miraculously escaped much injury in my experiences with them up to the publication of my last story, "Tryst in Time" which was so mangled and dismembered that I could scarcely bear to look upon the bleeding remnants. Typographical errors ranged from the careless to the ludicrous—I remember a brook 'tickling' through a meadow, for one. And with the most uncanny precision they eliminated and ruined the only two parts of the story for which I felt real affection. My paragraph referring to the mysterious urge which drives races upon migration was left out entirely. I had mentioned the great prehistoric hegiras of our remote fathers across vast areas of Europe, perhaps over the land-bridge into America, the recent fever to "Go West" that burned in our immediate ancestors, and hinting wisely that mayhap the fever which my hero felt to travel in time might be the beginning of a new race-migration somewhere. It didn't mean anything much, but it was kinda fun and I bitterly resented its omission. And in the last of the story a sentence whose "well-greased perfection", to quote yourself, gave me a great joy was utterly butchered. I had it, "Wherever you adventured the knowledge of my presence tormented you, and through all my lives I waited for you in vain." Perhaps it verges on blank verse in its extreme unctuousness, but who are they to cut it in their vandalism to—"Wherever you adventured the knowledge of my presence tormented you—and I waited in vain!"??? If they don't like the way I write why don't they go back where they came from? I am burning up.

It's a great delight to find more of your stories appearing in WT. With Howard gone Wright is going to be definitely hard-up for material. I shuddered as zestfully at "Thing on the Doorstep" in print as I did in manuscript form. Finlay's drawing was as beautiful as usual. (By the way, I had a letter from him recently, thanks to you.) And wasn't his drawing for that frightful degenerate-story, the Miller of Kobold's Keep,[13] a joy to behold? I know as surely as one can without actual proof that the author of the tale wrote it after he heard that story that's going the rounds concerning the census-taker in Tennessee. I've had every intention of telling it to you before now, and believe I have, but remind me if I omitted it. You'd love it. I never realized until my brother's intended told it to me how closely allied is mirth and horror. My almost painfully violent amusement was compounded of equal parts of each, inextricably intermingled.

I've had bad luck with Haunter of the Dark all around. Missed seeing the ms., and misplaced my copy of WT which contained it and which probably nothing but a thorough housecleaning will reveal. So I am not qualified now to comment intelligently on it. In fact, I may never be, for I am becoming more and more convinced that there is at 2547 an invisible doorway into the fourth dimension. Things vanish now and then with the most baffling completeness. A large box of my last year's hats absolutely evaporated this spring, for instance. It isn't the sort of thing you'd absent-mindedly carry out and lose, yet within the four walls of the house it completely disappeared and has never to this day been discovered. I do hope my copy of Haunter of the Dark is not slowly circling around that hat-box somewhere in the fourth dimension. I dread the day when some member of the family will unwittingly stumble through that gateway and vanish from human ken.

I'm returning your pages which deal with present social and political conditions.[14] I'd be interested to know if you ever do work the material into a general article, for it seems to me extremely well-organized and convincing. I must admit it's no great feat to convince me, for practically anyone can induce me to believe anything for awhile. I am, as I've often said, a direct spiritual descendant of the White Queen, who could believe three impossible things before breakfast.[15] The whole panorama of the background which your arguments cover is a little too big for me to grasp—perhaps too big for anyone to understand fully; and suggested reforms must necessarily deal with aspects of the whole whose repercussions might well travel so far and affect so many other angles of the situation, each with its own individual solution, that the entire prospect seems to me a bit hopeless for any human mind to solve. In fact, I am very little interested in the question except when confronted with such lucid and graphic explanations as yours. That is, of course, a wholly reprehensible attitude, but represents pretty well, I suppose, the outlook of the great majority. Very few of us have minds which, like yours, enclose the whole scope of the political-social situation and can look ahead past individuals. Most of us are like me, who have *got* to have money which can only be earned by daily work and who do not question the source of the salary so long as it's forthcoming. I can understand but not share your subtle scorn of the capitalist's parasite who, accepting the polluted gold as a means of providing bread and butter for dependents, feels no responsibility for the luckless majority whom the capitalistic system dooms beyond a mild regret that such things happen; and certainly is not imbued with the desire to throw up the job, let dependents starve and go forth crusading for the adoption of a new system, even though it might result eventually in greater happiness for the crusader himself. Most of us are so tied down with hostages to fortune that we have not even the desire to destroy the system which sustains us though we may recognize it as pernicious for the majority. That in itself is a poisonous sort of situation, but I can think of no way out. It rises from the primary quality of human nature—selfish interest. Reform when it comes will probably arrive in spite of us, certainly not through us. And after all, there's the comforting thought, "what could *I* do, as an individual, even if I tried, toward overthrowing the system which provides my livelihood? I bitterly regret the unhappiness which that system imposes on others, but what change could I make in it, myself? Why even think of it, since the only result is personal distress?" And that point of view results in just the present situation of laissez-faire. What the world needs is more people like you who can see the whole thing from a distance. I and my fellow parasites can't see the woods for the trees. It reminds me of a stanza from Kipling:

> Singing: Break bread for a starving folk
> That lie about the field;
> Give them their food as they take the yoke,
> And who shall be next to yield, good sires,
> *To such a bribe to yield?*[16]

The sort of world which would result from a projection of Utopia of the New Deal sounds pretty marvelous. I can understand now what had not occurred to me before—that gentlemen are the product of leisure and assured social position, however that security and leisure may have been achieved and through whatever social system may at the time be in power. I am afraid, however, that I shall not live to see the new order of gentlemanly socialists—it will take a few generations after the new order is well established to produce them—and shall have to go on regarding such men as my much admired bankers as the highest social type of my time. The year of transition, when such petty government tyrants as the bank examiners I've warred with are in the high places, is going to be very nasty indeed and I hope I do not live to see it.

The low literary standards of today must, I suppose, be blamed on the same supine masses which submit to present social situations. As I have said before, editors refuse work of genuine merit not from fiendish malevolence on their part but because they've got to give the public what it wants. I wonder just how far an editor's duty to educate his public extends. Surely not so far as to try vainly to cram meritorious literature down the reluctant gullets of people who simply continue buying trash from others until the commendably motivated but bankrupt editor has to fold up and quit. So very many of us must live so very fast, in accordance with the tempo of the times, that our reading hours are too limited for anything but brevity and action in literature. In fact, I wonder if the tremendous changes in living and the entire social structure of civilization in the last generation or so have not wrought changes in literature as great as in the fundamentals of government and business. It's possible to imagine that what we regard as to inflexibly right and beautiful in literature seems as outmoded and slow and futile to readers of action pulps as the backward-yearning Republican stick-in-the-mud political ideals seem to you of the new era. Perhaps all merit is comparative and beauty in the eye of the beholder.

Truly meritorious pictorial art can be appreciated by pulp readers perhaps because it simply doesn't take time to enjoy. One can see at a glance that Finlay's drawings are far superior to the work of other WT artists, but to appreciate fully The Willows one must sit down alone, dismissing all outside influences, close one's ears to the noise of traffic and lose oneself in the pale yellow horror of the flooding river and the wooded islands terrible with unseen presences.

I read the Sinclair Lewis article in Reader's Digest, and fully agreed with it.[17] The ideal thing would be to have a private income and devote leisure days to the composition and polishing and enjoyment of really good writing. Next best is to have a job, like me, and squeeze in among the few leisure hours of evenings time to write as one likes. To have one's daily bread depend, as Price's does, upon the number of words he can grind out, can certainly be nothing but detrimental to the quality of the work produced. But I question the advisability of writing only for the few who appreciate good literature and making no concessions whatever to editorial strictures. The answer to a "take it or leave it" attitude on the part of the author would almost certainly be "leave it!" And the world might never see works of very real beauty. The thing that Price and Long and I and all the others are striving for, of course, is to achieve such recognition in the pulp fields that the slicks will accept us and we will be released at least, after long labor in the mines, to write the best that's in us. That seems to me the only way that our good work can be circulated and appreciated. Very few of us are such geniuses that even excellent work would be snapped up on sight by the few high-grade magazines that print good stuff, when the author was unknown. You've got to climb the ladder by long and painful processes if you ever hope to be free to write as you want. If the processes ruin you—well, it's too bad, but the loss is no greater than if you'd continued living and starving in a garret and writing beauty and wonder which no editor would accept and no public ever read.

I can think of no greater delight than a book of your stories illustrated by

Finlay. I do most fervently hope that it may come about, though I have often been told that books of short stories almost never sell very well. (Said Polly-anna brightly.)

The Price photographs sound amazingly interesting. And what a curious coincidence the Stuart Morton Boland data is! Within the last month I have myself had a communication from this same St. Boland, though prosaically signed with the full name, very generously presenting me with a small book on Corot,[18] illustrated with lovely reproductions of the misty paintings he produced. One line in the book impressed me greatly in its observation that there is in Corot paintings a serenity and peace which makes the picture seem to extend far beyond the frame and casts a beautiful hush over all things near it. Mr. B. was generous and insincere enough to explain the gift by likening my stories to the paintings. I wrote him gratefully, but have had no reply. Whether he intended the gift to remain a sort of manna descending from the vasty unknown, or whether he proposes to enter into correspondence I do not yet know, but I hope to hear more from him now that you tell me of his interesting and unusual qualities. Don't fail to let me know about the "peculi-ar objects". I hope that they may not prove to be products of Barbara Hut-ton's famous stores, but that, though genuine, they don't carry any frightful curses from the abyss to blast you.[19] A correspondent of mine, Thurston Torbett of Texas, friend of REH's, has been regaling me with passages from books on the occult which state that all the dreadful things we imagine must have had origin in fact or we would be unable to picture them. If one reverses that, then by the very act of writing of Cthulhu (spelling right?) and Sham-bleau we must conjure them into vague life, and you will doubtless eventually wind up the victim of your own ingenuity. I hope that your aunt does not some morning find you a mass of black putrescence on the floor, still clutch-ing in your melting stumps of fingers the "peculiar objects" which the elder gods, via Boland, have sent for your destruction.

I am horribly shocked at your dissipations on ice-cream. From being able to take it or leave it alone you are, I fear, rapidly approaching the point where you cannot do without it, and may wind up in a padded cell, a mass of skin and bones and jangled nerves, plucking at your hair with trembling, claw-like fingers and shrieking in a high monotone of ice-cream—ice-cream—ICE-CREAM! So does the insidious demon gain ascendance over its victims. Two quarts of it! Reason totters. I once found myself in a position of having to eat a quart or see it melt slowly away into ruin, and almost perished in the at-tempt to save the 35 cents or so involved, so I can understand what capacity must be involved in the devouring of two quarts. In fact, on second thought I just don't believe it. No human creature could do it. I shall one day make a trip to Providence if for no other reason than to prove you a braggart and a fibber. Better start training now, for the hour is coming when you will have to sit down under my sceptical eye and do away with two quarts of ice cream, or face the world a perjured man.

Your visitors and social activities during the late autumn sound like fun. What a lot of people seem to pass through Providence. You sound extremely busy—60 hours of work without rest sounds pretty awful. I hope it doesn't happen often.[20]

I can imagine how pleased you were to discover in the local astronomer-group such interest and intelligent knowledge of their subject. You would probably enjoy a membership if you could find time to attend. *** Just inspected the telephone book to see if any such organization exists here. I found nothing, but was sidetracked for about five minutes by the pleasant results, noticed before now but always amusing, of transposed names. Bright, Violet, for instance, leaped out of the page and transfixed me with delight. Bright Sarah, too, must have been a close relation to Pollyanna. On the other hand, Black Harry sounds like some sinister baron of old England. Then we have White Marguerite, unquestionably a martyred queen. Black Joan is most certainly a witch, while Black Grace sounds like a Sabbat. Christian George calls up visions of the saint and his dragon, while Blue Sherwood is twilight over the ancient forest with robber bands moving down the long evening aisles and the sound of a bugle shivering faintly through the leaves. Then we have Grave Paul, and I've just remembered in a blaze of glory that I went to school with a Forrest Bowman. Oh, that can't be! But no, I remember distinctly and can't imagine why it never struck me before now. The dictionary is likewise full of the pleasantest surprises. For instance, the other day I discovered that the potato is a member of the nightshade family, while the sweet potato belongs to the morning glory group. Shade of night and glory of morning. How ducky.

What I did want to say before forsaking the topic of astronomy (though too late now, I fear) was that I don't see how I can possibly wait until the new big telescope is finished. Imagine the sensations of the people who look through it for the first time, seeing things that no man on earth ever saw before.

The Witches' Tales which you mention I have recently observed on local news stands.[21] Thurston Torbett sent me a copy about a month ago, and it's quite ordinary. From the information in the magazine I gathered that it was a publication of stories broadcast over the radio on a program presumably called "The Witches' Tales". I never heard of it, but have been hearing persistent rumors among friends, of weird stories dramatized on some radio program or other. (Usually with the comment, "Just the sort of thing *you* like!") Also I had the impression that most of the tales in the magazine are written by one man, who likewise prepares the material for the broadcast. I suppose that if the mag keeps on the market they will have to procure new stories from other writers, but it's just a thriller like Horror and Terror and the like.[22] WT, with all its faults, continues to print the best of fantasy—that best consisting of a story or two every several months which seems really worth reading. Not a high percentage considering the millions in the country.

I wish I could express to you Mother's delight in the Coggeshall data. We are eternally indebted, and are hoping for an opportunity to render some similarly useful favor in the future. Yes, I'm sure that there must be full genealogies somewhere; the fragments of information which we have gleaned are too detailed not to have been derived from some such publication. I am wondering if there may not be an error in our mysterious Caleb's birth date. 1709 seems such an awkward year to fit him in. We could learn only from a full genealogy, however, for we know nothing except that date. The similarity in names must be very confusing. (Incidentally, my brother's intended is named Catherine too. It's going to lead to much bafflement when there are two Catherine Moores in the same family. Though I had my fortune told the other day and learn that I am to marry in a couple of years, so it won't last long.) It was pleasant to find my Coggeshall ancestors so well regarded in Nantucket. I've always wanted badly to visit 17th century New England and get acquainted with them. I wonder if the people of a former day would really outrage our modern spirits as strongly as happened in "Berkeley Square". I was so impressed by the line referring passionately to "this filthy little pig-sty of a world" that I shall not soon forget it. My grandmother, searching back among her dimming memories for local color, recalls a gambler uncle who brought money home from all-night sessions in buckets sometimes. He must have carried a rabbit's foot. And a progenitor of her own who, leaving his wife alone for the week end in a wilderness cabin, chalked a cross on the door to guide her in case robbers tried to break in. And they did, and she fired the family gun right through the target and he returned to find her swooning on the floor inside and the robber defunct on the doorstep. Then there was Grandfather Moore, Dr. Henry, who left medical school to enlist in the Civil War, and wandered about the battlefields after hours patching up the wounded out of goodness of heart, so that the doctors at the hospital stations, finding among the streams of incoming victims an occasional soul professionally bandaged, back-tracked to Grandfather Henry and snaked him out of the ranks into the their [*sic*] service. I wonder why my ancestors had to live in such colorful surroundings, while nothing ever happens to me? Though I'd probably be the first one to howl bloody murder if robbers came hammering at the door or battlefields opened up before my horrified gaze.

Anyway, countless thanks for what you have been able to discover anent Coggeshalls. Please don't trouble yourself unduly to gather further data, though anything you can pick up casually will be tremendously appreciated. I'm glad the discovery of the marriage date of John Rathbone and the fair Anne Dodge resulted from your efforts on our behalf. Possibly the elusive Caleb's birthdate is the result of another such error in our own line. Wasn't it nice of Jack and

Anne to marry while North Kingstown was Rochester? I'll bet they fumed over the high-handedness of their modern politics as violently as we do today.

I suppose by now that winter has set in about you, and you have retired into hibernation for the season. When you wrote your last letter you were basking in the last warm days of Indian summer, and mentioned the newly accessible woods you had discovered. It must be lovely to make such explorations. I wish I were free during the day to go on similar adventures. Hope the two little kittens you met are doing well still. I wonder if they did not represent the attempt of some squeamish local family, unexpectedly blessed with feline increase, who took the infants out and abandoned them instead of using chloroform or the water bucket. I cannot imagine myself having too many cats, but if that day ever arrives I hope I shall repair to a vet and have him exterminate them humanely, for the idea of small kittens abandoned and slowly starving makes me purple with anger. It would be so lovely to have lots of cats and pups. Someday I shall—God willing—have a nice big farm near an ocean, with a house bulging with modern conveniences and a kennel for dog-breeding and a cattery full of large sleek fluffy cats in all stages of kitten- and cathood. And will feel like a slave-dealer whenever one is sold.

Well, at long last I seem to have covered most of what I want to say and can begin to consider mailing this. I have a shameful confession to make, though. After sending back the last batch of books to you, I discover among loans from other benefactors a stray Dunsany volume which unaccountably escaped. I shall send it back this week with all my embarrassed apologies. If I ever do that again and you notice it, please take me sternly to task about it. In fact, I have a guilty feeling that in your last letter were some "please return" items. I shall search when I wrap the book and send back anything I find.

Everything from rush orders for stories to service on Christmas party committees and illness from bad colds has combined to delay this letter inexcusably, but I have stuck to it like a little man and am proud to report its completion at last. Please don't punish me as I deserve by as long a delay in your reply. I must also apologize for the ignorance of this typewriter, a new one which hasn't yet learned to space properly.

Try to control these ice-cream debauches, and please forgive my irresponsible negligence.

Abjectly,

Catherine Moore

[Notes by HPL on CLM's envelope, X'd out; front, next to image of The Fletcher Trust Company / Indianapolis] Pinnacled Pharos of Petrological Profundity[23]

[back]

   Acknowledgement

pg 2—Charleston trav. offer Loan WT————p 8

p 12  no hurry about Dunsany

    pp 7–8   Tryst in time

       text mangling

---

   Witches Tales

   current WT material

   census-taker anecdote

   Haunter

   Doorstep—illus

   Finlay

   verses—CAS exhib.

   Pickman reprint

p. 10  Boland

   Fan magazines— SFC, Fanciful, Frome, Telegram, England

   Innsmouth

   p. 9—literary standards

      policies

---

p. 8  social & political

   Rabbi Wise

   Election Nov. 3

p. 6—King Edward—

p. 5  national renaissance

   Indians

   Mayans

   Peruvians?

   Polynesians

   niggers

   Mongol &c aesthetics

   cause of racial aspect

   diet rats

   Trench

p. 11—genealogy

---

p. 4  dialect-spelling

p. 3  quaint honey & cheese merchant

p. 3  Housman

   Chivers

p. 7      Ste. Margerie poem
p. 7      ascetic impulse

---

pp. 1–2  cinemas
   Leiber
p. 10    Ice cream
   Ast. Soc. large telescope p. 11
   Wmsburg & philos. lectures
   Tel. Book delving
p. 4   –parks &c
p 12 Outings—wood—kittens
   Oct 28 Neutaconkanut
   Thanksgiving—Hibernation
   Christmas—skull  ~~lectures~~
   ~~? astronomy~~

————Sorry to hear of colds

Ansd

*Notes*

1. CLM may be referring to *Dimples*, an American musical film directed by William A. Seiter released 16 October 1936, or *Poor Little Rich Girl*, another musical directed by Irving Cummings released 24 July 1936.

2. *A Midsummer Night's Dream* (Warner Bros., 1935), directed by Max Reinhardt and William Dieterle; starring Ian Hunter, James Cagney, Mickey Rooney, Olivia de Havilland, Joe E. Brown, and Dick Powell.

3. "Miracle in Three Dimensions."

4. "Goodnight."

5. Franklin Pierce Adams, "The Coward," in *The Melancholy Lute* 32.

6. Untitled prefatory poem, ll. 5–8.

7. From John Philip Sousa, "The Stars and Stripes Forever."

8. *The Lincoln Library of Essential Information* (Buffalo, NY: Frontier, 1924; many subsequent rev. eds.).

9. CLM found this in her *Lincoln Library of Essential Information*.

10. CLM refers to the furor surrounding King Edward VIII of England's desire to marry the American divorcée Wallis Simpson, a move strongly opposed by Prime Minister Stanley Baldwin. On 11 December 1936 Edward VIII abdicated, making way for his brother, George VI (r. 1936–52), to take the throne.

11. English nursery rhyme, folk song, and playground singing game that first appeared in its modern form in *Mother Goose's Melody* (c. 1765).

12. From the nonsense poem "Sainte Margérie," ll. 1–5.

13. G. Garnet, "The Headless Miller of Kobold's Keep" (*WT*, January 1937).

14. Probably "A Layman Looks at the Government" (dated 22 November 1933).

15. Actually six. See CLM 15.

16. "Russia to the Pacifists."

17. Sinclair Lewis (1885–1951), "A Double Life for Writers," *Reader's Digest* 29, No. 4 (October 1936): 71–72; a reprint from *Yale Literary Magazine* centennial number 101, No. 6 (February 1936): 46–47.

18. Possibly Sidney Allnut, T. Leman Hare, and Jean-Baptiste-Camille Corot, *Corot: Masterpieces in Color* (New York: Frederick A. Stokes Co., 1910). 79 pp.

19. See HPL to E. Hoffmann Price, 13 October 1936 (ms., JHL): "Boland says he visited Teotihuacan this summer, & that he is about to send me some 'peculiar objects' which he secured there near the Pyramid of the Sun. Iä! Shub-Niggurath! What alien entities are about to enter the ancient portal of #66? Did they come up out of that gaping chasm amidst the palaeogean megalithic masonry? Are they shapes of a sort intelligible to mankind—or *something else?* My curiosity is piqued . . . . I am vaguely & subtly disquieted . . . . . Or are the 'peculiar objects' mystical trinkets derived from the counters of Frank Winfield Woolworth or his equivalents & vended to a gullible touristry by an obliging peasantry?" Barbara Hutton was heiress to Woolworth, the retail tycoon.

20. HPL had noted that he had recently spent 60 hours without a break in revising Renshaw's *Well Bred Speech*. Anne Tillery Renshaw, *Well Bred Speech*. HPL's work was for naught, since most of his revisions and additions were omitted from the published version. These portions were first published as "Unpublished Parts of *Well Bred Speech* as Written by H. P. Lovecraft," in *Letters to Elizabeth Toldridge and Anne Tillery Renshaw*. The essay now titled "Suggestions for a Reading Guide" was first published in *The Dark Brotherhood and Other Pieces*. Galleys of *Well Bred Speech* corrected by HPL survive at JHL.

21. *The Witch's Tales* (November and December 1936; 2 issues) was a short-lived weird magazine edited by Tom Chadburn and published by the Carwood Publishing Co.

22. *Horror Stories* (Popular Publications, 1935–41) and *Terror Tales* (Popular Publications, 1934–41), two weird-menace pulp magazines.

23. This is the salutation of HPL's last letter to James Ferdinand Morton [December 1936?–February? 1937]. HPL had written it next to the image of the Fletcher Trust Company, on the envelope CLM had used from her place of employment.


[38]   [AL, leaves 3-9, 17 only]

[7 February 1937]

[. . .]

Regarding the low or eccentric literary standards of today—I believe they are chargeable to several more or less dissociated factors, social & intellectual, which unhappily operate simultaneously & in the same direction. It may be that these separate factors all have an ultimate philosophic connexion, but for the purposes of a brief survey they may well be regarded as independent. The major factors seem to be three in number—two affecting serious non-commercial creation, & the third touching the frivolous & negligible (though quantitatively overwhelming) morass of commercial slop including both "slicks" & "pulps". These do not include the special element you mention—the speed of living which you say "must" be pursued "in accordance with the tempo of the times"—because I regard that as a decadence-phenomenon touching at least two of the basic factors. That is, two of the three great factors involve this principle. Overspeeded living is the reaction of sheep-like ninnies to certain commerce-fostered ideals too cheap to be worth spitting on. No one "must" meet the conventional "tempo of the times", & the independent spirit resolutely refuses to conform, no matter how great the material cost. Actually, I believe fewer people grovel to this vulgar speed fetish than is commonly supposed. Young persons, if not philosophic by nature, succumb for a brief period; but I fancy most of them develop out of it as they mature. The cheap gadgets—aeroplanes & all that—persist, but it is not always the same people who keep on using them. And the great bulk of the people are going to fight to the finish before they will allow coarse slave-drivers like the motor magnates to chain them to a speeded-up industrial peonage. Times are changing in more directions than the one leading toward increased speed! Nevertheless, of course, the fetish of speed *is* an active present influence affecting both the sincere artistic decadent & the cheap commercial hack—& its results, divided equally betwixt the output of these two types, may or may not involve permanent harm.

The serious, non-commercial aesthetics of today suffers, as I have suggested above, from two distinct maladies—the irrational & solipsistic freakishness of the subjective decadent, & the prosaic propagandism of the social theorist. The decadent concedes the existence of such a thing as disinterested art, but allows the futilities & absurdities & paradoxes & contradictions of the dying capitalist culture to disorganise him to such an extent that he can reflect nothing but chaos, paradox, hallucination, & ironic contrast. The theorist, on the other hand, refuses to admit that any such thing as art exists as an independent entity. To him (& he is usually an orthodox Marxist who reads an economic motive into everything from the motions of binary stars to the sighing of the wind in the trees), every human activity must have a direct bearing on the technical problem of organising human society for the optimum fulfilment of the majority's physical needs; & art is justifiable only so far as it promotes the successful operation—or hastens the adoption—of a rational social order. Betwixt the two types, we get a sorry enough mess of nonsense & mediocrity. One gives us diagrams of scrambled conic sections or nightmares with locomotives floating in the sky over landscapes of skyscrapers twisted into spirals & dollar-signs, whilst the other gives us undistinctive photographic likenesses of Lenin & Stalin, educational posters urging children to brush their teeth, or grotesquely ironic murals shewing the triumph of machinery or the woes of the Mexican peon. To me, both of these attitudes seem essentially absurd. Each grows, I think, out of an excessively literal &

exaggerated application of the idea that an artist should (or necessarily does) reflect something of his environment . . . . . although the Marxist position is part of a more elaborate maze of theory. This idea itself has always struck me as only loosely & partly true—& I certainly think that any attempt of the artist *to keep it constantly in mind* is ruinous to his work. We can produce real art only when we forget all about theory. It may be that our spontaneous results will indeed reflect something of our period & of our social sympathies in an unconscious way—but if we start out consciously with the idea of reflecting the period or airing our economic doctrines, we shall not get very far as artists. Of course, a person is now & then so naturally gifted with artistic genius that he cannot help producing real art as a by-product even when his conscious theories are of the most ridiculous & arid kind. Thus a surrealist crank or commercial hack or social propagandist may, by accident, evolve many a thing of undoubted power & authenticity. But even in such a case as this, the amount of *waste* is cruelly great. No matter how often the theory-handicapped or commerce-crippled artist manages to produce something good, we are always aware of how much better his results would be without the handicap. The real fact is that no artist ought to tie himself too completely or definitely to any particular period or aera. After all, the environment in which he develops is not merely that of one brief point in the time-stream. It is, rather, the sum of all that the ages have contributed to his civilisation. To the modern European, the sculpture of Phidias & Scopas & Praxiteles, the architecture of Ictinus, Callicrates, Metagenes, Dinocrates, Polyclitus, Hippodamus, & Apollodorus, the painting of Botticelli, Michelangelo, Leonardo, & Raphael, & the music of Handel, Bach, & Beethoven, are just as vital & immediate & personally present as are the latest creations of his own chronological period; & any attempt to erect a new art without reference to such foundations must necessarily be hollow, barren, & fallacious. Our particular age is indeed one of decay & chaos & transition, so that it can probably contribute less fresh material to art than can most others—but why should this force all artists either to devote themselves to the job of portraying decay & chaos, or to forswear self-expression & become social & political propagandists? Are the existence & presence of the past annulled by the momentary disturbances of a readjustment-period? Is a Gothic cathedral less beautiful because we have ceased to believe what the builders of Chartres & Lincoln & Salisbury believed about the governance of the cosmos? Are the landscapes of Ruysdael & Hobbema ugly or meaningless because they were painted amidst a bourgeois-capitalist civilisation whose social & economic values we no longer accept? Suppose we *do* have our grain harvested by machinery & ground in complex mechanical plants with tangles of tall smokestacks? Does that alter the fact that over a great part of our racial history we used scythes & wind & water mills, or annul the powerful appeal of pictures laying stress on these ineradicable cultural landmarks? Up to a relatively recent time, no one thought of questioning the equal artistic value of themes pertaining to our past (no matter how outmoded) & themes pertaining to our present (which will soon enough be merely another phase of the outmoded past!)—both forming equal influences in the shaping of the long cultural steam. Though we did not *use* Egyptian pyramids or Greek galleys or Roman chariots, or *believe* in centaurs & mermaids, we found all these things of vital significance in art—as bearing on the life & beliefs of those ancestral ages which moulded & gave rise to ours. Why, then, must we suddenly proceed to claim that a painting of a windmill is alien & meaningless because we no longer depend on windmills—or aver that we must depict a placid meadow or woodland as a jumble of cubes & cog-wheels because (a) we feel that the chaos of a dying social order & (b) are more used in an urban-mechanical culture to seeing cubes & cog-wheels than to seeing trees & kine & hedges & distant spires? To my mind, the ultra-moderns have (as in the surrender of some of the less sensitive & courageous & determinedly individual spirits to the now tottering Golden Calf of Mammon) simply flown off the handle—letting their heads become turned by the admitted rapidity & completeness of certain current mutations which really do not differ in kind from dozens of mutations of the past. Certainly, our daily lives (assuming that we have many contacts & employ the various useful or useless devices evolved by machinery) differ from those of our grandfathers. But so did theirs differ more or less from those of *their* grandfathers. What if the gap is *quantitatively* wider in our case? Where is the radical cleavage in *essence* betwixt the one gap & the other? Suppose our ideas of society & religion & property do differ from those of the 19th century? Did not the 19th century's ideas of these things differ nearly as much from the corresponding ideas of the 13th century? Yet did the 19th century aesthetically repudiate the 13th as completely as our ultra-moderns would aesthetically repudiate the 19th & all preceding? The extremists forget that the mere phenomenon of change does not necessarily abrogate the principle of continuity. There are no basic eternal things—but there are always sources & antecedents & mnemonic deposits which cannot lightly be disregarded.

*Commercialism* forms the third aesthetically degrading factor of the present age, but is a parallel evil of different origin & nature. Instead of vitiating honest efforts at self-expression, as do decadence & social propagandism, it *simply removes human energy altogether from the field of honest expression*, & shackles it to a greedy & aesthetically & intellectually dishonest sort of charlatanry having no connexion with art. It is an older disease than chaotic decadence & systematic propagandism, & will persist as long as bourgeois capitalism remains a factor to be coped with. It was not so marked in the agrarian aristocratic age, because at that period the most unimaginative, philistinic, & under-educated elements did little or no reading or conscious artistic contemplation. When they did reach out aesthetically, they copied educated gentlefolk. Bourgeois capitalism gave artistic excellence & sincerity a death-blow by enthroning cheap *amusement-value* at the expense of that *intrinsic excellence* which only cultivated, non-acquisitive persons of assured position can enjoy. The determinant market for written, pictorial, musical, dramatic, decorative, architectural, & other heretofore aesthetic material ceased to be a small circle of truly educated persons, but became a substantially larger (even with a vast proportion of society starved & crushed into a sodden, inarticulate helplessness through commercial & commercial-satellitic greed & callousness) circle of mixed origin numerically dominated by crude, half-educated clods whose systematically perverted ideals (worship of low cunning, material acquisition, cheap comfort & smoothness, worldly success, ostentation, speed, intrinsic magnitude, surface glitter, &c.) prevented them from ever achieving the tastes & perspectives of the gentlefolk whose dress & speech & external manners they so assiduously mimicked. This herd of acquisitive boors brought up from the shop & the counting-house a complete set of artificial attitudes, oversimplifications, & mawkish sentimentalities which no sincere art or literature could gratify—& they so outnumbered the remaining educated gentlefolk that most of the purveying agencies became at once reoriented to them. Literature & art lost most of their market; & writing, painting, drama, &c. became engulfed more & more in the domain of *amusement enterprises.* Hence the *Saturday Evening Post,* the Hearst press, the "art" of Maxfield Parrish, the fiction of Robert W. Chambers (*after* his "King in Yellow" period!) & Kathleen Norris, the happy ending tacked on to the cinema version of "Winterset"[1] (to say nothing of the aimless mess of flickers which I drowsed through while waiting for "Winterset" to come on!), the heterogeneous pseudo-Colonial & pseudo-Tudor villas of our smart real-estate developments, the persistent sale of the late O. Henry's collected charlatanries, &c. &c. &c. And when bourgeois capitalism found it profitable to reach down to the still-submerged elements & cater to their crippled, repressed, & grotesquely unformed tastes with tabloid news rags, pulp "confession", "spicy", "love", "western", "horror", "scientifiction", & "G-man" magazines, & the like, the opening-up of this huge new market merely aggravated the trend away from real excellence toward showmanship & charlatanry. The suave bosses of a business "civilisation" have no wish to improve the masses— rather the reverse. Certainly, the spineless clod who sells himself into a pulp editorship under the present degenerate set-up cannot attempt to educate his circle of yokels & half-wits, or seek to cram meritorious literature down the reluctant gullets of people who simply continue buying trash from others. If he has chosen a cheap showman's job, he must stick to the pandering standards of his underworld or get out & make an honest living at some really constructive job of another sort if he can find such in a bourgeoise world. Capitalism says, 'work the poor devils as cheaply as possible (throwing 'em out to starve when they're superfluous), & cash in on their present dwarfed tastes & faculties by selling 'em all the tabloids & Macfadden rags their decreasing store of pennies can pay for.['] Thus the noble culture of well-mannered bank presidents, of Messrs. Hoover, Mellon, Mills, Al Smith,[2] &c., & of other idealistic & disinterested upholders of our Sacred Constitution of the Founding Fathers. No wonder the Marxists exaggerate a *trend or influence* into an *immutable law*, & proclaim the eternal linkage of art & economics!

Actually, the aesthetic outlook is not quite 100% hopeless. Let us grant that most profit-motivated writing & other forms of creation must be counted out. Also, that much of our sincere aesthetic or pseudo-aesthetic endeavour becomes sidetracked through the decadent & propagandist tendencies previously noted. Nay, more—that the restricted area of non-eccentric, non-propagandist material still aimed at gentlefolk (*Harpers**, *Atlantic,* Alfred Noyes, Edith Wharton, Frank Brangwyn,[3] Boston Symphony Orchestra, &c.) is increasingly lifeless, sterile, mannered, preoccupied with form, & obviously linked with obsolescent attitudes & interests & perspectives. Does this indeed mean the death of all normal & vigorous self-expression for its own sake? I hardly think so. The human instinct for creation—manifest from Cro-Magnon times onward—is too hardy & powerful to be downed by even as formidable a combination as that of all the forces here mentioned . . . . & this duly allowing for the ever-increasing diversion of human energy from imaginative synthesis to scientific analysis as brought about by new light on the universe. Counting all handicaps, I think there will always be a residue of honest & powerful aesthetic expression—some of it from unhampered & undeluded artists, & some from naturally gifted creators who cannot help evolving beauty despite various conscious fallacies & handicaps. There are great living novelists—Rolland, Mann, Dreiser, Undset, Lagerlof, &c.—& with Masefield, MacLeish, & others poetry is not dead. O'Neill & Maxwell Anderson give really substantial drama, & in painting Matisse & Zuloaga are still on deck—whatever one may think of Dali or Picasso or Diego Rivera. In architecture, despite all the "functional" horrors, Cram still holds the fort for Gothic, whilst the classic shade of Cass Gilbert may yet outlive Frank Lloyd Wright. This continuing body of soundness cannot be wholly without effect on the younger generation; & despite the lure of eccentricity, the dogmata of Marx, & the death-struggle of a blind & doomed commercialism, there will surely be a strong minority conscious of their heritage & determined to express themselves. And the more private commerce, industry, & finance become curbed & absorbed—as they must if civilisation is to survive without an explosion—the less mighty will bulk the cheap ideals of speed, quantity, ostentation, surface amusement, &c., which form one of the worst influences. Under a better controlled economic system, with Federal encouragement of mass-education (even if the first few sets of government adult-instruction commissioners lack perfect drawing-room manners), an appreciable rise in

---

*I refer only to the *fiction* in *Harpers.* In its *articles,* H's shews admirable vitality as contrasted with the well-bred vapidities of the smug & anile *Atlantic.*

public taste may well be expected. It is probably as non-profit projects of some sort—governmentally subsidised or otherwise—that really meritorious magazines in fields as narrowly specialised as the weird will exist . . . . if they ever do exist. Capitalism had no place for this kind of thing—& in pre-capitalistic ages such special products depended upon the caprice of royal or other powerful patrons. The war between honest human expression & the profit motive is eternal & truceless.

As you may see, I disagree totally & violently with your belief in making concessions in writing. One concession leads to another—& he who takes the easiest way never comes back. They all say they *mean* to come back some day—but they never do. Belknap is gone. If Sultan Malik ever pulls out of charlatanry it will be purely the individual & non-representative triumph of a singularly keen objective intellect. Abe Merritt—who could have been a Machen or Blackwood or Dunsany or de le Mare or M. R. James (*they* never gave in & truckled to the Golden Calf! . . . . why *should* one if he can get food & decent clothing & warmth & shelter in any less ignominious way?) if he had but chosen—is so badly sunk that he's lost the critical faculty to realise it. And so on—& so on. The road does *not* lie through any *magazines* . . . . that is, the road for a fantastic writer. The "slicks" are just as tawdry & insincere as the "pulps"—with merely a different kind of tawdriness & insincerity—& the reputable magazines (*Harpers, Scribners, Story* &c.) virtually never handle fantasy. The road to print for the serious fantaisiste is through *book-publication* alone—save for those *incidental* magazine placements which lie along the way. And if one can't make the book grade in the end, he is better off with his work largely unpublished—able to look himself in the face & know that he has never cringed nor truckled nor sold his intellectual & aesthetic integrity. He may go down, but he'll go down like a free & unbroken gentleman with sword untarnished & colours defiantly flying. Britons never shall be slaves! Actually, all technical training for the popular magazines is in *precisely the wrong direction* so far as aesthetic expression is concerned. The better magazine hack one is, the less chance one has of ever doing anything worth doing. Every magazine trick & mannerism must be rigidly unlearned & banished even from one's subconsciousness before one can write seriously for educated mental adults. That's why Merritt is lost—he learned the trained-dog tricks too well, & now he can't think & feel fictionally except in terms of the meaningless & artificial clichés of 2¢-a-word romance. Machen & Dunsany & James *would not learn* the tricks—& they have a record of genuine creative achievement beside which a whole library-full of cheap "Ships of Ishtar" & "Creep, Shadows" remains essentially negligible. It is much better never to have anything published than to cringe to cheap tradesmen—yet in practice the determined anti-concessionist often lands a story. True, he doesn't land as many as the truckler lands—but that was *never* his object. He wrote what he wrote because he wanted to write it—& the feat of mood-crystallisation itself was its own reward. If he had merely written what some grasping editorial clown wanted, where would his satisfaction have been? When it comes to a question of industrial production to suit a market demand, it's rather more dignified to let the commodity be something staple & useful—wheat, oranges, coal, furniture, & so on—than to let one's production-programme mock & parody the basic human impulse of aesthetic creation. However, as I have said, an enormous percentage of honestly & uncompromisingly written material can often be professionally & remuneratively placed. Many cases on actual record prove it. Klarkash-Ton's period of concessions was very brief, yet he has landed story after story—the real stuff, & no tailored-to-measure shoddy mixture. Then, too, we note with tragic wistfulness the many readily-published sincere *early* stories of writers who later sold themselves & slid down the toboggan to commercial success & rabble popularity. God! what Burks could have done if he'd stuck to the mood & manner of his early Haitian stuff & his "Bells of Oceana"! But human psychology is a complex & devious thing—& the influence of a dying but still greed-breeding capitalistic order is what it is. I'll cut my evangelical career short in its infancy, & let the dysoptic world go to hell in its own divinely-condemn'd way. But for commerce & all its ideals & conditions & ramified consequences—one lingeringly thumbed nose & one reverberant Bronx cheer!

Speaking of aesthetic expression—so many Manhattan correspondents wrote me about the recent display of fantastic & surrealistic painting at the Museum of Modern Art that I'm hoping its travelling residue will include ancient Providence on its route. The group of elder sources—pictorial fantasistes as far back as El Greco & Hell-Fire Bosch—would have especially fascinated me . . . but I fear it won't be included in the migratory aftermath. In general, though, I am not a surrealistic enthusiast, for I think the practitioners of the school give their subconscious impressions too much automatic leeway. Not that the impressions are not potentially valuable, but that they tend to become trivial & meaningless except when more or less guided by some coherent imaginative concept. A thing like Señor Dali's humorously-dubbed "Wet Watches"[4] tends to become a reductio ad absurdum of the fantastic principle, & to exemplify the aesthetic decadence discussed in the foregoing pages. However, I surely concede that this form of expression should be adequately recognised; since many of its products undoubtedly do possess a powerful imaginative reach & freshness, whilst the whole movement cannot but make important & revivifying contributions to the main stream of art. There is no drawing a line betwixt what is to be called extreme fantasy of a traditional type & what is to be called surrealism; & I have no doubt but that the nightmare landscapes of some of the surrealists correspond, as well as any actual creations could, to the iconographic horrors attributed by sundry fictioneers to mad or daemon-haunted artists. If there were a real Richard Upton Pickman or Felix Ebbonly,[5] I am sure he would have been represented in the recent exhibition by several blasphemous & abhorrent canvases! Better than the surrealists, though, is good old Nicholas Roerich—with his special museum in N.Y. at Riverside Drive & 103d St. I seldom let a Manhattan trip go by without at least one extended visit to Old Nick's place.[6] There is something in his handling of perspective & atmosphere which to me suggests other dimensions & alien orders of being—or at least, the gateways leading to such. Those fantastic carven stones in lonely upland deserts—those ominous, almost sentient, lines of jagged pinnacles—& above all, those curious cubical edifices clinging to precipitous slopes & edging upward to forbidden needle-like peaks!

Thanks immensely of the return of those pages with social & political arguments—though I don't know whether I'll ever have occasion to use them after all. Events move swiftly, & the smashing victory of last November has so routed the enemy that I do not believe the barbaric Republican point of view will ever be seriously regarded hereafter in the United States. Civilised goals will have become so thoroughly taken for granted by 1940 that the bulk of the people will never again be bamboozled into voting for injustice, famine, & misery. It is not merely that they would revolt if Hooverism were put over on them. It is that they will never more allow Hooverism to be put over on them. The only way the handful of defeated greed-worshippers could ever regain power would be through a shrewdly organised fascist movement based on primitive emotional appeals of the religio-hysteric type (waving the flag, rousing nominal Christians against "Jewish intellectualism", exciting native-Americans against "Catholic–Irish–Jewish [or whatever foreign element predominates in any particular section] democracy", exciting Catholics against "materialistic communism", exciting provincial pride against "decadent European innovations" &c. &c.), or through an armed revolt with foreign backing like that of Gen. Franco in Spain. Granting the scant probability of a Franco-like revolt of the Hoovers & Mellons & polite bankers, & conceding that—despite Coughlinism, the Black Legion, & the Silver Shirts, & the K.K.K.—the soil of America is hardly very fertile for any variant of Nazism, it seems likely that the day of free & easy plutocracy in the United States is over. It has taken the people generations to discover how they have been fooled; but once disillusioned, they are much less likely to be fooled again. Republicanism of the old type is out for good—though of course its confused & embittered remnants will long constitute a more or less harmless muttering minority like the Royalists in France & the Jacobites in 18th century England. The *real* issues of tomorrow lie betwixt the adherents of a controlled capitalism (Roosevelt; La Follette) which may or may not [it probably will, though many present liberals deny it] evolve into rational socialism, & the adherents of a sudden violent move toward some form of orthodox Marxian communism. A tremendous amount of the best thought of the younger generation is on the side of a communist move—Little Whiskerando & Kid Sterling[7] are the latest converts in the fantasy circle—since sociologists of a certain type believe that the obstructionist element of the dying order will always form a fatal barrier to permanent progress unless violently deprived of mischief-making opportunities. I, however, do not agree with this position; for I believe that a slow, peaceful revolution in thought & perspective is already under way amongst the majority, so that the obstructive reactionaries will never gain more than the horse-laugh which they gained last November. They will be a nuisance & drag, but hardly a danger—& meanwhile it is the part of wisdom to choose a peaceful & gradual evolution instead of a culturally destructive upheaval. Better let the capitalists hang on (under proper governmental control & taxation) a generation or two more than to plunge the nation into bloodshed & risk the destruction of the many sound factors in our hereditary culture. Industry should be socialised by degrees, & only as soon as the mass of the people are ready to back up the various absorptive moves. The government must dictate hours & wages, & see that employment is universally spread. If private industry can meet such rigidly enforced demands, well & good. If not—& it probably can't—absorption will be in order. And after it has been proved that nothing but absorption will perpetuate endurable conditions, the masses will so overwhelmingly endorse absorption (as they would not today) that no amount of private greed can obstruct its peaceful adoption. It will come, no doubt, in various ways. Now & then a private industry will be purchased by the government at a reasonable price—now & then a socially & legally culpable industry will be seized after a due trial now & then the government will find it advisable to enter a certain field as competitor & eliminate private industries through non-profit sales at lower prices. One at a time—& without any disruption of the normal stream of American life. No seizure of homes or any private non-industrial holdings of reasonable amount [investors in private industries can be properly compensated in government bonds when absorption occurs], no interference with free scholarship & research & intellectual & aesthetic tradition, no official inculcation of grotesque & fallacious scientific theories, no invasions of personal dignity or impositions of arbitrary punishment, no attempts to dissociate extent of recompense from extent of service, no campaign against the refinements of civilisation [instead, a dissolution of the fallacious linkage of the concepts of cultivation & economic advantage, aided by mass education of unprecedented scope, thoroughness, & discrimination], & above all, no wasteful slaughter & widespread misery of the sort lately prevailing in Russia & still prevailing in Spain. There will be plenty of corruption & routine friction—but the net result can't help being better than either the crazy orgy of moribund capitalism (where the chief corruption is actually *legalised* under the name of private profit) or the sanguinary shambles of a regulation Marxist revolution. It is toward such a goal that I prefer to work—& I believe the odds against achieving it are not insuperably great. The main fight will not be so much against the dupes of absolute capitalism as against the hotheads of extreme radical movements—& even here there is something hopeful in the willingness of some radicals to adopt compromise positions. It is the Popular Front idea which will win in the end. *All* progressives against reaction. Rather than see Hoover fascism gain, we conservatives would yield a point or two to the communists, whilst they would yield a point or two to us. Anything except allowing plutocracy to regain its loathsome hold. That once disposed of—as it ought to be soon—the main struggle will be regarding the rate & extent of social change . . . . & here I am on the side of the moderates.

The attitude which you outline—of a blind clinging to whatever immediate conditions give one the most luxuries & the most congenial social contacts in business hours, irrespective of the consequences to the bulk of the population—is indeed a very typical one, but I don't think it is of much ultimate significance because the immediate needs of *most people* (not merely most *nice* people or most *smart* people) are *not on the side of reaction, but are on the side of rational change.* For every well-fed Caspar Milquetoast whose personal advantage is served by the prosperity of the utility company which gives him a fat salary, there are a thousand or two John Smiths whose personal advantage (indeed, whose endurable existence) depends on the governmental regulation of that company's hours & wages & rates . . . & perhaps on the government's absorption & non-profit operation of that company. Now that the John Smiths are beginning to know where their advantage lies, they will act just as Caspar does—blindly upholding what will personally serve them best—& when the millions of votes are counted against those of the Caspars, the result is not hard to predict. The trend is further promoted by the fact that not *all* fat-salaried beneficiaries of capitalism *are* Caspars. A few can reason, & can see that capitalism is *automatically* doomed by the natural course of economics unless upheld by fascist bayonets (although of course some of these reasoners merely shrug their shoulders & cry *apres nous, le deluge*); a few realise that their expert services will be just as well recompensed under government operation (even if the officials wear jarring neckties & have uncultivated accents) as under private profit-grabbing operation; whilst a few possess real social vision & share the disgust of the scholar & aesthete & gentleman at a tottering, unstable equilibrium founded on lies & delusions & hypocrisy & involving the equal negation of common human decency & long-range common sense. The number of these last is not to be sneezed at—for despite the complacent position of the typical bourgeois the ranks of social thinkers are constantly recruited from all the comfortably-situated classes . . . . gentry, plutocracy, professional, salaried commercial, official, & so on. The whole policy of *Harpers*—a magazine of frankly aristocratic appeal—is slanted at an intellectual type of about the New-Deal degree of political leftness, whilst the real thinkers of all collegiate classes since 1930 are overwhelmingly liberal. Virtually *all* the reputable authors & critics in the United States are political radicals  Dreiser, Sherwood Anderson, Hemingway, Dos Passos, Eastman, O'Neill, Lewis, Maxwell Anderson, MacLeish, Edmond Wilson, Fadiman—

but the list is endless. It would be shorter & easier to compile a list of first-rate writers who are *not* leftists! In the ranks of gentry & plutocracy & officialdom one young thinker after another comes out for social change great or moderate—Corliss Lamont, Oliver Baldwin, the son of Pres. Justo of Argentina,[8] &c. &c. &c.—here again one has only to pause for recollection in order to fill a page with illustrious surnames. The cream of human brains—the sort of brains not wrapped up in personal luxury & immediate advantage—is slowly drifting away from blind class-loyalty toward a better-balanced position in which the symmetrical structure & permanent stability of the whole social organism is a paramount consideration. What happened just before the French & Russian revolutions is happening now—the thinkers & artists & scholars are changing sides, abandoning their support of a dead order, & preparing to be the leaders & guides & administrators of the people in a general struggle for desperately-needed readjustment. When the plutocrats make their last stand—assuming that they have enough vitality remaining to make a last stand—they will find that their old-time advantage is gone. No more will a horde of helpless, uneducated, disorganised mental children be at their mercy. Instead, they will be faced by an increasingly awakened army of determined citizens, encouraged, supported, & officered by the best brains & executive ability of the nation—by a staff of socially-conscious leaders sprung from & trained amidst the governing gentry & plutocracy & professionaldom.

I cannot accept your point about a natural reluctance "to destroy the system which sustains us", because no rational reformer *wants* to destroy any system which sustains any honest worker. As I see it, your mistake lies in assuming that it *is* the dying plutocratic set-up which sustains you—a very basic & crucial mistake, when one comes to think of it. Actually, nothing could be further from the truth. So far as your own individual case is concerned—if I judge correctly, you are an expert in certain forms of finance & accountancy & administration, whereby your services are important in any enterprise involving the receipt, disbursement, exchange, or comparison of commodities, or the maintenance of complex industrial or administrative operations. Now do you suppose that such services are any the less necessary, or that they would be less reasonably rewarded, in a government-controlled or government-owned enterprise than in a private profit-grabbing scheme? What difference would it make to you whether your just return for high-grade mental work comes from the American government or from a courteous private financier? The only losers in a move toward rationalisation would be the dividend-drawers who now get something for nothing, & the few top executives whose present salaries are disproportionately padded beyond all relationship to the extent of their actual services. Would such a rationalisation form an "overthrowing of the system which provides your livelihood"? I can't see that it would. I can't see that socialism would hurt anybody who is willing to work & who expects a just return for the work he performs—

including guarantees of proper security in old age & in times of necessary unemployment or disability. Then, of course, it must be remembered that the moderate road avoids even the principal minor ills of readjustment. The communism of Sonny Belknap & Little Bobby & Little Mr. Sterling means some rather disconcerting bumps—but there is nothing of destruction or violent dislocation in the orderly progressivism whose various stages are represented by the New Deal, the La Follettes, & Norman Thomas.

But the real joke of course is, that all this isn't a matter of choice anyhow! Capitalism is dying from internal as well as external causes, & its own leaders & beneficiaries are less & less able to kid themselves. I'm no economist, but from recent reading I've been able to form a rough picture of the dilemma—the need to restrict consumers' goods & to pile up a needless plethora of producing equipment in order to maintain the irrational surplus called profit—which has caused orthodox economists like Hayek & Robbins[9] to admit that only starvation wages & artificial scarcity could stabilise the profit system in future & avert increasing cyclical depressions of utterly destructive scope. Laissez-faire capitalism is *dead*—make no mistake about that. The only avenue of survival for plutocracy is a military & emotional fascism whereby millions of persons will be withdrawn from the industrial arena & placed on a dole or in concentration-camps with high-sounding patriotic names. That or socialism—take your choice. In the long run it won't be the New Deal but the mere facts of existence which will be recognised as the real & inevitable slayer of Hooverism. Nobody is going to 'destroy the system'—for it has been destroying itself ever since it evolved out of the old agrarian-handicraft economy a century & a half ago.

All this from an antiquated mummy who was on the other side until 1931! Well—I can the better understand the inert blindness & defiant ignorance of the reactionaries from having been one of them. I know how smugly ignorant *I* was—wrapped up in the arts, the natural (not social) sciences, the *externals* of history & antiquarianism, the *abstract* academic phases of philosophy, & so on—all the one-sided standard lore to which, according to the traditions of the dying order, a liberal education was limited. God! the things that were *left out*—the inside facts of history, the rational interpretation of periodic social crises, the foundations of economics & sociology, the actual state of the world today . . . & above all, the *habit* of applying disinterested reason to problems hitherto approached only with traditional genuflections, flag-waving, & callous shoulder-shrugs! All this comes up with humiliating force through an incident of a few days ago—when young Conover, having established contact with Henneberger, the ex-owner of W T, obtained from the latter a long epistle which I wrote Edwin Baird on Feby. 3, 1924, in response to a request for biographical & personal data.[10] Little Willis asked permission to publish the text in his combined *SFC–Fantasy*, & I began looking the thing over to see what it was like—for I had not the least recollection of ever having penned it. Well . . . . I managed to get through, after about 10 closely typed pages of egotistical reminiscences & showings-off & expressions of opinion about mankind & the universe. I did not faint—but I looked around for a 1924 photograph of myself to burn, spit on, or stick pins in! Holy Hades—was *I* that much of a dub at 33 . . . only 13 years ago? There was no getting out of it—I really *had* thrown all that haughty, complacent, snobbish, self-centred, intolerant bull, & at a mature age when anybody but a perfect damned fool would have known better! That earlier illness had kept me in seclusion, limited my knowledge of the world, & given me something of the fatuous effusiveness of a belated adolescent when I finally *was* able to get about more around 1920, is hardly much of an excuse. Well—there was nothing to be done . . . . . except to rush a note back to Conover & tell him I'd dismember him & run the fragments through a sausage-grinder if he ever thought of printing such a thing! The only consolation lay in the reflection that I *had* matured a bit since '24. It's hard to have done all one's growing up since 33—but that's a damn sight better than not growing up at all. Here's hoping that Henneberger (quite a get-rich-quick Wallingford[11] in his way) won't try to blackmail me with the letter!

As for the November victory—I expected good results, though the *extent* of the landslide surprised & delighted me. Late in October I attended a highly interesting New Deal rally, with the eminent Rabbi Wise of New York as principal speaker.[12] He sized up the changes in the national mind with phenomenal penetration & wit—so that I can well imagine the polite Nazis of Wall St. cursing him as a blasphemous non-Aryan intellectual! I guess I mentioned seeing F D R himself on Oct. 20. On the eve of the election I did—for the second time in a long life—what I did on the night of Nov. 7–8, 1916, when the fortunes of Hughes & Wilson hung in the balance ["he kep' us outa war"][13] . . . . went to a late cinema show where election returns were announced. The national results were early manifest, but the state & city figures (a clean Democratic sweep) took longer to settle. By the time the performance closed—2:45 a.m.—there was no danger of any contrary report next day as there was 20 years ago. On that occasion, as you may have read, the nation retired believing Hughes elected, but had that belief shattered the next day. All in all, the recent triumph is pretty significant in what it implies. The feeble arguments, obvious hokum, absurd accusations, & occasional underhanded tactics of the enemy reacted against them, while some obscure instinct of common sense seemed to hold the extreme radicals to the Popular Front & keep them from wasting their votes on obviously hopeless tickets. It amuses me to see the woebegone state of the staid reactionary reliques with whom I am surrounded—the Providence old-family clique away from whose past-drugged ideology it is impossible to pull my aunt. Around election time I came darned near having a family feud on my hands! Poor old ostriches! Trembling for the republic's safety, they actually thought their beloved Langston or Langhorne or

Lemke (or whatever his name was) had a chance![14] However, the intelligent university element was not so blind. Indeed, one of the professors said just before the election that his idea of a bum sport was a man who would actually *take* one of the pro-Lansdowne (or whatever his name was) bets offered by the white-moustached constitution-savers of the Hope Club easy-chairs. Well—even the most stubborn must some day learn that the tide of social evolution can't be checked for ever. The shade of old King Canute will again speak his famed command to the waves, & teach the economic royalists of this age the lesson which he taught the courtiers of his own.

Regarding the recent royal upheaval—one may only feel sad from many angles. Not that the identity of the sovereign is in this age ever likely to have far-reaching consequences, but that so much tension & hypocrisy & disappointment exist all around. On the one hand one is sorry that Edward had to have such cheap tastes in entertainment & companionship all through his youth—but on the other hand one is even more furious at the sorry hypocrisy of those who came forth with sanctimonious cant the moment the poor chap *did* want to settle down in a sedate, middle-aged way. For those canting hypocrites were in some cases the very same individuals who blandly condoned the under-cover antics of Edward VII, & in all cases the spiritual descendants of those who stood for Henry VIII, Charles II, Georges I, II, & IV, & William IV. Apparently, with these stuffed shirts, anything goes until it is brought into the light. Charles II's lady friends were all right . . . . but when a more honest monarch proposes to make a relatively respectable gentlewoman the Queen—or even a morganatic legal consort—there's hell to pay. Doddering old bishops whine about the theological implications of a divorced status, & double-chinned dowagers wonder how they could stand the sight of an *unsuitable person* at a royal reception! Horse feathers! And for this they have forced from his birthright a man who, despite all defects, had more genuine social vision & orientation to this age than any other occupant of a European throne; a man who, though limited in technical power, could have been an inestimably valuable influence in guiding the Empire through the coming evolution toward a rational economic & political condition. Probably a fear of Edward's enlightened social outlook added zeal to the moral fervour of his opponents. Edward's own attitude is hard to fathom, & the future will put various interpretations on his course. That, at his age, any vast romantic devotion to an equally middle-aged & not-especially ornamental lady was the determinant factor, one might at first doubt—but after all, psychology has its curious twists. More plausible is the idea that the Simpson incident was merely a starting-point—& that the real issue was whether a monarch must take dictation from Parliament over any matter not involving state policy. However, both of these aspects may have seemed fused together in Edward's mind—& the more the opposition, the more his determination. Probably Mrs. Simpson does happen to be very congenial to the one-time playboy; understanding his tastes & providing a sort of homelike, restful environment for one rather fed up on youth & beauty & ready for the slippers & easy-chair of the middle years. His wireless farewell address—which I heard in full—was certainly one of the most poignant oral documents in modern history . . . . & an utterly incredible thing as judged by the standards of the past. Fancy, in any other age, the spectacle of a worldwide throng listening to the most intimate personal sentiments of the planet's mightiest monarch, in his own voice & speaking directly for their benefit! A stronger character like Henry VIII might have held out & told parliament to go to the devil. A weaker character might have given in & taken orders from parliament. Being what he is, I fancy Edward did the wisest thing possible—leaving the throne with dignity & preserving the right to shape his own career. I hope he won't regret his course—indeed, the red tape of kingship never seemed to please him very well. Whether his autumnal romance will become literary material in the Lancelot–Guenivere & Romeo–Juliet tradition, remains to be seen. The present milieu is perhaps less favourable to the weaving of such legends than was that of the Middle Ages & Renaissance. But in any case I hope he'll derive some happiness from his coming marriage, & that the latter may prove above the average in permanence. Meanwhile the most loyal & friendly sentiments should go forth to the new Monarch, a person of undoubted conscientiousness & high character whose fortunate social & domestic tastes fit him eminently for his office. His lack of a brilliant personality & acquiescence in outworn customs may well be pardoned—& if he fails to be the sociological leader which Edward might have been, others from the people's ranks will see that such a function is not left undischarged. As a focus of sentiment, & embodiment of the virtue & integrity of our race, we may ask no better figure than he who has chosen to bear the name of GEORGE THE SIXTH. God Save the King! Incidentally, though, I perceive that there are still a few who would tend to ask, *which* King, & to repeat the famous lines of John Byrom:

> "God blefs the KING, I mean the Faith's Defender;
> God blefs—no Harm in bleffing—the Pretender:
> But who Pretender is, or who is King—
> God Blefs us all—that's quite another Thing!"[15]

You will find the enclos'd cutting of much interest—if indeed you have not previously met with the item in other papers. Just as there are still some Republicans in America, so are there still some Jacobites at home—& like the Republicans they exalt that which is an enemy of their nation . . . for the present "King over the Water"—Rupert the First, by the Grace of God King of England, Ireland, & Scotland, Defender of the Faith—is none other than that doughty old standby of the Kaiser, Kronprinz Rupprecht von Bayern, whose leadership of a German army on the Western Front made him a field-marshal in 1917. Hoch der König! The theoretical pretendership of Rupprecht well illustrates how far afield the Stuart succession has gone since the death of Cardinal York ("Henry IX") in 1807. Indeed, owing to some shadowy dual interpretation of the succession, Kronprinz Rupprecht (whose claim rests on his descent from Elizabeth, daughter of James I & mother of that older Prince Rupert who came to England, fought for the Cavaliers at Edgehill & Marston, & was first Governor of the Hudson's Bay Co.) is not the only Jacobite pretender today; his rival being Princess Maria Theresa of Modena ("Queen Mary III"), a descendant of Charles I.

Regarding the phenomenon of national renaissance—morale rebuilt through the exaltation of a racial goal in which the people *really* believe—you are, I think, correct in tracing the present movement from Russia through Turkey to Italy and finally Germany. Japan is a little out of the stream—because its national unity & purpose are of older growth. Indeed, it is not a renaissance but the original article, since Japan has never been really decadent as yet. Whether Spain will be the next re-born nation depends on whether the liberal government can triumph over Franco's Germano-Italian-backed Hooverites. It is making a magnificent stand, but the determined backing of the fascist nations may precipitate a rebel sweep & complete relapse to barbaric reaction & continued unrest—if indeed it doesn't start a whole world war! If Germany & Italy decide that the struggle to prop up Franco isn't worth the trouble & prestige, we shall see first [. . .]

[. . .] every-day life—could really brood seriously over what the Christians called "consciousness of sin" or "need of personal salvation"—seems almost incredible today; & yet there is evidence that such a condition existed even among the educated in Western civilisation until a generation or two ago, & that it survives even now among the ignorant on the one hand and the cultivated hysteric-neurotic type (Buchmanites,[16] Popish converts, pious old ladies, perverted over-emotional subjects, &c.) on the other hand. Thus orgiastic self-torture has always possessed an overwhelmingly powerful backing. Truly, as Lenin said in connexion with a totally different aspect of it, "religion is the opium of the people."[17] H. G. Wells points out the profound nature of this self-mutilating fixation after thousands of years of its inculcation in the young—shewing that at a certain age small children have a distinct & sometimes powerful tendency to torture & mutilate themselves, so that it is unsafe to leave them in a room with fire, scissors, jack-knives, &c. Dr. Carrel is rather a dupe of primitive concepts—laying aside his ordinarily acute reasoning powers when he approaches the domain of hereditary superstition—but he is right in assuming that religious orgiasticism is on the wane. The rabble are less repressed as to the conscious expression of instinct & emotion, hence this poisonous perversion is less necessary or inevitable as an outlet. The old hysteria is now more healthily expressed in "hot jazz" among those who need such expression, whilst more & more persons are being raised by rational education to a plane somewhat above the primitively emotional, so that they no longer have so many seething & turbulent emotions to express. And of course the *ethical* emotions have virtually shaken themselves free of religion's putrescent carcass. Nowadays we know that "sin" does not exist, & that we have no need of "personal salvation"—(but we also know that if we want to develop our highest faculties to the full, & to live in the way most harmoniously gratifying to our aesthetic senses, we must coöperate diligently in the moulding & maintenance of a social order favourable to collective growth & involving a minimum of subsistence-struggle & mutual encroach-ment among individuals. In other words, we have exchanged the fake called "personal holiness" for the tangible & practical reality of sound, materialistic *social morality*. Whatever natural ethical enthusiasms & indignations we may have, have ceased to be wasted in sterile & frivolous self-titillations & have gone into the great group-struggle for better social conditions. Hence the vio-lent rebirths in Russia, Turkey, Italy, Germany, & Spain, & the less explosive but equally determined drives for real, collective progress in New Deal Amer-ica & elsewhere. I can't say that I share your fondness for religious ritual— Popish, Mahometan, Anglican, Buddhistic, or any other sort. To me there is something profoundly *disgusting & malodorous* in the notion of grown & poten-tially rational beings whining & grovelling like savages around the symbols of *things which are not so & never were so.* The Jesus-myth always left me cold, & even my worship of beauty & mystery in the form of Apollo, Pan, Artemis, Athena, & the fauns & dryads ended when I was 8. The only things I deem worth the worship of free, rational, & enlightened men are *truth* (the gratifica-tion of the species' most complex & evolved instinct) & *beauty* (the gratifica-tion of a second instinct scarcely less complex & evolved)—the latter of course embracing that form of harmony known as *ethics,* whereby we learn the art of adjusting ourselves to one another in such a manner as to ensure maximum evolution-possibilities for each. The scraps of gross superstition handed down from ages of primitive ignorance, & inculcated in each new generation through a disgusting & dishonest process of mental & emotional crippling in helpless early childhood, have nothing to offer us as a whole in our quest for these twin realities. All are founded on assumptions so basically absurd, & are entwined with such infantile fallacies regarding the nature of man, the identity of human values & motives, & the nature & governance of the cosmos, that they have nothing but confusion & obstruction to offer in a world of clear-cut needs & problems demanding reason & reason alone. One is just about the same as the other—Islam, Buddhism, Popery, Judaism, Prot-estantism, Shintoism, Brahmanism, & so on. If in any there exist useful ethi-cal precepts, we shall find all those precepts duplicated in a clearer & more effective way amidst the sound scientific fabric of sociology & social ethics. It is time for the hysterics & perverts & mystics to put away their tops & marbles & either go home or go to the asylum. But of course I'm no advocate of violence. Let religion die a natural death. I approve of the suppression of active religious arrogance, such as that of popery in Spain & Spanish-America, & of the Greek Church in Czarist Russia, but I would not close the churches as long as there are old fools enough to attend them. Merely root religion out of government, & out of such education as the state can control without imposition of a Nazi-like or Catholic-like tyranny, & let nature take its course.)

Well—now for that aforementioned *second* element in the general phenomenon of sacrificial self-injury or self-denial. Here we have something vastly less primitive than propitiatory or expiatory sacrifice—something less connected with abnormality & orgiasticism, & indeed not without a shadowy counterpart in rational social discipline. I refer, needless to say, to the *ascetic principle* in its purest sense—the ideal of a regimen *whose object is not pain-infliction or deprivation for its own sake*, but merely *the minimisation of such physical sensations & goals as interfere with the operation of the more complex & delicate parts of the human personality*. In practice, of course, the traditional religious superstitions mix this principle up inextricably with the grosser & older one of orgiastic sacrifice; yet its actual separateness & infinitely higher level are obvious. It undoubtedly appeared in human folkways tens of thousands of years later than its primitive analogue—indeed, it could not have appeared until after the development of religions involving very ethereal imaginative concepts & very profound & subtle intellectual speculations. It appears to be distinctly Oriental at the start, & may have had its origin in India alone—although it involves psychological laws so basic & universal that its simultaneous appearance in dissociated groups at the same cultural stage is not inconceivable. [. . .]

## Notes

1. *Winterset* (RKO, 1936), directed by Alfred Santell; starring Burgess Meredith, Margo Ciannelli, and Eduardo Ciannelli. Based on the play by Maxwell Anderson.

2. Although Alfred E. Smith (1873–1944) was the Democratic candidate for president in 1928, he became hostile to FDR and joined the American Liberty League, which opposed many New Deal programs.

3. Sir Frank William Brangwyn (1867–1956), Anglo-Welsh artist, painter, water colourist, engraver, and illustrator.

4. *The Persistence of Memory* (*La persistencia de la memoria*, 1931), known by some as "Melting Clocks" or "Wet Watches," is the most famous painting by Salvador Dalí (1904–1989).

5. Characters (artists), respectively, in HPL's "Pickman's Model" and Clark Ashton Smith's "The City of the Singing Flame."

6. HPL frequently visited the Nicholas Roerich Museum (now at 319 West 107th Street), devoted to Roerich (1874–1947), the Russian painter, writer, archaeologist, and theosophist. Roerich is mentioned six times in *At the Mountains of Madness*, as HPL suggests that the city of the Old Ones is reminiscent of Roerich's paintings of Himalayan monasteries.

7. I.e., R. H. Barlow (who was now sporting a mustache) and Kenneth Sterling.

8. Corliss Lamont (1902–1995), American socialist philosopher and director of the ACLU (1932–54); Oliver Baldwin (1899–1958), British socialist and son of prime minister Stanley Baldwin; Agustín Pedro Justo (1876–1943), president of Argentina (1932–38), who instituted numerous economic measures to counter the effects of the Great Depression.

9. Friedrich Hayek (1899–1992), Austro-Hungarian social philosopher; Lionel Robbins (1898–1984), British economist at the London School of Economics.

10. Published in part in *SL* 1.294–304 and complete in HPL and Willis Conover, *Lovecraft at Last* 200–211. HPL incorporated portions of the essay "A Confession of Unfaith" (1922) into the letter (see *CE* 5.145–48).

11. HPL refers to George Randolph Chester (1869–1924), *Get-Rich-Quick Wallingford* (1907), a novel about a con artist that was later adapted as a play (1910) and as two silent films (1916, 1921).

12. Rabbi Stephen Wise (1874–1949), a leading figure in more than a dozen Jewish organizations, and probably the most influential and well-respected American Jew of his generation.

13. In the presidential election of 1916, many parts of the country believed that the Republican Charles Evans Hughes had been elected, but results from the West Coast, available only the next day, confirmed that Woodrow Wilson had been re-elected. Wilson's campaign slogan was "He kept us out of war," referring to the United States' nominal neutrality in the early years of World War I. In April 1917 the US entered the war on the side of the Allies.

14. HPL makes fun of the Republican challenger Alf Landon (letter 34n2) and the third-party candidate William Lemke (letter 34n1).

15. John Byrom (1692–1763), "An Epigram."

16. HPL refers to Frank Buchman (1878–1961), an American Protestant evangelist who went to England and formed the Oxford Group, whose members were devoted to the public confession of sins.

17. The statement is actually by Karl Marx.

*Robert Bloch in his father's wheelchair, pushed by Henry Kuttner during a visit from Los Angeles.*

# Letters to Henry Kuttner

[1]    [Trans., WHS]

66 College Street
Providence, R.I.
Feby. 16, 1936

Dear Mr. Kuttner:—

I was very glad indeed to receive yours of the 10th—& feel extremely flattered by what you say of my fiction attempts, & of their effect on your own productions in the same line. Bloch mentioned you not long ago, & I read your "Ballad of the Gods" in the recent W T with genuine pleasure. These verses may indeed be hasty & casual—but they certainly have the right kind of swing, atmosphere, & punch. I hope to see some of your more serious efforts some time . . . . if they're much better than this, they must be fine indeed.

Congratulations on the story acceptances! The younger generation surely is coming into its own, with Bloch already a W T fixture, you following fast, & young Rimel (whom you may know through the "fan" magazines) placing his first story last month.[1] I shall await "The Secret of Kralitz", "The Grave-yard Rats", & "It Walks by Night" with keen interest, & hope also to see the rejected items some time. By the way—speaking of the latter (or such of them as you don't intend to re-work for Wright)—why don't you try them on the "fan" magazines? No pay, of course, but you can thereby get your work before a sympathetic audience of reasonable size, & secure many criticisms & suggestions otherwise unobtainable. Most seem to find these humble & struggling sheets quite an encouraging influence. In case you don't know all of them I'll list those which I recall—

*Marvel Tales,* William Crawford, 122 Water St., Everett, Pa.
*Fantasy Magazine,* Julius Schwartz, 255 E. 188th St., N.Y. City
*The Phantagraph,* Donald A. Wollheim, 801 West End Ave., N.Y. City
?*Nuggets,* B. C. Black, Box 53, Upland, Indiana.

I prefix a question-mark to this last because I'm not sure whether it is a regular fan magazine. All I know about it is that its editor has just asked me for an article on horror fiction.

From the hints you give anent your various tales, I am inclined to think they must be very powerful & absorbing. I surely am curious to see some of them! I appreciate the compliment implied in the use of some of my settings & dramatic entities. Clark Ashton Smith & I frequently use each other's hell-ish books & devil-gods—giving Tsathoggua & Yog-Sothoth a change of environment, as it were! Some time I'll quote darkly from your "Book of Iod"—

which I presume either antedates the human race like the Eltdown Shards and the Pnakotic Manuscripts, or repeats the most hellish secrets learnt by early man in the fashion of the Book of Eibon, *De Vermis Mysteriis,* the Comte d'Erlette's *Cultes des Goules,* von Junzt's *Unaussprechlichen Kulten,* or the dreaded & abhorred *Al Azif* or *Necronomicon* of the mad Arab Abdul Alhazred.[2] "The Salem Horror"[3] sounds very alluring. I know old Salem quite minutely—quite a number of houses of the 1692 witchcraft period are still standing in good condition. Salem is, very roughly (though it has no college) the prototype of my imaginary "Arkham"—just as Marblehead is of "Kingsport" & Newburyport of "Innsmouth". You probably recall these names from sundry yarns of mine. Sorry Wright didn't take the "Horror", but don't let his rejections discourage you. He is very capricious, & has rejected my best tales—sometimes asking for them again, sometimes not. He seems to have a prejudice against my kind of work—for he will never take a *long* story from me, although he uses endless serials by others. He rejected the "Mts. of Madness", now appearing in *Astounding.* Glad you can grind out salable commercial stuff (I can't), & hope it won't hurt your serious fictional style. Congratulations on the "Bamboo Death" sale.

Your references to my attempts are very gratifying to the ego. I like "The Colour out of Space" best of all my stuff, & "The Music of Erich Zann" second. I haven't much use, though, for "The Horror at Red Hook"—which gets cheap & melodramatic in spots. Yes—I've written a reply to Bloch's "Shambler" called "The Haunter of the Dark".[4] Bloch leaves me as a mangled mass of organic tatters—& I leave him a rigid corpse staring out a west window with an expression of cosmic, soul-shattering fear on its decomposing face. Amenities of authorship!

The last two W T issues are nothing remarkable—a Moore story being in each case the chief redeeming feature.[5] However—"Norn",[6] in this current number, is rather remarkable in its way. I have an idea that the tale is by the old standby Everil Worrell—did you notice that LIREVE is Everil spelled backward? Why the pseudonymity, I'm sure I don't know. I wish someone would found a *really good* weird magazine—handling standard work of the calibre of Machen, Blackwood, Dunsany, M. R. James, de la Mare, Wakefield, &c. &c. I don't believe there'd be any trouble in getting material—for all the masters just listed are still alive. The trouble, I suppose, would be getting readers enough—since unfortunately the number of civilised persons craving a weird magazine is lamentably small. Hence Wright's energetic efforts to cater to the uncivilised.

William Crawford of Everett, Pa., is planning to publish my "Shadow over Innsmouth" as a booklet very soon. This is one of the things Wright rejected. Another rejected item—"The Shunned House"—will be issued by R. H. Barlow, Box 88, De Land, Florida.[7] Speaking of swell books—here's a circular mentioning something by a friend of mine—Samuel Loveman—which may interest you as a poet.[8] These verses aren't overtly weird, but they have wistful overtones of wonder in them. You ought to have a verse collection published some time.

Well—I'm very glad to have heard from you, & hope to see specimens of your fiction soon. Your correspondent Bloch is a tremendously bright youth, & has progressed strikingly in the last couple of years. Apparently you are following the same route. Had you been writing long when Brother Farnsworth let down the bars for the first time?

With every good wish, & again expressing my appreciation of your references to my efforts, I am

Yours most cordially & sincerely,
H. P. Lovecraft

*Notes*

1. Duane W. Rimel, "The Disinterment" (*WT,* January 1937), revised slightly by HPL.

2. HPL wrote no more fiction and so never referred to the *Book of Iod.* The other titles are fictitious: Eltdown Shards (Richard F. Searight), Pnakotic Manuscripts and *Necronomicon* (HPL), Book of Eibon (Clark Ashton Smith), *De Vermis Mysteriis* and *Cultes des Goules* (Robert Bloch), and *Unaussprechlichen Kulten* (Robert E. Howard).

3. See also HK 2.

4. "The Shambler from the Stars" (*WT,* September 1935) features a character based on HPL. In "The Haunter of the Dark" (*WT,* December 1936), the main character Robert Blake (= Robert Bloch) dies under mysterious circumstances. Much later, Bloch wrote yet another sequel, "The Shadow from the Steeple" (*WT,* September 1950).

5. C. L. Moore, "The Dark Land" (January 1936) and "Yvala" (February 1936).

6. Everil Worrell [as "Lireve Monet"], "Norn" (*WT,* February 1936).

7. Wright rejected "The Shadow over Innsmouth" upon its surreptitious submittal by August Derleth in 1933. He rejected "The Shunned House" twice, but published the story in October 1937 following HPL's death. Crawford published *The Shadow over Innsmouth* near the end of HPL's life. Barlow planned to issue *The Shunned House* (sheets of which had been printed by W. Paul Cook but not bound or distributed), but only distributed about 8 copies. The rest were distributed in 1959–61 by Arkham House.

8. *The Hermaphrodite and Other Poems.*

[2]    [ALS, WHS]

66 College Street
Providence, R.I.
March 12, 1936

Dear Mr. Kuttner:—

This will be a very inadequate reply to yours of the 26th, since I am writing under a rather bad handicap. Not only is my own programme crowded beyond endurance, but at present my aunt[1]—who presides over this household—is down with an illness of undetermined duration, so that I am bound to service for a long period as a sort of combined nurse, secretary, butler, & errand-boy. However, I must acknowledge your material with gratitude & appreciation, & make at least a few comments.

"The Salem Horror" gave me much pleasure, & I certainly think it is a great deal better than much of the stuff which Wright continually prints. My own criticism would be that the tale is a little *vaguely motivated*. Just *what* started the major phenomena at the particular time they did start? Surely Carson was not the first to occupy the old witch's room—& yet one can hardly imagine a repetition of this sort of phenomena [*sic*] every time someone lights a fire in the fireplace. In stories where nameless entities are evoked from the abyss it is always well to attribute their summoning to some *specific* act or circumstance which has never occurred before (or has never occurred without a similar result), yet whose occurrence seems to come naturally & inevitably as a result of preceding events. I've largely forgotten my own "Witch House", but I think I had my student-victim dabbling in mathematico-magical formulae of a rare kind, which eventually reached a dangerous parallelism with those of the bygone witch—hence placed the two in rapport. Or have I got this mixed with some other yarn of mine? Another criticism I'd make is that the colour is laid on too thickly—strange things come too rapidly in succession, & with too great abruptness. In some cases there is not enough gradualness & emotional preparation. The best & most potent horror is the *subtlest*—what is *vaguely hinted* but never told. A certain kind of *sensation of disquiet* is usually more effective than a scaly, tentacled monster—& in the greatest weird story ever written—Algernon Blackwood's "The Willows"—*virtually nothing visibly & openly happens*. **Atmosphere** is the one supreme desideratum of the weird tale. Another point—you need to give *Salem* a little more research in order to make the setting ring true. Modern Salem is a city of 43,000, & despite the large percentage of ancient houses still standing, there is very little hushed whispering about witches today. Gabled houses of the witchcraft period are very rare—not more than a half-dozen surviving in recognisable shape. Some have been altered to later types—especially during the 2nd quarter of the 18th century, when peaked roofs were changed to the gambrel type all over New England. There may be, in all, some 20 or 25 houses in Salem which were standing in witchcraft times (1692). Incidentally, there was never any witchcraft reported in Salem after 1692. The most famous old houses of Salem are of the 18th & early 19th century—the age of maritime greatness, when witchcraft was largely forgotten. There are no white-washed chimneys. Regarding burying-grounds—the really ancient cemeteries, where the witchcraft-period burials occurred—have no caretakers, & have not been used for new burials for fully a century. They are the Charter St. Burying Ground—on a bluff which once overlooked the harbour (this part now filled in) & which was once called "Burying Point", & the Broad St. Burying Ground. Hawthorne's fiancé [*sic*] lived in a house whose rear abutted on the Charter St. Burying Ground, & it is this building which he describes in "Dr. Grimshawe's

Secret". Of newer cemeteries, the Howard St. Burying Ground was established in 1801, & the Greenlawn Cemetery in 1807. This is still used, & can be described as having a caretaker. It is somewhat out of the centre of the city. Harmony Grove Cemetery, a suburban area established in 1840, is the principal modern burying ground. More—the Salem waterfront is no longer used for shipping. Nothing but an occasional coal barge ever lands. The greatest of the wharves of maritime days was Derby Wharf at the foot of a short street near the old Custon House. The Essex Institute (a great antiquarian society with two large museums on opposite sides of Essex St. (the main business street)[)], may soon restore this abandoned wharf to its colonial appearance.

1. House of the Seven Gables—1669
2. Custom House—1816
3. Hawthorne's Birthplace
4. "Grimshawe" House & Charter St. Burying Ground
5. Site of Old Witchcraft Gaol
6. So-called "Old Witch House", where the magistrate Jonathan Corwin, who lived there, questioned suspected witches.

Salem streets aren't narrow, & you won't find any tall houses leaning over them. The neighbouring town of *Marblehead* is really much more spectral-looking.

Essex Street is the main business street. Its intersection with Washington above the railway station is the centre of the town—Town House Sq. Derby St. is a slum inhabited by Polish immigrants—mill workers. On the westward side of Salem Common some of the finest houses of the 1800 period are seen. Chestnut St. is lined on both sides with such houses. Federal St. has picturesque houses of the 18th century. The place where the 19 convicted witches were hanged—Gallows Hill, a rocky eminence—is about a mile west of the central district—still largely rural. The greatest number of very old houses can be found around Essex & Derby Sts. east of Derby Wharf. There aren't as many "quaint cobbled alleys" as one might wish, & very few houses are tall. The different general types of houses are something like this: Those built before 1700 generally have an overhanging second story & diamond-paned casement windows—or *did* originally.

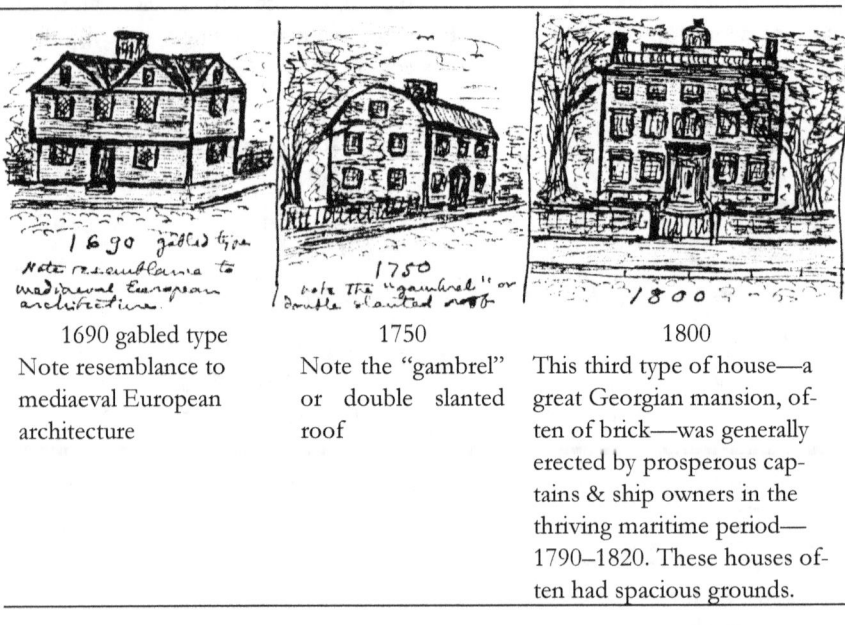

1690 gabled type
Note resemblance to mediaeval European architecture

1750
Note the "gambrel" or double slanted roof

1800
This third type of house—a great Georgian mansion, often of brick—was generally erected by prosperous captains & ship owners in the thriving maritime period— 1790–1820. These houses often had spacious grounds.

By sending 35¢ to *The Essex Institute, Salem, Mass.,* you can get an excellent guide book[2] full of pertinent information. If you are really interested in mastering Salem atmosphere, architecture, topography, &c., I'll be glad to lend you postcard views from my collection. The 1760–1820 mansions of Salem are noted for their classic colonial doorways—with pillars & pediments. The net impression which Salem gives is really not as sinister & ancient as that which the imaginative history student hopes for. The best old streets really reflect the classic & beautiful 18th century rather than the spectral 17th. But the ancient burying grounds really are a bit spectral—with their old slate slabs. Slabs from 1660 to around 1750 generally have a winged skull as a device. From 1750 to 1780 a fat-cheeked winged cherub-face predominates. After that the urn & weeping willow form the most popular carvings.

Various types of old Salem tomb & monument. *Crosses* are never found in old New England burying grounds, because of the intense Protestantism of the colonists.

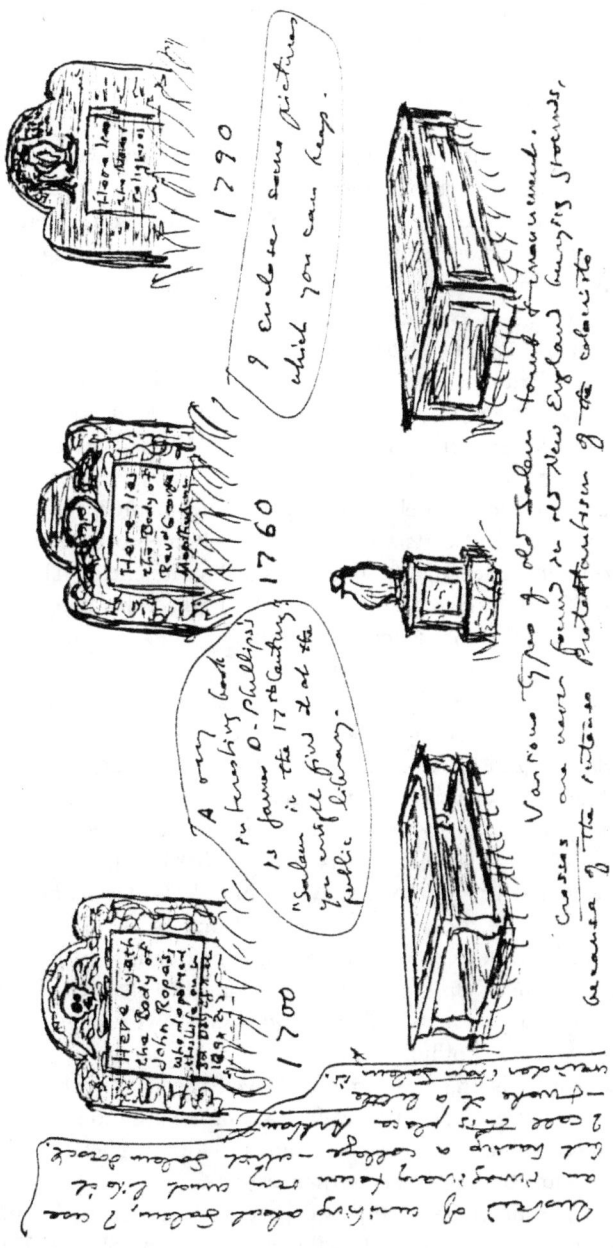

Instead of writing about Salem, I use an imaginary town very much like it but having a college—which Salem doesn't. I call this place *Arkham*—& make it a little weirder than Salem is.

A very interesting book is James D. Phillips's "Salem in the 17th Century". You might find it at the public library.

I enclose some pictures which you can keep.

The idea of *two* horrors—one from the sky & one from the earth—is very good. One or two more incidents might have helped—but *don't* emphasise action. It doesn't belong in a weird tale. Don't pile on characters, either. The *phenomena*, not any persons, are the real protagonists of a spectral story. Your climax—having the discovery of a small, inconspicuous object imply a hideous revelation—is excellent. You have great skill in weaving a tense *atmosphere*—don't lose it in efforts to be laconic & journalistic. I like your "Graveyard Rats" in the current W T very much—it has an excellent & ironic climax. Congratulations on the acceptance of the "Wolf" ballad. Spirited & vivid—& unusually smooth for a quarter-hour's job! You are surely making a good start—keep it up!

"The Book of Iod" surely sounds promising in prospect. In writing of Druid Britain be sure of certain historic points. Remember that it was *not* the Druids who built Stonehenge & the other great stone circles. These megaliths date back to 2000 B.C. or so, & are the work of a neolithic people of Mediterranean race. The Celts (Gaelic) entered around 1800 to 1600 B.C. & had nothing to do with the works of the dark race they conquered. Stonehenge has probably been deserted for 3500 years. Also—after 61 A.D., when the troops of C. Suetonius Paullinus wiped out the Druidic headquarters on the isle of Mona (Anglesey), British Druidism must be *secret* & struggling.

Regarding "fan" magazines—they really form a very encouraging influence, & have no relation to "gyp" enterprises where the editor—& only the editor—makes cash. They are all struggling as hard as the writers they welcome, & are mostly run at a loss. The best one—*The Fantasy Fan*—failed because the losses were too great for the publisher to stand.[3] Your ability to remodel ideas for various types of pulp magazine ought to prove quite a meal ticket in the course of time. I can't do anything like that. Glad your experiments aren't spoiling your style. About rejections—I've always run up against them. Wright will take nothing subtle.

I know that California has some finely weird scenic effects. Clark Ashton Smith speaks often of Crater Ridge, & has sent me a curious stone fragment picked up thereon—a thing like a pre-human eidolon. Death Valley & Terminal Island[4] must be full of spectral suggestions!

No—my "Haunter" is hardly a real sequel to Bloch's "Shambler". The entity which gets the young artist in the end is not the Shambler, but something from an altogether different pocket of space.

No—*Kirk Mashburn* is not a pseudonym for Single-Plot Hamilton. On the contrary, Mr. W. Kirk Mashburn is a very genuine & gifted native of Louisiana, now living in Texas. Price knows him well & visits him now & then. The one alias of Hamilton which I know of is "Hugh Davidson". Hamilton's best story—& a splendid one—was his first. He wrote "The Monster God of Mamurth"[5]—& then the pulp formula got him!

I have never made efforts to market stories in England, but several have been reprinted in anthologies there. There is a weird anthology series—"Not at Night"—appearing every year in London, & several of my tales have been in that.[6]

Loveman was, in a way, a protege of Bierce's. He met the old boy in person in Washington, D.C., & Bierce often tried to aid in popularising Loveman's poetry. Loveman has edited & published the 21 letters he received from Bierce—these including the last letter Bierce is known to have written before his disappearance in 1913.[7] Our gang is also acquainted with that amusing old charlatan Adolphe de Castro—formerly Gustaf Adolf Danziger—who was so close a friend of Bierce in the 80's and 90's. Frank B. Long—whose tales you doubtless know—revised de Castro's Bierce biography & wrote the preface.[8] I've revised many a tale for Old 'Dolph myself . . . . he's had 2 or 3 in W T, as you may know.[9]

Well—I must cut short & get busy. Hope to see more of your work in W T & elsewhere, & trust you'll make an increasingly big thing of writing. Your skill in extemporaneous verse is really remarkable in one who is predominantly a prose writer, & both of the specimens I have seen stand far above the usual W T standard.

All good wishes—

Yrs most cordially & sincerely,

H. P. Lovecraft

## Notes

1. Annie E. P. Gamwell (1866–1941), who had moved into 66 College Street with HPL in May 1933. At this time she was hospitalized for breast cancer.

2. By T. F. Hunt.

3. The *Fantasy Fan* (September 1933–February 1935) was edited and published by Charles D. Hornig.

4. Terminal Island is a largely artificial island in Los Angeles County, between the neighborhood of San Pedro in Los Angeles and the city of Long Beach. It is the location of the Federal Correctional Institution, Terminal Island.

5. See CLM 1n1.

6. "The Horror at Red Hook," in *You'll Need a Night Light;* "Pickman's Model," in *By Daylight Only;* "The Rats in the Walls" and HPL's revision of Zealia Bishop's "The Curse of Yig," in *Switch On the Light;* HPL's revision of Hazel Heald's "The Horror in the Museum," in *Terror by Night;* and "The Curse of Yig," "Pickman's Model," and "The Horror in the Museum," in *The "Not at Night" Omnibus.* All the anthologies were edited by Christine Campbell Thomson and published by Selwyn & Blount (London).

7. Actually, the last known letter by Bierce is dated 26 December 1913 (See *A Much Misunderstood Man: Selected Letters of Ambrose Bierce*, ed. S. T. Joshi and David E. Schultz [Columbus: Ohio State University Press, 2003], 244–46). The last letter to Loveman is dated 10 September 1913.

8. *Portrait of Ambrose Bierce*. The preface is signed "Belknap Long."

9. De Castro had only two stories in *WT*, both ghostwritten by HPL: "The Last Test" (November 1928) and "The Electric Executioner" (August 1930). HPL elsewhere speaks of a third tale revised for de Castro (*SL* 3.204); R. H. Barlow identified it as "In the Confessional," but apparently it has been lost. It is unlikely that HPL revised any more stories than these three.

[3]     [Trans., WHS]

66 College Street
Providence, R.I.
April 16, 1936

Dear Mr. Kuttner:—

I am reprehensibly tardy in acknowledging yours of March 23, & even now will have to reply very inadequately. My aunt's illness increased, so that she has had to be successively at an hospital & a nursing home—& during her absence my duties have increased rather than decreased. She will probably be back within a week, since she is now recovering finely—but my programme is so utterly tangled up that I see no hope of an early return to normality. Letters remain unanswered—duties have to be transferred—revision jobs are returned unperformed—borrowed books accumulate unread—indeed, if I ever get straightened out it will have to be through neglect & repudiation rather than through accomplishment. I understand how the European countries feel about their international debts! A hanging-on of bad health, too, has not helped matters.

Sorry to hear of the recent illnesses in your household, & hope both you and your mother are now fully recovered. Thanks exceedingly for the local views, which I shall add most gratefully to my extensive but loosely classified geographical gallery. I have never been in the west, but delight to get amidst the subtropical vegetation of the south whenever I can. Indeed, my favorite city is the ancient & beautiful seaport of Charleston, S.C., where the palmetto, magnolia, oleander, fig, camellia, azalea, & oleander [*sic*] flourish luxuriantly, & where the twisted live-oaks bear grotesque festoons of grey Spanish moss. In Florida, where I sometimes visit, I encounter the larger species of palms—while as for *cacti* . . . you ought to have seen me helping my host rid his front lawn of them last year! Enclosed are a few views of Providence which may prove of interest. This is a very interesting old town, nearly as full of colonial architecture as Salem, though it also has extensive modern sections. Some of your California structures must be fascinating—especially the missions & the surviving Spanish haciendas. There is even some Russian architecture at Ft.

Ross, north of San Francisco, where a Russian trading & military post tried to take root around 1810. That house near San Jose must be curious—though I should think the credulous owner could have secured the *sound of hammers* more cheaply by simply hiring somebody to pound on a piece of timber during the appropriate hours![1] Later—as soon as I have a moment to assemble it—I will lend you a representative set of Salem views ... with some of ancient Marblehead, its visually far quainter neighbour. Marblehead *looks* more as you originally fancied Salem to be, & is the original of the "Kingsport" I sometimes mention in stories. By the way—thanks extremely for the drawing of your curious pet from R'lyeh. Glad he thrives on dry land—or does he have to take a plunge into an aquarium now & then? Bloch & Barlow occasionally send me samples of their malign art—which is largely derived from that of your gifted fellow-Californian Clark Ashton Smith. Have you ever seen much of CAS's work? If not, I'll lend you some specimens. He has recently taken to miniature *sculpture,* producing some marvellously grotesque figurines from the softer stones of his native region (Auburn).

Interested to hear that you've read the "Mts. of Madness". As to the relative merits of exotic & mundane settings—I fancy it depends on both writer & reader. Actually, there is room for each—though some *do* the one better than the other, while others *like* the one better than the other. A serious weird tale is, necessarily, not so much a chronicle of events as simply a picture or crystallisation of a certain human mood. Since our moods include both utter strangeness & strangeness linked to familiar scenes, it follows that both types of fantasy have a legitimate place. However, because moods with a mundane setting are more common, it is undoubtedly easier to create an effective story on that pattern. This, indeed, is the guiding principle of M. R. James—& Blackwood's & Machen's best work seems to bear it out. But in the long run each author has to write exactly what's in him. By the way—"The Turn of the Screw" is not by Blackwood, as you seem to imply, but by the verbose, over-precise, & not usually weird *Henry* James. "The Wendigo" is a good story, but its concreteness & tangibility rob it of that ultimate touch of utter perfection which characterises "The Willows". Blackwood is a very uneven writer—much of his output is really pitiful sentimental slop. And yet he stands absolutely unapproached as a delineator of the subtler shadings of our illusory sense of the unreal. I'm not sure that you're right, by the way, in advocating the actual appearance of horrors in stories. To my mind the most effective method is to *suggest* certain things through unmistakable evidences, & let the reader do his own imagining. I haven't often practiced what I preach—but a better writer than I could get the effects I mean. Some of Bloch's ghoul stories are splendid—he'll be a figure to reckon with if he doesn't go commercial or get diverted to wider phases of literary endeavour. Your own recent yarns—"The Little Ones" & "Horror at San Xavier"—sound extremely alluring, & I'm sure the use of authentic local colour will enhance your effects. I don't agree about the importance of plot.

Indeed, I believe that—because of the foundation of most weird concepts in dream-phenomena—the best weird tales are those in which the narrator or central figure remains (as in actual dreams) largely passive, & witnesses or experiences a stream of bizarre events which—as the case may be—flows past him, just touches him, or engulfs him utterly. It must be remembered that the canons of cheap pulp fiction have absolutely nothing to do with good writing. The two fields are for the most part definitely antagonistic, & he who seeks deliberately to write salable stories is lost to literature. That is the tragedy of good old Merritt. He *could* have been a real author like Blackwood. Instead, he chose the path of commerce & became an idol of the herd—with glimpses of his potential greatness breaking through only occasionally.

I was greatly interested in the further details anent the Book of Iod. This must be the ⳩ ⳩⳩⳩⳩ ⳩ ⳩⳩⳩ mentioned on the seventh Eltdown Shard—& very possibly the "volume that cannot be" hinted at in the *Necronomicon* (ix, 21—p. 598 of the black-letter German copy (in Latin) in the library of Miskatonic University.) Some day I must bring pressure to bear & borrow that Negus translation (into Latin, I presume) in the Huntington Library.

Shub-Niggurath is a female daemon—wife of Yog-Sothoth & mother of the hellish entities Nug & Yeb. Her worship—the symbolic rite of the Goat with a Thousand Young—was one of the most monstrous legacies taken over by the human from the pre-human world.

Work on "Innsmouth" progresses slowly. Crawford has secured 4 fine illustrations from Frank Utpatel of Mazomanie, Wis.—whose designs for Derleth's work you doubtless know. Probably they'll be the only redeeming thing about the volume!

April W T is not as bad as it might be—Jacobi, Derleth, & Bloch all doing well. The Price reprint,[2] though not weird, is a splendid item I have always admired. Wish good old Sultan Malik could take a vacation from commercial stuff & write such things now!

I hope to see more of your work in the course of time. Don't hesitate to send along a MS., even though I may not be able to give very prompt comment on it. So far your products seem to me extremely good, & I hope you will not entirely desert the field of weirdness for domains of wider possibilities.

Yours by the Black Tower of Leng,

H. P. Lovecraft

*Notes*

1. The Winchester Mystery House, a mansion in San Jose once the personal residence of Sarah Winchester, the widow of gun magnate William Wirt Winchester. Construction on the house continued without interruption from 1884 until Mrs. Winchester's death on 5 September 1922. Mrs. Winchester used no architect and added to the building haphazardly, so that there are doors and stairs that lead nowhere, windows

that overlook other rooms, and stairs with odd-sized risers.

2. *WT* 27, No. 4 (April 1936): Carl Jacobi, "The Face in the Wind"; August Derleth and Mark Schorer, "They Shall Rise"; Robert Bloch, "The Druidic Doom"; E. Hoffmann Price, "The Rajah's Gift" (orig. January 1925).

[4]    [Trans., WHS]

66 College Street
Providence, R.I.
May 18, 1936.

Dear Mr. Kuttner:—

I trust that the disordered state of my affairs may form a sufficient excuse for this tardy reply to yours of 22nd ult. My aunt, I am glad to say, is steadily improving—having left the hospital for a convalescent home on April 7, & having returned to the ancient corridors of #66 on the 21st. She now takes walks on every sunny afternoon, & has had one motor ride through the vernal countryside. However—she still needs much coöperation in household tasks; so that my added duties are by no means over. A raw, cold spring has combined with my various other burdens to keep my energies at a low ebb—but I shall feel better when continuous hot weather gets here. Not till April 28th was there a really warm day. Since then I have been able to take my work out to Prospect Terrace (a little park on the ancient hillside a few blocks north of here—with a magnificent view of the outspread town & of the distant hills beyond) several times. The landscape is now a captivating spectacle with its new verdure & abundant blossoms, & I hope to find time for some rural walks ere long. Barlow has invited me down to De Land again, but I greatly doubt my ability to accept.

On May 4th the Rhode Island Tercentenary observances began with a parade on colonial costume which started at the college gate—just a stone's throw from here. Later there was a mock-session of the rebel legislature of May 4, 1776—held in costume in the selfsame room of the ancient colony-house (1761) where the original session was held. In this, each old-time deputy was impersonated by a lineal descendant. The acting & costumes were so convincing that one could easily fancy the bygone period returned—with the intervening 160 years merely a bad dream. I was one of the few spectators lucky enough to get into the colony-house & witness the proceedings. In the afternoon—in a ceremony at the State House which I did not attend—Gov. Curley of Mass. presented to Gov. Green of R.I. a copy of the recently adopted resolution of the Massachusetts General Court, rescinding the banishment imposed by that august body upon Roger Williams in Octr. 1635. After 300½ years, Mr. Williams no doubt highly appreciates this delicate mark of consideration!

No—the Providence cards were *not* to be returned. Before long I will send the loan-exhibit of Salem & Marblehead views, which I trust you will find of interest. Marblehead adjoins Salem—being a peninsula southeast of it. A 20-minute trolley ride connects the centres of the two places. Unlike Salem, Marblehead never became a sizeable city; its 1930 population being only 8668. But it is the most perfectly preserved 18th century town in the U.S.—with steep, winding, occasionally sidewalkless streets, ancient houses, & picturesque waterfront. Artists & tourists invade it in summer—but in winter it becomes itself & drowses venerably, dreaming of old sea-days & forgotten faces. Keep these views—when they come—as long as you like; & when you've finished with them you might forward them to Miss C. L. Moore, 2547 Brookside Parkway, South Drive, Indianapolis, Indiana—the gifted creator of "Shambleau" having expressed a wish to see these glimpses of crumbling "Arkham" & "Kingsport". Under separate cover I am sending some Klarkash-Ton Iconography—though sadly conscious that these small specimens do not represent the artist at his best. CAS is weak on perspective & on the human figure, but strong on utter strangeness as expressed in grotesque heads & morbid, non-terrestrial *vegetation*. Some day you ought to get in touch with him & have him lend you a few of his better pieces. His address is Box 88, Auburn, California. Have you his booklet of six short stories entitled, "The Double Shadow"? If not, you ought to get a copy. The author himself can supply you for the modest sum of 25¢ postpaid.

Yes—I recall hearing that Wright is a Californian. That fact has not, however, prevented him from turning down some of Klarkash-Ton's best work on the ground that it was "too poetic" or "not convincing" . . . . indeed, CAS could heartily appreciate (as I do) your clever limerick on the editor & the ghoul! Glad you find the pulp market easy to make—and that good writing helps you with the commercial stuff. Most, alas, find this latter thing just the other way around—serious effort disqualifying them for the formula-writing demanded by cheap editors, & formula-writing disqualifying them for serious composition. So far, I've never seen anybody but Derleth ride both horses at once with any degree of success—& even he is thinking of giving up pulp junk for a while. Quinn, Long, Price, Wandrei, Hamilton, & many others are virtually lost—it would take them years to get back to the mood of sincere creative effort again.

Don't harbour too high expectations of "Innsmouth", for the submarine part is very slight—merely a sort of background of allusion & menace. I don't know when Crawford will ever get it published—though Utpatel's illustrations are finished, & are extremely good.

As to an *absolutely non-mundane* story—of course, it would have to have a certain amount of human filtration or interpretation (the events being witnessed by a human being, or roughly translated into parallel events comprehensible to mankind), but I still think it could be written by the right author & made a tremendously powerful thing. I don't know anyone who could do it *now* (Blackwood comes the nearest), but believe the suitable genius might arise in the course of time. All that is necessary to provide the sought-for artistic quality or emotional effect is a potent conveying of the impression of *liberation & strangeness*—of transcended boundaries, or suspended or infracted natural laws. There need be no connexion with man, earth, solar system or galaxy so long as the abstract idea of liberation—escape—contravention—can find some pseudo-concrete embodiment or parallelism capable of human comprehension. As to the preferability of a pictorial over a printed medium—in some cases this might be true, although there is really nothing which words cannot capture if employed by the right artist. What is more—there are many things which *nothing but words* can capture. Pictures are useful only as long as the given concepts remain dominantly *visual*—but in the handling of remote themes none of the senses of terrestrial mammals might be involved. Your suggestion that certain unrealities are best hinted at by *their effects on familiar objects* is a very sound one. Indeed, that is the *only* way in which certain classes of inconceivable phenomena can be convincingly handled. How closely an "outside" tale needs to bring in ordinary events depends upon many things. Bloch is certainly right in saying that a tale does not need to be written from the standpoint of conventional human values & emotions (which are themselves largely artificial & fictitious)—indeed, the main trouble with cheap weird junk is that it *does* adhere to these values & emotions. The result is commonplaceness. I have long wished that someone might write a tale from the angle of one opposed to the existence of mankind—or something of that sort. This would not necessarily be *incomprehensible* to human readers. The basic alienage would make it all the more convincing, because there is always an aura of theatrical unreality about representations of non-human, non-terrestrial beings with commonplace human desires, perspectives, standards, social institutions, & even *names*. I can imagine a magnificently powerful story written—though not by me—from the angle of Wilbur Whateley's utterly non-human brother.[1]

Your mention of "The Frog" interests me greatly, for it looks like one of my favourite sort of tales. If Wright rejects it, I trust you'll let me see the MS.—for I don't want to miss the kind of item this appears to be! The atmosphere of dream-pursuit is surely ideal for anything of this nature. Glad Crawford has some of your material, & hope he'll be able to get it into print within the next few years. I read "The Herd"[2] with great interest, & like it exceedingly. It has the sort of atmosphere which most weird attempts lack. You will note my various observations & criticisms on the margin of the MS., & I have also supplied an outline for what seems to me a more definite motivation & simplification. You can use this outline or not—just as you choose—in preparing a second version. Or you can modify it in any way to suit yourself. At most, it is a mere bit of suggestion. The idea of a "drug of devolution" which you suggest, does not seem to fit in very well. It requires explanation & motivation itself. However—you can use your own judgment. Just get all the suggestions you can from various persons, & then choose what seems to work best—most naturally. I'll be interested to see the final version of the tale—which I hope will eventually get published.

No—Wright has nothing of mine awaiting publication. He has rejected all my longer & better things, & I doubt whether I shall submit anything more till I have a lot of junk on hand. Whether that will ever come to pass, I don't know. Other things clamour for attention, & various criticisms have somewhat dampened my creative ardour by making me distrustful of what I write. The only thing that will ever start me writing again is ample leisure, & complete withdrawal from the pulp arena. I'll have to forget critics & readers, editors & formulas, & recover the complete lack of self-consciousness which I had at first. And even then, nothing of any value may result.

Bloch is certainly coming along finely—his improvement from year to year being almost spectacular. "The Druidic Doom"[3] is a splendid piece of work. I always encourage him not to drop or subordinate his serious weird fiction, & caution him against letting haste & commercial concession permeate his best attempts. Perhaps he will be able to resist the pulp influence as Derleth has resisted it.

As for the matter of university training—I don't think you need to worry. At least half of the weird writing group have never attended college—this half including Clark Ashton Smith, A. Merritt, Robert E. Howard, H. C. Koenig, Bloch, Barlow, Hornig, &c. I haven't, either—since I was "all in" with a nervous breakdown at the time I ought to have been in Brown. But we ignorant guys seem to plug along somehow, picking up loose odds & ends of information along the way in a haphazard fashion! Perhaps, late in life, I shall soak up a few ideas through living on the very edge of the Brown campus—in a house owned by the college & having its steam heat & hot water piped in from the college engineering plant ... or if the steam & hot water don't turn the trick, the *lectures* may—recent performances in that line including subjects as diverse as Plato's "Republic", modern painting, Chinese contributions to modern culture, Gilbert Stuart, R.I. Silversmiths, archaic Greek art influences, early classical sculpture, philosophy & poetry, Mayan ruins, & the Michelson–Morley experiment.

Before I forget it I must thank you for that splendid folder of California desert views. Really, I had no idea your arid spaces were so captivatingly brilliant! I wish I could see such things some time—but all that depends on finances.

And now I must get to work. Hope my remarks on the story may prove useful. Salem & Marblehead views will come later. Return CAS stuff at your convenience.

All good wishes—yrs by the Windowless Tower—
E'ch-Pi-El

*Notes*

1. A reference to HPL's "The Dunwich Horror."

2. "'The Herd' was one of my early stories sent to Lovecraft for his opinion. I didn't work on it at the time, but intend to do so eventually, as Lovecraft's notes on the manuscript were copious and valuable" [note by Henry Kuttner]. The story is apparently unpublished.

3. *WT,* April 1936.

[5]   [Trans., WHS]

Bottomless Well of Yeguggon
—Hour that the Snout appears
[c. 15 June 1936]

Dear Archimage Khut-N'hah:—

I duly received & appreciated yours of June 4 with enclosures, & am revelling in the century-old atmosphere of Niles' Register.[1] Those old papers certainly do bring back the intimate texture of a bygone age about as well as anything could. I shall be very careful of the volume (whose cover is none too solidly attached), & will ultimately return it with the keenest & sincerest thanks. Meanwhile I trust the Salem & Marblehead material is proving of interest. Keep this stuff as long as you like, and then kindly forward it to Miss C. L. Moore. Enclosed herewith you will find the two stories you wish to see—these to be kept as long as you like, & ultimately returned to me. Hope they won't disappoint you. I also send a list of *all* my stories in case you've missed—& would like to see—others. If you'll return this list with the desired items checked in pencil, I'll probably be able to lend you copies of the latter. There are only 2 or 3 things of which I lack available copies. But meanwhile let me thank you most sincerely of those splendid *Arkham* lines[2]—which I read with the utmost appreciation & admiration. This is really an enormously vivid piece of verse, & I surely hope it may ultimately adorn the pages of W T. Your skill in adapting horror to metre seems to excel that of anyone else of the weird group. Some day I hope you can assemble a collection of these Avernal chants.

You are lucky, incidentally, to be able to grind out commercial potboilers without effort & without spoiling your style. Hope both your recent efforts land. I couldn't write a mechanical formula yarn if my life depended upon it. Long can & does do it—but only with severe effort, & at the cost of his once-promising career in serious literature.

Glad you enjoyed Klarkash-Ton's pictures, & that you obtained "The Double Shadow". His genius & style are of a highly individual sort, so that he undoubtedly ranks with Robert E. Howard—& perhaps C. L. Moore—as one of the supreme leaders of the W T group. Have you read much of his poetry? I can lend you his various volumes if you'd like to see them. Barlow is planning to publish another CAS collection[3]—& I wish he'd hurry up about it! Smith is, as you say, unlike Dunsany at bottom. I haven't read the latest Dunsany book—but the recent specimens differ greatly from the early work.[4] They are excellent in their way—but what chiefly fascinates me is the old fantasy of 30 years ago; the period of "Time & the Gods" & "A Dreamer's Tales".

Thanks for your tip regarding the Merritt story in *Wonder*.[5] I missed it, but must get on the trail of the magazine. Despite good old Abe's concessions to the pulp formula, he still retains a trace of his own innate genius which makes one wish to read all his products. I hope to see his new novel when it appears.[6] As for his *style*—I'll admit that I don't like its recent manifestations. He has fallen into pulpish tricks—including the brisk, cheerful, short-sentenced jargon which means absolute death to true weirdness of atmosphere. However—there's a buried substance somewhere which keeps him miles above the mere Hamiltons & Williamsons. If he had never seen nor heard of a cheap magazine he would be in the class of Machen & Blackwood. He has their imaginative gifts—but lacks their austere immunity to the lure of the profit motive.

By the way—he has just done young Hornig (late editor of *Wonder* & publisher of the much-lamented *Fantasy Fan*) a very good turn—securing him a newspaper job in San Francisco. I surely hope the venture will prove successful.

Glad you liked "The Shadow out of Time"—the printed version of which had relatively few errors despite the insane style sheet (which overpunctuates & overcapitalises to a grotesque extent). *Astounding* utterly ruined the "Mts. of Madness"—correction of whose printed text was a prodigious job.[7]

Your story observations all contain a great element of soundness. Too close analysis—or too detailed explanation—of mysteries is in most cases a weakening factor. As for my own efforts—the only thing to do at present is to *rest,* & see what happens to my creative psychology. If a period of freedom from criticism reawakens the impulse of 15 years ago, well & good. If not, that's all right too. No work is better than forced or harassed work.

Thanks very much for the various reading tips—on which I hope I'll be able to act in the course of time. I've undoubtedly missed many valuable weird works in the course of my lifetime—& some of the lacunae may never get filled. For example—the almost classic "Lodger" by Mrs. Belloc Lowndes escaped me for years, & is even now lying on my library table as a still-unread loan.

Your recent dream was surely a memorable affair, & I hope you'll be able to make definite fictional use of it. Dreams are generally too vague & incoherent for literary exploitation, but once in a while something almost ready-made comes along. I am a very vivid dreamer, & have frequently made use of dreams in stories. "The Statement of Randolph Carter" is virtually a literal transcript of a nightmare I experienced in December 1919. Another singular dream of mine (Oct. 1927) about Roman Spain has been incorporated by Long into his 2-part "Horror from the Hills". In other tales I have used fragments of less complete nocturnal visions—& other dreams are jotted down in my notebook for possible future use.

I doubt if I can get to Florida—or anywhere in particular this year, & am accordingly irritated. Unlike you, I am extremely fond of travel—antiquarian exploration from Quebec to New Orleans & Key West being my favourite diversion. I hope you can some time conquer your antipathy sufficiently to let you get east—visiting various Black Mass centres & seeing ancient Salem first hand. When that time comes, don't fail to include ancient Providence in your itinerary—for we have here many of the brooding marks of time which distinguish "Arkham" & "Kingsport" & "Innsmouth". For example—on the hill only a few blocks north of #66 is a completely hidden churchyard weird & shadowy enough to delight the heart of any Graveyard Rat. I can't resist enclosing some photographs taken last year—which I'll ask you to return at your leisure along with "Cool Air" & "The Picture in the House".

My programme is still tangled and overcrowded—all the more so because I was forced by the prevailing chaos to devote 4 solid days (including 2 nights of sacrificed sleep) to the devastating process of file-cleaning. I must have thrown away a couple of tons of old letters, cuttings, &c. Among other items in my attempted conquest of chaos was a reading-up of the contemporary W T issue. R. E. Howard's serial is really splendid. Yuggoth, how that bird can surround primal megalithic cities with an aura of aeon-old fear and necromancy! His "Black Canaan" is likewise magnificent in a more realistic way—reflecting a genuine regional background & giving a clutchingly powerful picture of the horror that stalks through the moss-hung, shadow-cursed, serpent-ridden swamps of the far south. Bloch is doing finely—following up his "Druidic Doom" with "The Faceless God" & "The Grinning Ghoul". Comte d'Erlette's "Telephone in the Library" is excellent, & Hamilton has escaped his formula a bit in "Child of the Winds". Burks spoils his "Room of Shadows" with a certain hack treatment. M. J. Bardine's "Harbour of Ghosts" has promise & atmosphere. So has Harold G. Shane's "Lethe".[8] But, at best, the percentage of meritorious matter is pitifully small!

Well—once more let me thank you for "Arkham", the loan of the *Register*, &c. &c. &c. Don't hurry about any of the material sent.

Yours by the Elder Sign

—E'ch-Pi-El

P.S. Just heard a report of the suicide of Robert E. Howard.[9] It seems incredible—I had a long normal letter from him written May 14. He was worried about his mother's health, but outside of that seemed quite all right. This is a blow indeed—he was the most *vital* & spontaneous of all the group!

*Notes*

1. *Niles' National Register,* a magazine published in Philadelphia (1811–49).

2. Apparently unpublished and nonextant.

3. Barlow never did publish *Incantations,* but Smith included the poems more or less selected for the book under that heading in his *Selected Poems.*

4. Probably a reference to the novel *Up in the Hills* (1935), a non-supernatural comic novel set in Ireland. The US edition had appeared in February 1936.

5. "The Drone Man" (*Thrilling Wonder Stories,* August 1936). First published in *Fantasy Magazine* (September 1934).

6. Evidently *The Fox Woman,* to have been written in collaboration with Max Brand. It was never completed in Merritt's lifetime.

7. HPL refers to his making many (but not nearly all) corrections to the serialization of *At the Mountains of Madness* in three copies of *Astounding.*

8. Robert E. Howard, "The Hour of the Dragon" (December 1935–April 1936), "Black Canaan" (June 1936); Robert Bloch, "The Druidic Doom" (May 1936), "The Faceless God" (June 1936); August Derleth, "The Telephone in the Library" (June 1936); Edmond Hamilton, "Child of the Winds," and Arthur J. Burks, "Room of Shadows" (May 1936); M. J. Bardine, "The Harbor of Ghosts," and Harold G. Shane, "Lethe" (June 1936).

9. C. L. Moore had notified HPL by postcard that Robert E. Howard committed suicide. See CLM 31.

[6]     [Trans., WHS]

66 College Street
Providence, R.I.
July 29, 1936

Dear Khut-N'hah:—

I have just completed the assembling of the various items in which you expressed interest. Thanks for the postage. The MSS. go in this envelope first class. Flat printed matter fills another envelope. And a third package, to go by parcel post, contains the thickish books & magazines. No hurry about any of this—but the following are to be returned at your convenience:

> All Klarkash-Ton material
> All MSS.
> The six issues of *Home Brew* (a lousy rag!)
> The Shunned House (loose sheets)
> Feby. 1934 *Fantasy Fan* with "Polaris".

You may—if you have any especial use for such—permanently retain the following:

> Oct. '34 F F with "Beyond the Wall of Sleep".
> June '34 F F with "From Beyond".
> *Marvel Tales* with "Celephaïs".

Of these latter items I have a considerable stock of duplicates. I'm not sending "The Thing on the Doorstep" or "The Haunter of the Dark" because

(a) I haven't any MSS. left, & (b) these are the two items to be published in W T. Schwartz of the F M has some wild idea of getting MSS. of mine reprinted in England (probably nothing will come of it), & in connexion with this venture I sent my only 2 unsubmitted stories to W T in order to exhaust their cisatlantic possibilities. I expected instant rejection—but to my astonishment Wright took the damn things! Glad you are going to have the "Innsmouth" book when—or if ever—it is issued. I have bad luck with book ventures. You'll notice that "The Shunned House" consists of unbound sheets. These represent a small book which a friend of mine was about to publish back in 1928. After the printing various delays occurred, & in 1930 the publisher—Cook—suffered a nervous & financial breakdown from which he has never fully recovered. For four years the loose sheets of about 250 copies lay in a bindery in Boston, but eventually Cook salvaged them & sent them down to Barlow in De Land, Fla. Barlow planned to bind & circulate them—but is going so slowly that most orders are still unfilled. Probably the thing will never be really circulated. Incidentally, this tale describes an actual house in Providence[1]—on the ancient hill only a few blocks N. of #66. In reality, however, there are no sinister events connected with the forbidding-*looking* place. "Herbert West"—the series in *Home Brew*—is my one & only attempt at the sort of hack writing you grind out with such left-handed ease. It nauseated me so badly that I could never do it again. Don't regard these things as *stories*—they are merely more or less picturesque items of low-grade Americana. Another but less intentionally rotten thing is "From Beyond". Also pretty bad is the mawkish, pseudo-Dunsanian effort, "The Quest of Iranon". And speaking of Dunsaniana—"Celephaïs" isn't so hot! "The Tree" is so poor that I may soon repudiate it—scratch it off my list of acknowledged products. I don't recall your having seen "The Nameless City"—but it will appear in the coming Wollheim–Shepherd venture *Fanciful Tales*. I didn't see any of the yokel comment on "The Shadow out of Time", but Sterling told me that the "Mts. of Madness" was badly received.[2] The wonder is that a magazine catering to non-literary kids should ever have taken these tales. But the joke is on Tremaine, who paid $630.00 for the pair of 'em! When I corrected my printed copies early in June & saw the hellish mutilations which ruin the "Mts. of Madness" (I now consider that story *unpublished*), I resolved never to send another damn thing to Street & Smith. Now I realise they probably wouldn't take anything if I *did* send it! Glad "Cool Air" & "The Picture in the House" held interest for you. W T is going to reprint the latter soon. As to the source of "Cool Air"—while "M. Valdemar" has always been a favourite of mine, I don't think it was the primary element behind the tale. The genesis was less direct. One idea was to embody the general repulsiveness of New York's run-down sections—a theme also manifest in "He" & "Red Hook". That place in 14th St. is a portrait from life of a seedy joint on whose ground floor my friend George Kirk had a book shop (he still conducts the business—long ago moved to 58 W. 8th St.).[3] More than that—I wanted somehow to embody the terrible (though not wholly new) idea of a person needing some constant artificial aid in order not to lapse into some grotesque & hideous state. If any one tale unconsciously influenced me, it was probably Machen's "White Powder" (in "The Three Impostors") rather than "M. Valdemar". Yes—I think the idea of *decadence from some familiar norm* tends to be more horrible than that of *sheer alienage to the normal. Decay* links the horror more closely to the familiar world around us, & to the beings of that world.

Glad you enjoyed the Salem–Marblehead stuff, & that it has been duly sent along. Glad also that the hidden churchyard proved interesting. No—you could scarcely expect an old-fashioned churchyard in California, unless one happened to exist around one of the old Spanish missions. I've heard of Forest Lawn—in fact, someone once sent me a booklet about it.[4] I believe it contains a reproduction of the old Stoke-Poges church in whose yard (or about whose yard) Gray wrote his Elegy . . . . although it lacks the yard itself. Gray would probably feel more at home in the Providence churchyard—which does not differ in any important respect from the ancient God's-Acres of Old England.

Sorry you've been overburdened with work—& hope the sales curve will rise. I myself have been utterly swamped with unremunerative tasks—& in rather poor health except for a week of very hot weather. I *need* extreme heat as much as you dislike it   & am certainly an ass to live in this northern climate. My aunt, on the other hand, likes cool weather, & is doing finely.

The July W T is memorable only for the items by Klarkash-Ton & C L M—unless poor old Two-Gun's serial (I never read serials till they're done) turns out to be remarkable.[5] REH certainly stood high in its preceding issues. Yes—I read "The Ship of Ishtar" as a serial a decade or so ago, & later as a book. It didn't impress me vastly, although Merritt agrees with you in rating it high. Yes—I read "The Moon Pool" both in original novelette & expanded form, & like the former much better. As it originally ran, the story ended with Throckmartin's disappearance from the ship after his first set of unexplained adventures. There was little or nothing of the really pulpish in it, & the reader could let his imagination run riot. Then Abe had to tack that voluminous second part—vastly longer than the first—on, & the thing was sunk. All the familiar clichés & adventure hokum. I never obtained the bound book, although I have the full text in three crumbling issues of the early *Amazing*. I also have the original novelette from the *All-Story* (June 7, 1918)[6]—which I treasure. Certain touches were left out when this section was saddled with the anticlimactic ¾—hence I hang on to the first edition. I didn't get around to the cinema version of "Burn, Witch"[7]—for these alleged horror films seldom amount to anything. The one cinema I do want to see is the Wellsian "Things to Come". I seem to recall one or two tolerable items in "Jorkens Remembers Africa", but it is the *old* Dunsany whom I chiefly value.[8]

The loss of Robert E. Howard is the worst blow of all. *There* was a real titan—always distinctive & vigorous no matter what he wrote; always himself no matter how much he outwardly catered to cheap editorial caprice. We shall never, alas, have another like him. His suicide is as surprising as it is distressful, for ol' Two-Gun Bob always seemed to be a particularly hard-boiled egg. The moody streak manifest in his bitter hatred of civilisation must have run deeper than we ever suspected—so that he could not accept philosophically that inevitable passing of the elder generation to which most of us are perforce resigned. The shock to poor old Dr. Howard must be atrocious—wife & splendid only child gone at one stroke—but he is bearing up like a true pioneer. Perhaps you know that he is giving his son's library to the latter's alma mater—Howard Payne College in Brownwood—as the nucleus of a Robert E. Howard Memorial Collection. Obituaries will appear on every hand—including a sizable one by me in *Fantasy Magazine*. Barlow has written a fine elegiac sonnet which Wright has taken for W T.[9] This is Ar-E'ch-Bei's first professional acceptance, & it is surely melancholy that his debut should have so tragic a background.

No real trips for me this year, I imagine—but I hope you'll have better luck getting east. Local news scarce & tame. Had a pleasant call from young Sterling (now in Lynn—near Salem & Marblehead—& recovering finely from his spring operation) June 30, & shewed some other out-of-town friends the local countryside in mid-July. During the hot spell—week of June 8—I was feeling very active; cleaning up a lot of work, being outdoors much of the time, & taking a trip to ancient Newport—where I roamed through colonial streets & did considerable writing on the high, rocky sea-cliffs with nothing but a saline solution betwixt me & the strife-torn Iberian peninsula. July 22 I saw the new Peltier comet at the Ladd Observatory a mile north of here. Just a small disc with a hazy, fanlike stub of a tail.

But the most recent event of all is Barlow's arrival in Providence for an indefinite sojourn.[10] Some property adjustments about the De Land place are occurring, & Ar-E'ch-Bei thought this would be a good time to pay the Old Gentleman a visit & make his headquarters in ancient New England for a while. I surely am glad to see him—no lack of congenial conversation from now on! He was my host in Florida in 1934 & 1935. He has taken quarters in the boarding-house just across the garden from #66, & is full of literary plans.

All good wishes,

Yours by the Black Goat,

E'ch-Pi-El

*Notes*

1. The John Mawney House (c. 1764) at 135 Benefit Street.

2. All letters commenting on HPL's stories in *Astounding* are reprinted in *A Weird Writer in Our Midst: Early Criticism of H. P. Lovecraft*, ed. S. T. Joshi (New York: Hippo-

campus Press, 2010), 210–18.

7. Kirk's Chelsea Book Shop operated briefly at 317 West 14th Street. HPL helped Kirk move into the building in August 1925. Kirk stayed there only two months before moving to 365 West 15th Street, then to 58 West 8th Street.

4. Forest Lawn Memorial Park, an immense cemetery in Glendale, CA, a suburb north of Los Angeles.

5. Clark Ashton Smith, "Necromancy in Naat" and C. L. Moore, "Lost Paradise" (*WT*, July 1936); Robert E. Howard, "Red Nails" (*WT*, July–October 1936).

6. The novelette version of "The Moon Pool" appeared in the *All-Story Weekly* for 22 June 1918 (*LL* 26); expanded as *The Moon Pool* (New York: Putnam's, 1919).

7. *The Devil-Doll* (MGM, 1936), directed by Tod Browning; starring Lionel Barrymore, Maureen O'Sullivan, and Frank Lawton. Based on Merritt's *Burn, Witch, Burn!*

8. Dunsany published numerous short stories narrated by Joseph Jorkens, a raconteur who frequented the fictional Billiards Club in London and spun fantastic stories if someone would buy him a large whiskey and soda.

9. "R. E. H." (*WT*, October 1936).

10. Barlow visited HPL in Providence from 28 July to 1 September.

[7]     [Postcard][1]

[Postmarked Providence, R.I.,
August 1936]

*Notes*

1. Nonextant. See HPL to E. Hoffmann Price, 3 December 1936 (ms., JHL): "To shew how small the world is—when old de Castro was here last August I happened to mention Kuttner as a rising figure, & old 'Dolph was instantly all attention. He had known a Henry Kuttner years ago, & knew that he had a son of the same name— hence inferred that our energetic young colleague was that infant grown up. We at once dropped Kuttner a card—& it turned out that old Dolph's guess was right. Kuttner's late father—a bookseller—was indeed a pal of the venerable scholar's 20 years ago. Since the reëstablishment of the link Kuttner & de Castro have become regular & interested correspondents."

[8]     [Trans., WHS]

The Ancient Hill
August 29, 1936

Dear Khut-N'hah:—

        I enjoyed yours of Aug. 14, & am very grateful for the glimpse of the Combe–Rowlandson "Dance of Death". These quaint early 19th century products have always held a peculiar charm for me—"Dr. Syntax" having been encountered at an early age. I wish I had acquired a whole set of these red-covered reprints when they were cheap. As it is, I have only the first "Syntax" book.[1] The macabre subject-matter of the present volumes adds to their interest. Hope my overcrowded programme won't cause me to detain them too long. Eventually I'll return them safely along with Niles' Register—which is itself a splendid sidelight on the early (or fairly early) 19th century.

Your ancestral link with early San Francisco is surely interesting. I suppose the present city has relatively little quaint or old-time material, & yet it seems to fascinate most persons. The very striking topography—bay, hills, headlands—& the dramatic local traditions supply a glamour which makes up for the lack of architectural appeal. The fog, with its outline-softening tendency & its element of mysterious suggestion, must be a decided asset.

Thanks exceedingly for the Wrightwood cards—which seem to depict a highly attractive region. Hope your vacation was uniformly pleasant. In one detail I'd appreciate this region less than you—for I have no use for cold or cool weather. The cold utterly disintegrates me mentally & physically, & I've become wholly unconscious at plus 14°. It really isn't safe for me to be exposed to anything under plus 20°, & I can't manage my muscles well enough to write under 75° or so. My favourite temperature-range is 80°–90°, & I don't know what it means to be too hot.

Glad the batch of stories contained some interesting material. Wright twice rejected "The Shunned House", & I don't believe it will ever be really published. The loose sheets of about 250 copies are stored among Barlow's effects (he took them when W. Paul Cook became unable to handle them), but I don't know when he'll be ever able to bind or circulate them.

Sorry you didn't finish your memorial poem to Two-Gun Bob. P. Schuyler Miller recently prepared a sort of history of Conan the Cimmerian, in which he listed all the Conan tales in proper chronological order, & added a running comment tracing the fortunes of the hero from his first appearance at 15 to his kingship of Aquilonia around the age of 40.

Glad that you & Mooney & Ackerman[2] had an enjoyable session. And so the boys thought Grandpa's handwriting was pretty bad, eh? Well—they're not the first to slander the Old Man's scrawl! I really ought to use a typewriter—though I hate the damn things like hell!

As to the hashing-up of my tales by S & S—it was my own fault to the extent that I didn't tell them in advance to follow text or return the MS. I sell to Wright only on condition that not so much as a comma be changed. The "Colour" in *Amazing* was not intentionally butchered, but the sundry accidental misprints made it a sorry mess. I've heard from others of S & S's dislike of having their authors write for other magazines.

On August 15 we visited ancient Newport, & on the 20th Barlow & I went the rounds of Salem & Marblehead. Your recent reading of the guidebooks will give you an idea of what we saw in centuried Arkham & Kingsport. We explored the House of the Seven Gables & other venerable edifices, & sat for a long time on one of the tombs in the Charter St. Burying

Ground—where, by the way, we saw that slab half-engulfed by the giant willows which figures in "The Unnamable". We were accompanied by young Kenneth Sterling—then staying in Lynn near the scene of our explorations. Sterling is now well recovered from his serious operation of last spring, & has passed his Harvard entrance examinations with highest honours. Enclosed are a couple of Salem cards which you may retain.

All good wishes,

Yours by the Nighted Eidolon

E'ch-Pi-El

*Notes*

1. *The Tour of Doctor Syntax in Search of the Picturesque.*
2. James Mooney (1919–2008), an artist, and Forrest J Ackerman (1916–2008), a science fiction fan, both in the Los Angeles area.

[9]    [Trans., WHS]

The Ancient Hill

October 15, 1936.

Dear Khut-N'hah:—

I received & appreciated both the mountain postcard & the interesting letter of Sept. 12. Your Poe acrostic[1] is really splendid a good deal closer to actual, spontaneous poetry than any of its predecessors! It is curious how this idle half-hour's pastime has aroused echoes. Up in Milwaukee my friend M. W. Moe (a teacher in West Division High School—who visited here last July & saw the churchyard) composed another sonnet of the series, & has conceived the idea of incorporating all the specimens (I must send him yours) into a hectographed booklet for use in his English classes.[2] Furthermore—he sent his sonnet to Derleth, & the latter is incorporating it into a Wisconsin state anthology which he is writing for the publisher Henry Harrison![3]

As to the activities of nocturnal Things in that hillside necropolis—very few extreme phenomena have been *reported,* but persons who have visited the spot shortly after midnight have failed to reappear in the world. Corpse-lights sometimes leap above certain very ancient graves, while signs of stress & breakage *from within* deface many of the centuried tombs. Skeleton hands have been seen to reach up out of certain thickets, while some have complained of white, gelatinous objects which wriggle across the path in the twilight & vanish in hidden burrows & tomb-crevices. Then there is that inexplicable rattling from within sometimes heard at the nameless tomb on the eastward slope—but it were better not to speak of *that!* Glad you haven't seen any horrors amongst your local tombstones. Probably the Los Angeles graveyards are too new to have developed *certain features,* & to have attracted a certain kind of denizen *to the surface.*

It certainly is tragic that your father did not live longer, for he would obviously have formed the most congenial & inspiring of companions. To grow up in a bookshop & imbibe lore from its presiding genius would have been the most felicitous of fates! But it's something to be in touch with bookdom even indirectly, & I'm sure you must have plenty of opportunities. I used to haunt the bookshops of this city—& I guess I told you how much time I spent in the attic of my old home—with a candle in a sinister window-less room, where I found all the brown-backed 18th century volumes which had been banished from the more elegant shelves downstairs. I learned the rules of poetry from a book printed in the long ſ—hence my lifelong addiction to the 18th century & everything connected with it. My father died before I could more than vaguely remember him, but I was greatly influenced by an uncle—or, rather, my elder aunt's husband—who was a classicist & antiquarian of really solid attainments. I have his books & many of his things still—indeed, the desk & chair I am now using were his. Some day I wish I could get his Virgil published—a blank verse translation of everything but the Eclogues, which (together with other MSS. of his) I have always carefully treasured.[4]

Yes—I think my California likes would run to San Francisco for atmosphere & imaginative stimulation, but to San Diego for climate. I fancy I'd like old Mexico as well—especially such towns as retain a maximum of Spanish colonial atmosphere. The Aztec & Mayan ruins in the south would furnish that added touch of remoter antiquity which one gets from Roman ruins in England.

Glad to hear of cheques & acceptances—even though some of these imply a wearisome grind of pure hack writing. I wish I had a dependable meal-ticket like that, but I simply *can't* do it. In revision you have to work harder & get less. The other day I plugged 60 hours without sleep on a hell of a rush revision job—& won't get as much from it as from a short story of average length.[5]

Thanks for your generosity with *Register* & D of D. Both are certainly fascinating. Much of the attraction exerted on me by the late 17th & entire 18th centuries is also exerted by the early 19th .... indeed, any age from around 1680 to 1850 seems fairly homelike to me. But I won't detain these volumes indefinitely and weigh down your car with them next summer.

I haven't had many chances to read anything lately, & in the October W T I've read only "The Secret of Kralitz".[6] In spite of the suggestion of youthful overcolouring in spots I like it immensely. It had the Gothic atmosphere touch that I supremely relish—the one intangible element which makes a weird story really potent & fascinating in my eyes. It is a pity that most "weird" tales lose this fundamental quality in an effort to be modern & sprightly. I read Seabury Quinn's pages of brisk, cheerful, up-to-date conversation (when I stop to read them at all) with a polite yawn & an academic admiration of his cleverness in handling the conventional technique of fiction. Of any real sense of weirdness there is none—because nothing in the style has served to build up any emotional preparation for the marvels or horrors so glibly stuck in toward the end or prosaically catalogued throughout the text. Everything is sprightly, mechanical, & puppet-like, & nothing reaches that inner region of perception & response which gives birth to the true sense of fear. That's what these pulp hacks get for repudiating the foundations of the old Gothic tradition & trying to compete with the casual, half-flippant best-seller boys. And so I always appreciate reading anything in the good old main tradition—something which makes the style contribute to the ultimate effect. I can forgive a lot of immaturity when I see the author headed in the right direction! Glad you liked RHB's elegiac sonnet—an opinion which I'll surely relay to the author. Too bad Bob's first professional acceptance had to have such a melancholy background.

About good old Two-Gun Bob's characters—odd as it may sound, I doubt whether Conan was, in spirit & intent, a typical pulp hero. He *resembled* such externally, but actually I fancy he was a type or projection of the sort of lawless rover REH himself longed to be. There was more of sincere & ardent wish-fulfilment than of conventional copying in the mighty Cimmerian—& that is why he always seemed to me more *alive* than the jointed marionettes of Hamilton & all the other hacks. Solomon Kane reflected another side of Two-Gun—the brooding ethical sense which made him furious over injustices & oppressions. How he used to storm over the maltreatment of prisoners by policemen, the high-handed outrages of absentee oil corporations in Texas, & latterly the absorption of Abyssinia by Italy! But after all, the human characters are the least part of weird fiction. REH had a strange atmospheric power which manifested itself in more subtleties of description than even he himself realised, & which leaves in the reader's mind a menacing, mist-wreathed image of Cyclopean walls in the jungle, smothered in unwholesome vines, & hiding hellish secrets older than mankind.

I've recently been hearing from young Finlay, W T's gifted new illustrator, who got my address from Bloch. He is really a picturesque & remarkable figure—poet as well as artist—& I believe he has the stuff to take him a long way. He is doing the heading for my "Haunter of the Dark".

The advance of autumn has ended my outdoor sessions of reading & writing, but I still get out for occasional rural walks. Lately I have taken to exploring a wooded hill—Neutaconkanut—on the western rim of the town (& visible in the distance from my window) whence a series of marvellous views of outspread city & adjacent countryside & blue bay may be obtained. I had often ascended it before, but have only recently examined & appreciated the exquisitely mystical sylvan scenery—curious mounds, flower-starred meadows, & hushed hidden valleys—beyond its crest. It shall henceforth be a favourite goal of mine.

The other night I attended a meeting of the local organisation of amateur astronomers—"The Skyscrapers"—which functions more or less under the auspices of Brown University—& was astonished at its degree of development. Some of the members are almost serious scientific observers, & the society is contemplating the purchase of a well-known private observatory (the Seagrave Obsy.—whose presiding genius died recently)[7] in the western part of the state. It has separate meteor, variable star, moon, planet, comet, &c. sections, & enjoys the use of the college observatory. Surprisingly systematic work is done—largely in the variable star & meteor fields—& the enthusiasm of the 70 or 80 members seems to be immense. It brings back my early astronomical interests so vividly that I'm half-tempted to apply for membership. At the recent meeting there was an address (by an amiably ignorant grammar school principal, in a toupee too brown for his greying fringe, who didn't know what an orrery is) on early Rhode Island astronomy, & the reflecting telescope of Joseph Brown—used to observe the transit of Venus on June 3, 1769 & owned by the college since 1780 or so—was exhibited. It is really curious how radically the general public's interest in astronomy has increased since my day. When I was young no layman seemed to give a damn about the cosmos & its mechanism & phenomena!

Have lately been hearing from a chap in San Francisco—one Stuart Morton Boland—who says he is a librarian & has seen lots of books like the Necronomicon! Widely travelled, apparently.

Best wishes—& thanks for all items.

Yours,

Abdul A.

*Notes*

1. "Where He Walked."

2. See CLM 35n2. Moe's hectographed booklet *Four Acrostic Sonnets on Edgar Allan Poe* (1936) did not contain Kuttner's poem.

3. August Derleth, ed., *Poetry out of Wisconsin* (New York: Henry Harrison, 1937), 191.

4. Dr. Franklin Chase Clark (1847–1915). See HPL to Richard F. Searight (31 May 1935): "My late uncle Dr. Clark made a pentameter blank verse translation of the Æneid & Georgics, but died before getting at the Eclogues. It has never been published, but I have the typed MS. Wish I could publish it some day—finishing the Eclogues myself" (*Letters to Richard F. Searight* 59). Clark's papers are held by the Manuscripts Division of the Rhode Island Historical Society.

5. See CLM 37n20.

6. By Kuttner.

7. The private observatory of Frank Evans Seagrave (1859–1934) was located at 119 Benefit Street; it is now at 47 Peeptoad Road, North Scituate, R.I. Seagrave died on 15 August 1934. His executor, Wayne F. Angell, died on 7 July 1936.

[10]   [Trans., WHS]

The Lair on the Ancient Hill
November 30, 1936.

Bolivar Twirp, Esq.[1]
    Executor, Estate of Henry Kuttner, Esq.,
        Beverly Hills, California, U.S.A.

My Dear Mr. Twirp:—

It is with sorrow that I learn of your distinguished client's disappearance—such a promising young man! And the attendant circumstances are such as to cause profound disquiet. That tentacle suggests very ominously one which groped fumblingly about my own study eighty years ago, upon the one occasion when I attempted to read the *entire* Aklo ritual. I paused in time—but I shudder to think of what may have happened to a younger man too bold, too curious, or too enthusiastic to cease at the right moment. Poor Mr. Kuttner! What a writer he might have been! Of course, he *may* return—but what I know or suspect of the daemon "R. B." does not incline me to optimism. My greatest hope is that he may have found the door to complete oblivion . . . the alternative is not pleasant to contemplate!

Let me thank you most sincerely for sending Mr. Kuttner's parting message to the world, as well as his vivid posthumous story "Hydra". I have read the latter with the keenest enjoyment, & hope that the learned editor of *Weird Tales* may share my favourable opinion.

\* \* \*

I described myself as "Ward Phillips" in the tale collaborated with Price[2]—& the reader is at liberty to assume or reject the identity of the two Providence occultists. Before long, by the way, Bloch and I will be getting quite used to violent deaths. This is his second. Long killed me off in 1930 or thereabouts in "The Space Eaters". Judging from the standard of the felidae of which I am so fond, I have six more deaths betwixt me and permanent oblivion.

I trust the sturdy vehicle you mention may ere long bear the astral projection or zombie or undead corpse of the late Mr. Kuttner eastward to the necropolitan haunts of his fellow-ghouls! The Margulies–Weisinger group of magazines forms a very reliable market financially, as Long appreciatively attests.[3] I may try things on them under a pseudonym if I ever get to writing again—but for the present other tasks have me hopelessly chained. As for 60-hour sessions—I couldn't manage them *often,* but once in a while I can stand such a thing if the impelling motive is powerful enough to keep me keyed up. A parallel case where pleasure rather than duty is the stimulus is afforded by my southern trips. To save hotel bills at intermediate places I shoot straight down to Charleston from here—spending two nights on buses & doing no more than drowse. I start from Providence around 11 a.m. & arrive in Charleston 48 hours later. Well—I'm usually so eager to poke around the by-ways & churchyards of the ancient Carolina metropolis that I generally stay up through the day after a refreshing shower & change of linen at the Y. Of course I'd be drowsy if I tried to do any substantial mental work—but I'm good until evening with only sightseeing & postcard writing on the pro-gramme. However, when I *do* finally hit the hay it would take an earthquake or fire brigade to bring me back to earth for 8 or 9 hours—or even longer sometimes. I never tried cutting out a *third* night and riding straight to Flori-da, since I couldn't bear to pass through Charleston without stopping there. That's the town of all towns for me! As for revision—I hate it venomously, & am more exhausted by it than by anything else. I wish to Gawd I never had to see a page of it again!

No more Poe acrostics to date—but after the existing specimens are printed there may be further echoes. Have I the estate's permission to send the late Mr. Kuttner's lines to a fan magazine, or did he dispose of them him-self before his sinister vanishment? About "Nemesis"—it is a longish piece of my own verse, published in WT back around 1924. Of all my metrical effu-sions, it is probably the least lousy. Wish I had a copy outside the magazine to lend. (Have just looked it up. It was April, '24.)

I learn with great interest of the various old California graveyards, & hope that enough may be found of the missing Mr. Kuttner to ensure his in-terment in one or more of them. By the way—has that bottomless, luminous, & upward-flowing lake been dragged? It might reveal much! I'd enjoy Death Valley—one of whose inhabitants, I am told, shivered at a temperature of 110° in the outer world & expressed a wish to get back to a place where one didn't have to wear a coat.

Thanks, by the way, for the loan of the Blavatsky opus—which I shall read with the most intense interest.[4] I've never read any of the classics of the-osophy, though I've always been meaning to. I wonder if anybody has ever tried to isolate the real Oriental folklore in them from the 19th century fakery & interpolations? I may have fumbled that allusion to the Book of Dzyan,[5] since all I know about it is something in a letter of Price's which spoke of the early parts as having been brought from an older solar system than ours. Of course the text ridiculed in the *Necronomicon* is the merest imitation! Speaking of the good old *Necro*—Wright's recent statement was of course made to promote the peace of mind of certain timid readers.[6] A judiciously censored version of whatever history Koenig might write would probably be safe enough for the limited & initiated clientele reached by the Shepherd–Wollheim publications. Incidentally, I am told that a review of a new translation of the *Necro* recently appeared in the newspaper of a small town near New York

City.[7] Shepherd, I think, is duly cautious—& by the way, those remains in the vault at Miskatonic U. Library may be traceable to some influence *other* than the *Necronomicon*. The old Arkham college harbours many strange volumes— & in an early issue of the new *Science-Fantasy Correspondent* you will read of an incident there connected with the monstrous & unmentionable *Ghorl Nigral*.[8]

Now is the season when I'm envying you your climate! The autumn here, however, was not of the most extreme severity, & my occasional outings extended over the line into November. As I possibly mentioned last month, I succeeded in discovering several splendid rural regions within a 3-mile radius of here which I had never seen before. One is a wooded hill on the western rim of the town, whence a series of marvellous views of the outspread city & adjacent countryside may be obtained. I had often ascended it before, but the exquisitely mystical sylvan scenery beyond the crest—curious mounds, hummocked pastures, & hushed, hidden valleys—was wholly new to me. Oct. 20 & 21 were phenomenally warm, & I utilised them in exploring another hitherto untapped region down the east shore of Narragansett Bay—finding a highly fascinating forest called the Squantum Woods, where there are great oaks & birches, steep slopes & rock ledges, & marvellous vistas beyond the trees. Our autumn, though, was notably lacking in visual splendour. Half the trees were swept bare by heavy rains as soon as they began to turn, while the other half remained green for an anomalous length of time—the leaves then falling almost as soon as they did turn.

I don't think I've ever seen "The Creeper in the Crypt",[9] but shall look for it in W T. "The Shadow over Innsmouth" has at last appeared—with 33 misprints.[10] The one good thing about the book is the set of Utpatel illustrations.

Alas, my lives are rapidly being used up. Since I began this epistle I've received from young J. Vernon Shea (a bright chap—his address, in case you'd like to exchange fantasy ideas with him, is Halter Apts., #3, 4779 Liberty Ave., Pittsburgh, Penna.) a new tale called "The Necronomicon",[11] in which I am minutely described & left as a clean-picked skeleton. Shea also reminds me that Bloch has killed me off *twice* (leaving a hog-snouted, taloned Thing where I ought to be in the second instance)—the last time in "The Dark Demon".[12] Only four more lives left, then!

Snow as early as Nov. 24—quite a record even for this subarctic hell! Not a very pleasing augury for the winter! Possibly I shall freeze to death once or twice before the hellish season is over, thus cutting down my quota of lives still more dangerously. In one of my early "pomes" I summarised winter with considerable sincerity if less than classic eloquence, as:

> "The mad time of unreason,
>     The brain-numbing days
> When winter, white-sheeted & ghastly, stalks onward to torture & craze."[13]

By the way—I pulled another pome the other day in writing Finlay. He had lamented the decline of the days when (as in the Renaissance & the 18th century) people wrote versified tributes to one another's work, so I prepared some prosodical comment on his splendid "Faceless God" picture, just to shew him that the 18th century lived in me. Here's the result:

TO MR. FINLAY
UPON HIS DRAWING FOR MR. BLOCH'S
TALE, "THE FACELESS GOD"

In dim Abyſſes pulse the Shapes of Night,
　　Hungry and hideous, with ſtrange Mitres crown'd;
Black Pinions beating in phantaſtick Flight
　　From Orb to Orb thro' ſunleſs Voids profound.
None dares to name the Coſmos whence they course,
　　Or gueſs the Look on each amorphous Face,
Or ſpeak the Words that with reſiſtleſs Force
　　Wou'd draw them from the Hells of outer Space.

Yet here upon a Page our frighten'd Glance
　　Finds monſtrous Forms no human eye ſhou'd ſee;
Hints of thoſe Blaſphemies whoſe Countenance
　　Spreads Death and Madneſs thro' Infinity.
What Limner he who braves black Gulphs alone
And lives to make their alien Horrors known?

Speaking of the 18th century—anachronisms concerning it are painfully numerous. One instance that vastly pained me was in the story "The Album"[14] in the Dec. W T. Here we had a tacit assumption that successful photography existed in the 18th century (actually, nothing like a permanent photograph existed before Niepce's achievement of 1814), & an absurd lot of gibberish supposed to be a warning written in the late 18th century. That piece of supposed 18th century English is a pathetic thing—as bad as some of the kindred anachronisms of W H Hodgson & Seabury Quinn. What gets into these birds? Haven't they read Gibbon & Goldsmith & Boswell & Johnson & the Declaration of Independence? The 18th century is fairly recent, & yet they drag down from the remoter reaches of antiquity a cobwebbed jargon more Chaucerian or Elizabethan than anything else, & serve it up as the living speech of the 1700's! Actually, that message in "The Album" should have run something like this:

To Whomsoever may Open This Book

This is set down as a Warning to you, Sir or Madam, that you are not to open this Book beyond the Place mark'd by a red Riband. It wou'd be better for you to throw the whole Book unopen'd into the Fire; but being unable to do so myſelf, I cannot hope that you will. I do nevertheleſs adjure you to look nowhere in it beyond the Riband, leſt you loſe yourſelf to this World, Body & Soul; for truly, it is a Tomb for the Living.

Well—pray let me know if anything (anything, that is, which the human brain can bear) is heard of your missing client Kuttner.

Yours by the Outer Void,

E'ch-Pi-El

## Notes

1. Note by Henry Kuttner: "This particular letter requires some explanation, I think, in order to appreciate fully Lovecraft's whimsical humor. In my preceding letter, which was written on Halloween night after finishing the story—'Hydra'—to which this letter refers, I ended jokingly with a semi-frantic scrawl to the effect that 'they' were creeping up on me. I typed a postscript by one 'Bolivar Twirp' declaring that I had unaccountably disappeared, and that my letter was being sent along to HPL."

2. "Through the Gates of the Silver Key." HPL had earlier used that pseudonym for some poems published in the amateur press.

3. HPL refers to Leo Margulies (1900–1975) and Mort Weisinger (1915–1978), who edited many pulp magazines in the weird, detective, and science fiction fields, including *Thrilling Mystery, Thrilling Wonder Stories,* and *Startling Stories.*

4. Helena Petrovna Blavatsky (1831–1891), founder of theosophy. The book may have been *The Secret Doctrine* (1888). HPL probably did not read it.

5. HPL refers to the mention of the *Book of Dzyan* in "The Haunter of the Dark." In referring to this and other "forbidden" books, HPL notes: "They were the black, forbidden things which most sane people have never even heard of, or have heard of only in furtive, timorous whispers; the banned and dreaded repositories of equivocal secrets and immemorial formulae which have trickled down the stream of time from the days of man's youth, and the dim fabulous days before man was" (*CF* 3.460). Blavatsky claimed that *The Secret Doctrine* was based on ancient esoteric Tibetan writings, but the claim has been subject to debate. See letter 214 to CAS in *Dawnward Spire.*

6. *WT* (December 1936) contained a letter by one Arthur Mink, inquiring whether the *Necronomicon* was a real book, to which Farnsworth Wright appended the following: "The *Necronomicon,* that book by the mad Arab Abdul Alhazred, so often referred to by WT writers, is part of the Lovecraft mythology, being a fictional invention of H. P. Lovecraft's fertile brain.—The Editor" (p. 636).

7. Donald A. Wollheim's spoof "review" of the *Necronomicon* appeared under the "Book Chats" column of the *Branford Review and East Haven News* 8, No. 24 (12 September 1935): 7; rpt. *Lovecraft at Last* 102–3. In *Lovecraft Annual* No. 9 (2015): 218–20.

8. An imaginary book conceived by Willis Conover. It does not appear that any story involving it appeared in Conover's fanzine, the *Science-Fantasy Correspondent.*

9. Robert Bloch (*WT,* July 1937).

10. Cf. HPL to John J. Weir (31 December 1936; ms., private collection): "There are about 50 errors in Crawford's edition of my 'Innsmouth'. I found about 35, but the

eagle-eyed Stickney spotted (too late, alas, for the printed list of errata!) many that I had overlooked." HPL lamented that even the errata sheet contained several misprints.

11. Published many years later in *Dragon & Microchips: Le Seul Fanzine Qui Rêve*.

12. *WT*, November 1936.

13. From HPL's "The City" (1919).

14. By Amelia Reynolds Long.

[11]    [Trans., WHS]

The Ancient Hill
February 8, 1937.

Dear Khut-N'hah:—

I was pleased to see your Mooney-illustrated story in the Feby. W T, & liked the touch of originality at the end. Mooney did very well with the picture. Haven't had time to read all of Jan. & Feb. W T as yet, so can't report on the Quinn opus. I did read Two-Gun's yarn, & liked it despite a certain stiffness & immaturity. Comte d'Erlette did very well in giving the old "beast with five fingers" idea a new twist. In the Jan. issue your "Eater of Souls" has some good touches, while Rimel makes a very auspicious professional debut. There is also a certain convincing atmosphere about the somewhat amateurish "Kobold's Keep". I was vastly pleased with Finlay's illustration to "Doorstep"[1]—and rejoice that Wright has honoured me with the originals of that & the "Haunter" design . . . which far surpass the cuts.

As for the Ghorl Nigral—it is a very hellish tome by a sinister German scholar,[2] but you'll have to apply to young Conover for details concerning it. The S F C will publish a terrible incident connected with the carefully guarded copy at Miskatonic. Glad the pictures interested you. Barlow surely gives CAS good competition as a sculptor! Regarding the windowless side of my ancient & crumbling dwelling . . . silence is indeed the best policy. It is only occasionally that any *fumes* escape. Here's another hour's work for you—mistakes not covered by the printed list of errata:

> p. 27, l. 13—period instead of comma after *Innsmouth*.
> p. 36, l. 9—insert *l* in *explained*
> p. 39, l. 4—for "fiinally" read *finally*
> p. 42, l. 5—for "house" read *houses*
> Correction given as for "p. 115, l. 11" should be for *p. 120, l. 11*
> p. 132, l. 2—for "croaakng" read *croaking*
> p. 141, l. 17—for "dilusion" read *delusion*

Most of these were spotted by the eagle-eyed young Corwin Stickney, printer of the S F C. Yes, before long I expect to see Klarkash-Ton's hellish casts. Glad you've heard from Shea—who is certainly quite a home-grown critic.

The accounts of cold weather—epistolary & journalistic—made me shudder in sympathy. CAS also spoke of the Pacific Coast's hellish visitation. The weird rain effects, though, must have been worth watching. The first half of our winter was exceptionally warm—temperatures sometimes in the 60's well into January. Some early exposures to the cold, however, put me rather in the bum—bringing out my usual winter malady of mountainously swollen feet. Added to this is a digestive disturbance & general weakness which may form a variant of the prevailing grippe. Still, it hasn't had me down as yet, & I get out for brief neighbourhood walks whenever the temperature is high enough. But I certainly would give a good deal to be in Key West or the West Indies right now!

At this point I must acknowledge, with the most appreciative obiesances, the honour paid me in the composition of your recent & extremely clever acrostic.[3] All apart from its ingenuity, this piece is really a splendid specimen of bizarre suggestion & imagery; & I'm glad it has found a niche in the appropriate publication. Again, my thanks & genuflections.

Glad to hear that you & C L M are collaborating on a dual masterpiece. The result certainly ought to be powerful enough! Staging a meeting betwixt the mediaeval Jirel & the future Northwest Smith will call for some of your most adroit time-juggling—but with two keen imaginations at work no obstacle is likely to be insurmountable.[4] Good luck to both of you aesthetically & financially! Bloch tells me that Satrap Pharnabeezer has looked favourably upon the revised "Black Kiss"[5] after his long vacillations. Good!

I trust your Yuletide was pleasant. Ours here was commendably festive—including a turkey dinner at the boarding-house across the garden, with a congenial cat meandering among the tables & finally jumping upon the window-seat for a nap. We had a tree in front of the hearth in the living-room—its verdant boughs thickly festooned with a tinsel imitation of Florida's best Spanish moss, & its outlines emphasised by a not ungraceful lighting system. Around its base were ranged the Saturnalian gifts—which included (on my side) a hassock tall enough to let me reach the top shelves of my bookcases, & (on my aunt's side) a cabinet of drawers for odds & ends, not unlike my own filing cabinets, but of more ladylike arrangement & aspect. Of outside gifts one of the most distinctive was perhaps that which came quite unexpectedly from young Conover—for lo! when I had removed numberless layers of corrugated paper & excelsior, what should I find before me but the yellowed & crumbling fragments of *a long-interred human skull!* Verily, a fitting tribute from a youthful ghoul to one of the hoary elders of the necropolitan clan! This sightlessly staring monument of mortality came from an Indian mound not far from the sender's home on the Maryland Eastern Shore—a place distinguished by many archaeological exploits on the part of the enterprising editor & his young friends. Its condition is such as to make its reassembling a somewhat ticklish task—so that I may reserve it for the ministrations of some expert mender like Barlow upon the occasion of a future visit. Viewing this shattered yield of the ossuary, the reflective fancy strives to evoke the image of him to whom it once belonged. Was it some feathered chieftain who in his day oft ululated in triumph as he counted the tufted scalps sliced from coppery or colonist foes? Or some crafty shaman who with mask & drum called forth from the Great Abyss those shadowy Things which were better left uncalled? This we may never know—unless perchance some incantation droned out of the pages of the Necronomicon will have power to draw strange emanations from the lifeless & centuried clay, & raise up amidst the cobwebs of my ancient study a shimmering mist not without power to speak. In such a case, the revelation might be such that no man hearing it could any longer live save as one of those hapless entities "who laugh, but smile no more".[6]

Thanks for the cutting of the Salem cinema,[7] which I shall endeavour to see. If the scenery is good, you'll recognise architectural types from pictures you've seen. Hope it isn't full of discouraging anachronisms.

Just skimmed the March W T. Peirce, Hasse, & Ludvig Prinn seem to carry off the honours.[8]

Yrs by the Carven Eibon,
E'ch-Pi-El

## Notes

1. Henry Kuttner, "I, the Vampire" (*WT,* February 1937; ill. Jim Mooney); Seabury Quinn, either "Children of the Bat" (January 1937) or "The Glove of Memories" (February 1937) [probably the February story]; Robert E. Howard, "Dig Me No Grave" (February 1937); August Derleth, "Glory Hand" (February 1937); Henry Kuttner, "The Eater of Souls," Duane W. Rimel, "The Disinterment," G. Garnet, "The Headless Miller of Kobold's Keep," and HPL, "The Thing on the Doorstep" (January 1937).

2. Willis Conover attributed the book to one Herrmann Mülder.

3. "H. P. L."

4. The result was "Quest of the Starstone."

5. By Bloch and Kuttner (*WT,* June 1937).

6. Poe, "The Haunted Palace," l. 48.

7. Probably *Maid of Salem* (Paramount, 1937), directed by Frank Lloyd; starring Claudette Colbert, Fred MacMurray, and Harvey Stephens.

8. Earl Peirce, Jr., "The Last Archer"; Henry Hasse, "The Guardian of the Book"; Robert Bloch, "The Brood of Bubastis."

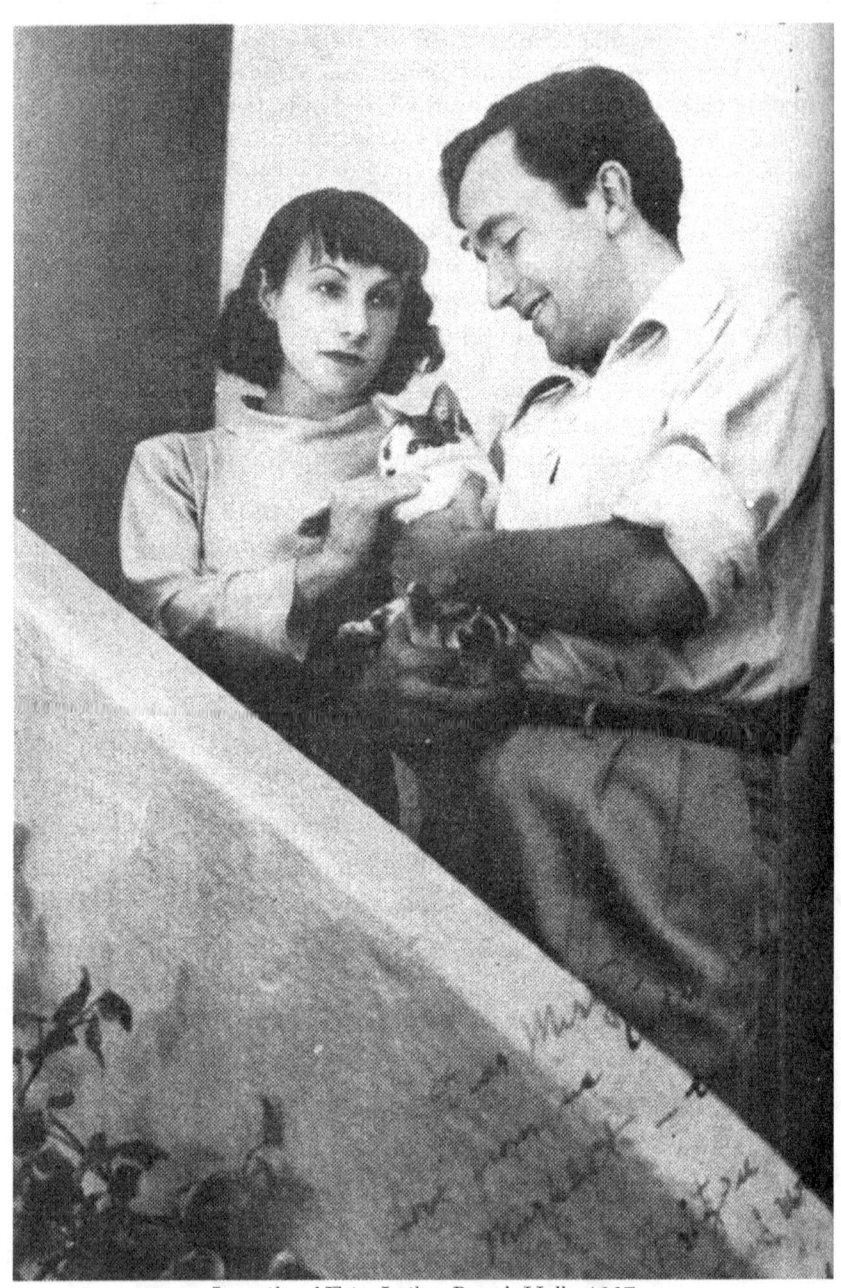

*Jonquil and Fritz Leiber, Beverly Hells, 1937*

# Letters to Fritz and Jonquil Leiber

[1]     To Jonquil Leiber [AHT]

66 College St.
Providence, R.I.,
Nov. 2, 1936.

My dear Mrs. Leiber:—

Your enquiry of Oct. 14, after some extremely devious wanderings, has reached me at last; & I must hasten to say how gratified I am to hear of the kind opinion of my fictional efforts held by you & your husband. My pleasure is the greater because of the admiration & appreciation with which I have always regarded the work of your father-in-law. In the earlier years of the century I saw him many times in Mr. Robert Mantell's[1] companies—in parts like Horatio, Iago, Mercutio, Bassanio, Edmund, & Faulconbridge—& delighted in his happy blending of classic traditionalism with the more refined & modulated technique of the present. His Faulconbridge was to me especially unforgettable, and I can still recall across the gulf of years his magnificent rendering of those stirring climactic lines (always prime favourites of mine):

> "This ENGLAND never did—nor never shall—
> Lie at the proud foot of a conqueror,
> But when it first did help to wound itself.
> Now these her princes are come home again,
> Come the three corners of the world in arms,
> And we shall shock them. Nought shall make us rue,
> If ENGLAND to itself do rest but true!"[2]

For a quarter of a century I have associated Mr. Leiber Sr.[3] with these lines, & these lines with Mr. Leiber. It surely pleases me profoundly to know that he has a son & namesake to carry on his tradition, & to find that that son regards my own fantastic attempts with a charitable eye!

[. . .]

*Notes*

1. Robert B. Mantell (1854–1928), a heralded Shakespearean stage actor who made several silent films.
2. See CLM 36n2.
3. Fritz Reuter Leiber, Sr. (1882–1949), American Shakespearean stage actor who also had a successful career in film.

[2]    To Fritz Leiber, Jr. [AHT]

Nov. 9, 1936

My dear Mr. Leiber:—

[. . .] Needless to say, your closely analytical remarks on my fiction gratify me immensely—doubly so because your singling out of specific points indicates that I have in certain cases more or less done what I was trying to do. It is vastly encouraging when anyone recognises as clearly as you do the *special direction* of my attempts—the wish to capture some phase of the mystery & terror clinging round the eternal presence & pressure of *the outside* . . . . The mentally & materially inaccessible gulfs of boundless space whose alien worlds & alien laws & values can never be known to us, & amidst which our earth & solar system & galaxy & conceivable cosmos may form the most negligible, untypical, transient, & diseased speck. I am tempted to quote from an old article of mine on Supernatural Horror in Literature—where I define my idea of what a weird story must be if it is to form any sort of a serious aesthetic attempt:

"The true weird tale has something more than secret murder, bloody bones, or a sheeted form clanking chains according to rule. A certain atmosphere of breathless and unexplainable dread of outer, unknown forces must be present; and there must be a hint, expressed with a seriousness and portentousness becoming its subject, of that most terrible conception of the human brain—a malign and particular suspension or defeat of those fixed laws of nature which are our only safeguard against the assaults of chaos and the daemons of unplumbed space."

I wish there were a really first-rate writer able & willing to do what I keep on stumblingly attempting—and I am always looking hopefully for the appearance of such. What I miss in Machen, James, Dunsany, de la Mare, Shiel, & even Blackwood & Poe, is a sense of the *cosmic*. Dunsany—though he seldom adopts the darker & more serious approach—is the most cosmic of them all, but he gets only a little way. Another lack which I constantly feel is that of *realism* or *convincing seriousness*. That is, the average weird author is essentially superficial & frivolous in his purpose. He wishes merely to entertain, instead of to reflect potently & artistically those deep-seated human instincts & moods which create & centre around the persistent illusion of violated natural law. Again let me quote from one of my articles—this time a more recent one.

"Atmosphere, not action, is the thing to cultivate in the wonder story. We cannot put stress on the bare *events*, since the unnatural extravagance of these events makes them sound hollow and absurd when thrown into too high relief. Such events, even when theoretically possible or conceivable in the future (as those of a science-fiction tale), have no counterpart or basis in existing life and human experience, hence can never form the groundwork of an adult tale. All that a marvel story can ever be, in a serious way, is *a vivid picture of a certain type of human mood*. The moment it tries to be anything else it becomes cheap, puerile, and unconvincing. Therefore a fantastic author should see that his prime emphasis goes into subtle suggestion—the imperceptible hints and touches of selective and associative detail which express shadings of moods and build up a vague illusion of the strange reality of the unreal—instead of into bald catalogues of incredible happenings which can have no substance or meaning apart from a sustaining cloud of colour and mood-symbolism. A serious adult story must be *true to something in life*. Since marvel tales cannot be true to the *events* of life, they must shift their emphasis toward something to which they *can* be true; namely, certain wistful or restless *moods* of the human spirit, wherein it seeks to weave gossamer ladders of escape from the galling tyranny of time, space, and natural law."[1]

The writer who comes closest toward creating these (as I view them) reasonable specifications is Algernon Blackwood *in his best moments*. He actually analyses & reproduces faithfully the details of the persistent human illusion of—& out-reaching toward—a misty world of vari-coloured wonders, transcended natural laws, limitless possibilities, delighted discoveries, & ceaseless adventurous expectancy. But he labours under three severe handicaps—an undistinguished journalistic style, a recurrent tendency to lapse into mushy sentimentality & infantile namby-pambyism of the most painful sort, & a credulousness regarding "occultism" which causes him to employ now & then a professional mediumistic jargon of woefully weakening effect. Of all Blackwood's voluminous output, only a golden minimum represents him at his best—but that is such a marvellous best that we can well forgive him all his slush & prattle. It is my firm opinion that his longish short story "The Willows" is the greatest weird tale ever written (with Machen's "The White People" as a good second.) Little is said—everything is suggested! Of his books, "Incredible Adventures", "John Silence", & "The Centaur" form the cream—though "Julius LeVallon" & the juvenile "Jimbo" are not to be despised. But heaven deliver us from crap like "The Extra Day", "The Wave", & (ugh!) "The Garden of Survival"! Next to Blackwood, Poe stands first in basic seriousness & convincingness—though his themes tend to centre in limited manifestations of the terrestrially gruesome, & in sinister twists of morbid human psychology. In *total effect* he probably *transcends* Blackwood, & indeed all rivals; that is, what he *does* tell is told with a potent art & daemonic force which no one else can even approach. One of my favourites is M. P. Shiel, whose "House of Sounds" is a marvellous tour de force comparable to its obvious Poesque prototype "The Fall of the House of Usher". The first half of Shiel's novel "The Purple Cloud" is also a veritably stupendous piece of work.

As for style & realism—I'm glad you think well of my stuff in that respect. I've always held two cardinal principles regarding weird fiction: that the structure & rhythm of the language should reflect & promote the tension, menace, gloom, dreamlike quality, cumulative mood-flow & climactic suspense of the theme; & that an air of absolute realism should be preserved (as if one were preparing an actual hoax instead of a story) *except* in the one limited field where the writer has chosen to depart (in a way consistent with actual human psychology & illusion as reflected in experience & folklore) from the order of objective reality. I haven't always succeeded in embodying these principles to the extent I'd like, but at least I've tried to do so. Commercial "pulp" fiction repudiates them altogether—glibly piling on extravagant marvels without the least relation to mankind's natural myth-making tendencies, & phrasing everything in a brisk, happy, casual, cheerful style which would be enough to kill even a good idea or plot! It is too bad that no magazine market for seriously intended weird fiction exists. One must either make the book good (which I can't) or be satisfied to have things in the pulp rags—whose editors accept a really serious story more in spite of its real merits than because of them. I see red every time I think of the number of finely-endowed fantaisistes who have been lured away from sincere writing by the rewards of the commercial magazine market. Most of them soon become so steeped in the cheap methods, puerile psychology, shoddy values, & stock characters & events of popular thrillerdom that they could never "come back" as serious literary artists even if they wished. The salient example of this kind of thing is of course *A. Merritt*—of "Moon Pool" fame. Azathoth, what a genius gone wrong! Today dishing out the usual sort of formula-tripe—yet now & then revealing flashes of descriptive or evocative power which tell the sort of titan he might have been had he elected to follow the path of Machen or de la Mare instead of that of the *Argosy* hacks!

    [. . .] I'm glad the geographical colour in some of my tales seems to ring true—as it ought to, since I was born less than a mile from this spot & have lived hereabouts all my life save for a trivial two-year period in New York City. The realistic side of me has always tended to soak up local atmosphere, & I think it's well to keep true to the characteristics of a region even when the place-names are fictitious. I like a solid, definite, visualisable, and even identifiable background behind certain types of weird fiction. In the "Haunter of the Dark" I accurately described my own abode (the old Georgian house on the hill), the westward view from my doesk window (I'm looking at that darkly-looming church right now—though I regret to say it lost its spire through a lightning-stroke last summer),[2] the general layout of Federal Hill, & various minor Providentiana. However—Arkham, Miskatonic University, Kingsport, Innsmouth, Dunwich, & certain other oft-mentioned localities (as well as poor old Abdul & his hideous *Al Azif* which the Byzantine monk Theodorus Philetas translated into Greek circa 900 A.D. as Το Νεκρονομικον are of the bubble or boil-like nature of those lands you have dreamed about—these places having slight & harmless intrusions on Massachusetts geography. Roughly speaking, "Innsmouth" (an exaggeration of quaint decaying *Newburyport*) is supposed to be on the marshy coast a bit south of the real Newburyport. "Arkham" (an idealisation of *Salem* plus a wholly gratuitous college) is a good deal south of that—a few miles inland up the imaginary river "Miskatonic", but not as far inland as Ipswich & Essex. "Kingsport" (a "stepped-up" reflection of ancient & fascinating *Marblehead*) is at the mouth of this imaginary river—bearing about the same relation to "Arkham" as that borne by the real Marblehead to the real Salem. "Dunwich" is far inland—near the headwaters of the mythical "Miskatonic". It is a sort of synthesis of the picturesquely retrograding Wilbraham country (near Springfield) with certain characteristics of southern Vermont. I have always been fond of maps & geographical details (I've drawn a map of "Arkham" to keep my local references straight), & my lifelong antiquarianism has caused me to lay zestful stress on historic backgrounds & traditional architectural minutiae. My one real avocation & hobby is the imaginative pursuit of the past—especially of the 18th century, to which I have a curious sense of inextricably belonging—& my chief avenue of century-spanning is the architectural. My supreme joy is to visit old cities where rich deposits of early architecture remain. I have never been to Europe (for ill-health in youth & bad finances in later life have severely circumscribed my travels), but I *have* managed to see—& absorb from the point of view of comparative architecture & antiquities—most of this continent's venerable cities from Quebec on the north to St. Augustine & Key West on the south & New Orleans & Natchez on the west. *Charleston* is probably my favourite of all cities.

I note your reference to the late Charles Fort—some of whose books I have read with extreme interest. I don't think his scraps of bizarre reporting made out much of a case against accepted science, but I do tremendously admire the zeal & consistency of his delvings. He makes magnificent weird source-material! As for *melancholy*—it is indeed, as old Burton realised, a fruitful field for exploration.[3] My own temperament, I should say, is one of *scientific indifferentism* (the solar system is a meaningless drop in an unknown & purposeless cosmos, but what the hell of it?) rather than melancholy—though I suppose my constant interest in fantasy expresses a subconscious dissatisfaction with objective reality which is not far from certain phases of the genuine article. I've always been fascinated, by the way, by that engraving of Dürer's.[4]

Well—I must apologise for this possibly boresome burst of verbosity! But genuine devotees of the weird are rare. I regret the geographical circumstances which postpone oral conversation.[. . .]

## Notes

1. "Some Notes on Interplanetary Fiction" (some portions originally appeared in "Notes on Writing Weird Fiction").

2. St. John's Catholic Church (1871) stood at 352 Atwells Avenue until it was demolished in February 1992.

3. Robert Burton (1577–1640), *The Anatomy of Melancholy* (1621).

4. In 1513–14, Albrecht Dürer (1471–1528) produced three well-known engravings, including *Melencolia I*.

[3]    To Jonquil Leiber [AHT]

Nov. 13, 1936

Dear Mrs. Leiber:—

[. . .] Pray convey my appreciative regards to "the governor" & tell him I shall be on the lookout for those two films. I can imagine how well he must interpret the austere Thomas Jonathan Jackson.[1] As a native of the Mother Land, you would surely be in a position to appreciate his magnificent delivery of that "King John" finale! Those lines—& Mr. Leiber Sr.'s rendering of them—reach me with a certain extra closeness because I am nearer to Old England on the paternal side than is the average Yankee. Whilst my maternal lines are of ancient Rhode-Island stock dwelling hereabouts for the past 2½ to 3 centuries, my own paternal grandfather was born in Devonshire in 1815; reaching these shores only in 1827 when brought by his father after a sort of financial annihilation. And the wife he later married was only one generation from

"This royal throne of kings, this sceptred isle,
This earth of majesty, this seat of Wars,
This other Eden, demi-paradise,
This fortress built by Nature for herself
Against infection & the bond of war,
This happy breed of men, this little world,
This precious stone set in the silver sea,
Which serves it in the office of a wall
Or as a moat defensive to a house,
Against the envy of less happier lands,
This blessed plot, this earth, this realm, this ENGLAND."[2]

Add to this the circumstance the fact that I am a natural-born antiquarian, prone to revel in dreams & pictures of the past & to cherish ancestral things, & one may readily see why it would take much more than a political cleavage a century & a half ago to make me anything but a British colonial at heart! And yet I have never seen Old England, & I do not know whether it will ever be financially possible for me to do so. I envy you the experience of that mouldy castle in Wales—Arthur Machen's enchanted west country "with the ancient woods hanging all about . . . & the wild domed hills, & the ragged land."[3] I long to see the great-boled oaks I dream about, & the grassy ridges that were once Roman roads stretching through the twilight of deep forests.

As for the matter of my years & aspect—I fear the snapshot your husband saw was either very archaic or very flattering. Even "the governor" (who must have realised that an admirer of his old-time Faulconbridge & Edgar could scarcely be a youth today!) underguessed my burthen of greying winters, since as a matter of ruthless fact I shall turn 47 on the 20th of next August. Nearly a semi-centenarian, but with all my teeth, & memory still fairly dependable. The enclosed pair of snaps* (all I can find & rather crude, but betwixt them not wholly unrepresentative) give an idea of the sort of scarecrow I am. I was very glad to hear details of Mr. Leiber's appearance, & hope to gain a pictorial glimpse in the course of time. His combination of physique, features, & genius should carry him far—& I can well imagine the joint pride which you & "the governor" must take in him!

With my best regards to you, & to the Messrs. Leiber junior & senior, [. . .]

*One of them includes my young friend Frank Belknap Long, Jun., whose work in W T you & Mr. L. must know. This reminds me to ask whether your household would care for the loan of a collection of snaps shewing what several of the W T authors look like. I'd be very glad to lend any such an array.

*Notes*

1. Thomas Jonathan "Stonewall" Jackson (1824–1863), a Confederate general during the American Civil War. Fritz Leiber, Sr. played him in the movie *Under Southern Stars* (1937).
2. Shakespeare, *Richard II* 2.1.40–50.
3. From "The Shining Pyramid."

[4]    To Fritz Leiber, Jr. [AHT]

Nov. 15, 1936

My dear Mr. Leiber:—

[. . .] Yes—damn it all!—you are only too correct in deducing that I have not seen your father in his more recent tours as an independent star. I have at times read of his later appearances, but they have never taken place in any city simultaneously with my presence therein. My great grudge against the cinema lies is the havock it has wrought with the stage in all but the largest metropolitan centres. Twenty years ago no company like your father's could possibly have neglected the old Providence Opera House—but today, alas! Indeed, the Opera House was torn down in 1931, & its manager (with a tragic timeliness worthy of the Muse whose temple he had tended) died the following year. Would that some future dispensation might bring a Leiber Lear or Macbeth to one of our still-surviving (if less historic) theatres! My tantalisation at hearing about your father's productions would have been greater had I known that better versions than Mantell's were used. I recall that many used to criticise Mr. Mantell's choice of texts—especially his use of the Cibber "Richard III".[1] (Personally, as a devotee of the 18th century, I forgave that—for what metaphorical periwig-wearer cou'd deem Richard truly himself without such savorous sallies as:

Th' aspiring Youth that fir'd th' Ephesian Dome (in Greek architecture!)
Outlives in Fame the pious Fool that rais'd it.[2]

or

> Hence, babbling Dreams; you threaten here in vain;
> Conscience, avaunt, Richard's himself again!
> Hark! the shrill Trumpet sounds, to Horse, away
> My Soul's in Arms, & eager for the Fray![3]

Certainly, a full or well-edited Lear comes close to forcing the high-water mark of modern (using the adjective in the sense of *non-ancient*) dramas, with its glimpses of the black, sardonic Outside pressing in upon the helpless figures driven before storms both literal & non-literal. Here is the spirit of Aeschylus & Sophocles with something added—& I pity the poor 'debunking' clod who can see in it no more than a petulant dotard backed up by John Dennis's thunder.[4] Not only do the characters & their onrushing fates suggest the background of infinity, but every visual picture contributes to the massed, subtle impression. Man against the Abyss—blind Gloster led up to the edge of the Dover cliffs in a scene which for me conveys the most dizzying picture in all literature . . . . a scene in which your father (& now, I learn, you after him!) spoke those peculiarly potent lines about the crews & choughs & samphire-gatherers. That whole episode of Gloster, blind & deluded (for his own good) as to what is really taking place around him ("Look up a-height—the shrill-song'd lark so far cannot be seen or heard . . . . his eyes were two full means; he had a thousand noses; horns whelk'd, & wav'd like the enridged sea.")[5] is ironically symbolic of man's whole place in the cosmic gulfs. What a picture—a blind old man racked by misery on the edge of a void & helpless to gain even the oblivion he chooses! I was indeed interested to know that you have played Edgar to your father's Lear. Certainly a noble apprenticeship! Speaking of *cutting* Lear—a friend of mine (Samuel Loveman, who now conducts the Bodley Book Shop at 104 Fifth Avenue., N.Y.C.) once went to the opposite extreme & wrote a scene (in diabolically clever Elizabethan language) to be interpolated in the tragedy![6] Taking the view of Sir Joshua Reynolds & Swinburne that Lear actually refers to the Fool & not to Cordelia (a view which seems doubtful, but which is at least interesting) when he says "And my poor fool is hang'd", Loveman invents a scene which in the play would break up the concluding scene somewhere betwixt the departure of Lear & Cordelia under guard & the subsequent entry of Lear bearing his dead daughter—a scene laid in the forest near the British camp, in which the Fool is brought in as a captive & killed in the presence of Lear & Cordelia, & in which Cordelia is killed before her father's eyes. Lear then departs with Cordelia's body, ready to reappear in the text proper with his memorable lines of anguish. A carping critic might pick flaws in this interpolation—but I would feel proud indeed if I could re-create the Elizabethan atmosphere as well. Loveman also did an interpolated scene for Macbeth—which I had the honour of publishing 15 or 16 years ago when I edited the official organ of the United Amateur Press Association.[7] It pleases me very much to know that

Faulconbridge was one of your father's favourite parts—indeed, I might have imagined it from the glow & spirit with which he delivered those memorable final lines. Your own very juvenile handling of the role—or parts of it—must at least have been picturesque—like the performance of the three-year-old hopeful of an English-teacher friend of mine, whose fond papa once discovered him (at a time when "Macbeth" was much under discussion in the household) with an ornate paper-knife (for he had a literal mind!) declaiming very gravely:

> "Ith dith a dagger w'ich I thee before me,
> De han'le toward muh hand? Tum, let me tlut de!"[8]

It has always seemed to me that Faulconbridge is the *principal* character in "King John"—at least, I must say that it is the one which makes the most impression on me. The bluff, wholesome impudence ("And hang a calf's skin on those recreant limbs!")[9] of the youth stands out notably amidst the welter of subtleties & villainies, & he leaves more of a concrete picture with the spectators than does the subtle, moody monarch—pathos, death, & all. At least, with a goodly number of the spectators, whatever be the judgment of the profound & sensitive critic. The least that can be said of Faulconbridge is that it is a nearly *equal* part—like Iago to Othello, or Antony to Brutus.

But I wander far from the weird! Let me return by saying how thoroughly I agree with you regarding Spengler's distinction betwixt the "Faustian" or modern western sense of infinity (which begins with a clearer idea of, & interest in, one's orientation in time & space) & the classical localism & lack of a time-sense. Spengler, I may add, produced a profound impression upon me when I first encountered him a decade ago[10]—and this despite my inability to endorse completely his view of a culture as a quasi-biological organism. His pointing out of the modern time-&-space consciousness as opposed to the Hellenic indifference to long cycles and sequences (when did the Greeks ever think of their world as a momentary dot in an endless line or curve? What mind was it which created conflicts of data in its leading myths, & established as fixed chronological relationships betwixt such cycles of events as the Seven against Thebes, Trojan War, &c. &c.?) gave me almost a *shock,* because it revealed so great a streak of the non-classical in myself, who have always felt so closely akin to the Graeco-Roman as opposed to the mediaeval. Of course I had always recognised my taste for Gothic mystery & shadow as something Northern & definitely *outside* my classic intellectual orientation; but I had not previously felt that this taste was so antithetically *opposed* to the foundations of classicism, & that my fascinated preoccupation with the element of *time* was *so much more than accidentally* differentiated from Hellenic timelessness. Yet I could not help being convinced & impressed—even at the cost of admitting that a dominant part of my personality was non-classical & even anti-classical.

Incidentally, this admission involves a sharp cleavage rather than a contradiction, since the purely philosophic side of me—plus a large amount of the aesthetic side—certainly *is* classical. I am a complete materialist in belief—of the line of the Ionians, Leucippus, Democritus, Epicurus, & Lucretius, & such moderns (Hobbes, Condillac, Comte, Dewey, Bertrand Russell, Santayana) as derive from this source. I abhor the mediaeval spirit of faith, dogma, & intellectual mysticism (how weary the exalters of the "great" 13th century—Cram, Chesterton, Belloc, et al.—make me!), & value as man's choicest possession the Greek spirit of free, sceptical enquiry. Moreover, in architecture (the art to which, apart from literature, I am most sensitive), decoration, sculpture & pictorial representation, my tastes run overwhelmingly to the Graeco-Roman (with, however, a parallel fondness for really *fine* Gothic design) & its Renaissance derivations. ("Functional" modernism nauseates me & makes me see red!) All this is joined to a curious *sense of identification* with classic *Rome* .... a psychological twist which a superstitious person would attribute to metempsychosis or something of the sort. This feeling—which runs parallel to my still stronger sense of identification with the 18th century, is independent of any intellectual appraisal of Rome on my part. I know damn well that Roman culture was infinitely inferior to its Hellenic source, & can even understand Spengler's passionate indictment of the Respublica .... yet not for a second can I emotionally grasp any human event anterior to 500 A.D. except through Roman eyes. Greece is "our" province of Achaia. The Orient is the scene of "our" Mithridatic wars. Egypt is the province which fell to "us" after Actium, & so on. When I run up against a person with a strong anti-Roman bias—like the late Robert E. Howard, who championed the northern barbarians—I feel an almost personal affront. I have not a drop of non-British blood, yet as I cast my fancy backward through time there comes a point when my blood-allegiance breaks, and my sense of identification & quasi-patriotism shifts from the Thames to the Tiber. In a conflict like that of the Saltus Teutobergiensis in A.D. 9 my instinct is not to exult with my blood-kinsman Arminius but to weep like Augustus for the lost legions of Quinctilius Varus. Naturally all this gives me a tremendous & particular interest in *Roman Britain,* where my two personalities, ancient & modern, meet. To think of a forum in London, of a Roman amphitheatre in Caerleon, & of the Respublica's roads & villas & camps & temples all over my ancestral soil, is intensely & peculiarly gratifying to me. The summit of my delight was reached when I read in the works of the late Arthur Weigall & other recent authorities that evidence now seems to point to the survival of vast amounts of Britanno-Roman & Roman legionary blood (largely Nordic, though, since the army was recruited most numerously in Gallia & Germania) in modern English veins. Thus it became a virtually literal certainty that blood forbears of mine have spoken Latin, worn togas, & borne names like C. Ulpius Silvanus, L. Valerius Celsus, P. Vicius Marcianus, A. Aufidius Olussa, L. Martius Senecianus (I quote from actual Britanno-Roman stelae) & so on. What a drama is that of Roman Britain—Britannia Prima et Secunda—& its slow crumbling before the Teutonic onrush! The forts of the "Saxon shore" (some still standing!)—the naval battles & massacres—the withdrawal of support from Rome—the gradual attrition & the heroic stands—Artorius, the Comes Britanniae ("King Arthur")—the final fight of Aurelius Candidanus at Durham in 582 A.D.—Ædepol! I don't wonder that Machen reverts again & again to the Britanno-Roman background motif! But I digress. In spite of all this sense of classic identification, I must admit the parallel presence of the opposite element—the feeling of nearness to the great Abyss which my hypothetical ancestors Ulpius Silvanus & Valerius Celsus never had—or having, derived from their Teutono-Celtic tribal stream & not from their acquired Roman culture. You repeat almost verbatim something I have many times pointed out when you speak of the function of religion in assuaging Nordic mankind's impatience of temporal & spatial bounds during ages of belief—& of the need of some substitute when supernatural belief declines. The fact is, I have again & again driven home this point in repelling the charge of inconsistency levelled at me for being a complete agnostic & materialist on the intellectual side, & a confirmed fantaisiste & myth-weaver on the aesthetic side. I have told my critics that in all probability the reason I *want* to write about circumventions of time, space, & natural law is that I *don't* believe in such! If I *believed* in the supernatural, I would not need to create the aesthetic illusion of belief. Indeed, the supernatural would not seem strange & fascinating to me. I am preoccupied with the invention of a desired thing which I can get *only* through invention. And as for the desire itself—the need to imagine a mastery of the cosmos & a satisfied curiosity anent the black outer voids—I am willing to acknowledge its alienage to the classic stream, & its characteristic position in modern western civilisation as a legacy of the northern blood side—the same Teutonic side which bequeathed us our major political principles & our tacit adoption of the *honour* (= pride in the open dealing of a strong, free man) concept in opposition to the ostensibly accepted (& really Hebraic) divine-will-&-justice concept as a primary motive in ethics.

Your remarks on my favourite writers interest me vastly, & as you now see, form an enlightening commentary on the parallel remarks in my own previous letter. Machen is a master of hints, & certainly holds the true cosmic concept in the back of his consciousness (I'll never forget that pillar raised by Flavius Senilis to Nodens, *Lord of the Great Abyss*),[11] but he was unfortunately strongly affected by the 1890-ism & Stevenson romantic tradition of his youth. He loves stylistic effects & melodramatic climaxes; & now & then his use of coincidence, & of jaunty Victorian mannerisms, vitiates what might otherwise be well-nigh perfect. Then too, as you remark, he is often a bit hasty in having things thrown terrifically into the flames after the merest glance! "The White People" needs no excuses. Even before one read Miss Murray's

"Witch Cult in Western Europe" it is disquieting; after such reading, it is diabolical. Or perhaps different temperaments would receive it differently in relation to a knowledge of the anthropological background—some finding its cosmic & sinister implications more profound in the *absence* of specific data about sabbats, estbats, & the like. Anyhow, it's a magnificent evocation of shadows from the abyss. Nowhere else, I think, have I ever seen a *landscape* so endowed with sentient evil as that series of fields through which the child advances toward the ancient wood. That picture—or phantasmagoria—haunts my memory even now. One can envisage meadows like that as meeting-places of the known & the black unknown … like the remote Scottish island in John Buchan's "Skule Skerry"—"Insula Avium quae est ultima insula *et proxima Abysso*."[12] If I could ever create a landscape like Machen's—or an island like the new Lord Tweedsmuir's—I'd consider that I hadn't written in vain! I think I said that I regard "The White People" as the second-greatest weird story ever written—with Blackwood's "Willows" alone ahead of it.

Your analysis of Blackwood really coincides with my own—though perhaps I am a little more sympathetic toward his serious treatment of the anatomy of our emotional out-reaching toward unreality. I agree that this treatment tends to lose effectiveness when it becomes *visibly scientific* or mixed up with the jargon of occultism—the old Lodge & Doyle & Flammarion & Chevreuil & Richet stuff.[13] But when this acute analysis is concealed—or manifested only in the description of sensations & events (as in "The Willows" & certain of the "Incredible Adventures" … yea, in "The Centaur" as well, though the *length* of this latter verges on tediousness)—the result is difficult to surpass. Blackwood's discouraging unevenness is his curse. It is fatally easy to misjudge him if one first approaches him through his pseudo-occult chronicles or his infantile sentimental slop. But taking "The Willows", "Incredible Adventures", "The Centaur", the tales (except the first & last) in "John Silence", & such occasional shorts as "The Wendigo", we find a body of weird writing whose authentic power proclaims its creator a master no matter what else he has perpetrated!

Dunsany has a peculiar appeal for me. Casual and tenuous though any one of his fantastic flights may seem, the massed effect of his whole cycle of theogony, myth, legend, fable, hero-epic & dream-chronicle on my consciousness is that of a most potent & particular sort of cosmic liberation. When I first encountered him (through "A Dreamer's Tales") in 1919 he seemed like a sort of gate to enchanted worlds of childhood dream, & his temporary influence on my own literary attempts (vide "Celephaïs", "The Doom That Came to Sarnath", "The Quest of Iranon", "The White Ship", &c) was enormous. Indeed, my own mode of expression almost lost itself for a time amidst a wave of imitated Dunsanianism. There seemed to me to be in Dunsany certain poetic adumbrations of the cosmic lacking elsewhere. I may have read some of them in myself, but am sure that a goodly number must have been there to start with. Dunsany knows a certain type of dream & long-ing and vague out-reaching natural to the Nordic mind & shaped in child-hood by the early folklore and literary impressions afforded by our culture—the Germanic fairy-tale, the Celtic legend, the Biblical myth, the Arabian-Nightish Orientale, the Graeco-Roman epic, and so on. This vision or long-ing or out-reaching he is able to crystallise in terms of certain elements drawn from all these simple & familiar sources, & the result has an odd universal magic which few can deny. The philosophy behind his work is essentially that of the finer minds of our age—a cosmic disillusion plus a desperate effort to retain those fragments of wonder & myth of significance, direction, & pur-pose which intellectual progress & absorption in material things alike tend to strip away. Of course Dunsany is uneven, & his later work (despite the differ-ent sort of charm in "The Curse of the Wise Woman") cannot be compared with his early productions. As he gained in age & sophistication, he lost in freshness & simplicity. He was ashamed to be uncritically naive, & began to step aside from his tales & visibly smile at them even as they unfolded. In-stead of remaining what the true fantaisiste must be—a child in a child's world of dream—he became anxious to show that he was really an adult good-naturedly pretending to be a child in a child's world. This hardening-up began to show, I think, in "The Book of Wonder"—say around 1910. It was very perceptible in "The Last Book of Wonder"—though it did not creep in-to the plays so soon. A decade later it relaxed slightly in the novels "Chroni-cles of Rodriguez" and "The King of Elfland's Daughter", but it shews at its worst in the "Jorkens" tripe. Alas that no writer can ever keep up to the level of his best! When I think of Dunsany, it is in terms of "The Gods of the Mountain", "Bethmoora", "Poltarnees, Beholder of Ocean", "The City of Never", "The Fall of Babbulkund", "In the Land of Time", and "Idle Days on the Yann".

"The Worm Ouroboros" is indeed a familiar friend & cherished posses-sion of mine. What a chronicle of dream! When it was first circulated around 1927 half our gang were swearing great oaths by Koshtra Pivrarcha! Some may think the interest flags in spots, but it does not flag for me. It leaves the same massed impression of a gateway to dream (though I do think the sup-posed setting on Mercury is a bit clumsy) that the best works of Dunsany leaves. Eddie has written other things—a Norse saga called "Styrbion the Strong", & a very recent social allegory of some sort which I haven't seen. But never again has he struck the heights of Ouroboros. Koshtra Pivrarcha, alas, can be scaled only once!

You are right in remarking how few can enter into the mood of the cos-mically weird. I notice the element of preoccupation with local human con-cernments which pervades most of the attacks on my attempts. Material with a cosmic angle—in which *phenomena*, not the local inhabitants of a single neg-ligible sphere, are the protagonists—never reaches the average man in the street. He wants something "folksy", as his more homespun representatives frequently express it. I can't seem to cater to that demand. Trends, impacts & adventures of whole culture-streams, millennial cycles of development or decay, clashes of man as a whole with the principle of time or with the terror of the outer dark—these things have always interested me more than individual biography & character-analysis. And who can write effectively or meaningfully if he has to fake an interest? So far as weird fiction is concerned, I always insist that the emphasis be kept on *the wonder of the central abnormality itself.* As I wrote once in an article, any violation of what we know as natural law is *in itself* a far more tremendous thing than any other event or feeling which could possibly affect a human being. But Holy Yuggoth, how the old man runs on! [ . . . ]

*Notes*

1. *Richard III* (1699) is an adapted version of Shakespeare's history of the same name (1591), reworked by Colley Cibber (1671–1757). It remained the standard stage version until well into the 19th century.

2. *Richard III* (Cibber version) 3.2.459–60.

3. *Richard III* (Cibber version) 5.4.239–42.

4. John Dennis (1658–1734) was a British dramatist and critic who in *Essay on the Genius and Writings of Shakespeare* (1712) generally praised Shakespeare but sharply criticized him for failing to adhere to neoclassical rules for writing tragedies.

5. *King Lear* 4.6.58–59, 69–71.

6. "A Scene for *King Lear*," *Sprite* 8, No. 3 (August 1917): [2–10]. In *Out of the Immortal Night* 136–41.

7. "A Scene for *Macbeth*," *United Amateur* 20, No. 2 (November 1920): 17–19. In *Out of the Immortal Night* 141–45.

8. *Macbeth* 2.1.33–34 ("Is this a dagger which I see before me, / The handle toward my hand? Come, let me clutch thee"), as if spoken by Maurice Moe's young son Donald.

9. *King John* 3.1.199 ("his" for "those").

10. HPL read the first volume of Spengler's *The Decline of the West* around March 1927 (see *Essential Solitude* 78). He apparently never read the second volume.

11. From Machen, "The Great God Pan." HPL mentions Nodens in "The Strange High House in the Mist" and *The Dream-Quest of Unknown Kadath*.

12. "The Island of the Birds, which is the outermost island and near the Abyss."

13. Sir Oliver Lodge (1851–1940); Sir Arthur Conan Doyle (1859 –1930); Camille Flammarion (1842–1925); Léon Chevreuil (1852–1939); and Charles Richet (1850–1935), all proponents of spiritualism and other pseudo-sciences.

[5]     To Fritz Leiber, Jr. [AHT]

November 18, 1936

My dear Mr. Leiber:—

[. . .] I was much interested in your allusion to the meteor-deposited strangers, the burrowing lizard-men, & the Creatures of the Peaks. I wonder how much of this is authentic (i.e., relatively diffused & spontaneous) folklore, & how much the imaginative product of your friend? Speaking of Coronado & Cibola—I once used the idea of a subterrene region beneath the southwest, peopled by the descendants of Atlanteans *& others,* into which strayed one of Coronado's men—one Panfilo de Zamacona y something-or-other.[1] It was not in a tale of my own, but in one I ghost-wrote for a revision-client. By the way, though strange as it may seem, I did *not* invent the Mi-go or Abominable Snow Men. This is genuine Nepalese folklore surrounding the Himalayas, & I picked it up in most unscholarly fashion from the newspaper & magazine articles exploiting one or another of the attempts on Mt. Everest. Probably you are familiar with at least two stories in which this concept is very advantageously employed—E. F. Benson's "The Horror-Horn" in "Visible & Invisible", & H. R. Wakefield's "The Cairn" in "Others Who Returned". Kadath in the Cold Waste is, however, my invention. In one of my repudiated efforts—a novelette written in the winter of 1926–7 I made it my central theme, but the result was not successful.

Yes—as I said in last Sunday's instalment—I do not think our estimates of Blackwood, Machen, & Dunsany are in any sense antipodal. No one regrets more than I do the limitations besetting Blackwood, & I have often sighed at Nature's inability to effect a sort of synthesis of him & Machen—giving the composite genius Blackwood's vision & understanding of man's out-reaching emotions & illusions, plus Machen's definitely literary perspective & self-critical faculty. Machen, with all his faults, knows literature & style. He is often trivial & insipid, but never awkward nor mawkish nor silly. You make an excellent point regarding Poe. His infinity was indeed *within*—the wall of horror & darkness which is the true though unrecognised human spirit. "There are moments", he says, "when even to the sober eye of Reason the world of our sad Humanity may assume the semblance of a Hell—but the imagination of a man is as Carathis, to explore with impunity its every cavern. Alas! the grim legion of sepulchral terrors cannot be regarded as altogether fanciful—but, like the Demons in whose company Afrasiab made his voyage down the Oxus, they must sleep, or they will devour us—they must be suffered to slumber, or we perish."[2] Today our sense of mystery & infinity shifts to a less personal realm for many reasons—a prominent one being the gradual dissociation of most of our subjective feelings into simpler & less impressive components by the processes of modern psychology. Then again, as you point out, the cheerful prosaicism of recent scientific social thinkers really invites a reaction in favour of the external, the indefinite, & the uncontrollable. Modern science may or may not leave out important elements in its view of the universe—but in either case the *emotional* revolt against prosaic certainty & limitation cannot be downed.

In my view of the universe I probably side more—objectively & intellectually—with the material man of science than with the mystic; but my repudiation of unverified trimmings causes me to reject unjustified extrapolations & dogmata on one side as well as on the other. Certainly, I have nothing but rueful & sardonic laughter of the political economist who insists that future history *must* necessarily follow this or that course (no two agree, but each one is sure of himself!), or for the biologist who (like J. B. S. Haldane) maps out a certain line of marvellous upward development for the race. I don't believe in any "cosmic consciousness" or purpose or direction, nor in any "spiritual" order of entity coexisting with the universe of electrons. But I do see existence filled with an infinity of *unrecognised* (not supernatural) & *incalculable* factors—factors involving the relationship of everything we know to the totality of space-time—whereby all supposed certainties & long-term calculations must be called into question so far as any absolute sense is concerned. We don't know what we are in time & space, or what will happen to us before our kind of matter & energy will cease to exist. Organic life is only a momentary incident—whether a local & unique accident or a widespread cosmic principle often repeated, we can never know. We can never know how far our kind of natural law holds good in the gulfs of space & time, or when some manifestation of it will change. Nor can we interpret it well enough to calculate the future of life & of the universe even if it does not change. So far as future history is concerned, I'm damned if I know what lies ahead. Probably certain philosophic historians & sociologists have a *limited* rightness in pointing out rough general trends—such as that from capitalism to *some* form of collectivism under the impact of widespread mechanisation—but the moment they try to prophesy in detail as the Marxists do they are merely weaving myths. Any one of a dozen possible courses may await mankind. Nobody knows what factors will pop up to prove the decisive ones. What will the next war bring—& leave? How much of existing knowledge & technology will survive—or leave recoverable keys—through the next dark age? How fatal will be the decadence or collapse toward which both western & eastern cultures seem to be moving? Will the modified behaviour-patterns created by the lapse of certain traditional beliefs produce unforeseen results? To what extent will a new dark age restore or duplicate the early attitudes & superstitions of mankind? In connexion with this sort of speculation no one ought to miss reading W. Olaf Stapledon's "Last & First Men", published some six years ago. Probably you *have* read it. If not, make a bee line for library or bookstall! To give a personal guess—I look for a sharply-divided world with intervals of terrific warfare taking the general level of civilisation lower & lower each time. I doubt the probability of a general worldwide explosion—for most great decays have been gradual. Indeed, I fancy the saner nations will have many intervals of relative placidity & decency. The northern & western countries seem to have a knack of readjusting their government, economics, & society to meet changing needs without explosive disaster, & if they can be left free to evolve without encroachment, they probably have quite a future. I don't look for any social upheavals of prime magnitude in America or Great Britain (or any part of the Empire) or Scandinavia, & believe that their dangers lie in external wars. How well can they resist the encroachments of more violent neighbours? How wisely will they combine their interests & defences, & arrange their economic contacts? I don't know. Nor will I try to rival the aforementioned Mr. Stapledon in conjecturing what will come out of the next general dark age. In that matter I haven't even a guess to offer. But that a kind of dark age will come in 1000 years I feel reasonably certain. Nor will it be without its compensations, as hinted by Dunsany in his "Prayer of the Flowers" in "Fifty-One Tales".

Regarding Charles Fort—I'm not against the principle that no observed phenomenon should be ignored merely because it fails to harmonise with existing knowledge & existing ideas of natural law. Indeed, I don't think any truly scientific thinker is. It is only from the observation of numberless varied phenomenon that we have formulated "natural laws", & when we strike a new phenomenon at once clearly established & definitely irreconcilable with our "laws", we know that we must seek new explanations & draw up a new code of conjectural principles. Thus perished Laplace's nebular hypothesis, the Ptolemaic system, the theory of "phlogiston",[3] & so on. In every case the old doctrine was shelved as soon as the contrary evidence became conclusive. The thing which makes men of science hold out in certain cases is a grave doubt of the authority & conclusiveness of the contrary evidence. They know how deceptive appearances are, how spontaneously yet realistically myths arise & spread, and how minutely & painstakingly they & their predecessors had to verify, purge of illusions, & sift out from among endless examples of false appearances the body of evidential phenomena on which existing ideas are based. Knowing this, they have a right to ask that each bit of evidence challenging such ideas be examined & analysed just as thoroughly as were the evidences whence the ideas were formulated. When an overwhelming weight of tested evidence points in one direction, any lone phenomenon seeming to point in the contrary direction must surely be taken very much on probation—not brushed aside, but analysed very carefully, & not regarded too seriously until analysis & verification have established it as a certainty necessitating a general re-casting of existing ideas. My opinion of Fort as an interesting rather than intellectually revolutionary figure arises from the casual & unverified nature of his reports. He assembles odd statements of so loose & un-authoritative an origin (I speak from memory, not having read him ("The Book of the Damned", "New Lands") in a decade.) that one does not see why they form a serious challenge to existing ideas. We are all too familiar with the anthropological & sociological processes which customarily give birth to irresponsible statements of this general nature. Of course, no one would claim that all such statements ought to be dismissed without an investigation. Indeed, investigation of all strange phenomena not obviously fictitious should be encouraged. But until these reports—or some of them—have been shewn to be different from the run of wild canards common to folklore & the press, a good many solid thinkers will decline to attach too much importance to them. That, however, doesn't mean a closed frontier. See what repetitions of the Michelson–Morley experiment have done to our most cherished conceptions of time & space—& what further repetitions (as now conducted by Prof. Dayton C. Miller)[4] may do the equally cherished relativity ideas of the moment! See how respectfully (note the article in the current *Harpers*) the general scientific public is beginning to listen to the experiments of Prof. Rhine at Duke University[5] touching on telepathic & clairvoyant (but not, of course, really "supernatural") principles! I don't think science is quite as ruthless & arbitrary as Fort maintained. One *must* guard the frontiers of accepted learning against casual delusion & charlatanry—suppose academic authorities were to endorse phrenology, animal magnetism, psychic vibrations, ectoplasm, & all the rest of the pseudo-science peddled down the ages by fanatics & pretenders! But I get your point—& realise that there are indeed many narrow men of science whose closed minds justify all the Fortian invective. It is well, I doubt not, that healthy irritants like Fort appear from time to time to rouse the guardians of human learning from a stultifying complacency & cocksureness. By the way—I envy you the intellectual vigour & activity implied in the list of some of your studies and pursuits. I lag far behind—so that I really don't enjoy mental activity per se, but employ it only as a means to the end of gratifying curiosity about the cosmos & the phenomena. Thus I never maintained any enthusiasm for chess—though for that matter I don't care for *any* games ... intellectual, physical, or fortuitous. I lack most completely the competitive or sporting instinct.

I appreciated extremely the criticisms of my various tales, & believe I agree completely with all of them. *Characterisation* is undeniably a woefully weak point with me, & I am usually so intent on depicting or suggesting *phenomena* that I lack the patience to develop and motivate the human figures (of no interest to me except as indices of the phenomena) as I should in order to make the total picture convincing. The weakness is also aggravated by the *dream-attitude* which habitually underlies my attempts to crystallise moods & cosmic adumbrations. The way I think of strange phenomena & outside intrusions is as a dreamer helplessly & passively watching a panorama flit past him, or floating disconnectedly through a series of incredible pictures. Everything connected with motive & action is absent—a mad universe obeys strange new laws, & the spectator has no wish but to watch, & no acts save to stare. If the panorama or pictures happen to contain people, what they do or why they do it remains shrouded in mystery—this mystery contributing to the dream-concept part of its essential force. Of course I realise that I can't get this over to any reader, hence have to invent characters & motives. But these puppets & excuses are so objective & artificial, & so little related to what I'm really trying to do, that I tend to become weary & slight them. I felt the weakness particularly in "Whisperer", & believe I tried (albeit clumsily) to have him explain his apparently anomalous helplessness in one of his letters. In the "Haunter" I think I also tried to suggest some reason for the victim's passiveness—implying that the experience almost paralysed his will & that the Entity was exchanging personalities with him, but I know I did it badly & listlessly. I surely must pay more attention to this point. Regarding the other point—springing marvels before I've sufficiently prepared the reader—I recognise that, too. This is without question a result of my constant writing for a pulp rag like W T. The insidious influence of the cheap shocker gets at me despite my conscious efforts to exclude it. Recently I've felt this defect very keenly, & have made efforts to break away from it—though there are no results so far. I'm glad indeed to have these points emphasised, & shall double my alertness to avoid the usual kind of error. Glad you've seen "Cthulhu"—a product of 1926 which I regard as only so-so. I'll have some things to lend as soon as I get that checked list— quite a batch of previously lent material returned yesterday. [. . .]

*Notes*

1. Panfilo de Zamacona y Nuñez, in "The Mound," ghostwritten for Zealia Bishop.
2. "The Premature Burial."
3. Johann Joachim Becher postulated that a firelike element called phlogiston is contained within combustible bodies and released during combustion.
4. Dayton C. Miller (1866–1941), American physicist and astronomer and opponent of Einstein's theory of relativity.
5. J. B. Rhine (1895–1980) established the Duke University Parapsychology Laboratory in 1935 for the scientific study of psychic phenomena.

[6]    To Jonquil Leiber [AHT]

November 29, 1936

Dear Mrs. Leiber:—

[. . .] Descending from the sublime to the ridiculous, I am interested in the impression conveyed to you & Mr. Leiber by the snap of my own grotesque & senescent mug. I lately suggested to the *Weird Tales* illustrator Finlay, to whom I had sent the same snap in response to his request, that he use it as a model for one of those nameless cosmic horrors from outside—such as he drew in his memorable design for Bloch's "Faceless God" in the issue for last May. The reading of Puritanic & witch-hanging (no witch-suspect was ever *burned* in New England) characteristics into my grim & forbidding features suggests a number of curious lines of research—ethnological, biological, psychological & what-not—in view of the fact that with one exception not a single line of my ancestry tarried for more than a few years in that part of New England where the dour Puritan theocracy held sway—Rhode Island being a colony founded by & maintained for the opponents of—& refugees from—that arrogant theocracy. Why, then, the undeniable resemblance to the popular picture of the conical-hatted whiner of tunes from the Bay Psalm-Book[1]—a resemblance infinitely greater than that of most of the actual psalm-singers & witchcraft-judges of 17th century Massachusetts (Cotton Mather was a plump, cheerful-looking soul beneath his full-bottom'd periwig)? Excluding the fact that precisely one-half of my ancestry never touched New England till a couple of years before my birth (an exclusion justified by the fact that my features seem wholly of maternal derivation), why should a Rhode-Islander look like the folklore concept of a Bay Colony Puritan? Was it (a) origin from a similar element in Great Britain (& variations, local & social, in British ethnology are a study in themselves—as Sir Arthur Keith[2] could attest), (b) climatic & dietary similarities in New England, promoting similar glandular functioning, (c) *rough* similarities in psychological life despite the differences between the beliefs of those within & outside the Mass.–Conn. theocracy, (d) an *individual* dourness of the Mass. type, or (e) combinations of any two or three or all four of the foregoing influences? Well—I don't know. As to the first count, I think there did tend to be a vague similarity of source in the Massachusetts & Rhode Island colonists (East Anglian lines predominating, though exceptions were bewilderingly many)—a tendency accentuated by the fact that many Rhode Islanders were either refugees from Massachusetts or of known kinship to Massachusetts families. In my own ancestry a good many lines—Perkins, Rathbone, Dyer, Place, Whipple, Field, & others I could think of if I stopped to get out my charts—did cross the sea as Massachusetts colonists (coming therefore from the usual Mass. sources), though they paused only transiently (save Perkins, which didn't reach R. I. till the 18th century) in the Bay. These names represent regions as far apart as Warwickshire & the West Riding of Yorkshire, but two are from Norfolk, & some of my non-Massachusetts lines are also East Anglian. There is, then, an undeniable East Anglian bias, like Massachusetts', in my maternal & feature-determining lineage. This argues perhaps a basis for facial differentiation—about which a first-hand student of the Eastern counties could tell better than I. Probably East Anglians, coming from the old "Litus Saxonicum" which the Teutonic invaders first occupied, have more of the tribal Teuton direct from the north of Europe, & less of the Celt & Britanno-Roman, than other English stocks—although the more southerly natives of Kent & Sussex should by the same token have at least as much. The second point—climatic & dietary similarities between Mass. & R.I.—may also be significant. The two regions are close together, & colonial eating habits were very similar. Physically, all southern N.E. colonists met a similar milieu. As the psychological element—here I think the parallelism grows weaker. Whilst Rhode-Islanders undoubtedly shared the general New-England preoccupation with ethical & theological matters, they had nothing of the savage Massachusetts approach. They fought not for the narrow enforcement of one creed but for the tolerance of all. We welcomed Jews in Newport as early as the 1670's & their synagogue of 1763 still remains in use. Not a single case of witchcraft prosecution ever occurred on our soil, & Quakers—the bane of the Bay—flourished in our midst. The Church of England became predominant in our southern counties about the time of William & Mary, & so remains to this day. These southern counties likewise diverged from the rest of New England in social & economic organisation & way of life—developing large plantations with negro slaves in the manner of the southern colonies, & fostering a patriarchal agricultural life surprisingly like that of old England, or rather (considering the colour & status of the labour) like that of Virginia or the South Carolina low country. These more or less squirearchical plantation families represented something very far from the Puritanism of the Bay—& about half of my maternal lines stem from them more or less directly. The plantation system largely collapsed with the revolution; some representatives of the planter houses being able to remain on their own lands, whilst others (many of my own forbears among them) took smaller holdings in the undeveloped region to the northward & mingled with the westward-pushing element from Providence. All of which argues a life & psychology widely different from the more narrowly centred Massachusetts type. If *only* psychological influences moulded the "Puritan face", one would not expect to find it in the people of Rhode Island. So far as the *individual* element goes—I'm not much of a Bay-Colony theocrat. Whilst I *do* share the basic New-England respect for an orderly life & social organisation (as did also Plato, John Locke, & many other non-Yankees), I have no belief in any religion, nor any use for any state policy imposing the least curb upon intellectual & aesthetic (or religious, if anybody wishes to retain the legends of yesteryear) freedom. I likewise oppose the Puritan concept of ethics in art & literature—believing ethics itself to be an independent art & not logically miscible with any other. Any vestigial philosophic resemblance I may have to the bygone Puritan is perhaps contained in my general belief (a mere personal opinion, whose application by force I would violently oppose) that a contemplative & imaginative life is of somewhat more evolved quality, & likely to confer richer ultimate rewards upon persons of highly organised sensibilities, than is a more elemental life with its concentration on the primitive, the more simply emotional, & the orgiastic. In a word, I seem to favour the Apollonian over the Dionysian ideal as a general policy—though for purely aesthetic & scientific reasons, & without the least wish to incorporate it Nazi-fashion into a civic doctrine. Whether this perfectly tolerant attitude tends toward the creation of a Puritan bigot's physiognomy, I can't say. Possibly I am what George Santayana would call a Puritan in decay[3]—although I lack the sense of abstract *duty* (as distinguished from the aesthetic satisfaction in symmetrical & adequate completion) which he & others find still dominant in the Puritans' agnostic descendants. As for the mere gleam of a sulky temperament or bad digestion—which so often produces the illusion of piety, asceticism, & moral fervour—I must record as a prosaic fact that I scarcely have even this. Though in very poor health prior to the age of 30, I have never been able to cultivate a picturesque melancholy. Indeed, it has never even occurred to me to try. Instead, though scarcely of a boisterous or ebullient disposition, I am a distinctly good-natured old cuss, with a kind of mild paternal benevolence toward the external world, & with no constitutional inability to twist the grim line of my mouth at least slightly in the direction of a fairly amiable & non-sardonic smile. I have also laughed aloud on at least four occasions within a memory extending back to 1892. I would not, in all probability, qualify as a Falstaff—yet scarcely fancy my temperament alone could have determined the sourness of my phiz. No—referring back to the classification near the bottom of p. I, 1—I fancy the Judge Hathorne[4] visage must be attributed to point (e) in the end . . . . a combination of causes, & these more physical (selective ancestry & climatic-dietary milieu influencing the feature-deciding half of my lineage) than psychological. But even so, the habit of occasional (though scarcely savage or morose) analysis & reflection may have played its subtle part. It does not do to be dogmatic. However, I will say that a map like mine is more likely to *give* its possessor melancholy (unless, as I do, he avoids mirrors as much as possible) than to be a *result* of melancholy!

Proceeding to answer the questions in your letter (& trusting perhaps overconfidently that the foregoing garrulous & egocentric comment has left you with enough patience & consciousness to hear the not-quite-so-garrulous (I hope)* replies thereto)—I may say that (a) I haven't any especial claims to the title of "student", being not even a university graduate (health broken down during years which should have been collegiate), & being more or less superficial & fragmentary about everything. Whether a sort of curiosity about things in general—impelling informal dabblings in bits of history, a few of the sciences, & so on—would win me an unofficial or non-commissioned status as semi-student or pseudo-student, I really don't know. But my ignorance always impresses me more than any ill-coördinated acquirements which I may have picked up in an aimless way. As to (b) my matrimonial status—you are right to the extent that I am not married *now,* although I was from March 3, 1924 to March 25, 1929.[5] I am very much in favour of an harmonious wedded state, but mistook superficial for basic congeniality. Small similarities did not, as expected, grow greater; nor did small differences, as expected, grow less. Instead, the reverse process occurred in both cases—aided no doubt by that financial insecurity which is ever the foe of domestic adjustment. Aspirations & environmental preferences diverged increasingly, until at length—albeit without real blame or

---

*Later—how vain are the hopes of mankind!

even bitterness on either side—the Superior Court of Providence County was permitted to exercise its corrective & divisive function, & the old gentleman was ceremoniously reënthroned in a dour celibate dignity. My household is now presided over by my sole surviving aunt—my only close relative. Whether (c) I am very reserved or not depends upon one's interpretation of 'reserve'. Certainly I am not gratuitously gregarious, or prone to seek conversation whether or not I have anything to say; & consequently, I might by some be regarded as a crusty hermit. On the other hand, as various victims of my epistles can attest, I am positively loquacious whenever any topic of interest to me is to be discussed. I was not a hermit at all during the period when I lived within reach of a group whose interests were akin to mine (that was in N.Y.—but I loathed the place as a whole so vehemently that I couldn't stand it even for the sake of pleasant individual associations), & am more or less so now merely because I don't discover many thoroughly kindred spirits hereabouts. (d) The picture of me as alternately pottering over a desk ("The Haunter of the Dark" accurately describes this house & the position of my desk at a west window commanding a view) & taking long walks ((in warm weather—my optimum temperature is 80° to 90°; I can't write legibly under 75° (some cynical souls declare I can't at *any* temperature) & am very badly affected by real cold—under about +20°)) through ancient streets & slightly agrestic & sylvan scenes is a perfectly correct one—although on hot days I take my work along in a black bag & perform it in various selected scenic spots along my chosen line of march. (e) As to what the neighbours (at present, very largely the youthful denizens of the contiguous fraternity-houses, plus the elderly respectables inhabiting the boarding-house across the back garden in a parallel street) think of me—I have never taken the trouble to ascertain, & scarcely imagine I should feel greatly complimented if I did. Your estimate is probably correct! As to (f) how the wolf is kept from the door—I can only reply (without the least pique at the query) that I presume sheer luck is the deciding factor so far, & that in the future I can't guarantee that the fanged & furry menacer *will* be kept away! No one more annoyingly lacks the least rudiments of remunerative enterprise or commercial aptitude than I. I simply don't know how to gather cash except incidentally & accidentally. I made the mistake in youth of not realising that literary endeavour does not always mean an income. I ought to have trained myself for some routine clerical work (like Charles Lamb's or Hawthorne's) affording a dependable stipend yet leaving my mind free enough for a certain amount of creative activity—but in the absence of immediate need I was too damned a fool to look ahead. I seemed to think that sufficient money for ordinary needs was something which everyone had as a matter of course—& if I ran short, I "could always sell a story or poem or something". Well—my calculations were inaccurate! The kind of poems & stories & somethings I write (& I have no more skill in the saleable commercial sort of stuff* than has a coal-heaver) are *not* the kind one can translate into rent & nourishment with any degree of dependability—yet here I find myself in middle life with no trained commercial aptitude, & with the original resources of my youth disrupted & nearly exhausted. Such tales as I do sell—& more than that, such revisory & ghost-writing work as I perform—help to postpone the fatal day of reckoning; but when it comes, & I find no further trace of patrimonial reserve to draw upon, it will (in the prevailing sermo plebeius)[6] be just too bad. So far,* I haven't been able to make scattered returns even roughly equal the $10.00 or $15.00 per week which would meet my drastically (tho' gradually) minimised needs—but some trace of the blind & fatuous optimism of my youth remains, conferring the hope that at some time before the final crash I can somehow stumble stupidly upon some sort of a job paying about 10 or 15 berries hebdomadally. Being of an abstract cast of mind with no interest in—or prejudices concerning—sources of subsistence, I don't care what in thunder it is so long as it is honest, adequately performable by me, and capable of yielding the modest amount necessary to provide a roof for myself, my books, and the accustomed articles of furniture, statuary, paintings, etc. which survive from my old house & without whose familiar presence I could not possibly exist. Fortunately my aunt seems independently provided for—& my own needs have been whittled down with such scientific precision that even an annual $500 ought to float me if I am not too fastidious as to neighbourhood when the next move comes. I have reduced nourishment to $2 and $3 per week, and continue to wear the raiment of yesteryear (suits: 1925, 1925, 1925, 1928. Overcoats: 1915, 1932. Hats: 1931, 1935). Nor do I resent the process—which to one of my years and unworldly temperament has something of the amusing aspect of a game. Hence I merely keep enquiring as to the various sorts of jobs—editing, elevator-running, proofreading, night-watchmanning, revising or ghost-writing on a salaried basis, doortending, acting as publisher's reader or critic, sandwich-manning, &c.—which might be swung by an untrained & naively uncalculative but conscientious old goof whose years & physique render pickaxe-wielding or stevedoring slightly impracticable. So far my investigations have revealed little of definite value, since I have not the remotest idea how—or whom—or where—or when—one asks for a job. But like most shiftless dreamers (dislike of Victorian literature forbids me to introduce the inevitable comparison to Mr. Wilkins Micawber‡)[7]—I keep

---

*You're wrong in assuming that there isn't money in the pulps for those ingenious & case-hardened enough to sink personal repugnance & cater to the artificial, puerile needs of the cheap editors. Price & Long & Wandrei & Hamilton & others thrive on pulp writing. They are able to forget literary criteria & meet the market. It is my financial misfortune that I can't do likewise.

† Except last year, when the two *Astounding* items caused me to break even.

‡or even to the real-life figure of my happy-go-lucky fellow-Yankee, Amos Bronson Alcott, father of the celebrated author of "Little Women".

fancying that I shall stumble upon something—that something, as it were, will 'turn up' before I hit the relief rolls, or that I shall at length discover how 'jobs' are discerned & secured—hence refrain from the darksome wailing of lugubrious apprehension. And at that, certain 'breaks' *might* come. Conceivable changes in public taste & editorial policy might enable me to capture *every* year something like the $630 which my two novels in *Astounding* drew last year. Were that so, I would have no worries. Not that it is likely to be so, but that it might be. Or some really good revision opportunities might appear— or your letter to Mr. Rosenbach[8] might start a Lovecraft boom at once & make me (after the deduction of your commission as agent) a plutocrat over-night—or anything might happen. Incidentally—I'm sure *I* don't mind your enquiry to Mr. Rosenbach if *he* doesn't. It won't be *I* who will be sent off on a wild-goose-chase after the nugatory & ephemeral yarns of an undesired un-known, which in the end can scarcely net more than the dime or quarter each asked by such juvenile junk dealers as Mr. Forrest J. Ackerman! That ponder-ous treatise (whose austere dignity as a "first" is doubtless enhanced rather than impaired by its current reprinting in the "fan" press) catalogued by Janvier in '28 *might* bring today the $3.00 as it was supposed to bring then— but wouldn't the first enquirer be tacitly expected to buy the darned thing in the event that a stray copy actually *did* turn up? Therefore pray be cautious about seeming to investigate the ancient item. Not that *I* mind the sending of the catalogue-leaf to the Maison Rosenbach—but that if you did send it you might find yourself saddled with a tattered copy of the bygone *Recluse* plus a bill even greater (in view of the 'priceless item's' greater antiquity & presumable rarity) than the $3.00 quoted some eight years ago! Could even the nickname-laden regards of the eminent deter from the eternal profit-quest one who is, after all, a professional dealer?

Having inadvertently maundered on for some five pages in a more or less autobiographical strain, I will mercifully desist. I am sorry to learn that "Adept's Gambit" did not land with W T—I would suggest (out of a knowledge of Wright's capricious temperament) that it be resubmitted after a few months, perhaps with nominal emendations. Wright has a curious way of accepting things he has once rejected—especially if the rejection was reluctant or half-undecided, as is apparent in this case. Meanwhile I trust Mr. Leiber will let me see the MS., since I am eager to sample the creative efforts of one who comprehends so fully & profoundly the nature of true cosmic horror & alienage. Indeed, he promised me a glimpse in the event of its return.

I am greatly interested in your reference to your grandfather (who might *conceivably* have seen mine if he was of remembering age before 1827, though Devon & Cornwall represent quite a few square miles betwixt them!) & his menacing cone-topped Devil-Tower—& the strange whistles blown by no human lips & doubtless designed as signals to the Dark Ones of Outer Space. The astronomical phase appeals to me especially, since I have been interested in the heavens since the age of 12, have a 3″ refracting telescope, & used to write regular astronomical articles for the press. As a boy I used to haunt the Ladd Observatory of Brown University—looking through the 12″ refractor now & then, reading the books in the library, & probably making an unmitigated nuisance of myself through my incessant questioning of everybody present. Curiously enough, the assistant there was one of your grandfather's humbler compatriots—a Cornishman named John Edwards, whose capacity for misplacing h's was limitless. Scarcely less limitless was his mechanical skill, & in his infinite kindness he fixed me up all sorts of devices (a long-focus celestial camera, a set of photographic lantern slides, a diagonal eyepiece for my telescope, &c. &c) at no more than cost price. I still have the slides somewhere—as well as lunar & other photographs I took with the camera. He is dead now—as is Prof. Upton, the director in those days, our acquaintance with whom gave me my passport to that dark-domed enchanted castle.[9] My third victim there—Associate Prof. Slocum—is now head of the observatory at Wesleyan U. in Middletown, Conn.[10] I would have carried astronomy further but for the *mathematics*—but I hadn't quite the right stuff in me. Oddly enough, I have a real astronomer in my heredity—but I have to go back to Queen Elizabeth's reign to claim him. He was John Felde[11]—sometimes called "The Proto-Copernican of England" because of his "Ephemeris" of 1557 was the first English book to contain an account of the solar system's true motions. Two of his grandsons—John & William Field—settled in Providence in 1637, & I am descended from three of Grandson John's grandchildren.

But since I am back on autobiography I had better call a halt. I'd surely enjoy hearing of "Old Master Stebbins'" daemon-chasing & other-world-communing in the Dark Tower!

Again, my sincerest thanks for the pictures!

Best wishes to you & Mr. Leiber—your obt. servant,

H. P. Lovecraft

## Notes

1. The Bay Psalm Book, a metrical Psalter, was the first book printed in British North America, in Cambridge, MA, in 1640.

2. Sir Arthur Keith (1866–1955), Scottish anatomist and anthropologist.

3. See his novel, *The Last Puritan*.

4. John Hathorne (1641–1717), one of the most notorious of the Salem witchcraft judges and a direct ancestor of Nathaniel Hawthorne.

5. Since HPL did not sign the papers terminating his marriage to Sonia Greene, he technically was still married.

6. Vulgar Latin spoken by the common people.

7. A character in Charles Dickens's novel *David Copperfield* (1850) who was unable to earn a living and spent time in debtors' prison. Amos Bronson Alcott (1799–1888),

American teacher, writer, philosopher, and reformer, also experienced financial difficulties throughout his life.

8. Abraham Simon Wolf Rosenbach (1876–1952), American collector, scholar, and seller of rare books and manuscripts, credited with popularizing the collecting of American literature at a time when only European literature was considered collectable.

9. Winslow Upton (1853–1914), professor of astronomy at Brown University and director of the Ladd Observatory, where he allowed the young HPL wide access. HPL owned a copy of Upton's *Star Atlas* (1896).

10. Frederick Slocum (1873–1944), American astronomer. He joined the staff of Brown University as a mathematics instructor, then became an assistant professor of astronomy in 1900 under Winslow Upton. In 1914 he became the first professor of astronomy at Wesleyan University.

11. HPL customarily gives "Felde" as an alternate to "Field."


[7]     To Fritz Leiber, Jr. [ALS, JHL]

The Castle Called Mist[1]
(#66 *is* on the crest of a precipitous
hill—cf. "The Haunter of the Dark")
——Dec. 19, 1936.

My dear Mr. Leiber:—

I read yours of the 3d with the keenest pleasure, but have postponed my reply till after an unhurried & appreciative perusal of the simultaneously-arriving literary products. Let me say at once that the latter brought no disappointment. On the other hand, I am delighted & enthralled by the ever-present intimations of brooding & intrusive Outsideness, & by the vivid imagery, narrative skill, & apt, musical language with which each theme is developed.

Let me consider first the slighter & more impressionistic "Demons of the Upper Air." The whole sequence seems to me to possess the power which I noticed in the previously-quoted extract, & the graphic & unhackneyed choice of symbols throughout excites fresh admiration. Especially potent are the occasional changes of mood & cadence—& the concomitant changes in linguistic method. With the second section the free verse settles down into suggestions of iambic tetrameter, & with the third there appears rhyme, & the more traditional type of utterance with goes with it. Then in Section IV the chant becomes freer again—with long, resonant lines, & a splendid contrast of the real signs with the mere stage-properties of the Outer Darkness. In the fifth section something of the spirit of folklore appears, & the reader is prepared for the regular rhyme & meter when they come. At this point, though, I must pedantically remark that in one of the lines (p. 5—5th l. from bottom) the word *al-lies'* occurs in such a place as to make the accent seem to fall on the first syllable. This, I think, deserves straightening out—& I fancy you can do it without much trouble. I won't venture to recommend a definite alternative—though something like the following might do:

Ho! Wild, / misrul'd / allies / upon / the earth

Section VI extracts genuine power from a traditional medium—the ever-repeated *beyondness* furnishing a splendid effect. Here again, though, Grandpa's innate pedantry must crop out—for on p. 6 (ll. 11, 12) there is a *false rhyme* [*town—roun(d)*] which needs rectification. You know better than I, in all probability, how to eliminate it without loss of dramatic force. I might suggest:

Beyond, a factory city's *found*
With costly suburbs snuggled round.

Section VII presents a very effective "stepping-up"—& has something of the old Edda quality about it. The eighth & final division, with its interesting metrical shifts, forms an appropriate conclusion. Surveying the production as a whole, one cannot but adjudge it truly powerful, well-developed, & articulate with its chosen message. That old Satrap Pharnabazus of North Michigan Ave.[2] turned it down—if he did—forms no reflection on its quality; for of course no poem of this length & mood could conceivably find a place in what is, despite its superiority to the worst grade of pulp rags, essentially a sensational oaf-tickler. I hope most strongly that you can get this sequence published in some not too inappropriate medium.[3] Have you ever tried the so-called "little magazines"—non-paying, non-profit ventures which combine high standards with an absence of professional prejudices & taboos? The number of these is legion—though one might mention *Driftwind* (Walter J. Coates, N. Montpelier, Vermont) and *L'Alouette* (Charles A. A. Parker, 114 Riverside Ave., Medford, Mass.) among the all-verse specimens, & *Manuscript* (17 N. Washington St., Athens, O.), *Fantasy* (450 Huberton Ave., Pittsburgh, Pa.), *The Tanager* (Grinnell, Iowa), *American Prefaces* (Iowa City, Iowa), & *Literary America* (175 Fifth Ave., New York, N.Y.) among those which are less specialised. In any case, so fine a set of intimations of the Great Abyss ought not to languish indefinitely in manuscript!

But now I approach the piece de resistance—"Adept's Gambit"—& will proceed to give vent to remarks which . . . whether or not as peculiar as those of the palpitant Brother Farnsworth . . . . are likely to be at least sincere & appreciative. First, though, let me say, as of the poems, that pulp rejection can have no qualitative implications regarding a work like this. The cheap magazines have their set formulae, & this delectable fantasy simply doesn't happen to coincide with any of them. Magazines from the W T level down (& that there *is* a "down" no one who has seen the editorial products of one Rogers Terrill, or the happily defunct Macfadden *Ghost Stories,* can dispute) have no use for anything not simple, literal, & explicitly diagrammed enough to bore its difficult way through the densest cortical integuments of the gaping yokelry.

My appreciation & enjoyment of "Adept's Gambit" as a capturer of dark currents from the void form an especially good proof of the story's essential power, since the style & manner of approach are almost antipodal to my own. With me, the transition to the unreal is accomplished through humourless pseudo-realism, dark suggestion, & a style full of sombre menace & tension. You, on the other hand, adopt the light, witty, & sophisticated manner of Cabell, Stephens, the later Dunsany, & others of their type—with not a few suggestions of "Vathek" & "Ouroboros". Lightness & humour impose a heavy handicap on the fantaisiste, & all too often end in triviality—yet in this case you have turned liabilities to assets & achieved a fine synthesis in which the breezy whimsicality ultimately builds up rather than dilutes or neutralises the tension & sense of impinging shadow.

The farther I read into "Adept's Gambit" the more I enjoyed it. You succeed abundantly in the difficult art of emotional modulation—heightening the tension & making each fresh turn more impressive—never less—than the preceding one. The picaresque chronicle is always in an ascending key. As the Viking & Mouser leave the low seacoast for the highlands of Turkestan & the mountains beyond the Lost City the feeling of latent evil & immanent alienage mounts, & a fascination creeps increasingly on the reader. Then—on p. 55, where the Elobeth section begins—you let the tempo change a bit & subordinate the cheerfully whimsical to the poignantly pathetic. The shift comes at the right time, & conveys the effect of the opening of some inner door. It is well synchronised with the complete following of the *current,* the vanishment of Ningauble's urchin-emissary, the steeper ascent, the wilder & more precipitous landscape, & the coming of a flaming sunset & purple twilight. Nor is there any letdown. Despite recurrences of the whimsical mood, the tension is always on the increase. The scenes within the castle are magnificently replete with cosmic fear & the sense of encroaching order upon order of alien outsideness. Nor is the ending anticlimactic—for the escape of the adept's soul in the traditional form of a mouse blends perfectly with the massed nature of what has gone before. Indeed, all the developments are gratifyingly plausible & inevitable according to the laws of that fantasy-touched world which you have chosen to depict. I could name dozens of especially tense & powerful high spots—such as the terrified glances in the Adept's sarcophagus in the lost city, the discovery of what was suspended in the box in the castle, &c. &c. &c. If anything in the plot would be the better for changing, I think it is perhaps the matter of the Adept's (or power-beyond-the-Adept's) motive in imposing an ignominious spell on Fafhrd & the Mouser. This is of course suggested on p. 29—but in view of the later doubtfulness of the source of Isaiah ben Elshaz's volition I think the suggestion might well be a trifle more definite. Why was Isaiah—or That or Those behind him—interested in Fafhrd & his companion? Was it indeed because the Mouser's superficial magical dabblings had attracted attention? Of course the Grey One's own explanation—about having insulted the Adept in Ephesus—is ruled out, since Elobeth's story-within-the-story reveals that Isaiah cannot have walked abroad in his own body as a magician. As for possible re-proportioning—if any sections would bear condensation, it is probably those referring respectively to the action of the spell in Tyre (the story's first 8 pages) & to the conversation & combat with the Adept's corpse in the Lost City. This latter section, however, should (as just stated) contain a very specific hint of the reason for the spell cast on the adventurers. However—all these observations are very minor matters. The novelette is really very much all right just as it is!

Certainly, you have produced a remarkably fine & distinctive bit of cosmic fantasy in a vein which is, for all the Cabellian or Beckfordian comparisons, es-sentially your own. The basic element of allegory, the earthiness & closeness to human nature, & the curious blending of worldly lightness with the strange & the macabre, all harmonise adequately & seem to express a definite mood & personality. The result is an authentic work of art—& I certainly hope it can eventually get published somewhere even though its genre makes it the hard-est conceivable sort of thing to place. Picaresque fantasy of this type generally appears only in book form—which is of course a significant commentary on the vapid formula-following of even the best periodicals. I'll be very much interested to hear your own remarks—as well as Wright's—on this not-merely-promising bit of accomplishment.

And now for a few pedantic observations on certain points in the text which I jotted down as I came to them. Some of these observations may seem trivial—others will perhaps prove helpful in correcting minor slips.

*Page 1*—would *Hittites*\* have a separate identity in the great Syrian amalgam as late as Hellenistic times? Look the matter up. *General orthographical notes*—note spelling of *sistrum*. One stores water in a *cistern,* but it's a *sistrum* that one rattles! The sistrum was *Egyptian* & connected with the cult of Isis, but the spread of Egyptian influence to the Syrian region proba-bly justifies its mention in this tale.

*pp. 3 & 53* The country in Asia Minor is *Cilicia* (Κιλικια), not *"Cilesia"*. *Silesia* is a region in Europe grabbed from Austria by Frederick the Great & with pieces now chipped off & allotted to Czechoslovakia & Poland.

*p. 4 Philistines* as a separate people† are less & less heard from as the Hellenistic age advances. The last specific men-tion of them is in the Book of Maccabees—2nd cent. B.C.

*Regarding any possibly anachronistic national names— you could substitute another known to belong to the Hellenistic period—such as Idumaean or Cydonian or Rhodian or Cyprian or Chalcidian or Libanian or Sabaean.*

---

\*Last-minute conclusions after combing my library a bit: I think the name *Hittite* could *not* have survived to Hellenistic times. No classical text known to me records it, & the last mention of the race seems to be in Assyrian inscriptions far antedating the Greek period in the East.

†though they left their name *geographically* in the word Παλαιστινα or Palaestina.

But your reference is all right.

*p. 9*—I fear that the allusion to Tamerlane's later building of Samarcand must come out, since this ancient city was in existence & already venerable in the Hellenistic age of Fafhrd & the Grey Mouser. The town antedates the recorded history of its region, & appears in Persian days as *Maracanda,* capital of Sogdiana. It was a thriving place, with walls extending 90 stadia. Alexander the Great destroyed it—but it survived & did well in the days of the Graeco-Bactrian kingdom. In Arabic times it appears under its corrupted name *Samarcand*—being captured by Kataiba ibn Moslim in A.D. 712 . . . the period of my fictitious *Necronomicon* author Abdul Alhazred. It became a mighty metropolis & seat of Saracenic culture under the Arabs, but was destroyed by Genghis Khan in 1219. Nearly a couple of centuries after that, Tamerlane made it his capital & (together with his successors) adorned it with fine buildings & institutions—but as you may see, it can scarcely be considered as *built* by him. So far as our historic vision can reach, we always find a great city on the site.

*p. 14.* Here is something a bit puzzling to an old gent not so quick on the uptake. You have the Mouser speak of a supposed work whose title is the

[d]

*Duocedahe[d]ron of Artemi"s"orus*—these names having been altered in the text from a better to a worse state—but I can't quite figure out the intention. Is the Mouser supposed to be inventing names with a clumsiness & erroneousness greater than usual? What holds me up is that the erroneousness is *too great to be convincing.* *Artemidorus* (gift of Artemis—Αρτεμιδορος) was too common a Greek name (especially in the Orient)—too typical in form—to be mis-rendered as "Artemisorus" by anyone who had knocked about the Hellenistic world as the Mouser presumably had. I'm not sure of your chronology—but if the period is as late as B.C. 100 (which I doubt) the great geographer Artemidorus of Ephesus ought to be on the scene. The name of the book is another tough nut. I assume that the intent is to give a corruption of *Dodecahedron* (Δωδεκαέδρον) or its possible variant *Duokaidecahedron* (Δυοκαιδεκαέδρον) [for δυο-και-δεκα or two-and-ten often subbed for δωδεκας twelve]—"The Twelve-Sided Thing"—but here again the problem of *degree of illiteracy* comes up. Δωδεκαέδρον [I never saw the δυοκαιδεκα substitution applied to this particular word, though I suppose it could be done] was a very well-known & typical word, so how could the Mouser very well hash it up so badly? Wouldn't it be more in character for him to invent a *fictitious work,* but have the title & author in *correct Greek?* Thus I'd vote for the *"Dodecahedron* (Or Duokaidecahedron) *of Artemidorus"* as the supposed title. Incidentally—I haven't yet figured out the Mouser's nationality. Fafhrd calls him "scum of wit-weighted culture", so I put him down as some sort of Levantine or Hellenistic half-Greek. Anyhow, I seem to envisage him as speaking Greek very glibly & reasonably correctly. By the way—*Artemidorus* was a favourite name in Ephesus, because of the deeply-seated cult of Artemis (or rather, of an earlier Asiatic goddess whom the Greeks identified with Artemis) there. "Great is Diana of the Ephesians". There was a later Artemidorus born there (2nd cent. A.D.) who wrote a learned treatise on the interpretation of dreams. Pardon all this vacuous rambling—& use your judgment about the name of the supposed treatise & its author.

*p. 15*—avoid the non-existent "thusly" for *thus.*

*p. 19*—here's a fine point. You speak of the "Endless Caverns"—but are you sure this won't arouse jarringly prosaic associations based on the fairly well-known Endless Caverns near New Market, Va., U.S.A.? I can testify that the Caverns in Virginia are the very reverse of prosaic—Ædepol, what a subterrene world of wonder!—but there is always a suggestion of anticlimax when a name supposed to figure in an ancient & exotic scene duplicates something in the modern & nearby world.[4]

*p. 20*—& elsewhere. Avoid split infinitives in spite of all the modern libertarian ballyhoo in their favour.

*p. 23*—*insignia* should not be used in the *singular.*

*p. 24*—*went* should be *gone.*

*p. 25*—note correct spelling of metamorphosed. I never heard the form "metamorphised".

*p. 42*—The names *Arachni* and *Altaeoni* sound somehow off-key to me as Greek. *Arachne* is a name figuring in mythology (with an etymological significance), but you ought to have something less weighted with associations. How about *Aganippe* and *Authemius* for the two names?

*p. 44*—avoid ultra-modern coinages like *recontacted. Contact* really ought never to be used as a *verb*—the recent custom in "business English" to the contrary notwithstanding. Why not say *rediscovered?*

*p. 52*—use of verb *typed* doubtful. Better say "whom they instantly classified as a street gamin". This change also eliminates another error (the insertion of a redundant "that of") which needed attention.

*p. 65*—I hate to see the modern twisted use of *intrigue* as a verb meaning to interest or fascinate. It really ought to be discouraged. Could you substitute *fascinating* or *intriguing?* Of course, this use of "intrigue" is sadly widespread— but in the present novel the quasi-archaic, traditional tone of the style makes it seem doubly inappropriate.

*pp. 70 & 72*—lack of uniform usage in name of Ishtar–Astarte. You say *Astarte* in other places, so better not say *Istarte* here.

*p. 75*—no such word* as *"constrictious".* Why not say constrictive?

---

*Whenever I say "no such word" in so apparently pontifical a manner, I mean merely that *I don't know of it,* & that I can't find it in either of the two dictionaries—a Stormonth & an 1890 Webster's International—which I possess. In some cases a recent unabridged *p. 82*—"react" for respond in a general sense is a somewhat needless modernism. Why not say *respond?*

*p. 83*—no such word (as far as I know) as *necrous.* Try *necrose, necrosed,* or *necrotic.* Never mind the medical connotation.

*pp. 92 & 95*—*activated* was in old English, but long ago disappeared. The use of this resurrected word by scientific students has spread until ultra-moderns are dragging it into the general field—but such an extension has nothing to recommend it. Better say *moved.*

*p. 99*—there is no such word as *"unbeknownst"*—this form being merely a comic coinage. Even *"unbeknown"* is wholly colloquial. The best thing to say is *unknown.* Pardon all this pedantry—but I spent most of the summer & autumn revising & partly ghost-writing a manual on "Well-Bred English" for a private school in Washington, D.C., & I can't get the damned influence out of my system!

Realising its connexion with the Fafhrd–Mouser myth-cycle, I saved the extract from Mr. Fischer's letter to read *after* my perusal of "Adept's Gambit"—a thing I am very glad I did, since it gave me a truer perspective of the background out of which the epistolary fragment grew. Needless to say, I enjoyed the episodic bit tremendously, & conceived an instant admiration for the gifted creator. A two-way correspondence full of these isolated episodes must surely be a test of creative fancy—an even better form of literary exercise than the participants consciously realise. Both of you ought to keep carbons of these beginningless & endingless passages—some day coördinating them & developing them into a series of mood-studies for publication. It is easy to see how "Adept's Gambit" grew out of this play & interchange of fancy, & I do not wonder at the graceful dedication—which must surely be greatly appreciated by its object. Let us hope that your mental collaboration will give rise to a long sequence of tales about Fafhrd & the Mouser—figures which I somehow visualise as stylised & exaggerated projections of the two unquenchable correspondents—projections, at least, so far as basic outlines & imaginative flights are concerned. Mr. Fischer's style has a marked kinship to that of your own more whimsical passages—& I suppose the nature & typical actions of Fafhrd, the Mouser, Ningauble, & perhaps other recurrent characters are equally well-known to you both through the long exchange of imaginings such as this. It interested me greatly (as when I met my old pal Cthulhu in "Adept's Gambit")[5] to come across an Entity whose name synthesised two of my own geographical creations . . . the mountain Kadath in the Cold Waste, & the vague trans-galactic hell called Yaddith. Kaddith would seem to have been (or should I still use the present tense despite what happened to the soul-image?) an extremely formidable Entity, & I shudder to

---

dictionary might reveal such a word as existing—but even in that case I'd be inclined to consider it a bit too obscure or modern for a style as traditional as the novel's.

think of what would have become of the Mouser had that "scum of wit-weighted culture" been less adroit or less protected! Some later episode, I hope, will chronicle the Small Grey One's fortunes after his emergence from the Place of Black Stones—his Asking of the Questions, & his presumable rescue of Fafhrd from captivity. Indeed, an added note on the MS. leads one to think that such a hope may not be wholly vain. This picaresque kind of writing has a strong fascination, & I once attempted it myself (1926–7) in a long novelette called "The Dream-Quest of Unknown Kadath" . . . . of which the central figure was that rather shadowy & flexible dummy Randolph Carter. The tale did not, however, satisfy my critical sense when completed, so I marked it off my list & did not type it. Years later my young friend Barlow asked for the MS., & proposed to type me a copy (for preservation as a sort of quarry of imagery & incidents for possible future tales) in exchange—but although I gave him the rough draught, he has so far returned less than half of the text in typed form. Barlow suggests that my attempt might make a passable *juvenile* item—but I have my doubts as to whether it's good for anything in its present form. Thanks immensely for Fischer's address. I am dropping him a line of appreciation anent his fragment—& the myth-cycle behind it—& shall surely be more than delighted to hear from him directly. The fragment itself I return to you herewith—for I fancy you will want it for your permanent archives. Incidentally—I hope those tales about the godlet in the Chicago Aquarium, the penultimate goblin, & the god-isolating mortal will all eventually get written. As the Mouser himself says, the possibilities of professional publication for such elusively fantastic material are sadly limited; but that does not lessen the joy of creation, or imply that ways of reasonable circulation cannot in the end be found. About Mr. Fischer's non-appreciation of music—I suppose my own case is not very remote from his. I am by no means indifferent to some forms of melody, but have no power of discrimination betwixt the classically good & the tawdry. I am like a person who could read Balzac, the *Saturday Evening Post,* & *Wild Western Stories* with almost equal relish & emotional response. My lines of preference ignore quality, but include *some* good music, *some* mediocre music, & *some* tin-pan tripe (the latter all antedating 1910 or so). Much of what I *think* is musical liking is merely *associative*—I like this or that piece because it gratifies a patriotic emotion ("Rule, Britannia", "The Star-Spangled Banner", &c.), evokes some folklore vista of yesterday ("Suwanee River", "Ben Bolt", &c.), or calls up memories of my own youth ("Sweet Adeline", tunes from "Floradora", "The Burgo-master", & so on).[6] By chance, I may be strongly moved by some genuine classic—Wagner, MacDowell,[7] Schubert, Beethoven—but other classics of equal reputation either leave me cold or actually repel me. I remember *tunes* with fair tenacity, but am very bad at correlating them with their *names*. Some of my friends refer familiarly to the so-and-so'th movement of what's-his-name's $N^{th}$ Symphony—& I don't know what the hell they mean, although I could probably identify the tune if they whistled it recognisably. Nor do I have the *craving* for music which some people speak of. I like an occasional ditty, but I could do without the sound of kalipac, tittibuk, & zootibar[8] indefinitely without getting badly steamed up. On the other hand, I'd be utterly sunk—or driven to tearing the anaemic grey lint that fringes my bald spot—if I were cut off from books, opportunities to write, or the sight of certain forms of architectural, decorative, pictorial, & landscape art. Decidedly, Grandpa is an eye-man & not an ear-man! If any one thing killed my musical taste it was the violin-lessons I took betwixt the ages of 7 & 9. Back in '97 I thought I liked music, but a year or two of classico-academic drill on a ¾ size fiddle soured me completely. They wouldn't let me scrape the tunes I wanted, but confined me to useful exercises & insipid folk-tunes out of a book. As a result, practicing became a hell, & the whole damn business drove me so close to nervous exhaustion that two physicians (I was little short of a neurotic semi-invalid as a kid) told my mother that a halt would have to be called. Thus ended the Kreislerian[9] career of the Old Man Without a Beard.[10] Today I can scarcely tell one end of a violin from another, & don't recall a cursed thing about reading music except that the spaces spell F-A-C-E, & that the lines represent the initials of the phrase Every Good Boy Does Finely. My only spontaneous melodic memories of that age are of "Sweet Rosie O'Grady", "Dolly Gray", & Paul Dresser's "Banks of the Wabash" [whose chorus the now-eminent Theodore Dreiser wrote to help out his brother Paul][11] & "Just Tell Them That You Saw Me", & a few assorted coon songs like "Oh, Oh, Miss Phoebe".[12] Well—who knows? Perhaps some of my native folklorish recollections are more significant than classic recollections would be . . . for did not those old coon-songs form the birth of *syncopation*— a principle perhaps destined (under various modified & elaborated forms) to become dominant in the future music of Western Civilisation? Let no cultural snob scorn me because of the vividness with which I recall fat Peter F. Dailey[13] (today I suppose they've forgotten even the cigar named after him) cavorting over the boards & unctuously intoning "Cindy" or "Mah Sunflower Sue"! But I don't believe I quite share Mr. Fischer's refined *nasal* discrimination. While I *am* peculiarly repelled by unpleasant odours, I have no vast hankering after perfumes, & always urge barbers not to smell up my old bean with patent citified lotions. I like the fresh scent of springtide on the hills, & the August aura of new-mown hay, but I'd never go to the trouble of building an organ of olfactory notes—with perfume-phials for pipes—as did des Esseintes in the tenth chapter of "A Rebours"! I surely hope that your recently intensified sensitiveness to music may yield adequate returns in pleasure & aesthetic creation. It flatters me to learn that a passage in my "Witch-House" has evoked an experiment in musical composition from you—& I hope the projected piece may develop successfully. *Weird music* is a subject all in itself— & one of which the *idea* fascinates me tremendously. I've dragged allusions to such into many of my tales—the impression being derived from composite memories of Saint-Saëns' "Dans Macabre", Grieg's "Peer Gynt" suite, & other stuff by Tchaikowsky, Rimsky-Korsakov, Debussey, Sibelius, et al. Incidentally, two of my "Fungi from Yuggoth" ("Mirage" & "The Elder Pharos") were set to weird music a few years ago by someone in your neighbour-town of Los Angeles—one Harold S. Farnese (a native of Monaco, trained in Paris & specialising in fantastic airs), Dean of the local Institute of Musical Education. Unfortunately, I never had a chance to hear his compositions.[14] He had an idea at one time of writing an opera bringing in my synthetic pantheon of Yog-Sothoth, Cthulhu, Nyarlathotep, Nug, Yeb, Azathoth, &c. (in fact, he first asked me to attempt the libretto, though I knew damn well I couldn't swing such an enterprise without experience), but I don't know whether he ever developed it or not. It must be a couple of years since I last heard from him.

I'm glad the small magazines safely arrived, & that you found my contributions therein tolerable. If you get the new *Fanciful Tales* pray let me know, & I will send you a table of errata listing the 59—count 'em—59 bad boners in the text of my "Nameless City." Glad you liked "Sarnath", although I see a good deal of the merely picturesque & imitative in it. Certainly, that kind of style is almost inevitable if one is to parallel Dunsany's themes—but alas! not everyone can tread those paths as successfully as Edward John Moreton Drax Plunkett! "The Dunwich Horror" attempts a certain composite realism in setting—engrafting certain characteristics of Southern Vermont upon the retrogressive countryside of the region near Springfield, Mass. It is, in a way, an echo of a visit to Wilbraham, Mass. in 1928, during which my hosts related much of the local traditions, & had much to say of the state of the contemporary peasantry. "The Thing on the Doorstep" is, contrary to my usual practice, more of a character study than a geographical study. I'll be interested to learn of the reason for your particular interest in it. Here, possibly, the reason why the terror-ridden character doesn't break away sooner is less obscure than in other tales of mine. But regarding those other cases—as you agree, the problem has many aspects. What really should be done is to provide a proper motivation without rubbing it into the reader. Let the vague, dream-like impression remain, but see that troublesome questions are unobtrusively anticipated. A more careful story-teller than I ought to be able to do that.

I am delighted to know that somebody besides myself likes good old Colley Cibber's "Richard III" version! To my mind, the borrowing of material from "Henry VI" adds vastly to the unity of the thing, & I don't wonder that it has persisted as an acting text. I've tried off & on to get a copy for the past 35 years, but haven't succeeded. Evidently it is now to be commonly found only in sets of the British Dramatists. I read it in an early collection of the sort belonging to the public library. However—other Shakespearian dramas did not fare well in the classick aera, as the operatick fate of "The Tempest" at the hands of Dryden & Davenant,[15] the *rhymed* "Macbeth" & "Julius Caesar" of Davenant alone,[16] the "improved" "Timon of Athens" of Shadwell,[17] the stepped-up "Troilus & Cressida" of Dryden[18] [in the prologue to which he speaks of Avon's Bard as "Untaught, unpractis'd, in a barb'rous Age"], & the cheerful Tate "King Lear" with a new fifth act mournfully attest.[19] In considering poor "Lear" I blush to think that my Phillips great-great-grandfather has a Tate & Brady epitaph on his tombstone: "The sweet Remembrance of the Just / Shall flourish when he sleeps in Dust."[20] Lear was certainly pretty well mangled by the time decorous Mr. Winter prepared his version for Edwin Booth.[21] Incidentally—if you like, I'll be glad to lend you the old amateur papers containing Loveman's interpolated "Lear" & "Macbeth" scenes. I hope you will some time attempt the possible Goneril–Regan scene before the battle!

It interests me immensely to learn that your father has varied artistic endowments outside the dramatic field, & I surely hope you will let me see photographs of his recent sculptural achievements. No one, surely, is better qualified than he for any task depending upon a sympathetic understanding of Shakespeare's characters! I hope—& am led to believe by the word *casting*—that his process is of a sort to permit of duplication, rather than one yielding only a single copy of the embodied item. Did I mention that the weird writer Clark Ashton Smith is also a sculptor of sorts, & that an exhibition of his grotesque & fantastic statuettes (one of which, I learn with becoming pride, is a monstrosity 11 inches tall entitled "Cthulhu's Child") will next month be held at the Crocker Art Gallery in Sacramento? Virgil Finlay—the gifted new WT artist—also experiments in carving & modelling.

I am delighted to hear that classic Rome forms your favourite historic period, even though you have not that curious sense of personal membership in it which has always haunted me. Incidentally, very few seem to have that acute feeling of belonging to some remote age, race, & region. The closest parallel to myself in that respect whom I have known was the late Robert E. Howard, with his veritably atavistic participation in the life of ancient tribal Gaul & Britain. I appreciate very strongly the force of the dramatic contrast formed by those occasional contacts of the classical & northern worlds which history records—Goths in the Euxine & Mediterranean lands, the Massilian Greek Pytheas in Iceland in the time of Alexander the Great, &c. &c. &c. Just as you think of Vikings in the Hellenistic-Roman world, so do I think of Roman navigators in strange & distant parts—washed across the Western Ocean to unknown shores, camping on the future site of Providence & fighting the coppery predecessors of the Narragansetts & Wampanoags, or captured by the soldiers of the Mayas & forced to escape from ornately carven dungeons in Guatemalan jungles . . . . . or circumnavigating Africa & sampling the exotic marvels of India, China, & lost Polynesian lands of which there remain today only the vine-grown megaliths of Ponape & the cryptic eidola of Easter Island . . . . or trading overland with vanished peoples in the Gobi, & perchance for a moment glimpsing immemorial Shamballah behind its curtain of oblivion . . . . . . or penetrating south into Africa beyond the mark set by Maternus, skirting the Niger, threading through steaming jungles, fighting savages, pygmies, & apes, killing lions & rhinoceroses, & finally coming upon that Kingdom of Elder Horror whereof there survives today only the ruined masonry of the Great Zimbabwe. . . . A knowledge of the hellish Dianic cult that festered underground in Europe adds to the fascination of the pageant—& one might add hints of straggling Neanderthal survivors in some of the great limestone cavern systems . . . . survivors whom stray legionaries encounter sane, but from whom they escape as madmen. I'm glad you've secured "The Witch-Cult in Western Europe", which certainly throws a clear light on many aspects of Machen, Blackwood, & others. The theories of Miss Murray regarding the source of the cult have been attacked from different angles by scholars as antipodal as Joseph McCabe[22] & the Rev. Montague Summers, but I still think they are as plausible as any yet advanced. You will, I think, appreciate "The White People" anew upon giving it a post-Murray re-reading. What I like about it is its subtlety & slow, cumulative convincingness—qualities in which, to my mind, it excels "The Black Seal."[23] The device of a child-narrator for the most hellish parts is exceedingly clever—& those sinister landscape-descriptions can wring a shudder from me even after numberless re-readings:

> "I looked out from them & saw the country, but it was strange. It was winter time, & there were black terrible woods hanging from the hills all round; it was like seeing a large room hung with black curtains, & the shape of the trees seemed quite different from any I had seen before. I was afraid. Then beyond the woods there were other hills round in a great ring, but I had never seen any of them; it all looked black, & everything had a voor over it. It was all so still & silent, & the sky was heavy & grey & sad, like a wicked voorish dome in Deep Dendo. I went on into the dreadful rocks."[24]

I hope you'll write that play about the Caesars—& meanwhile I am intensely interested in your present epic of Fafhrd & the Mouser in the Julio-Claudian world. I note that you have them *reincarnated* rather than preserved from the earliest Hellenistic period through the action of some cryptical elixir. Which reminds me—about what *is* the approximate period of "Adept's Gambit"? You seem to suggest a Hellenised Orient—which fixes the time as after Alexander—but introduce an allusion to Italy as rustic or provincial, which places things well before the Mithridatic wars . . . . & perhaps before the Macedonian & Syrian wars as well, since Asiatics would not be likely to speak patronisingly of Rome after Magnesia. Perhaps, then, we may call the period around B.C. 250—is this reasonably correct? As I have said before, I fear that the mention of *Hittites* as a living nationality as late as Greek times (the period is conclusively fixed as post-Socratic on p 6) constitutes an anachronism. Most of the ancient separate races had then so far coalesced, &

had been so overridden by the Persian & (if post-Alexandrine, as seems indicated) Greek civilisations, that only a few of the very ancient distinctions then held good. Jews & Phoenicians were distinct, & Philistines were only just dissolving. But I doubt the survival of the Hittites. And yet it does not do to be dogmatic. This matter is worth a bit of special research on your part—or I'll transmit any conclusive information which may come my way.

All of which brings me to your question about the status of anachronisms in general, as occurring in the course of historical romances with invented characters. In reply, I would say that *small* slips do not generally seem like grave defects, though very flagrant errors (such as the "Ephesian Dome" which our friend Cibber engrafted on the stamping-ground of Fafhrd & the Mouser, or some representation of a Persian Empire [other than the Parthian region which revolted in B.C. 250 & became a new Persian Empire under the Sassanidae in A.D. 224] after Alexander the Great) are to be frowned upon. When we come upon too many—or too great—lapses from what we know to be fact, we tend to find a narrative less convincing than it would otherwise be. Shakespeare gets away with such things because in him the setting is only a vague background for character-studies—but in any ordinary tale, anachronisms ought to be kept within bounds. However—that does not mean that one needs to retreat to a fantastic or prehistoric dream age, or to a Dunsanian realm beyond the edge of the world. Some types of fiction thrive much better in genuine historic settings—& I believe this is true of your projected novel. The thing to do is to meet the difficulty with a bit of special reading, & with the critical advice of a few qualified scholars. It is not hard to brush up passably on a given period—& with such a passable brushing-up one may easily avoid such major errors as would affect the main plot & action. It is well, of course, to take care that these elements depend as little as possible on any historical or antiquarian details which might be called into question. Refer knotty points to specialists—in this case, teachers of ancient history—when it seems necessary, & let such authorities go over your rough draught after its completion. With such precautions, you are pretty sure of escaping any mistakes so bad as to imperil the success of the story. "Adept's Gambit" is all right except for the few small points mentioned, & there is no reason why the Julio-Claudian novel should not be the same. I certainly vote for the Roman setting—the advantages of which are easily obvious.

Now as to the books* on this subject which would help to eliminate anachronisms. First of all, perhaps, one ought to brush up by reading the relevant sections of some popular text-book like *Myers' "Ancient History".** That gives a fresh general hang of the age, & the relative time of occurrence of the

---

*Books marked with an asterisk are owned by me, & at your disposal as loans. I have also the large Harper Dictionary—but I need that so often myself that I wouldn't dare lend it, lest I be caught in a tight place.

various major events. It provides a framework of freshened connected knowledge on which to drape the more detailed & atmospheric results of later researches. Then it would be a good idea to absorb some general manuals on Roman life under the Empire—of which there are fortunately a good number. The best starter that I know of is *"Roman Life in Pliny's Time"**, by *Maurice Pellison*. Never mind the later period—the essentials will hold good for the Julio-Claudian as well as the Domitiano-Trajanic age, & you can check up on details with larger works. This gives a fine generalised picture—& they used to use it in the old Chautauqua reading courses. Read also the useful little *"Roman Antiquities"** by *A. S. Wilkins* in the old Science Primer series. I've seen *Thomas's "Roman Life"* recommended, but haven't read it myself. Also *Davis's "A Day in Old Rome"*. Of the formal encyclopaedic & statistical manuals you can't beat that old standby—Fiske's translation of *J. J. Eschenburg's Manual of Classical Literature**. It is about as thorough as anything I know, & the century-ago scholarship is not such as to mislead. It may be hard to get hold of now, but my grandpaternal copy (1846) is at your disposal. Of shorter manuals James S. S. *Baird's Classical Manual** is probably the best, although the *"Classical Handbook"** of T. P. & W. F. Allen* is not to be despised. These latter are very concise, & have some extremely useful tables. In Baird there is a table by which any modern date can be translated into its Roman equivalent—thus a glance shews that today, Dec. 19, is A.D. XIV. KAL. IAN. (A.D. signifying *ante diem*, not *anno Domini*). All these general manuals have sections on classical geography which would save one from bad boners, but I find it fascinating to read separate works on ancient geography—in fact, such works are really necessary if one is to speak in much detail of this or that region in Italia or the provinces. The best such work—by an infinitely wide margin—is *Charles Anthon's "System of Ancient & Mediaeval Geography"**. (1850) Good old Charlie! He certainly started classical scholarship in America, & compares well with many a European figure! Shorter & less thorough is *Mitchell's Ancient Geography*—with its running-mate *Mitchell's Ancient Atlas*. I used to have the atlas, but it was lost during a household removal. (Three removes, said old Dr. Franklin, are as bad as a fire!) For the geography of the *city of Rome*—hills, topography, nature & location of streets, buildings, fora, statues, &c.—nothing can excel *"Rome of Today & Yesterday: The Pagan City"**, by *John Dennie*. However, John was pre-Mussolini, so take the "today" descriptions with reservations. Archaeology has done its stuff since then! Meanwhile arrange to have constant access, throughout the composition of the story, to some inclusive & convenient reference-work such as *Harper's Dictionary of Classical Literature & Antiquities*.[25] That's a volume without which I could not exist. Ædepol, the questions it settles every day! I have also two smaller reference volumes which, added together, make a very passable substitute—& these (*Smith's Smaller Classical Dictionary** & *Smith's Smaller Dictionary of Greek & Roman Antiquities**)[26] I'd be glad to shoot along for a long-term loan. With such a handy reservoir of facts at one's side as a guide in moments of doubt, the chances of falling into serious errors are vastly decreased. Oh, yes—& in order to be sure of accuracy in architectural or other art matters, better get some good classical museum handbook or some such brace of popular manuals as *Tarbell's "History of Greek Art"** & *Goodyear's "Roman & Mediaeval Art"*". I could also lend you *Smith & Slater's "Classic Architecture*"*, a rather more thorough work within its field, & very useful if you have occasion to describe any building (especially a *fictitious* building, where fancy might otherwise run riot) in detail. [I also have the companion Gothic & Renaissance work.] Well—so much for the groundwork. Now as for added atmosphere—there are a few modern novels which help pretty well to evoke the spirit of Roman times, & which are distinctly worth reading. Avoid the conventional "Quo Vadis" junk,[27] with its mawkish & distorted emphasis on early Christianity. Take only such novels as shew the Roman scene normally through Roman eyes. *"A Friend of Caesar"**, by *William Stearns Davis*, is a bit insipid, but nevertheless worth going through. *Desider Kostolanyi's "The Bloody Poet"*—a study of the emperor Nero— also reflects its time & theme very well. Better still, as I am told (though I haven't yet read them), are the two recent companion novels *"I, Claudius"*, & *"Claudius the God"*, by *Robert Graves*. But the finest modern fictional reflections that *I've* ever seen—the most Roman-like re-creations of the daily life & manners—are the two novels by *Edward Lucas White* (also a *weird* author. Poor old duffer—he committed suicide two or three years ago) *"The Unwilling Vestal"* & *"Andivius Hedulio"**. This latter, a picaresque novel of great length & wide scope, forms a magnificent pageant of every phase of life, urban & rural, in Imperial Italy. Read it by all means if you don't know it already. Both of these tales are laid in the age of the Antonines—rather late for your purposes—but even within them there is enough explicit differentiation betwixt the permanent & the new to make them extremely useful. Now for a little more concrete & specific historic dope—read *Suetonius' "Lives of the Caesars"** & the relevant parts of *Velleius Paterculus*[28] (remembering, however, that the former runs to slander, & the latter to flattery). Of modern works, try *Bury's "Student's Roman Empire"*, *Capes' "The Early Empire"*, *Merivale's "History of the Romans Under the Empire"*, & *Inge's "Society in Rome Under the Caesars"*. Bits of *Montesquieu* & *Michelet*[29] are also useful, & for heavier dope don't forget *Mommsen's "Provinces of the Roman Empire from Caesar to Diocletian"*. Well—all this takes you pretty well along. For the most minute details, & such valuable colour-touches as the names of consuls in given years, there's nothing like going back to the two *original* authorities who best cover the period—*Tacitus** & *Dio Cassius*.[30] I have Murphy's Tacitus, & would give a good deal to get hold of a translated set of Dio Cassius, which I've read at the library. As a final word—all Roman imperial themes bring in the Hellenistic world to a great extent, so don't fail to keep brushed up on the late-Greek dope. Your best guide, I think, will be good old *Mahaffy*—the following three works by whom you ought to peruse:

*"Survey of Greek Civilisation"\**, *"Old Greek Life\**", & *"The Greek World Under Roman Sway"*. So much for bibliography. Of course you don't have to read *all* of these items—& indeed, if you secure good critics of the manuscript, you could whittle your preparation down to a minimum. One might suggest a *short* reading course something like this:

West's "Ancient History\*
Pellison's "Roman Life in Pliny's Time"\*
Wilkins' "Roman Antiquities"\*
Baird's "Classical Manual\*"
Anthon's "Anc. & Med. Geog.\*"
Dennie's "Rome\*"
Harper's Dictionary (or equivalent\*)
White's "Andivius Hedulio\*"
Capes' "The Early Empire"
Access to Tacitus & Dio Cassius for consultation
Mahaffy's "Old Greek Life\*"

Another fine sidelight—Lecky's "History of European Morals\*"

Edgar Saltus's "The Imperial Purple" is pleasant—if somewhat sketchy, flashy & over-"smart"—reading in this line. Ed was a sort of Manhattan Suetonius & Petronius in one.

Even the longer course isn't as dry & pedantic as it sounds, since the whole subject is so damned interesting & full of unparalleled drama that sheer fascination & historic curiosity keeps one's nose glued to the various enlightening authorities. Even more fascinating to me is the sturdy republican age of ruthless expansion when Spain, Carthage, & the East fell before the Roman eagles, & "Mare Nostrum"[31] became a living reality. Also there is a melancholy magic about the final period of decay—when national ennui & administrative & economic complexities lowered the Roman morale, & the vast Imperium began to crumble, decline in art & scholarship, & finally dissolve before the Teutonic inroads—leaving only its eastern half to revert to the Hellenism (or, rather, *remain in* the Hellenism—or Byzantine successor to Hellenism) from which it had never been wrenched. I am fascinated by such questions as that of *when Latin ceased to be spoken in this or that place* . . . when Constantinopolis became *thoroughly* Greek, when the patois of increasingly Teutonised Gaul became openly known as *Lingua Romana* instead of *Lingua Latina* [have you never seen the text of the Strasburg Oath, A.D. 842?]\*, & when men in Italy habitually called themselves *Tullio, Varrone,* & *Luigi* instead of *Tullius, Varro,* & *Lucius*. What pathos in the brief semi-comebacks toward the last—when the Eastern Empire under Justinianus (one of the last Imperatores who really spoke Latin as a mother-tongue) reconquered North Africa from the Vandals, & in A.D. 553 regained Italia itself . . . as the "Exarchate of Ravenna"! Even a bit of Hispania was reclaimed from the Visigoths—but how long did it all last? The Spanish conquests were merely nominal, & were

---

\*in a dialect curiously midway between Latin & what we now call French.

lost within 70 years. North Africa—& with it Egypt & Syria—was gone to the Arabs within a century & a half. And in two centuries the last Italian fragment had been detached by Franks & Lombards, & the way paved for the ironically named "Holy Roman Empire" (neither holy nor Roman, & seldom a true empire) of Charlemagne & his successors! There is a fascination in this decay—but a sad one. And what a confusion & complexity of manners & customs, with dozens of nations intermixing, & the folkways of each one of them in a state of rapid flux! Here, truly, even the greatest student must unconsciously wallow in anachronisms if he try to depict the age in fiction or drama!

I'm glad to hear of your perusal of "The Last & First Men"—a volume which to my mind forms the greatest of all achievements in the field that Master Ackerman would denominate "scientifiction". Its scope is dizzying—& despite a somewhat disproportionate acceleration of the tempo toward the end, & a few scientific inferences which might legitimately be challenged, it remains a thing of unparalleled power. As you say, it has the truly basic quality of a myth, & some of the episodes are of matchless poignancy & dramatic intensity. This work has evoked dozens of imitations in the pulp magazines—the least absurd of which is a novelette by the brothers Binder, whose title eludes my memory.[32] It is itself perhaps an echo of the spacious speculations of Prof. J. B. S. Haldane regarding the future of mankind both on & off this planet. Have you ever seen the two little books—"Daedalus" [this ably answered by Bertrand Russell in "Icarus"] & "The Last Judgment"—in which Haldane gives free rein to his speculative imagination? Verily, they might form a source-book for dozens of romances enthralling to the "scientifan"! I have both, & would be glad to lend them if you'd like. As for Shiel—his unevenness is surely enough to reduce one to sulphureous eloquence! It would be difficult to find anything more trivial, affected, & flamboyant than his worst stuff—or more vivid, menacing, & genuinely moving than his two high spots—"The House of Sounds" [which represents a 1907 recasting of a florid 1896 attempt whose title I forget][33] & the first part of "The Purple Cloud." Sorry the "Cloud" seemed a bit disappointing—but possibly I laid the superlatives on too thick when describing it. It is of course riddled with crude & extravagant spots, & the occasional prosaic explanations tend to jar. Likewise, its concluding portions flop miserably into callow romance. But with all its faults it remains great stuff! That panorama of a dead world has no parallel in literature. I own "The Purple Cloud", but "The House of Sounds" has so far eluded my acquisitive attempts. It occurs in a volume called "The Pale Ape & Other Stories", published in London by T. Werner Laurie in 1908. When Knopf & the Vanguard began reviving interest in Shiel a decade ago—reprinting several of his works—I hoped that "The Pale Ape" might be offered in a new edition—but the boom collapsed before they got around to it. I'm thankful enough that "The Purple Cloud" was reissued in time! Yes—I wish the *right* person might illustrate "Ouroboros"—what a chance for somebody like Sime! If the new W T artist Virgil Finlay (age 22) lives up to his present promise, he'll be a logical candidate for the job in a decade or so. He has his lapses—I didn't care much for that text-belying design for my "Haunter"—but at his best he can knock all rivals sou'sou'west for a triple colonnade of Ceylonese snow-shovels! His drawing for Bloch's "Faceless God" (which Wright has framed for the W T office) is his high spot, but the one for my "Doorstep" is no slouch. Some of the illustrations inflicted upon W T writers are indeed pathetic—almost as bad as the stories! The give-away heading of my "Whisperer" has me still seeing red after 5 years & more! No—I don't think weird illustrations should be detailed. They should have the vagueness & suggestions of instability & mutation characteristic of true dreams. That is why, in W T, I have always preferred Hugh Rankin to others who are better draughtsmen. Finlay, as he matures, is acquiring the right idea—which I think his "Doorstep" design embodies to a perceptible extent. Here's something, by the way, which I lately ground out about Finlay's masterpiece:

>     To Mr. Finlay, *upon his Design for*
>     Mr. Bloch's *Tale,* The Faceless God:

In dim Abysses pulse the Shapes of Night,
　　Hungry and hideous, with strange Mitres crown'd;
Black Pinions beating in phantastick Flight
　　From Orb to Orb thro' sunless Voids profound.
None dares to name the Cosmos whence they course,
　　Or guess the Look on each amorphous Face,
Or speak the Words that with resistless Force
　　Would draw them from the Hells of outer Space.

Yet here upon a Page our frighten'd Glance
　　Finds monstrous Forms no human Eye shou'd see;
Hints of those Blasphemies whose Countenance
　　Spreads Death and Madness thro' Infinity.
What Limner he who braves black Gulphs alone,
　　And lives to make their alien Horrors known?

　　I learn with great interest of Messrs. Nemo & Murphet Leiber, & wish my own household were able to harbour their counterparts. As it is, my aunt & I have reluctantly agreed that our very light scale of housekeeping—involving irregular hours & occasional long absences (as when I paid 2 & 3 month visits in Florida in '34 & '35) on my part—render the tenure of any non-inorganic companions impracticable. Consequently, I am forced to content myself with playing occasional host to varied felidae of the neighbourhood—especially the inhabitants of the boarding-house in a parallel street whose rear abuts on

N.B. Do you know the work of William Hope Hodgson? It is very obscure, yet almost makes the Machen & Blackwood grade. You ought to read "The Boats of the Glen Carrig", "The House on the Borderland", & "The Night Land". If you wish, I'll have the owner of these books put your name on the list of borrowers among our back garden. For this purpose I always have a supply of catnip on hand, & many an afternoon as I sit writing I have some black or tiger or grey or black-&-white caller racing around the floor after spools or chewing the papers on my desk or alternately purring & dozing in a neighbouring easy-chair, according to his age & temperament. The little garden beside & behind this house is so completely cut off from the world that it forms a favourite congregating-place for local Mousers, grey or otherwise—who tend to choose as their social centre the roof of a small shed directly in line with my west windows. This group of shed-sprawlers has so many of the earmarks of a definite organisation that I have come to regard it (on the analogy of the numerous Greek-letter fraternities which form our neighbours on the ancient hill) as the Providence Chapter of the earthwide Kappa Alpha Tau society—an institution whose initials may be interpreted as the words Κομπσων Αιλουρων Ταξις (band of elegant or well-dress'd cats), though low punsters persist in reading a shorter & more phonetic meaning into our corporate initials K.A.T. Of this band, notwithstanding the inapplicability of the adjective to me, I consider myself an honorary member by virtue of my lifelong regard for the feline species. I am sure that Nemo & Murphet are high officials of the Southern California Chapter—just as Mother Simaetha, the incredibly aged coal-black witch-cat of Clark Ashton Smith, heads the Ladies' Auxiliary of the Central California Chapter. Enclosed you will find a small tribute which the Providence K.A.T. is sending, with its compliments, to Nemo & Murphet. I believe you have not seen this tale—or at least, that you do not have it permanently—hence I trust that its new furry owners will permit you to glance through it at least once or twice. It is rather a favourite of mine, as my own junk goes, & last Christmas my young friend Barlow astonished me with this special edition of 40 copies, which he sent to most of our circle in lieu of a greeting card.[34] He gave me several, but unfortunately my duplicates have narrowed down to the present rather seedy copy which borrowers have harshly handled, & for whose condition I must very sincerely apologise. I ought not to have allowed this gift-edition to piece out my battery of W T lending copies . . . . . but I am sure that Nemo & Murphet have a generous share of civilised tolerance. By the way—I hope to read at some time of Yanquisaga & his War-Cats, who respond to the summons of a silver whistle. They remind me of some of the characters in my repudiated fantasy "The Dream-Quest of Unknown Kadath". The peculiar charm of the felidae is a composite thing difficult to analyse. It seems to arise on the one hand from the utter grace & harmony of the cat—a perfect eurythmy pervading outlines & motions alike—plus those marks of cool, superior independence & self-sufficiency which remove Sir Thomas from the realm of human satellitism & make him the aristocratic exponent of another order of being—proud, alien in motives, values, & objectives, & linked with the mysteries of those black outer gulfs whence surely the first terrestrial felines lithely sprang long ago when Mu & Hyperborea were young. The ardent ailurophile is in good company, for does he not number eminent men as varied as Mohammed, Richelieu, Dr. Johnson, Poe, Baudelaire, & Vilfredo Pareto among his fellows?

As for the attitude of rational men of science toward the marvellous—the whole thing goes back into the remotest beginnings of epistemology. What do we know? How do we know we know it? Where the hell do all our ideas & impressions & perspectives come from, anyhow? Obviously, our traditional heritage of beliefs is of no use as a guide to truth, since it is predominantly an indiscriminate mass of primitive personifications, childish animistic pseudo-explanations, & ignorant inferences made from a background of subjective emotions & typical mental illusions—the whole developed & crystallised at a prehistoric date when the race knew nothing of the facts behind its environment, of cause & effect as related to terrestrial & celestial phenomena, or of the workings of its own consciousness & feelings. In an honest attempt to learn what the cosmos is, how it works, what its trends & directions are, & what relation to it is borne by organic life (including ourselves), religion & folklore are absolutely out [save as illustrations of human psychological processes]. Our only possible method is to observe the phenomena of the external world at first-hand—excluding all hereditary or preconceived ideas—& to form from an accurate study of these phenomena a set of inferences based on those same dependable & verifiable principles of cognition whereby we recognise intrinsic similarities & differences in immediate things such as temperature, degree of light, colour, odour, texture, sound, taste, & so on. It is of course understood that such an inferential process necessarily involves not only a minute biological study of those human channels through which our impressions come, but likewise a close survey (so far as our position & limitations allow) of those cognitive functions whereby we unconsciously select & emphasise & classify impressions, & draw conclusions from them. In these latter studies we must be prepared to realise that our images of things are arbitrarily limited by the accidents of our physical equipment (we, a spider, a snake, & a bird see & hear & feel & smell & taste altogether different things when experiencing the same objective environment), & that the concepts we deduce from these images are themselves altogether dependent upon a physiological state of things conditioned by racial history & swayed by numberless obscure factors. Ability to perceive & infer, a quality at first developed solely in the interest of primitive needs & gratifications, is constantly at the mercy of the crude instincts & emotions which called it forth, & can only with the most supreme difficulty be dissociated from the irrational hereditary delusions, material interests, & childish desires & perspectives with which it has for hundreds of thousands of years—or countless millions, if we go behind the human & primate & mammal stages—been inextricably intertwined. The stimulation of a nerve-centre, the hypertrophy or atrophy of an endocrine gland, the prior presence of a given concept or impression—any of these things may, wholly apart from truth or from any legitimate evidence, totally alter the conclusions which a given mind will draw from a given set of external impressions. Our subjective life is an utter, unreliable chaos from which no truth may be extracted, & which we must examine with the utmost closeness—studying its principles & characteristic tendencies—in order to allow for its effect on the objective concepts that we try to form. It is, then, no wonder that rational observers are cautious in advancing claims of the marvellous which on the one hand bear a suspicious resemblance to traditional notions of known erroneousness, & which on the other hand are sustained only feebly or not at all by any genuine or verifiable evidence in the external world. Of course, there are iconoclastic zealots who *overdo* the matter of caution—tending to minimise the evidence in behalf of things which seem at first sight unusual or opposed to the recognised scheme of Nature, & to magnify the defects & unreliability of our cognitive apparatus—but it is not the conclusions of these pedantic enthusiasts which triumph in the long run. Normal scientific progress generally makes steadily for increased truth—hence the tragedy of those new philosophies, so popular in totalitarian dictatorships, which exalt unreason & demand that scholarship be used only to serve preconceived propagandist ends. Nor will science ever be able to kill the feeling of wonder in the human spirit. The mystery of the black outer gulfs, & of the deepest cognitive processes within us, must always remain unplumbed—& against these limitations the ego-driven restlessness of the human consciousness & imagination must always frantically pound. It is phlegmatic complacency or a callous absorption in material things, which—rather than scientific truth—forms wonder's greatest foe. ¶ And now let me apologise for this extreme & tedious verboseness. Pray convey my compliments to Mrs. Leiber, whose interesting letter of the 8th I am about to answer. ¶ Yr obt Servt—The Old Man Without a Beard

P.S. As per instructions, I am holding the two MSS. for further discussion. I hope they may—if not destined for early publication—be circulated (as has other similar material) among a choice circle of the elect—such as Barlow, Clark Ashton Smith, Miss Moore, H. C. Koenig, & so on. Koenig (450 E. 80th St., N.Y. City) is the owner of those W. H. Hodgson books which I'm suggesting that you borrow from him if you can't get them locally.

*Notes*

1. A reference to a site in Leiber's "Adept's Gambit."
2. I.e., Farnsworth Wright, editor of *Weird Tales*.
3. R. H. Barlow eventually published the poem in *Leaves*.
4. HPL visited the Endless Caverns in 1928. See "Observations on Several Parts of North America" (1928; *CE* 4.28–29).

5. Leiber removed the reference in the published story.

6. "Old Folks at Home" (1851; sometimes called "Suwannee River"), a song by Stephen Foster (1826–1864). "Ben Bolt" (1848), a song by Nelson Kneass (1823–1868), based on a poem (1843) by Thomas Dunn English (1819–1902). "Sweet Adeline" (1904), a song by Henry W. Armstrong (1879–1951), with words by Richard H. Gerard (1876–1948). *Floradora* (1899), a musical comedy (book by Owen Hall [pseud. of Jimmy Davis], music by Leslie Stuart, additional songs by Paul Rubens). *The Burgomaster* (1900), a musical (book and lyrics by Frank S. Pixley, music by Gustav Luders).

7. Edward Alexander MacDowell (1860–1908), American composer focusing on compositions for piano and songs.

8. Imaginary instruments cited in Lord Dunsany's "Bethmoora."

9. Friedrich "Fritz" Kreisler (1875–1962), Austrian-born violinist and composer.

10. A character in Leiber's "Adept's Gambit."

11. The noted American author Theodore Dreiser (1871–1945) was the younger brother of Paul Dresser (born Johann Paul Dreiser, Jr.; 1857–1906), an American singer, songwriter, and comedic actor of the late nineteenth and early twentieth centuries.

12. "Sweet Rosie O'Grady" (1896), a song by Maude Nugent. "Goodbye, Dolly Gray" (c. 1900), a song by Will D. Cobb (lyrics) and Paul Barnes (music). "On the Banks of the Wabash, Far Away" (1897), a song by Paul Dresser. "Just Tell Them That You Saw Me" (1895), a song by Paul Dresser. "Oh! Oh! Miss Phoebe" (1900), a song by Andrew B. Sterling (words) and Harry von Tilzer (music).

13. Peter Francis Dailey (1868–1908), an American burlesque comedian and singer who became popular during the Gay Nineties.

14. Farnese's compositions were first recorded in 2015, on Fedogan and Bremer's remastered and expanded recording of HPL's *Fungi from Yuggoth*.

15. *The Tempest; or, The Enchanted Island* (1667), a comedy adapted by John Dryden (1631–1700) and Sir William Davenant (1606–1668) from Shakespeare's comedy. The musical setting was probably by John Weldon (1676–1736).

16. The Dryden–Davenant *Macbeth* dates to 1664. An adaptation of Shakespeare's *Julius Caesar,* attributed to both Dryden and Davenant (not Davenant alone), published in 1719, is probably by neither author.

17. Thomas Shadwell (1642?–1692) adapted Shakespeare's *The History of Timon of Athens the Man-Hater* in 1678.

18. Dryden's *Troilus and Cressida* dates to 1679.

19. *The History of King Lear* (1681), an adaptation of Shakespeare's *King Lear* by Nahum Tate (1652–1715). It concludes with a happy ending in which Lear regains his throne.

20. HPL refers to the collaboration of the poets Nahum Tate and Nicholas Brady, *New Version of the Psalms of David* (1696). The lines are from Psalm 112. They appear on the headstone of HPL's maternal great-great-grandfather Asaph Phillips (1764–1829). See *Essential Solitude* 210.

21. HPL refers to the American actor Edwin Booth (1833–1893) and the author William Winter (1836–1917), who adapted *King Lear* for Booth in 1888.

22. Joseph McCabe (1867–1955) was a well-known philosopher, historian, and free-thinker, author of such works as *The Evolution of Mind* (1910) and *The Story of Evolution* (1912). He also translated Ernst Haeckel's *The Riddle of the Universe* (1900).

23. I.e., "Novel of the Black Seal," an episode in Machen's *The Three Impostors.*

24. Arthur Machen, "The White People," in *The House of Souls* (New York: Alfred A. Knopf, 1923), 128–29.

25. Ed. Henry Thurston Peck.

26. HPL has erred on the title, which is *A School Dictionary of Greek and Roman Antiquities* (1846).

27. A popular historical novel by Henryk Sienkiewicz.

28. M. Velleius Paterculus (19 B.C.E.?–31 C.E.?), a Roman historian. His *History* covered the period from the end of the Trojan War to the death of Livia (wife of the Emperor Augustus) in 29 C.E.

29. Charles-Louis de Secondat, Baron de La Brède et de Montesquieu (1689–1755), *Considérations sur les causes de la grandeur des Romains et de leur décadence* (1734; *Considerations on the Causes of the Greatness of the Romans and Their Decline*). Jules Michelet (1798–1874), *Histoire romaine: Première partie, république* (1831; *History of the Roman Republic*).

30. L. Cassius Dio (155?–235; formerly referred to as Dio Cassius), Roman statesman of Greek origin and noted historian who wrote in Greek. Dio published a history of Rome in 80 volumes, beginning with the arrival of Aeneas in Italy, then documenting the founding of Rome, the formation of the Republic, and the creation of the Empire, and onward.

31. "Our sea," i.e., the Mediterranean.

32. Probably Eando [Earl and Otto] Binder, "Dawn to Dusk." a serial in *Wonder Stories* (November 1934, December 1934 and January 1935).

33. The early version of "The House of Sounds" appeared as "Vaila" in *Shapes in the Fire* (1896). Both versions can be found in Shiel's *The House of Sounds and Others,* ed. S. T. Joshi (New York: Hippocampus Press, 2005).

34. I.e., *The Cats of Ulthar.*

[8]     To Jonquil Leiber [AHT]

December 20, 1936

Dear Mrs. Leiber:—

[. . .] Concerning the matter of prosaic toil—I can scarcely rejoice that I have not discovered & engaged in some more regular & remunerative form of it than free-lance revision, since the tangible results would be distinctly more helpful than the psychological atmosphere would be harmful! Instead, if ever I *do* stumble upon an opening, the picturesque conception of me as a non-time-clock-puncher will swiftly & ruthlessly vanish. However, I shall probably be available a decade hence—if still living at so advanced an age—for that good-weird-magazine editorship which Mr. Leiber has in mind! Such a magazine would surely be welcomed by a limited & devoted circle—though in harsh fact I gravely doubt its practicability as a commercial or even self-sustaining venture. The old W.T. group has many a time discussed something of the sort—pointing out that virtually all of the world's first-rate authors (for example—Henry James, Rudyard Kipling, Edith Wharton, F. Marion Crawford, Theodore Dreiser, Guy de Maupassant, &c. &c. &c) have at one time or another written weird material, & arguing that they would probably produce a great deal more if a definite & dependable market existed. With this potential source of contents (to which would of course be added the presumably increased output of such acknowledged fantaisistes as Blackwood, Machen, Dunsany, de la Mare, &c.), argued the optimists, the right sort of publisher might float a weird magazine of the very highest grade, commanding a select & dependable public, & reaching persons who would toss aside a cheap rag like W.T. with contempt. A pleasing picture! But there were not lacking pessimists to point out that this select & faithful public would of necessity be woefully small. After all, a taste for fantasy in large doses is a rather unusual thing. Most readers like it only occasionally—relishing a Machen book now & then, or faintly appreciating the timid & insipid bits (like "The House of the Laburnums" in the Dec. *Harpers*)[1] sparingly scattered through the conventional magazines, but becoming distinctly bored when confronted by a solid or frequent diet of shadow & bizarrerie. Hence the reluctance of book publishers to issue collections of weird short stories . . . . & hence, by inference, the impossibility of finding enough readers among the literate to keep a cosmic-spectral periodical alive. That Farnsworth Wright & his congeners recognise this dilemma is very obvious—for their output is deliberately designed to attract the limitless hordes of the crude & illiterate. They tap a class which a civilised magazine could not reach—the coarse sensation-seeker, the superstitious séance-devotee, & so on—& yet they manage to retain a small literate following through the insertion of a few passable yarns, & because of the fact that no other magazines of the like subject-matter exist. The editors are glad to hold this handful of the civilised if they can do so without alienating their bread-&-butter-yielding yokelry—but when it comes to a choice betwixt the two, the yokelry wins every time. Caeteris paribus, the cheap, sensational story is preferred to the sincere artistic effort. And the sad thing is that the editors are probably commercially right. That's what business is! If they tried to present an all-civilised programme of fiction their circulation would probably dwindle below the self-supporting limit. But let us hope—for the sake of weird literature as well as of that editorship—that conditions may somehow miraculously change before 1947. Good luck to the future *Leiber Fabularum Pavidorum* . . . . if one may attempt a base but classic example of paronomasia.[2]

I can appreciate the startling contrast which would have been afforded if—in consonance with the whimsical wish of Fafhrd the Viking—I had suddenly appeared, like some skeleton at the feast, at Mr. John Barrymore's Anacreontic gathering. That your genial host would have 'gone to pieces over me' (albeit for a far different reason than that which caused his disintegration over your distinguished 'governor's' visage) I can well imagine; for even the most potent distillate of the golden maize never produced a pink elephant quite so grotesque & terrifying as the thing he would have beheld! Alas that I was unavoidably absent—for might not the shock have permanently flung the ivy-wreathed genius upon a water-wagon destined to bear him to new heights of accomplishment? By such little slips is the course of history & of the arts sometimes irrevocably changed! Yes, indeed, I have frequently encountered Mr. Barrymore's name in the press, & must congratulate him on his ability to remain in touch with romance to an extent not common among those of our greying generation! It is only in an earlier & widely different phase that this luminary & I have any point of resemblance—this being our common difficulty in establishing contact with systematic toil. I have always appreciated that oft-repeated anecdote of his youth—when, as a somewhat elegant but scarcely industrious flaneur in '06, he was engulfed in the chaos of the San Francisco disaster. Along with others he was drafted into emergency rescue & ruin-clearing service by the military authorities in charge of the stricken area—upon hearing of which his illustrious uncle, Mr. John Drew, is reported to have exclaimed, "By god, it took an earthquake & the United States Army to put John to work!" And yet the parallel is by no means perfect, since there is no period of my life in which I could not have been driven into useful pursuits by an earthquake alone—or by an army without an earthquake! No use trying to compete with the great in colour or intensity!

Speaking of industrio-economic matters—let me assure you that a 2-or-3-dollar-a-week dietary programme need not involve even a particle of malnutrition or unpalatability if one but knew what to get & where to get it. The tin can & delicatessen conceal marvellous possibilities! Porridge? Mehercule! On the contrary, my tastes call for the most blisteringly highly-seasoned materials conceivable, & for desserts as close to 100% $C_{12}H_{22}O_{11}$ as possible. Indeed, of this latter commodity I never employ less than four teaspoons in an average cup of coffee. Favourite dinners—Italian spaghetti, chile con carne, Hungarian goulash (save when I can get white meat of turkey with highly-seasoned dressing). If this be asceticism, make the most of it! As for the expense element—to begin with, I eat only twice daily from choice . . . or rather, digestive advisability. I adopted this two-meal programme long before I had to economise. The rest is merely a matter of judicious and & far from self-denying choice. Let us investigate a typical day's rations.

(a) *Breakfast* (whether I eat it before or after retiring depends on whether I retire at 2 a.m. or 9 a.m. or 3 p.m. or 9 p.m. or some other hour. My programme of sleeping & waking is very flexible.)

Doughnut from Weybosset Pure Food Market .................................... 0.015
York State Medium Cheese (for sake of round numbers).................. 0.060
Coffee + Challenge Brand Condensed Milk + $C_{12}H_{22}O_{11}$.................. <u>0.025</u>
Total Breakfast....................................0.100

(b) *Dinner* (occurring vaguely betwixt 6 & 9 or 10 p.m.)
1 can Rath's Chili con Carne*.................................................................0.100
2 slices Bond Bread .................................................................................0.025
Coffee (with accessories as noted above).............................................0.025
Slice of cake or quadrant (or octant) of pie.........................................<u>0.050</u>
Total Dinner.............................................0.200
Grand Total for Entire Day...............0.30
7
Average Total per Week....................2.10

Occasionally, of course, extravagant additions occur—such as fruit with breakfast, or cheese with pie at dinner, or a chocolate bar or ice cream at an odd hour, or a meat-course costing more than a dime, or other sybaritic luxuries. But even the most Lucullan indulgence seldom tops an hebdomadal 3 bucks. And the old man still lives—in a fairly hale & hearty state, at that! Oddly enough, I was a semi-invalid in the old days when I *didn't* economise. Porridge? Not for Grandpa! [. . .]

[. . .] I can endorse with the most profanely fervent emphasis your appraisal of American Business Push! The fact is, an ideal of toil for its own sake, & an exaltation of the grasping, aggressively acquisitive type, have always seemed to me so self-evidently barbarous & ignominious that I have never quite been able to realise their existence as important factors. Commercial ideals are a trifle better camouflaged in New England than in other parts of America; & as one more disposed to draw ideas from books than to absorb the spirit of my physical environment, I managed to grow up with a European rather than pioneer-American scale of values regarding the individual & society. Not that I have ever scorned honest industry—for should not every person contribute all he can to society, in exchange for the organised benefits it extends him?—but that I have scorned the notion of industry *as an end in itself.* I cannot comprehend the exaltation of a mere *process* as distinguished from its *objects. Working to live* I can understand—but not *living to work!* And the poisonous, cheapening vulgarity of the commercial mind—the readiness to haggle, the tendency to relate all ideas & impressions to material advantage, & the rat-like intensiveness associated with 'business enterprise'—has always nauseated me so violently that the notion of a social order founded on it has seemed to partake of fantastic nightmare rather than sober reality. Yet I suppose such a reign of commercial ideals does exist—indeed, I see many evidences of it when I view the objective phenomena of today. But I fancy its triumph will be short-lived. Mechanisation of industry & diffusion of knowledge are laying the foundations

---

*(or Armour's Corned Beef Hash or baked beans from delic., or Armour's Frankfort Sausage or Boiardi Meat Balls & Spaghetti or chop suey from delicatessen or Campbell's Vegetable Soup, &c. &c. &c.)

for widespread change, & squirearchy & capitalism must alike go down in time before some planned society more rational & equitable than either. Let us only hope that in this part of the world the coming transition will be evolutionary rather than revolutionary—as indeed we may expect of any fabric whose cultural roots are of Northwestern Europe. But so far as the past & present are concerned, I would certainly be more at home in England than in America. Indeed—if I were not so wrapped up in antiquarianism that I virtually *am* in England spiritually, I would probably find my milieu psychologically unendurable. I get by because I have blinders on!

It is interesting to know that you have a touch of piracy in your ancestry! I have a *counterfeiter* as a great-great-grand-uncle[3] about whom I'll tell you some time. He was also a silversmith—with pieces surviving in the Metropolitan Museum of N. Y., the Boston Museum of Fine Arts, & elsewhere. He'd have been hanged in 1770 if his neighbours (who were probably implicated in the coining—such offences being lightly regarded in the colonies) hadn't effected a gaol-delivery. I am lineally descended from his elder brother, born in 1723. I wish I could see your ancestral crag of St. Michael's Mount—descriptions of which have always fascinated me. If pictures speak truly, the castle on its summit must be one of the loveliest & most ethereally fantastic objects outside the pages of Dunsany—to which is added the charm of its long history, & the rumour that a giant's skeleton was discovered in a secret dungeon beneath it a century or so ago. The appearance of the Mount with its pinnacled citadel under certain lighting & atmospheric conditions—as, for instance, outlined against an orange sunset—must be exquisite beyond description. And the little village on the shore doubtless shares that fascinating quality which all Cornish seaports seem to possess. (Which reminds me—I suppose you have read E. F. Benson's splendid weird tale "Negotium Perambulans", which is laid in a typical Cornish village betwixt the sea & an overshadowing crag.) Mount's Bay, I believe, still reveals at low tide the spectral black trunks which bespeak its former life as a forest above the water. One can imagine dark and curious things in connexion with a wood beneath the waves! All told, I believe that Cornwall must form the most picturesque & fascinating spot in England, with its plenteous reliques of the past, its bold topography, its ancient villages, its tenacious folkways, its suggestions of subtropical vegetation (this in the latitude of northern Newfoundland—so potent are the subtler elements of climate-formation!), & its legends of dim yesterdays & of the sunken land of Lyonesse. I have several ancestral lines which remotely extend back to Cornwall—Carew, Edgecome, Trefusis—hence feel that it is no alien soil. It is in ancient Damnonia, however, that Lovecrafts are chiefly scattered—largely in the valley of the Teign near Newton-Abbot. Historically, Cornwall & Devon are pretty much a unit. Both may have known the footstep of the Phoenician trader as far back as 100 B.C.—& in Egypt tin vases, perhaps of Cornubian origin, have been found in tombs even older than that.

That is the kind of contrast which ought to appeal to Fafhrd the Viking. And not very far from your St. Michael's Mount—at St. Hilary on the mainland—there is a stone with a Roman inscription—FLAVIO. IVLIO. CONSTAN-TIN. PII. CAESARI. DVC. CONSTANTINI. PII. AUGUSTI. FILIO—dating from A.D. 307 & bringing the region vividly into the stream of classical history. Truly, a fitting locale for Adrian Stephens & his Devil-Tower!

I note with great interest the list of Mr. Leiber's Novanglian lines, & regret that none of them are in my own ancestry. My aunt knows *Bronsons* in this city—indeed, until recently two maiden ladies of that name conducted Providence's most select school for small children. The Bronson School was in Hope St.—next the Hope St. High School which I attended 1904–8—& in those days we used to tell fellow-students whose egos we wished to deflate that they were in the wrong building—implying that they belonged over at the Misses Bronson's with the five-year-olds! *Temple* is also represented hereabouts—indeed, if the rain lets up this afternoon my aunt & I are going to hear a lecture on old textiles at the School of Design half way down the hill by one who combines a Temple line with our *Casey* line—the latter the one on which the counterfeiter of 1770 occurs. Rather odd, by the way, to find an Irish name like Casey in early Rhode Island. That's my only line of ancestry outside England and Wales. The Caseys—seated in Tyrone & of the Anglo-Irish Protestant persuasion—were engulfed in the massacre of 1641, & of this branch only a 6 year old boy named Thomas survived. He was rescued by his nurse & taken to his mother's family in Gloucestershire, whence he emigrated to Newport, Rhode Island, in 1658. Sam the Counterfeiting Silversmith (b. 1724) & my ancestor John (b. 1723) were his grandsons. Other descendants appear elsewhere in history. Capt. Wanton Casey fought with the rebels in the trouble of 1775–83. Gen. Silas Casey was the author of a book of military tactics & died in the Mexican War. Another of them was the engineer who either started or finished (I forget which) the Washington Monument, whilst a later scion was (may gawd forgive him) the architect of Washington's baroque & bedizened Library of Congress. Foine bhoys, ahl av thim, aven if wan av thim did go a bit wrong toward the end of the 1760's, & misapply his talent in constructing near-silver bas-reliefs of the reigning Bourbons & Broganzas (the *corpora delicti* were fake Spanish milled dollars & Portugese Moidares). The lecturer we are (perhaps) about to hear is Miss Elizabeth Temple Casey,[4] Asst. Curator of the School of Design Museum. [. . .]

  Yr. Obdt &c.   H P L

*Notes*

1. Mollie Panter-Downes, "The House of the Laburnums," *Harpers* 174, No. 1 (December 1936): 42–45; rpt. *The Ash-Tree Press Annual Macabre 1997*, ed. Jack Adrian

(Ashcroft, BC: Ash-Tree Press, 1997). Panter-Downes (1906–1997) was a British writer and author of the bestselling novel *The Shoreless Sea* (1923).

2. HPL's coined Latin phrase would mean "Book of Frightening Stories," with *Leiber* being a punning reference to *Liber* (Book).

3. Samuel Casey (1724?–1770+), brother of HPL's great-great-great-grandfather John Casey (1723–1794). Casey was a silversmith in Kingstown, RI, who was arrested for counterfeiting.

4. Elizabeth Temple Casey (1901–1991), assistant curator of the Rhode Island School of Design Museum (1926–35), curator of textiles (1935–43), and curator of the Lucy Truman Aldrich Collection of European porcelain figures (1950–78).


[9]    To Fritz Leiber, Jr. [AHT]

DATA. PROVIDENTIAE.

VIII. A. K. FEBR.

Jany. 25, 1937

FLAVIUS. SENILIS. P. CORNELIO. SCIPIONI. S. P. D.

The reprehensibly late date of this bulletin may be charged jointly to the plethora of tasks currently pressing on me, & to the reduced amount of energy available for their performance. For the past month I have been more or less on the semi-invalid list—with a recurrent winter malady manifested in swollen feet & ankles, plus a curiously persistent combination of intestinal indigestion & general weakness perhaps allied to the prevailing grippe. Not that I've been laid flat—indeed, I've managed to take regular walks for my health on warm days in a pair of cut & stretched old shoes, & have attended most of the recent college lectures . . . on subjects as diverse as Peruvian antiquities, Italian Romanesque architecture, biological implications in philosophy, modern French painters, & Greek astronomical hypotheses. But I've had to rest frequently, & it has taken me a hell of a while to get anything done. Meanwhile I have heard most interestingly from the grey mouser of Louisville (who I hope is still above water despite the floods now visiting his section)—his latest epistle being a marvellously brilliant document accompanied by a generously proportioned pastel drawing of our curious friend Ningauble from the crayon of his gifted wife.[1] In an earlier epistle the Gray One most kindly quoted for my benefit the opening paragraphs of the Fafhrd-Mouser cycle, which gave a certain feeling of orientation regarding the series as a whole. [. . .]

[. . .] It is with the greatest interest that I learn of your plans for revising the "Gambit", & I shall surely welcome the new version when it reaches me. The plan for greater indefiniteness in allusions will surely dispose of all the anachronisms—though if you wished to avoid an excess of compound words you could call a "scientist" either a *philosopher* or a *cunning artificer,* depending on which side of his activities you wished to emphasise. Your suggestion for an era-fixing first paragraph sounds very fruitful—& that possible allusion to Hamilcar & his small son at the end provides another distinctly fascinating link with the historic stream. Regarding the basic plot & motivation changes—these all seem eminently in the right direction. It is one of my fictional axioms that, although a writer should feel perfectly free to change his plot or characters or emphasis during the course of composition, he ought to be scrupulously careful to go over the finished MS. & reconcile very part with the dominant design finally adopted. I don't believe your revision will injure the style, since you seem to have a natural & easy mastery of the chosen type of prose rhythm. Naturally, the later sections will need but little change. Would you like your original MS. returned directly? It seems as if you might use many of the pages & avoid retyping. Let me know. I am very grateful for permission to circulate the MS. among a select circle, & will take pains to confine the list to the extremely appreciative—thus avoiding both delay & wear & tear on the MS. Your notes on Fafhrd's & the Mouser's possible antecedents are extremely interesting—& I wish good old Two-Gun Bob Howard were alive to see this echo of his virile & adventurous heroics. Some day I surely hope a great deal of the Fafhrd cycle will get into print—leading off with "Adept's Gambit". I fancy you are wise, after all, in choosing an imaginary age for the forthcoming story—especially since you wish to include dealings with monarchs & leaders. R E H had a splendidly self-consistent world of pre-history mapped out for his King Kull & Conan tales, & he made it vital & vivid despite his very unfortunate use (how vainly Price & I have lectured him on this point!) of a nomenclature fraught with misleading historical suggestions Have you seen the issues of the little *Phantagraph* containing Howard's own serial account of his legendary lands—"The Hyborian Age"? If not, you really ought to get hold of them. Only about a quarter has yet appeared, but the size of instalments may be increased. I'll gladly lend you the issues in question—or you can get them permanently from Donald A. Wollheim, 801 West End Ave., N. Y. City. Not that you'll want to copy anything, but that you'll take pleasure in the vigour & lifelikeness of the coördinated pseudo-historic picture, & will appreciate the Conan tales all the more for having imbibed it. Klarkash-Ton, High Priest of Tsathoggua, likewise has two very well-coördinated mythical worlds—the *Hyperborea* of the fabulous past & the *Zothique* of the infinite future—in addition to his enchanted mediaeval-French world of *Averoigne*—which latter is a sort of European "Arkham country" of 800 years ago. I have helped C A S give *Averoigne* a pseudo-history extending back to Gallic days, when the *Averones* trickled in from a sunken western land & brought with them the hellish tome known in later years as Liber Ivonis or Livre d'Eibon. This dark people set up the worship of Tsathoggua, Sadagai, or Sadoqua in the region where they settled, so that by the Gallo-Roman period the *Regio Averonum* or *Averonia* was feared as the abode of a black and unearthly sorcery. Especially dreaded were the towns of Simaesis (Ximes) & Avionium (Yvones), where certain cults obscurely flourished. Timid references to the Averones & Avernia occur in certain unknown Gallo-Roman authors such as Flavius Alesius (whose "Annales" tell of the Dark Ones' coming) & the poet Valerius Trevirus. Trevirus, in his hideously necromantic poem "De Noctis Rebus" (circa. A.D. 390), thus alludes to the Averones:

NIGER. INFORMISQUE. VT. NUMEN. AVERONUM. SADOQUA.

—which, in Theobald's privately printed English translation (1711), runs:

> Black & unform'd, as pestilent a Clod
> As dread Sadoqua, Averonia's God.[2]

Merovingian & Carlovingian legends hold dark allusions to the Averones, & by the 11th century the Catholic hierarchy of Averoigne was thoroughly tainted with diabolism. For accounts of mediaeval conditions in this shadowy land, C A S is a better authority than I. As you know, Gaspard du Nord's translation of the Liber Ivonis (whether from the corrupt Latin text or from the accursed Hyperborean original we cannot be sure—his accomplishments were dark & obscure) into mediaeval French in the 12th century brought about frightful consequences—the popular diffusion of certain rites & incantations causing Averoigne to receive that shadow of concentrated necromancy from which it has never quite emerged.[. . .]

*Notes*

1. Martha McElroy Fischer (1912–1991)
2. First propounded in HPL's letter to Clark Ashton Smith, [13 December 1933], and HPL's initial preparatory notes. *DS* 498 and 494, respectively.

# Letters to Harry O. Fischer

[1]    [*SL* 927]

Unknown Kadath—
[late February 1937]

Valiant & (I fervently trust) Undrownèd Mouser:—[1]

Regarding the element of *fear*—I don't think I share your immunity. I am a middle-grounder, with *heights* as my weak point. Lacking any natural sense of balance (some of those curious equilibrating devices in the inner ear must be weak or absent in me), I become dizzy in lofty & difficult places, & could easily fall to a pulpy doom (in more than the figurative, literary sense) if I tried to duplicate some of the stunts which others perform as a matter of course. Just about a decade ago I began refusing to take dares—beginning with the time a friend challenged me to walk along the foot-wide & not-quite level parapet of upper Riverside Drive in New York, with a 500-foot perpendicular drop to ragged rocks & railway tracks on one side. In other fields, however, I'm an especial Caspar Milquetoast—being willing to take a chance where there really *is* a chance. I'm not especially set on living for ever, although I'd dislike meeting a messy or disintegrative end. I don't bear pain well, & dodge it whenever possible. However, I endeavour not to do my yelling out loud. In infancy I was afraid of the dark, which I peopled with all sorts of things; but my grandfather cured me of that by daring me to walk through certain dark parts of the house when I was 3 or 4 years old. After that, dark places held a certain fascination for me. But it is in *dreams* that I have known the real clutch of stark, hideous, maddening, paralysing *fear*. My infant nightmares were classics, & in them there is not an abyss of agonising cosmic horror that I have not explored. I don't have such dreams now—but the memory of them will never leave me. It is undoubtedly from them that the darkest & most gruesome side of my fictional imagination is derived. At the ages of 3, 4, 5, 6, 7, & 8 I have been whirled through formless abysses of infinite night & adumbrated horrors as black & as seethingly sinister as any of our friend Fafhrd's "splatter-stencil" triumph's. That's why I appreciate such triumphs so keenly. *I have seen these things!* Many a time I have awaked in shrieks of panic, & have fought desperately to keep from sinking back into sleep & its unutterable horrors. At the age of six my dreams became peopled with a race of lean, faceless, rubbery, winged things to which I applied the home-made name of *night-gaunts*. Night after night they would appear in exactly the same form—& the terror they brought was beyond any verbal description. Long decades later I embodied them in one of my *Fungi from Yuggoth* pseudo-sonnets, which you may have read. Well—after I was 8 all these things abated, perhaps because of the scientific habit of mind which I was acquiring (or trying to acquire). I ceased to believe in religion or any other form of the supernatural, & the new logic gradually reached my subconscious imagination. Still, occasional nightmares brought recurrent touches of the ancient fear—& as late as 1919 I had some that I could use in fiction without much change. "The Statement of Randolph Carter" is a literal dream transcript. Now, in the sere & yellow leaf (I shall be 47 in August), I seem to be rather deserted by stark horror. I have nightmares only 2 or 3 times a year, & of these none ever approaches those of my youth in soul-shattering, phobic monstrousness. It is fully a decade & more since I have known *fear* in its most stupefying & hideous form. And yet, so strong is the impress of the past, I shall never cease to be fascinated by *fear* as a subject for aesthetic treatment. Along with the element of cosmic mystery & outsideness, it will always interest me more than anything else. It is, in a way, amusing that one of my chief interests should be an emotion whose poignant extremes I have never known in waking life!

Of the celebrated "phobias" of the modern psychologists (or of things like them) I have only *one;* & that, amusingly enough, is one I have never seen cited or named. Probably it *has* a name & record, but my very superficial knowledge of psychology (a subject which fails to fascinate me greatly, despite its grotesque fictional possibilities) does not include any glimpse of it. I know about *claustrophobia* & *agoraphobia,* but have neither. I have, however, a cross betwixt the two in the form of a distinct fear of *very large enclosed spaces.* The dark carriage-room of a stable—the shadowy interior of a deserted gashouse—an empty assembly-room or theatre-auditorium—a large cave—you can probably get the idea. Not that such things throw me into visible & uncontrollable jittery spasms, but that they give me a profound & crawling sense of the sinister—even at my age. I'm not sure of the source of this fear, but I believe it must link up somehow with the black abysses of my infant nightmares. Anyhow, I keep it in mind to deflate my ego when I tend to feel superior about the illogical aversions & timidities of others. Grandpa must not forget his Achillean heel!

The name "Abdul Alhazred" is one which some adult (I can't recall who)[2] devised for me when I was 5 years old & eager to be an Arab after reading the Arabian Nights. Years later I thought it would be fun to use it as the name of a forbidden-book author. The name *Necronomicon* (νεκρος, corpse; νομος, law; eikon, εικον image = An Image [or Picture] of the Law of the Dead)[3] occurred to me in the course of a dream, although the etymology is perfectly sound. In assigning an *Arabic* author to a *Greek-named* book I was whimsically reversing the condition whereby the monumental astronomical work of the *Greek* Ptolemy (Μεγαλε Συνταξις Της Αστρονομιας) is commonly known by the *Arabic* name *Almagest* (or more truly, Tabrir al Magesthi), which was evolved from a corruption of the original title when the Arabs made their translation (μεγιστε is the superlative of μεγαλε, & the Arabs probably found it in common use to distinguish the work from another of Ptolemy's). It was not until later that I took the trouble to hunt up a genuine Arabic title (Al Azif—a word which I found in Henley's learned notes to *Vathek*. I use the term correctly, though at second-hand) for old Abdul's *original* version of the Byzantinely translated Νεϰρονομιϰον.

I can well comprehend the vague impression of aloneness or differentiation which you have always had in some degree. Such, I imagine, is always the concomitant of a very active imagination & highly individualised personality. The bulk of the human race lives very little in the imaginative realm; hence can seldom grasp the goals, motives, & aspirations of anyone with whom subtle perspectives, symbolic associations, & obscure mental correlations form important emotional factors. Such a one must inhabit a quasi-solipsistic world of his own even more completely than the average individual, & he is always fortunate when he encounters others of a cast sufficiently similar to appreciate the existence, general principles, & typical laws of his private universe. This general comprehension of separate worlds & their workings is usually as sound a basis of congeniality as that rarer & perhaps wholly non-existent phenomenon of an *identity* of private universes. At least, what makes me feel cordial & at ease toward anyone is not so much an identity of tastes & beliefs & perspectives, as an assurance that my own tastes & beliefs & perspectives are not regarded as insane, incomprehensible, or non-existent!

Yrs by *still*-sunken R'lyeh—
        Grandpa Cthulhu

*Notes*

1. HPL alludes to the fact that Fischer and and his family had been enduring the Ohio River Flood of January–February 1937 at his home in Louisville.

2. Elsewhere HPL identifies this person as the family lawyer, Albert A. Baker.

3. HPL's derivation is almost entirely erroneous. See S. T. Joshi, *Lovecraft and a World in Transition* (New York: Hippocampus Press, 2014), 420.

# Letters to Frederic Jay Pabody

[1]  [ALS, JHL]

66 College St.,
Providence, R.I.,
Feby. 28, 1936.

Frederic Jay Pabody, Esq.,
1367 E. Sixth St.,
Cleveland, Ohio.

Dear Mr. Pabody:—

Your enquiry regarding the source of the name *Pabodie* in my recent story[1] has just been forwarded by Street & Smith. In reply let me say that—although I am not personally acquainted with anyone of this patronymic—I chose it as a name typical of good old New England stock yet not sufficiently common to sound conventional or hackneyed. I try very much to be realistic in fictional nomenclature—to select every-day names characteristic of the regions in which they are supposed to occur, & to avoid the cheap practice of using overdone, ambiguous, or pseudo-romantic names supposedly "appropriate" to the various characters. Thus instead of having a central figure named "Jack Strong" or "Richard Manly"[2] or "John Cavendish", I try to have him named something like "Walter F. Hazard" if he comes from Rhode Island's South County, "Daniel P. Gilman" if he comes from Rockingham County, N.H.,[3] "Nicholas A Freer" if from Ulster County, N.Y., "Henry S. Valentine" if from the neighbourhood of Richmond, Va., "Thomas B. Rhett" if from the Carolina low country, "Charles N. Sanchez" if from St. Augustine, "John R. Legris" if from New Orleans,[4] &c. &c[.] &c.* It is also my aim to avoid having all central figures young, bold, dashing & handsome, & to avoid the arbitrary division of characters into "hero", "villain", & so on. In other words—the whole battery of popular clichés, & the whole ideology of the popular plot-&-action story, are anathema to me. But pardon the digression.

I suppose I hit upon the name *Pabodie* by a very indirect process. Most of my tales centre in an imaginary Massachusetts town (vaguely reminiscent

---

*I also use a realistic proportion of names of later immigrant stock where such are called for—in such cases having them appropriate to the region, occupation, & social situation concerned. . . . French-Canadians, Italians, Portugese, Irish, Poles, &c. in New England, Jews in N.Y. City, Slavs & Germans in the Middle West, Scandinavians in the Northwest, Mexicans in the Southwest, &c. However—the *antiquarian* element in most of my tales causes me to deal mainly with old American stock.

of Salem, but with an imaginary college—"Miskatonic"—added) called "Arkham", in Essex County, hence I am rather partial toward Essex surnames—Pickman, Ropes, Derby, *Peabody*, Keezar, Wingate, Upton, &c. &c. It was probably this Essex County leaning which made me think—at first—of *Peabody* for my engineering professor; but upon reflection I decided that the great fame of this name (in museums, philanthropic foundations, &c.) made it a little too conventional for the realistic atmosphere I wanted. So I turned to a variant of it which used to be quite well represented in my own city, & which even now is not wholly extinct here. . . . the name which, with a slight orthographical variation, you have the honour to bear.

Probably all Peabodys, Pabodies, & Pabodys have an origin in common—from the *"Peabodie"* which you cite. I am not enough of a genealogist to trace the Providence *Pabodies* back other Massachusetts *Peabody* stock from which they are probably derived, though an hour in the library of the R.I. Historical Society would probably clear everything up. Since that august institution is less than a full-sized block from my door, I'll be glad to look at the records if you find nothing definite from \the surviving Pabodie whose address I am about to give.

The earliest Providence Pabodie whose name I have encountered is a friend of Edgar Allan Poe, at whose house the poet used sometimes to stop when in this city. This *William J. Pabodie* was one of the witnesses to the tentative marriage contract drawn up between Poe & Mrs Sarah Helen Whitman in 1848, & was in close touch with Poe throughout his brief & frustrated romance with the local poetess. Data concerning this Pabodie ought to be relatively easy to find. In the 1850's there was a dealer in hats—B. G. Pabodie & Co.—at 13 Arcade in this city.

I next encounter the name of Pabodie in the 1890's, when the engraving & publishing firm of *C. A. Pabodie & Son* rose to prominence & became the local leaders in this branch of industry. This firm issued Providence & Rhode Island maps, directories, street-guides, &c., becoming a formidable rival to the older firm of Sampson, Murdock, & Co., which has always handled such business—& still does. From 1890 or so until far into the 1900's, the Pabodie firm was the first choice of the average Providentian when social engraving—cards, invitations, announcements—was desired. At this same period my aunt (who survives as head of my household) was slightly acquainted with some elderly Pabodies—two maiden ladies & their brother (or possibly two brothers), who were friends of the parents of one of her friends. They were shadowy figures to one then of the younger generation, but she seems to recall that they were of the engraver's immediate family—if, indeed, the remembered brother were not the engraver himself. Today, so far as I can judge from the telephone book, the firm of Pabodie no longer exists. Its last address that I can recall—circa 1904—was 139 Mathewson St., Providence.

Coming now to the present—although I do not personally know any Pabodies, I find one (residential) entry of the name in the current telephone directory . . . . *C. Walter Pabodie, 54 Harvard Ave., Providence, R.I.* I would suggest that you write him for data, since it is only reasonable to suppose that he is an heir of the same line to which the earlier Providence Pabodies belong. It is more than likely that he is the "& Son" of the old engraving firm, now retired from business . . . . . . though of course this is merely a guess.

As the only male Lovecraft* (to my knowledge) outside England [my great-grandfather, Joseph Lovecraft, came to upper N.Y. State from Devonshire in 1827.[6] My *maternal* stock is colonial Rhode Island], I am greatly interested in what you say regarding the scarcity of American *Pabodys*. Does this known group of seven include persons using the spelling *Pabodie*, or is it restricted to those following the *Pabody* usage? If you are interested in *Peabody* (thus spelled) data, I would suggest that you write a good friend of mine [descended from John Peabody of England & Massachusetts though his son Lieut. Francis Peabody (1614–1698) & the latter's daughter Lydia (1640–1715)] who is a really encyclopaedic genealogist with oceans of statistics & records at his finger-tips—*James F. Morton,* [Curator of the] *Paterson Museum, Paterson, New Jersey.* He is usually very eager to help others out regarding their ancestral problems. Mr. Morton, by the way, is a grandson of the Rev. Samuel Francis Smith, who wrote "My Country, 'Tis of Thee."

Hoping that communication with Mr. Pabodie—& perhaps with Mr. Morton—may yield material of value to you, & rejoicing if my story should eventually prove the indirect means of your extending your family knowledge,

      I am

              Yours most sincerely,

                  H. P. Lovecraft

*Notes*

1. I.e., the recently published (not written) *At the Mountains of Madness.*
2. HPL used the name "Jack Manly" in the satirical story "Sweet Ermengarde."
3. But cf. the Gilman family and Gilman House cited in "The Shadow over Innsmouth" (1931), taking place in that fictitious Massachusetts backwater.
4. HPL's "The Call of Cthulhu" has a character named John R. Legrasse.
5. *WT* 23, No. 6 (June 1934): 783.
6. The actual year was 1831.

---

*A letter signed "Edgar Lovecraft, Martinsburg, W. Va." appeared in the readers' department of *Weird Tales* 2 years ago,[5] but since communications to this person were returned unclaimed, I have concluded that the surname was a pseudonym—chosen because of the frequent occurrence on the contents table of the magazine.

[2]    [ALS, JHL]

Out on Prospect Terrace
June 19, 1936.

My dear Mr. Pabody:—

       Your letter & story both safely arrived, & I wish to congratulate you very sincerely on the excellence & appealing qualities of the latter. In view of your modest depreciation of it, I read it with eyes alert for flaws & weaknesses—but as I went along I found it very hard to discover the looked-for defects! The fact is, I like it tremendously. It catches a certain wistful aspect of weak human nature in symbols of refreshing concreteness & verisimilitude. Poor Stanley is not sentimentalised, but the mere chronicle of incidents befalling him makes him a living character evocative of the reader's pity. I do not feel that it is unimaginative, because the central figure seems truly envisaged. You have succeeded in getting inside a certain character & sharing his individual perspective—& in a *consistent* way which leaves no hint of artificiality. And I think you emphasise the *universal* element in the person & situation to the extent necessary in serious literature. Stanley is not just a grotesque & comic Polack, with qualities based on the external mannerisms of his kind, but a representative of weak, timid, ineffective, vainly dreaming youth the world over. The absence of artificial "plot" is to my mind an asset—for I despise nothing more than the unreal, theatrical event-juggling of commercial fiction. And so far as "significance" goes—I rejoice in the lack of any effort to give conscious embodiment to some philosophical, ethical, or political principle. The purpose of fiction is not to teach, but simply to *express*. What is wanted is a glimpse of life itself—with the permanent essentials of character & vital drift *embodied*, but not annotated with diagrams & sermons. With the new school of "socially motivated" or "proletarian" literature I am not in agreement. While of course a strong emotion in behalf of those injured by the slowly dying capitalistic order may well colour & animate a depiction of life, it is only a source of weakness when a writer deliberately selects events & human traits in order to illustrate a social or economic thesis. An orthodox Marxian would demand that Stanley's thoughts & doings & fate be twisted into a clear proof of the accumulating stresses which kept his father crudely undeveloped, which gave the boy his timidity & limited horizons, & which precipitated some of his specific embarrassments. Such a critic—like many now reigning in literary circles—would almost gauge the merit of a story by the degree to which it fulfilled this function. But to me all this is on the wrong track. Proof of sociological theories belongs to the essay or the treatise—not to the story. If a story is so vivid & so true to life that it does indeed illustrate a social principle, well & good. But such illustration cannot well be more than a by-product. The moment it becomes an end in itself the vitality of the story is lost. Events & traits manipulated for didactic purposes are just as hollow & unreal & unconvincing as events & traits manipulated for cheap melodramatic or bourgeois tickling purposes. In either case the discriminating reader feels that he is not seeing an actual fragment of life, but that he is merely witnessing an indifferently managed puppet-show. The fictionist's only purpose should be to draw life & character in their natural proportions & with their natural shadings—irrespective of whatever principle they may illustrate. Only in that way will he ever create anything of genuine vitality & importance. Well, as I have said, I like "Inadvertently" extremely. It depicts a specific & universal human type, & does it vividly & well—using dozens of homely little incidents as illustrations. And that embodies enough "significance" for me. I really don't know what I could suggest in the way of improvement. It's a far better story of its kind than I could ever write. If I were you I'd aim high & send it to *Story,* which welcomes unhackneyed & non-machine-made character studies of this sort. If you'd like further criticism, I'd be glad to forward it to friends of mine who have some experience in this type of writing—especially August W. Derleth, whose "Place of Hawks" you may have seen reviewed last autumn or winter. But I'd try it on *Story* first. The editors—who are on the lookout for new writers—might give you a number of useful suggestions from the standpoint of the soundest modern critical trends—literary, not commercial. Incidentally, I can sympathise with your disinclination to revise material once it is in fairly definite shape. While I often write slowly & deliberately, with much correction *as I go,* I hate to disturb a product which I have left as finished. When I have to do such, I find it better to let a very long time elapse between the original writing & the siege of emendation. Well—good luck with the story, & congratulations on what seems to me its very substantial merit!

As for *typing*—it may be a little faster than careful script, though (as I clumsily practice it) scarcely ahead of the illegible racing hieroglyphics (designed for my own perusal alone) in which I set down the rough draughts of MSS. If there is any advantage of speed, that advantage is more than neutralised by the nerve-irritating nature of the process. Nothing exhausts & exasperates me more completely than a session at the machine, & I never use the thing except under compulsion—as when preparing material for an editor, or writing someone with poor eyesight or poor deciphering ability. I couldn't possibly write anything important on a typewriter. The process impairs my creative imagination & prevents the instant & detailed revision which I always apply to material destined for publication. I have only a huge & archaic (non-visible-writing) Remington which I bought as a rebuilt machine in July, 1906. If I used a typewriter much, I'd have to get a portable specimen—since so great a proportion of my work & correspondence is done outdoors (as today) in summer.

About Atlantis & kindred matters—you seem to be ahead of me in data on this point. I can't recall any allusion in Herodotus,[1] although I read him through once & have dipped into parts again on other occasions. The *Atlantes* referred to in Book IV, 184 (who are vegetarians & who *never dream*) are merely the North-African tribes around the Atlas Mountains. After receiving your

letter I thumbed over my old copy of the Father of History (Beloe's translation—1855), but failed to come across any Atlantean tales in the vivid "Eu-
terpe" section. Possibly my aim was careless—in any event, if you can recall
the precise part of Herodotus containing the allusion, I'd be tremendously
grateful to know of it. And just to reveal the abysmal depths of my ignorance—I never even heard of Nicander Nucius before! Who was he?[2] The
only Nicanders I know of are the very ancient Spartan king & the Colophoni-
an physician-poet of the 2nd century B.C. I suppose Nicander Nucius was an
early geographer—but I'll admit I've missed him so far. Here, again, any information will be vastly appreciated. The principal classical references to Atlantis that I know of are in Plato's "Timaeus" & in Diodorus Siculus. Plato
represents Critias as having heard from his grandfather that Solon learned
about Atlantis from the Egyptian priests as Saïs. Accounts of a *still-existing*
western land—perhaps springing from such vague knowledge of America &
only slightly overlapping the standard Atlantis myth—are more common in
the Graeco-Roman writers. Those are mixed up with the notion of "Fortunate Isles" in the west—a notion which antedates the historic discovery of
the Canary, Madeira, & Cape Verde Islands, but which caused these groups to
be associated with it. Homer's Ogygia or Isle of Calypso belongs in the class
of fabulous western lands, as do the Isles of the Hesperides mentioned frequently beginning with Hesiod. Aristotle heard Carthaginian accounts of a
western *continent* (De Mir. Anc. 84) & Diodorus repeats the account—
carefully distinguishing it from the Fortunate Isles or Hesperides. Seneca
(Suasoria I) accepts the idea as a matter of course, saying "Fertiles in Oceano
jacere terras, ultraque Oceanum rursus alia littora, alium nasci orbem."[3] &c.
Plutarch attempts to place both Ogygia & the great western continent & adds
that the inhabitants of the latter regard the old world as merely a small island.
By the beginning of the middle ages these vague hints of western regions had
begun to fuse with certain Celtic myths & give rise to the well-known mediaeval conception of the Isles of the Blessed where departed spirits dwell—the
Hy-Brasil, Flath Innis, or Thir-na-n'og of Irish legend, so delicately woven
into Dunsany's recent novel, "The Curse of the Wise Woman". Avalon—
though really the quasi-island in the windings of the river Brue on which
Galstonbury is situated—has also been identified with the Blessed Isles. The
Byzantine historian Procopius seems to be the first who fused the classic with
the Celtic legends of western lands. Probably both have an origin in pure mythology—the notion of a glorious western land of happiness (after death or
otherwise) arising from the glories of the sunset—although I suspect they
were coloured by prehistoric rumours of both America & such islands as Iceland, the Canaries, the Madeiras, & the Cape Verdes. It would have been almost odd if such navigators as the Phoenicians & Carthaginians had not
heard of these regions or perhaps come across them. Aristotle & Diodorus
assume that the Carthaginians were in free communication with the western

continent. There is very little possibility that any western land has sunk beneath the sea since the period of man's existence began. In past geologic ages, of course, land & water area were constantly shifting; but a comparison of the fauna & flora of America, of the West Indies, of the Canaries & Madeira, & of Europe & Africa, proves almost conclusively that they have been widely separated throughout the age of mammalian dominance. Thus I feel sure that the Platonic Atlantis is a sheer myth (based on America, perhaps)—unless, as recent scholars have suggested, it is a case of *confused identity* . . . with some region in North Africa, of which parts became inundated by the encroachment of the Syrtis Major (just as the sea washes away the east coast of England, parts of Cape Cod & Nantucket, & the island of Jamestown, Va.) as a basis. If the new theory is correct, Atlantis must have been somewhere in the Tunis region. One may add that these European legends have nothing to do with the early Hindoo myths on which the theosophists draw. The identification of the lost world *Kusha* with "Atlantis" was a mere gesture of the 19th century mystagogues. According to eastern lore—as doctored by theosophist interpreters—"Kusha" included a great part of the world both existing & sunken. It embraced northern Asia—above the great sea now the Gobi desert—& extended eastward to include China & Japan; then occupying the North Pacific basin nearly as far as the present American West Coast. In the south it coincided with India, Burma, & Malaysia, & westward it included Persia, Arabia, Syria, & the Red Sea, & Il Duce's new Abyssinian province. It filled the present Mediterranean Sea & covered Italy & Spain—&, in projecting out to sea from Ireland & Scotland, stretched westward over the present Atlantic to cover that area & much of North & South America besides.

The shaded area in this rough Mercator's Projection chart gives a rough idea of what "Kusha" or the Third Land was supposed to be. Just how much real Hindoo myth there is in this, I can't say; since the sly dopesters of the Blavatsky-

Besant–Leadbeater tribe[4] touched up the supposed outlines in order to give them a vague conformity to 19th century geological ideas of former systems of continental distribution.

Those cases of recent strange events which you cite—the accursed ground near Bremen & the photographable marine ghosts—are certainly vivid & interesting, & ought to make good story material. They remind one of the incredible reported marvels in the late Charles Fort's curious compilations ("The Book of the Damned", "New Lands", "Lo!", &c.), & of the occult reports in Jung-Stilling, Chevreuil, & Flammarion.[5] The secret of most of these things is that they are mis-reported. Some little twist is left out or put in. As given, they never happened. Very few people realise the extent to which mere myth-making & folklore repetition consistently give rise to new false beliefs & legends which become widely accepted as fact. The legends that the ghosts of England's old archers of Crecy & Agincourt came to the aid of the British army at the Battle of Mons in 1914 have become universally swallowed by the credulous—so much so that the late Harold Begbie wrote a book defending it.[6] Actually, it came from a newspaper story of Arthur Machen's. Deep & implicitly accepted folk-beliefs arise every year from the flimsiest errors or from nothing at all. Press despatches set the gullible agog with all manner of marvels—& many of these find a permanent lodgment in folklore (helping to create a mass mood favourable to occult stories) simply because nobody bothers to investigate & explode them. A classic example of a *newly evolved* myth is a certain *subsidiary* product of the famous "Indian rope trick", whereby a Hindoo fakir is supposed to throw a rope into the air, have it remain standing—stretched taut, & extending up out of sight—& have a boy climb up it out of sight & never come down again . . . the rope then falling limp as before. This supposed trick is itself sheer folklore—*for no one has ever seen it performed at first-hand* [it is always *someone else* who "saw" & told of it . . . or who was told of it by Col. X or Major Y, who lately died]—but in the 19th century it was accepted as genuine legerdemain & tentatively explained in various ways. The favourite theory was *mass hypnotism;* & it was said that many persons had *photographed* the "trick" *& found nothing but the performer in an inert pose* on the developed plates, thus proving the hypnotic nature of the performance. Well—the truth is that *this story was just as much a folklore illusion as the "trick" itself*—albeit one of spontaneous contemporary growth. No one had ever photographed the "trick"—because no such "trick" ever existed save in imagination & legend. Track down half the "cases" reported in Flammarion or Fort & you'll find them more or less of this nature. A few will be lies—conscious or unconscious—whilst others will form various sorts of misinterpretations of actual natural occurrences. In most cases the *traditional nature* of such "manifestations" makes their character obvious.

Good luck with the magnum opus—& may the sales of policies cease to be a rarity as time passes! I'm enclosing something about your Little Compton progenitors which came to light in a recent titanic file-cleaning. Please return it some time. Hope you can see Little Compton soon. ¶ Best wishes—

Yrs most sincerely——H P L

*Notes*

1. Herodotus mentions Atlantis by name in referring to the body of water into which it sank. In his *History* (1.202), the waters beyond the Straits of Gibraltar are referred to as the Atlantis Sea.

2. Nicander Nucius was not a classical author, but a writer from the era of Emperor Charles V of the Holy Roman Empire (r. 1516–56). Two books of his *Travels* survive.

3. "[They say that] in the Ocean there lie fertile lands, while beyond it in turn are born new shores, a new world." Seneca the Elder (54 B.C.E.–39 C.E.), *Suasoriae* 1.519M.

4. HPL refers to the Theosophical writers Madame Helena Petrovna Blavatsky (1831–1891), Annie Besant (1847–1933), and C. W. Leadbeater (1854–1934).

5 See Leiber 4n13. HPL owned Jung-Stilling's *Theory of Pneumatology* and Flammarion's *Haunted Houses*.

6. In his book *On the Side of the Angels* (1915), Edward Harold Begbie (1871–1929) defended the reality of the alleged apparition of the Angels of Mons and attacked Machen for claiming it derived from his story "The Bowmen."

[3]     [ALS, JHL]

66 College St.,

Providence, R.I.,

June 26, 1936.

My dear Mr. Pabody:—

The address of *Story* is as follows: *Story Magazine, Inc., 432 Fourth Ave., New York City.* Being a magazine of quality rather than a best-seller, it is not usually found on ordinary news stands. Contributors *are* paid for—though perhaps not at rates as lavish as those of the Philistine "slicks". The number of tales chosen from this magazine for citation in the O'Brien anthologies is a pretty good index of its literary standing. Here's hoping "Inadvertently" lands—for a foothold in *Story* is a tremendous asset to the developing fictionist.

I shall be on the lookout for data anent Nicander Nucius, & will meanwhile comb Herodotus with greater care for the elusive Atlantean passage. No—the usual form of the Atlantis tale could not be reconciled very well with any geological theory (either yours or the Wegener–Joly theory mentioned in my "Mts. of Madness")[1] which regards the European-African & American coast-lines as the edges of some rift in a former single land mass. The hypothesis of the moon's birth from the Pacific was, I think, first advanced by the great tidal student George Howard Darwin (son of the immortal Charles) a generation ago.[2] It is a very arresting idea—for the great size of the moon (as compared with that of other satellites in proportion to their primaries) seems to argue some extraordinary antecedent condition. I believe, however, that mathematical physicists (calculating stresses from the known masses & motions of earth & moon) have attacked it in recent years . . . how successfully, I can't say.

I am glad the newspaper article on the early Pabodies proved of interest—& hope you will feel in no haste about returning it. The present tenant of the old house would undoubtedly be delighted to welcome a descendant of the builder from far away—especially one with the same name. If typing isn't too tedious for you, I should think you would want a copy of the article—for it surely gives a delightful reconstruction of the life & scenes amidst which your ancestors moved! Just now—as part of my endless task of reading up borrowed books—I'm immersed in very similar scenes through the pages of Mrs. Easton's splendid biography (1930) of Roger Williams. In this volume I note many references to the boundary questions which we recently discussed.

Coming down just half way from 1636 to the present—I enclose a folder which may be of some interest. Very recently two of Providence's most notable colonial mansions—the John Brown & Edward Carrington houses—were thrown open as public museums[3] . . . albeit at exorbitantly high admission rates. Last week I explored both of them, & was not disappointed. The Brown house excels in sheer magnificence any mansion I have ever explored—from Quebec on the north to St. Augustine & New Orleans on the south. The closest parallel, perhaps, is the Brewton–Pringle house in Charleston. The Carrington house (built 1809) is less classical in its symmetry, but is remarkably homelike. With its stables, courtyard, coach-houses, & extensive grounds it forms one of the finest domestic units of the early-republic period now on exhibition. This estate has been given to the R.I. School of Design by the last of the family (who lives in another colonial mansion coming down through another ancestral line) as a permanent museum . . . with all its original furniture, china, &c. undisturbed. I could not obtain any pictures of this place, though it is said that some will be available later.

You have my sympathy regarding the Cedar Point experience—for although this spot did not form part of my Cleveland itinerary in '22, I have met with its counterparts elsewhere in the course of a long life! To me a picnic is enj[oy]able only when held in a really wild & deserted region—& even then I prefer to cut the nourishment down to a minimum. What I enjoy is nature itself—with meals at home before & after the trip. The nearest approach to Cedar Point which I can recall in Cleveland is Gordon Park—on the shore of Lake Erie—where our group spent an afternoon. We went out on the lake—where I had my first rowing experience in 7 years. I'll never forget how at one juncture we struggled against some unknown obstacle, only to discover that the man at the stern (one George W. Kirk, now of N.Y. but then residing at 1894 Charles Road, out in East Cleveland) had forgotten to draw the anchor in! Golden days!

I was shocked to learn lately of the suicide (for no discoverable reason) of the splendid writer Robert E. Howard, whose powerful magazine work you doubtless know. It seems almost incredible—I had a long normal letter from him in mid-May. This is weird fiction's worst blow since the passing of Henry S. Whitehead 4 years ago.

All good wishes—yrs most sincerely,

H P Lovecraft

*Later*

Before I sealed this epistle, yours of the 24th arrived with the returned article. I am surely glad that the description proved of interest to your family, & wish that your father's plan for the purchase of the old Pabodie house might materialise. I believe I agree with him rather than with you concerning its restoration & establishment as a national point of interest—for its importance both to Pabodie descendants & as the home of the first white woman born in New England (not *America*, since . . . Counting out the non-English whites . . . that distinction goes to Virginia Dare of the ill-fated Roanoke colony, born in 1587) seem to mark it out as a natural shrine of some sort. Establishment as an historic landmark does not mean the vulgarisation of a place— or its overrunning by the rabble. Actually, very few of the sort of people who clutter up Cedar Point ever bother to seek out the publicised landmarks of early America . . . . especially if they are apart from the main lines of tourist travel. By a kind of automatic elimination the visitors to a colonial museum house are generally limited not only to old-stock Americans, but to the relatively small & thoughtful section of the latter who take an active interest in the past. I have visited many of these rural shrines—places like "Whitehall", the residence of Dean Berkeley near Newport in 1729–32, or like the farm-house of the Salem witchcraft victim Rebecca Nurse near Danvers, Mass.—& have always found the quiet country atmosphere still undisturbed. The only cases of excessive exploitation which I can think of are Mount Vernon in Virginia & the Wayside Inn in Sudbury, Mass.[4]—& both of these cases are the result of special conditions . . . the fame of Genl. Washington on the one hand, & the deliberate publicity campaigns of Henry Ford on the other hand. A good sample of an historic house well preserved & displayed is the ancient Fairbanks homestead on the edge of the village of Dedham, about ¾ths of the way from Providence to Boston. This is the oldest dwelling-house of English construction in North America, having been erected just 300 years ago, in 1636. It is owned by a society of Fairbanks descendants, to which the last private occupant bequeathed it, & forms not only a shrine for the family (where meetings of descendants are held), but a valuable relique of early 17th century life for the inspection of such discriminating students as take the trouble to seek it out. The Alden–Pabodie house[5] could very well serve an analogous function.

Regarding the present ownership of the Pabodie house—I know nothing at all. I have never been in it nor met Miss Gray, for I am always hesitant about pushing into places which are not specifically open to the public. It occurs to me that the best place to begin enquiries would be the *Rhode Island Tercentenary Committee, Providence, R.I.,* for this body has made a special investigation of all the ancient buildings in the state—at least, so I judge from what I was told by the old lady in the Clemence house last month. (I believe I wrote you about the latter—built in 1654 & oldest in the state). If the committee lacked the actual information, it would certainly refer you to some better informed source. The prices for old houses of this sort are surprisingly low. If I recall aright, the old Clemence house could be purchased for something like $5000 . . . . . though unfortunately no interested individual or society seems able or disposed to expend that sum at the present moment. If ever any miracle were to grant me a fortune, the bulk of it would certainly go into purchases & restorations of this sort. All too swiftly the tangible links with the early days are disappearing!

Your method of writing the novel—in detached sections rather than continuously—is one which has been successfully followed by many authors. It pays each individual to experiment with methods until he has found that which best suits him personally. I shall be delighted to look over the chapter when it is finished—especially now that a perusal of your short story has taught me what to expect.

I wish I might see the Great Lakes Exposition—especially if it has avoided the nightmare architecture of the Chicago affair. The only exposition of any sort which I have ever visited is the Philadelphia Sesquicentennial a decade ago—a failure so far as attendance was concerned, yet having some marvellous colonial reproductions. An entire street of old Philadelphia was reproduced in the "Midway"—& it grieved me prodigiously that so exquisite a thing should be merely temporary. It caught the spirit of the past in every detail. In 1939 I believe there will be a large exposition in New York—held in the new open marshlands on Long Island between Corona & Flushing. I shall probably see that—unless the buildings are so modernistic as to nauseate me.

Again, all good wishes—& hoping that some day your family may be instrumental in making a permanent historic shrine of the Alden–Pabodie house!

——Yrs most cordially——HPL

*Notes*

1. HPL was a supporter of the continental drift theory, at this time doubted by many geologists. The German geologist Alfred Lothar Wegener (1880–1930) became the theory's chief proponent: he delivered a paper in 1912 on the subject and then published a book, *Die Enstehung der Kontinente und Ozeane* (1915), translated in 1924 as *The*

*Origins of Continents and Oceans.* The theory was developed by Frank Bursley Taylor (1860–1938) and John Joly (1857–1933). Cf. *At the Mountains of Madness:* "it is likely that they came not long after the matter forming the moon was wrenched from the neighbouring South Pacific" (*CF* 3.100).

2. Sir George Howard Darwin (1845–1912), fifth child of Charles Darwin, became Plumian Professor of Astronomy and Experimental Philosophy at Cambridge. He propounded the theory that the material forming the moon was pulled from the earth by tidal action from the sun.

3. See CLM 35n22.

4. HPL visited both sites: see *CE* 4.27 and 64–66.

5. Elisabeth (Betty) Alden (1623–1717) of Plymouth, MA, was the daughter of *May-flower* pilgrims John and Priscilla Alden. She married William Pabodie in Duxbury, MA, around the age of twenty and gave birth to thirteen children. In her sixties, she, William, and two of their children moved to Little Compton, RI.


[4]    [ALS, JHL]

66 College St.,
Providence, R.I.,
August 6, 1936.

My dear Mr. Pabody:—

Thanks for the stamps—but there was really no need of bothering about them. Sorry "Inadvertently" didn't land—but of course *Story* is an exacting publication, & is probably offered so much good material that choice becomes difficult. Regarding further potential havens for the tale—I'm not very well up on general markets, but am writing for information from a friend who knows such things minutely—August W. Derleth of Sauk City, Wis., whose tales you may have seen. Most of the receptively inclined publications are probably non-remunerative "little magazines"—but encouragement from these is not to be despised. They are generally of really high quality, & aid in building up a new writer's standing. Editors of standard magazines see them & notice the work of their best contributors. It was through a reputation obtained in the "little magazines" that Derleth eventually broke into *Scribners* & others of that calibre—& he still floods these friends of his youth with contributions.

I am sorry your chapter in the adjuster cycle doesn't satisfy you—for resemblance to life (which this story *has*) is what makes fiction worth reading & preserving. But of course commercial junk is another matter. The superficial herd demand their stock characters & situations & their trick endings—& the mechanic clever enough to juggle the desired artificialities in the flashiest way is the lad who cops the dough! It is to build up commercial mechanics of this sort that most of the professional agents strive—& when the victim is willing to sacrifice serious artistic aims, the best of them have marvellous success in moulding him into a cash-gathering instrument. Probably the greatest of all these agents is the rather well-known *Otis Adelbert Kline* of 4333 Costello Ave., Chicago. The fellow is a veritable wizard in showing apt & adaptable pupils how to crash the paying markets, & has put chaps like E. Hoffmann Price & Frank Belknap Long (both of whom *used* to do serious work before Mammon got them) on the road to financial success. Kline is likewise a very successful fictional hack himself. He surely knows every ramification of all the popular formulae!

Sorry the heat has such an exhausting effect on you—but in the long run you are luckier than I, since a year contains many more of the cold days on which *I* suffer, than of the hot days on which *you* suffer! Hope your vacation proved a decided relief. Your mention of Cleveland's lake breeze sets me shivering—for I recall what it did to me in '22. My visit was in late July & early August, & most of the days were magnificently hot. Then, about 5 o'clock, the windows (of the public library—where I generally was at that hour. The library was then temporarily housed in an office building) would begin to rattle & the temperature would begin to fall. In 15 minutes I would be shivering miserably—scarcely able to keep my teeth from chattering—& all the evening I would generally need a gas heater in order to keep comfortable. I can't use the muscles of my hand for legible handwriting under 75° or so.

I shall be interested to hear results from the R.I. Tercentenary Committee, & hope you may in the end be able to add one more to our state's historic museums. Incidentally—Newport's old stone mill *is* the "Viking Tower" found in folklore & alluded to in Longfellow's "Skeleton in Armour".[1] There is nothing else of the kind (except modern reproductions of *it*) in the country—& it is undoubtedly the one you have heard of. A glance at your map will show that Newport isn't so prohibitively far from the island of Martha's Vineyard. This mill was erected by Gov. Benedict Arnold (great-grandfather of the traitor) about 1660. There is not a single authentic Norse relique on the North American continent, & no one knows where the "Vineland" of the Sagas was. It may have been anywhere from Newfoundland to North Carolina. The legend about the Newport mill arose in the 1830's as the result of an erudite hoax in the *Providence Journal*. The public—including the eminent Danish historian Prof. Rafn[2]—"bit", & the result is an enduring piece of local mythology. Similar myths have arisen about other fragments of early colonial masonry—such as the farmhouse foundation-walls near the Charles River in Massachusetts, which have been "identified" with the Norse settlement of Norumbega. Another "Norse" vestige is the curious carving on a rock in the Taunton River near Brighton, Mass.—now believed to be a composite (remarkable enough in itself!) of inscriptions scratched by Indians, by early English colonists, & by the lost Portugese explorer Miguel Cortereal in 1509.

Your Maugham-like story about the calendar picture sounds very ingenious, & I would surely be glad to look at it when it's ready. The mere *reading* of a story is always pleasant—never an imposition. What takes the energy out of one is the task of *actual revision.*

July 18–19 I had an enjoyable visit from an old friend (M. W. Moe—a poet & teacher of Milwaukee) & his son. They came in the latter's car, & in the all-too-brief span of 2 days we covered quite a bit of scenic & historic ground. We sought the quaint quondam fishing village of Pawtuxet (on a picturesque cove 6 m S. of Providence's civic centre—now overtaken by the expanding network of city streets), ascended old Ft. Independence (W. shore of bay, with a magnificent view of the city skyline on the N. & of the blue water & green shores on the S.), wound through the foliage-shaded driveways of Roger Williams Park, traversed the deep woods & colonial farmlands N. of the city, & as a climax descended the E. sore of the bay to the stately old seaports of Warren & Bristol. Weather favoured us greatly, for we had warmth & sun throughout—whereas the very next day was cold & rainy, forcing me to crouch blanketed over an oil stove.

Had an interesting view of Peltier's comet on July 22 at the Ladd Observatory of Brown University (on high ground a mile N. of #66)—through a 12″ refracting telescope. The object shewed a small disc with a hazy, fanlike tail. I could have seen it through my own small (3″) glass were the northern sky less cut off from this neighbourhood by roofs & foliage.

Am now acting as semi-host to a literary friend from Florida (R. H. Barlow—whose weird work shows increasing merit. I visited him in De Land in '34 & '35), who has come to Providence for an indefinite sojourn & has taken quarters at the boarding-house just across the garden from #66. Plenty of congenial conversation—& I hope I shan't wear the poor chap out showing off local antiquities. A lineal ancestor of his—Dr. Barzillai Hayward (well-known Massachusetts physician whose patronymic supplies the "H" in R H B's own name)—graduated in 1807 from the college only a stone's throw from here .... though Bob seems to retain no hereditary memory of the place! True, the neighbourhood is a bit changed; but the same old main college edifice (1770) is here, & even this house is a survivor of those times. Barzillai Hayward's wife Hannah was a daughter of the Rev. Valentine Rathbone—whose grandfather, John Rathbone (b. 1658) of Block Island, is my lineal ancestor in the 7th generation. Thus Barlow & I are 6th cousins.

¶ Letter from Derleth recd. since I began this. He says the best "little magazines" to which to send "Inadvertently" are *Manuscript* (17 W. Washington St., Athens, Ohio), *Fantasy* (950 Haberton Ave., Pittsburgh, Pa.), *The Tanager* (Grinnell, Iowa), *American Prefaces* (Iowa City, Iowa), & *Literary America* (175 Fifth Ave., New York, N.Y.). Hope you'll decide to try some of these—& that the story may yet appear in print.

Enclosed is a picture of the old Pabodie–Alden house which appeared in the rotogravure section of last Sunday's Journal. The front door, bay window, &c. are relatively modern changes which a thorough restoration would abolish. The square-paned windows are probably of the 18th century—17th century windows having generally been diamond-paned.

All good wishes——Yrs most cordially—H P L

*Notes*

1. HPL refers to the Old Stone Mill in Touro Park, Newport, the remains of a windmill probably built by Benedict Arnold (colonial governor of Rhode Island, 1663–66, 1669–72). Longfellow's poem "The Skeleton in Armor" (1842) hints of Norse origin.
2. Carl Christian Rafn (1795–1864), Danish antiquarian and early advocate of the theory that the Vikings had explored North America centuries before Columbus and Cabot.

[5]    [ALS, JHL]

66 College St.,
Providence, R.I.
Aug. 25, 1936.

My dear Mr. Pabody:—

Congratulations on your approaching entry into the married state! On the whole, no form of social & emotional adjustment is even comparable in psychological, practical, & civic value to marriage at its best—& he who is able to achieve & permanently maintain such an adjustment is indeed fortunate. It ought to form a marked incentive to literary creation—& I trust the coming autumn & winter may witness an exemplification of that principle in your case! Again, my sincerest congratulations & good wishes.

Very glad to see "The Calendar." It is extremely well-written, & is distinctly novel in the way it handles the persistent escape-urge latent in all human types. The formula-bound critic would of course complain that it is a single narrative of change, without the artificial plot complications & interactions which constitute the conventional "short-story"—but that sort of complaint means nothing to me. I think the tale ought to be eminently acceptable to one or another of the "little magazines". If there is anything potentially unconvincing in it, it is perhaps the extent to which the calendar affected a man's entire life. This detail, however, is really only incidental & symbolic—*typifying* a revolt which would no doubt have occurred anyway. It doesn't seem a real fault to me—nor do I deem the title at all inept. I yet hope to see this in print—as well as "Inadvertently." By the way—I've made one or two suggestions for changes in the text—in each case a very trifling emendation.

Glad the picture of the Pabodie or "Betty Alden" house proved of interest, & hope there will be no difficulty in getting a supply. The view appeared in the *Providence Sunday Journal* for Aug. 2, & I fancy a letter to *The Providence Journal Co., Fountain St., Providence, R.I.* would bring results. The Sunday paper is 10¢ per copy  & it also occurs to me that the *Journal* might arrange to supply real photographic prints at a nominal cost. The negative no doubt reposes in the company's official "morgue". Such a picture ought to be of interest to Pabodies & Pabodys all over the country. Whether good old Bill Pabodie the Town Clerk was called "Mr. Alden" in his lifetime is surely a natural question in the light of today's ballyhoo—but actually I fancy he had little idea of the aura of romance which the future would cast about the Alden name. [Even the protagonist in Santayana's much-read "Last Puritan" is called "Oliver Alden"!] Probably he was mildly & proudly conscious of the fact that his spouse was the first white girl born in New-England, but it remained for Prof. Longfellow & the sentimental 19ᵗʰ century to apotheosise Mrs. Pabodie's amiable & affectionate parents, & thus cast a reflected glow upon that lady herself. I'd wager a good deal that in 1700 or 1800 or 1836 the staunch old dwelling was known simply as the "Pabodie place". Also, what a heritage of feminine sentiment the lace-trimmed Victorian age wished on to New England antiquarian nomenclature! Bustled or Dundrearied dabblers raked up all the stale romantic legends they could find, & covered the map of these colonies with names like "Agnes Surriage's Well", "Hannah Robinson's Rock", "the Evelyn Bray house", &c. &c. &c. Poor old Bill! Why did Henry W. have to hang such a publicity stunt on his parents-in-law?

Your vacation sounds quite ideal—& the intimations of *heat* arouse my envy. Deserted beaches have a charm not to be found in the populated sort—the best specimen I know being on Anastasia Island near St. Augustine, Florida.

Providence has had some decently warm weather at last, so that I'm not as run down as I was earlier in the season. Barlow is still here, & last week the party was augmented by an old revision client of mine—Adolphe de Castro, who in the 1880's & '90's was quite a friend & associate of Ambrose Bierce. We made the usual museum rounds, & on one occasion Barlow, de Castro, & I sat on a tomb in a hidden hillside churchyard just north of here & wrote rhymed acrostics on the name of *Edgar Allan Poe*—who 90 years ago used to wander in that selfsame churchyard when on visits to Providence. On Aug. 15 Barlow & I visited ancient Newport, & on the 20th we went the rounds of Salem & Marblehead in company with other friends.

Every good wish, & renewed congratulations. Yrs most sincerely—

H P L

[6]     [ALS, JHL]

66 College St.,
Providence, R.I.,
Sept. 17, 1936.

My dear Mr. Pabody:—

Glad the remarks on "The Calendar" proved useful. Here's wishing you luck with the *Amazing* item. I haven't kept track of that periodical in recent years, but presume you know something of its requirements & customs.

The sudden death of your friend must surely have been a shock—comparable to the effect of Robert E. Howard's recent suicide (he shot himself June 11, upon learning that his mother was about to die) upon our fantasy group. The tragic event is heightened by his recent marriage—& I can imagine how bewildered & incredulous everyone must feel. 1936 has been a black year for an astonishing number of persons—but fortunately there are more than a few felicitous happenings to preserve the balance.

Speaking of the latter—let me again congratulate you on your approaching union. I'm sure you'll find it a stabilising & inspiring influence, even though the other half of the venture isn't a devotee of ponderous literature. Time & constant companionship will probably bring about a gradual moulding of your wife's taste in the direction of your own. The fact that this taste is largely unformed, rather than definitely developed in directions antagonistic to your own, is all in your favour. The one thing which leads inevitably to Reno is a case of two utterly hostile sets of perspectives, values, responses, sensitivenesses, & preferences, each highly developed & ingrained in its possessor. When *that* occurs, we have the spectacle of a couple in whom every incident of the day, every item in the news, every book read or lecture heard, every chance remark in company, &c. &c. &c. awakes two totally different sets of associations, sympathies, visions, aspirations, & judgments; & the more evolved & scholarly the persons are, the more acutely these differences will irritate them & frustrate the growth of that complete psychological harmony which ought to characterise marriage. The hell of it is that such couples are often found—the possession of a common intellectualism or aestheticism having attracted them in the first place, but an analysis of the *basic nature* of that intellectualism or aestheticism having been postponed until after marriage. Lucky, then, is the youth whose fiancee is not steeped in a mental life definitely alien & opposed to his own. Sorry the high rent is going to eat so considerably into your budget, but one can of course economise in other ways. It is easier to do without certain recreational or dietary frills than to live in the slums!

I envy you the warm weather—though not the recent hurricane. Likewise do I envy you the Louisiana trip which will prolong your summer. I like to augment my summers at the *other* end—getting south in the early spring. This suits me better, since I'd hate to come up from comfortable weather into the subarctic hell of a northern late autumn or winter. The natural coming of autumn is bad enough—I feel its blighting influence already. Would that I might find some way to transplant a bit of Rhode-Island's scenery & architecture to Cuba or Jamaica!

Our friend Morton was here Sept. 11–12–13, & brought me a new ancestor as a present . . . . one Sylvester Eveleth, first encountered in Boston in 1643. This gentleman—whose daughter Elizabeth married John Perkins Jr. of

Ipswich, the most recent common ancestor of Morton & myself—turned up during J F M's latest genealogical researches in Lynn. Morton attended the Harvard Tercentenary exercises after his sojourn here . . . . & just prior to his advent he distinguished himself by winning the U.S. crossword-puzzle championship (for which he will receive an impressive silver loving-cup) at the Boston convention of the Puzzlers' League.

Enclosed is a Little Compton item which may be of some interest. You have had distinguished cousins, it seems, right on the old home ground!

I'm having a tough wrestle with an exacting revision job[1]—which seems all the harder because cold weather have drained all the energy out of me. Hades, but I wish the mercury would never drop below 80°! ¶ Congratulations & best wishes—

Yrs most sincerely,<br>
H P Lovecraft

*Notes*

1. *Well Bred Speech* by Anne Tillery Renshaw.


[7]     [ALS, JHL]

66 College St.,<br>
Providence, R.I.<br>
Dec. 1, 1936.

My dear Mr. Pabody:—

Your account of the New Orleans trip interested & tantalised me vastly—for I fervently wish I were headed in that direction at the present moment, with no compulsion to see the north again until next June! As coincidence would have it, the Monteleone is where I first stopped in 1932—although I later found a humbler place (the Orleans—quite a way out St. Charles toward the library) which suited my purse better & enabled me to prolong my stay. You are right, I think, in regarding the Vieux Carré as the only extensive foreign urban development in the U.S. Of course St. Augustine & Santa Fé afford many specimens of genuine Spanish architecture, but they are not large enough to present the overpowering & saturating impression which old Nouvelle-Orleans presents. To parallel it, one must cross the international boundary-line & see something like Quebec or the more unspoiled towns of Mexico. The one other U.S. city which saturates the visitor in a purely local & distinctive architecture is *Charleston*—but of course this architecture is not basically foreign. Whilst the houses of New Orleans reflect a Franco-Hispanic mixture evolved without English influence & on soil then actually alien, Charleston's architecture is at bottom our own English Georgian—plus a group of added influences originally foreign but here greatly modified & developed within an English-traditioned community. Charleston's houses are English, but modified by certain French influences brought by the Huguenots, & by other characteristics imported by West Indian planters. Tiled pointed roofs, stucco walls, abundant wrought-iron grille work, curved eaves, notched gables, many-storeyed side porches with street door in an end wall, spacious walled gardens with ornate wrought-iron grates, curved double flights of steps to front door, with iron railing & archtec tunnel beneath, &c. &c. &c.—all these things bespeak old Charleston. Yet the groundwork is really English, as rayed fanlights, classic pediments, decorative details, & dozens of major & minor characteristics clearly shew. And the public buildings & churches are altogether English—hardly distinguishable from many in Providence. Charleston, I think, fascinates me more than any other place I've ever seen. Were it not for the pull of early associations, I'd make an effort to move thither. It is curious to reflect how many foreign architectural traditions are represented to a greater or lesser degree on our own soil. French touches affect New Orleans & Canada & the Huguenot settlement of New Paltz, N.Y. New York & New Jersey are full of Dutch houses—although these are now exclusively rural. In colonial times New York City & Albany were very Dutch in appearance, being full of houses with stepped gables; but the last such urban edifice disappeared 80 or so years ago. Pennsylvania is full of German colonial houses—mostly of stone—& in Delaware several steep-roofed Swedish houses remain from the 17th century. Another influence which is at least a bit outside the *major* English tradition is the *Welsh* touch in Pennsylvania houses, whereby heavy cornices are carried around the gable end. In Florida, of course, St. Augustine gives plenty of Spanish Colonial specimens, while French & Franco-Hispanic architecture is encountered in Mobile, New Orleans, & Natchez. The Southwest gives abundant Spanish & native Indian specimens, & in California (N. of San Francisco) there are several *Russian* buildings remaining from a fort & trading post established around 1810. Alaska (in Sitka) also has Russian houses & a church. As for *recent* foreign architecture in the United States (i.e., the genuine spontaneous work of immigrants & not the conscious exoticism of romantic American architects), we have in Providence an abundance of really fine Italian churches with campaniles, erected in the vast Italian colony on Federal Hill, whilst I understand that in Minnesota an abundance of spontaneous Scandinavian architecture exists.

I can well imagine how you enjoyed Nouvelle-Orleans—although my overwhelming lifelong loathing for sea-food in any form causes me to view your restaurant reports with interest rather than envy. Gastronomy is a great tradition in the Crescent City—but my aesthetic sensitivenesses have generally centred in other fields, so that I was quite content to heed my flat pocketbook & absorb a plebeian nutriment at various beaneries along Royal & St. Charles Sts—mostly members of the Gluck & Thompson chains!

Your route to Mobile seems roughly to have parallelled mine on the 'bus. I missed that Pascagoula legend, & am glad to have it supplied—albeit

4½ years late! I liked Mobile very much, although to me it didn't have the intense pull of old *Natchez*. Natchez, indeed, was the high spot of my trip—in some respects overshadowing New Orleans. I shall never forget the great columned facades of the neo-classic plantation-houses, the quaint little buildings of the town proper, the arcaded suken roads of yellow clay (& yellow *dust!*), & the great woods of moss-bearded live-oaks—which Chateaubriand (once a sojourner there) reflected in his "Atala". My route from the north was Washington–Roanoke–Knoxville–Chattanooga–Memphis–Vicksburg, & the whole trip was an unending delight. It was curious to pass from one definite zone into another—thus there was no Spanish moss in Vicksburg, but much around Natchez . . . & no palm-like growths (except miniature scrub palmettoes in one or two gardens) in Natchez, though such abounded in Baton Rouge. On the return trip I took in Montgomery, but thereafter diverged from your route—going through Atlanta, Charlotte, Winston-Salem, & Danville to Richmond, where I paused a while amidst the scenes of Poe's boyhood. I have a curious fondness for old Richmond, even though much of its quaintness has departed. By the way—you are right in pointing out the undistinctiveness of main highways. That is the one regrettable element in 'bus travel—although forced detours often give the passengers gratuitous glimpses of the unspoiled hinterland!

Meanwhile let me congratulate you upon the beginning of a domestic career—which I feel sure will more than justify the dietary shift from cavair to beans & round steak. Come to think of it, I doubt whether old Bill Pabodie & Betty Alden had very delicate fare in their sturdy Little Compton abode!

Sorry all the MSS. returned—but that is the common lot of all. Only the other day I was informed that the Morrow firm did *not* wish to handle a collection of my tales . . . . this being my 6th or 7th turn down of that kind since 1928. Better luck this winter—indeed, I'm sure you'll begin to land stories in the course of time.

Yes, indeed—the blighting touch of winter is in the air! However, I managed to take occasional trips to the woods & fields throughout October & even over the line into November. As I possibly mentioned in my last letter, I succeeded in discovering several splendid rural regions within a 3-mile radius of here which I had never seen before. One is a wooded hill—Neutaconkanut—on the western rim of the town, whence a series of marvellous views of the outspread city & adjacent countryside may be obtained. I had often ascended it before, but the exquisitely mystical sylvan scenery beyond the crest—curious mounds, hummocked pastures, & hushed, hidden valleys—was wholly new to me. Late in October I explored this region still further—including the country west of Neutaconkanut & the western slopes of that eminence itself. This terrain is full of magnificent views of rolling meadows, ancient stone walls, hoary groves, & distant cottage roofs to the west & south. I crossed the hill (it is really a small plateau or table-land) eastward to the parts I knew before, occasionally skirting the wooded edge where dark valleys slope down to the plain below, & huge balanced boulders on rocky heights impart a spectral, druidic effect as they stand out against the twilight. Finally I came to more familiar ground—where the grassy ridge of an old buried aqueduct gives the illusion of one of those vestigial Roman roads which traverse the woods & fields of England—& stood once more on the cityward slope which I have always known. Country like this—high & rocky, in utter contrast to the low-lying, windmill-studded sea plains of your ancestral Little Compton—well illustrates the extreme geographic diversity possible within Rhode Island's minute area! Oct. 20 & 21 were phenomenally warm, & I utilised them in exploring a hitherto untapped region down the east shore of Narragansett Bay (toward, but not very far toward, Little Compton), where the Barrington Parkway winds along the high bluff above the water. I found a highly fascinating forest called the Squantum woods—where there are great oaks & birches, steep slopes & rock ledges, & marvellous westward vistas beyond the trees. On both occasions there was a fine sunset—then glimpses of the crescent moon, Venus, & Jupiter . . . & the lights of far-off Providence from high places along the parkway. On the expedition of the 20th I ran across two tiny kittens in the heart of the woods (they doubtless belonged to a nearby hospital), & they trotted companionably after me as a sort of body-guard or retinue during the entire hour & a half I was there! Our autumn, though, was notably lacking in visual splendour. Not as prematurely cold as I had feared, but with the dullest foliage of any October within my memory. Half the trees were swept bare by heavy rains as soon as they began to turn, whilst the other half remained green for an anomalous length of time—the leaves then falling almost as soon as they did turn. *Red* hues were especially rare. The result was a tremendous loss of glamour—although we heard of gorgeous foliage at points not many miles inland, while the Vermont & New Hampshire leafage is said to have been of unparallelled magnificence. Derleth also told of riotous autumn colours in Wisconsin. Snow first came Nov. 24— very early for R.I.—& there have since then been some atrociously cold days. Hibernation must now be my lot till April or May!

All good wishes——Yrs most sincerely, H. P. Lovecraft

[8]     [ALS, JHL]

66 College St.,
Providence, R.I.,
Dec. 20, 1936.

My dear Mr. Pabody:——

Thanks extremely for the picture of Cleveland's "Black Day". Curiously enough, despite my acquaintance with many Clevelanders, I never before heard of this typical phenomenon—nor did I encounter anything like it during my 17-day sojourn in your metropolis fourteen years ago. New England had a famous "Dark Day" in 1780, & a scarcely less famous "Yellow Day" about a century after that.[1] I should think the city would turn on the street lamps on such an occasion—I see by the picture that at least one bank & one hotel made the most of their electric signs. Hope you'll get a good story out of the "Invasion of Night" idea!

Congratulations on your ground-floor entry into the laboratory equipment boom! The new invention seems like something which ought to sell very widely—as indeed early returns would seem to indicate. I trust that your high-school or college chemistry remains enough in the foreground of your memory to facilitate the technological research you are having to make—& I hope that the whole enterprise may prove a gateway to financial comfort.

About the Betty Alden matter—you Pabodys will have to organise a campaign for juster nomenclature . . . even at the risk of having war declared on you by various Alden family associations. Point out that the Lucy Stone League wasn't organised in the 17th century—& ask why the mere romantic glamour cast on an Alden by a rather tenuous sentimental poem should count so heavily as contrasted with the galaxy of genius, philanthropy, & general distinction formed by the Pabody–Pabodie–Peabody clan!

I was greatly interested in your account of recent weird reading, & trust you will continue the process. Glad you've encountered Blackwood's "Willows"—which I consider the best weird story ever written. Read also Blackwood's "John Silence" & "Incredible Adventures" if you can get hold of them. Of Arthur Machen's tales read at least "The White People", "The Great God Pan", "The Three Impostors", "The Terror" & (for atmosphere) "The Hill of Dreams". Try to get all the short stories of M. R. James, & don't miss Walter de la Mare's "Mr. Kempe", "A Recluse", "All-Hallows", "The Return", & "Seaton's Aunt." For sheer grimness read Ambrose Bierce's two collections—"In the Midst of Life" & "Can Such Things Be?"—& as a taste of sheer poetic fantasy try Lord Dunsany—especially "Time & the Gods", "A Dreamer's Tales", "The Sword of Welleran", "The Book of Wonder", & the play "The Gods of the Mountain["]. Another hellishly powerful thing is Robert W. Chambers' "The King in Yellow". Read also M. P. Shiel's "The Purple Cloud", & (if you can get hold of "The Pale Ape & Other Stories") his short masterpiece "The House of Sounds." Also look up the tales of William Hope Hodgson—especially "The House on the Borderland". If you go in for systematic weird reading I can lend you many items—while my fellow-enthusiast H. C. Koenig, 540 E. 80th St. N.Y. City, would be glad to lend others which I lack. And if you care for a reading guide, I'll lend you (when someone else returns it) my long article or treatise of a decade ago—"Supernatural Horror in Literature"—which the old *Fantasy Fan* started reprinting, & which the new *Science-Fantasy Correspondent* is about to continue from the point where the first-named magazinelet failed, thereby cutting it off abruptly.

You are certainly right in assuming that the primary function of the *seriously artistic* weird story is not to describe grotesque monsters or re-hash stereotyped ghost-legends, but simply to present a powerful & subjectively realisable picture of man's deeply-ingrained emotions—largely a fascinated fear—concerning the unknown, or of man's persistent illusions of a circumambient world of unreality. I'll quote an article of mine on the subject:

> Atmosphere, not action, is the thing to cultivate in the wonder story. We cannot put stress on the bare events, since the unnatural extravagance of these events makes them sound hollow & absurd when thrown into too high relief. Such events, even when thoroughly possible or conceivable in the future (as in the case of some science-fiction), have no counterpart nor basis in existing life & human experience, hence can never form the groundwork of an adult tale. All that a marvel story can ever be, in a serious way, is *a vivid picture of a certain type of human mood.* The moment it tries to be anything else it becomes cheap, puerile, & unconvincing. Therefore a fantastic author should see that his prime emphasis goes into subtle suggestion—the imperceptible hints & touches of selective & associative detail which express shadings of moods & build up a vague illusion of the strange reality of the unreal—instead of into bald catalogues of incredible happenings which can have no substance nor meaning apart from a sustaining cloud of colour & mood-symbolism. A serious adult story must be true to something in life. Since marvel tales cannot be true to the *events* of life, they must shift their emphasis toward something to which they *can* be true; namely, certain wistful or restless *moods* of the human spirit, wherein it seeks to weave gossamer ladders of escape from the galling tyranny of time, space, & natural law.[2]

This, as you see, is all opposed to the minute description of Nameless Tentacled Things & cavorting corpses—though now & then a writer *can* effectively break the rule & give the reader at least a momentary glimpse of some Entity which Should not Be. One of the best such exceptions that I've ever seen is the very story you mention—Perceval Landon's "Thurnley Abbey"[3]—where the narrator comes to grips with the singular & unpleasant skeleton, & where the temporarily defeated Thing collects itself in a highly disconcerting fashion. The secret of this story's success is its emotional tension. As I have always said—aye, shouted—to young writers, it is impossible to produce a really convincing weird story with the brisk, cheerful, casual, matter-of-fact "action" style affected by most of the pulpists. That is one of the reasons why the bulk of pulp fantasy is merely lifeless crap appealing only to the mentally immature. To create a genuine sense of the unreal, the *emotional preparation* is all-important. *Everything* lies in the "build-up"—without which the events are simply a meaningless series of ridiculous & extravagant statements. The first law of weird fiction is that *the emotional atmosphere must overshadow the weird events.* If you want to write in a quiet, reserved style, you must confine the weird events to the most delicate & elusive hints. The only way to "get away" with obviously extravagant events is to "step up" the emotional tension in preparation—keeping the mood, as expressed in the prose rhythm, vocabulary, & visible effect of the action on the characters, always definitely ahead of the events. Of course, beyond certain limits the law of diminishing returns gets in its work, & you *can't* step up the mood any higher without slopping over into the ignominious realm of unconscious comedy. Even a whole page of "O Gawds" & shrieks & convulsions & "Gawd! take it away's" can't float too heavy a burden of visible extravagance; & after a time the super-feverish "Oh, my Gawds" get to be ridiculous in themselves. You've got to be able to envisage the limit of effectiveness in heightening the tension—but within that limit, see that the tension looms above the events. In "Thurnley Abbey" the limit is approached more closely—& more adroitly—than in any other horror-tale of classic calibre which I've ever seen. The *events in themselves* are *essentially comic*—the perfect stuff of burlesque & parody. How, then, does the author manage to give them a really poignant aura of clutching fear? Obviously, by stepping up the *mood* to the limit of phobic hysteria. And how does he accomplish that without becoming melodramatic & absurd? By *art*—damned skilful art—the kind of thing that none of the pulpists possess in more than rudimentary degree. He is able to "lay it on thick" because he lays it on *gradually & indirectly*. First, the apt device of *indirect narration*. The steamship, & the strong man riven with a haunting, undying fear—& the later jump back to a realisation of that setting when the concentrated horrors are about to be unfolded. Then the excellently realistic descriptive parts, providing a foil & compensation for the high spots & preserving an *average of sanity* in the net impression. Besides this, the explicit & powerful description of the stark, mad fright felt by the characters at the grotesque & hellish phenomena. Seeing the effect of the horror upon them, we experience a reflected panic—half-irrespective of the *source* of the fright—ourselves. And of course a thousand little details connected with the *order of unfolding events,* the choice of descriptive devices, & so on, help to promote the effectiveness & convincingness of the story. It would be a hard sort of tale for a beginner to achieve successfully—yet you see what a truly accomplished story-teller made of it. Once one *can* get such a concrete thing across, it perhaps leaves a sharper immediate impression than any subtler tale can leave; though after all, it is the subtler tale which most closely approaches the condition of true literary art.

There is no question but that weird fiction offers much greater artistic possibilities than science fiction, though [except for one able to conquer aesthetic scruples & cater to the insufferable rabble-press represented by *Terror Tales* & *Horror Stories*] science fiction [with *Astounding, Amazing,* & *Wonder* as steady markets, & magazines like *Argosy* & *Blue Book* cautiously opening the gates to a limited amount] certainly offers the best *financial* returns. Science fiction *could* be a medium of serious expression if authors would get rid of the cheap action-&-adventure element, tone down the half-baked use of incomprehensible technicalities, & buckle down to the real task of crystallising our imagination-pictures of other worlds, other aeons, & other orders of being— but who the hell except H. G. Wells, S. Fowler Wright, & W. Olaf Stapledon ever *has* followed this course? However, even at its best, the science-fiction field could scarcely offer the depth & scope & variety offered by the weird.

As to the local writers' club—you could probably tell better whether you would or wouldn't like it after attending a meeting or two as guest. It might be a useful assemblage of persons with real literary interests to discuss—or it might be a herd of Babbitts talking about current detective-&-western prices & new markets—or it might be a flock of lisping, posing Greenwich-Village egomaniacs. All three sorts exist—though the rarity of Sort I is deplorable! Sorry your indispensable typewriter has been out of reach lately. That, to me, would be no handicap except in preparing MSS. for publication; since I couldn't compose anything original on a machine if I wanted to. I hate the damned things—they exhaust me nervously & physically in almost no time, whereas I can use pen & ink indefinitely without fatigue. I never use a typewriter except under compulsion—though I guiltily realise how troublesome my lousy script must be to such correspondents as possess neither a cryptographic eye nor a Rosetta stone. However—I never could swing my enormous correspondence if I had to handicap myself with a mechanical medium I detest. It's a question of writing as I do or not at all.

I don't envy you your local autumn. Our temporary whitenesses of Nov. 24 & 28 were bad enough—but a full foot of snow on Thanksgiving Day (I saw a rotogravure picture of it—brrrr!) is past the limit! That nearby -1° temperature doesn't sound very inviting, either. Our lowest so far has been +14°—itself highly unusual for the early winter or late autumn. Seaboard R.I. is reasonably mild as northern regions go. Our all-time low in history is -17° (Feby. 9, 1934)— the next lowest being -12° (Dec. 30, 1917). But of course our official records date back only to 1904. In general, zero or below is very rare in Providence. I can't safely stand exposure to any temperature under +20°—respiratory, digestive, cardiac, & renal complications (including alarming swelling of feet & ankles) attending such exposures. Nor am I really comfortable under 80°.

Your Arboretum walks & other rural rambles must have been delectable—though I would have had to cut out the winter ones. Odd that solitary walking should be regarded as so extraordinary nowadays—I don't think it was considered at all freakish or uncommon in my day! At any rate, lone scenic exploration was just as much of a specialty of mine in youth as it is now— cycling trips being my favourite amusement. This habit put me in touch with New England scenery & farm & forest atmosphere to an extent not altogether common among urbanites—but then, my old home was itself near the easterly limit of the compact town's expansion; so that I could look westward over solid lines of roofs & streets, yet reach the open country in two or three blocks of northeastward walking. Today all that open country is built up solidly with residential streets—for the city spreads like a cancer. An oasis, however, survives in the form of a city park which covers the high wooded bluff of the Seekonk River & a ravine extending inland therefrom—near my old home, & about a mile east of here. This area is still pretty much as I knew it in my infancy & youth. Another curious oasis is an ancient farm about a mile northeast of the old home.[4] This tract of land with its 1735 house has been inherited in unbroken line from its original proprietor, & has never been sold nor changed. There it is still—with barns & byres & stone walls & orchards—just as it was when all the region was rolling countryside; though it is hemmed in on all sides by smart residences & paved streets. Providence has other overtaken farmhouses in its compact area—though none can rival this old farm in respect to adjacent land & outbuildings. One very picturesque farm cottage lies only a little way down the hill from 66 College St.[5]

Glad you liked "The Haunter of the Dark"—whose geographical references are all scrupulously correct except for the immediate environment of the sinister church. The College Hill house described is this one—& the westward view of Federal Hill with its darkly-silhouetted church tower is the one at which I am now gazing as I raise my eyes from the page. This story—in which a figure very much like young Robert Bloch is killed off—forms a kind of revenge for the two vicarious deaths which this rising fantaisiste has inflicted on the old gentleman. In both "The Dark Demon" & "The Shambler from the Stars" Bloch has a figure modelled more or less after me come to a hideous end. Well—I've survived other fictional deaths—Long having left me as a charred cinder on the floor of my apartment over a decade ago in "The Space-Eaters". In a recent unpublished MS. Kuttner kills off Bloch, himself, & myself under thin disguises . . . . slaughter de luxe! I am decapitated—but my head is later found with its teeth buried in his carotid artery. Nice, wholesome ideas the boys have!

As for more data about me—under separate cover I'm sending one of the "fan magazines" with a sort of write-up plus a portrait which looks somewhat as a son or nephew of mine might.[6] My existence has been so prosaic & uneventful that a blank-book would make an excellent biography. I was almost a nervous invalid when young, & could attend school only irregularly. Indeed, I never went to a university, since I was virtually in the midst of a breakdown after the high-school period & throughout the years which would normally be collegiate. My knowledge is very erratic, one-sided, & irregularly picked up. Antiquarianism has been a dominant interest of mine since I was very small—indeed, I have always felt myself peculiarly a part of the 18th century. I'd feel more at home in periwig, knee-breeches, & three-cornered hat than I do in modern costume. This taste dates from my earliest years—when I used to rummage around in a windowless attic room at home & exhume dusty 18th century books long banished from the shelves downstairs. Out of one of these—a text book* stereotyped in 1797[7] & used by my great-grandfather about 1810—I first learned the principles of versification. I never cared for games or sports, but was outdoors a good deal & played about the average amount with other children—favouring diversions that involved the following-out of dramatic plots . . . wars, outlaw & police adventures, &c. I had also an almost exaggerated interest in transportation—especially electric cars. At one time I knew the wording of every side of the signs on every car line in Providence, & could place any car (make, type, line used on) in town by its number. Golden days—eheu fugaces! My father died when I was very young, & I grew up at the home of my maternal grandfather. I was sent to a Baptist Sunday School, but saw no more reason for being a Christian than for being a Mohammedan like the people in my beloved Arabian Nights. When I turned to Graeco-Roman mythology as an interest, I adopted the old Graeco-Roman religion & made sacrifices to Jove, Pan, Diana, Apollo, & Athena . . . . but since the age of 8, when I turned to the sciences, I have had no belief in any religion. I am strictly a scientific materialist like Haeckel, Huxley, Bertrand Russell, George Santaytana, &c.

When you speak of *occupation* you hit my weakest point. I have none save writing—mostly in the form of revision, criticism, & ghost-writing—but it doesn't make a living. There's a gold mine in the pulps, but I can't turn out the lifeless artificialities they want. If I try, I merely sink down in a welter of disgust. My fragmentary income from sporadic revision & accidentally placed stories is not adequate to even the barest subsistence (a level to which I have gradually accustomed myself during the past decade) except when I place long things as I did in *Astounding* last year, & when the last microscopic remnants of the patrimonial residue vanish—as they will in 2 or 3 more years—I shall simply have to stumble accidentally off a dock unless I can land some sort of situation in the interim. I have worked out a technique for getting by on about $600 per year—aside from the trips I used to take—& if I could be sure of even $10.00 or $15.00 per week I would be safe. Perhaps I shall find some humble opening before the danger-zone is reached. All I want in a financial way is enough to keep me fed & warm (I don't say *clothed* because I keep on wearing the same clothes . . . I'm in a 1925 suit now!) & secure in the hire of a room or rooms large enough to house my books & a few of the paintings & pieces of furniture from the old home—without which I could not exist. I am absolutely uncommercial & have no interest in money except as a preserver of life & of the salient environmental landmarks I need. My serious writing can never, except by accident, be a gainful factor—since it is not of the sort which sells. I must have a non-literary subsistence-job of a routine sort which can be put out of my head after working hours, leaving me free for my own non-commercial work. How to get one, I have not the slightest

---

*"The Reader", by Abner Alden, A.M. Pardon my dragging in *Aldens* again!

idea—but I hope I can gather enough suggestions & data to enable me to find one before the otherwise-inevitable crash of the future.

My great mistake was in not preparing for some routine occupation in youth. I was, however, completely naive & ignorant regarding industrial conditions; & was not then in need of money. I spent freely in those days, but attached no importance to the matter, since I had not the slightest interest in wealth, ostentation, or a parade of commercial competence. When in later years I *had* to economise, I did so without a pang. Material luxuries meant nothing to me when I had them, & mean equally little now that I don't have them. I had the ancient Aryan contempt for the psychology of trade & acquisitive aggressiveness. Of course I expected to earn reasonable sums when I grew up—but I thought that whatever scientific or literary pursuit I might elect to follow would give me enough to piece out my heritage in meeting my very modest needs. Also—I little knew how existing finances would shrink, or how little return would be yielded by the sort of literary endeavour to which chance & temperament would direct me! Hence my mistake. Had I known how devoid of profit my chosen field was, I would have speedily mastered some routine clerical accomplishment enabling me to get the needed weekly pittance yet leaving some time & energy for serious aesthetic endeavour. *Then*—when I was young—it would have been easy. *Now*—at 46 & growing older instead of younger—it is another matter! Well—we shall see. Unexpected turns might enable me to get by on writing—or some minor lifesaving job suited to an untrained man of my age and paying $10.00 to $15.00 per week might turn up. I have no interest in prosperity, but merely wish to be certain of keeping some of the old familiar objects—the tables & chairs & bookcases & vases & statues & paintings & candlesticks & clocks &c. which I grew up with & without which I should feel lost—around me. I could do that (with a slight—or perhaps less than slight—sacrifice of neighbourhood) in a $5.00-per-week large room & alcove—& my food bill is down to $2.50 or $3.00 per week. Ironically enough, my present situation gives no visible key to the desperate state of my finances—for I am doubled up with an aunt (my only surviving close relative) in an apartment of which she pays half the miraculously low rent of 40.00 per month. (This brings me down to the 5-a-week level of the foregoing estimate.) This apartment—in an ancient house after my own heart—is a sheer stroke of luck. Belonging to the college, it is situate almost on the edge of the campus—in a court next the John Hay Library—hence involves no "come-down" in neighbourhood. Being an entire upper floor & attic, it allows my aunt & me to spread out our residue of the old home furnishings in a very adequate fashion—so that the visitor, passing a colossal marine painting on his way up the colonial staircase & beholding Georgian rooms with ample furnishings & decorations well-suited to the house & family alike (despite a seediness whose effect is more mellow than repulsive), could form no idea of the poverty lurking beneath. My aunt has just enough to get by, considering the probable number of years ahead, so that my own fix is separate from hers. Thus the worst crash—in case I don't find some source of regular income—is still to come. Despite the tobogganing, I have never *yet* lived in a common neighbourhood, or apart from the books & pictures & furniture & objets d'art amongst which I grew up, or in any physical discomfort. With my sober & old-fashioned tastes in dress, I don't even *look* particularly tramp-like on the outside (but you ought to see the *linings* of some of my junk) myself. But that is only *so far.* How many years before the smashup? Well—time & the gods will tell. Discovery of a job would save me, & so would certain not wholly inconceivable turns in the fantastic fiction market.

But I should have trained for a routine standby—like Charles Lamb's East-India clerkship or Hawthorne's Salem custom-house job—in youth. With such a foundation, even the explosion of original resources would not have left me in peril or even necessitated the drastic economies which I have gradually come to accept as matters of course. I might even have been able to sustain an independent domestic establishment, with a wife & with children to whom to pass down the books & heirlooms & traditions to which I cling so tenaciously. With my characteristic lack of foresight in youth I *did* get as far as the wife; but originally-understimated differences in outlook & temperament grew with the years, & aggravated the even-then-uncomfortable financial tension—so that in the end the Superior Court of Providence County was called upon (albeit with neither blame nor even bitterness on either side) to restore the status quo ante. There were no children, so that I slipped back into the old routine with less & less each year to remind me that I had ever been out of it. And by the time that I saw how impracticable my uncommercialism made all further matrimonial plans, I was too old to consider such plans (being without the romantic illusions of such fellow-elders as Mr. John Barrymore & His erstwhile Majesty) anyhow!

Well—so much for senile reminiscence & philosophising. Returning to the question of whether one can actually make a living writing for the pulps—my answer (not applicable to myself because of my utter loathing for pulp standards, my lack of mechanical cleverness in slinging cheap fictional formulae, & my general absence of every trace of commercial psychology) is *emphatically yes.* Of course certain natural qualifications probably have to be present. Not every generally intelligent & adaptable person can seem to turn the trick. One must have a sort of inborn knack at discerning dramatic situations & ways of unfolding events, plus a profound comprehension of low-grade herd psychology & an almost intuitive knowledge of the primitive, conventional stimuli to which the herd most readily respond. More—he must be sympathetic enough with the herd-perspective to put at least a little spontaneous zest into his writing, & indifferent enough to literature not to gag & rebel at the utter mockery & charlatanry of the whole process. Given these qualifications, there is no limit to the cash a brilliant & energetic pulpist can make. Arthur J. Burks is virtually a plutocrat through pulping alone. Others set $400. per week as a reasonable income. This, however, applies to an unusual group who make slaves & machines of themselves. But I know or know of many a man who lives in comfort from pulping alone—E. Hoffmann Price, the late Bob Howard, the Wandrei boys, Edmond Hamilton, Paul Ernst, Jack Williamson, & dozens of others. Long is rapidly getting into this class. These writers have probably killed their real talent by selling themselves into charlatanry. They will never again (as a few of them once did) produce a work of serious value. But they know where their next year's rent money is coming from. Most of them employ agents who egg them on with tips & suggestions—Otis Adelbert Kline & August Lenniger being the two best-known ones. (I can find you their addresses if you're interested) As for the kind of *information* needed by pulpists—ordinary scholarship is almost useless. That isn't what's wanted. The dope that sells cheap fiction is modern data on certain fields of especial herd interest—police, detective, & court procedure; criminal & underworld lore; western life; legal & medical details; colour & atmosphere of certain flashy strata of contemporary life (stage, cinema, night-clubs, &c.); customs of strange (especially Oriental) lands; details of certain hazardous occupations (war, aviation, &c.) & of certain modern industries in which the readers are likely to be engaged or otherwise interested; conditions & language of business & finance, especially "Wall Street" stuff; theories & vocabulary of modern science—so far as the latter relates to spectacular concepts of other worlds & aeons & dimensions, or of radical changes in terrestrial life & living-conditions; &c. &c. &c. Of all this, as you may see, only a small part pertains to the body of ordinary academic or literary scholarship. It is more a matter of "sophistication" than of what is commonly regarded as education, My almost total lack of this sort of knowledge, & the concomitant lack of interest which makes its acquisition difficult, would alone be enough to debar *me* from success in pulpdom—although most commercially trained & even moderately worldly persons have a great deal of it instinctively, automatically, & as a matter of course. Naturally, one doesn't have to be intimately versed in *all* the fields here enumerated. A few—or even one or two—are all that any one writer generally tries to follow. Thus Price concentrates on the Orient, the police, & the underworld; Donald Wandrei on detective procedure & [usually erroneous] scientific borderlands; Howard Wandrei on the gangster underworld; Carl Jacobi on Borneo geography & anthropology; Edmond Hamilton on cockeyed astronomy; Seabury Quinn (who edits an undertaker's magazine as his main support) on occult folklore & medico-legal details (he's an ex-lawyer); Hugh B. Cave on abnormal psychology & sadism; &c. &c. &c. In any of these fields a good bluff at knowledge is as effective as knowledge itself—& even the needed smattering of real knowledge is easy for most if they have any real interest in the chosen fields. Certainly, a thorough education is the very last thing pulpdom demands! Of technical writing skill, however, it demands a great deal—for its whole success depends on the adroit manipulation of certain puppet-like stock figures in just those hackneyed ways which most acutely tickle the emotions of the mentally undeveloped herd. One must be a shrewd psychologist, able to envisage his audience & cater expertly to their foibles, prejudices, & ignorance. This applies equally to the writer for the popular "slicks" (*Cosmopolitan, Sat Eve Post* &c.), whose material is just as artificial & insincere as pulp junk, despite its "slanting" toward a group of clods with more cash, formal education, shrewdness, & surface sophistication. No dub ever succeeded in popular writing. It is not an art, but it is a major branch of commerce—requiring the same qualifications as those required by industry, banking, shopkeeping, &c. That's why I'm no good at it. Incidentally, I believe the various writers' magazines (of which *The Writers' Digest* is probably the best) tend to be extremely helpful to the incipient pulpist—furnishing lists of current markets, & containing articles on various live problems of method & technique in the commercial writing field. The different mechanical plot-casting devices (charts, dials, &c.) so widely advertised are also potentially useful for the manipulation of formula-stories. No one need despise pulping too acutely. If I *could* do it, I would. It is not art, but it is an honest trade. If it carries with it something of the cheap aura of charlatanry & the amusement industry, one must reflect that the amusement of the masses is a necessary social function. One can't leave the *circenses* out of the essential *panem et circenses.* And any needed productive industry is a lot less ignominious than some of the highly-regarded speculative businesses which merely juggle resources without adding to them, & which perform no social service.

Well—here's to good luck & a milder winter!

Yrs most sincerely—H P Lovecraft

*Notes*

1. The "Dark Day" occurred on 19 May 1780, when an unusual darkening of the day sky was observed over New England and parts of Canada. The cause appears to have been a combination of smoke from forest fires, a thick fog, and cloud cover. The *Providence Daily Journal* for 7 September 1881 reported that the previous day, the atmosphere throughout New England was "pervaded with a yellowish light, which lends a strange appearance" (p. 1) to the landscape. The cause of the atmospheric effect was attributable to smoke that had travelled eastward from the "Thumb Fire" that had burnt more than a million acres of woodlands in Michigan's Thumb Area. Note that this event antedates the eruption of Krakatoa in the Dutch East Indies on 26 August 1883. Cleveland's "Black Day" has not been identified.

2. "Some Notes on Interplanetary Fiction" (some portions copied from "Notes on Writing Weird Fiction").

3. Perceval Landon (1868-1927) was an English writer and journalist. His story is in *50 Years of Ghost Stories* (no ed. named), which HPL owned.

4. HPL refers to the Justice Richard Brown House (1731) on the grounds of Butler Hospital. See Cady, pp. 32–33 (photo on p. 32).

5. Probably the Governor James Fenner House at 41 Waterman Street.

6. HPL sent Pabody a copy of *Fantasy Magazine* containing F. Lee Baldwin's "H. P. Lovecraft: A Biographical Sketch." The "portrait" is a linoleum cut of HPL by Duane W. Rimel, from a photograph taken by R. H. Barlow in 1934 when HPL visited him in Florida.

7. HPL is in error: Abner Alden's *The Reader* was first published in 1802.


[9]     [ALS, JHL]

66 College St.,

Providence, R.I.,

Jany. 20, 1937.

My dear Mr. Pabody:—

I greatly enjoyed your letter of Dec. 22, with its varied comments & interesting autobiographical glimpses. The verbal self-portrait sounds to me just a bit over-modest—indeed, I doubt whether a photographic revelation could be quite so formidable as your imply! As to that linoleum cut allegedly of myself—if I ever get a new supply of prints from the chap who took the prototypical photograph, I'll let you see the hellish reality behind the printed illusion. You're right—the anaemic grey lint which imperfectly covers an increasing natural tonsure is by no means so abundant as linoleumist Rimel charitably implies. When you behold the snapshot, you can judge how correct or incorrect your previous impression was. As for the magazine—if you have a file of such material you're welcome to it; though I could probably use it to better advantage than the waste-basket if it came to a choice between the two.

The notes on your career are interesting indeed, & would seem to me to imply exceptionally good foundations for further progress. I imagine that the "Wonder World" set must be something like the much-advertised "Book of Knowledge"[1]—both being evidently of very high value to the unfolding mind. I regret that nothing of the sort existed in my own early days. Your interval of ill health may have been a handicap in one way, but was probably a stimulus & incentive in other directness. Too bad the pain & nightmares were so poignant—yet the latter doubtless figured, along with Verne & Wells, in your imaginative development. Your recurrent forest-dream reminds me of one of my own—the latter based upon a picturesque wooded ravine (now filled in) near my home. In this dream strange & non-human brown things (like small monkeys, but curiously different in details) used to wriggle out of burrows in the steep ravine-walls & perform unholy ceremonies around an altar-stone in the centre of the hollow. I have twice used this theme in verse,[2] but never in prose so far. Your early editorial experience surely formed a good literary apprenticeship—as did the reporting & the fictional case-history. And of course the varied reading & wide experience in different industrial fields are assets of great value. So, too, is your ability to endure the typewriter—an instrument so closely linked nowadays with all authorship for publication.

I am surely glad that you know & like "The Hill of Dreams"—which is an imaginative education all in itself. Machen's work is doubly fascinating to me because of his frequent allusions to *Roman Britain*—a phase of history in which my interest has always been intense. "The Great God Pan" has a classic reputation, but looks a bit mechanical—with its tremendous dependence on coincidence—today. But "The White People" is magnificent—perhaps the second-greatest weird story in existence [Blackwood's "The Willows" being the greatest]—while some of the episodes in "The Three Impostors" come close to the head of the list.

"The Eighth Green Man"[3] is good as pulp products go, but has a certain crudity & naivete none the less. One reflects with a sigh how much *more* Machen or Dunsany or de la Mare could have made of a theme like this. I surely hope that you will, despite the lure of more immediately profitable types, persist in your ambitions to create material of this kind. That it is not wholly unsalable is proved by the printing & reprinting of "The Eighth Green Man" itself.

However, the ideas you outline for earlier use are surely fruitful enough. The "hyper-hypnosis" theme is full of possibilities—& its exterior has, as you point out, the added advantage of scientific plausibility. And I believe the vine-forest dream of childhood would also make splendid material. One could write quite a thesis on the *terrible forests* in weird literature—mentioning those in Bierce's "Halpin Frayser", Dunsany's tale of the Gnoles, Buchan's "Witch Wood", &c. &c. &c.

Glad you think you'll find the Lake Shore Author's Club reasonably helpful. Similar organisations—including the American Fiction Guild—have proved quite useful to many in marketing pulp material . . . . through market tips, suggestions as to trends & demands, inside information on editorial policies, & so on. The Guild is nationwide, & has active local chapters—E. Hoffmann Price being very active in it on the Pacific coast. Of course pulp-writing is the very opposite of authentic literary expression, & often ruins a person as a real author. Only a few can escape the contamination of its methods. I'd never advise anyone to go into it unless (a) he has no wish to become a sincere writer, or unless (b) he feels sure of the possession of a compartmented mind like (for example) Derleth's, which permits him to follow two conflicting lines of endeavour at the same time without mutual interference. The people who really ought to do the pulping are those who care nothing for literature but who are clever, resourceful, & adaptable in the mechanical handling of clichés & expected & oversimplified verbal efforts. It is a business & not an art—in fact, it is more definitely hostile to artistic feeling that are most businesses.

About the marketing of those stories you mention—the David–Bathsheba & "true confessions" & detective episodes—my very vague knowledge of the field is hardly sufficient to make my advice worth taking. If the given themes happen to be handled in just the style of certain publications, they might land—yet a different treatment would earn the same basic material a rejection slip. With luck, or a well-known name, one might place frothy matter (as you describe the David–Bathsheba sketch) in some self-consciously "smart" periodical of the *Esquire* order. More naive material—with similar luck—could perhaps get into the very popular *Liberty*. In the pulp field I believe the Munsey publications—*Argosy*, &c.—might offer the best chances. Wandrei (1152 Portland Ave., St. Paul, Minn.) or Price (Route 2, Box 100-U-5, Redwood City, Calif.) or Long (230 W. 97th St. N.Y.C.) or Derleth (Sauk City, Wis.) could tell you much more than I about such matters. I have nothing to do with commercial fiction, & never see the periodicals in question. To hit the very aptest markets, it is well to employ a literary agent at first—the best I know of being Otis Adelbert Kline [old address, 4333 Costello Ave., Chicago—from which mail would undoubtedly be forwarded to his present N.Y. address, which I don't know. Long could give you his present address.] Writers' magazines are also a vast help, being full of hints anent markets, methods, formulae, "slants", & other matters vital to the commercial writer. The best of these, I think, is *The Writers' Digest*. All these magazines are full of advertisements of books & devices to aid the financially ambitious pulpist—including volumes of the sort of occupationally or socially specialised information & phraseology which I recently mentioned as being in demand. Under separate cover I'll send a copy of a recent pamphlet advertising the *Writer's Digest*, & composed of specimen articles & advertisements from the latter. I think you'll find it a fairly interesting key to further data regarding commercial possibilities. By the way, I'm interested to learn of your good opinion of Wandrei's story in *Esquire*[4]—which I haven't read. He spoke of having something there, but I never have time to follow the popular magazines—whose glib artificiality most distinctly does not appeal to my taste.

As for a collection of my tales in book form—I'm pretty sure nothing of the kind will ever appear. Despite my utter repudiation of pulp standards, my complete refusal to "slant" anything at the request of commercial editors, the poison of cheap writing seems to have tainted my stuff through the subconscious influence of submitting things to W T & sometimes getting them accepted . . . . . & as a result, my stories are not good enough for book publication. Six times or more I have been approached by publishers on the subject of a collection, & at their request have sent in a representative array of material for consideration. In each case the matter has ultimately come to nothing. At present an agent is hawking some of my tales in England, but I have no expectation of any results. Incidentally, O'Brien never *reprinted* any of my stories in his collections. He merely *cited* certain specimens for honourable mention—three-starring "The Colour out of Space" & "The Dunwich Horror" & giving others lesser notice.[5] Fantastic books, as you remark, are hard to find in public libraries—but I fancy the reason is lack of demand rather than censorship. There is nothing in the weird classics that calls for censorship according to any standard—however Victorian & artificial—but there is a profound public apathy which acts in the same way. How to reconcile this with your report on the demand for Bierce &c. in Cleveland I don't know—but perhaps Bierce has a special glamour in himself. And some of the newer collections have been fairly well publicised by reviews. Be that as it may, I am constantly told of the lack of demand for weird stuff, & of the financial failure of most weird anthologies—with the possible exception of "Creeps by Night" (containing my "Music of Erich Zann"), which has [largely on the *name*-strength of contributions by William Faulkner, Stephen Vincent Benet, Conrad Aiken, &c.] gone into a dollar reprint.

Regarding religion—it is to my mind simply a primitive survival from early stages of mental & emotional evolution. It represents the awe & fear & orgiastic response of an ignorant species confronted by phenomena which it does not understand & into which it reads a fictitious personality, with pseudo-mammalian consciousness, will, & objectives, like its own. Today it seems to me completely meaningless, irrelevant, & even frivolous. It has nothing to do with anything we really know or really are. The fact that certain branches of it have gratuitously annexed the task of preaching & enforcing ethics (a subject which belongs jointly to utilitarian sociology & to aesthetics) is without significance. Indeed, under the changed ethical needs of today we often find religion an obstructive & anti-social force rather than a beneficent influence. I can sympathise with all anti-clerical moves so far as they leave untouched the field of private opinion.

Religion, so far as I can see, is simply a sort of emotional self-tickling—or mutual tickling among bands of the voluntarily blind. Its survival very obviously depends upon the simple principle of *emotional crippling*—attacking the infant mind with propaganda before it has developed a critical rationality, & thus permanently warping the subject's perspective. There is nothing in the universe which in the light of modern knowledge could even vaguely suggest such a thing as religion. All the supposedly "natural" inclinations of man toward religious belief & ecstasy are obviously the result of inherited propaganda acting on emotional complexes well (& materialistically) known to contemporary psychologists. The whole fabric is a decadent vestige—without relation to truth, & antagonistic to the pursuit of truth.

As for truth in itself—that is another matter, & one which can be successfully approached only with a mind completely free of traditional preconceptions. Your positivism is right—we can *know* nothing. But we can compare what slight scraps of impressions we *do* receive from the external world, & form guesses as to the *relative probability* of certain hypotheses. Such a process of comparison reveals all traditional religious concepts as so purely gratuitous & unrelated to anything actually known or existing around us that we may safely dismiss such concepts from consideration.

Of the ultimate constitution & operation of the universe we shall never be likely to know anything. But we *can* see how silly it is to assume that the cosmic fabric has a definite "author" (if so, who is the author's author?), a definite "consciousness", a definite "purpose", a definite set of principles of "good", "evil", &c., a definite relationship to the momentary planetary phenomenon called organic life, &c. &c. &c. All this childish imagining is simply an example of the so-called "pathetic fallacy"—reading human emotions & mental processes into objects & phenomena which have nothing to do with them. The closer to a human being any theory makes the cosmos seem to be, the more likely that theory is to be completely cockeyed.

So far as probability goes—there is no reason to impute any beginning or ending to "infinite creation". The cosmos shews no sign of being other than *a basic & eternal condition*—a field of force in which occurs infinite rearrangement according to fixed patters of least resistance, but which has no "direction", "collective consciousness", "purpose", "meaning", or anything else except sheer existence. That those local phenomena which (like the more complex mammals) have built up fields of impression-registration (= consciousness) have any especial relation to the fabric of the whole ("human dignity", "moral law", "immortality", "soul", &c. &c) is a notion so basically silly & unjustified by any real indication that it scarcely needs serious attention. Man had better stop playing with infantile myths & turn his attention to the scientific realities which will enable him to utilise his energies & capacities to better social advantage.

As for the public's reaction to reports of strange & unnatural occurrences—you would tend to sympathise with the basic position of Charles Fort, who collected thousands of such reports into his famous compilations ("The Book of the Damned" &c.) & drew fantastic theories from them. But while there is something to be said for this side, I tend to see the opposite side rather vividly—the incurable myth-making, lie-peddling, & fact-twisting capacity of the human animal. Anthropology, in tracing the origin of folk-beliefs, sheds a strong light on these modern reports of marvels—most of which never occurred in the first place, & others of which represent vague distortions of events not in themselves so basically inexplicable. However—well-authenticated oddities ought always to be investigated very thoroughly.

Hope you had an enjoyable Yule. We had a tree, & the weather was gratifyingly mild. Of gifts, the most distinctive was perhaps that which came from one of the youthful "fan magazine" editors—one Conover of Cambridge, Md.—for lo! when I had unwrapped the bundle what should I find but the yellowed & crumbling fragments of *a long-interred human skull!* It came from an Indian mound near the donor's home. One strives to evoke the image of him to whom it once belonged. A sanguinary chief? A crafty medicine-man? Who knows?

Best wishes for 1937—H P L

*Notes*

1. HPL refers to the encyclopedias *Our Wonder World: A Library of Knowledge* (Chicago: Shuman & Co., 1918; 10 vols.) and *The Book of Knowledge* (New York: Grolier Society, 1928; 20 vols.).
2. Probably "The Eidolon" and "Recognition" (*Fungi from Yuggoth* IV).
3. G. G. Pendarves, "The Eighth Green Man" (*WT,* March 1928; rpt. January 1937).
4. "The Eye and the Finger," *Esquire* 6, No. 6 (December 1936): 70, 319–20.
5. Edward J. O'Brien's *The Best Short Stories of 1928* (New York: Dodd, Mead, 1928) gave "The Colour out of Space" a 3-star rating and printed a brief autobiography by HPL in the "Biographical Notices" section (p. 324). *The Best Short Stories of 1929* (New York: Dodd, Mead, 1929) gave a 3-star rating to "The Dunwich Horror" and a 1-star rating to "The Silver Key." *The Best Short Stories of 1924* (Boston: Small, Maynard, 1924) gave a 1-star rating to "The Picture in the House."

[10]    [ALS, JHL]

66 College St.,
Providence, R.I.,
Feby. 17, 1937.

My dear Mr. Pabody:—

I enjoyed your letter very much & am grateful for the clever bit of 'hot-doggerel' which you contributed to the Robinson column.[1] I agree in censuring your oversight in not stamping out the unpleasant new form of matter which has so virulently overrun the entire planet—although even if you'd stepped on it it might have formed itself again. Those hardy, primitive organisms can take a lot! It interests me to follow the new discoveries regarding the behaviour of filterable viruses & their tentative identification with usually-non-alive proteins—which would seem to indicate the closest approach yet to a bridge between life & non-life.

Hope you'll have luck with your short-short weird story—which might be made very convincing with the right sort of atmosphere despite the apparently slender theme. I trust, too, that your longer W T product will develop successfully. It seems to me that you don't need to make so many popular concessions in writing for W T, since Wright takes many an atmospheric bit without the conventional action & hokum. Still, if you throw in the junk you'll be able to submit the tale to other markets in case of Wrightian rejection! From your description, I judge that the creeping death lacks nothing in hideous picturesqueness. Now it remains merely to provide such trifles as "who done it & why". Glad you've found a capable-seeming agent, & don't see why he can't prove a worthy rival of the widely-revered Kline. His presence in your own city makes him a more convenient & logical choice than anyone at a distance. Postage is no joke when many MSS. are involved.

No—I hadn't heard of "Law Under England",[2] & am greatly interested. It sounds like just my kind of stuff, & would have to be pretty badly written in order not to fascinate me. I shall certainly look it up at the very first opportunity—meanwhile abundant thanks for the tip. Have just had another book recommended to me—"The Undying Monster"[3]—which is said to contain considerable horrific colouring despite a flat ending.

Surely you are welcome to that *Fantasy Magazine* with the writeup of me—I have several duplicates left. Beginning with the next issue, F M will merge with another little "fan mag"—*The Science-Fantasy Correspondent*—& the first combined issue will have *another* writeup with the same tedious subject . . . . this time a very informal account by E. Hoffmann Price of our two get-togethers in New Orleans & Providence. Price sent it to me for censorship, but the only thing I changed was an allusion to the colour of my hair. Price—he hasn't seen me since July '33—said it was *dark* . . . . but such are the rapid changes of the last 3½ years that I had to set the present status down as *grey*.[4] I'll be glad to see that future snap of you when it is ready—& can assure you that I will leave me unterrified. Four decades & more of familiarity with the mirror have hardened me to confront the very worst in the domain of quasi-human features. You will appreciate the singular & drastic thoroughness of this hardening when I get hold of a print of that portrait whose details the linoleum artist mercifully veiled.

I surely hope you'll be able to get that car & arrange for that Eastern vacation, & that circumstances will dictate a choice of the Providence–Little Compton–Boston itinerary. You certainly couldn't find a more picturesque field for exploration—all apart from special ancestral reasons—than the New England coastal region from Portsmouth on the north to Narragansett Bay on the southwest.

Glad to hear of the varied & substantial boons which Yuletide brought. I had *one* turkey dinner—but that's more than I could cope with right now, since my digestion is all shot to hell in connexion with this lingering semi-grippe. At present, pea or ox-tail soup with bread forms my preferred heavy meal of the day . . . the "preference", needless to say, being a purely forced & emergency one! I've been very grateful, though, for the generally mild winter—which has allowed me to get outdoor air & exercise, whereas a really cold season would have clamped the lid of absoluteness on my hibernation. Still, I wish I were in Florida!

Later—down at last! Intestinal symptoms worse. Doc has me taking 3 nostrums & up only a little while each day. Affairs in chaos!

All good wishes———Yrs sincerely—H P L

P.S. A request or some astronomical articles has caused me to do a lot of brushing up on that science.[5] The changes of the last 20 or 25 years are bewildering—but there is an abundance of excellent popular treatises now.

*Notes*

1. Edwin Meade "Ted" Robinson (1878–1946) at the time was a columnist for the *Cleveland Plain Dealer*. Pabody apparently contributed some verse to Robinson's "Philosopher of Folly" column. Robinson once mentioned HPL his column when Samuel Loveman's Colophon Club voted "Hypnos" among the dozen or so best short stories in the world. See "The Philosopher of Folly: A Journalistic Journal." *Cleveland Plain Dealer* (13 March 1923): 10.

2. Unidentified.

3. By Jessie Douglas Kerruish.

4. E. Hoffmann Price, "The Sage of College Street," *Amateur Correspondent* 2, No. 1 (May–June 1937): 6–7. The memoir was originally titled "H. P. Lovecraft: Viewed by E. Hoffmann Price" and was somewhat longer than what appeared in *Amateur Correspondent*. Price had initially written "His hair is dark"; HPL had revised this to read "His greying hair was until recently dark." See *Lovecraft at Last* 156–59.

5. Charles Blackburn Johnston, the Barlows' handyman in DeLand, Florida, now "connected" with Stetson University and its astronomical society, asked HPL for a series of "elementary articles on the heavens for the local paper" (see *SL* 5.422). HPL resurrected his series "Mysteries of the Heavens" (1915) for that purpose, but never revised the articles.

# Appendix

## *Verse by C. L. Moore**

The girls who died for Dalmar, [/] tonight they sleep a-chill—[/]they honey lips are dust now, [/] the throbbing throats are still, and peace is on the high hearts [/] that beat for him so warm, [/] and peace is on the sleek heads [/] that lay on Dalmar's arm. [/] Their hearts have ceased from sorrowing, [/] their tears no longer fall—[/] the narrow bed, the cold bed [/] the grave enfolds them all. [/] Oh, girls who died for Dalmar, [/] and ligh tonight so low—[. . .]

Oh, gay the swinging chorus the marching army sings,
And gay the spurs are jingling and brave the armour rings,
And bright the plumes and pennants beneath the blue spring sky
As southward, south to Rivah, King Jamin's men go by.

*   *   *

King Jamin marches homeward beneath the blue spring skies,
A tattered Dragon Banner from Rivah's ramparts flies. . . .

Toll the bells for the Dragon King who never wore a crown,
Sing a dirge for the Black Lorane, the monarch of the drowned . . .
Over my green and golden land the headlong ocean broke. . . .

High o'er Alisia's level land
The castled crags of the Sun-born stand,
And over the country, near and far,
The bloody tracks of the Dragon are.

10 September 1934

No Title as Usual.

Where have they gone? The great, the splendid ones,
Monarch and warrior, baron, beggar, king,
Living and loving under long dead suns,
Hark to the jingling mail, the rumbling guns,
That faintly, faintly down the ages ring.

---

*from her letters to R. H. Barlow

Furled are the Dragon's wings.

The pirate banner rides the wind no more,
Amar and Luc-delar are dust and gone;
Peace reigns triumphant on the Umar shore.
Where are the Gentlemen of shining yore?
Deep in the Sea-Maid's arms they slumber on—

Romance is dead and gone.

Where are the splendors of the ancient days?
King Jamin rode to Rivah, long ago.
The Red Prince fell beside the watch-tower's blaze,
The marching feet of armies on the ways
That lead to war ring low.

The mists of years between us ebb and flow.

Still are the dancing blades that sang of war,
Muted and still the pulsing golden throats
Of Amorette and Dalmar, and that far
Call of the bugle 'neath the falling star.
The lightning blazes on the pirate boats—

The death-black banner floats.

We gave our sons the silver wings to fly,
But that is over—dead and ended now.
We watched Prince Malne soar, we watched him die—
His flaming ship swept screaming down the sky,
Dead with Malne and the Dragon vow—

Over and ended, now.

Our day is ended: downward sweeps our star,
The golden throats are dust.
Faintly the silver bugles sang of war,
Thundering hoofbeats gallop, faint and far,
Down the bright years, to dust.

We die, because we must.


This Sea-Maid's Song is interminable and very ancient. Any reference in history to the Song means this.

"My heart belongs to the Sea-Maid, lads, and she is my only love,

She holds my soul where the long waves roll
And the sky is blue above

I'll follow the Sea-Maid's Song, my lads, as long as my life shall last,
I'll hear her song tho the miles be long
That part me from the mast.

Keep your castles and fields and towns, for we forsake them all
Who know the tides that our vessel rides
And follow the Sea-Maid's call.["]

etc. etc. The Sea-Maid is really our patron saint, and there are innumerable songs dealing with her from chanties like "Hé, ho,

> The salt winds blow,
> Kiss me, sweet, and let me go,
> For the Sea-Maid calls me home"

to more formal efforts such as,

Farewell to whitewalled Albion, farewell to sunny Spain,
My ship is hungry for the wind that sings across the main.
The Sea-Maid calls across the waves a far-flung cry to me,
I'm off to launch a white-winged flight across the singing sea.

And then there was a topical ditty made about a high-born gentleman who had pirated under the *carmagliom,* the black flag, until his marriage, and who later left his wife and "Went down to Valden" again, which means he met his old friends at the notorious pirate rendezvous, the little town of Valden:

"The Captain's left his castles, the Captain's left his crown,
The Captain's left his fair young wife and all his friends in town;
The Captain's left his duties, his troubles and his bride
And hied him south to Valden, to Valden by the tide.

The Captain's gone to Valden, across the hills to Valden,
He's southward bound to Valden, upon the ocean side.

Oh, duties may be irksome and wives be sharp of tongue,
And husbands may be handsome, and restless too, and young;
The Sea-Maid's call is luring; the merchant ships are fat;
*Carmaglios* are flying—we ask you, what of that?

The Captain's gone to Valden, across the hills to Valden,
He's southward bound to Valden—we ask you, what of that?["]

There is supposed to be a famous song called "We'll All Go Down to Valden" but I have never got around to writing it.

And here's a love-song: [. . .]

Of all the girls in Coronel there's none like Pretty Sali,
She's sweeter than the ruffled rose that blooms along the valley.
I would not rule the pirate ships that loot the fleets of Spain;
I'd rather dwell beside the brook that threads the singing valley,
And all the world would envy me who shares the Spring with Sali.

And there was the sailor's song I made to go to the tune of Oh Susannah:

Oh, Cleona, unbar the door to me,
I'm coming home with silks and gold
From sailing round the sea.

I've fought against the Dragon Flag with good King Nedri's men,
I've fought beneath the Dragon's gold, and then the Hawk again.
I've sailed the seas the Luc-delar, I've sailed against him too,
But now I'm back from oceans far, I'm coming home to you.

Oh, Cleona, unbar the door to me—etc. That goes on forever, too.

And a lament from ancient history, made into opera now:

I ride behind stallions along the white sea-sand
Valhadra hath strewn for the feet of her queen,
They gather me garlands from gardens and trees, and
They hail me with singing on highway and green:
etc.
But all the night-tide I am weeping and weeping
(Valhadra's proud princes and darling as I—)
That on a far hillside eternally sleeping
My father and brothers in loneliness lie,
And there amid ashes and stark vigil keeping,
The ruins of Farale look up at the sky.

This would probably continue for hours, so I will give one more and quit. It's all about the woes of one lady Niki j'Dracen, who was terribly in love with Dalmar:

She closed her eyes in weariness and pain
And turned into the shadowed room again
Where gilded hangings glimmered on the wall.
She heard the singing fountain's rise and fall,

She heard the night wind in the swaying trees.
She turned her back.

       In silence, on her knees.
Her forehead bowed against her folded hands,
She learned these sounds as landsmen know their lands;
Seeking thru pain the bitter road to peace.

She found no magic for her soul's surcease.
The silver Mary turned her eyes away.
Deep in her heart she knew she did not pray
That haloed God so many ages dead.
Deep in her heart that other haloed head
Ringed with its coronet of deadly gold
Glimmered behind the slipping beads she told.

"Oh Blessed Mary, give my prayers thy head,
From Heaven's high throne, in this my hour of need—
*(These are the arms that closed his shoulders' spread,*
*To this dark hair he bent his gilded head—*
*This is the mouth that answered to his kiss—*
*My heart was his—and is—and all of this. . . .)*

["]Dear Lord, Thy mercy like a fountain streams—
Guard me from sin by daylight and by dreams—
For his dear sake who died upon the Tree—
*(Send my crowned lover back to me! . . .)*["]

P.S. Just one more and I promise I'll quit. Got to remembering the Sea-Maid's Call made to fit more or less that song from ["]Show-Boat"[,] the Lonesome Road:

"Come down—come down—into my arms—thou rover of the sea,
Come down—come down—into my arms—and rest for aye with me—
My heart grows weary—weary waiting—waiting here below—
Come down, come down, my only love—why do you tarry so. . . . ? (on second thought maybe I didn't make that up at all. It's fearfully reminiscent of the original song. Oh, well.)

                                       31 December 1934

I am that Helen, that very Helen,
Of Leda born in the days of old,        (was she the fledgling out of that
Men's hearts as inns that I might dwell in  divine egg born to Leda and the Swan?)
Homeless I wander tonight, and cold.
Because men loved me no gods take pity,

My ghost goes wailing where I was queen—
Alas, my palace in Troy's tall city,
My ghost goes wailing where I was queen—
Alas, my palace in Troy's tall city,
My gilded arches, my hangings green!
Waste with fire are the halls they built me,
And sown with salt are the ways I trod,
There flowers they scattered and spices spilt me,
Alas that Zeus is a jealous god!          (doesn't sound very paternal if she was
Swiftly I went on my sandals golden,     indeed hatched from that fabulous Egg)
Of love and laughter I had my fill,
With Paris' kisses my lips were holden,
Nor guessed I, when life went at my will
That the fates behind me went softlier still.

February 24, 1936

*    *    *

Your second summer underground:
The sun still dapples through the trees,
The leaves still wink in sun and breeze
And still the wheeling world goes round.
Though you sleep sound.
And half reluctantly I feel
The scars of heartbreak slowly heal.

Those scars still pull, as scars must do
When in forgetfulness I strain
The heart that's almost whole again
In sudden memory of you,
But pain is through.
Relentlessly it ebbs away
A dark low tide that will not stay.

I feel it ebb, I feel it go,
This living link between us two,
This last strong bond from life to you,
And as it ebbs away I know
You too will go.
You too will dim and fade and cease,
So high a price we give for peace.

Once there was silence when we met
Of hearts too full for common speech;
Then heaven itself was just in reach

Remembering now, my eyes are wet.
I shall forget.
The hot, sweet months swing slowly round:
Your second summer underground.

August 1937

\*   \*   \*

I was flung full length upon the ground before
Castilles' umeasured miles of dust and gold
Which autumn bathed in mysteries untold.
A great clear sun sank down beyond the floor
Of furrowed earth; the slow plough opened wide
Furrow and channel to hold the dormant seed
Bestowed by honest hands; and taken, heed
Of this sweet scene I turned my gaze inside.
I thought to search my heart and learn unshamed
Its content; <text excised>

[c. 6 October 1938?]

\*   \*   \*

Here is deep summer, with a touch of rot.
    In every loosening flower and bronzing green,
Summer for Arthur and for Camelot
    And for the full-blown beauty of the Queen.

Were happiness our human lot
    It should be mine today;
But none knows better it is not—
    Here dawns the first of May

And here my heart runs full once more
    With well remembered pain
And all the hurt I knew before
    Would be my own again

Had I not learned in other springs
    On rainbow heights I trod
To shun like death this beat of wings,
    This small and deadly god.

I know the hurt his harrows deal
    And I shall walk apart—

It is no happiness to feel
    This tremor shake my heart—

My heart that stumbles when we meet
    In warning to beware
Of love and spring and things too sweet
    For mended hearts to bear . . . .

6 June 1939

## Henry Kuttner

### For H. P. Lovecraft

The pain is a little less now
    For a wound may heal with time,
But because of a wound that may never quite heal
    I make this rhyme.

Not with a sure and skilful hand
    But because of a word you said,
I have tried to count the world's loss
    Now you are dead.

And the world's loss is a great loss,
    With fame at the long road's end,
But the world knew you through your words:
    You were my friend.

And the flame of art shall be brighter
    For the strange fire you lend,
And many shall mourn the Titan:
    I mourn my friend.

April 1937

## Fritz Leiber

### My Correspondence with Lovecraft

I read "The Colour out of Space" when it first appeared in *Amazing Stories* and its dismal gray horror chilled my dreams for weeks. Some years later I gulped down in two nights most of Lovecraft's published stories, preserved in magazine tearsheets by a college acquaintance. I read "The Shadow out of Time" and "At the Mountains of Madness" when they came out in *Astounding Stories*.

These tales gave me a wonder, mystery, and delightful terror I found in no other writing. They were sensational yet studious, weird as a theosophist's cosmos yet with no touch of charlatanry. It was the dream come true of meeting the mysterious scholar who tells one, yes, there are forbidden books, secret cults, undreamed eras of history, nonhuman intelligences, and all the rest of it. I imagine this acute effect was due to the channeling, both in me and the stories, of several powers: discounted mystical aspects of a hampered sexual urge, the wonder of science beyond all dull textbooks and elementary laboratory courses, the culturally deep-rooted love and dread of secret societies, the intoxication of metaphysics, the simple joy of excitement and surprise which Lovecraft himself referred to as "adventurous expectancy."

In 1936 these stories had maintained their spell over me to such a degree that I was searching second-hand magazine stores for them, chiefly to have them for rereading and permanent possession, though there were a few I had missed. I remember purchasing from Forrest J. Ackerman tearsheets of "The Silver Key" and "The Whisperer in Darkness."

Then in the late summer my wife, with a bold directness I had been unable to conceive for myself, wrote a letter to Lovecraft care of *Weird Tales*. A few days later the great man replied with what we thought was a long letter, until we had received some of his average-sized communications. That was the beginning of an orgy of letter-writing which lasted the few short months until his death. My wife wrote more letters herself and shortly we were joined by my friend and fellow enthusiast for the fantastic, Harry O. Fischer, then of Louisville, Kentucky. Our letters were returned to us by Mrs. Gamwell afterwards. The entire correspondence was excerpted by Derleth for the volume of letters and later borrowed and retained, permanently as yet, by another individual who shall remain nameless here.

The first things that struck me about Lovecraft from his letters were the wide range of his interests and his courteousness and great helpfulness, always tactful yet always ready. In his first letter he recalled at length my father's spirited Philip Faulconbridge in a performance of *King John* early in the century and quoted in full the speech that begins, "This England never did, nor never shall, lie at the proud foot of a conqueror, . . ." When I merely mentioned to him my intention of writing a novel set in Roman times, he sent me several thousand words of highly pertinent advice, including a longer and shorter bibliography for researching the period. Now, setting to work on such a novel twenty years later, I am helped by his remembered instructions. Ancient Rome, I discovered then, was the historical period with which Lovecraft identified himself most intensely, next to Restoration England.

Lovecraft's famous handwriting, which packed so very many words on a page or card, yearning toward all four edges sometimes by way of interlineations and balloons, was only superficially crabbed and difficult. Every tiny graceful hieroglyph for the simpler words was abbreviated and shaped exactly the same each time. With a bit of practice his handwriting made for fast easy reading. Lovecraft was a writer in many senses, not all of them current; in particular, the production of many pages of fine impromptu prose each day (chiefly in letters) was to him the breath of life.

He asked to see my own writing, none of it published, as soon as I told him about it. I sent him a long fantasy and a set of poems, "The Demons of the Upper Air." He praised and criticized both in detail, correcting each spelling error and infelicity, and carefully debating each dubious word-choice. He was particularly hard on such ponderous affectations as "activate" for "move." The fantasy was afterwards published by Arkham House as "Adept's Gambit" in my collection *Night's Black Agents*. This action on his part, crazily generous by hard-headed standards, influenced me permanently toward greater care in the polishing and final preparation of manuscripts.

His criticisms were not solely literary. When I praised Charles Fort for poking holes in scientific theories, he replied at once with a carefully reasoned, convincing defence of the dogmatism of the professional scientist. Fort's books, he said, were not to be taken seriously, though amusing enough and a great source of materials for the writer of fantasy and science fiction.

And he was unsparingly and I think excessively critical of his own writings, quite as harsh in fact as Edmund Wilson. He thought most of his stories were labored, unhumorous, wanting in lively human portraits, and heavy with a sort of pseudo-realism and with intentional partial repetitions designed to build atmosphere. He told me of his practice of disavowing from time to time stories which he found aesthetically wanting and he sent me a list, of which I still have a copy, of stories not disavowed as yet, "Herbert West— Reanimator" was still on the list but, he said, it was about to get the ax.

For my part, I think that Lovecraft, besides writing some excellent short stories somewhat in the manners of Poe, Dunsany, Machen, Hoffmann, and Bulwer-Lytton, and in addition to giving fiction with solid New England background a unique spectral note, did more than any other author to establish the science-fiction story as a vehicle for supernatural horror—a clear-cut and valid story form. Occasionally overshadowed by timelier, catchier, more chameleonlike fantasy and science fiction, such tales as "The Whisperer in Darkness," "The Dunwich Horror," "The Colour out of Space," "The Shadow out of Time," and "The Dreams in the Witch House" will live.

Besides setting me in his letters an enduring example of honest scholarly criticism, Lovecraft did something of equal importance for my future. He circulated the fantasy and poems I sent him among several other congenial correspondents. As a result I met Robert Bloch, Henry Kuttner, and later several other writers in the fantasy field. I came to think of myself as at least potentially a professional author.

Lovecraft is sometimes thought of as having been a lonely man. He made my life far less lonely, not only during the brief half year of our correspondence but during the twenty years after.

Yet those six precious months did have a special magic. Here are some examples. Inspired by Lovecraft's stories I produced several pictures in a medium I called splatter-stencil: star-fields splattered on black paper silhouette monstrous forms and structures. I sent a set to Lovecraft and he liked them. And I recall I was going to play Scipio Africanus in a drama about Hannibal that had a short life on the stages of San Francisco and Los Angeles. In the end I did not get the part, but we had a fine time commenting in our letters on this unexpected intrusion of old Rome. And there was talk of a volume of Lovecraft's short stories being published in hard covers, though he discounted the possibility since it had more than once occurred and failed to materialize before.

There seemed no reason why our stimulating and fruitful relationship would not go on indefinitely. Although he sometimes referred to himself as the Old Gentleman, Lovecraft had only become 46 years old on August 20th—"in my 47th year" was his way of putting it. His letters proved that his reserves of energy were prodigious, his interest fresh, his attitudes youthful—how many middle-aged men make friendships of the temperamental, unreserved, impractical sort by mail? To us, there was every indication that a long life remained to Lovecraft.

Yet there were disturbing hints that the situation was not quite like that. With more of her directness, my wife asked Lovecraft about his diet. The Old Gentleman obliged us with his College Street menu: chiefly coffee and a doughnut for breakfast, coffee and bread and cheese or a small can of beans or supper.

In the winter there was a brief hiatus in his replies. Then he wrote that he had been in a hospital for a few days,* but was out again and taking his regular walks, though in slippers or in shoes that had been cut out to accommodate his swollen feet.

Again his replies ceased. In Los Angeles my wife and I hid our fears from each other. In a Louisville attic, where his family had been driven by the Great Ohio Flood that opened 1937 (and destroyed a set of my splatter-stencils), Harry Fischer noted down, in a letter he had no way of sending me at the time, that something must be done to provide Lovecraft with fresh vegetables.

It was a little late for vitamins. Shortly afterwards Mrs. Gamwell informed us of her nephew's death. Only then did we realize that his letters to us newcomers were, beyond their other values, an example of truly smiling fortitude, of the enjoyment of life in the face of the greatest adversity.

---

*[Actually, HPL did not enter the hospital until 10 March 1937, five days before his death.—ED.]

# Glossary of Frequently Mentioned Names

**Forrest J Ackerman** (1916–2008), American agent, author, editor. Ackerman had been a science fiction fan since the late 1920s; he corresponded sporadically with HPL from around 1931 onward.

**Baird, Edwin** (1886–1957), first editor of *WT* (March 1923–April 1924), who accepted HPL's first submissions to the magazine. Also editor of *Real Detective Stories*.

**Barlow, R[obert] H[ayward]** (1918–1951), author and collector. As a teenager he corresponded with HPL and acted as his host during two long visits in the summers of 1934 and 1935. In the 1930s he wrote several works of weird and fantasy fiction, some in collaboration with HPL. HPL appointed him his literary executor. He assisted AWD and DAW in preparing the early HPL volumes for Arkham House. In the 1940s he went to Mexico and became a distinguished anthropologist. He died by suicide.

**Blackwood, Algernon** (1869–1951), prolific British author of weird and fantasy tales whose work HPL greatly admired when he read it in 1924.

**Bloch, Robert** (1917–1994), author of weird and suspense fiction who came into correspondence with HPL in 1933. HPL tutored him in the craft of writing during their four-year association.

**Boland, Stuart M[orton]** (1909–1973), librarian in San Francisco who corresponded with HPL in the 1930s, as recounted in his memoir, "Interlude with Lovecraft" (1945).

**Burks, Arthur J.** (1898–1974), voluminous contributor to *WT* and other pulp magazines.

**Cave, Hugh B[arnett]** (1910–2004), prolific author of stories for the pulp magazines. Lived for a time near HPL in Pawtucket, RI. They corresponded briefly but never met.

**Conover, Willis** (1920–1996), weird fiction fan who edited *Science-Fantasy Correspondent* (1936–37) and was a late correspondent of HPL.

**Crawford, William L[evy]** (1911–1984), editor of *Marvel Tales* and *Unusual Stories* and publisher of the Visionary Publishing Company, which issued HPL's *The Shadow over Innsmouth* (1936).

**de Castro, Adolphe (Danziger)** (1859–1959), author, co-translator with Ambrose Bierce of Richard Voss's *The Monk and the Hangman's Daughter*, and correspondent of HPL. HPL revised his "The Last Test" and "The Electric Executioner."

**de la Mare, Walter** (1873–1956), British author and poet who wrote occasional weird tales much admired by HPL for their subtlety and allusiveness.

**Derleth, August W[illiam]** (1909–1971), author of weird tales and also a long series of regional and historical works set in his native Wisconsin. After HPL's death, he and Donald Wandrei founded the publishing firm of Arkham House to preserve HPL's work in book form.

**Dunsany, Lord (Edward John Moreton Drax Plunkett, 18th baron Dunsany)** (1878–1957), Irish writer of fantasy tales whose work notably influenced HPL after HPL read it in 1919.

**Edkins, Ernest A[rthur]** (1867–1946), amateur journalist associated with the "halcyon days" of the National Amateur Press Association (1885–95). He came in touch with HPL in 1932.

**Finlay, Virgil** (1914–1971), one of the great weird artists of his time and a prolific contributor of artwork to the pulps; late correspondent of HPL.

**Hamilton, Edmond** (1904–1977), popular and prolific author of "weirdscientific" stories for WT.

**Henneberger, J[acob] C[lark]** (1890–1969), founder of *College Humor* (1922) and the original publisher of *WT*.

**Hodgson, William Hope** (1877–1918), British author of weird fiction whose work had fallen into obscurity until it was rediscovered in the 1930s, largely through the efforts of H. C. Koenig.

**Hornig, Charles D[erwin]** (1916–1999), editor of the *Fantasy Fan* (1933–35) and associate editor of *Wonder Stories*.

**Howard, Robert E[rvin]** (1906–1936), prolific Texas author of weird and adventure tales for *Weird Tales* and other pulp magazines; creator of the adventure hero Conan the Cimmerian. He and HPL corresponded voluminously from 1930 to 1936. He committed suicide when he heard of his mother's impending death.

**Jacobi, Carl** (1908–1997), prolific author of weird, weird menace, and science fiction stories for the pulp magazines. He published three collections of tales with Arkham House.

**James, M[ontague] R[hodes]** (1862–1936), celebrated British writer of ghost stories much admired by HPL. His *Collected Ghost Stories* appeared in 1931.

**Kirk, George [Willard]** (1898–1962), member of the Kalem Club. He published *Twenty-one Letters of Ambrose Bierce* (1922) and ran the Chelsea Bookshop in New York.

**Kline, Otis Adlebert** (1891–1946), prolific writer for *WT* and other pulp magazines; also a literary agent for C. L. Moore, Robert E. Howard, and others.

**Koenig, H[erman] C[harles]** (1893–1959), late associate of HPL who spearheaded the rediscovery of the work of William Hope Hodgson.

**Long, Frank Belknap** (1901–1994), fiction writer and poet and one of HPL's closest friends and correspondents. Late in life he wrote the memoir, *Howard Phillips Lovecraft: Dreamer on the Nightside* (1975).

**Loveman, Samuel E.** (1887–1976), poet and longtime friend of HPL and DAW as well as of Ambrose Bierce, Hart Crane, George Sterling, and Clark Ashton Smith. He wrote *The Hermaphrodite* (1926) and other works.

**Lumley, William** (1880–1960), eccentric late associate of HPL for whom HPL ghostwrote "The Diary of Alonzo Typer" (1935).

**Machen, Arthur** (1863–1947), Welsh author of weird fiction. He corresponded sporadically with AWD.

**Mashburn, W[allace] Kirk[patrick], Jr.** (1900–1968), frequent contributor to *WT* in the mid-1930s; later an insurance salesman.

**Merritt, A[braham]** (1884–1943), writer of fantasy and horror tales for the pulps. His work was much admired by HPL in spite of its concessions to pulp formulae. His late novel, *Dwellers in the Mirage* (1932), may have been influenced by HPL.

**Moe, Maurice W[inter]** (1882–1940), of Appleton and Milwaukee, WI. Amateur journalist, English teacher, and longtime friend and correspondent of HPL.

**Moe, Robert Ellis** (1912–1992), one of Maurice W. Moe's two sons (the other was Donald), who began corresponding with HPL in 1934 and met him on several occasions.

**Morton, James Ferdinand** (1870–1941), amateur journalist, author of many tracts on race prejudice, free thought, and taxation, and longtime friend of HPL.

**Price, E[dgar] Hoffmann** (1898–1988), prolific pulp writer of weird and adventure tales. HPL met him in New Orleans in 1932 and corresponded extensively with him thereafter.

**Quinn, Seabury** (1889–1969), prolific author of weird and detective tales to the pulps, notably a series of tales involving the psychic detective Jules de Grandin.

**Rimel, Duane W[eldon]** (1915–1996), weird fiction fan and late associate of HPL, who revised some of his early tales.

**Schwartz, Julius** (1915–2004), editor of *Fantasy Magazine* who acted as HPL's agent in marketing *At the Mountains of Madness* to *Astounding Stories*.

**Shea, J[oseph] Vernon** (1912–1981), young cinema and weird fiction fan from Pittsburgh who began corresponding with HPL in 1931.

**Shepherd, Wilson** (1917–1985), amateur printer and publisher of the *Phantagraph, Fanciful Tales,* and HPL's *A History of the Necronomicon* (Rebel Press, 1937).

**Shiel, M[atthew] P[hipps]** (1865–1947), British author of weird fiction, including the short story "The House of Sounds" and the novel *The Purple Cloud* (1901; rev. 1929).

**Smith, Clark Ashton** (1893–1961), prolific California poet and writer of fantasy tales. He received a "fan" letter from HPL in 1922 and corresponded with him until HPL's death.

**Sterling, Kenneth** (1920–1995), young science fiction fan who came into contact with HPL in 1934. He later became a distinguished physician.

**Stickney, Corwin F.** (1921–1998), copublisher with Willis Conover of *Science-Fantasy Correspondent* (1936–37), later titled *Amateur Correspondent* (1937f.), edited by Stickney alone.

**Sylvester, Margaret** (1918–2010), correspondent of HPL (1934–37). She had written to HPL in care of *WT,* asking him to explain the origin and meaning of the term *Walpurgisnacht.* She married and became Margaret Ronan, writing the preface to a school edition of HPL's tales, *The Shadow over Innsmouth and Other Stories of Horror* (Scholastic Books, 1971).

**Utpatel, Frank** (1905–1980), artist friend of AWD who illustrated some of AWD's work for *WT* and later did many jackets and interiors (primarily woodcuts and line drawings) for Arkham House; late correspondent of HPL.

**Wakefield, H[erbert] Russell** (1890–1964), British author of ghost stories.

**Wandrei, Donald** (1908–1987), poet and author of weird fiction, science fiction, and detective tales. He corresponded with HPL from 1926 to 1937, visited HPL in Providence in 1927 and 1932, and met HPL occasionally in New York during the 1930s. He helped HPL get "The Shadow out of Time" published in *Astounding Stories.* After HPL's death he and AWD founded the publishing firm Arkham House to preserve HPL's work. For their joint correspondence, see *Mysteries of Time and Spirit* (Night Shade Books, 2002).

**Wandrei, Howard** (1909–1956), younger brother of Donald Wandrei, premier weird artist and prolific author of weird fiction, science fiction, and detective stories; correspondent of HPL.

**Whitehead, Henry S[t. Clair]** (1882–1932), author of weird and adventure tales, many of them set in the Virgin Islands. HPL corresponded with him and visited him in Florida in 1931. HPL wrote a brief eulogy of Whitehead for *WT.*

**Wollheim, Donald A[llen]** (1914–1990), editor of the *Phantagraph* and *Fanciful Tales* and prolific author and editor in the science fiction field.

**Wright, Farnsworth** (1888–1940), editor of *Weird Tales* (1924–40). He often rejected HPL's work of the 1930s, only to publish some of it after HPL's death upon submittal by AWD.

# Bibliography

## A. Works by H. P. Lovecraft

*Books*

*The Ancient Track: Complete Poetical Works*. 2nd ed. Edited by S. T. Joshi. New York: Hippocampus Press, 2013.

*The Annotated Supernatural Horror in Literature*. 2nd ed. Edited by S. T. Joshi. New York: Hippocampus Press, 2012.

*The Cats of Ulthar*. Cassia, FL: Dragon-Fly Press, Christmas 1935.

*Charleston*. [New York: H. C. Koenig, 1936.] In *CE* 4.

*Collected Essays*. Edited by S. T. Joshi. New York: Hippocampus Press, 2004–06. 5 vols. [*CE*]

*Collected Fiction*. Edited by S. T. Joshi. New York: Hippocampus Press, 2015, 17. 4 vols. [*CF*]

*Dawnward Spire, Lonely Hill: The Letters of H. P. Lovecraft and Clark Ashton Smith*. Edited by David E. Schultz and S. T. Joshi. New York: Hippocampus Press, 2017.

*E'ch-Pi-El Speaks: An Autobiographical Sketch*. Saddle River, NJ: Gerry de la Ree, 1972.

*Essential Solitude: The Letters of H. P. Lovecraft and August Derleth*. Edited by David E. Schultz and S. T. Joshi. New York: Hippocampus Press, 2008. 2 vols. (numbered consecutively).

*Fritz Leiber and H. P. Lovecraft: Writers of the Dark*. Edited by Ben J. S. Szumskyj and S. T. Joshi. Holicong, PA: Wildside Press, 2003.

*Further Criticism of Poetry*. Louisville, KY: George G. Fetter, 1932. See "Notes on Verse Technique."

*Letters to Elizabeth Toldridge and Anne Tillery Renshaw*. Edited by David E. Schultz and S. T. Joshi. New York: Hippocampus Press, 2014.

*Letters to Richard F. Searight*. Edited by David E. Schultz and S. T. Joshi. West Warwick, RI: Necronomicon Press, 1992.

*Lovecraft at Last* (with Willis Conover). Arlington, VA: Carrollton-Clark, 1975. New York: Da Capo Press, 2002.

*A Means to Freedom: The Letters of H. P. Lovecraft and Robert E. Howard*. Edited by S. T. Joshi, David E. Schultz, and Rusty Burke. New York: Hippocampus Press, 2009. 2 vols. (numbered consecutively).

*O Fortunate Floridian: H. P. Lovecraft's Letters to R. H. Barlow*. Edited by S. T. Joshi and David E. Schultz. Tampa: University of Tampa Press, 2007.

*Selected Letters*. Edited by August Derleth, Donald Wandrei, and James Turner. Sauk City, WI: Arkham House, 1965–76. 5 vols. [*SL*]

*The Shadow Over Innsmouth*. Everett, PA: Visionary Publishing Co., 1936.

*Fiction*

*At the Mountains of Madness. Astounding Stories* 16, No. (February 1936): 8–32; 17, No. 1 (March 1936): 125–55; 17, No. 2 (April 1936): 132–50. In *CF* 3.

"Beyond the Wall of Sleep." *Pine Cones* 1, No. 6 (Oct. 1919): 2–10. *Fantasy Fan,* 2, No. 2 (October 1934): 25–32. In *CF* 1.

"The Cats of Ulthar." *Tryout* 6, No. 11 (November 1920): [6–11]. *WT* 7, No. 2 (February 1926): 252–54. In *CF* 1.

"The Call of Cthulhu." *WT* 11, No. 2 (February 1928): 159–78, 287. In *Beware After Dark! The World's Most Stupendous Tales of Mystery, Horror, Thrills and Terror,* ed. T. Everett Harré. New York: Macaulay, 1929. 223–59. In *CF* 2.

"Celephaïs." *Rainbow* No. 2 (May 1922): 10–12. *Marvel Tales* 1, No. 1 (May 1934): 26, 28–32. In *CF* 1.

"The Colour out of Space." *Amazing Stories* 2, No. 6 (September 1927): 557–67. In *CF* 2.

"Cool Air." *Tales of Magic and Mystery* 1, No. 4 (March 1928): 29–34. In *CF* 2.

"Dagon." *Vagrant* No. 11 (November 1919): 23–29. *WT* 2, No. 3 (October 1923): 23–25. In *CF* 1.

"The Doom That Came to Sarnath." *Scot* No. 44 (June 1920): 90–98. *Marvel Tales of Science and Fantasy* 1, No. 4 (March–April 1935): 157–63. In *CF* 1.

*The Dream-Quest of Unknown Kadath.* In *CF* 2.

"The Dreams in the Witch House.'" *WT* 22, No. 1 (July 1933): 86–111. In *CF* 3.

"The Dunwich Horror." *WT* 13, No. 4 (April 1929): 481–508. In *CF* 2.

"From Beyond." *Fantasy Fan* 1, No. 10 (June 1934): 147–51, 160. In *CF* 1.

"The Haunter of the Dark." *WT* 28, No. 5 (December 1936): 538–53. In *CF* 3.

"Herbert West—Reanimator" (as "Grewsome Tales"). *Home Brew:* 1, No. 1 (February 1922): 84–88 ("From the Dark"); 1, No. 2 (March 1922): 45–50 ("The Plague Demon"); 1, No. 3 (April 1922): 21–26 ("Six Shots by Moonlight"); 1, No. 4 (May 1922): 53–58 ("The Scream of the Dead"); 1, No. 5 (June 1922): 45–50 ("The Horror from the Shadows,"); 1, No. 6 (July 1922): 57–62 ("The Tomb-Legions"). In *CF* 1.

"The Horror at Red Hook." *WT* 9, No. 1 (Jan. 1927): 59–73. In *You'll Need a Night Light,* ed. Christine Campbell Thomson. London: Selwyn & Blount, 1927. 228–54. In *CF* 1.

"The Hound." *WT* 3, No. 2 (February 1924): 50–52, 78. *WT* 14, No. 3 (September 1929): 421–25, 432. In *CF* 1.

"The Music of Erich Zann." *National Amateur* 44, No. 4 (March 1922): 38–40. *WT* 5, No. 5 (May 1925): 219–34. In *Creeps by Night: Chills and Thrills,* ed. Dashiell Hammett. New York: John Day Co., 1931. 347–63. In *Modern Tales of Horror,* ed. Dashiell Hammett. London: Victor Gollancz, 1932. 301–17. *Evening Standard* (London) (24 October 1932): 20–21. *WT* 24, No. 5 (November 1934): 644–48, 655–56. In *CF* 1.

"The Nameless City." *Wolverine* No. 11 (November 1921): 3–15. *Fanciful Tales* 1, No. 1 (Fall 1936): 5–18. In *CF* 1.

"The Outsider." *WT* 7, No. 4 (April 1926): 449–53. *WT* 17, No. 4 (June–July 1931): 566–71. In *CF* 1.

"Pickman's Model." *WT* 10, No. 4 (October 1927): 505–14. In *By Daylight Only*, ed. Christine Campbell Thomson. London: Selwyn & Blount, 1929. 37–52. *WT* 28, No. 4 (November 1936): 495–505. In *The "Not at Night" Omnibus*, ed. Christine Campbell Thomson. London: Selwyn & Blount, [1937]. 279–307. In *CF* 2.

"The Picture in the House." *National Amateur* 41, No. 6 (July 1919 [*sic*]): 246–49. *WT* 3, No. 1 (January 1924): 40–42. *WT* 29, No. 3 (March 1937): 370–73. In *CF* 1.

"Polaris." *Philosopher* 1, No. 1 (December 1920): 3–5. *National Amateur* 48, No. 5 (May 1926): 48–49. *Fantasy Fan* 1, No. 6 (February 1934): 83–85. In *CF* 1.

"The Quest of Iranon." *Galleon* 1, No. 5 (July–August 1935): 12–20. In *CF* 1.

"The Rats in the Walls." *WT* 3, No. 3 (March 1924): 25–31. *WT* 15, No. 6 (June 1930): 841–53. In *Switch On the Light*, ed. Christine Campbell Thomson. London: Selwyn & Blount, 1931. 141–65. In *CF* 1.

"The Shadow out of Time." *Astounding Stories* 17, No. 4 (June 1936): 110–54. In *CF* 3.

"The Shadow over Innsmouth." In *CF* 3.

"The Shunned House." In *CF* 1.

"The Statement of Randolph Carter." *Vagrant* No. 13 (May 1920): 41–48. *WT* 5, No. 2 (February 1925): 149–53. In *CF* 1.

"Strange High House in the Mist." *WT* 18, No. 3 (October 1931): 394–400. In *CF* 2.

"The Thing on the Doorstep." *WT* 29, No. 1 (January 1937): 52–70. In *CF* 3.

"The Tree." *Tryout* 7, No. 7 (October 1921): [3–10]. In *CF* 1.

"The Whisperer in Darkness." *WT* 18, No. 1 (August 1931): 32–73. In *CF* 2.

"The White Ship." *United Amateur* 19, No. 2 (November 1919): 30–33. *WT* 9, No. 3 (March 1927): 386–89. In *CF* 1.

*Poetry* [all poems in *The Ancient Track*]
"August." *Tryout* 4, No. 8 (August 1918): [3]. *National Enquirer* 6, No. 21 (22 August 1918): 10. *Californian* 5, No. 1 (Summer 1937): 25.

"The City." *Vagrant* No. 10 (October 1919): 6–7 (as by "Ward Phillips"). *Weird Tales* 42, No. 5 (July 1950): 48–49.

"The Eidolon." *Tryout* 4, No. 10 (October 1918): [3–6] (as by "Ward Phillips").

*Fungi from Yuygoth.*

    IV. "Recognition." *Driftwind* 11, No. 5 (December 1936): 180.

    XX. "Night-Gaunts." *Providence Journal* (26 March 1930): 15. *Interesting Items* No. 605 (November 1934): [6] (as "Night Gaunts"). *Phantagraph* 4, No. 3 ([June] 1936): 8.

  XXIII. "Mirage." *WT* 17, No. 2 (February–March 1931): 175.

XXVII. "The Elder Pharos." *WT* 17, No. 2 (February–March 1931): 175.

"A June Afternoon." *Tryout* 4, No. 6 (June 1918): [1]. *National Enquirer* 6, No. 12 (20 June 1918): 10. *Vanity Fair* No. 13 (September 1919): 8.

"March." *United Amateur* 14, No. 4 (March 1915): 68. [Providence] *Evening News* 52, No. 66 (1 March 1918): 7.

"Nemesis." *Vagrant* No. 7 (June 1918). *WT* 3, No. 4 (April 1924): 78.

"Ode for July Fourth, 1917." *United Amateur* 16, No. 9 (July 1917): 121. *National Magazine* 45, No. 10 (July 1917): 616 (as "Ode to July 4th: 1917"). [Providence] *Evening News* 51, No. 26 (3 July 1917): 3.

"On an Unspoil'd Rural Prospect." *Crypt of Cthulhu* No. 21 (Eastertide 1984): 36–37.

"Ode to Selene or Diana." *Tryout* 5, No. 4 (April 1919): [8] (as "To Selene"; as by "Edward Softly").

"Quinsnicket Park." *Badger* No. 2 (June 1915): 7–10. [Providence] *Evening News* (8 February 1916): 8.

"To Mr. Finlay, upon his Drawing for Mr. Bloch's Tale, 'The Faceless God.'" *Phantagraph* 6, No. 1 (May 1937). *Weird Tales* 30, No. 1 (July 1937): 17.

*Nonfiction*

"An Account of a Trip to the Antient Fairbanks House, in Dedham, and to the Red Horse Tavern in Sudbury, in the Province of the Massachusetts-Bay." In *CE* 4.

"In Memoriam: Robert Ervin Howard." *Fantasy Magazine* No. 38 (September 1936): 29–31. In *CE* 5.

"A Layman Looks at the Government." In *CE* 5

"Letters to Farnsworth Wright." Ed. S. T. Joshi and David E. Schultz. *Lovecraft Annual* 8 (2014): 5–59.

"Mysteries of the Heavens Revealed by Astronomy." *Asheville* [NC] *Gazette-News* (16 February–17 May 1915).

"Notes on Verse Technique." Published as *Further Criticism of Poetry*. Louisville, KY: George G. Fetter, 1932. In *CE* 1.

"Notes on Writing Weird Fiction." *Amateur Correspondent* 2, No. 1 (May–June 1937): 7–10. In *CE* 2.

"Objections to Orthodox Communism." In *CE* 5.

"Robert Ervin Howard: 1906–1936." *Phantagraph* 4, No. 5 (August 1936): 4–5.

"Some Dutch Footprints in New England." *De Halve Maen* 9, No. 1 (18 October 1933): 2, 4. In *CE* 4.

"Some Notes on Interplanetary Fiction." *Californian* 3, No. 3 (Winter 1935): 39–42. In *CE* 2.

"Suggestions for a Reading Guide." *The Dark Brotherhood and Other Pieces*. Sauk City, WI: Arkham House, 1966. *CE* 2.

"Supernatural Horror in Literature." *Recluse* No. 1 (1927): 23–59. Rev. ed. in *Fantasy Fan* (October 1933–February 1935). In *CE* 2.

"Unpublished Parts of *Well Bred Speech* as Written by H. P. Lovecraft." In *Letters to Elizabeth Toldridge and Anne Tillery Renshaw* 403–38.

*Revisions and Collaborations*

"The Challenge from Beyond" (with C. L. Moore, A. Merritt, Robert E. Howard, and Frank Belknap Long). *Fantasy Magazine* 5, No. 4 (September 1935):
221–29 (Lovecraft portion pp. 223–27). In *CF* 4.

"The Mound" (with Zealia Bishop). *WT* 35, No. 6 (November 1940): 98–120
(abridged). In *CF* 4.

"Through the Gates of the Silver Key" (with E. Hoffmann Price). *WT* 24,
No. 1 (July 1934): 60–85. In *CF* 3.

# B. Works by C. L. Moore

*The Best of C. L. Moore.* Edited by Lester del Rey. Garden City, NY: Nelson
Doubleday, 1975. *Contains:* Shambleau; Black Thirst; The Bright Illusion;
Black God's Kiss; Tryst in Time; Greater than Gods; Fruit of
Knowledge; No Woman Born; Daemon; Vintage Season; Afterword:
Footnote to "Shambleau" . . . and Others.

"The Black God's Kiss." *WT* 24, No. 4 (October 1934): 402–21.

"Black Thirst." *WT* 23, No. 4 (April 1934): 424–48.

"Bright Illusion." *Astounding Stories* 14, No. 2 (October 1934): 120–37.

"The Cold Gray God." *WT* 26, No. 4 (October 1935): 441–60.

"The Dark Land." *WT* 27, No 1 (January 1936): 53–71.

"Greater Glories." *Astounding Stories* 16, No. 1 (September 1935): 111–29.

"Happily Ever After." *Vagabond* 7, No. 1 (November 1930): 28–30 (as by
"Catherine Moore").

"Lost Paradise." *WT* 28, No. 1 (July 1936): 75–90.

"Miracle in Three Dimensions." *Strange Stories* 1, No. 2 (April 1939): 85–94.

"Nymph of Darkness" (with Forrest J Ackerman). *Fantasy Magazine* 4, No. 5
(April 1935): 118–27; WT 34, No 6 (December 1939): 49–58.

"Quest of the Starstone" (with Henry Kuttner). *WT* 30, No. 5 (November
1937): 556–74.

"Semira." *Vagabond* 7, No. 3 (March 1931): 19–23 (as by "Catherine Moore").

"Shambleau." *WT* 22, No. 5 (November 1933): 531–49.

"Two Fantasies." *Vagabond* 7, No. 1 (April 1931): 15–17 (as by "Catherine
Moore").

"Tryst in Time." *Astounding Stories* 18, No. 4 (December 1936): 10–27.

"Werewoman." *Leaves* No. 2 (Winter 1938–39): 81–96. HPL owned a typewritten ribbon copy, bound in half morocco and heavy paper-covered boards,
by R. H. Barlow. Inscribed by Moore and with an additional inscription
on an adhesive label affixed to front fly. One of three copies.

"Yvala." *WT* 27, No. 2 (February 1936): 148–67.

## C. Works by Henry Kuttner

"Arkham." Nonextant.

"Ballad of the Gods." *WT* 27, No. 2 (February 1936): 147.

"Ballad of the Wolf." *WT* 27, No. 6 (June 1936): 719.

"Bamboo Death." *Thrilling Mystery* (June 1936): 28–35.

"The Bells of Horror" [i.e., "The Horror at San Xavier"]. *Strange Stories* 1, No. 2 (April 1939): 115–26 (as by "Keith Hammond").

"The Black Kiss" (with Robert Bloch). *WT* 29, No 6 (June 1937): 678–90.

*The Book of Iod.* Edited by Robert M. Price. Oakland, CA: Chaosium, 1995. Contains: The Secret of Kralitz; The Eater of Souls; The Salem Horror; The Black Kiss (with Robert Bloch); The Jest of Droom-Avista; Spawn of Dagon; The Invaders; The Frog; Hydra; Bells of Horror.

"The Frog." *Strange Stories* 1, No. 1 (February 1939): 102–11.

"The Eater of Souls." *WT* 29, No. 1 (January 1937): 93–94.

"For H. P. Lovecraft." Previously unpublished.

"The Graveyard Rats." *WT* 27, No. 3 (March 1936): 359–63.

"H. P. L." *WT* 30, No. 3 (September 1937): 359. In *Marginalia* by H. P. Lovecraft et al. Sauk City, WI: Arkham House, 1944. 371.

"Hydra." *WT* 33, No. 4 (April 1939): 98–109.

"I, the Vampire." *WT* 29, No. 2 (February 1937): 159–70.

"It Walks by Night." *WT* 28, No. 5 (December 1936): 616–20.

"The Little Ones." Nonextant.

"Master of the Damned." Part 1: *Fantasmagoria* 1, No. 2 (July 1937: 16; Part 2: 1, No. 3 (Winter 1937): 6; Part 3: 1, No. 4 (November 1938): 4.

"The Salem Horror." *WT* 29, No. 5 (May 1937): 575–85. In *Tales of the Cthulhu Mythos,* ed. August Derleth. Sauk City, WI: Arkham House, 1971.

"The Secret of Kralitz." *WT* 28, No. 3 (October 1936): 361–65.

"Where He Walked." *Crypt of Cthulhu* No. 57 (St. John's Eve 1988): 28.

## D. Works by Fritz Leiber

*Adept's Gambit: The Original Version.* Ed. S. T. Joshi. Welches, OR: Arcane Wisdom, 2014.

*The Demons of the Upper Air.* Glendale, CA: Roy A. Squires, 1969.

*Fritz Leiber and H. P. Lovecraft: Writers of the Dark.* Edited by Ben J. S. Szumskyj and S. T. Joshi. Holicong, PA: Wildside Press 2003. *Contains:* Introduction by Ben J. S. Szumskyj; H. P. Lovecraft: Letters to Fritz and Jonquil Leiber; STORIES AND POEMS BY FRITZ LEIBER: Adept's Gambit; The Demons of the Upper Air; The Sunken Land; Diary in the Snow; The Dreams of Albert Moreland; The Dead Man; A Bit of the Dark World; To Arkham and the Stars; The Terror from the Depths. ESSAYS BY FRITZ LEIBER: The Works of H. P. Lovecraft: Suggestions for a Critical

Appraisal; Some Random Thoughts About Lovecraft's Writings; Leiber on Onderdonk; A Literary Copernicus; My Correspondence with Lovecraft; Lovecraft: A Symposium; The "Whisperer" Re-examined; Through Hyperspace with Brown Jenkin; The Cthulhu Mythos: Wondrous and Terrible; Lovecraft in My Life; Afterword by S. T. Joshi.

*H. P. Lovecraft: A Symposium* (with Robert Bloch, Sam Russell, Arthur Jean Cox, and Leland Sapiro). [Los Angeles:] Riverside Quarterly/Los Angeles Science Fantasy Society, 1963.

*Night's Black Agents.* Sauk City, WI: Arkham House, 1947. *Contains:* Foreword; Smoke Ghost; The Automatic Pistol; The Inheritance; The Hill and the Hole; The Dreams of Albert Moreland; The Hound; Diary in the Snow; The Man Who Never Grew Young; The Sunken Land; Adept's Gambit.

*Sonnets to Jonquil and All* (with Jonquil Stephens). Glendale, CA: Roy A. Squires, 1978. *Contains:* JONQUIL STEPHENS: The Scarlet Frock; Behemoth over the Hill; The Midnight Wall; The Awakening; To a Dead Lover; Notes (Sonnets to Jonquil and All, essay by Fritz Leiber); Pendaren's Song. FRITZ LEIBER: The Midnight Wall; 5447 Ridgewood Court; The Other Side; Past Druid Guards; The Voice of Man; Poor Little Ape; The Gray Mouser: 1; The Gray Mouser: 2; Santa Monica Beach at Sunset; 1959: The Beach at Santa Monica.

"Adept's Gambit." In *Night's Black Agents.* Sauk City, WI: Arkham House, 1947.

"The Cthulhu Mythos: Wondrous and Terrible." *Fantastic* 24, No. 4 (June 1975): 118–21.

"The Demons of the Upper Air." *Leaves* No. 2 (1938): 113–17.

"Leiber on Onderdonk." Letter to the Editor. *Fantasy Commentator* 1, No. 7 (Summer 1945): 163.

"A Literary Copernicus." In *Something about Cats and Other Pieces* by H. P. Lovecraft et al. Sauk City, WI: Arkham House, 1949. 290–303.

"The Lords of Quarmall" (with Harry Otto Fischer). *Fantastic Stories of Imagination* 13, No. 1 (January 1964): 6–51; 13, No. 2 (February 1964): 52–91.

"Lovecraft in My Life." *Journal of the H. P. Lovecraft Society* 1 (1976): [5–9].

"My Correspondence with Lovecraft." *Fresco* 8, No. 3 (Spring 1958): 30–33.

"Some Random Thoughts about Lovecraft's Writings." *Acolyte* 3, No. 1 (Winter 1945): 20–21. [Incorporated into "A Literary Copernicus."]

"Through Hyperspace with Brown Jenkin: Lovecraft's Contribution to Speculative Fiction." *Shangri-L'Affaires* No. 66 (September 1963): 8–12. In *The Dark Brotherhood and Other Pieces* by H. P. Lovecraft et al. Sauk City, WI: Arkham House, 1966. 164–78.

"Two Sought Adventure." *Unknown* 1, No. 6 (August 1939): 99–124.

"The 'Whisperer' Re-examined." *Haunted* 2, No. 2 (December 1964): 22–25. In *The Book of Fritz Leiber.* New York: DAW, 1974. 143–47.

"The Works of H. P. Lovecraft: Suggestions for a Critical Appraisal." *Acolyte* 2, No. 4 (Fall 1944): 3–5. [Incorporated into "A Literary Copernicus."]

## E. Works by Henry Otto Fischer

"The Childhood and Youth of the Gray Mouser." *Dragon* 3, No. 4 (September 1978): 28–29, 31.

"The Finzer Family: A Tale of Modern Magic." *Dragon* 2, No. 2 (July 1977: 8–12, 14–17, 19–20; No. 3 (September 1977): 7–9, 12–14, 18–20.

"The Grey Mouser and the Game." [nonfiction] *Silver Eel* (1978): 8, 10.

## F. Works by Others

Adams, Franklin Pierce (1881–1960). *The Melancholy Lute: Selected Songs of Thirty Years*. New York: Viking Press, 1936.

Alden, Abner (1758?–1820). *The Reader: Containing the Art of Delivery, Articulation, Accent, Pronunciation,* [etc.]. <1802> 3rd ed. Boston: Printed by J. T. Buckingham for Thomas & Andrews, 1808. (LL 25)

Allen, Hervey (1889–1949). *Anthony Adverse*. New York: Farrar & Rinehart, 1933.

Allen, T. P. (1822–1868), and William F. Allen (1830–1889). *Handbook of Classical Geography, Chronology, Mythology, and Antiquities*. Prepared for the Use of Schools. Boston: Swan, Brewer & Tileston, 1861. (LL 29)

Anthon, Charles (1797–1867). *A System of Ancient and Mediaeval Geography for the Use of Schools and Colleges*. New-York: Harper & Brothers, 1850. (LL 45)

Baird, James S. S. *The Classical Manual: An Epitome of Ancient Geography, Greek and Roman Mythology, Antiquities, and Chronology*. New York: Sheldon & Co., 1871. (LL 69)

Baldwin, F. Lee. "H. P. Lovecraft: A Biographical Sketch." *Fantasy Magazine* 4, No. 5 (April 1935): 108–10, 132. In *Lovecraft at Last* (q.v.).

Beckford, William (1759–1844). *Vathek*. With an Introduction by Ben Ray Redman. Illustrated by Mahlon Blaine. New York: John Day Co., 1928.

Benson, E. F. (1867–1940). *Visible and Invisible*. New York: George H. Doran, 1923 or 1924. [Contains "The Horror Horn" and "Negotium Perambulans."] (LL 90)

Bierce, Ambrose (1842–1914?). *Can Such Things Be?* <1893> New York: Boni & Liveright (Modern Library), 1918. [Contains: "The Death of Halpin Frayser."] (LL 98)

———. *In the Midst of Life: Tales of Soldiers and Civilians*. <1891> Introduction by George Sterling. New York: Modern Library, 1927. (LL 99)

———. *Twenty-one Letters of Ambrose Bierce*. Edited with a Note by Samuel Loveman. Cleveland: George Kirk, 1922. (LL 101)

Birkhead, Edith (1889–1951). *The Tale of Terror*. New York: E. P. Dutton, 1921. (LL 105)

Blackwood, Algernon (1869–1951). *The Centaur*. London: Macmillan, 1911.

———. *The Extra Day*. London: Macmillan, 1915.

————. *The Garden of Survival.* London: Macmillan; New York: E. P. Dutton, 1918.

————. *Incredible Adventures.* London: Macmillan, 1914. New York: Macmillan, 1914. [Contains: "A Descent into Egypt."]

————. *Jimbo: A Fantasy.* New York: Macmillan, 1909. (*LL* 106)

————. *John Silence—Physician Extraordinary.* London: Eveleigh Nash, 1908. Boston: John W. Luce, 1909. London: Macmillan, 1912. New York: Vaughan & Gomme, 1914. New York: Knopf, 1917. New York, E. P. Dutton, [1920]. (*LL* 107, 108)

————. *Julius LeVallon: An Episode.* London: Cassell, 1916. New York: E. P. Dutton, 1916. (*LL* 109)

————. *The Listener and Other Stories.* London: Eveleigh Nash, 1907. New York: Vaughan & Gomme, 1914. New York: Knopf, 1917. [Contains: "The Willows."]

————.*The Lost Valley and Other Stories.* London: Eveleigh Nash, 1910. [Contains: "The Wendigo."] (*LL* 110)

————. *The Wave: An Egyptian Aftermath.* London: Cassell, 1916. New York: E. P. Dutton, 1916.

Buchan, John (1875–1940). *The Runagates Club.* Boston: Houghton Mifflin, 1928. [Contains "Skule Skerry."] (*LL* 141)

————. *Witch Wood.* London: Hodder & Stoughton, 1927.

Bury, J. B. (1861–1927). *The Student's Roman Empire: A History of the Roman Empire from Its Foundation to the Death of Marcus Aurelius (27 B.C.–180 A.D.).* London: John Murray, 1893.

Cady, John Hutchins (1881–1967). *Civic and Architectural Development of Providence.* Providence, RI: Book Shop, 1957.

Capes, W. W. (1834–1914). *Roman History: The Early Empire, from the Assassination of Julius Cæsar to That of Domitian.* New York: Charles Scribner's Sons, 1888.

Carrel, Alexis (1873–1944). *Man, the Unknown.* New York: Harper & Brothers, 1935.

Carroll, Lewis (pseud. of Charles Lutwidge Dodgson, 1832–1898). *Alice's Adventures in Wonderland.* London: Macmillan, 1866.

Chambers, Robert W. (1865–1933). *The King in Yellow.* New York: F. Tennyson Neely, 1895. (*LL* 184)

Clayton, John (pseud. of Henry Bertram Law Webb, 1885–1939). *Dew in April.* London: William Heinemann, 1934.

Combe, William (1742–1823). *The English Dance of Death: From the Designs of Thomas Rowlandson, with Metrical Illustrations.* London: J. Diggens, 1815–16. 2 vols.

Davis, William Stearns (1877–1930). *A Day in Old Rome: A Picture of Roman Life.* Boston: Allyn & Bacon, 1925.

————. *A Friend of Caesar: A Tale of the Fall of the Roman Republic, 50–47 B.C.* New York: Macmillan, 1900. (*LL* 240) de Castro, Adolphe (1859–1959). *Portrait of Ambrose Bierce.* Preface by Belknap Long. New York: Century Co., 1929.

de la Mare, Walter (1873–1956). *The Connoisseur and Other Stories.* London: Collins, 1926. New York: Alfred A. Knopf, 1926. [Contains "All Hallows" and "Mr. Kempe."] (*LL* 243)

———. "A Recluse." In *The Ghost Book,* ed. Cynthia Asquith. London: Hutchinson, 1926.

———. *The Return.* London: E. Arnold, 1910.

———. *The Riddle and Other Stories.* <1923> New York: Alfred A. Knopf, 1930. [Contains: "Seaton's Aunt."] (*LL* 244)

Dennie, John. *Rome of To-day and Yesterday: The Pagan City.* 5th ed. New York: G. P. Putnam's Sons, 1914. (*LL* 246)

De Quincey, Thomas (1785–1859). *Confessions of an English Opium-Eater and Selected Essays.* <1822> Edited with Notes by David Masson. New York: A. L. Burt, n.d. (*LL* 247)

Derleth, August (1909–1971). *Place of Hawks.* New York: Loring & Mussey, 1935. (*LL* 250)

Dunsany, Edward John Moreton Drax Plunkett, 18th baron (1878–1957). *The Book of Wonder* (1912) [with *Time and the Gods* (1906)]. New York: Boni & Liveright (Modern Library), [1918]. [Contains: "In the Land of Time," "How One Came, as Was Foretold, to the City of Never," and "How Nuth Would Have Practised His Art upon the Gnoles."] (*LL* 288)

———. *The Chronicles of Rodriguez.* London: G. P. Putnam's Sons, 1922. New York: G. P. Putnam's Sons, 1922 (as *Don Rodriguez: Chronicles of Shadow Valley*). (*LL* 289)

———. *The Curse of the Wise Woman.* London: William Heinemann, 1933. New York: Longmans, Green, 1933.

———. *A Dreamer's Tales and Other Stories.* New York: Boni & Liveright [Modern Library], [1917], [1919], or [1921]. [Contains: "Poltarnees, Beholder of Ocean," "Bethmoora," and "Idle Days on the Yann" and also *The Sword of Welleran.*] (*LL* 290)

———. *Fifty Poems.* London & New York: G. P. Putnam's Sons, 1929.

———. *Fifty-one Tales.* London: Elkin Mathews, 1915. (*LL* 291)

———. *Five Plays: The Gods of the Mountain; The Golden Doom; King Argimēnēs and the Unknown Warrior; The Glittering Gate; The Lost Silk Hat.* <1914> Boston: Little, Brown, 1923. (*LL* 292)

———. *The King of Elfland's Daughter.* London: G. P. Putnam's Sons, 1924. (*LL* 294)

———. *The Last Book of Wonder.* Boston: John W. Luce, 1916. (*LL* 295)

———. *Mirage Water.* London: Putnam, 1938. Philadelphia: Dorrance & Co., 1939.

———. *Mr. Jorkens Remembers Africa.* London: William Heinemann, 1934. New York: Longmans, Green, 1934 (as *Jorkens Remembers Africa*).

―――. *The Sword of Welleran and Other Stories.* London: George Allen & Sons, 1908. [Contains "The Fall of Babbulkund."] See *A Dreamer's Tales and Other Stories.*

―――. *Time and the Gods.* See *The Book of Wonder.*

Easton, Emily M. *Roger Williams, Prophet and Pioneer.* Boston: Houghton Mifflin, 1930.

Eddison, E. R. (1882–1945). *Mistress of Mistresses: A Vision of Zimiamvia.* London: Faber & Faber; New York, E. P. Dutton, 1935.

―――. *Styrbiorn the Strong.* London: Jonathan Cape, [1926].

―――. *The Worm Ouroboros: A Romance.* New York: Albert & Charles Boni, 1926. (*LL* 309)

Eschenburg, Johann Joachim (1743–1820). *Manual of Classical Literature.* From the German of J. J. Eschenburg . . . with Additions . . . by N. W. Fiske. 4th ed. Philadelphia: E. C. Biddle, 1843. (*LL* 319)

Field, John (1520/1530–1587). *Ephemeris anni. 1557. Currentis iuxta Copernici et Reinhaldi canones fideliter per Ioannem Feild Anglum, supputata ac examinata ad meredianum Londinensem qui occidentalior esse indicatur a Reinhaldo quam sit Regij Montis, per horam. 1. Scr. 50. Adiecta est etiam breuis quædam epistola Ioannis Dee, qua vulgares istos ephemeridum fictores merito reprehendit. Tabella deniq[ue], pro cælesti themate erigendo iuxta modum vulgariter rationalem dictum, per eundem Ioannem Feild confecta, Londinensis poli altitundini inseruiens exactissime.* Londini: [In ædibus Thomæ Marshe], M.D. LVI. [1556] Septembris. XII.

*50 Years of Ghost Stories.* London: Hutchinson, [1935]. (*LL* 333)

Flammarion, Camille (1842–1925). *Haunted Houses.* Tr. Edmund Edward Fournier d'Albe. London: T. Fisher Unwin, 1924. (*LL* 340)

Fort, Charles (1874–1932). *The Book of the Damned.* New York: Boni & Liveright, 1919.

―――. *Lo!* New York: C. Kendall, 1931.

―――. *New Lands.* New York: Boni & Liveright, 1923.

Garstin, Crosbie (1887–1930). *The Coasts of Romance.* London: William Heinemann, 1932.

Goodyear, W. H. (1846–1923). *Roman and Medieval Art.* Meadville, PA: Flood & Vincent, 1897. (*LL* 393)

Graves, Robert (1895–1985). *Claudius the God and His Wife Messalina.* London: Arthur Barker, 1934. New York: Harrison Smith & Robert Haas, 1935.

―――. *I, Claudius.* London: Arthur Barker, 1934. New York: Harrison Smith & Robert Haas, 1934.

Haggard, Audrey (1896–). *The Double Axe: A Romance of Ancient Crete.* London: J. M. Dent; New York: E. P. Dutton (Everyman's Library), 1929. (*LL* 410)

Haldane, J. B. S. (1892–1964). *Daedalus; or, Science and the Future: A Paper Read to the Heretics, Cambridge, on February 4th, 1923.* London: Kegan Paul, Trench, Trübner & Co., 1924 *or* New York: E. P. Dutton, 1924. (*LL* 413)

————. *The Last Judgment: A Scientist's Vision of the Future of Man.* New York & London: Harper & Brothers, 1927.

Hamilton, Cicely (pseud. of Cicely Mary Hamill, 1872–1952). *Lest Ye Die: A Story from the Past or of the Future.* New York: Charles Scribner's Sons, 1928.

Hawthorne, Nathaniel (1804–1864). *Dr. Grimshawe's Secret.* Boston: J. R. Osgood, 1883.

Herodotus (fl. 5th c. B.C.E.). *The Ancient History of Herodotus.* Translated from the Original Greek by Rev. William Beloe. With the Life of Herodotus by Leonhard Schmitz. New ed., rev., & cor. New York: Bangs Brothers, 1855. (*LL* 446)

Hodgson, William Hope (1877–1918). *The Boats of the "Glen Carrig."* London: Chapman & Hall, 1907.

————. *The House on the Borderland.* London: Chapman & Hall, 1908.

————. *The Night Land.* London: Eveleigh Nash, 1912.

Housman, A. E. (1859–1936). *More Poems.* New York: Alfred N. Knopf, 1936.

————. *A Shropshire Lad.* London: Kegan, Paul, Trench, Trübner & Co., 1896.

Howard, Robert E. (1906–1936). "Black Canaan." *WT* 27, No. 6 (June 1936): 662–83.

————. *The Hyborian Age* [with *A Probable Outline of Conan's Career* by P. Schuyler Miller and John D. Clark, Ph.D.]. Los Angeles: LANY Cooperative Publications, 1938. Rpt. in Robert E. Howard, *The Coming of Conan.* New York: Gnome Press, 1953.

————. "The Queen of the Black Coast." *WT* 23, No. 5 (May 1934): 530–49.

————. "Worms of the Earth." *Weird Tales* 20, No. 5 (November 1932): 604–24.

Hunt, T. F. (1841–1898). *Visitor's Guide to Salem.* Salem, MA: Essex Institute, 1916.

Huysmans, J.-K. (1848–1907). *Against the Grain [A Rebours].* <1884> Tr. John Howard, introduction by Havelock Ellis. New York: Albert & Charles Boni, 1930. (*LL* 483)

Inge, William Ralph (1860–1954). *Society in Rome under the Caesars.* London: John Murray, 1888.

James, Henry (1843–1916). *The Two Magics: The Turn of the Screw; Covering End.* <1898> New York: Macmillan, 1911. (*LL* 498)

James, M. R. (1862–1936). *Ghost-Stories of an Antiquary.* London: Edward Arnold, 1904. [Contains "Count Magnus"] (*LL* 499)

————. *A Thin Ghost and Others.* <1919> London: Edward Arnold, 1925. (*LL* 501)

Joshi, S. T. *Lovecraft's Library: A Catalogue.* New York: Hippocampus Press, 2002; rev. ed. 2017.

Jung-Stilling, Johann Heinrich (1740–1817). *Theory of Pneumatology, in Reply to the Question, What Ought to Be Believed or Disbelieved concerning Presentiments, Visions, and Apparitions, According to Nature, Reason, and Scripture.* Translated from the German, with Copious Notes, by Samuel Jackson. London: Longman, Rees, Orme, Brown, Green & Longman, 1834. (*LL* 521)

Kerruish, Jessie Douglas (1884–1949). *The Undying Monster: A Tale of the Fifth Dimension.* New York: Macmillan, 1936.

Kosztolányi, Dezsö (1885–1936). *A véres költö.* <1921> Tr. by Clifton P. Fadiman as *The Bloody Poet: A Novel about Nero.* As by "Desider Kostolanyi." With a prefatory letter by Thomas Mann. New York: Macy-Masius, 1927.

Kurath, Hans (1891–1992), ed. *Linguistic Atlas of New England.* Providence, RI: Brown University, 1939–43. 3 vols. in 6.

Lecky, W. E. H. (1838–1903). *History of European Morals from Augustus to Charlemagne.* <1869> 3d ed., rev. New York: D. Appleton & Co., 1881. 2 vols. (*LL* 555)

Leith, W. Compton (pseud. of O. M. Dalton, 1866–1945). *Sirenica.* <1913> With an Introduction by William Marion Reedy. Portland, ME: Thomas Bird Mosher, 1927. (*LL* 560)

*The Lincoln Library of Essential Information.* Buffalo, NY: Frontier Press, 1914. Numerous rev eds.

Long, Frank Belknap (1901–1994). *The Goblin Tower.* Cassia, FL: Dragon-Fly Press, 1935.

———. *The Horror from the Hills. WT* (January and February–March 1931). Sauk City, WI: Arkham House, 1963.

———. "The Space Eaters." *WT* 12, No. 1 (July 1928): 49–68.

———. "The White People." *WT* 10, No. 5 (November 1927): 633.

Lounsbury, Thomas R. (1838–1915). *History of the English Language.* New York: Henry Holt & Co., 1879. (*LL* 584)

Loveman, Samuel (1887–1976). *The Hermaphrodite and Other Poems.* Caldwell, ID: The Caxton Printers, 1936. (*LL* 594)

———. *Out of the Immortal Night: Selected Works by Samuel Loveman.* Ed. S. T. Joshi and David E. Schultz. New York: Hippocampus Press, 2004.

———. "A Scene for *King Lear.*" *Sprite* 8, No. 3 (August 1917): [2–10]. Introductory note by Harry Edward Martin, pp. [1–2].

———. "A Scene for *Macbeth.*" *United Amateur* 20, No. 2 (November 1920): 17–19. Editor's note by H. P. Lovecraft, p. 17.

Lowndes, Marie Belloc (1868–1947). *The Lodger.* London: Methuen, 1913.

Machen, Arthur (1863–1947). *The Hill of Dreams.* London: Grant Richards, 1907. New York: Alfred A. Knopf, 1923. (*LL* 617)

———. *The House of Souls.* <1906> New York: Alfred A. Knopf, 1923. [Contains "The Great God Pan" and "The White People."] (*LL* 618)

———. *The Shining Pyramid.* London: Martin Secker, 1925. (*LL* 621)

———. *The Terror.* London: Duckworth, 1917.

———. *The Three Impostors.* <1895> New York: Alfred A. Knopf, 1930. (*LL* 623)

Macleod, Fiona (pseud. of William Sharp, 1855–1895). "The Sin-Eater." <1895> In *The Best Psychic Stories*, ed. Joseph Lewis French (1858–1936). New York: Boni & Liveright (Modern Library), [1920]. (*LL* 356)

Mahaffy, J. P. (1839–1919). *The Greek World under Roman Sway from Polybius to Plutarch*. London, New York: Macmillan, 1890.

———. *Old Greek Life*. New York: D. Appleton & Co., 1879. (*LL* 633)

———. *A Survey of Greek Civilization*. Meadville, PA: Flood & Vincent, 1896. (*LL* 634)

Mason, A. E. W. (1865–1948). *The Three Gentlemen*. London: Hodder & Stoughton, 1932.

Merivale, Charles (1808–1893). *A History of the Romans under the Empire*. London: Longman, Brown, Green, & Longmans, 1850.

Merritt, A. (1882–1943). *Burn, Witch, Burn! Argosy* (22 October–26 November 1932). New York: Liveright, 1933.

———. *Creep, Shadow!* Garden City, NY: Crime Club/Doubleday, Doran, 1934.

———. *The Face in the Abyss*. New York: Liveright, 1931.

———. "The Moon Pool." *All-Story Weekly* (22 June 1918). (*LL* 26)

———. *The Moon Pool*. New York: G. P. Putnam's Sons, 1919.

———. *The Ship of Ishtar*. Los Angeles: Borden, 1924.

———. "Through the Dragon Glass." *All-Story Weekly* (24 November 1917).

Meyrink, Gustav (1868–1932). "Bal Macabre." <1908> *Strange Tales of Mystery and Terror* 2, No. 3 (October 1932): 375–79.

———. *Der Golem* [*The Golem*]. <1915> Tr. Madge Pemberton. London: Gollancz; Boston: Houghton Mifflin, 1928.

Mitchell, Samuel Augustus (1790–1868). *Mitchell's Ancient Atlas, Classical and Sacred*. Philadelphia: Butler, 1844.

———. *Mitchell's Ancient Geography*. Philadelphia: Cowperthwait, DeSilver & Butler, 1855. (*LL* 665)

Mitchison, Naomi (1897–1999). *Black Sparta: Greek Stories*. New York: Harcourt, Brace, 1928; rpt. 1933.

———. *The Corn King and the Spring Queen*. London: Jonathan Cape, 1931.

Mommsen, Theodor (1817–1903). *The Provinces of the Roman Empire from Caesar to Diocletian*. Tr. William P. Dickson. London: Richard Bentley, 1886. 2 vols.

Mundy, Talbot (1879–1940). *Tros of Samothrace*. New York: D. Appleton-Century Co., 1934.

Murray, Margaret A. (1863–1963). *The Witch-Cult in Western Europe*. Oxford: Clarendon Press, 1921.

Myers, P[hilip] V[an] N[ess] (1846–1937). *Ancient History*. Boston: Ginn & Co., 1904. (*LL* 698)

Peck, Harry Thurston (1856–1914), ed. *Harper's Dictionary of Classical Literature and Antiquities*. New York: American Book Co., 1896. (*LL* 746)

Pellisson, Maurice (1850–1915). *Roman Life in Pliny's Time*. As by "Maurice Pellison." Translated from the French by Maud Wilkinson. With an Introduction by Frank Justus Miller. Meadville, PA: Flood & Vincent, 1897. (*LL* 747)

Phillips, James D. (1876–1954). *Salem in the Seventeenth Century*. Boston: Houghton Mifflin, 1933.

Prevot, Francis C. (1887–1967). *Ghosties and Ghoulies*. Chelsea, UK: Chelsea Publishing Co., 1933.

Railo, Eino (1884–1948). *The Haunted Castle: A Study of the Elements of English Romanticism*. New York: E. P. Dutton, 1927.

Renshaw, Anne Tillery. *Well Bred Speech: A Brief, Intensive Aid for English Students*. [Washington, DC: Standard Press, 1936.] (*LL* 796)

Russell, Bertrand (1872–1970). *Icarus; or, The Future of Science*. New York: E. P. Dutton, 1924.

Saltus, Edgar (1855–1921). *Imperial Purple*. New York: Brentano's, 1906.

Santayana, George (1863–1952). *The Last Puritan: A Memoir in the Form of a Novel*. London: Constable, 1935. New York: Charles Scribner's Sons, 1936.

Sayers, Dorothy L. (1893–1957). *The Nine Tailors: Changes Rung on an Old Theme in Two Short Touches and Two Full Peals*. New York: Harcourt, Brace, 1934.

Scarborough, Dorothy (1878–1935). *The Supernatural in Modern English Fiction*. New York: G. P. Putnam's Sons, 1917.

Sherwood, Robert Emmet (1896–1955). *The Virtuous Knight*. New York: Charles Scribner's Sons, 1931.

Shiel, M. P. (1865–1947). *The Pale Ape and Other Pulses*. London: T. Werner Laurie, 1911. [Contains: "The House of Sounds."]

———. *The Purple Cloud*. <1901> New York: Vanguard Press, 1930 (*LL* 871); rpt. in *The House of Sounds and Others*, ed. S. T. Joshi. New York: Hippocampus Press, 2005.

Sienkiewicz, Henryk (1846–1916). *Quo Vadis: A Narrative of the Time of Nero*. Tr. Jeremiah Curtin. Boston: Little, Brown, 1896.

Smith, Clark Ashton (1893–1961). *The Double Shadow and Other Fantasies*. Auburn, CA: Auburn Journal Press, 1933. [Contains: "The Voyage of King Euvoran"; "The Maze of the Enchanter"; "The Double Shadow"; " A Night in Malnéant"; "The Devotee of Evil"; "The Willow Landscape."] (*LL* 880)

———. *Ebony and Crystal: Poems in Verse and Prose*. Auburn, CA: [Auburn Journal,] 1922. (*LL* 881)

———. *The Star-Treader and Other Poems*. San Francisco: A. M. Robertson, 1912. (*LL* 884)

Smith, T. R. (1830–1903). *Architecture, Gothic and Renaissance*. New & rev. ed. London: Sampson Low, Marston & Co., [189-?]. (*LL* 887)

Smith, T. R., and John Slater (1847–1924). *Architecture, Classic and Early Christian*. London: Sampson Low, Marston, Searle, & Rivington, 1890. (*LL* 888)

Smith, Sir William (1813–1893). *A School Dictionary of Greek and Roman Antiquities*. Abridged from the Larger Dictionary. With Corrections and Improvements by Charles Anthon. New-York: Harper & Brothers, 1846. (*LL* 892)

———. *A Smaller Classical Dictionary of Biography, Mythology, and Geography.* Abridged from the Larger Dictionary by William Smith. New York: American Book Co., [1852?]. (*LL* 893)

Spengler, Oswald (1880–1936). *Der Untergang des Abendlandes.* <1918–22? Tr. by Charles Francis Atkinson as *The Decline of the West.* New York: Knopf, 1926–28. 2 vols.

Stapledon, W. Olaf (1886–1950). *Last and First Men.* London: Methuen, 1930.

Stern, Gladys Bronwyn (1890–1973). *The Matriarch: A Play in a Prologue and Three Acts.* London: Samuel French, 1931.

Stormonth, James (1824–1882). *A Dictionary of the English Language.* <1871> The Pronunciation Carefully Revised by the Rev. P. H. Help. New York: Harper & Brothers, 1885. (*LL* 928)

Suetonius (C. Suetonius Tranquillus) (69–130?). *The Lives of the Twelve Caesars.* An unexpurgated English version edited with notes and an introduction by Joseph Gavorse. New York: Modern Library, 1931. (*LL* 934)

Summers, Montague (1880–1948). *The Geography of Witchcraft.* London: Kegan Paul, Trench, Trübner; New York: Alfred A. Knopf, 1927.

———. *The Vampire: His Kith and Kin.* London: Kegan Paul, 1928.

Syntax, Doctor [pseud. of William Combe, 1742–1823]. *The Tour of Doctor Syntax in Search of the Picturesque.* <1812> New ed. New York: D. Appleton & Co, 1903. (*LL* 941)

Tacitus, P. Cornelius (56?–115?). *The Works of Cornelius Tacitus.* With an Essay on His History and Genius, Notes, Supplements, &c., by Arthur Murphy. New ed. New York: Bangs, Brother & Co., 1855. (*LL* 942)

Tarbell, Frank Bigelow (1853–1920). *A History of Greek Art, with an Introductory Chapter on Art in Egypt and Mesopotamia.* Meadville, PA: Flood & Vincent, 1896. (*LL* 945)

Taylor, Rachel Annand (1876–1960) *Invitation to Renaissance Italy.* New York: Harper & Brothers, 1930.

Thomas, Emile (1843–1923). *Roman Life under the Caesars.* New York: G. P. Putnam's Sons, 1899.

Thomson, Christine Campbell (1897–1985). *By Daylight Only.* London: Selwyn & Blount, 1929. (*LL* 960)

———. *Switch On the Light.* London: Selwyn & Blount, 1931. (*LL* 965)

———. *Terror by Night.* London: Selwyn & Blount, 1934.

———. *The "Not at Night" Omnibus.* London: Selwyn & Blount, 1937. (*LL* 964)

———. *You'll Need a Night Light.* London: Selwyn & Blount, 1927. (*LL* 966)

Trench, Richard Chenevix (1807–1886). *On the Study of Words: Five Lectures.* London: John W. Parker & Son, 1851.

Wakefield, H[erbert] Russell (1890–1964). *Others Who Returned: Fifteen Disturbing Tales.* New York: D. Appleton, 1929. [Contains "The Cairn."] (*LL* 1003)

Webster, Noah (1758–1834). *Webster's International Dictionary of the English Language.* Now Thoroughly Revised and Enlarged under the Supervision of Noah Porter. Springfield, MA: G. & C. Merriam, 1891. (*LL* 1024)

Weigall, Arthur (1880–1934). *Wanderings in Roman Britain.* London: Thornton Butterworth, 1926. (*LL* 1025)

Wells, H. G. (1866–1946). *The Shape of Things to Come.* New York: Macmillan, 1933.

West, Willis Mason (1857–1931). *Ancient History to the Death of Charlemagne.* Boston: Allyn & Bacon, 1902. (*LL* 1032)

White, Edward Lucas (1866–1934). *Andivius Hedulio: Adventures of a Roman Nobleman in the Days of the Empire.* New York: E. P. Dutton, 1923. (*LL* 1035)

———. *Lukundoo and Other Stories.* New York: George H. Doran, 1927. (*LL* 1036)

———. *The Unwilling Vestal: A Tale of Rome under the Caesars.* New York: E. P. Dutton, 1918.

Wilder, Thornton (1875–1959). *Childe Roland to the Dark Tower Came. Yale Literary Magazine* 84, No. 6 (June 1919): 238–40. In *The Angel That Troubled the Waters.* New York: Coward-McCann, 1928.

Wilkins, Augustus S. (1843–1905). *Roman Antiquities.* (Classical Antiquities II.) London: Macmillan, 1877. (*LL* 1054)

Williams, Charles (1886–1945). *The Greater Trumps.* London: Faber & Faber, 1932.

———. *The Place of the Lion.* London: Faber & Faber, 1931.

# Index